Sovereignty and Jurisdiction in the Airspace and Outer Space

Sovereignty and jurisdiction are legal doctrines of a complex nature, which have been subject to differing interpretations by scholars in legal literature. The tridimensionality of state territory recognised under customary international law subsists until the present but there are other territories that do not or cannot belong to any state or political entity and these must also be accounted for in legal theory. The issues surrounding sovereignty and jurisdiction are likely to become ever more pressing as globalisation, growing pressure on resources and the need for energy and national security become acute, and the resolution of spatial delimitation disputes seems likely to become a vital question in the twenty-first century. As a result of the fast pace of technological developments in air and space activities and the massive increases in air transportation, satellite communications and space exploration, the need for scholars and practitioners to sharpen their appreciation of the legal and political issues becomes crucial.

This book will focus primarily on the issues of sovereignty, jurisdiction and control in airspace and outer space and their effects on public and private activities, but it will also look at related issues pertaining to the seas and Antarctica. Commercial exploitation, resource control and the international regime regulating contractual obligations in relation to transportation of goods and services over all forms of territory will be examined to the extent that they are necessary to explain jurisdictional rights and duties over territory. Older problems of international law such as crimes in the air and airspace trespass are considered along with newer developments such as space tourism as well as growing demand for private ownership and involvement in outer space exploitation.

The book goes on to consider the distinction between airspace and outer space and puts forward legal criteria which would allow for the resolution of the spatial delimitation dispute. These criteria would determine where in spatial terms the exclusive sovereignty of airspace ends and where outer space – the province of all mankind – begins, and contribute to the jurisprudence of territorial sovereignty and jurisdiction.

Gbenga Oduntan is a Lecturer in Law at the University of Kent, UK.

Routledge Research in International Law

Available:

International Law and the Third World
Reshaping Justice
Richard Falk, Balakrishnan Rajagopal and Jacqueline Stevens (eds)

International Legal Theory
Essays and Engagements, 1966–2006
Nicholas Onuf

The Problem of Enforcement in International Law
Countermeasures, the Non-Injured State and the Idea of International Community
Elena Katselli Proukaki

International Economic Actors and Human Rights
Adam McBeth

The Law of Consular Access
A Documentary Guide
John Quigley, William J. Aceves and Adele Shank

State Accountability under International Law
Holding States Accountable for a Breach of Jus Cogens Norms
Lisa Yarwood

International Organisations and the Idea of Autonomy
Institutional Independence in the International Legal Order
Nigel D. White and Richard Collins (eds)

Self-Determination in the Post-9/11 Era
Elizabeth Chadwick

Participants in the International Legal System
Multiple Perspectives on Non-State Actors in International Law
Jean d'Aspremont

Sovereignty and Jurisdiction in the Airspace and Outer Space
Legal Criteria for Spatial Delimitation
Gbenga Oduntan

Forthcoming titles in this series include:
The Law on the Use of Force
A Feminist Analysis
Gina Heathcote

International Law in a Multipolar World
Matthew Happold (ed.)

International Law, Regulation and Resistance
Critical Spaces
Zoe Pearson

The ICJ and the Development of International Law
The Lasting Impact of the Corfu Channel Case
Karine Bannelier, Théodore Christakis and Sarah Heathcote (eds)

Antarctic Security in the Twenty-First Century
Legal and Policy Perspectives
Alan D. Hemmings, Donald R. Rothwell and Karen N. Scott (eds)

The Right to Self-determination Under International Law
"Selfistans," Secession, and the Great Powers' Rule
Milena Sterio

The Cuban Embargo under International Law
El Bloqueo
Nigel D. White

Threats of Force
International Law and Strategy
Francis Grimal

Sovereignty and Jurisdiction in the Airspace and Outer Space

Legal Criteria for Spatial Delimitation

Gbenga Oduntan

Routledge
Taylor & Francis Group
LONDON AND NEW YORK

First published 2012 by Routledge

2 Park Square, Milton Park, Abingdon, Oxfordshire OX14 4RN
52 Vanderbilt Avenue, New York, NY 10017

Routledge is an imprint of the Taylor & Francis Group, an informa business

First issued in paperback 2019

British Library Cataloguing in Publication Data
A catalogue record for this book is available from the British Library

Library of Congress Cataloging in Publication Data
A catalog record has been requested

ISBN: 978–0–415–56212–6 (hbk)
ISBN: 978–0–367–86504–7 (pbk)

Typeset in Baskerville
by Keystroke, Station Road, Codsall, Wolverhampton

TO MY CHILDREN

Jimi, Ifeoluwa Max, Fela-Oyuwa Chidozie Richard and Omotoduntan Kamsiochukwu Oduntan

Per aspera ad astra
That they might aspire beyond the stars

Contents

Acknowledgements xv
List of abbreviations xvii
Table of cases xxi
Table of treaties, conventions and statutes xxv
Preface xxxiii

Introduction **1**

1 Preliminary considerations: sovereignty, jurisdiction and control in international law **11**
1.1 Territory and territorial acquisition in international law and relations 11
1.2 Delimitation and demarcation of international territories 19
1.3 The principle of territorial sovereignty 20
1.3.1 Sovereignty and property rights 26
1.3.2 Spatial dynamics of sovereign equality 29
1.4 The principles of territorial jurisdiction and territorial integrity 30
1.4.1 Quasi-territorial jurisdiction 36
1.4.2 Personal jurisdiction 37
1.5 Criminal jurisdiction of states 39
1.5.1 The territorial principle 42
1.5.2 The nationality principle 44
1.5.3 The protective (or security) principle 45
1.5.4 The passive personality or passive nationality principle 48
1.5.5 The universality principle 48
1.6 *Jurisfaction* and *jurisaction* 51
1.7 Control as a determinant of rights and liabilities 52
1.8 Summary and conclusions 54

2 The legal status of the airspace **57**
2.1 Nature and character of rights over airspace 57
2.2 Development of the concept of sovereignty over airspace 58
2.3 Nationality principle and control over aircraft in flight 66
2.3.1 Nationality principle and the question of what an aircraft is 71
2.3.2 Nationality of aircraft and the question of "genuine link" 75
2.4 Obligations with respect to state aircraft, civil aircraft and piloted/pilotless aircraft 80
2.5 Summary and conclusions 82

3 Jurisdiction over crimes in the airspace and on board aircraft **85**
3.1 Development and patterns of national responses to crimes in airspace 85
3.2 Hierarchy of sources of jurisdiction over crimes committed in flight 91
3.3 Jurisdiction over common crimes and unruly passengers 93
3.4 Control over unlawful interference with civil aviation 102
3.5 The regime of multilateral treaties 114
3.6 The regime of bilateral treaties and other regional arrangements 121
3.7 The problem of state-sponsored crimes against the safety of aircraft 122
3.8 Summary and conclusions 128

4 Jurisdiction and control in the airspace over international spaces **132**
4.1 International straits 133
4.2 Contiguous zone 134
4.3 The exclusive economic zone 135
4.3.1 Military activities over the EEZ 138
4.4 The continental shelf 141
4.5 The high seas 143
4.6 Airspace over Antarctic territories 145
4.7 Airspace over polar territories 146
4.8 Summary and conclusions 146

5 Sovereignty and trespass in territorial airspace **148**
5.1 Involuntary entry of aircraft 151
5.2 Deliberate intrusion by state aircraft 152
5.3 Aerial intrusion by civil airliners 158
5.3.1 Trespass by foreign-based dissident, terrorist and activist groups 162
5.4 The controversial practice of no-fly zones and trespass over national territory 166
5.5 Summary and conclusions 171

6 Jurisdiction and control in outer space **174**
6.1 Exploitation and use of outer space: achievements and prospects 175
6.2 Jurisdiction and control in outer space: relevance of property and possession to the higher grounds 177
6.3 Summary and conclusions 188

7 Legality of the common heritage of mankind principle in space law **191**
7.1 Outer space – *res nullius* or *res extra commercium*? 195
7.2 The scope of application of the CHM principle in space law 197
7.3 The CHM principle and the arguments for and against property rights in space 199
7.4 Summary and conclusions 205

8 Jurisprudential basis for common ownership **207**
8.1 Jurisprudential basis for common ownership, possession and control over outer space 207
8.1.1 The significance of morality 215
8.2 Summary and conclusions 217

9 Jurisdiction and control *rationae instrumenti* and *rationae personnae* in outer space **220**
9.1 Jurisdiction and control over national and international space stations 220
9.2 Nature of jurisdiction over space stations 222
9.3 Nationality and registration over space stations 225
9.4 Civil jurisdiction over space stations 229
9.5 Civil jurisdiction and intellectual property in the operation of space stations 232
9.6 Criminal jurisdiction over space stations 239
9.7 Jurisdiction and control *rationae personae* in outer space 245
9.7.1 Terminological confusion 245
9.7.2 Cases of unsettled jurisdiction 247
9.7.3 Liability over aerospace objects 250
9.7.4 The legal status of astronauts 253
9.7.5 Civil and criminal jurisdiction over envoys of mankind 257
9.7.6 Jurisdiction and control over mixed nationality crews 259
9.7.7 Socio-scientific considerations in the exercise of criminal jurisdiction in spatial territories 261
9.8 Summary and conclusions 264

10 Contemporary trends and threats to the regime of outer space law **266**
10.1 Illegality of the militarisation of space 266
10.2 Jurisdiction and control over remote sensing operations: questions surrounding clandestine remote sensing from outer space 269
10.3 Liberal commercialism and entrepreneurship as driving force of international space tourism 273
10.4 Summary and conclusions 280

11 The never ending dispute: legal theories on the spatial demarcation boundary plane between airspace and outer space **282**
11.1 The no-present-need theory 285
11.2 The present need school 290
11.3 The criteria of space activities or the functional approach 293
11.4 The aerodynamic lift theory 297
11.5 The Bogota Declaration view 301
11.6 The *usque ad infinitum* theory 305
11.7 The national security and effective control theory 306
11.8 The lowest point of orbital flight theory 306
11.9 Theories of arbitrary distances 309
11.10 Developing a conclusive theory on a legal spatial demarcation boundary plane between airspace and outer space 310

12 General conclusion **314**

Appendices **322**
Appendix I: Table AI.1 Chronology of notable military and diplomatic responses to aerial intrusions 1946–1999; Table AI.2 Chronology of allegations of Cuban airspace violations by aircraft of US nationality 1992–1996 322

Appendix II: Sample of letters of protest and denial between Cyprus and Turkey – (a) Letter dated 5 December 2010 from the Permanent Representative of Cyprus to the United Nations addressed to the Secretary-General; (b) Letter dated 10 January 2011 from the Permanent Representative of Turkey to the United Nations addressed to the Secretary-General 342

Appendix III: Sample of letters of protest by Iraq against the USA, Britain and France. Letter dated 11 February 2002 from the Chargé d'affaires a.i. of the Permanent Mission of Iraq to the United Nations addressed to the President of the Security Council 350

Appendix IV: Diagrammatic representation of sovereignty and jurisdiction over maritime, air and outer spaces 358

Appendix V: States and their position of choice in response to the spatial demarcation boundary plane question 360

Index 362

Acknowledgements

I wish to express sincere gratitude to the duo of Professor Wade Mansell, who supervised the thesis on which this book is based at the University of Kent, and Professor Nick Grief, who was the external examiner at the viva. Many years later, they were both further saddled with reading the scripts of the book and provided the usual fatherly advice. I remain grateful to Dr Yutaka Arai (Reader in Law) for advisory services and for constantly encouraging me to publish this and other works. Much appreciation to Dr Akalemwa Ngenda (Lecturer, Brunel Law School) for many hours of intellectual stimulation and for being a bouncing board for many academic thoughts and insights.

I owe a lot of gratitude to the staff and services of the Templeman Library, the Kent Law School and the entire staff and administration of the University of Kent at Canterbury who have provided excellent facilities for me through which to engage in this research under the best of collegial conditions.

Completing a scholarly piece like this can only be enriched with the reality check of the cries and banter of my youngest children, Fela and Duntan, aged around two years and 9 months at the time of completing the manuscript. Jimi's intermittent visits from Germany, also provided additional colour and meaning to my life. Much gratitude to them and to my sweet wife, Obianuju Evelyn Oduntan. Uju obviously deserves special kudos for having being lumbered with a husband who decides to write a monogram in the first three years of marriage. This can only be the sign of better and more exciting times to come. Eternal gratitude to my parents, Reverend Dr and Reverend Mrs E.K. Oduntan for offering me a solid foundation across the board and a sure start in life.

Gbenga Oduntan
Canterbury
December 2010

List of abbreviations

AC	Law Reports: Appeal Cases
ADIL	Annual Digest and Reports of Public International Law Cases
ADIZ	Air Defence Identification Zone
AER	All England Law Reports Reprint
AFDI	Annuaire Français de Droit International
AFRAA	African Airlines Association
AICG	Aviation Insurance Clauses Group
AJCL	American Journal of Comparative Law
AJIL	American Journal of International Law
ALF	Aviation Liaison Forum
All ER	All England Law Reports
AOC	Air operator certificate
ASIL	American Society of International Law
ATS	Australian Treaty Series
BYIL	British Yearbook of International Law
CAOC	Combined Air Operation Centre
CATSA	Canadian Air Transport Security Authority
CL	Current Law
CLP	Current Legal Problems
Cmnd	United Kingdom Command Papers
COSPAR	Committee for Space Research
CrAppR	Criminal Appeal Reports
Crim LQ	Criminal Law Quarterly
Crim LR	Criminal Law Review
CSIS	Canadian Security Intelligence Service
DOHSA	Death on the High Seas Act
DOT US	Department of Transportation (DOT)
EASA	European Aviation Safety Agency
EEA	European Economic Area
EEZ	Exclusive Economic Zone
ESA	European Space Agency
EU	European Union

FAA	Federal Aviation Administration
FCO	Foreign and Commonwealth Office
FIR	Flight Information Region
GA	General Assembly
GAOR	UN General Assembly Official Records
GSO	Geostationary orbit
HL	House of Lords
HSC	High Seas Convention
Hudson	International Legislation (Hudson)
IAF	International Astronautical Federation
IATA	International Air Transport Association
ICAO	International Civil Aviation Organisation
ICJ	International Court of Justice
ICLQ	International and Comparative Law Quarterly
ICLYB	International Law Commission Year Book
ICSU	International Council of Scientific Unions
IGA	Intergovernmental Space Stations Agreement (1988)
IGY	International Geophysical Year
IISL	International Institute of Space Law
ILC	International Law Commission
ILM	International Legal Materials
ILR	International Law Reports
ITU	International Telecommunications Union
JALC	Journal of Air law and Commerce
LFN	Laws of the Federal Republic of Nigeria
LME	Large Marine Ecosystem
LNTS	League of Nations Treaty Series
LOSC	Law of the Sea Convention
LT	Law Times
MEZ	Maritime Exclusion Zone
MMW	Millimetre Wave
MOU	Memorandum of Understanding
NASA	National Aeronautics and Space Administration
NATO	North Atlantic Treaty Organisation
NILR	Netherlands International Law Review,
NY Times	New York Times
OPC	Office of the Privacy Commissioner
OR	Official Records
PCIJ	Permanent Court of International Justice
PIA	Privacy Impact Assessments
Proc Coll	Proceedings of the (. . .)st/nd/th Colloquium on the Law of Outer Space
QRA	Quick Reaction Alert
RCMP	Royal Canadian Mounted Police

RdC	Recueil des Cours de l'Académie de droit international de la Haye
RFDA	Revue Français de Droit Aérien
RIAA	Reports of International Arbitral Awards
SAS	Scandinavian Airlines System
SC	Security Council
STO	Surface to outer space
STS	Surface to surface
TIAS	Treaties and other International Agreements of the United States
TIDE	Terrorist Identities Datamart Environment
TLR	Times Law Reports
TSA	Transport Security Administration
TSC	Territorial Sea Convention
TSDB	Terrorist Screening Database
UK	United Kingdom
UKTS	United Kingdom Treaty Series
UN	United Nations
(UN) COPOUS	(United Nations) Committee on the Peaceful Uses of Outer Space
UN Doc.	United Nations Document
UNGA	United Nations General Assembly
UNISPACE UN	Conference on the Exploration and Peaceful Uses of Outer Space
UNTS	United Nations Treaty Series
US	United States
USTS	United States Treaty Series
WBI	Whole Body Imaging
WLR	Weekly Law Reports

Table of cases

Abu Dhabi Arbitration (1951) 18 ILR 144
AG of the Government of Israel v. Eichmann (1961) 36 ILR 5 District Court of Jerusalem
Aerial Incident of November 7, 1954 (United States v. USSR) ICJ Reports 1959
Aerial Incident of October 7, 1952 (USA v. USSR) ICJ Pleadings 29, 1956
Aerial Incident of September 4, 1954 (USA v. USSR) ICJ Pleadings 19, 1958
Aerolinas Perunas S.A. Permit Case, 31 International Law Report, p. 416
Alleman v. Omni Energy Services Corp., 75, Journal of Air Law and Commerce 1 (2010): 181, 187
Alvarez-Machain v. United States, 331 F 3d 604 (9th Cir 2003)
Appalachian Insurance Co. v. McDonnell Douglas, Journal of Space Law, Vol. 18 (1990), pp. 41–44
Application for Revision of the Judgment of 11 September 1992 in the Case concerning the Land, Island and Maritime Frontier Dispute (El Salvador/Honduras: Nicaragua intervening) (El Salvador v. Honduras) (2002);
Armed Activities on the Territory of the Congo (New Application: 2002) *(Democratic Republic of the Congo v. Rwanda)* (2002);
Asahi Metal Indust. Co. Ltd v. Superior Court, 480 US 102 (1987)
AT&T v. Martin Marietta, Journal of Space Law, Vol. 23 (1995) pp. 177–83
Aviateca, S.A. v. Friedman, 678 So. 2d 387 (Fla App 1996)
Barcelona Traction Case, ICJ Reports 1958, p. 308
Boardman v Phipps [1967] 2 A.C. 46, at 123
Case Concerning the Questions of Interpretation and Application of The 1971 Montreal Convention Arising from the Aerial Incident At Lockerbie (Libya Arab Jamariya v. United Kingdom); Case Concerning Questions of Interpretation and Application of the 1971 Montreal Convention Arising from the Aerial Incident At Lockerbie (Libya Arab Jamariya v. United States of America) ICJ Reports 1992
Chaudhry v Prabhakar & Anor [1988] 3 All ER 718.
Cox v. Army Council [1963] AC 48
Cutting Case (1887) US for Rel, p. 751
Day v. Trans World Airlines, 528 F. 2d 31 (2nd Cir 1976)
Day v. TWA, Inc., 528 F. 2d 31(1975), Cert Denied 429 US 890
Dispute regarding Navigational and Related Rights (Costa Rica v. Nicaragua) (2005); *Duru v. Police* [1961] 1 All NR p. 44

DPP v. Boot [1973] AC 807
Duru v. Police [1961] 1 All NR p. 44
Frontier Dispute (Benin/Niger) (2002)
Gardner v. Howe (1865) 9 F.Cas. 1157 (CCD Mass. 1865).
Gartside v. Outram (1856) 26 LJ Ch. 113
Go-Video, Inc., v. Akai Elec Co. Ltd, 885 F.2d 1406. 1414 (9th Cir. 1989)
Harunami v. Borno Native Authority [1966] All NLR 22-23;
Helicopter Sales (Australia) Pty Ltd v. Rotor-works Pty Ltd, High Court of Australia; 1 Air Law, pp. 189–90
Her Majesty's Advocate v. Abdelbasset Ali Mohmed Al Megrahi and Al Amin KhalifaFhimah Prisoners in the Prison of Zeist Camp (Kamp van Zeist) the Netherlands in the High Court of Justiciary at Camp Zeist Case 1475/99
Hernandez v. Air France, 545 F. 2d 279 (1976)
Husserl v. Swiss Air Transport Co. Ltd, 12 CCH Avi 17, 367 at 17, 370 (DCNY, 1972) *re Air Disaster at Lockerbie, Scotland on December 21, 1988*, 928 F. 2d 1276 (2nd Cir), Cert Denied 502 US 920, 112 S Ct 331 (1991)
Ibeziako v. Commissioner of Police 12 WACA 363
Initial Services v Putterill [1968] 1 QB 396;
International Shoe Co. v. Washington, 326 US 310 (1945)
Island of Palmas Case (1928) RIAA: 2 829
Joyce v. DPP [1946] AC 347
Justiciary at Camp Zeist Case 1475/99 http://www.pixunlimited.co.uk/guardian/pdf/0131lockerbieverdict.pdf
Keppel v. Wheeler 1927 1KB 557
Krystal v. BOAC, 403 F Supp. 1322 193 (1975)
Land and Maritime Boundary between Cameroon and Nigeria (Cameroon v. Nigeria) paras 64, 68 , 70, 219, 223. Judgments, cases and materials of the ICJ are available at www.icj.org.
Laroche v. Spirit of Adventure (UK) Ltd Court of Appeal of England and Wales, [2009] EWCA Civ. 12.
Lotus Case, PCLJ Reports 1927 Series A. No. 10
Mangrui v. Compagnie Nationale Air France, 549 F. 2d 1256 (1977) Cert Denied, 45 Law Weekly, (1977) p. 380
Marconi Wireless Telco v. USA (1942) 53 USP.Q 246 (Ct. Cl. 1942).
Maritime Delimitation in the Black Sea (Romania v. Ukraine) 2004
Maritime Dispute (Peru v. Chile) (2010)
Martin Marietta Corporation v. International Telecommunications Satellite Organisation (Intelsat) Journal of Space Law, Vol. 19 (1991), pp. 173–6
McDonald v. Mabee, 90 US 230 (1916)
Military and Paramilitary Activities in and Against Nicaragua. (Nicaragua v. United States of America) 1986 IC] Rep. 14
Nain Malvan v. Attorney-General for Palestine Case, 1948 AC 351 at pp. 369–70
Nottebohm Case, Second Phase (Guatemala v. Liechtenstein) ICJ Reports (1955), pp. 4, 23
Parker v. Parker 1954 AC 15 at 22

Proceedings jointly instituted by Burkina Faso and the Republic of Niger (Burkina Faso/Republic of Niger)
R (on the Application of Bancoult) v. Secretary of State for the Foreign and Commonwealth Office [2001] QB 1067
R v. Bow Street Metropolitan Stipendiary Magistrate, ex p. Pinochet Ugarte (Amnesty International intervening) (No.3) [1999] 2 All ER 97
R v. Dudley and Stephens (1884) LR 14; (1884) 14 QBD
R. v. Horseferry Road Magistrates Court, ex p. Bennet [1994] 1 AC 42, HL
R v. Kent JJ, ex p Lye [1967] 1 All ER 560, at 564, 565.
R. v. Martin and ors [1956] 2 QB 272
R v. Naylor [1962] 2 QB 527
R v. Secretary of State for Transport, ex p. Pegasus Holidays (London) Ltd 1989 2 All ER 481
R v. Whitehouse (Neil) [2000] Crim LR 172 (2000) 97(1) LSG. 22 Times, December 10, 1999; Independent, December 14, 1999
Re Ownership and Jurisdiction over Offshore Mineral Rights, 65 DLR 2d (1967) 353; ILR 43, 93
Re Piracy Jure Gentium [1934] AC 589
Samuel Leiser, Claimant, Appellant, v. United States of America, Libelant, Appellee No. 5098. 234 F.2d 648.
Schooner Exchange (1812) 7 Cranch 116 (US)
Skiriotes v. Florida, 313 US 69, 73 (1941)
Sovereignty over Pedra Branca/Pulau Batu Puteh, Middle Rocks and South Ledge (Malaysia/Singapore) (2003);
Sovereignty over Pulau Ligitan and Pulau Sipadan (Indonesia/Malaysia).
Stanford & Others v. Kuwait Airways & Others 25 AVI 17, 511 1996
State v. Okpegboro [1966] All NLR 17;
Tomoya Kawakita v. US, Reported in Vol. 46 AJIL (1952), p. 147
Territorial and Maritime Dispute (Nicaragua v. Colombia) (2001)
US Mexican General Claims Commission, United Nations Reports of International Arbitral Awards, Vol. 4, pp. 119, 121–22
US v. Aluminium Co. of America, 148 F. 2d 416 (1945)
US v. Alvarez-Machain (1992) 119 LEd 2d 441
US v. Archer (1943)
US v. Holmes Fed. Cases 360, No. 15, 383 (US Cir. Ct. E. Pa., 1842)
US v. One 1980 Cessna II Aircraft, US District Court, Southern District of Florida 15 Dec. 1997, 26 Avi 15, 459; Vol. xxiv Air and Space Law No. 6 1999
US v. Rezaq, US Court of Appeals District of Columbia Circuit 6 February (1998), Avi 15, 404
US v. Roduguez, 182 F Suppl. 479 (1960)
US v. Yunis 681 F Supp. 896 US District Court, DDC February 12, 1988 . . . 681 F Supp. at 901, 902
US v. Watchmakers of Switzerland Information Center Inc., 133 F Supp. 40 (1955); 134 F
USA v. Cordoba and Santen (1950) USA v. R 1: 3 Avi 17, 306
Warton –Pitt [1991] 92 Cr App R 136

Wedding v. Meyler 192 US 573, 584 (1904)
Yasuda Fire & Marine Insurance Co. of Europe v. Orion Marine Insurance Underwriting Agency 1995 2 QB 174
Zicherman v. Korean Airlines 116 S. Ct 629 (1996).

Table of treaties, conventions and statutes

[The treaties referred to in this book are listed in chronological order. Where possible, reference to the source and particular articles, sections or parts referred to are supplied. Information as to the place, date of signature, date of entry into force and, in respect of multilateral treaties, the number of parties (or contracting states if the treaty is not in force) is supplied, where applicable, in the footnotes.]

1804	French Civil Code (1804) Article 544
	Norway (General) Penal Code, 1902 as amended
	UK Aerial Navigation Act 1911
1905	Protectorate Treaty (Second Korea-Japan Agreements, Eulsa joyak) signed 1905 Nov. 17.
1913	UK Aerial Navigation Act 1913: 2 & 3 Geo. 5 C22
	Convention relating to the Regulation of Air Navigation of October 13 (1919 League of Nations, Treaty Series, 174, 1919 . . . Articles 1, 6, 32
	Paris Convention on Aerial Navigation, 1919 Treaty Series (No. 2/1922) HM Stationery Office, London (1922) Cmd. 1609; 9 Hudson International Leg. (1989) p. 359 . . . Article 1, Annex A
1920	Dangerous Drugs Act 1920 10 and 11 Geo V C40 (UK)
1920	Death on the High Seas Act (DOHSA) 46 USC 761.
1923	United States–Mexican General Claims Convention 1923, 4 RIAA, p. 11
	France (Air Navigation Act 1924)
1926	Ibero-American Convention of Madrid 1926
	Bustamante Code, Convention on Private International Law adopted in 1928 LNTS vol. LXXXVI, No. 1950
	Pan-American Convention on Commercial Aviation Signed at Havana on 20 February 1928 Text in Spanish and English 6th International Conference of American States, Report of the Delegates of the United States to Department of State, Washington (1928) 177–1189. See 3 Journal of Air Law (1932) p. 411 . . . Article 1, 7, 8, 9
	Convention for the Unification of Certain Rules relating to International Carriage by Air, signed at Warsaw on October 12th, 1929 . . . Article 17

	Hague Convention on Certain Questions relating To the Conflict of Nationality Laws 179 LNTS 89 . . . Article 4
1930	Italy Penal Code 1930
1930	Philippines Penal Code 1930
1932	Poland Penal Code 1932
1935	Harvard Draft Convention. Text of the Draft convention with Respect to Crime in Vol. 29 AJIL (1935) Supp. 443 p. 439
	Cuba Code of Social Defence 1936
1936	Guatemala Penal Code 1936
	Romania Penal Code 1936
	Belgium Air Navigation Act 1937
	Brazil Air Code 1938
	Ecuador Penal Code 1939
1941	Costa Rica Penal Code 1941
1942	Italy Navigation Code 1942
1942	Uruguay (Aviation Codes 1942)
1943	The Lebanon (Penal Code 1943)
1944	Chicago Convention on International Civil Aviation (1944) 78 UKTS 8 1953 Cmd. 8742; UNTS 295 . . . Articles 1, 2, 3, 4, 5, 6, 8, 11, 12, 17, 18, 19, 30, 31, 32, 77, Art 3 bis, Art 83 bis, Art 93, Annex 7, Annex 17
1944	Venezuela Civil Aviation Code 1944
	Charter of the United Nations San Francisco, 26 June 1945; Documents on the UN Conference on International Organisation, vol. 15, p. 336 . . . Articles 2, 102
1945	Truman Proclamation on the Continental Shelf (1945) Presidental Proclamation No. 2667 28th September 1945
1948	Luxembourg Air Navigation Act 1948
	Switzerland Federal Air Navigation Act 1948
	International Convention for the Regulation of Whaling, UKTS 5 (1949) Cmnd. 7604; 161 UNTS 72
1949	Syria Penal Code 1949
1950	Greece Penal Code 1950
	Honduras Aviation Law 1950
	Hungary Penal Law 1950
1953	The Outer Continental Shelf Lands Act of 1953 (OCSLA) (67 Stat. 462)
1953	UK Dangerous Drugs Regulations 1953; . . . section 3
1954	UK Air Navigation Order 1954
1955	Protocol to Amend the Convention for the Unification of Certain Rules Relating to International Carriage by Air, Signed at Warsaw on 12 October 1929, Done at The Hague on 28 September 1955 (The Hague Protocol 1955) 478 UNTS 371
1955	Protocol to Amend the Convention for the Unification of Certain Rules Relating to International Carriage by Air, Signed at Warsaw on 12 October 1929, as Amended by the Protocol Done at The Hague on 28

September 1955, Signed at Guatemala City, on 8 March 1971 ATS 1998 No. 10

1958 Nigerian Air Navigation (Safety of Navigation) Act Cap. 8 of the 1958 edn of the Laws of Nigeria. section 17, 51

1958 Geneva Convention on the Continental Shelf 499 UNTS 312–321 . . . Art 3

Geneva Convention on the High Seas (1958) UKTS 5 (1963) Cmnd. 1929; 450 UNTS 82 (1958) 52 AJIL 842 . . . Articles 1, 2

1958 Geneva Convention of 1958 on the Territorial Sea UKTS 3 (1965),Cmnd. 2511; 516 UNTS 205; (1958) 52 AJIL 751 . . . Article 24

High Seas Convention (1958) 450 UNTS 82 . . . Article 5

(US) National Aeronautics and Space Act Pub. L. No. 85-568, as Amended

1959 Antarctic Treaty Signed at Washington, December 1959 UKTS 97 (1961), Cmnd. 1535, 402 UNTS 71; (1960) 54 AJIL (1960) 477 . . . Articles 1, IV, V, VI, IX, XII

1960 (UK) Air Navigation (General) Regulations 1960

1960 (UK) Air Navigation Order, 1960, Art 2

1960 (UK) Civil Aviation Act 1960

1961 (UK) Carriage by Air Act 1961 9 and10 Eliz. E, 27C

1961 Convention Supplementary to the Warsaw Convention for the Unification of Certain Rules Relating to International Carriage by Air Performed by a Person other than the Contracting Carrier (Guadalajara Convention 1961)

1961 Vienna convention on Diplomatic Relations 1961 UKTS 19 (1965), Cmnd 2565; 500 UNTS 95

1962 (UK) Carriage by Air (Supplementary Provisions) Act 1962

1962 South African Aviation Act 1962 (Act No. 74 of 1962)

1963 UNGA Resolution 1962 (XVIII). Declaration of Legal Principles Governing the Activities of States in the Exploration and Use of Outer Space (1963); . . . Declarations 1, 3, 7

1963 Tokyo Convention (1963) UKTS 126 (1969), Cmnd. 4230; 704 UNTS 219 . . . Articles 3, 4, 5, 6, 7, 8, 9, 10, 11, 13, 16

1963 Treaty Banning Nuclear Weapon Tests in the Atmosphere, in Outer Space and Under Water 1963 UNTS Vol. 480 (1963) p. 45 ff.

1963 Vienna Convention on Consular Relations Vienna 24 April 1963. 523 UNTS 117

1964 Agreed Measures for the Conservation of Antarctic Fauna and Flora (1964); Done at Brussels 2 June 1964

1964 (Nigerian) Civil Aviation Act 1964, No. 30 LFN 1990 . . . Sections 1, 2, 3, 17

1964 UK Continental Shelf Act 1964, C29

1965 Nigerian Civil Aviation Act 1965 Cap. 51, LFN 1990

1966 Montreal Inter-Carrier Agreement 1966

1967 Convention Establishing the World Intellectual Property Organization. 21 U.S.T. 1749. 828 U.N.T.S. 3.

1967 Treaty on Principles Governing the Activities of States in the Exploration and Use of Outer Space, including the Moon and Other Celestial Borders (1967) (18 UST 2410, 610, UNTS 205) . . . Article I, II, III, IV, V, VII, VIII, IX, XII

1968 Agreement on the Return of Objects launched in to Outer Space 1968 UKTS 56 (1969), Cmnd. 3997; (1969) 63 A.J.I.L. 382 . . . Articles 1, 2, 3, 4, 12

1970 UN General Assembly Declaration on Principles of International Law concerning Friendly Relations and Co-operation among States in accordance with the Charter of the United Nations Adopted by Resolution 2625 (XXV) of October 24, 1970. See UNGA Official Records: Twenty-Fifth Sess., Supp. No. 28 (A/8028) . . . Article 1

Declaration of Principles Governing the Sea-Bed and the Ocean Floor, and the Subsoil Thereof, Beyond the Limits of National Jurisdiction GA Res. 2749 (XXV), December 17, 1970 (1970). (1971) 10 ILM 220

Hague Convention for the Suppression of Unlawful Seizure of Aircraft of December 16 1970 ILM, Vol. 10 1971 p. 133 . . . Articles 2, 4, 7, 8, 9, 10

1971 Montreal Convention (1971). UKTS 81 (1983), Cmnd. 9100 (1979) 18 Convention for the Suppression of Unlawful Acts Against the Safety of Civil Aviation ILM 1456. In force 1983 . . . Articles 1, 10

Organization of American States Convention to Prevent and Punish Acts of Terrorism Taking the Form of Crimes against Persons and Related Extortion that are of International Significance of February 2, 1971. ILM Vol. 18 (1979), 1457

1972 Convention for the Conservation of Antarctic Seals UKTS 45 (1972), Cmnd. 8714; 1080 UNTS 176; 11 ILM 251

1972 Convention on International Liability for Damage caused by Space Objects 1972 UKTS 16 (1974), Cmnd. 5551; 961 UNTS 187; 10 ILM 965

International Telecommunication Convention (ITU Malaga – Torremolinos Convention) (1973) 28 UST 2495, TIAS No. 8572

1973 United Nations Convention on the Prevention and Punishment of Crimes against Internationally Protected Persons, including Diplomatic Agents of December 14, 1973 UNTS Vol. 1035, p. 167

1974 Charter of Economic Rights and Duties of States (1974) GA Res. 3281 (XXIX) (1975) 14 ILM 251 . . . Article 2

UN Charter of Economic Rights and Duties of States (1974) GA Res. 3281 (XXIX)

1975 Additional Montreal Protocol No. 4 of 1975.

1975 Convention for the Establishment of a European Space Agency 30 May 1975 1297 UNTS 161, 14 ILM 855.

1975 European Space Agency Convention May 1975, Basic Texts of the

European Space Agency, Convention and Rules (1980); US Congress, US Congress, Space Law and Related Documents, 101st Congress 2 d Sess., Committee Print, S. Print No. 101-98, GPO, Washington, DC 1990

Convention on Registration of Objects Launched into Outer Space (1975) UNTS 187; 14 ILM 43; UKTS 70 (1978) . . . Articles I, II

1977 European Convention on the Suppression of Terrorism Done 27 January 1977; UNTS Vol. 1137, 93.

1977 UK–US Air Services Agreement in 1977 UKTS No. 76 (1977) Cmnd. 7016

1977 European Convention on the Suppression of Terrorism of January 27 1977 UNTS Vol. 1137, 93

1978 Extradition Treaty between the United States of America and the United Mexican States, May 4, 1978, U.S.-Mex., 31 U.S.T. 5059

1978 Bogota Declaration of 1976, Journal of Space Law, Vol. 6 No. 2 (1978) . . . Article 2

Bonn Declaration on International Terrorism (1978) 17 ILM 1285; UKMIL 1978; (1978) Vol. 49 British Year Book of International Law. 423 . . . Paragraph 1

US Commercial Space Launchings Act (CSLA) of 1978

Agreement Governing the Activities of States on the Moon and Other Celestial Bodies (1979) (GA Res. 34/68, UN GAOR, 34th Sess., Supp. No. 46 at 77, UN Doc. A/34/664 (1979) . . . Articles 2, 4, 5, 6, 7, 9, 10, 11, 12, 15, 18

Carriage by Air and Road Act 1979 (Commencement No. 2) Order 1997, Statutory Instrument1997 No. 2565 (C97) ISBN 0 11 065088 3

1979 International Maritime Organization (IMO), International Convention on Maritime Search and Rescue, 27 April 1979, 1403 UNTS.

1979 United Nations Convention against the Taking of Hostages of December 18, 1979 ILM, Vol. 18 (1979) p. 1457 . . . Article 10

Air Navigation Order 1980, SI 1980 No. 1965 . . . Article 45

1981 Declaration of Montebello in 1981; ILM, Vol. 20 (1981) 956

1982 The Principles Governing the Use by States of Artificial Earth Satellites for International Direct Television Broadcasting (resolution 37/92 of 10 December 1982);

1982 Convention on the Conservation of Antarctic Marine Living Resources (CCAMLR) (1980) 19 ILM 841. Convention entered into force on 7 April 1982 . . . Article IV

1982 (UK) Civil Aviation Act 1982: 1982 C16 . . . Sections 60, 61

1982 United Nations Convention on the Law of the Sea, Montego Bay, 10 December 1982 xxi ILM 1245 (1982) . . . Articles 1, 33, 78, 86, 87, 91, 101, 136, 140, 150, 153, 246

1982 US Invention Secrecy Act 1982 35 USC Sections 181–188

1982 US Patent Act. 1982 35 USC ssc. 101 *et seq.*

1983 UK–Egypt Air Services Agreement (UKTS No. 52 (1983)) Cmnd. 9025

1983 UK–New Zealand Air Services Agreement (UKTS No. 5 (1983)) Cmnd. 8784

1984 UK–Cameroon Air Services Agreement (UKTS No. 4 1984)) Cmnd. 9124

1984 UK–Korea (UKTS No. 47 (1984)) Cmnd. 9263

1985 Canada Privacy Act (R.S.C., 1985, c. P-21)

1985 Canadian Aeronautics Act as amended in 2004 Aeronautics Act (R.S.C., 1985, c. A-2).

1985 Criminal Code (RS 1985, C46) (Canada) . . . Part 1 Sections 1, 4

1985 Memorandum of Understanding Between the National Aeronautics and Space Administration and the European Space Agency for the Conduct of Parallel Detailed Definition and Preliminary Design Studies (Phase B) Leading Toward Further Cooperation in the Development, Operation and Utilization of a Permanently Manned Space Station, June 3, 1985

UK–Antigua and Barbuda, which came into force on 25 March 1985 UKTS No. 29 (1985) Cmnd. 9556 . . . Article 8

1986 Internal Revenue Code of 1986 (Pub. L. No. 99-514, § 2, 100 Stat. 2095 [Oct. 22, 1986]).

1986 The Principles Relating to Remote Sensing of the Earth from Outer Space (resolution 41/65 of 3 December 1986

1988 International Government Agreement (IGA), Done at Washington, DC, 29 September 1988. See IGA Proceedings of the Colloquium on Manned Space Stations – Legal Issues, Paris 7–8 November 1989, ESA SP-305, ISBN 92 9092 062 9, Jan 1990 . . . Articles 5, 11, 12, 16, 21

1988 Protocol for the Suppression of Unlawful Acts of Violence at Airports Serving International Civil Aviation, Supplementary to the Convention for the Suppression of Unlawful Acts Against the Safety of Civil Aviation Done at Montreal on 23 September 1971. Signed at Montreal on 24 February 1988, UNTS Vol 1598 474

1990 UK Aviation and Maritime Security Act (1990) C31

1991 Convention on the Marking of Plastic Explosives for the Purposes of Detection 1991 30 ILM 721.

1991 Protocol on Environmental Protection to the Antarctic Treaty 1991 30 ILM 1455 . . . Articles 2, 3, I, II III, IV, V

1991 US Code of Federal Regulations Title 14 – Aeronautics and Space Part 1211 Extraterrestrial Exposure Friday April 26 1991 56 FR 19259 . . . 1211.102, 1211.108

1992 Council Regulation (EEC) No. 2407/92 of 23 July 1992 on Licensing of Air Carriers
Official Journal L 240, 24/08/1992

1992 Principles Relevant to the Use of Nuclear Power Sources in Outer Space A/RES/47/68 85th plenary meeting 14 December 1992

1993 South African Space Affairs Act 1993 (Act No. 84 of 1993)

1993 (UK) Air Navigation (General) Regulations 1993, Stationery Office: ISBN 01 103 4622 X

1995 IATA Intercarrier Agreement on Passenger Liability (IIA) of 31 October 1995

1996 Agreement on Measures to Implement the IATA Intercarrier Agreement (MIA) 1996.

1996 Declaration on International Cooperation in the Exploration and Use of Outer Space for the Benefit and in the Interest of all States, Taking into Particular Account the Needs of Developing Countries (1996) A/RES/51/122 . . . Declarations 2, 3

1996 UK Civil Aviation Amendment Act 1996 . . . section 92

1998 Agreement among the Government of Canada, Governments of Member States of the European Space Agency, the Government of Japan, the Government of the Russian Federation, and the Government of the United States of America Concerning Cooperation on the Civil International Space Station Agreement signed at Washington 29 January 1998. Treaties and Other International Acts Series 12927

1998 Australian Space Activities Act 1998 (Cth)

1998 International Government Agreement (IGA) signed on 29 September 1998; see Journal of Space Law, Vol. 26 (1998), pp. 90–98

1998 (UK) Aviation Security Act C36. Halisbury's Statutes of England and Wales 4th edn 1998

1998 US Commercial Space Act of 1998 signed into law October 28, 1998

1999 Declaration Adopted by the Council of the International Civil Aviation Organisation at the Ninth Meeting of its 156th Session on 10 March 1999 . . . Declarations 1, 2, 3, 4, 5, 7

1999 Patents in Space Act 35 USC 105; Journal of Space Law Vol. 18 No. 1 1999

2001 HR 2177 – the Invest in Space Now Act of 2001 – was proposed in the House of Representatives on 14 June 2001.

2001 Space Tourism Promotion Act of 2001.R. 2443 on July 10th, 2001

2001 Air Navigation (Dangerous Goods) (Amendment) Regulations 2001

2004 Intelligence Reform and Terrorism Prevention Act (IRTPA). (Public Law 108-458, 118 Stat. 3638-3872)

2004 Commercial Space Launch Amendments Act (CSLAA) Public Law 108–492 108th Congress, 23 December 2004 [HR 5382]

2004 Kiribati Civil Aviation Act 2004. Available at http://www.parliament.gov.ki/acts/2004/ CivilAviationindex.pdf (accessed 10 October 2010) ss 139–144.

2005 Guidelines for Navigation and Overflight in the Exclusive Economic Zone May 2005 http://www.sof.or.jp/en/report/pdf/200509_20051205_e.pdf

2006 Nigerian Civil Aviation Act 2006.

2009 UK Air Navigation (Amendment) Order 2009 (SI 2009/1742).

Preface

Sovereignty and jurisdiction are legal doctrines of a complex nature that have been subject to differing interpretations by scholars in legal literature. The relationship between the two with respect to all the manifestations of territory has also not been fully worked out by lawyers. The tridimensionality of state territory recognised under customary international law subsists up to the present. The idea of sovereignty and jurisdiction over the airspace has developed over the centuries and is even older than the history of human flight. Under prevailing treaties on air law, particularly the Chicago Convention (1944), the principle of complete and exclusive sovereignty over the superincumbent airspace is unassailable. Airspace sovereignty is delimited *ratione loci* in respect of the space above national territories and not *ratione materiae* in respect of the air, which may at any given time be filling this space. Quasi-territorial jurisdiction and personal jurisdiction may, however, be exercised by other states with respect to aircraft, spacecraft and their citizens to which they have granted legal personality even when found in foreign airspace. However, unsettled jurisdictional problems persist in relation to control over aircraft, spacecrafts and space objects, criminal jurisdiction in spatial territories and airspace trespass.

While national sovereignty and exclusive jurisdiction can be exercised over the airspace relating to all parts of national territory, sovereignty is completely inapplicable to outer space and its celestial bodies. Certain comparable jurisdictional competencies found in air law are also exercisable in outer space in relation to spacecraft, scientific stations, instrumentalities and personnel. Central to the discussion of the application of jurisdiction and control in outer space is the concept of "common heritage of mankind", a political and legal doctrine that reinforces outer space as the province of mankind. This creates ideological problems among lawyers and statesmen particularly across the developing and developed states divide regarding the operation of familiar notions of ownership and possession.

The legal distinction between airspace and outer space and the two bodies of law governing them is not only factual but also ultimately necessary. In spite of the acknowledged commercial, strategic, political and environmental importance of air and space activities, the province of the applicable laws has not been determined. What remains to be done is to determine where in spatial terms exclusive sovereignty ends and where the province of all mankind begins. Indeed the determination of a demarcation line is primarily of legal significance. Views and literature on the subject abound; however, no satisfactory consensus has been reached. It is from this medley of ideas that the book attempts to distil and formulate legal criteria for the resolution of the spatial delimitation dispute.

Introduction

In 2009 within a year of similar communications from Germany, the UK, Denmark and Brazil another space-active nation with immense and important investments in outer space wrote to the UN COPUOS in very clear terms stating its intention to continue its massive investment and involvement in outer space. It was stated that this country:

> [h]as been utilizing both air- and space-based platforms for information and communications, and has developed air-based surveys using sophisticated aircraft equipped with the necessary imaging instruments. Moreover [. . .] prospectively plans to launch a multi-mission geostationary satellite for telecommunications, telebroadcasting, information technology-based functioning and microwave remote sensing devices, in addition to telecommunications instruments. The geostationary satellite data will be used for meteorological applications such as monitoring cyclones, rainfall, floods and cold waves, which are regularly occurring phenomena in [. . .]. The development of an air-based survey system, polar orbiting and geostationary satellites is very important for [. . .].[1]

That country was Bangladesh, a state with 40% of its population living below the national poverty line according to the World Bank[2] and one of 49 countries that are currently designated by the United Nations as "least developed countries" (LDCs).[3] Yet its concern about outer space exploration and utilisation is both

1 Bangladesh communication to COPUOUS of 27 October 2009 as quoted in United Nations, General Assembly, Committee on the Peaceful Uses of Outer Space, Questions on the Definition and Delimitation of Outer Space: Replies from Member States January 2010, A/AC.105/889/Add.5 11. Available online at: http://www.unoosa.org/pdf/reports/ac105/AC105_889Add5E.pdf (accessed 18 June 2010).

2 The World Bank, "Bangladesh at a Glance" (12/9/09). Available online at: http://devdata.worldbank.org/AAG/bgd_aag.pdf (accessed 18 June 2010).

3 UNCTAD, *The Least Developed Countries Report 2009: The State and Development Governance* (New York and Geneva, The UN, 2009): 4. Materials relating to the UNCTAD are available online at: http://unctad.org/en/docs/ldc2009_en.pdf (accessed 18 June 2010).

commendable and indeed imperative if it is to emerge from underdevelopment. This certainly underscores the importance and reality of aerospace exploration to all modern states and the need for the law to continue its relentless catching up game with technological advancements and the accelerating developments in outer space exploration.

Today, nearly six decades after the first space flight in 1957, there exist good grounds for the proposition that international space law has become a branch both of science and of international law in its own right. Air law also prescribes the rules and principles of international law regulating the activity of states in the use of national and international airspace. Both branches of law have grown nearly independent of one another and have different legal and historical development. Air flight by powered manned aircraft is at least a century old but the law regulating it has, from its inception, been principally dictated by the technologically advanced states. By the same token, international regulation of outer space activities is barely five decades old. However, it has developed rapidly, due to the overriding influence of the technological powers.

From the outset of space exploration in 1957 the following queries have been presented: What is outer space from a legal point of view? What are the permissible acts of jurisdiction allowed therein? Where does outer space begin? Where do the principles and rules of international airspace law cease to operate? The separate laws developed to regulate both airspace and outer spaces respectively have tended to be very general in nature. So also has the treatment of the rules in legal literature. It is to be noted that there is a huge difference between the legal status of the airspace and that of outer space. Sovereignty and exclusive jurisdiction is granted in the former whereas in the latter there can be no exercise of sovereignty. Outer space generally remains not only the "province of all mankind" but parts of it such as the Moon are regarded by states as the "common heritage of mankind". However, it is crucial to note that current international documents that establish the regime of airspace have not determined the upper limit to the spread of a state's sovereignty over its airspace. Likewise the international treaties that establish the regime of outer space have not pinpointed the exact lower limits of outer space or its outer limits. Thus, while there is today an appreciable amount of literature on air and space law, there has been very little work done connecting these two branches of international law within the scope of the principles of state sovereignty and jurisdiction, on one hand, and the resolution of the spatial demarcation of boundaries problem, on the other. Whereas the resolution of these issues is assuming increasing and immediate importance due to an upsurge in air and space activities the central problems remain of divisive value among states and scholars. Aerospace activities having a bearing on different aspects of public international law presently span commercial transportation, military and defence activities, meteorite mining, satellite communications, remote sensing, reconnaissance, space manufacturing, scientific exploration and so on. Yet the exact geophysical scope of the application of both air law and space law will appear not to have been determined. It is an indisputable fact that undefined frontiers only create a potential source for confusion and conflict in the international system.

This book attempts to render a rich and dependable account on the manifestation of sovereignty (as it relates to territorial extents of a state) and jurisdiction (as it relates to the competences of states in all forms of territory). It does not, and cannot, examine all the areas in which the legal concepts of sovereignty and jurisdiction have relevance. The legal and semantic senses of sovereignty and jurisdiction in law are too numerous to be meaningfully treated in any single volume and there will be little merit in attempting to do so.

As a book on jurisdiction in international law, especially as regards the competence to regulate, administer and resolve disputes relating to the airspace of states as well as in the outer space, this work will assume that the trend towards commercial exploitation and use of the airspace and outer space is of universal interest. This includes the belief that if well managed and kept within the confines of international law and with the democratic input of as many states as possible, air and outer space law can be a force for universal good and will serve the benefit of all nations and their peoples.

As telecommunications and satellite technology assume a greater importance globally, the rights to use outer space will be challenged and, doubtless, international disputes will arise. The demarcation of spheres of influence and activities will also become of crucial importance as more states begin to utilise free space (for placement of satellites) and visit celestial bodies for scientific research and other uses. This scholarly analysis is, therefore, an attempt to discuss the legal principles that have been the guiding light of mankind in the land territories as well as in the regulation of all common spaces, which have also by analogy been extended to outer space. These principles are likely to have a strong influence on the way in which such disputes might be resolved in the coming years. They will also guide the nature, extent and scope of man's investment in airspace and outer space activities.

The "resolution of spatial delimitation disputes" is likely to be a vital question in the 21st century as globalisation, growing pressure on resources and the need for energy and national security become acute. Ultimately, the central aim is to propose a solution to the problem of demarcation between airspace and outer space, employing the dictates of classic public international law approaches to maritime and polar regions along with pragmatic legal, political and moral considerations.

It is hoped that the treatment of these issues will have a broader impact in allied areas of academic discourse especially as it relates to increasing human occupation and commercial exploitation of previously inaccessible zones such as Antarctica and the polar territories. The usefulness of a book like this to students and practitioners in the field of public international law is manifest. As Professor Bin Cheng, perhaps the doyen of air and space lawyers in the UK, explained: "I find that . . . the pursuit of special interests can in turn greatly enhance one's understanding of the entire international legal system."[4]

4 Bin Cheng, *Studies in International Space Law* (Oxford, Clarendon Press, 2004): vii.

Space law as conceptualised in this book represents a functional classification of those rules of international law and of municipal law relating to outer space or affecting outer space. In other words, these are rules of international space law and rules of space law belonging to the various municipal systems.[5]

We would adopt the sense of space law that refers in the main to international space law, because, in the matter of boundaries between airspace and outer space, it is international law that is controlling. Indeed, municipal law matters in most cases only to the extent to which it throws light on the situation in international law.[6] Similarly, air law, in respect of this book, refers to the principles of international air law as maintained within international law and not the national rules regulating the airspace. References, however, will be made to municipal rules regulating the airspace for illustrative purposes.

The significance of academic study of the aerospace environment and the activities that occur therein cannot be overstated. The value of space science and exploratory activities include massive improvements in emergency response,[7] international cooperation and education,[8] among others. Satellite technology has applications in medical aid, international healthcare and telemedicine. With satellite link-ups technology such as the European Healthware project, people living in remote areas where healthcare professionals are unavoidable or unable to leave their homes may receive advanced healthcare. Medical professionals also discuss cases and tap into specialisations without expensive transfers. Success stories in the area of teleconsultation healthcare have been demonstrated in Cyprus, France, Greece, Czech Republic, Poland and United Kingdom.[9] Thus, outer space

5 Cf. Cheng 2004: 429.

6 Cf. ibid.

7 The increasing severity of natural disasters demands the utilisation of space applications in ways that were previously thought impossible. The year 2008 proved historical as a year with one of the highest numbers of victims of natural catastrophes. Chinese victims of the earthquake in the province of Sichuan, the cyclone in Myanmar, and several other natural catastrophes in the first part of the year alone claimed the lives of more than 150,000 people. The previous year had recorded 960 disasters and events, the largest number in recorded history. Celestino Gomez, "SAFER and GMES Emergency Response Core Service: One step closer to full-scale operational deployment", available online at: www.kpk.gov.pl/ (accessed 10 June 2010). Note should also be made of the planned framework of the United Nations Platform for Space-based Information for Disaster Management and Emergency Response (A/AC.105/929). The COPOUS endorsed the workplan of the United Nations Platform for Space-based Information for Disaster Management and Emergency Response (UN-SPIDER) for the biennium 2010–2011 (A/AC105/937). See also United Nations, Report of the Committee on the Peaceful Uses of Outer Space, General Assembly Official Records Sixty-fourth Session Supplement No. 20, United Nations New York, 2009, paras 100–4, 117–25: 18.

8 Earth observation classes are taught to science students, broadband communication via satellite communication has improved university and other education across the globe.

9 The Healthware system uses a communications format known as digital video broadcasting return channel via satellite (DVB -RCS) which does not depend on a physical cable. See European Commission, DG enterprise and Industry, EU: Connecting People through satellite-based Telemedicine Connecting People Through satellite-based Telemedicine Solutions: Scenarios

activities can also be a valid instrument of diplomacy and development aid. Matters relating to remote sensing of the Earth by satellite and monitoring of the Earth's environment are applications with particular relevance to developing countries.[10]

The interconnectedness of all nations in the world in relation to airspace transportation was dramatically portrayed by the events of the natural disaster of volcanic eruption in early 2010. The potential of aerospace science to help reduce the severity of such events was also made transparent. The potentials of science to assist in repairing the earth and normalising human and international relations is just beginning to be understood in clearer terms. Most of the grave environmental problems facing the world are of international significance and demand co-ordinated scientific response requiring space applications. An account shows that: "The fastest growing city in China in economic terms is Shanghai. Since 1996, it has shown an increase in tropospheric nitrogen dioxide of 29%, which is not good news for anyone in China, Europe or the rest of the world." Part of the solution to this universal concern interestingly comes from the unlikely effort of space scientists in the Netherlands where the Royal Netherlands Meteorological Institute (KMNI) has developed an integrated information system for monitoring and forecasting tropospheric pollutants over China.[11] Nevertheless, it must be conceded that large-scale engagement in space activities by potentially close to 200 independent states and thousands of private enterprises present its own unprecedented dangers particularly in the areas of space debris, environmental pollution, climate change and international conflict.[12]

This book is, therefore, undertaken as a pre-emptive exercise to raise pertinent questions of theory and practice before they become of crucial importance. It also aims to compare and contrast the application of sovereignty and jurisdiction to the

and Practical Experiences from the Healthware project, available online at: http://www.epractice.eu/files/media/media1916.pdf (accessed 11 June 2010).

10 The operational production, distribution and the effective use of environmental, remote sensing and Earth observation data are of enormous benefit to sustainable development in the developing world. The VGT4 Africa project is but one of the developmental projects that allows African states to access satellite technology for vegetation monitoring, food security, early warning crop estimation, livestock modelling and better management of biodiversity. The VGT4 Africa partners are VITO, JRC-IES and MEDIAS-France, collected and communicated data derived from the VEGETATION instruments on board SPOT Satellites to states including countries within the Southern Africa Development Community (SADC), Sudan, Rwanda, Ivory Coast, Kenya, Ethiopia, Senegal, Congo-Brazzaville, Mauritania, The Gambia, Tunisia and the Democratic Republic of Congo. Tim Jacobs and VGT4AFRICA Partners: "VGT4 Distribution of Vegetation Data in Africa through EUMETCast, Final Publishable Activity Report", available online at: http://www.vgt4africa.org (accessed 12 June 2010); UN COPOUS OPCIT (2009), paras 103–4: 16–17.

11 See GMES info, "Space for a Safer World: Reinforcing the European Emergency Response Capacity", No. 6, *Research EU*, June 2010: 18.

12 Scientific projections of the effects of space tourism show that with a conservative estimate of 1,000 suborbital flights per year rubber-burning engine crafts would produce soot that could disrupt the stratosphere and send temperatures soaring at the poles. Editorial, "Space Tourism's Toll on Climate", *New Scientist*, 30 October 2010: 5.

conduct of air and space activities. Further, it compares and draws analogies between the "aerospace" regimes and other international territories – Antarctica, high seas, high seabed and the nonsovereign parts of the Arctic. In sum, the book sets to determine five central questions:

1 legal status of the airspace
2 legal status of outer space
3 possibilities of attaining workable criteria for the legal demarcation between the two territories
4 relationship and commonalities between the episteme surrounding notions of international territories
5 law and politics of development as it relates to international territories and common spaces.

A central problem to the resolution of issues in relation to international spaces is the opposing views of the developing and developed states particularly in relation to commercialisation, exploitation and delimitation/demarcation. The book seeks to consider their diverse positions and present the sometimes conflicting legal and scientific theories and considerations that have been proffered by leading authorities on the subject of permissible manifestation of sovereignty in airspace and outer space and the precise scope of their applicability. The desired aim is to synthesise the divergent positions as found in all forms of international territories into a single, consistent legal theory, which would not only satisfy air lawyers and space lawyers, on the one hand, but also bridge the perennial divide between developing and developed states on the issue, on the other.

The book seeks to offer alternative views to some of the central assumptions in air law and space law that are based on or at least represent evidence of the political realities inherent in prevailing international law. Such an enquiry is topical in light of the noticeable trend among scholars both from the developed and developing world to question the content of international law. In any case, what is regarded as law whether municipal or international has been, in many instances, exposed as the product of vested interests. Therefore, in a study like this we are obliged to consider whether or not the present rules of air law and space law perpetuate the myth of legal objectivity and political neutrality in a world where the law is increasingly identified as ideology and as politics facilitating a capitalist world.[13]

13 For wider perspectives of this issue, see the following: W. Mansell, A. Thomson and B. Meteyard, *A Critical Introduction to Law* (London: Cavendish Publishing Ltd, 1995): 1–27 *et passim*; P. Sinha Surya, *Legal Polycentricity and International Law* (Durham, NC: Academic Press, 1996); N'zatioula Grovogusi Siba, *Sovereigns, Quasi-sovereigns and Africans: Race Self-determination in International Law* (Minneapolis: University of Minnesota Press, 1996) R. Falk, B. Rajagopal and J. Stevens, *International Law and the Third World*, London: Routledge. As a writer puts it, "a major research theme that unites this diverse anti-colonial intellectual tradition is its primary focus on arguing about the limits within which the newly independent nations of Africa would embrace an international; law that was Eurocentric in its geographic origin". James Thuo Gathii, 'Review Essay: International Law and Eurocentricity: Introduction', Vol. 9 *European Journal of International Law* No.1 (1997): 185.

Effort is exerted to present the views and contributions of the developing states and legal scholars therefrom on the developments in air and space law. It is also hoped that the case would be made for the rights of protection for nations, which are at present not sufficiently technologically advanced to be able to launch space objects into orbit or that cannot at present meaningfully participate in aerospace activities. More importantly, the virtual monopoly of the regulation of air and outer space by technologically advanced countries for their commercial use and social convenience is critiqued. If the book succeeds in creating awareness for an urgent need to arrest the virtual monopoly of legal and scientific discussion over air and outer space activities by the Western nations, as well as presenting a coherent theory for resolving the demarcation problem, it will have achieved its purpose. Furthermore, it aims to foment the necessary discussion that will, it is hoped, draw attention to the crucial need for lawyers, researchers and legal advisers to study the applications and dynamics of sovereignty, jurisdiction and control over the airspace and outer space prior to the happening of the inevitable events that will stimulate and agitate the interest of states and governments in the 21st century. In the final analysis, the usefulness of a book like this will be its assistance as a trustworthy reference on the pertinent points in issue.

The territorial scope of the research naturally embraces all sovereign states since there is no state without a supervising airspace and an accompanying natural and legal entitlement to outer space. The scope of the book includes an examination of the development of the concepts of sovereignty and jurisdiction particularly in relation to air law and space law. Thus, the first chapter of the book deals with the epistemology of the terms and their legal and political connotations. However, the concepts receive continuous examination throughout the book.

The regime governing sovereignty and jurisdictional spheres in the airspace and in the conduct of aviation activities is one of the most important areas of contemporary international law. These considerations present in microcosm nearly all the fundamental problems of international law as a whole. These include: the relationship of states and other international legal entities, nationality, unification of private laws, many problems of conflict of laws, crimes on board aircraft, liability for damage to third states, aerial warfare and trespass. Judge Moore, while pointing out the consequences of the "protective principle" of nationality in his individual opinion in *The Lotus* in 1927, very aptly said: "[I]n this way an inhabitant of a great commercial city in which foreigners congregate may in the course of one hour unconsciously fall under the operation of a number of foreign criminal codes."[14] It would appear that without being aware of it, he was, in fact, prophetically describing the legal quagmire of criminal jurisdiction inherent in present-day civil aviation activities.[15]

14 PCIJ Series A 10, 92.

15 Going by the much touted "floating island theory" used to explain the quasi-territorial jurisdiction over national crafts and vessels, an aircraft may by a corresponding legal fiction be regarded as a city in which people of various nationalities congregate. If this were so, then in one hour, an aircraft may indeed traverse many territories, each with its own unique criminal laws. The imagination can thus, hardly conjure to the fullest the possible complexities of criminal jurisdiction, which may

Thus, Chapters 2 to 5 examine the development of legal jurisdiction over national airspace, questions of nationality of aircraft,[16] jurisdiction over crimes committed in the airspace, jurisdiction over international airspace and the permissible response to aerial trespass.[17] The connecting thread between these aspects is that while they have attracted an immense wealth of jurisprudence in legal literature and in various attempts at legal regulation, the resolution of the crucial issues therein are far from complete and still generate a lot of controversy in air law. The ultimate resolution of these controversies is a *sine qua non* to the peaceful conduct of international relations in the 21st century. The aim is to determine if international legal rules governing these matters are sufficiently explicit and whether or not the present regulations are based on equitable solutions involving the necessary balance between national and the general international interests.

Chapters 6 to 9 deal with the core aspects of jurisdiction and control in outer space. Working on the basis of the impressive network of treaties developed since 1963 by the United Nations to govern man's activities in outer space, state practice and some national legislation, the book makes a comparative analysis with the regime in air law. Examination of the jurisdictional aspects of achievements and prospects of space exploration is made. Jurisdiction and control over persons and flight instrumentalities is discussed in comparative analysis with the regime of air law. The book questions the relevance and applicability of ownership, possession and property over outer space in the absence of the concept of state sovereignty in outer space. The legal validity, import and relevance of the concept of "common heritage of mankind" is examined not only in relation to outer space territories but in terms of its development in international law and in analogous situations. In view of the restiveness of the technologically advanced states to embark on

arise in a "simple" international flight. The significance of the escalating wave of aerial hijacking (since the 1950s) and the increasing incident of violent behaviour of passengers and persons on board aircraft must not be lost to us. The new century was entered with a plane hijack incident still unsolved. Pakistan-based terrorists hijacked Indian Airlines flight 814 over the yuletide period. Within the first two months of the new millennium another aircraft hijack occurred. An Ariana Afghan Airlines hijacked on an internal flight in Afghanistan ended up in London Stansted airport. The horrific events of the September 11 terrorist hijackings for suicidal attacks on the United States may just signal another development in the long list of problems that air law will have to cope with in this century.

16 Since almost every question of air law assumes some international dimensions and the primary subject of international law is the state, nearly all legal issues relating to aircraft have to do with the principle of nationality. This book, thus treats the principle of nationality of aircraft as the chief determinant of control in relation to state jurisdiction over aircraft.

17 Nowhere else has the significance of the concepts of nationality and jurisdiction over aircraft as well as criminal actions in aerial territories been brought into sharper focus than in the reaction of states to trespass in their airspace. Sharp disagreements often occur as to the status and standards of treatment to be accorded to such intruding aircraft. Is such an aircraft completely at the mercy of the territorial sovereign? Does the right to destroy the aerial intruder logically inhere in complete and exclusive sovereignty? Or does international law impose considerable restraint on the territorial state in dealing with aerial intruders?

large-scale exploitation of outer space resources the book argues for the development of a progressive utilisation regime for outer space-based resources based on equitable considerations and taking into account the needs of developing countries. The argument in favour of maintaining a moratorium on mining on celestial bodies is made.

Finally, Chapter 10 presents the legal theories on the spatial demarcation boundary plane between airspace and outer space. The arguments of the various schools of thought on the spatial demarcation problem are summarised and discussed with a view to eliminating the solutions least likely to be successful in law and in practice. The special problem of the Geostationary Orbit (a special flight path for satellites) is treated in relation to the developing versus developed states divide. This orbit is directly above the equator, at which satellites circle at the same speed as the earth rotates. Just three satellites are enough for continuous coverage of the whole globe at this height. However, since it is the only orbit capable of providing these services, it is a finite resource and a strong point of controversy between developed and developing states on matters of jurisdiction and control. The book, therefore, ends on a prescriptive note with a theory that takes into account the major arguments and forms a synthesis of the positive ideas inherent in the submissions of writers on the subject.

1 Preliminary considerations: sovereignty, jurisdiction and control in international law

1.1 Territory and territorial acquisition in international law and relations

> The territorium is the sum of the lands within the boundaries of a community [civitatis]; which some say is so named because the magistrate of a place has the right of terrifying [terrendi] that is exercising jurisdiction, within its boundaries.[18]

Territory is both a political and legal term and concerns the relation between sovereignty, land and people.[19] Territory derives its roots from the Latin *terra* meaning land or terrain and the compound *territorium*, which, by the prefix *orium*, denotes "the place of something" or surrounding something. The etymology of *territorium* according to the Oxford English Dictionary is "unsettled". It is described as:

> usually taken as a deriv[ative]: of terra earth, land (to which it was certainly referred in popular L[atin]. When altered to *terratorium*); but the original form [*territorium*] has suggested derivation from *terrere* to frighten.[20]

Territory is, therefore, both spatial and locational in referring to "the place surrounding an area".[21] In this sense, we can envisage that the location of such an "area", at least in our modern world, can indeed be maritime, aerial or celestial as long as it is a space, place or sphere of physical activities capable of being occupied

18 Pomponius Manual in the Digest of Justinian cited in Stuart Elden, *Terror and Territory: The Spatial Extent of Sovereignty* (Minneapolis: London, 2010): v.

19 A critical interpretation of the basis for the emergence of this concept in the way it is recognised has been explored elsewhere. See Stuart Elden, "Missing the Point: Globalisation, Deterritorialisation, and the Space of World", *Transactions of the Institute of British Geographers* 30, 1 (2005): 8–19 and "Governmentality, Calculation, Calculation, Territory", *Environment and Planning D: Society and Space* 25 (2007): xxvi et seq. Elden notes at 578 "Territory is more than merely land, but a rendering of the emergent concept of 'space' as a political category: owned, distributed, mapped, calculated, bordered, and controlled".

20 J.A. Simpson and E.S.C. Weiner, *The Oxford English Dictionary*, 2nd edn (Oxford: Clarendon Press, 1989), Vol. XVII: 819.

21 Elden (2010) op. cit.: xxix.

by use of or for passage. It is interesting that territory has in time, however, acquired a popular meaning of a "bounded space". One of the problems that emanate from such a view has been adduced to by the query "what is space" and how is it bounded?[22] It is for this reason that one author concluded quite persuasively that:

> A properly critical political theory of territory needs to investigate the quantification of space and the role of calculative mechanisms in the commanding of territory, and the establishment of borders.[23]

René Descartes also helpfully suggested that geometry is the science that best allows us to conceptualise spatial territory. Analytical geometry and the entire gamut of scientific methodology of spatial measurement have indeed provided the techniques to map out the various terrains known to mankind including deserts, arctic, polar and even celestial bodies and the geostationary orbit.[24] It is for this reason that this book proceeds from the *a priori* position that determination of territorial extents by objectively verifiable criteria is both an attribute of human instinct and a legally obligatory act. It makes good policy in both the domestic and international legal orders for there to be distinct territories and a fundamental understanding of the juridical nature of all forms of physical and extraterrestrial territories. A corollary position of this view is that, wherever possible, the precise distinction in terms of delimitation and demarcation of all territories must always be attempted even if not achieved.

There is a total of 351 separate geographic entities in the world today. This includes 194 independent states;[25] several dependencies and areas of special

22 Ibid: xxvii.

23 Ibid: xxvii.

24 Ibid: xxvi. Elden points out that advances in the time of Descartes, which include analytic geometry that he pioneered using algebra and equations partnered with developments in cartography and land surveys as well as more accurate means of measuring time, allowed for the accurate determination of longitudes and latitudes.

25 The independent states are: Afghanistan, Albania, Algeria, Andorra, Angola, Antigua and Barbuda, Argentina, Armenia, Australia, Austria, Azerbaijan, the Bahamas, Bahrain, Bangladesh, Barbados, Belarus, Belgium, Belize, Benin, Bhutan, Bolivia, Bosnia and Herzegovina, Botswana, Brazil, Brunei, Bulgaria, Burkina Faso, Burma, Burundi, Cambodia, Cameroon, Canada, Cape Verde, Central African Republic, Chad, Chile, China, Colombia, Comoros Island, Democratic Republic of the Congo, Costa Rica, Cote d'Ivoire, Croatia, Cuba, Cyprus, Czech Republic, Denmark, Djibouti, Dominica, Dominican Republic, Ecuador, Egypt, El Salvador, Equatorial Guinea, Eritrea, Estonia, Ethiopia, Fiji, Finland, France, Gabon, the Gambia, Georgia, Germany, Ghana, Greece, Grenada, Guatemala, Guinea, Guinea-Bissau, Guyana, Haiti, Holy See, Honduras, Hungary, Iceland, India, Indonesia, Iran, Iraq, Ireland, Israel, Italy, Jamaica, Japan, Jordan, Kazakhstan, Kenya, Kiribati, Kosovo, Kuwait, Kyrgyzstan, Laos, Latvia, Lebanon, Lesotho, Liberia, Libya, Liechtenstein, Lithuania, Luxembourg, Macedonia, Madagascar, Malawi, Malaysia, Maldives, Mali, Malta, Marshall Islands, Mauritania, Mauritius, Mexico, Federated States of Micronesia, Moldova, Monaco, Mongolia, Montenegro, Morocco, Mozambique, Namibia, Nauru, Nepal, Netherlands, New Zealand, Nicaragua, Niger, Nigeria, North Korea, Norway, Oman, Pakistan, Palau, Panama, Papua New Guinea, Paraguay, Peru, Philippines,

sovereignty, such as the Australian – Ashmore and Cartier Islands, Christmas Island, Cocos (Keeling) Islands, Coral Sea Islands, Heard Island, the McDonald Islands; and areas of indeterminate sovereignty, such as Antarctica, Gaza Strip, Paracel Islands, Spratly Islands, West Bank and Western Sahara.[26] The land boundaries in the world total add up to approximately 251,060 km (and that is where effort has been expended to prevent the counting of shared boundaries twice). Most states share boundaries with multiple land or maritime neighbours.[27] Nearly a quarter of all independent states are landlocked. Liechtenstein and Uzbekistan are, in fact, doubly landlocked (countries that are not only landlocked but are completely surrounded by other landlocked countries). Africa has two interesting examples – Zambia, which is completely surrounded by eight states (Angola, Botswana, Congo DRC, Malawi, Mozambique, Namibia, Tanzania and Zimbabwe), and Lesotho, which is not only landlocked but country locked as it is completely surrounded by South Africa.[28] Virtually all states have access naturally to their airspace and a potential direct access to outer space depending only on their level of rocket technological acquisition or interest in procurement of launches through other states' vessels.

Territory may be acquired by many means and there is much truth in the statement of Brownlie that the student of the materials on the acquisition of title to territory is apt to erroneously feel that he is studying the history of a class of disputes instances of which are unlikely to arise in future. He wrote:

> [I]n one sense at least law is history and the lawyer's appreciation of the meaning of rules relating to acquisition of territory and of the manner of their application in historical cases will be rendered more keen by a knowledge of the historical development of the law . . . In other words, the principles developed in relation to the normal territorial areas provide useful analogies for those engaged in building a legal regime for any international space.[29]

Poland, Portugal, Qatar, Romania, Russia, Rwanda, Saint Kitts and Nevis, Saint Lucia, Saint Vincent and the Grenadines, Samoa, San Marino, São Tomé and Principe, Saudi Arabia, Senegal, Serbia, Seychelles, Sierra Leone, Singapore, Slovakia, Slovenia, Solomon Islands, Somalia, South Africa, South Korea, Spain, Sri Lanka, Sudan, Suriname, Swaziland, Sweden, Switzerland, Syria, Tajikistan, Tanzania, Thailand, Timor-Leste, Togo, Tonga, Trinidad and Tobago, Tunisia, Turkey, Turkmenistan, Tuvalu, Uganda, Ukraine, United Arab Emirates, United Kingdom, United States, Uruguay, Uzbekistan, Vanuatu, Venezuela, Vietnam, Yemen, Zambia, Zimbabwe. See CIA, *The World Factbook* available at https://www.cia.gov/library/publications/the-world-factbook/docs/notesanddefs.html (accessed 10 September 2010).

26 Ibid.

27 China and Russia, for instance, border 14 other countries each.

28 The list of currently recognised 45 landlocked states and territories are: Afghanistan, Andorra, Armenia, Austria, Azerbaijan, Belarus, Bhutan, Bolivia, Botswana, Burkina Faso, Burundi, Central African Republic, Chad, Czech Republic, Ethiopia, Holy See (Vatican City), Hungary, Kazakhstan, Kosovo, Kyrgyzstan, Laos, Lesotho, Liechtenstein, Luxembourg, Macedonia, Malawi, Mali, Moldova, Mongolia, Nepal, Niger, Paraguay, Rwanda, San Marino, Serbia, Slovakia, Swaziland, Switzerland, Tajikistan, Turkmenistan, Uganda, Uzbekistan, West Bank, Zambia, Zimbabwe.

29 Ian Brownlie, *Principles of Public International Law*, 5th edn (Oxford: Oxford University Press, 1970): 125–6.

In reality, there is a continuing relevance of the classical modes of territorial acquisition and the entire question of modes of territorial acquisition is of current legal significance and will remain so for a considerable length of time. A cursory glance at the work of the International Court of Justice in the last ten years alone will reveal that the Court is occupied with disputes arising out of territorial questions. Many of these are as a result of controversy over the applicable root of title and can only be resolved with reference to them.[30] It would appear that a surprising proportion of frontiers taken for granted as settled are actually dormant disputes waiting to erupt. States may at any time be called on to prove territorial title or defend their territorial sovereignty. The need to do so may, in fact, be on the increase in the 21st century for many reasons. These include conflict over natural and energy resources,[31] challenge of inchoate titles and the consequences of rapid and previously unimaginable changes in technological advancements. Developments in shipping technology, aviation and space technology continue to break down zones of inaccessibility to mankind and put valuable resources within the reach of corporations and businesses. All these make it necessary for the modern-day lawyer (even the air and space lawyer) and decision maker to remain familiar with the issues and nuances surrounding the legal modes of territorial acquisition including, of course, the possible causes of loss of sovereignty over territory.

Even the ancient concept of *terra nullius* (i.e. land belonging to no one), which arguably can no longer rear its head in modern times having been exposed as a political tool for acquisition of territory by stealth in Africa and Asia by the European powers, somewhat unfortunately remains relevant in legal analysis as root of previous titles and in the resolution of disputes between states.[32]

30 Territorial and boundary-related disputes that have been litigated before the court in the last decade are as follows: *Proceedings jointly instituted by Burkina Faso and the Republic of Niger (Burkina Faso/Republic of Niger)*; *Maritime Dispute (Peru v. Chile)* (2010); *Dispute regarding Navigational and Related Rights (Costa Rica v. Nicaragua)* (2005); *Maritime Delimitation in the Black Sea (Romania v. Ukraine)* 2004; *Sovereignty over Pedra Branca/Pulau Batu Puteh, Middle Rocks and South Ledge (Malaysia/Singapore)* (2003); *Application for Revision of the Judgment of 11 September 1992 in the Case concerning the Land, Island and Maritime Frontier Dispute (El Salvador/Honduras: Nicaragua intervening) (El Salvador v. Honduras)* (2002); *Armed Activities on the Territory of the Congo (New Application: 2002) (Democratic Republic of the Congo v. Rwanda)* (2002); *Frontier Dispute (Benin/Niger)* (2002); *Territorial and Maritime Dispute (Nicaragua v. Colombia)* (2001). Note also celebrated cases such as *Land and Maritime Boundary between Cameroon and Nigeria*; *Territorial and Maritime Dispute (Nicaragua v. Colombia)*; *Sovereignty over Pulau Ligitan and Pulau Sipadan (Indonesia/Malaysia)*.

31 According to International Energy Agency (IEA) forecasts, global energy demand will grow 45% between 2006 and 2030. See Communication and Information Office, "New Energy Realities – WEO Calls for Global Energy Revolution Despite Economic Crisis", 12 November 2008 London, available at https://www.iea.org/press/pressdetail.asp?PRESS_REL_ID=275 (accessed 5 May 2010); cf. International Energy Agency, World Energy Outlook 2008 Executive Summary: 13, available at http://www.worldenergyoutlook.org/docs/weo2008/WEO2008_es_english.pdf (accessed 6 May 2008). Aside from territorial sovereignty there may also be issues of indigenous rights and control to consider. See also Al Gedicks, *The New Resource Wars: Native and Environmental Struggles against Multinationals* (Boston, MA: South End Press, 1993): 13–15, 156–60.

Territory may be transferred or acquired in one of several ways but the methods are now restricted by present international law. Some methods are now of completely historical interest and some that are still employed are quite controversial and are reminiscent of the "old international law".

Occupation is one means of territory acquisition. Under this method, a territory that is not controlled by another state is taken over by way of occupation. Up to the 19th century, Europeans denied statehood to territories outside Europe with a few exceptions. Thus, if they did not have the military power to adequately defend themselves, they could be subjugated and their territory occupied by the first European power that moves in that direction. The Permanent Court of International Justice later laid down the constituent ingredients of effective occupation in the *Eastern Greenland Case* as (i) the intention to act as sovereign and (ii) adequate exercise of display of sovereignty.[33] An issue of current relevance regarding this mode of acquisition relates to the contiguity theory advanced by Canada and the USA to claim sectors in the Arctic. In 2008 Russia dramatically staked a claim to parts of the Arctic by planting a flag at the bottom of the sea. The penchant for flag planting by states continued in 2010 when China staked its flag at the bottom of the contentious South China Sea. This theory as well as that of historical ties has traditionally been used to explain situations in which it is not clear exactly how much territory was subject to occupation. It is, however, clear that the theory as well as the maintenance of sector claims over an area increasingly regarded as international commons remains controversial.

Cession is where the possession of certain territory as a sovereign right is conferred by agreement between intending grantor and grantee. Cession may take the form of a treaty, sale, gift exchange or grant provided sovereignty is transferred. A ceding state cannot give more than it has; defects in title as well as servitudes and other rights survive the cession.[34] Spain ceded the Caroline Island to Germany in 1899; France ceded Louisiana to USA in 1803 for 60 million francs and Lombardy to Italy in 1859 gratuitously. In 1902 and 1926 Britain made interval transfers of Ugandan territory to Kenya, then both under British rule. There is no reason to believe that this form of territorial transfer will not remain relevant in the 21st century. Indeed, the right to transfer territory is an attribute of sovereignty. It is, however, clear that if such cession be acquired by duress or force, other rules of international law will operate to nullify it.

Accretion, erosion and avulsion refer to the increase of territory through geographical formations. Thus, in the simple case, deposits on a seacoast may result in an extension of sovereignty. In the case of avulsion, the change comes through sudden, forcible and significant changes in river courses. For this class, no formal acts of

32 Note for instance, that the *terra nullius* doctrine came to be tested and was mentioned directly 16 times in the determination of Singapore's sovereignty over Pedra Branca in the case *Sovereignty over Pedra Branca/Pulau Batu Puteh, Middle Rocks and South Ledge.*

33 Norway–Denmark, PCIJ Ser A/B (1933) No. 53.

34 *Island of Palmas Case* 2 RIAA (1928): 89.

appropriation are required, however, any addition will relate to areas already under effective occupation. Indeed, because of the slow and gradual nature of the process involved it is clear that it is only a matter of time before discussion of this mode returns to relevance in particular cases. For instance, echoes of accretion and avulsion are to be found in the arguments presented before the boundary commission in the *Eritrea–Ethiopia Boundary Dispute Arbitration*, which began in 2000.[35] Where accretion, erosion or avulsion has added to affected territorial extents the effects will occur in a tridimensional manner and increase the airspace of the affected state.

Conquest or annexation is the acquisition of enemy territory after its conquest and a declared intent to annex. For this mode of title to be effective, military conquest is not enough; it must be followed by the *intent to annex*. There must be the declaration or other act of sovereignty by duly authorised and competent persons intended to provide unequivocal evidence of annexation. Italy formally annexed Ethiopia after its conquest in 1936. The Allies expressly disclaimed this act after their victory in the Second World War. Japan, for instance, established total control over Korea through a gradual process that began at the end of the 19th century and accelerated in the early years of the 20th century, leading to the 1905 Protectorate Convention and to the formal annexation in 1910. Questions as to the legality of this under international law divided lawyers for decades as many claimed that the position will have to include examination of both the state of international law at the time at which *these* events took place and international law as exists today.[36] The question will appear to have been well answered by the unequivocal apology made by Japan in 2010. In more recent times Iraq invaded Kuwait for the purposes of annexation in 1990 but UN resolutions and enforcement actions under Chapter VII of the Charter were brought to nullify and correct the illegality. It is perhaps safe to conclude that the current state of international law does not permit the use of this mode of acquisition any longer. As the case of Israeli occupation of Palestinian territories demonstrates, and has been restated in countless UN resolutions, occupation of conquered territory no matter for how

35 Submitted under the aegis of the Permanent Court of Arbitration as a result of the 12 December 2000 Agreement Between the Government of the Federal Democratic Republic of Ethiopia and the Government of the State of Eritrea

36 This raises the problem of "intertemporal law". Jon M. van Dyke, "Reconciliation between Korea and Japan", Vol. 5 *Chinese Journal of International Law*, 1: 215–39. The forcible annexation of the territory of non-European states was never considered "occupation" within the meaning of the laws of occupation (such as under the Hague Regulations of 1907). Indeed, when Asian and African states were annexed by Western imperial powers this was done either on the basis of alleged mutual agreement (for instance, an annexation treaty between local chiefs/kings and the British Empire) or by simple invasion as a matter of gunboat diplomacy. The laws of war were deemed simply inapplicable to colonial conquest. Kingdoms in Uganda were in this way incorporated into the British Empire while the Kingdom of Hawaii was forcibly annexed by the USA. If the same happened in "civilised nations" in Europe, North America or as in Cecile Rhode's South Africa (1899–1901), it was called "occupation", which was governed by laws of war (in particular, laws of occupation). See, further, the powerful critique made by A. Anghie, *Imperialism, Sovereignty and the Making of International Law* (Cambridge: Cambridge University Press, 2004): Chapters 1 and 2.

long cannot confer legitimate title to the occupied territories. Conquest as a mode of acquisition is, therefore, purely of historical value.

Prescription results from peaceful exercise of *de facto* sovereignty for a long time, which either confirms an existing title or extinguishes a prior title. Some jurists express the doubt whether prescription confers a good title. *The Island of Palmas Case*,[37] the *Anglo-Norwegian Fisheries Case*[38] and the *Eastern Greenland* Case[39] are, however, in support of this principle. Prescription was actually used expressly or impliedly to support occupation in these cases. Prescription features strongly in the arguments of Nigeria in its claims over the Bakassi Peninsula although its use in that case was unsuccessful.[40] Johnson stressed, in support of prescription, that the territory must be held under a claim of sovereign title, peacefully, publicly and uninterruptedly for a long time.[41] Fifty years was regarded long enough in the British Guyana–Venezuela dispute.[42]

Renunciation or *relinquishment.* A state may readily relinquish territory or deny continuous or further sovereignty or ownership over it. This may take the form of recognition that another state now has title or recognition of, or agreement to confer, a power of disposition to be exercised by another state or group of states. It is clear that an option open to Israel in the future with regard to the occupied territories under its control is that of renunciation or relinquishment of possession. This may be appropriate in the face of international consensus expressed through widely supported UN Security Council and General Assembly Resolutions, particularly Resolutions 242 of 22 November 1967 and 348 of 22 October 1973, affirming Israel's obligation to withdraw from occupied territories.

Adjudication. The award of a tribunal is certainly a valuable root of title but the award is not of itself dispositive. In other words, the existence of a pre-existing root of title acquired through another mode is presumed.

Abandonment and dereliction is the negative counterpart of effective occupation in that in the face of competing activity and claims by another, a state by conduct or by express admission acquiesces to the extension of its competitor's sovereignty. In very rare situations, a state may intend to abandon as well as formally and expressly renounce its title to a piece of territory.

Discovery whereas mere discovery, i.e. visual apprehension, could not give a valid title, symbolic acts of taking possession could have this result.[43] This mode would seem quite adaptable to the realities of outer space exploration. In practice,

37 op. cit.: 829.

38 ICJ Rep (1951) 116.

39 PCIJ Ser. A/B (1933) No. 53.

40 *Land and Maritime Boundary between Cameroon and Nigeria (Cameroon v. Nigeria)*, paras 64, 68 , 70, 219, 223. Judgments, cases and materials of the ICJ are available at www.icj.org.

41 D.H.N. Johnson, "Acquisitive Prescription", *British Yearbook of International Law* (1950): 345. Johnson identifies four conditions that must be present for acquisitive prescription to operate: the possession of the prescribing state must be exercised *à titre de souverain*; the possession must be peaceful and uninterrupted; the possession must be public; the possession must endure for a certain length of time. See pp. 343–8.

42 Britain–USA 89 BFSP (1896) 57.

43 Brownlie op. cit.: 127.

discovery may be accompanied by symbolic acts such as the planting of a flag. The Americans actually did plant their flag on the moon but according to present day international law that does not give them title to the moon. It may be suggested, therefore, that flag-planting exercises may have lost their potency as proof of occupation or first landing as it may have had in antiquity. Today it appears to serve no more a value than love for the "motherland".

Papal grant was recognised in the 15th century. In this instance, the Pope had power to grant or transfer territory. This mode of title is clearly obsolete in modern times and its return to relevance is so highly unlikely as to be considered impossible.

It must be noted that international law no longer confines itself to regulating state territory. The notion of territory today encompasses state territory, sea territories, Antarctic territories, polar territories, outer space territories, orbital territories, lunar territories and so on. Some of these territories fall under the jurisdiction and sovereignty of states, while others come under the category of "international spaces". The unifying factor is that all are subject to international law. The emerging concept of common heritage of mankind along with other formulas, such as the province of mankind, operate to prevent many of the traditional modes of acquisition from operating in relation to the high seas Antarctica and outer space. While there are useful analogies, some of the traditional modes such as conquest and occupation, stand rather more as a warning of how the law must not be allowed to develop than otherwise.

Orthodox analysis, indeed, does not account for the full range of interaction between the various categories of territorial acquisition. There is always the danger of doctrinal confusion over the modes of acquisition, which may lead to miscarriage of justice in present and future international territorial adjudication. This is more so when the question relates to any of the newer and common territories in Antarctica, polar regions and, within very strict legal limits, outer space. Therefore, lawyers must remain knowledgeable on the older categories. By the same token, a rigid attachment to the classic "models" as legally unrelated or incompatible may lead to unhappy conclusions. In fact, the issue of territorial sovereignty or title over territory is by its very nature complex and involves the application of various principles of law, both historical and modern. The process of reconciling them cannot be ascribed to any single dominant rule or mode of territorial acquisition. Disputes arising from the various means of territorial acquisition are not entirely unlikely to repeat themselves, even if in new and novel contexts such as in Antarctica and outer space.

It must be stated that there is no rule that state territory must at all times be contiguous and there have indeed been many cases of small and large non-contiguous sovereign territory. The territorial state in such instances will enjoy the full complements of coterminous territorial jurisdiction. This was certainly true of Germany's right over East Prussia (1919–1945), East and West Pakistan before 1971 and of US territory of Alaska. Fragmentation may be an indication of other debilitating disability but it is not determinative of statehood. Neither does fragmentation affect the full complements of the tridimensional nature of territory. As aptly summed up by Crawford: "Sovereignty comes in all shapes and sizes."[44]

1.2 Delimitation and demarcation of international territories

One of the central questions this book aims to address is that of the lack of demarcation in law and practice between airspace and outer space. It is a fortunate fact that few international territories share this lack of specificity. Delimitation of territory or territorial spheres is indeed one of the determinative characteristics of human societies. Even where territory is indeterminate as to its precise extents it is still important that firm ideas as to the juridical arrangement that governs the territory. Literarily hundreds of bilateral and multilateral treaties and legal instruments govern the maritime, oceanic, Antarctic, air and outer spaces. It is arguable that these were developed both in response to practical necessity of regulating activities in these areas as well as in response to a primordial legal instinct that is shared among all human civilisations which dictates delimitation and demarcation of territory. The legal instinct to delimit and demarcate is so strong that to ignore its imperative nature will be to completely disregard the impetus for much of the occurrence of international behaviour as practised within the overarching scope of sovereignty and jurisdiction. Sophisticated legal regimes both of a domestic and international nature may become near meaningless wherever doubt exist as to precise geographical boundaries and territorial extents on the occurrence of certain events.

Differentiated regimes within singular environments based on geographical or geological features are also observable human necessities. Hence the significant differences about what is permissible or impermissible within certain distances and strata of the seas, Arctic and Antarctic regions, aerial or cosmic territories. These sometimes rigid, sometimes fluid sets of complementary or contradictory areas/regimes of differentiation are some of the most fundamental principles permitting the human enterprise to be in motion and in constant progressive interaction. The precise place of occurrence of an event such as plane crash, sea collision or space accident may be dramatically significant in terms of legal consequences both in public and private international law. The position of a ship, vehicle, aircraft or aerospace object at the time of an incident may have international effects or produce effects only in relation to the laws of a single state or both. For instance, one of the issues that arose in the US TWA 800 crash in the ocean near Long Island in 1996 was the effects of the precise place the aircraft crashed on the right of the passengers to compensation.[45] As described in the US House Report, *Non-applicability of Death on the High Seas Act to Aviation Incidents*:

44 James Crawford, *The Creation of States in International Law*, 2nd edn (Oxford: Clarendon Press, 2007): 47. States like São Tomé and Principe consist of many small land areas separated by vast amounts of maritime territory.

45 Following the decision of the US Supreme Court in *Zicherman v. Korean Airlines* 116 S Ct 629 (1996). It was clear that the family of a deceased passenger could receive payments in damages for the wages that the person would have received but not for the pain and any suffering of that person or for the loss of companionship of loved ones due to the applicability of the Death on the High Seas Act (DOHSA) 46 USC 761. DOHSA applies to lawsuits that arise out of an aircraft crash in the ocean more than a marine league (about three miles) from land. The effect of this decision is

> Given the nature and speed of air travel, it is often as matter of happenstance as to where an aircraft crashes. The result is that a family's rights under the law depend on pure chance. At the Subcommittee's hearing on the issue, parents noted that where DOHSA applied, the life of their child was made to appear practically worthless in the eyes of the law.[46]

Suffice to state at this point that agreement about delimitation and demarcation (where it is physically possible) of international territories is very rarely achieved without serious disagreement and the process is usually fraught with politics. Yet, as we shall show later, impressive progress and final delimitation has been achieved in many zones of international importance including international land boundaries, maritime zones and in the law of the seas. The precise reasons why agreement is fraught with difficulties in relation to the airspace and outer space will be dealt with later in this book.

1.3 The principle of territorial sovereignty

Territorial sovereignty and jurisdiction are the very basic tools on which any realistic understanding of the relationship between a state and a territory may be expressed. This is more so where a state seeks to exercise any powers of ownership or exercise any form of public control. One of the fundamental differences between air law and space law is that, in the former, a state possesses absolute and exclusive sovereignty over its airspace whereas, in the latter, national appropriation by claim

to treat families very differently depending on whether the relative died in an aircraft that crashed into the ocean (and further than three nautical miles) or one that crashed into land. If an aircraft crashes into the land or within three miles from land the family can successfully claim non-pecuniary damages. If, however, the aircraft crashed into the ocean the family can only claim pecuniary damages.

46 William Shuster, *Non-applicability of Death on the High Seas Act to Aviation Incidents*, HR Rep. No. 105-201, at 2–3 (1997), available at http://www.thomas.gov/cgi-bin/cpquery/T?&report=hr201&dbname=105& (accessed 10 November 2010). The Commercial Aviation Exception was enacted by Congress as an amendment to the DOHSA in response to the TWA flight 800 crash and others like it and it changed the law to allow a recovery of loss of companionship – non-pecuniary damages in the case of commercial aviation disasters. For a comprehensive treatment of this legislative response, see Stephen R. Ginger, "DOHSA's Commercial Aviation Exception: How Mass Airline Disasters Influenced Congress on Compensation for Deaths on the High Seas", 75 *Journal of Air Law and Commerce* 1 (2010): 148–152, 160. Furthermore, in *Alleman v. Omni Energy Services Corp.*, the Fifth Circuit held that the Outer Continental Shelf Lands Act (OCLSA), rather than the DOHSA, applied. In December 2004 the defendant's helicopter crashed into the Gulf of Mexico while trying to land on an offshore oil platform but negligent storage on the helipad caused a manoeuvre that led into the helicopter's skidding into the water leading to the eventual death of a passenger. The fact that the injury could have occurred on the OCSLA-governed platform was determinative, in spite of the fact that further injuries and death actually occurred in the water governed by DOHSA. Amy Cawthon Bellah, "Jurisdiction – Determining the Line between OCSLA and DOSHA – in an Already Murky Area of the Law, the Fifth Circuit Leaves Open More Questions than Answers", 75, *Journal of Air Law and Commerce* 1 (2010): 181, 187.

of sovereignty over outer space is prohibited. Importantly, however, jurisdiction as a legal term applies both to the airspace and outer space. This necessitates an examination of these two concepts with a view to distinguishing their applicability in various situations in international law.

Sovereignty in law is often considered to be the essence of the state. It explains the powers of a state over its entire territories and its inhabitants. The normal complements of state rights, including the typical case of legal competence, are described commonly as sovereignty.[47] The concept is political in conception and is popularly symbolised by the Leviathan of Hobbes. It implies the supreme authority of a state, which recognises no higher authority in the region.[48] Bodin developed the concept in terms of internal strength and external limitation of power.[49] Jowitt picks up on this theme and defines sovereignty as: "[t]he power in a state to which none other is superior".[50] As the respected jurist Max Huber wrote in his opinion in the Island of Palmas Arbitration between the USA and the Netherlands: "[S]overeignty in the relations between states signifies independence. Independence in regards to a portion of the globe is the right to exercise therein to the exclusion of any other the functions of a state."[51] The connection between sovereignty and jurisdiction is, thus, so strong that the term "sovereignty" is sometimes used in place of "independence" as a basic criterion of statehood. However, sovereignty is said to have another more satisfactory meaning as an incident or consequence of statehood, namely, the plenary competence that states, *prima facie*, possess. Crawford impressively draws the conclusion that since the two meanings are distinct it is better to use the term "independence" to denote the prerequisite for statehood and "sovereignty" the legal incident.[52] Accordingly , one of the senses of the term sovereign is that which indicates plenary authority with respect to internal or external affairs. This view also helpfully clarifies that plenary authority is not in all cases coterminous with independence. Thus, Cyprus under *its* 1960 constitution was an independent state but it was not sovereign. This is because the pertinent constitution left a significant number of important powers and competences beyond the state's powers.[53] Sovereignty in essence refers to the "supreme authority and control over policy" within any delimited political space.[54]

47 Ian Brownlie, *Principles of Public International Law* (Oxford: Clarendon Press, 1998): 106.

48 G.S. Sachdeva, "Sovereignty in the Air – A Legal Perspective", 22 *Indian Journal of International Law* (1982): 398.

49 Imre Anthony Csbaffi, *The Concept of the State Jurisdiction in International Space Law: A Study in the Development of Space Law in the United Nations* (The Hague: Martinus Nijhoff, 1971): 50.

50 *Jowitts Dictionary of English Law*, 2nd edn, Vol. 2, ed. John Burke (London: Sweet & Maxwell, 1977): 1678.

51 *Island of Palmas Case* (1928) RIAA: 2829.

52 Crawford (2007) op. cit.: 89. The distinction between sovereignty and independence was carefully maintained by C. Rousseau, "Independance de l'Etat dans l'Ordre Internationale", 73 *HR* (1948): 171.

53 Crawford (2007) op. cit.: 89.

54 Kal Raustiala, "Rethinking the Sovereignty Debate in International Economic Law", 6 *Journal of International Economic Law* (2003): 852.

In modern literature, the term sovereignty has been employed in four different ways, which do not necessarily overlap in the sense that a state can have one and not necessarily the other. They are, namely, international legal sovereignty, Westphalian sovereignty, domestic sovereignty and interdependence sovereignty. Reference to international legal sovereignty denotes the practices that are associated with mutual recognition, usually between territorial entities that possess formal juridical independence. Westphalian sovereignty refers to political organisation, which is based on the exclusion of external actors from authority structures within a specific territory. Domestic sovereignty explains the ability of a state to exercise effective control within its territory and the competence to construct formal organisation of political authority within the polity. Finally, interdependence sovereignty is used in reference to the ability of public authorities to regulate the flow of information, ideas, goods people, pollutants or capital across the borders of their state.[55]

The principle of sovereignty is also embodied in various important treaties. Article 2(1) of the UN Charter gives effect to the concept.[56] It is further elaborated on in the provisions of the 1970 UN General Assembly Declaration on Principles of International Law concerning Friendly Relations and Co-operation among States in accordance with the Charter of the United Nations, as follows: "All states enjoy sovereign equality . . . Each state enjoys the right inherent in full sovereignty."[57] However, Schwarzenberger rightly describes this emphasis on complete independence as negative sovereignty. Negative sovereignty means non-recognition of any superior authority. On the level of legal relations, this situation may be expressed in terms of a right, or freedom, not to have to recognise any superior.[58] The hypothesis of negative sovereignty to date offers a particular attraction to those elements in the nation state that prefer the absence of limitations on the options and actions that may be open to independent states generally but particularly in international matters. This is probably what is reflected in the commentary:

55 International legal sovereignty and Westphalian sovereignty centre on issues of legitimacy and authority but exclude control. However, they are both based on what Krasner calls "certain distinct rules or logic of appropriateness". The rule for international legal sovereignty is that recognition is extended to territorial entities that possess formal juridical independence, while the rule for Westphalian sovereignty is the exclusion of external actors, both *de facto* and *de jure*, from state territory. Domestic sovereignty, by way of contrast, involves both authority and control in the sense that it encompasses the specification of legitimate authority within a given state and the extent to which that authority may be exercised. Interdependence sovereignty is concerned exclusively with control and not authority as it explains the inherent capacity of the state to regulate movements across its borders. See Stephen D. Krasner, *Sovereignty: Organised Hypocrisy* (Princeton, NJ: Princeton University Press, 1999): 3–4.

56 It reads thus: "The Organization is based on the principle of the *sovereign* equality of all its Members." Charter of the United Nations San Francisco, 26 June 1945, in force 24 October 1945. Documents on the UN Conference on International Organisation, Vol. 15: 336.

57 Adopted by resolution 2625 (XXV) of 24 October 1970. See UNGA Official Records: Twenty-Fifth Sess., Supp. No. 28 (A/8028).

58 G. Schwarzenberger, "The Forms of Sovereignty", Vol. 10 *Current Legal Problems* (1957): 264.

> [M]ost (but not all) of the time that "sovereignty" is used in current policy debates, it actually refers to questions about the allocation of power; normally "government decision-making power". That is, when someone argues that the United States should not accept a treaty because that treaty infringes upon U.S. sovereignty, what the person most often means is that he or she believes a certain set of decisions should be made, as a matter of good governmental policy, at the nation-state (U.S.) level, and not at the international level.[59]

It is indeed true that the limitation of sovereignty to its absolute extreme is as little justified as the attribution of a necessarily absolute character to any other notion. In fact, "the very contrast of sovereignty of God with any form of worldly sovereignty powers proves sufficiently the necessarily relative character of any type of sovereignty claimed by a temporal authority".[60] The dictates of our modern-day international society seem to incline towards interdependence of states more than undue exercise of sovereign powers.

On another level of legal relations, a complete lack of sovereignty over a territory or environment may be dictated by international law. For instance, Article 137 of the Convention on the Law of the Sea 1982[61] states that no state shall claim or exercise sovereignty or sovereign rights over any part of the area or its resources, neither shall any state or natural juridical person appropriate any part thereof. Thus, while older writers such as Schwarzenberger speak of *negative sovereignty* in terms of absolute and complete independence, modern-day international law is popularly regarded as actually moving in the direction of *negativing* sovereignty. However, wherever sovereignty cannot be exercised, jurisdiction is not excluded. It is a trite observation that in as much as sovereignty remains an abstraction, serious impact has been made on the principle by a host of factors in the modern-day international society. Thus, international lawyers are beginning to speak more in terms of "globalisation". This term was, until fairly recently, unknown to international law but it may, in fact, be argued that it is a natural consequence of the development of that body of law itself. The clear impression wherever we look is that the omnipotent nature of sovereignty is in recession. Whether the focus is on human rights, exchange rates, monetary policy, arms control, chemical weapons, landmines, warfare, environmental control or minority rights, the policy options open to states in any real sense have become increasingly constrained. Challenges to the traditional international law system of sovereignty can be seen in increases in depth and density of rules promulgated by intergovernmental organisations. These organisations are becoming more assertive vis-à-vis individual sovereign states both in rule making and in implementation. National courts, administrative agencies and perhaps even parliamentary bodies are said increasingly to function

59 John Jackson, "Sovereignty-Modern: A New Approach to an Outdated Concept", *American Journal of International Law* 97, 3 (October 2003): 782–802.

60 Schwarzenberger op. cit.: 276.

61 UN Doc. A/CONF. 62/122 (1982) 21 ILM 1261.

as parts of cooperative regulatory and enforcement transgovernmental networks and no longer simply as parochial national institutions.[62]

Some authors, however, present a very persuasive argument that the very interconnectedness of sovereignties rather than weakening the concept actually strengthens it. This is because the exercise of such authority and control in a world that has become so interconnected that people, politics, and pathogens are virtually able to disregard borders requires institutionalised cooperation and intervention. The institutionalisation of cooperation and coordination, therefore, makes each sovereign stronger in its effective reach over its nationals and even foreign nationals under legitimate circumstances and situations. Hence, Raustiala claims, international institutions "actually serve as a means to reassert sovereignty".[63] Organisations such as the United Nations, *a fortiori*, are "sovereignty-strengthening institutions" and fit neatly into what Chayes and Chayes and Marie Slaughter ascribe the notion of "the new sovereignty".[64] This new sovereignty describes the right and the capacity to participate in international institutions that allow their members, working together, to accomplish ends that individual governments alone could once never hope to accomplish.

The end of the territorial state as predicted has not materialised and is unlikely to do so. Indeed, the idea of an end to territorial sovereignty has not been unchallenged in literature.[65] A writer persuasively opines of the so-called decline of political sovereignty: "[E]ven if globalisation and European integration might

62 See Phillip Alston, "The Myopia of the Handmaidens: International Lawyers and Globalisation", *European Journal of International Law* 3 (1997): 435. See also Benedict Kingsbury, "Sovereignty and Inequality", 9 *European Journal of International Law* 4 (1998): 611. Other authors such as Krasner believe that international legal sovereignty and Westphalian concepts of sovereignty have always been characterised by "organised hypocrisy". He agrees with the mainstream view, that with changes to the basic nature of the international system, the scope of activities over which states can effectively exercise control is declining. These include atmospheric pollution, terrorism, the drug trade, currency crisis and the acquired immunodeficiency syndrome (AIDS). He notes, for instance, that technological changes have drastically reduced the costs of transportation and communication, which, in turn, has prompted independent states to enter into conventions and contracts (a manifestation of international legal sovereignty), some of which have led to a compromise of their Westphalian sovereignty by establishing external authority structures such as international institutions. He thinks, however, that contemporary scholars are overstating the newness of globalisation in that: "Rulers have always operated in a transnational environment; autarky has rarely been an option; regulation and monitoring of transborder flows have always been problematic . . . There is no evidence that globalisation has systematically undermined state control or led to the homogenisation of policies and structures. In fact, globalisation and state activity have moved in tandem." Krasner op. cit.: 12, 222–3.

63 Kal Raustiala, "Rethinking the Sovereignty Debate in International Economic Law", 6 *Journal of International Economic Law* (2003): 842.

64 Anne-Marie Slaughter, "Security, Solidarity, and Sovereignty: The Grand Themes of UN Reform", 99 *American Journal of International Law* (2005): 629. See, generally, Abram Chayes and Antonia Handler Chayes, *The New Sovereignty: Compliance with International Regulating Agreements* (Cambridge, MA: Harvard University Press, 1995).

65 Scholars who attest to the continuous relevance of sovereignty over territory in its old sense include: P.Q. Hirst and G. Thompson, *Globalisation in Question: The International Economy and the Possibilities of*

conceivably have reduced the importance of proximity as never before, this in itself does not mean that territory has lost its significance in politics."[66]

International law and international relations would, therefore, for the foreseeable future continue to ascribe the force of law to territorial sovereignty and the strict determination of territorial extents will also remain relevant. Accordingly a theorist persuasively concludes:

> It does not make much sense to speak about de-territorialisation (territory matters less) or territorialisation (territories matters more) in a general imprecise way. The intricate and complex reconfigurations and reconceptualisations of political relations within states, regions and evolving Euro-polity merely allow us to utilise the concept of reterritorialisation (territory matters differently). The important point here is to emphasise that territory always matters somehow in some way.[67]

It appears, therefore, that the death knell has not been sounded on the doctrine of state sovereignty. Sovereignty remains a crucial element in today's world and its manifestation remains particularly relevant within the airspace. Conceptualisation of sovereignty is definitely not a zero-sum game. What a state loses in one respect in the exercise of its sovereignty it obviously gains in some other respect. For instance, the *Lockerbie Case* shows that the reach of state power to deal with the perpetrators of aerial crimes is becoming more formidable even as we lament the decline of sovereignty.[68] This paradox is aptly captured in the interesting submission

Governance (Cambridge: Polity Press, 1995) and M. Keating, *The New Regionalism in Western Europe: Territorial Restructuring and Political Change* (Cheltenham: Edward Elgar, 1998).

66 C. Ansell, "Territoriality, Authority and Democracy" in C. Ansell and G. Di Palma (eds) *Restructuring Territoriality: Europe and the United States Compared* (Cambridge: Cambridge University Press, 2004): 225–45). In other words, the relevance of territory and territoriality in Europe has not necessarily anything to do with the uniquely progressive regionalism that take place among the participating European state. See also Michael Burgess and Hans Vollaard, "Analysing Westphalian States in an Integrating Europe and Globalising World" in *State Territoriality and European Integration* (Oxford: Routledge, 2006): 3–4.

67 Burgess and Vollaard op. cit.: 7.

68 Questions of Interpretation and Application of the 1971 Montreal Convention arising from the Aerial Incident at Lockerbie (*Libyan Arab Jamahiriya v. United Kingdom*) (*Libyan Arab Jamahiriya v. United States of America*). On 3 March 1992 Libya filed two applications in the registry of the World Court instituting proceedings against the United Kingdom and the United States of America concerning disputes on the interpretation or application of the Convention for the Suppression of Unlawful Acts against the Safety of Civil Aviation signed in Montreal on 23 September 1971. Libya referred to charges made by the Lord Advocate of Scotland and an American Grand Jury against two Libyan nationals suspected of having caused the destruction of Pan-Am flight 103 over the town of Lockerbie, Scotland, on 21 December 1988, in which 270 people died. Following these charges, the United Kingdom and the United States had demanded that Libya surrender the suspects for trial in either Scotland or in the United States. The Security Council of the United Nations subsequently adopted three resolutions (731, 748 and 883, two of which imposed sanctions) urging Libya "to provide a full and effective response" to the requests of the United Kingdom and the United States "so as to contribute to the elimination of international terrorism").

of a text writer who wrote that sovereignty should not be thought of: "[A]s the object of some kind of zero sum game, such that the moment x loses it y necessarily has it. Let us think of it rather more as of virginity, which can in at least some circumstances be lost to the general satisfaction without anybody else gaining it."[69]

1.3.1 Sovereignty and property rights

It may be of crucial importance to other states and international actors to be able to ascertain beyond doubt when a state does or does not possess the necessary quality of sovereignty over a piece of territory. On this certainty may lie significant consequences for the legality of actions by other states.[70] Investors and multinationals would need to be sure about the right to territory as this may affect their economic fortunes especially where issues of energy exploitation over the piece of land or maritime territory is involved.[71]

It is important to realise that international law maintains a distinction between rights of sovereignty and property rights. International courts have always made it clear that the latter do not always include the former. Hence a sovereign power may allow a land grant in favour of another state or corporation for the sole purpose of erecting a lighthouse,[72] a base,[73] farmland[74] or for scientific research without

After a protracted case, the parties agreed to a novel procedure, which is a significant victory for the long arms of national courts. This witnessed the transfer to the Netherlands, for trial by a Scottish court, of the two Libyan nationals suspected of having caused the Lockerbie incident. See also *infra*, Chapter 3.

69 Alston op. cit.: 435, note 4. For further discussions on the shrinking of the concept of sovereignty in modern day international relations, see Neil MacCormick, "Beyond the Sovereign State", 56 *Modern Law Review* (1993): 1 at 16; Walter B. Wriston, *The Twilight Of Sovereignty: How the Information Revolution is Transforming Our World* (New York: Maxwell Macmillan International, 1992); J.-M. Guehenno, *The End of the Nation State* (Minneapolis: University of Minnesota Press, 1995): 435.

70 Such as the contribution of forces by member states of the UN with regards to enforcement action against Iraq during its invasion of Kuwait.

71 Chayes and Chayes op. cit.: 4.

72 Witness the Pulau Pisang island arrangement memorialised in 1885 and backed with a 1900 indenture between the Sultan of Johor and the Governor of the Straits Settlements (British authority), which allowed the construction and operation of a lighthouse without transfer of sovereignty over the island. See *Sovereignty over Pedra Branca/Pulau Batu Puteh, Middle Rocks and South Ledge Case* (*Malaysia/Singapore* para. 141).

73 A controversial example of the grant of a dominium territory to another state may be found in the emptying and "unpeopling" of the Chagos Island by the UK, in favour of the creation of US military bases. Judicial assent for this grant appears to have been given in *R (on the Application of Bancoult) v. Secretary of State for the Foreign and Commonwealth Office* [2001] QB 1067, wherein it was stated that: "It is unarguable that the purposes of the BIOT Order and the Ordinance were to facilitate the use of Diego Garcia as a strategic military base and to restrict the use and occupation of that and the other islands within the territory to the extent necessary to ensure the effectiveness and security of the base." Those purposes were (or could at least reasonably be described as) of great benefit to the United Kingdom and the Western powers as a whole. Criticisms of this instance have been raised elsewhere based on possible violations of the principles expressed in Articles 8 and 13 of the Universal Declaration of Human Rights (GA Res. 217A (III), UN Doc. A/810 at 71, adopted 10 December 1948) as well as the provisions of the Magna Carta. See, further, G.

parting with sovereignty. Conversely, the existence of property rights over a base or installation *simplicta* may not confer sovereignty over the territory over which such property or feature may be situated. A state may thus, have real property or a *res* situated in another state or over a *res* or specified station in a place belonging to no state and/or incapable of belonging to any sovereign (such as outer space) without having any sovereignty over the place itself. But it is clear that a lot depends on the intention of the parties to such arrangement as made manifest by any treaties between them and the surrounding circumstances.[75] In this case, states ought to address their minds to the gravity of the matter when dealing with territorial arrangements between themselves. This is also the case even with corporate interests (since the issue of diplomatic protection may arise) such as in the grant of extensive farming land to foreign corporations or the operation of foreign airbases or military camps. The International Court of Justice, indeed, considers that the "the intention to acquire sovereignty may appear from the conduct of the Parties, particularly conduct occurring over a long period".[76]

There are two modes by which a state could acquire derivative title. First, title may be derived through the tacit agreement that may arise from or be reflected in the conduct of the parties. Second, title may pass onto a state as a result of the failure of the one state to respond to conduct *à titre de souverain* of the other where also such failure to respond amount to behaviour that the other state may interpret as consent.[77] Judge Huber concluded, in the *Island of Palmas Case*, that ignoring concrete manifestations of the display of territorial sovereignty by another state may become opposable to the state that latter claims to have originally possessed sovereignty.[78] The absence of reaction may well amount to acquiescence. In other words, the concept of acquiescence "is equivalent to tacit recognition manifested by unilateral conduct which the other party may interpret as consent" (*Delimitation*

Oduntan, "International Laws and the Discontented: How the West Underdeveloped International Laws" in Archana Parashar and Amita Dhanda (eds), *Decolonisation of Knowledge: Whose Responsibility?* (London: Routledge, 2009): 116.

74 Gulf states have in recent years spearheaded the lease of territory abroad for agricultural purposes. The lessee states and their private bodies have increased efforts to buy or lease land in developing nations such as Tanzania to secure food supplies and minimise the impact of food inflation. Africa News Network, "Gulf Firm seeks Long-term Lease on Tanzanian Farmland", available at http://www.africanagricultureblog.com/2010/01/gulf-firm-seeks-long-term-lease-on.html (accessed 5 September 2010); Friends of the Earth, "Africa: Up for Grabs", available at http://farmlandgrab.org/ 15110 (accessed 5 September 2010).

75 Hence in the *Sovereignty over Pedra Branca/Pulau Batu Puteh, Middle Rocks and South Ledge Case*, the court was unable to determine whether the Sultan of Johor had, in 1844, ceded sovereignty over Pedra Branca because there was no clear and formalised documentation witnessing this (see para. 148). Surrounding circumstances are important but they may be confusing. As the court said in this case: "Symbolic acts accompanying the acquisition of territory are very common both generally and in British practice. They are not however always present" (para. 149).

76 *Sovereignty over Pedra Branca/Pulau Batu Puteh, Middle Rocks and South Ledge*, para. 149.

77 Ibid, paras 120–1.

78 *Island of Palmas Case (Netherlands/United States of America)*, award of 4 April 1928, RIAA, Vol. II: 839.

of the Maritime Boundary in the Gulf of Maine Area (Canada/United States of America), Judgment, ICJ Reports 1984, p. 305, para. 130). In the view of the World Court, "silence may also speak, but only if the conduct of the other State calls for a response".[79]

The significance of these judicial authorities go well beyond contests over state territory but can extend to territory that is unconnected to the state but over which a state claims sovereignty. In this way, it is clear that sovereign maritime territory and far flung islands are included within the rule. The extent to which the rule applies to Antarctic and polar territories will be considered controversial depending on the validity of the territorial claim under international law in the first instance. The tridimensionality of state territory must be borne in mind when considering the extent of the state that may become affected by conduct *à titre de souverain*. Thus, continuous use of sovereign parts of the airspace without permission that is not responded to may amount to ignoring concrete manifestations of the display of territorial sovereignty. This is perhaps why the issue of legal response to trespass over airspace remains a lively area of international relations (see Appendices II and III). Although the question will be of scant relevance in relation to outer space territories it may nevertheless be pointed out that in the near future, conduct in the specified areas of scientific operations on celestial bodies and/or space stations may also require response to prevent usurpation of authority and jurisdiction but not sovereignty since contemporary international law does not recognise state sovereignty over outer space or parts thereof.

The requirement for vigilance in the maintenance of territorial integrity is based on the fact that most states retain the right to determine their territorial extent and the declaration of sovereignty over territory may not, in fact, be based on contiguity. Whereas international law has not expressly defined what is territorial airspace to any satisfactory extent, it does provide a clear treaty-based explanation of what the territorial sea is in the Law of the Sea Convention. Despite this fact, it belongs, in the first instance, to each state, the right to assert its territorial extent on which calculations of airspace territory or territorial waters delimitation may be derived. Hence, it was decided per Lord Parker CJ:

> I have come to the conclusion that, in the absence of any definition of "territorial waters" the expression in the Act of 1949 [Wireless Telegraphy Act 1949] must be read as meaning "territorial waters from time to time"; and rather than to say that the determination is governed by international law, I would prefer to say that it was governed by declarations of sovereignty from time to time by the Crown.[80]

79 *Sovereignty over Pedra Branca/Pulau Batu Puteh, Middle Rocks and South Ledge*, para. 121.

80 *R v. Kent JJ, ex p. Lye* [1967] 1 All ER 560, at 564, 565. See, further, the definition of territorial waters provided in John B. Saunders, *Words and Phrases Legally Defined*, Vol. 5 (London: Butterworths, 1970).

Eternal vigilance is, therefore, the mantra of custodians of territorial sovereignty and those charged with the maintenance of territorial integrity. They must within the legitimate exercise of international law based, inter alia, on treaties, agreements, customary practice, the result of international adjudication and negotiations determine their territorial extents and assert their territorial integrity from any or all competing claims. This is true of all forms of territory, whether subterranean, terrestrial or aerial, including the legitimately held dominions of the nation state.

1.3.2 Spatial dynamics of sovereign equality

A manifestation of state sovereignty of great relevance in the discussion of airspace and outer space is the concept of sovereign equality. International law operates on the principle that each sovereign has absolute power and control over all persons biological or juridical within its territory; it therefore follows that relationships of dominance, subjugation or subordinations cannot be allowed legitimately to exist between independent states.[81] The regime created by the United Nations charter post the Second World War is supportive of this principle of equality of sovereign state and remains one of the most closely guarded devices of international law and relations to date. The principle functions on the basis of Article 2 (7) of the UN Charter:

> Nothing contained in the present Charter shall authorize the United Nations to intervene in matters which are essentially within the domestic jurisdiction of any state or shall require the Members to submit such matters to settlement under the present Charter; but this principle shall not prejudice the application of enforcement measures under Chapter VII.

At face value this appears not to address rights over territory or territorial integrity but this provision does much more than that because it grants states the autonomy to utilise their territory in a manner that prevents other states from interfering with their ability to take actions or undertake activities in their national interests within their own territory as well as in non-sovereign spaces to which they have access under applicable international laws. It is in this latter sense that developing states particularly assert the importance of the need to secure international agreement on the spatial demarcation boundary plane between airspace and outer space as well as equitable international regimes over Antarctica, the high seabed and Arctic territories that are beyond national sovereignty.

In terms of spatial territory, the equality principle is useful in two ways. First, it delimits appropriately the territorial airspace in which national domestic jurisdiction operates. Second, it identifies the outer space in which sovereign states and, increasingly, their corporate nationals can participate in space activities on an equal

81 Wade Mansell, Belina Meteyard and Alan Thompson, *A Critical Introduction to Law*, 2nd edn (London: Cavendish, 1999): 139.

basis. It may be fair to note that, as one of the significant features of modern international law is that it limits sovereign power because it ensures that "the people whom sovereignty protects" are not entirely left "at the mercy of the internal acts and politics" of their sovereign without protection of other sovereigns under international law, it also increases the power of sovereigns by allowing the territorial sovereign to participate in the discovery exploration and exploitation of newer territories with other states on an equal basis and with peaceful means in ways that would have been completely unimaginable to the sovereign of as recent a time in world history as a mere century ago.[82]

In accordance with the equality principle, a state may not use coercive power to enforce its rules outside its territory. As Ryngaert notes, stating the contrary would mean shattering the sacrosanct principle of sovereign equality of nations. Neither may a state legitimately use military force to compel another state to abide by its laws.[83] When the so-called Allied nations imposed no-fly zones over Iraq, they were not claiming to do so in Iraqi airspace so as to implement or impose their own national laws but purported to be acting in furtherance of international laws, including possibly UN Security Council resolutions.[84]

1.4 The principles of territorial jurisdiction and territorial integrity

Many writers have attested to the difficulties of defining "jurisdiction".[85] One writer put it quite perplexedly: "what is certain is that jurisdiction somehow relates to sovereignty". In a world composed of equally sovereign states, any state is entitled

82 See H.G. Maier, "Jurisdictional Rules in Customary International Law" in K.M. Meessen (ed.), *Extraterritorial Jurisdiction in Theory and Practice* (The Hague: Kluwer Law International, 1996): 64, 66; Cedric Ryngaert, *Jurisdiction in International Law* (Oxford: Oxford University Press, 2008): 25. See also our discussion later in this volume.

83 Ryngaert ibid: 23. Note *Alvarez-Machain v. United States*, 331 F 3d 604 (9th Cir 2003). When the United States justified its abduction of the *Alvarez* in Mexico pursuant to its alleged authority to apply US criminal laws albeit extraterritorially and under the Controlled Substances Act, 21 USC § 878(a)(3), the Ninth Circuit disapproved of the argument and stated that the US Congress did not authorise US agents and agencies to embark on the unilateral, extraterritorial enforcement of the provisions relied on in foreign countries. Hence it was held that "[e]xtraterritorial application, in other words, does not automatically give rise to extraterritorial enforcement authority".

84 The Secretary of State for Defence Geoff Hoon, in the House of Commons (Hansard, 26 February 2001), betrayed the difficulties attesting these arguments when he strenuously argued: "The legal justification for the patrolling of the no-fly zones does not rest on Security Council Resolution 688. That has not been the government's position. In terms of humanitarian justification, we are entitled to patrol the no-fly zones to prevent a grave humanitarian crisis. That is the legal justification in international law. It does not rest on Resolution 688, although that Resolution supports the position we have adopted." HC Deb, 26 February 2001, Vol. 363, cc 620-34. See also submission of the Ministry of Defence Ministry of Defence of 6th November 2009 before the Iran inquiry available at http://www.iraqinquiry.org.uk/media/38010/mod-no-fly-zone-r1.pdf (accessed 2 October 2010).

85 Ryngaert op. cit.: 5; B.J. George, "Extraterritorial Application of Penal Legislation", 64 *Michigan Law Review* (1966): 609, 621.

to give shape to its sovereignty or *imperium* by adopting laws,[86] and to perform *ius dicere* functions (i.e. to state what the law is relating to persons, activities, or legal interests).[87] Jurisdiction, therefore, becomes not only a concern of international law but also perhaps the very basis on which international law is practised and realised. Furthermore, because it denotes the authority to affect legal interests, jurisdiction is also one of the most important basis on which all international activities, no matter where conducted, are to be tested.[88]

The doctrine of jurisdiction emerged in the 17th century from the concepts of sovereignty and territoriality. Its development led through *statute theory* to the *Huber Storyan maxim* and it became established in the 19th century.[89] Jurisdiction in a strict legal sense denotes the particular rights or accumulations of rights quantitatively less than the norm, which the omnibus term of sovereignty covers. In other words, while the term "sovereignty" covers the total legal personality of a state, jurisdiction refers to particular aspects of the substance, especially rights (or claims), liberties and powers.[90] Thus, jurisdiction is the authority a state exercises over natural and juristic persons and property within it. It mainly concerns the exercise of this power on a state territory or quasi-territory; however, some states exercise a measure of their jurisdiction both ex-territorially and extraterritorially. States that claim ex-territorial jurisdiction threaten punishment for certain acts either against the state itself, such as high treason, forging banknotes and the like, or against its nationals, such as murder, arson, libel and slander.[91] States that claim extraterritorial jurisdiction, chiefly the United States, have taken the view that whenever activity abroad has consequences within the state that are contrary to local legislation, then

86 H.E. Yntema, "The Comity Doctrine", 65 *Michigan Law Review* (1966): 9, 19 (referring to "the principle definitively established by Justinian, that the first attribute of the *imperium* is the power of legislation").

87 This is also what *jurisdictio* originally meant to the Romans: "the power of a magistrate to *ius dicere*, that is, to determine the law and, in accordance with it, to settle disputes concerning persons and property within his forum (sphere of authority)". J. Plescia, "Conflict of Laws in the Roman Empire", 38 *Labeo* (1992): 30, 32.

88 Joseph Beale, "Jurisdiction of a Sovereign State", 36 *Harvard Law Review* (1923): 36); C.L. Blakesley, "United States Jurisdiction over Extraterritorial Crime", 73 *Journal of Criminal Law & Criminology* (1982): 1109.

89 One of the leading Roman jurisconsults of the early 3rd century AD, Paulus, formulated the term *statute theory* and it has for a long time influenced the doctrine of jurisdiction. In Italy, the concept of *statutum non ligat nisi subditos* became accepted around 1200 AD. In effect, it denied the absolute power of *lex fori* and around the 16th century writers such as Bertrand d'Argentre spelt out the essence of statute theory by distinguishing between *potestas* and jurisdiction. The *Huber Storyan maxim* refers to the theory developed in Ulricus Huber's work, *De conflictu legum diversarum in diversis imperiis*, written in 1948. In terms of the Storyan maxim, territorial jurisdiction means that each state has exclusive jurisdiction within its own territorial domain over persons, property, things and legal transactions done within it, including the extraterritorial activities of such persons. See Csbaffi op. cit.: 49–51, notes 51–2.

90 Brownlie op. cit.: 85.

91 See L.F.L. Oppenheim, *International Law: A Treatise*, Vol. I, 8th edn (London: Longman, 1963): 331. See also U.O. Umozurike, *Introduction to International Law* (Lagos: Spectrum Publishing, 1993): 85.

that state may make orders requiring such things as the disposition of patent rights and other property of foreign corporations, the reorganisation of industry in another country or the production of documents.[92] It need only be said that this sort of jurisdiction (mostly in the context of economic issues) is a source of serious controversy between the very few states that practise it or acquiesce to its exercise and the majority of states, which are opposed to it.[93]

Beale defined the concept of jurisdiction in the following words: "The power of a sovereign to affect the rights of persons whether by legislation, by executive decree, or by judgement of a Court."[94] This definition is narrow in that it restricts jurisdiction to powers over persons alone. In *McDonald v. Mabee*,[95] Justice Holmes said that the ultimate basis of jurisdiction is "physical power" and in *Wedding v. Meyler*,[96] he equated jurisdiction with "authority". It can, thus, be said that state jurisdiction refers to the capacity of a state to exercise certain powers. That is the state's right to regulate or affect by legislative, executive or judicial measures the rights of persons, property acts or events within its territory. But such actions are not always entirely and exclusively of domestic concern.[97] Fawcet, thus, correctly noted that in exercise of its sovereignty a state has the jurisdiction to forbid the entry into any part of its territory any person or thing such as aircraft or pesticide. In equal manner, such jurisdiction is forbidden outside territorial limits especially within the jurisdiction of another state without its consent.[98] Jurisdiction, therefore, encompasses several discrete concepts, including jurisdiction to prescribe, jurisdiction to adjudicate, and jurisdiction to enforce.[99] These assertions inevitably bring

92 See, for example, *US v. Aluminium Co. of America*, 148 F. 2d 416 (1945) and *US v. Watchmakers of Switzerland Information Center, Inc.*, 133 F. Supp. 40 (1955): 134 F.

93 See Brownlie op. cit.: 310–12; M.N. Shaw, *International Law*, 4th edn (Cambridge: Grotius Publications, 1997): 483–4.

94 Beale op. cit.: 24.

95 90 US 230 (1916).

96 192 US 573, 584 (1904).

97 Csabafi op. cit.: 49.

98 It is recognised that in the 21st century migration – both forced and voluntary – is increasing the world over. People move around within and between states in larger numbers more quickly and to more distant destinations than at any other time in history. The implications for health and security of populations are immense and the sovereign has a real impetus to exercise control and an maintain an interest in the reception or repulsion of foreigners whether they arrive by land, sea or air or, in some instances, by means of underground tunnelling (such as Mexican smuggling tunnels). See J. Fawcet, "Domestic Jurisdiction", 132 *Recuell des Cours* (1971): 431. See also Manuel Carballo and Aditi Nerukar, "Migration, Refugees and Health Risks", 7, 3 *Emerging Infectious Diseases* (2001): 556; Xiushi Yang, "Temporary Migration and the Spread of STDs/HIV in China: Is There a Link?", 38, 1 *International Migration Review* (Spring 2004); IOM, 36, 4, *Migration and Aids* (1998): 445–68. Randal C. Archibold, "Smugglers Build an Underground World", *New York Times*, 7 December 2007: A18; Harriet Sherwood, "Palestinian Tunnel Tycoons Feeding Demand for Banned Goods: Boom in Illicit Trade in Motorbikes, Dismantled in Egypt and Smuggled into Gaza, Brings Deadly Consequences", *Guardian*, Tuesday 15 December 2009, available at http://www.guardian.co.uk/world/2009/dec/14/palestine-israel-smuggling-in-gaza (accessed 16 October 2010).

99 Susan W. Brennerl and Bert-Jaap Koops, "Approaches to Cybercrime Jurisdiction", 4, 1 *Journal of High Technology Law* (2004): 5.

us to a discussion of state territory within the context of the principle of state territorial supremacy or sovereignty.

Territorial jurisdiction is seen as the sum total of the state's powers in respect of a portion of *terra firma* under its governmental authority including all persons and things therein, and the extraterritorial activities of such persons.[100] It denotes the power of legislation, executive and judicial competence over a defined territory.[101] It is generally derived from territorial sovereignty, but it may also be derived from treaties, as in the case of mandated, trust or leased territories. It may also derive from *occupatio pacifica* or *bellica*.[102] The principle of territorial supremacy arises from the view that a state has absolute and exclusive authority over people, things and events within its own territory and, therefore, may exercise jurisdiction over them in all cases.[103] But the problem of what may properly be considered state territory for purposes of jurisdiction is not always clear. This brings us to the concept of territory itself.

The corpus of state territory and its appurtenances (airspace and territorial sea together with the population and government), comprise the physical and social manifestations of the state, which is the primary type of an international legal person.[104] The territory of a state is separated from those of other states by boundaries. A boundary may be natural or artificial.[105] Apart from land territory, which is permanently above low-water mark, territorial sovereignty may be exerted over all the geographical features associated with or analogous to land territory. Permanence, accessibility and natural appurtenance are naturally essential qualities. Furthermore, it is clear that no one knowledgeable in international law can deny that the territory of a state including its earth surface, "a sector of the earth below and a sector of space above",[106] are within the areas of exercise of jurisdiction permitted by international law. Indeed, the tridimensionality of state territory is recognised in customary international law. A state's territory is considered to consist of three sectors:[107]

100 B. Cheng, "The Extra-Territorial Application of International Law", *Current Legal Problems* (1965): 135.

101 Umozurike, op. cit.: 86.

102 Cheng (1965) op. cit.: 135.

103 Some authors like Starke choose to refer to these overwhelming powers as territorial sovereignty. The question then arises as to whether there is a possible distinction between territorial sovereignty and territorial jurisdiction. Oppenheim seems to have effectively answered this query by stating that he sees "Independence and Territorial as well as Personal Supremacy (which Starke seems to have referred to as territorial sovereignty) as aspects of Sovereignty" (brackets mine). *Cf.* Brownlie op. cit.:105–6. See J.G. Starke, *Introduction to International Law* (London: Butterworths, 1984): 151–2. Oppenheim op. cit.: 286. See also D.H. Ott, *Public International Law in the Modern World* (London: Pitman Publishing, 1987): 135.

104 Brownlie op. cit.: 107.

105 Umozurike op. cit.: 107.

106 J.C. Cooper, "High Altitude Flight and National Sovereignty", *Explorations in Aerospace Law: Selected Essays by John Cobb Cooper* (Montreal: McGill University Press, 1968): 157.

107 G.I. Tunkin (ed.), *International Law* (Moscow: Progress Publishers, 1988): 400.

- legitimately owned landmass within its borders, including the internal water territories, rivers, lakes, reservoirs, canals, territorial sea
- land mass below the surface of the soil (including its mineral resources) down to the centre of the earth
- airspace and atmosphere above ground level up to an extent that is still the subject of intense debate in academic circles.

In spatial terms, the law knows two other types of regime, which must be highlighted. They are the *res nullius* and the *res communis*. The *res nullius* is that land territory or environment legally susceptible to acquisition by states but not as yet placed under any state's territorial sovereignty. The European powers made use of this concept, which, albeit legal in form, was often political in application in that it involved the occupation of areas in Asia and Africa that were often the seat of previously well-organised communities.[108] There have also been some unsuccessful attempts to forge a link between this concept and outer space territory. In fact, it would appear that with or without the use of the technicality of *res nullius*, certain states are set to embark on the introduction of property rights over outer space-based resources for national and private ends, despite the position of current international law on this issue. The *res communis* is that territory or environment such as the high seas or Antarctica that are not capable of being legally placed under state sovereignty. In accordance with customary international law and the dictates of practical convenience, the airspace above and subsoil below each of the three categories, state territory, *res nullius* and *res communis*, are included in each category.[109]

Suffice it to mention that territorial jurisdiction also determines the appropriate forum in civil actions. A total lack of territorial connection may remove a dispute from the competence of a state. The Court in the US case of *Aviateca, S.A. v. Friedman*[110] issued a writ of prohibition that prevented a state court trial judge from hearing a wrongful death action brought against Aviateca arising from the crash of one of its aircraft. The court looked to Article 28(1) of the Warsaw Convention, which states that actions for damages that arise out of international air travel may be brought in one of four places:

1 domicile of the carrier
2 principal place of business of the carrier
3 carrier's place of business through which the contract of carriage was made
4 or place of destination.

The court rightly held that since, in this instance, the USA was not one of the four places, the trial court judge lacked subject matter jurisdiction over the matter.

As in the case of territorial sovereignty, we may pose the question of whether and to what extent territorial jurisdiction is affected by concessionary practice.

108 Brownlie op. cit.: 118.
109 Ibid: 98.
110 *Aviateca, S.A. v. Friedman*, 678 So. 2d 387 (Fla. App. 1996).

Territorial concessions do not in themselves extinguish formal independence of the territorial state. Accordingly, where formal independence is present, the formal territorial integrity of the state survives all forms of aerial, maritime or land territorial concessions. This distinction is becoming important in the current state of international relations where various forms of territorial concessions have become common. These include the grant of military and airbases, scientific bases, farmland territorial deals between states and transborder parks. Extensive territorial concessions were granted at different times by the North African states and China, which nevertheless preserved their territorial integrity as well as protected reversionary interests over the affected territory.[111] By implication, the grant of concessions over aerial territory does not separate that territory from the tridimensionality of the grantor state's territorial jurisdiction and integrity.

The question, then, is whether forcefully obtained concessions and indeed illegal intervention can grant territorial integrity in favour of the invading state. Just as concessions do not extinguish territorial integrity so are invasions and/or annexation of any form of territory previously belonging to another state incapable of extinguishing both the formal and actual independence of the territorial state.[112] It must be reiterated that this principle applies in all forms of territory – whether land, maritime, aerial or wherever else maintained. It will be consistent with international policy and customary law that invasion and annexation of space stations and facilities should have no place in the conduct of activities in outer space. In other words, such activities will not only be illegal but, more importantly, incapable of changing ownership or title over space-based facilities.

In the very worst-case scenario where a state's territorial integrity has being violated belligerently through occupation, territorial sovereignty and territorial jurisdictional rights continue to run even if difficult to see on the ground. James Crawford's seminal work, *The Creation of States in International Law* draws attention to this in the following words:

> Pending a final settlement of the conflict, belligerent occupation does not affect the continuity of the State. The governmental authorities may be driven into exile or silenced, and the exercise of the powers of the State thereby affected. But it is settled that the powers themselves continue to exist. This is strictly not an application of the "actual independence" rule but an exception to it, based on the maxim *ex factis ius non oritur* pending a settlement of the conflict by a peace treaty or its equivalent.[113]

111 Crawford (2007) op. cit.: 70; Rosemary Higgins, *The Development of International Law through the Political Organs of the United Nations* (Oxford: Oxford University Press, 1963): 32; J.H.L. Verzijl, *International Law in Historical Perspective*, Vol. II [1968]: 31–4, 482–8.

112 The Israeli and Syrian invasion of Lebanon; Vietnamese invasion of Cambodia; Soviet invasion of Czechoslovakia and Afghanistan; US invasion of Grenada, Panama, Afghanistan and, more recently, Iraq were at all times regarded by the international community as *de facto* situations that never could lead to right over territory or change sovereignty over the territories in question. Crawford (2007) op. cit.: 73.

113 Ibid: 73.

It is suggested here that illegal and belligerent occupation of the main territory of a state also does not itself change the sovereign rights or territorial jurisdiction the affected state may have over its non-contiguous territories – whether, land, and maritime, aerial or based elsewhere. The view that accords with international policy considerations is that the abhorrence of modern international law for belligerency as root to any form of state territorial title applies to all forms of territory.

1.4.1 Quasi-territorial jurisdiction

Where an incident occurs not within state territory, such as in foreign airspace or in outer space on a spacecraft, the powers of a state may be exercised quasi-territorially. Cheng aptly defines this as:

> The sum total of the powers of a state in respect of ships, aircraft and spacecraft (to the extent to which they are also granted legal personality) having its nationality. Its powers over pirate vessels *jure gentium* come also under this heading. Quasi-territorial jurisdiction differs from personal jurisdiction in that it extends not only to the craft in question but also to all persons and things on board the craft or elsewhere.[114]

Csbaffi Anthony correctly explains that "in this context we are concerned with the operations of rules of jurisdiction *ratione instrumenti*.[115] Vessels (i.e. ships, aircraft, spacecraft) bearing the flag of a state are subject to the jurisdiction of the flag state."[116] The flag flown by such a ship vessel establishes a *prima facie* presumption that the ship has the nationality of the state whose flag it carries.[117] Schwarzenberger, however, warns that only the ship (and by extension aircraft and spacecraft's) papers are real evidence of such nationality. In other words, such vessels must have been properly registered. That is the reason why it is left for every state to determine in accordance with its own municipal law to which ships and aircraft it is prepared to grant its own nationality. Such registration is usually granted to state-owned vessels and those owned by citizens or nationals of the state concerned. In conclusion, maritime vessels, aircraft and spacecraft that are navigating or flying under the legally assigned distinctive mark or flag of a given state and are located within international territory are viewed in a sense as state territory. Furthermore, by convention, pipelines and any other construction or equipment belonging to a state, located within the framework of international territory, are also viewed as state territory.[118]

114 Cheng (1965) op. cit.: 135.
115 Csabaffi op. cit.: 57.
116 Ibid.
117 G. Schwarzenberger, *Manual of International Law* (London: Stevens & Sons Ltd, 1952): 60.
118 Brownlie op. cit.: 401.

1.4.2 Personal jurisdiction

By this, we refer to the sum total of the powers of a state in respect of individuals or corporate bodies on business enterprises having its nationality or otherwise enjoying its protection or owing allegiance to it, wherever they may be situated. Pirates *jure gentium* may be said to come under the extraordinary personal jurisdiction of all states.[119] It is left to every state to determine to whom it wishes to grant nationality. International customary law, however, recognises that every state is entitled to protect its own nationals. Whenever such nationals are abroad and within the territory of another sovereign, the sovereign of their home state has to share its personal sovereignty with the territorial sovereign.[120] Personal jurisdiction and venue of criminal or civil action are thus, closely related. US agencies, for instance, will typically bring action over antitrust laws only if they conclude that personal jurisdiction exists under the due process clause of the US Constitution.[121]

In fact, it would seem not to matter under what circumstances the national finds himself in the territorial state. For the purposes of personal jurisdiction, involuntary extradition, while it may lead to considerable controversies between states, does not appear to be of much help to a defendant under municipal laws. Thus, in the fairly recent case of *US v. Rezaq*,[122] the fact that the defendant had been abducted from another country to the USA for the express purpose of prosecution for aircraft piracy did not warrant the reversal of his conviction for that offence. The court took the view that the fact that he had been brought within its jurisdiction involuntarily and by forcible abduction did not impair the jurisdiction of US courts. It was pointed out that neither the 1970 Hague Convention nor US piracy provisions created a statutory exception for such powers, since the US provision's applicability to defendants that are afterwards found in the US means only that the hijackers must be physically in the country and not that they must first be detected there.

This line of reasoning very clearly follows the Israeli decision in the celebrated *Eichmann Case*. Eichmann, a German national, was head of the Jewish Office of the German Gestapo during the Nazi era, under whose command a substantial part of the Final Solution was executed. This included acts of torture, murder, extermination, enslavement, starvation, deportation and other inhumane acts together amounting to crimes against humanity, which were committed principally against millions of Jews. He was apparently abducted by Israeli agents from Argentina and

119 Cheng (1965) op. cit.: 135.

120 Schwarzenberger op. cit.: 43.

121 See *International Shoe Co. v. Washington*, 326 US 310 (1945); *Asahi Metal Indust. Co. Ltd v. Superior Court*, 480 US 102 (1987). *Antitrust Laws and Trade Regulation Primary Source Pamphlet*, 2nd edn (New York: Mathew Bender & Co., Inc. 2000): 177. The Constitution requires that a defendant must have affiliating or minimum contacts with the USA, such that the proceeding therefore comports with "fair play and substantial justice". See *Go-Video, Inc. v. Akai Elec Co. Ltd*, 885 F. 2d 1406. 1414 (9th Cir 1989). Parties must equally be shown to have been properly served under the prevailing federal rules of civil procedure or other relevant authority.

122 US Court of Appeals District of Columbia Circuit 6 February 1998, Avi 15.404.

arraigned before an Israeli district court. The Supreme Court of Israel dismissed his appeal against the consequent conviction and death sentence on the following grounds, inter alia:

> [C]ontention of learned defence counsel was that the trial of the accused in Israel following upon his kidnapping in a foreign land is in conflict with international law and takes away the jurisdiction of this Court . . . [i]t is an established rule of law that a person being tried for an offence against the laws of a state may not oppose his trial by reason of illegality of his arrest or of the means whereby he was brought within the jurisdiction of that state.

It was added, quite revealingly, that:

> The courts in England, the United States and Israel have constantly held that the circumstances of the arrest and the mode of bringing of the accused into the territory of the state have no relevance to his trial, and they have consistently refused in all instances to enter upon an examination of these circumstances.[123]

The US courts, however, have been more consistent in their support for this expansive approach to the founding of jurisdiction. Even more recent cases, such as *US v. Alvarez-Machain*, continue to affirm this view. In that case, US Drug Enforcement Administration agents abducted a Mexican national to the USA from Mexico to face murder charges for the death of one of their officers. Mexico requested his return for trial. Although the Supreme Court expressed some level of displeasure at the abduction it went ahead in deciding that the exercise of criminal jurisdiction in the USA was not unconstitutional since there had been no breach of the US–Mexican extradition treaty (which did not prohibit abductions).[124] Although British courts had, indeed, held conflicting decisions on the point, the prevailing position is contained in the decision reached by the House of Lords in *R v. Horseferry Road Magistrates Court, ex p. Bennet.*[125] In that case, a New Zealand national who was wanted for fraud committed in England was found to be living in South Africa. With the collusion of the South African police force, he was forcefully brought back to England for trial without the benefit of any extradition process. Lord Griffiths view as held by the Court was that: "[W]here process of law is available to return an accused to this country through extradition procedures our courts will refuse to try him if he has been forcibly brought within

123 *A.G. of the Government of Isreal v. Eichmann* (1961) 36 ILR 5 District Court of Jerusalem. For further discourse, see D.J. Harris, *Cases and Materials on International Law* (London: Sweet & Maxwell, 1998): 280–88; James Fawcett, "The Eichmann Case", 38 *BYIL* (1962): 181; Schwarzenberger op. cit.: 248; Helen Silving, "In Re Eichmann: A Dilemma of Law and Morality", 55 *American Journal of International Law* (1961): 307.

124 (1992) 119 LEd 2d 441.

125 [1994] 1 AC 42, HL.

our jurisdiction in disregard of those procedures by a process to which our own police prosecuting or other executive authorities have been a knowing party." This represents a departure from the US position although Lord Griffiths tries to distinguish it from the *Alvarez Case* by saying that it ruled on the question of whether criminal jurisdiction was exercisable, whereas *Bennet* dealt with the exercise of judicial discretion not to take a case where jurisdiction, in fact, exists.

In the *Pinochet Case*, the issues are somwehat different. There was no forcible abduction of the infamous defendant. Rather, the central issues in this case border on whether any form of personal jurisdiction may be exercised on the person of a former head of state of another country for acts committed when he was in power that constitute "crimes against humanity". The answer to this legal riddle was given in *Pinochet Case* No. 3.[126] By an impressive vote of six to one, the House of Lords confirmed the earlier majority ruling, that a former head of state enjoys no immunity in extradition or criminal proceedings brought in the UK in respect of the international crime of torture. Warbrick and McGoldrick, however, argue correctly that the real ratio of this decision is that while territorial jurisdiction may be asserted as exclusive and comprehensive over all persons and acts within the territory it relates only to persons in breach of municipal law. This has been the position since Marshal CJ's judgment in the *Schooner Exchange.*[127] Thus, while British and US courts, in particular, may have taken very different views of the significance of how a defendant has been brought before the court, where the acts in question border on international crimes exclusive personal jurisdiction is no longer sacrosanct. In effect, the inability of the territorial state to exercise jurisdiction over another state or its officials in respect of acts committed outside its territory is not attributable to immunity but to lack of jurisdiction. Thus, a court that refuses to pronounce on the validity of the acts performed by another state does so not by reason of the latter's immunity but by reason of the forum state's incompetence to exercise territorial jurisdiction beyond its territory.[128] It is, therefore, to be noted that the jurisdiction of states under international law is exercisable in relation to domestic or municipal law and jurisdiction over subjects of municipal law and not over other states at all.

1.5 Criminal jurisdiction of states

International law does not actually impose restrictions on the civil jurisdiction of states' courts; it is their criminal jurisdiction that international law controls by evolving rules and principles of competence. It follows from this that, before considering crimes in the airspace and in outer space, it is necessary to concentrate

126 See *R v. Bow Street Metropolitan Stipendiary Magistrate, ex p. Pinochet Ugarte* (Amnesty International intervening) (No. 3) 1999 2 All ER 97.

127 (1812) 7 Cranch 116 (US).

128 Colin Warbrick and Dominic McGoldrick, "The Pinochet Case No. 3", 48 *ICLQ*, part 3 (1999): 698.

briefly on the criminal jurisdiction of the states under contemporary international law. The idea of criminal jurisdiction is based on the need to maintain the coercive instinct of society as it exists within and without its territory in order to protect its values that are backed by sanctions as it applies to persons the state may validly exercise jurisdiction over. The potential reach even to the farthest points of the universe and "terrifying" consequences of state criminal jurisdiction and its coercive nature has made imperative the elaboration of criminal jurisdiction under international law. Elden impressively attempts to capture the link between territorial reach and criminal jurisdiction thus:

> The link between terror and territory is more than merely coincidental . . . there is a relation suggested between "terrere" and "terra". There is therefore a direct link between "territory" and "terror". Terror like terrify is more nonproblematically derived from "terrere". Using this logic, "territorium" would be a place from which people are frightened, or where terror is exercised.[129]

This is probably what Pomponius meant when he described territory as the place where the "magistrate of a place has the right of terrifying".[130] In other words, "to occupy territory is to receive sustenance and to exercise violence and territory is a land occupied by violence."[131]

There are two emerging themes in the discussion of criminal jurisdiction within international law in the 21st century. First, the exercise or intention to apply criminal jurisdiction is capable of generating severe tensions and/or disputes among states. Second, the reach of states over alleged offenders appears to be increasing under international law. This is because states are increasing their criminal jurisdiction through national laws. Furthermore, and very important, the general trend of pertinent legislative output from the United Nations and other intergovernmental bodies is that of increasing the competence and jurisdiction of states over certain types of activity and person. Both of these themes are particularly manifest in the area of prevention or punishment of terrorism and in the treatment of aerial hijack and aviation-inspired offences. As a result, the jurisdictional quandary that an individual may face in the modern world of technological possibilities and innovations that allows people and ideas move rapidly across borders and through space and time zones may be quite bewildering. Many hypothetical and actual scenarios have been highlighted in legal literature in relation to the use of computers,[132] airspace transportation and, indeed, outer space activities.

129 Elden (2010) op. cit.: xxviii, xxix.

130 Pomponius Manual in the Digest of Justinian.

131 Elden (2010) op. cit.: xxvi.

132 Interesting scenarios that have been offered in the area of cybercrimes include the following: "A Web site in Germany caters to the adult market, and has done so happily for three years. Then, out of the blue, it finds itself indicted in Singapore because of spreading pornographic material in Singapore, even though the company has never done business with someone from Singapore.

It must be observed from the outset that the rules of international law on the criminal jurisdiction of the state are either permissive or prohibitive; they are not prescriptive. In other words, a state is normally not compelled by international law to exercise its criminal jurisdiction;[133] but when it decides to, it has to comply with these rules, which form the bases on which its courts will be competent to entertain criminal cases. This also applies by extension to the exercise of criminal jurisdiction over acts committed in the airspace and on board aircraft. There are, broadly speaking, five of these bases (also called principles or grounds) of criminal jurisdiction:

- territorial (or territoriality) principle
- nationality principle
- protective (or security) principle
- passive personality principle
- universality principle.

Since territory is relevant only in respect of the first basis, while all the others have to do (as we shall see shortly) with the person of the offender or of the victim, or with the character of the offence, some writers classify these bases into two major groups, namely, the territorial and the extraterritorial (or personal) grounds of jurisdiction. But the misleading nature of this latter expression should not be lost sight of. For if personal jurisdiction is, as Schwarzenberger defined it "the authority asserted by a sovereign over individuals on grounds of allegiance or protection",[134] it will be difficult to see how a person who has committed an offence such as piracy on the high seas or hijacking of an aircraft in international territory could be tried on the basis of the personal jurisdiction of the forum state. Therefore, it is really better to refer to the specific basis of jurisdiction relied on in each case rather than simply make reference to the blanket category of extraterritorial jurisdiction. These principles will now be considered individually.

To make things worse, the Web site owners are ordered to appear in court in Belgium, because some of the adult pictures are considered to be of 17-year-old minors, constituting the crime of child pornography (which, in Belgium, entails persons under 18 years of age; in Germany, the age limit is 14). The business is perfectly legal in Germany, but since it uses the Internet to conduct its business, it finds itself confronted with the criminal laws of all countries connected to the Internet—that is, all countries of the world." Unintentional damage may also be committed occasioning cross-border damage: "A script kiddie concocts a new worm and, without really thinking of the potential consequences, launches it on the Internet. To his amazement (and somewhat to his fear), he finds that he has blocked large portions of the Internet, causing significant damage in numerous countries around the world. Many countries have laws criminalising the spreading of worms, and so, in theory, he can be prosecuted by many countries, perhaps consecutively. In practice, however, perhaps no country will claim jurisdiction, thinking that surely other countries will have suffered more damage and hence will have priority in prosecuting." See Brennerl and Koops op. cit.: 3.

133 The possible exceptions to this rule exist as a result of treaty obligations voluntarily entered into by states such as in the prosecution of offenders with respect to the crime of unlawful interference with the safety of civil aviation as established in certain air treaties as discussed later.

134 Schwarzenberger op. cit.: 74.

1.5.1 The territorial principle

This principle operates on the basis of the aforementioned principle of territorial jurisdiction. It explains a state's exclusive and absolute criminal jurisdiction over persons, things and events within its territory. Therefore, once an offence is committed on the territory of the state, its courts are competent to entertain the case arising therefrom. It is generally agreed that this principle is the most basic one, as it seems more logical that a state on whose territory a crime is committed should assume jurisdiction over it.

There is no complication in the application of the territorial principle as long as the crime is wholly committed within the state's territory. But where due to the special nature of the crime it commences for instance in the airspace of one state and is consummated in the territory of another then a conflict of jurisdiction may arise. To resolve these sorts of problem, international lawyers have formulated the doctrine of constructive presence, the application of which enables both states to exercise jurisdiction. As the 1935 Harvard Draft Convention formulated it, a state may exercise territorial jurisdiction when a crime is committed "in whole or in part" within its territory.[135] Judge Moore, who dissented from the Permanent Court of International Justice decision in the *Lotus Case*, nonetheless, agreed that:

> It appears to be now generally admitted that where a crime is committed in the territorial jurisdiction of one state as a direct result of the act of a person at the time physically present in another state, international law, by reason of the principle of constructive presence of the offender at the place where his act took effect does not forbid the prosecution of the offender by the former state, should he come within its territorial jurisdiction.[136]

Elaborating further on the theory of constructive presence, writers have developed two sub-principles out of the territorial principle. They are the subjective territorial principle (according to which the state on whose territory the offender started committing or perpetrating the offensive act has jurisdiction); and the objective territorial principle (according to which the state where the offence was completed or had its effects has jurisdiction because, although the offender was not physically present on this territory when the crime started he may be considered present there when all the constituent elements of the crime are put together and for the purpose of his trial).

A good illustration of the foregoing is the often given hypothetical case of the gunman shooting from the territory of state A across the border and killing a person

135 See text of the Draft Convention with Respect to Crime in 29 *AJIL* (1935): 439. It is to be mentioned that the Harvard Research Draft Convention of 1935 was the product of the unofficial work of a number of American international lawyers. It is not as binding on states as a treaty and is not state practice. Yet it is widely accepted that the Draft Convention adequately reflects customary international law and its suggestions *de lege feranda* have been accepted as being of considerable value reflecting the thorough study that was put into the preparation of the text.

136 PCIJ Reports 1927 Series A No. 10.

in the territory of state B. In this case, state A possesses jurisdiction on the basis of the subjective territorial principle, whereas state B also has jurisdiction on the strength of the objective territorial principle, since the offender is seen as constructively present on state B's territory.

Thus, in *DPP v. Boot*,[137] the respondents, who were aliens, were convicted for the crime of conspiracy to import cannabis resin into the United Kingdom, even though the agreement, which amounted to conspiracy, was made outside the United Kingdom. In the process of carrying it out, the respondents were arrested in the UK. Justifying the jurisdiction of English courts, Lord Wilberforce said:

> [t]he present case involves "international elements" – the accused are aliens and the conspiracy was initiated abroad – but there can be no question here of any breach of any rules of international law if they are prosecuted in this country. Under the objective territorial principle (I use the terminology of the Harvard Research in international law) or the principle of universality (for the prevention of the trade in narcotics falls within this description) in both the courts of this country have a clear right, if not a duty to prosecute in accordance with our municipal law.

It must be observed that the scope of application of the objective territorial principle has greatly expanded since the *Lotus Case*. What the PCIJ said in this case was indeed that:

> [t]he courts of many countries . . . interpret criminal law in the sense that offences the authors of which at the moment of commission are in the territory of another, are nevertheless to be regarded as having been committed in the national territory, if one of the constituent elements of the offence, *and more especially its effects*, have taken place there.[138] (emphasis added)

As a result of this pronouncement, it became sufficient in order to invoke the objective territorial principle that the offensive act produces some effects on the territory of the forum state, whereas it was initially required that an actual element of the criminal act should occur in the territory of the forum state. David Ott notes that it can be argued that the effect principle is very difficult to control. This is because it "goes beyond the realm of direct physical injury in the affected state, it opens the door objectionably to an almost limitless exercise of jurisdiction, if any effect, however remote, can be found".[139]

It is necessary to note that there are certain exceptions from and restrictions on criminal jurisdiction founded on the territorial principle. The entities normally exempted include foreign states and heads of foreign states (i.e. sovereign

137 [1973] AC 807.
138 PCIJ Reports 1927 Series A No. 10.
139 Ott op. cit.: 137.

immunity),[140] diplomatic and consular agents of sovereign states,[141] public ships and aircraft of foreign states, armed forces of foreign states, as well as some international institutions. It may, thus, be asserted that a diplomatic agent would be exempt from the criminal jurisdiction of the receiving state if he commits a crime aboard an aircraft navigating in its territorial airspace or on board an aircraft having its nationality.[142]

1.5.2 The nationality principle

Jurisdiction here is assumed by the state of which the accused is a national. The competence of the state's courts is based on the allegiance owed by the accused who can be a physical or juristic person to his state of origin. It is generally admitted that jurisdiction may be founded on nationality at the time of commission of the offence or nationality at the time of prosecution, provided this does not violate the principle of non-retroactivity of criminal laws.

In cases of double nationality, both states have equal jurisdiction. Thus, in *Tomoya Kawakita v. US*,[143] the US Court of Appeal (9th Circuit) sentenced for high treason the accused who was a national of both the US and Japan and who was accused of having tortured US soldiers in Japanese prisons. Article 4 of the Hague Convention on the Conflict of Nationality Laws 1930 provides specifically that "a state may not afford diplomatic protection to one of its nationals against a state whose nationality such person also possesses".[144]

Some difference has been noted between common law countries and civil/continental law countries with respect to the extent to which they invoke the nationality principle to found jurisdiction. It would appear that in legal systems based on the civil European mode, the claim for jurisdiction on ground of nationality is more frequent than in legal systems of the common law tradition.[145] The latter would seem to reserve its use to offences considered as more serious, such as treason or murder. In *Skiriotes v. Florida*,[146] Hughes CJ stated that: "The

140 This is based on the principle that *par in parem non habet jurisdictionem* (two equals cannot be tried in one another's courts).

141 The immunities and privileges enjoyed by this category of people are regulated by the Vienna Convention on Diplomatic Relations 1961 (UKTS 19 (1965), Cmnd 2565; 500 UNTS 95) and the Vienna Convention on Consular Relations (of 24 April 1963. 523 UNTS 117, in force 19 March 1967, 126 parties), respectively.

142 For an interesting reading of the doctrine of sovereign immunity in relation to outer space activities, see Lauren S.B. Bornemann, "This is Ground Control to Major Tom . . . Your Wife would Like to Sue but there's Nothing We Can Do . . . the Unlikelihood that the FTCA Waives Sovereign Immunity for Torts Committed by United States Employees in Outer Space: A Call for Preemptive Legislation", 63, 3 *Journal of Air Law and Commerce* (1999): 517.

143 Reported in 46 *AJIL* (1952): 147.

144 1930 The Hague Convention on Certain Questions Relating to the Conflict of Nationality Laws 179 LNTS 89.

145 Shaw op. cit.: 466.

146 313 US 69, 73(1941).

United States is not debarred by any rule of international law from governing the conduct of its citizens upon the high seas or even in foreign countries, when the rights of other nations or their nationals are not infringed."

Under English case law, the possession of a British passport is sufficient proof of British nationality and duty of allegiance to Britain. Thus, in *Joyce v. DPP*,[147] the House of Lords allowed the hanging of the appellant for treason on the ground that, while in possession of a British passport, to which in reality he was not entitled, he went to the German side during the Second World War and made pro-Nazi propaganda broadcasts. With this case in view, Ryngaert's insistence that few crimes are amenable to the exercise of active personality-based jurisdiction and that punishment will, in practice, often be lighter than for territorial crimes is not entirely persuasive. His view is based on the assumption that harm to a state's public order might be smaller in case of extraterritorial offences.[148] In truth, severity of the punishment will always depend on the facts and the nature of the crime. What may appear not to affect the public order of the state of nationality may have serious implications for national welfare or security. For instance, although the prohibition of non-licensed pilots from flying aircraft is certainly for the public order and safety of a territorial state, where a national flies an aircraft abroad for terrorist purposes, it may well be in the interest of the state of nationality to reserve the severest punishment for such crimes as well.[149]

1.5.3 The protective (or security) principle

Here, a state assumes jurisdiction over aliens for acts committed on foreign territory but which affect the security or other interest of the forum state. Thus, currency, immigration and economic offences committed by aliens abroad are punished by the state offended. The protective principle works on the basis of the need to protect the concerned state from acts of foreign nationals perpetrated abroad that jeopardise its safety, sovereignty, territorial integrity or its right to political independence. Typically, such acts including economic sabotage, treason or felonious conduct may not be punishable in the state in which the acts or conduct originate, thus making the argument for exercise of protective jurisdiction by the state at which the acts are directed attractive. It has been persuasively argued that what distinguishes the protective principle from the objective territorial principle (or effects

147 [1946] AC 347.

148 Ryngaert op. cit.: 89.

149 Particularly in the sphere of aviation and space activities it may be argued that as long as it is clear that what is needed is for at least one state to assume jurisdiction over offences, which may even be of ongoing nature, then it is better that the law recognises control theory-based active personality principle. The facts over which criminal jurisdiction are necessary may be of a nature whereby the majority of affected states may face formidable challenges in mounting robust prosecutions Allowing exercise of the control theory-based jurisdiction under the active personality principle may, therefore, be the only realistic or preferable jurisdictional route. This is particularly justifiable where the state seeking the exercise of jurisdiction is the state of nationality of the corporation.

doctrine) is that the former does not require that actual harm need to have resulted from the offending actor conduct while the latter does.[150] The celebrated case of *Joyce v. DPP* represents a classic application of the protective principle. The appellant (primarily a US citizen by birth and of naturalised Irish parents) having been convicted for propaganda broadcast for the enemy in war time, his nationality was actually immaterial and the protective principle was also considered in the trial.

The protective principle has a long and interesting history which indeed spans many centuries but even in its present form it appears that there are differing perspectives and the common law view of the principle is said to be more reticent than that of the civil law states. Ryngaert points out this distinction thus:

> Continental European authors have traditionally considered the protective principle as deriving from a State's inherent right of self-defence. Common law authors, however, in whose home countries protective jurisdiction was historically non-existent, have rejected this justification, primarily because it is conceptually fallacious and prone to politicization and abuse. From a conceptual perspective, the self-defence justification has been criticized on the ground that protective jurisdiction is in fact exercised sometime after the (criminal) act has taken place. Self-defence is ordinarily only allowed as an inherent right when an armed attack actually occurs. Defence against a fait accompli may appear paradoxical.[151]

Thus, French criminal law is applicable to any felony, as well as to any misdemeanour punished by imprisonment, committed by a foreign national outside the territory of the French republic, where the victim is a French national at the time the offence took place.[152] French criminal law also applies to felonies and misdemeanours (that are violations of the fundamental interests of the nation, forgery and counterfeiting of state seals, of coins serving as legal tender, banknotes or public papers) and to any felony or misdemeanour against French diplomatic or consular agents or premises committed outside the territory of the French republic.[153] Note may also be taken of *US v. Archer* (1943) where a federal district

150 Ryngaert op. cit.: 96. M.R. Garcia-Mora, "Criminal Jurisdiction over Foreigners for Treason and Offenses against the Safety of the State Committed upon Foreign Territory", 19 *University of Pittsburgh Law Review* (1958): 567, 587. See also M.B. Krizek, "The Protective Principle of Extraterritorial Jurisdiction: A Brief History and an Application of the Principle to Espionage as an Illustration of Current United States Practice", 6 *Boston University International Law Journal* (1988): 337, 345.

151 Ryngaert op. cit.: 97. See also Garcia-Mora op. cit.: 585.

152 See the provisions of the French Penal Code Section II: Articles 113–7 Offences Committed outside the Territory of the French Republic.

153 Felonies and misdemeanours here are defined as violations of the fundamental interests of the nation and punishable under Title I of Book IV and under Articles 442-1, 442-2, 442-15, 443-1 and 444-1. For further provisions on the treatment of foreigners under French criminal law, see also Articles 692-2, 696-41, 706-73, 728-4, 706-73 of the Code of Criminal Procedure. French laws and their official translations are available at www.legifrance.gouv.fr.

court referred to the protective principle to justify a US statute that made it a crime for an alien to commit perjury before a US diplomatic or consular official outside US territory, even if this act might not be a crime in any other country.[154] The protective principle was so widely used in the 20th century that, as far back as 1935, the commentary of the Harvard Research Draft Convention on Jurisdiction with Respect to Crime (1935) stated that "in view of the fact that an overwhelming majority of states have enacted such legislation (i.e. legislation relying on the protective principle), it is hardly possible to conclude that such legislation is necessary in exercise of competence as recognised by contemporary international law".[155]

Perhaps, the most significant reading of this principle to date can be found in the law reports of the *Eichmann Case*, referred to earlier, in relation to personal jurisdiction. In this case, defence counsel had contended that the protective principle could not apply to the Israeli laws used against Eichmann because that principle is designed to protect only an existing state, its security and its interests, whereas the state of Israel did not exist at the time of the commission of the said crimes. In Eichmann's submissions, the same applied to the principle of passive personality, a corollary of the protective principle. In a forceful statement rejecting this argument, the court held that:

> In our view learned counsel errs when he examines the protective principle in this retroactive law according to the time of the commission of the crimes, as is usual in the case of an ordinary law. This law was enacted in 1950, to be applied to a specified period which had terminated five years before its enactment. The protected interests of the state recognised by the protective principle is in this case the interests existing at the time of the enactment of the law, and we have already dwelt on the importance of the moral and defensive task which this law is designed to fulfil in the state of Israel.

154 *US v. Archer* 51 F. Supp. 708 Dist. Court, SD California, 1943. Similarly, US courts relied on the protective principle to assume jurisdiction for the prosecution of aliens who outside the USA swear falsely before a US consul for the purpose of obtaining the necessary documents to enter US territory. See *US v. Roduguez,* 182 F. Suppl. 479 (1960). Cf. *Attorney-General of Israel v. Eichmann* (1961), where the Israeli court held that Israel, although not in existence during the Second World War, could exercise jurisdiction over a Nazi war criminal on the basis of the protective principle, because of the defendant's "crime against the Jewish people", which fact is the "linking proof" between the forum state (Israel) and the accused (Eichmann). Israeli agents, without the knowledge of the Argentine authorities, abducted Eichmann from Argentina in 1960. He was tried, convicted, sentenced to death and executed after his appeal to the Israeli Supreme Court was dismissed. The Bustamante Code, Convention on Private International Law, adopted in 1928 and in force between several South American states, also provides in Article 305 that "those committing an offence against the internal or external security of a contracting state or against its public credit, whatever the nationality or domicile of the delinquent person, are subject in a foreign country to the penal laws of each contracting state".

155 (1935) Vol. 29 *AJIL* Supp. 443.

The dynamics of the operation of the protective principle is underscored by its inclusion in treaties providing for multiple jurisdictional grounds relating to aerial offences, which shall be discussed later. Similarly with regard to space law, the protective principle forms the basis of the questionable insistence of some legal theorists that the territorial jurisdiction of states ought to extend infinitely in spatial terms.[156]

1.5.4 The passive personality or passive nationality principle

Under this principle, an alien may be prosecuted for acts done abroad that are harmful to the nationals of the forum state. This is the most controversial basis of criminal jurisdiction. In the *Cutting Case* (1887), a Mexican court exercised jurisdiction in respect of the publication in a Texas newspaper of material adjudged defamatory of a Mexican. Cutting, a citizen of the USA and the paper's editor was, thus, prosecuted in Mexico when he subsequently travelled there. The United States demanded his release, but the decision on appeal by which he was discharged from custody justified his release on grounds of public interest, as "the offended party . . . has withdrawn from the action".[157] It must be noted in this case that the USA protested against the court's assumption of jurisdiction until the court changed its theory to jurisdiction based on circulation of the libellous publication in Mexico.

All the dissenting judges in the *Lotus Case* rejected the passive personality principle (and the Harvard Draft Convention 1935 did not retain it either). In his dissenting opinion, Judge Moore said of the passive personality principle that it would mean that the national of one country, while travelling to another, takes with him for his protection the law of his own country, which is contrary to the well-established principle that such a visitor ought to put himself under the protection and dominion of the law of the receiving state, except that his government may intervene in case of denial of justice. Yet many states assert jurisdiction (through legislation) on the basis of the passive personality principle. This can be found, for example, in Article 4 of the Mexican Penal Code and Article 5 of the Swiss Penal Code. O'Connell, in supporting this basis of jurisdiction, wrote that it is "a corollary of the rule that any state may protect its own citizens abroad".[158] States are tempted to adopt this principle for various reasons, not least of which is their perceived laxity of the domestic laws of other states as compared to their own in certain matters.

1.5.5 The universality principle

In an increasingly globalised international society of states, criminal conduct of even a few persons may affect directly and indirectly the welfare and fortunes of vast swathes of human lives, their governments and national interests. As a result

156 *Infra*, Chapter 10.
157 (1887) US For Rel: 751.
158 D.P. O'Connell, *International Law*, 2nd edn, Vol. 2 (London: Stevens & Sons, 1970): 901, 902.

"the universality principle has gained a remarkable but contested ascendancy recently".[159] According to this principle, certain crimes are of such nature and seriousness as to justify their repression by all states as a matter of international public policy. Universal jurisdiction over piracy, for example, is well known under both customary and conventional international law: wherever committed and whatever the nationality of the criminal, a piratical act against a ship falls under the jurisdiction of any state that detains the pirate. Anybody who contributes to the committing of a piratical act is also a pirate.

The power to arrest pirate ships and watch out for them is based on the principle that there is a duty on all states to repress piracy. Piracy is defined in Article 101 of the Law of the Sea Convention (1982)[160] as consisting of:

> (a) any illegal acts of violence or detention, or any act of depredation committed for private ends by the crew or the passengers of a private ship or a private aircraft and directed: (i) on the high seas, against another ship or aircraft, or against persons or property on board such ship or aircraft, (ii) against a ship, aircraft, persons or property in a place outside the jurisdiction of any state;
> (b) any act of voluntary participation in the operation of a ship or of an aircraft with knowledge of facts making it a pirate ship or aircraft;
> (c) any act of inciting or of intentionally facilitating an act described in subparagraph (a) or (b).

Viscount Sankey LC, in *Re Piracy Jure Gentium*, has accurately expressed the total abhorrence of the act of piracy in international law thus:

> [W]hereas according to international law the criminal jurisdiction of municipal law is ordinarily restricted to crimes committed on its *terra firma* or territorial waters or its own ships and to crimes by its own nationals wherever committed, it is also recognised as extending to piracy committed on the high seas by any national on any ship, because a person guilty of such piracy has placed himself beyond the protection of any state. He is no longer a national, but *hostis humani generis* and as such he is justiciable by any state anywhere.[161]

In consequence of this, it was also held in this case that "actual robbery is not an essential element in the crime of *piracy jure gentium.* A frustrated attempt to commit a piratical robbery is equally *piracy jure gentium.*"[162]

159 Ryngaert op. cit.: 85.
160 United Nations Convention on the Law of the Sea, Montego Bay, 10 December 1982 xxi ILM 1245 (1982). Hereinafter referred to as LOSC (1982).
161 *Re Piracy Jure Gentium* [1934] AC 589.
162 Umozurike op. cit.: 112.

There have been efforts to extend the scope of application of the universality principle beyond piracy as it is known under customary international law to include other acts such as aerial hijacking and other acts regarded as *delicta jure gentium*. Such would include slave trading and genocide.[163] The number of such crimes is limited but admittedly appears to be growing. The most notable of possible newer categories are drug offences, aircraft hijacking, hostage taking and acts of terrorism. Arguments in favour of incremental criminalisation under the universal jurisdiction have been made in respect of crimes against telegraph and telephone cables, counterfeiting, trafficking in persons and in obscene publications and toxic substances.[164] It is possible to suggest possible extensions to cover similar acts that may occur on board spacecraft and on space stations.

The principle surely applies to war crimes. The United Nations War Crimes Commission stated in its *Digest of Laws and Cases* that: "According to generally recognised doctrine . . . the right to punish war crimes is not confined to the state whose nationals have suffered or on whose territory the offence took place, but is possessed by any independent state whatsoever, just as is the right to punish the offence of piracy."[165]

It is notable that in the *Eichmann Case* (1962), the Israeli courts relied not only on the protective principle, but also on the universality principle in trying the accused.

Universal jurisdiction is, therefore, arguably justified under the rationale of the common interests of states. The fact that the serious crimes in issue are by their nature of a common threat to all states becomes the rationale for universal recognition of a right to prosecute the wrongdoer(s).[166] This is why piracy was perhaps one of the first to establish itself in this manner. Since the 20th century international crimes such as genocide, crimes against humanity and grave forms of war crimes, as well as such treaty-based offences as torture and terrorism (hijacking) are included in this category.[167] It is clear that in the absence of treaties that expressly or by implication recognise or mandate universal jurisdiction over these crimes, it is difficult to reach agreement that they have transmuted into universal crimes. The specific crime of aerial hijacking and terrorism will, however, be dealt with later and the strong indications of its candidature as a crime on which universal jurisdiction may be necessitated will be considered.

163 *Infra*, Chapter 3.

164 H.F.A. Donnedieu de Vabres, *Les Principes Modernes du Droit Penal International* (1928): 64 (cited in Ryngaert op. cit.: 143).

165 Vol. XV Law Reports of Trials of War Criminals (1949): 26.

166 J.H. Marks "Mending the Web: Universal Jurisdiction, Humanitarian Intervention and the Abrogation of Immunity by the Security Council", 42 *Columbia Journal of Transnational Law* (2004): 445, 465–7.

167 M.T. Kamminga, "First Conviction under the Universal Jurisdiction Provisions of the UN Convention against Torture", *NILR* (2004): 439, 442; C. Ryngaert, ""Universal Criminal Jurisdiction over Torture: A State of Affairs 20 Years after UN Torture Convention", *Netherlands Quarterly of Human Rights* (2005): 571.

1.6 *Jurisfaction* and *jurisaction*

Cheng introduced two terminologies in the 1960s, which did not seem to have received sufficient analysis in academic literature. This, however, is not for the reason of the falsity of his analysis. In this discussion, however, it is appropriate to revisit these terms because they still represent a unique and important way of looking at jurisdiction. State jurisdiction as a whole, suggested Cheng, may be separated into two complementary elements:

1 jurisdiction to prescribe (prescriptive legislative jurisdiction or *jurisfaction*)
2 enforcement prerogative jurisdiction or *jurisaction* (that is jurisdiction to enforce).

Jurisfaction denotes the normative element of jurisdiction and it represents the powers a state has to adopt valid and binding legal norms and to concretise them with binding effect through its appropriate organs, whether judicial or otherwise. The spheres of validity or operative force of these norms may be realised *ratione loci* (territorial), *ratione instrumenti* (quasi-territorial) or *ratione personae* (personal).[168] *Jurisaction*, by way of contrast, is the formal element of state jurisdiction and it encompasses the powers a state possesses to, at any place or time, physically perform the acts of making, concretising or enforcing laws. That is, it may hold legislative assembly, set up courts or tribunals or even arrest wanted persons. From this point of view, "the validity of jurisaction presupposes jurisfaction, but it is possible to have jurisfaction without jurisaction".[169]

In respect of aircraft and spacecraft and all persons and things therein, including the activities of such persons, individuals or corporate bodies, state jurisdiction is exercisable quasi-territorially. The primary source of such jurisdiction is based on the principles of international customary law, which recognised state jurisdiction over flagged craft and even pirate vessels *jure gentium*. *Jurisfaction*, here, is on a par (i.e. in terms of hierarchy and precedence) with the other types of *jurisfaction* (i.e. territorial and personal) identified earlier, and the geographical scope is, of course, limitless. Therefore, it can be exercised on an aircraft or spacecraft whether on earth, airborne or in outer space. *Jurisaction* is also relevant in relation to flagships, national aircraft and spacecraft. In case of conflict between quasi-territorial *jurisfaction* and territorial *jurisaction* the latter overrides, but the former overrides personal *jurisaction*.[170] This, of course, is because although personal *jurisaction* may be exercised from outside territorial sphere or quasi-territorially, such jurisdiction is clearly limited to its legislative and judicial forms. As Cheng aptly puts it:

168 Cheng (1965) op. cit.: 136.
169 Ibid.
170 For a clearer picture of these submissions, see diagram on state jurisdiction by Cheng, (1965) op. cit.: 138–9.

> [A] state may, in its own territory (or in territorium nullius) pass laws applicable to its nationals who are in foreign countries or on board foreign craft that are not in its territory and even try them in absentia, but it may not send its officers to where they are in order to arrest them.[171]

1.7 Control as a determinant of rights and liabilities

Control in the sense which we mean in this work refers to those situations in which the connection between a thing, organisation, commercial entity or any actor leads to or causes legal consequences between it and a state. In the ordinary case, the presence of sovereign rights and jurisdiction confers control. The possession of sovereign rights over a territory justifies the exercise of control therein. Thus, sovereign rights over the extended continental shelf that most coastal states crave explains their control over marine scientific research, construction, operation and use of artificial islands and installations etc., as well as control over the delineation and placement of submarine pipelines. However, it is not in all situations that the occurrence, manifestation or exercise of sovereignty and territorial jurisdiction will be clear or possible but it will still be important to ascertain or assert legal control or more precisely jurisdiction. In these cases, extraterritorial jurisdiction of a sovereign state may become imputable as a result of the factual or presumed exercise of control. The vista for such determinations expands every day with thousands of payloads being uploaded into the environment of outer space and in the airspace with the increasing use of drones and other unmanned vehicles. Similarly, submersibles and underwater pipes and installations regularly call for identification and determination of nationality and control. The need to establish the connection of control may be by the controlling state in form of extraterritorial jurisdiction or due to the wish of others to establish an ultimate bearer of liability on the controlling state. The control theory is particularly renowned in the field of international economic and financial law whereby in consequence of the active personality principle, states may justify their jurisdiction over the business dealings of their corporations abroad. In the present state of international business transactions, where the nationality of multinationals may be obscured as they are subsumed in multinational networks, the nationality of a business concern may be crucial to determine but extremely difficult to ascertain. Indications of nationality such as place of incorporation, shareholder nationalities and corporate links to the forum may not be readily determinable especially where a sophisticated attempt has been made to obscure same.[172]

There is a need for better attention to be given in scholarly literature to the "control theory" wherein a state may justify its jurisdiction over business dealings and foreign operations of corporations emanating from its territory and having its nationality. In the brave new world of penetration of businesses into aviation and

171 Ibid: 137.
172 Cf. Ryngaert op. cit.: 91–2.

aerospace activities, this particular theory may acquire acute relevance. Although there has been quite limited recognition of this theory in the case law (international economic regulation with the rejection in the *Barcelona Traction Case* still being regarded as good law), it does appear that many of the reasons taken against the theory are no longer very convincing. Ryngaert's position is that:

> [F]rom an economic perspective, it appears rational not to accept the control theory, since the costs of identifying and initiating proceedings against US controlled foreign undertakings (i.e. enforcement costs) may outweigh any perceived benefits.[173]

Yet the reality as we shall show later on in this book is that with the aggressive presence of commercial entities in areas of activity such as outer space exploration, which were previously nearly completely engaged in only by states, it may be prudent to insist that multiplicity of jurisdictional competence of states ought to be increased rather than stunted.[174] As Ryngaert agrees:

> The "nationality" of a corporation may not always be readily established. Corporations could have different nationalities, since their nationality could be based on the State of incorporation, shareholder nationality as well as other corporate links to the forum.[175]

There is a clear and present danger particularly in the areas of airspace and outer space activities where the liability issues may be significant and dramatic, calling for a quick identification of where true liability lies. It is essentially in this area that the greatest worry may exist among aerospace lawyers. International lawyers appear to be caught unawares by the rapid speed at which corporate investment and actions are penetrating the aerospace environment. This is particularly true in the orbital satellites industry and space tourism. The propensity of risks and the universal nature of their potential effect arguably demands much more closer attention than it receives in law, insurance, politics, international relations and other fields. It is, however, safe to say that the pertinent, contemporary aerospace international legal regime is in favour of placement of the duty of control and liability on at least one state. In the current era of joint scientific teams, designing, producing and operating aerospace objects such as the Airbus A380,[176] space

173 Ryngaert op. cit.: 92

174 See *infra*, Chapter 4.

175 Ryngaert op. cit.: 91.

176 The Airbus A380 is a double-decked, wide-body, four-engine airliner manufactured by the European corporation Airbus, a subsidiary of EADS. Visit the official website of the Airbus at www.airbus.com. It is currently the largest passenger airliner in the world. China and Pakistan jointly produce and market the K-8 (JL-8) basic/advanced jet trainer and the JF-17 Thunder jet fighter aircraft. Wendell Minnick, "China Leaps into Global Aircraft Market Targets Russia's Traditional Customer Base", 23 November 2009, available at http://www.defensenews.com/

tourism shuttles and international space stations, the imperative for elaboration and fine-tuning of the law regulating legal control, joint liability, risk management and insurance are clear. We shall be discussing these issues in more detail in later chapters. It needs only be mentioned at this stage that principles of public and private international law as well as national laws may be used to determine control and liability over the use, conduct and operation of aircraft and spacecraft/space objects.

1.8 Summary and conclusions

Territory is fundamental to the human enterprise. The conceptualisation of territory, its apportionment in a tridimensional manner is the basis on which most legal realities are based and on which both national and international rule by law is possible. Territory is, therefore, about law and human law is scarcely possible without reference to the idea of territory. Cut to its barest essence, law is territorial and territory is law. The idea of sovereignty and jurisdiction over territory cuts clearly as a determinable concept across time and space. The study of the various forms of geophysical territorial space in a sense is, therefore, the most noble of all international studies. The importance of the study of territory and law is one of the single most underrated facts of international life. The imperative of multi-disciplinary study of the notion of aerial and outer space territories is again one of the most sacred duties of international lawyers. Similar duty of devotion to the topic ought to be demanded of experts in history, international relations, politics, sociology, linguistics and other social sciences as well as science and humanities. All knowledge is again relativised by its connections and interconnections as well as manifestation with territory. Clear understanding of territorial spaces and their permutations in terms of legal realities (delimitation, demarcation, criminal and civil jurisdiction) is, therefore, one of the imperatives of the modern prince just as much as it has always been throughout history. The bases for legitimate territorial acquisition are still deserving of study. They are also of interest to the aerospace lawyer based on the general principle that whenever territory has being acquired or lost under legitimate circumstances, the tridimensionality of territory principle ensures that there will have been a corresponding increase or decrease in the airspace of the affected state(s).

Sovereignty and jurisdiction are legal doctrines of a complex nature, which have been subject to differing interpretations by scholars in legal literature. Both concepts have been central to the development of international law. The relationship between the two with respect to all the manifestations of territory has also not been fully worked out by lawyers. Yet there exists a basic kernel of understanding as to

story.php?i=4387781 (accessed 10 August 2010); Indiaserver.com, "Pakistan-China to Jointly Produce JF-17 Jet Fighter", available at http://www.india-server.com/news/pakistan-china-to-jointly-produce-jf-17-6470.html (accessed 10 August 2010).

these two concepts in international law. While the term "sovereignty" covers the total legal personality of a state, jurisdiction refers to particular aspects of the substance, such as rights, liberties and powers of a state. Sovereignty explains the authority of the state over its populace, territory and affairs and operates in the international system along with the principle of equality of states.

Sovereignty and property rights are not always coterminous. Sovereignty may be possessed over the land on which foreign property rights exist. Sovereignty does not always confer property. Property does not confer sovereignty. Property may exist in areas in which no sovereignty at all may ever exist. Propertisation may also be forbidden in entire provinces in which no sovereignty may be exercised. We shall later come to see the workings of these concepts in relation to areas that are considered the common heritage of mankind and on which sovereignty cannot be exercised (e.g. outer space and to differing extents the high seas and significant parts of the Arctic as well as Antarctica) or property made from the resources of constituents thereof.

Jurisdiction also explains the right of the courts of a state to hear civil and criminal matters such as that which may arise with respect to damage caused during travel through airspace or by space activities or by acts committed on board aircraft and spacecraft. Due to the usefulness of the concepts of sovereignty and jurisdiction and the wealth of jurisprudence developed in relation to them over the centuries, it is inevitable that useful analogies will link them to control over the sea, Antarctica, the airspace and outer space. Hence, it is necessary to compare and contrast the manifestations of the concepts in these areas. Such exercises will not only reveal similarities but will also help fill any possible lacunae that exist in the development of the law in any of these areas.

In the treatment of crimes in airspace as well as outer space, it is necessary to accept the continuing relevance of the common bases of criminal jurisdiction of states which are: territorial principle, nationality principle, protective principle, passive personality principle and the universality principle. It is probably crucial for states to ascertain the specific basis of jurisdiction relied on in each case when they desire to exercise jurisdiction. Furthermore, immunities and privileges, dual citizenship and the total abhorrence of piratical acts are to be taken into consideration by states when exercising jurisdiction over persons and activities in the airspace and outer space.

It is clear that sovereignty has traditionally been claimed over *res nullius*. However, once a territory is recognised as *res communis*, the exercise of sovereign rights is out of the question. In the nature of things, it is doubtful that there remains any territory on earth, or indeed anywhere else, that is *res nullius*. In any case, the legal status of a territory as *res nullius* or *res communis* is determined promptly after discovery. In other words, there can be no change in the legal classification of any territory once it has been recognised as falling into one of the two categories. With particular reference to outer space and its celestial bodies, the significance of these findings is that the legal status of outer space has already been determined on the commencement of outer space activities. Since it has been the practice in international law to grant the status of *res communis* to all international commons[177] such as the high seas and Antarctica, it is reasonable to conclude at this stage that *res communis* also applies to outer space. Any attempt to introduce activities therein, which cannot be properly founded within this principle, will be difficult to reconcile with international law.

The tridimensionality of state territory recognised under customary international law subsists up to the present. The idea of sovereignty and jurisdiction over the airspace has developed over the centuries and is even older than the history of human flight. The operation of this principle, however, presupposes that at some point there is an upper ceiling to the dimensions of a state's territory. That point, however, has yet to be determined under international law.

Certainty over the geophysical extents of state territory, the determination of state boundaries and the legitimate exercise of extraterritorial jurisdiction are crucial issues in the 21st century much as they were since the decisive events of the peace treaties of Westphalia in 1648. This assertion does not in any way detract from the eminence and incremental relevance of globalisation and transgovernmentalism and their effect on international law. The study of sovereignty and territorial jurisdiction and the acceptance of their eminence does not detract from the possibility of celebrating international cooperation and cross-border cooperation in all senses between territorial sovereigns. Globalisation, cross-border cooperation and the sharing of international commons, indeed, confirm the existence of national sovereignties rather than deny them by ensuring the peaceful and progressive coordination of human societies.

177 International spaces have been defined by Kish (who was an early advocate of the development of a separate branch of international law for these spaces) as "the high seas, the polar regions and the cosmic spaces". The fundamental legal status of these spaces as international spaces, he explains, is in consequence of the incapability of national appropriation and the absence of effective national control. See John Kish, *The Law of International Spaces* (Leiden: A.W. Sijthoff International, NV, 1973): 196.

2 The legal status of the airspace

2.1 Nature and character of rights over airspace

The air is a gaseous substance of which the atmosphere is composed. It is transparent, perfectly elastic and highly compressible. Although very light, it has a perfectly definite weight in consequence of which it exerts pressure. The entire earth is enveloped by the airspace and may be considered as a gaseous sea at the bottom of which we all live and which extends upwards to a considerable height, which constantly diminishes in density as altitude increases.[178]

The airspace is an area that, for the most part of human existence, was not utilised for any reason other than breathing. Therefore, the early conceptions, as Borchard describes, it is that air is common public property, that which everybody may enjoy and which cannot be the object of exclusive right on the part of any individual or state; similarly, airspace has never been considered as commercial property. It cannot be considered as an object in strict legal terminology. In fact, property, according to Windscheid, can only mean "any singularised object (*Stück*) belonging to irrational nature".[179] Therefore, adopting this criterion, all property should be individualised as a phenomenon. It is more of an objective reality. For this reason, some jurists have found no difficulty in concluding that ownership of a given tract of airspace must be based on occupancy and possession.[180] In support of this view, Clement Bouve defines "ownership" as:

> based upon the possibility of becoming master of a thing, of taking possession of it, disposing of it at will; and when by virtue of characteristics peculiar to itself, a thing escapes from this appropriation further ownership in it is impossible.[181]

178 The term gaseous fluid represents the scientific fact that the atmosphere consists of several layers with different properties that flow into one another. G.S. Sachdeva, "Sovereignty in the Air – A Legal Perspective", 22 *Indian Journal of International Law* (1982): 397.

179 N.M. Matte, *Aerospace Law* (London: Sweet & Maxwell, 1987): 15.

180 B.K. Mukerjea, *The Problems of Air Law* (Calcutta: Hill Book Co., 1924): 60–1.

181 Clement L. Bouve, "Private Ownership of Airspace", *Air Law Review* (1930): 255.

Furthermore, he writes:

> But how much more true is this with respect to the aerial space above us . . . There is but one way of appropriating a portion of space, and that is by occupying it by means of building or plantings . . . Effective possession – that possession which manifests ownership can be accomplished in space only by works inherent to the soil and which in reality occupy a given tract of space.[182]

To Paul Fauchille, the conception of ownership with respect to any given portion of the superincumbent air column before occupying it by means of construction erected on the soil is out of the question: "For it is actual possession and not the possibility of it which creates ownership. The permanent possession of a thing is an essential prerequisite of ownership."[183]

These submissions by some European jurists (such as Bouve and Fauchille) can be accepted only with reservations. Their assertions may, at best, be pertinent if limited to the issue of private ownership of airspace. In reference to state ownership or sovereignty over superincumbent airspace, there need not be any form of overt effective occupation. Possessory rights reside implicitly in statehood. Thus, the correct emphasis is that pointed out by Cheng in holding that airspace sovereignty is delimited *ratione loci* in respect of the space above national territories and not *ratione materiae* in respect of the air that may at any given time be filling this space.[184] Thus, while Grotius remains correct in holding that since the air is not capable of being trapped it is, therefore, out of everyone's claim (indeed no one can hold the air just as no one can hold great expanses of water) that is not to say that ownership or sovereignty cannot be exercised over the oceanic space or airspace. Sovereignty, in this sense, does not really involve continual presence any more than possession does in private law. A state can exercise sovereignty over a huge desert or the summit of uninhabitable mountains, if it is in *de facto* control and is in a position to suppress internal disorder and repel external attack. Certainly in that sense, a state does own and control its airspace.

2.2 Development of the concept of sovereignty over airspace

The legal concept that a state has territorial rights above the earth is much older than the history of human flight. There is evidence that Rome did not hesitate to control the use of space whenever deemed necessary to protect public or private rights on the surface of the earth. The airspace over public highways and over sacred ground was kept open by law. Roman emperors limited the height to which buildings could be erected. Private rights in space above the landowner's property

182 Ibid.
183 Ibid.
184 Bin Cheng, "Recent Developments in Air Law", 9 *Current Legal Problems* (1956): 209.

on the surface were carefully kept and protected. The Roman state, indeed, made its law as effective above the surface of the earth as it did on the surface.[185] Roman law accepts private control of airspace above private property, because it considers it inherent in the ownership of the land itself and does not limit such control to low altitudes. It has been correctly suggested that:

> [T]he Romans could have met even the case of air navigation by permitting the aviator to cross a private air column, when it was not used by the land owner himself and provided such a crossing did not cause injury or damage to persons or to property . . . The upper control of airspace is nothing else but an extension of right of ownership a further exploitation of it, a higher use and enjoyment of property an extension of such use to upper zones. Therefore, the Romans would not have had any difficulty in admitting the private control of the airspace.[186]

The Romans, thus, developed the principle expressed in the maxim *cujus est solum ejus usque ad coelum et ad inferos* (whose is the soil, his is also that which is above it into infinity). In Anglo-Saxon law, the principle is found again: *cujus es solum ejus est usque ad coelum* (whose is the soil, his is also that which is above it).This principle derived undoubtedly from the existing knowledge of the possibility of the utilisation of space. However, scholars such as Arnoldo de Valles characterise the maxim as a principle simple in its absurdity and even opposed to the conception of ownership. To consider, says Grote, without qualification that the whole of aerial space is subject to property rights vested in the individual, community or the state, is in view of its colossal extent and in the absence of instrumentality competent to occupy a realm so infinite and so wholly, *sui generis*, a conception that is not only impossible at present but out of the question for all times.[187]

Again, while rejecting the view that aerial sovereignty should be based on effective occupation, the proposition cannot be accepted as advanced by some writers that international law has adopted *simpicta* the maxim *cujus est solum ejus usque ad coelum et ad inferos*. What international law today recognises is built on the maxim but is very different from the *ad inferos* (into infinity) and, therefore, *ad absurdum* nature of the Roman conception. The reason for the total nature of the earlier conception probably was that no one had any objection to the idea that everyone could stake out a claim in regions of space, for this was at that time, of course, a purely academic claim. Through time there have been numerous reasons advanced for determining the status of the airspace. Pufendorf, in the later part of the 17th century, remarked that: "Since man has been denied the ability to be in the air to the extent that he rest in it alone, and be separated from the earth he has been

185 Cooper op. cit.: 258; Alison J. Williams, "A Crisis in Aerial Sovereignty? Considering the Implications of Recent Military Violations of National Airspace", 42, 1 *Area* (2010): 53.

186 Francesco Lardone, "Airspace Rights in Roman Law", II *Airlaw Review* (1931): 150.

187 Bouve op. cit.: 250–1.

unable to exercise sovereignty over the air except in so far as men standing upon the earth can reach it."[188]

Thus, in his view, as is still held by some legal theorists today, national sovereignty in the air is limited by the ability for effective control. In other words, once control can be established through any means then sovereign rights can be claimed. Other writers such as Westlake, witnesses to developments in this century making it possible for man "to be in the air to the extent that he rest in it alone", have suggested that the necessity for extension of national sovereignty into the air exists because, "in the air, the higher one ascends, the more damage the fall of objects will cause on the earth".[189] For this reason alone, he concludes that: "the right of subjacent state remains the same whatever may be the distance". It needs be noted that concern for state security remains one of the reasons why there is still a blur today regarding the legal demarcation between national airspace and outer space. Therefore, any resolution of the spatial demarcation dispute will have to take into consideration the security concerns of states as well as their desire to retain complete sovereignty over territorial airspace.

In 1784 when the Montgolfier Brothers succeeded in constructing a balloon that could take people into the air and bring them back again, the law responded swiftly. On the occasion of the first ascent, 23 April 1784, a police order was issued in Paris defining in precise terms the conditions under which balloon flights could take place. The stated objective was the protection of the civil populace.[190] In essence, it represents one of the earliest concrete attempts to exercise lateral sovereignty and control over movements in the airspace. We may, in fact, posit that while lateral sovereignty is a much older concept, jurisdiction and control over movement in the airspace is a factor and an offshoot of the development of "aircraft".

McNair reports four theories on the legal status of the airspace prevalent until the early 20th century:

1 that the airspace is free, subject only to the rights of states required in the interests of their self-preservation
2 on the analogy of the maritime belt or territorial waters of each state there is a lower zone of territorial air space and a higher and unlimited zone of free airspace
3 that a state has complete sovereignty in its superincumbent airspace to an unlimited height, thus applying the *cuius est solum* maxim in its crude form

188 Cooper op. cit.: 258.
189 Quoted ibid.
190 Later developments include the 1911 and 1913 Aerial Navigation Acts of the UK, which instituted prohibited security zones along British coasts. In 1912 Russia hurriedly proclaimed an absolute prohibition to overfly its western frontiers. The Franco-German exchange of notes of 1913 (*infra*) established sovereignty over the airspace primarily between both countries. On the commencement of the First World War in 1914, Switzerland swiftly prohibited flights into its airspace by foreign aircraft (4 April). By November 1914 the USA forbade overflight over the Panama Canal. Sweden in 1916 also prohibited entrance of foreign aircraft. See Wybo P. Heere, "Problems of Jurisdiction in Air and Outer Space", xxiv, 2 *Annals of Air and Space Law* (1999): 70–1.

4 the fourth theory is the third with the addition of servitude of innocent passage for foreign non-military aircraft.[191]

The prevailing law differs in most respects from any of these theories. However, with the benefit of hindsight, it may be said that the first two theories remain alluring and the last two remain unacceptable propositions for all times.

In 1889 the first International Congress of Aeronautics was held in Paris on the occasion of the International Exposition with the participation of Brazil, France, Mexico, Russia, the UK and the USA. In 1890 there was a second International Congress of Aeronautics.[192] In 1900 Fauchille, in an address to the Institute of International Law, recommended that an international air code should be drawn up and as early as 1902 he presented a set of regulations consisting of 32 articles to the Institute of International Law, meeting in Brussels.[193] Fauchille, of course, was an ardent defender of freedom of the air and he was in disagreement with the Anglo- Saxon views presented by Westlake, who upheld the right of sovereignty of the underlying state while admitting the right of free peaceful transit.

In the conclusions of the International Law Association at its meeting in Madrid in 1911, the most widely held opinions among the jurists were expressed thus:

1 States have the right to regulate traffic over their territory (land and sea).
2 While reserving this right they should permit free transit to airships of all nations.[194]

In 1913 France and Germany signed the first treaty on air law. In it, sovereignty of the state over its airspace was maintained.[195] This development important as it was according to some modern legal historians did not go far enough since it did not result in a clear decision on the liberty of entering foreign airspace.[196] That same year in Madrid, the institute adopted a new theory in its resolution, which states:

191 Arnold McNair, *The Law of the Air*, 3rd edn (London: Stevens & Sons, 1964): 5.

192 Seara Vazquez, *Cosmic International Law* (Detroit: Wayne State University Press, 1985): 29.

193 Fauchille's arguments were simple enough. Echoing Pufendorf, he argued that real property of the air is impossible because we cannot appropriate it; the same applies to the possibilities of the state to dominate the air. Classically represented, it refers to the position that airspace is *res communis omnium* and *l'air est libre*. However, taking into consideration the arguments of the security school (as we may choose to call it) he approved a safety zone of the first 1,500 metres above the ground. Later on, apparently convinced of the correctness of his earlier convictions, he brought the ceiling down to 500 metres in 1910. See Paul Fauchille, *Le Domaine aérien et le régime juridique des aérostats* (Paris: 1901) as cited in Vazquez op. cit. See also Heere op. cit.: 22; Cf. *infra*, Chapter 11.9: Theories of arbitrary distances and my conclusions in Chapters 2 and 10.

194 Seara Vazquez op. cit.: 30. Having in effect agreed with Fauchille in1906 at its Gent meeting, the Institute in 1911 tried to avoid unnecessary disputes about the word "sovereignty" by adopting a resolution in which it was said that *la circulation aérienne est libre*.

195 There had been no agreement on the principle of sovereignty in the 1910–1911 conference. France and Germany agreed to recognise it in the 1913 conference.

196 Heere op. cit.: 71.

> It is the right of every State to enact such prohibitions restrictions and regulations as it may think proper in regard of the passage of aircraft above its territories and territorial waters. Subject to this right of subjacent States, liberty of passage of aircraft ought to be accorded freely to the aircraft of every nation.

This may very well mark the beginning of a limitation on territorial sovereignty in the airspace and the recognition of a servitude, which would, in any event, serve mostly the interests and be to the benefit of those states that have aircraft. It may well be wondered what the benefits of such a regime are to states that do not have aircraft at that stage of events and whether or not their interests were adequately considered. It is perhaps important to note that, at that time, most of the territories that are now independent states today were colonial possessions of the very states that designed the blueprint for what has today emerged as international air law.

The First World War of 1914–1918 brought about a realisation of the importance of aerial navigation as well as its potential danger to the subjacent state in military terms. Therefore, it was natural that henceforth the emphasis both in international treaties and by national legislation is on the theory of complete sovereignty in airspace subject only to mutual, carefully safeguarded and easily determinable right of free entry and passage for the non-military aircraft of foreign states.[197]

Therefore, when the first major multilateral treaty codifying the rules of air law was written in the guise of the Convention relating to the Regulation of Air Navigation of 13 October 1919[198] (which was signed by 33 states), the status of the airspace above national territory was stated as follows:

> The High contracting parties recognise that every power has complete and exclusive sovereignty over the airspace above its territory. For the purpose of the present convention the territory of a State shall be understood as including the national territory, both that of the mother country and of the colonies, and the territorial waters adjacent thereto.

This convention entered into force in 1922 and established two principles:

1 The full and exclusive sovereignty of each State over the atmospheric space above its territory. Each State has the right to open or close its airspace

197 Michael Akehurst, *A Modern Introduction to International Law*, 3rd edn (London: Allen & Unwin, 1980): 183.

198 To be referred to as the Paris Convention of 1919 League of Nations, Treaty Series, 174, 1919. See also Manley O. Hudson, *International Legislations* (New York: Oceana Publications, Inc., 1989): 359. The Convention was signed by Belgium, Bolivia, Brazil, the British Empire, China, Cuba, Czechoslovakia, Ecuador, France, Greece, Guatemala, Italy, Japan, Panama, Poland, Portugal, Romania, the Serb-Croat-Slovene State, Siam, the United States of America and Uruguay. Countries that later acceded include Peru, by declaration dated Paris, 22 June 1920; Nicaragua, by declaration dated Paris, 31 December 1920; Liberia, by declaration dated Paris, 29 March 1922; and Australia by declaration dated Paris, 1922.

including that above its territorial waters to foreign or domestic aircraft as it deems fit.

2 Freedom of peaceful transit for private planes of the contracting States in times of peace.

Note may be taken of the fact that exclusive sovereignty is granted over the airspace above "the colonies and the territorial waters thereto". This may be seen as verifiable evidence of the "Eurocentricity" of international law as was developed particularly in the 19th and 20th centuries. Even the principles of jurisdiction in air law were tailored to suit the prevailing Western interests and to legitimise the spoils of war.

The Ibero-American Convention of Madrid in 1926 was inspired by the same principles as that of Paris in 1919. This convention differed significantly from the Paris Convention not only in that it accounted for the principle of equal voting rights of its members (Article 34) but also quite significantly in that it recognised the right of a contracting state to permit the flight above its territory of an aircraft that did not possess the nationality of a contracting state (Article 5).[199] The Pan American Convention on Commercial Aviation 1928 in like manner conferred in Article I sovereignty over "atmospheric space" (*espace atmospheric*) while the latter, also in its Article I, recognises state sovereignty over the airspace (*espace areo*).[200]

These principles were again restated and incorporated in the Chicago Convention of 1944, which is the most important codification landmark in air law to date.[201]

The Convention provides thus:

Article 1: The contracting States recognise that every State has complete and exclusive sovereignty over the airspace above its territory.

Article 2: For the purposes of this convention the territory of a State shall be deemed to be the land areas and territorial waters adjacent thereto under the sovereignty, suzerainty, protection or mandate of such State.

It will be observed that the recognition of complete and exclusive sovereignty granted in Article 1 applies to "every state". In other words, it is not confined to contracting states. It is, therefore, clear that whatever controversy that may have

199 This Convention had a limited impact because of a poor record of ratifications. Whereas 21 states attended the Madrid Conference, only five States (Costa Rica, the Dominican Republic, Mexico, Paraguay and Spain) deposited their instruments of ratification.

200 Pan American Convention on Commercial Aviation signed at Havana on 20 February 1928, also referred to as the Havana Convention (1928). Text in Spanish and English 6th International Conference of American States, Report of the Delegates of the United States to Department of State, Washington (1928) 177-1189. See 3 *Journal of Air Law* (1932): 411.

201 78 UKTS 8 1953 Cmd 8742; UNTS 295. This Convention entered into force on 4 April 1947. Adherence by Nigeria to this treaty was on 14 November 1960. See Federal Ministry of Justice, *Nigeria's Treaties in Force: June 30 1969* (1971): 19.

existed as to the ownership, control and sovereignty over airspace and notwithstanding the influence of power politics in international relations, the question is now settled. The principle of complete and exclusive sovereignty over the superincumbent airspace by the underlying state is unassailable. Therefore, Vazquez concludes; "Airspace is that part of space subject to the sovereignty of a state."[202] McNair says: "Sovereignty in the superincumbent airspace reigns supreme."[203] Cheng sees the principle as "a well-recognised rule of international customary law".[204] For William J. Hughes, the principle is now a fundamental tenet of international law.[205] This universal principle underlies other numerous bilateral and multilateral conventions.

What becomes apparent from a study of the development of the regulation of the airspace is that it not so surprisingly reflects particular interests. Dominant scholars and countries dictate these interests from the perspective of prevailing ideas as well as political and economic interests. In fact, by sheer reason of colonial subjugation most countries that exist today did not have the opportunity to participate in the creation of air law.

Certain scholars from certain states have had more than a fair opportunity to shape air law at least within the principles of aerial sovereignty and jurisdiction. In fact, it may be suggested that the reason why the ensuing legal regime created for the airspace is not more blatantly unfair is due to competition among the few privileged aviation powers and not altruistic motivation or actual involvement of the majority of states. Again, it can only be said that the story of the development of the concept of sovereignty in the law of the air is not very different from the story of the development of international law itself, i.e. it is a product of the perceived interests of Western civilisation and other hegemonic interests.

Ironically, Britain and the USA were at cross-purposes around the middle of the 20th century over the conceptualisation of sovereignty and jurisdiction in the airspace. The Chicago Conference in 1944, coinciding as it was with the tail end of the Second World War, became the battleground for two opposing visions. At this time the USA possessed a virtual monopoly in the construction of aircraft big enough to navigate the world. Thus, the USA, which had not ratified the Paris Convention, suddenly found itself in the unenviable position of a leader without a following. It was not able to influence the shape of the law of the air beyond the Havana Convention of 1928.[206] Its agenda at the Chicago Conference for the principle of maximum freedom for civil aviation was viewed with suspicion by the UK, which neither possessed nor produced aircraft big enough to cross the oceans. The UK, therefore, pleaded for controlled use of the airspace. This became the

202 Vazquez op. cit.: 27.

203 McNair op. cit.: 15.

204 Bin Cheng, "From Air Law to Space Law", 13 *Current Legal Problems* (1960): 229; Cheng (1956) op. cit.: 208.

205 William J. Hughes, "Aerial Intrusions by Civil Airliner and the Use of Force", *Journal of Air and Commerce* (1980): 595.

206 *Supra*, note 200.

adopted position at the conference since the UK still had the then existing members of the Commonwealth behind its position and most of the colonial territories belonged to it.[207] Thus, the provision that passage through airspace and landing rights are at all times subject to the control of the territorial state became enshrined in Articles 1 and 6 of the Chicago Convention. It does not take much acumen to realise that from the position of developing countries the initial opposition of views between the "air powers" can be said to be very fortunate. Unity of views at that stage between them would have undoubtedly produced different results for the concept of jurisdiction over airspace. Exclusive control over aerial territory may have been whittled down to dangerous levels especially for weaker states. It is worthy of note that up to the present day the USA still aggressively promotes the principle of "open skies".[208] Starting in 1978 when its own internal aviation market was deregulated, the USA has offered liberal bilateral agreements to other states.

Of particular concern to us is the effect this policy will produce on the future of air law when it operates in conjunction with emerging European Union legislation. It was predictable that some of the most effective inputs towards the regulation of the international airspace (at least with respect to civil aviation) would be introduced via EU legislation. In 1987, 1990 and 1993, respectively, a liberal structure for civil aviation has been promoted and implemented by the European Commission. The implementation of these measures is based on the aviation policy devised by two memoranda of 1979 and 1984.[209] Thus, if from 1978 the USA and the EU have been pushing the agenda of deregulation and liberalisation, the tone is already set in an increasingly unipolar world for the operation of these principles on a worldwide basis. This, of course, is not necessarily a bad development. But it may also not necessarily be in the interest of the majority of developing states. For example, the airspace over national territories is becoming freer for big business to operate at a time at which the exploitation of outer space resources appears to be more and more the exclusive preserve of those states benefiting most from the "open skies".

The globalisation of the international airline long-haul operations industry produces an inescapable pull into which even developing states are drawn. The open skies agreement between Nigeria and the United States has, for instance, opened up Nigerian airspace for more serious competition from abroad.[210] Although, theoretically, Nigerian airlines ought to be able to explore opportunities open to them in the USA by open skies agreements the truth is, that without

207 The origins of the Commonwealth lie in Britain's former colonial empire. As the first colonies –Australia, Canada and New Zealand – evolved into self-governing dominions, they came to be seen as partners with Britain. The term seems first to have been used by Lord Roseberry in Adelaide in 1884, when he referred to the Empire as "a Commonwealth of Nations". Until 1949 the member states of the Commonwealth were united through common allegiance to the Crown. Information and materials about the Commonwealth are available at www.commonwealth-of-nations.org.

208 Heere op. cit.: 72.

209 Ibid.

210 "Chinedu Eze, BA: Open Skies has Made Nigeria's Airspace Competitive", *This Day* (Nigeria), Vol. 15, No. 5584 (2009): 29.

entering into global alliance arrangements, the business opportunities are merely illusory. Many of the available alliances were designed before the serious participation of airlines from developing states became possible and they indeed still face serious challenges in their ability to participate on equal terms. In a sense, therefore, north–south open skies agreements arguably work more to the advantage of the developed northern states and their businesses.

It would unfortunately appear that the majority of scholars particularly from developing counties have taken no studied position on these points. Complacency in this way is evidenced in the constructive exclusion of African airlines from much of the European Union airspace through a system of EU-wide blacklist that is revised periodically.[211] As the African Airlines Association (AFRAA) correctly notes: "The ultimate beneficiaries of the ban are European airlines which dominate African skies to the disadvantage of African carriers."[212] Contrariwise, it would appear that a much better solution is that bans in the form practised by the EU should be implemented by the International Civil Aviation Organisation (ICAO) as the only global regulator of aviation safety, which has a known track record of impartiality. Scholars in this area of studies do have to consider and evaluate the likely effects of the cocktail of trends – increased use of drones as well as no-fly zones and open skies policies – on the concept of exclusive national sovereignty and jurisdiction over national airspace.

2.3 Nationality principle and control over aircraft in flight

That state sovereignty to a large extent has territorial limitations has already been alluded to. Indeed, before a state can exercise unchallenged jurisdiction, present an international claim or confer rights and duties on a person, there must be a determination of nationality that is based on sovereignty.[213] With respect to aircraft

211 The EU regularly revises a list of international airlines that are blacklisted for want of compliance with EU regulations. Blacklisted companies as at 30 March 2010 included 111 companies from 11 sub-Saharan African states. Nik Ogbuile, "EU Grounds African Airlines", *Business World*, 27 September–3 October 2010: 12.

212 AFRAA noted and commented that in contrast to the position taken by the EU on African air safety challenges, the USA introduced the "Safe Skies for Africa" initiative aimed at upgrading capacity, developing skills and providing infrastructure to improve safety. All this is being done at a time when only a few US carriers are operating to Africa. See AFRAA, "AFRAA Responds to EU List of Airlines Banned from European Airspace", media release 6 April 2010, available at http://www.afraa.org/pressreleases.htm.

213 Despite challenges to the traditional international law system of sovereignty and equality that has been alluded to in Chapter 1, the traditional account of international law as law between states is still strong and serves useful purposes. "States" still represent the carving of the world into non-overlapping territorial units, vested with the authority to regulate their territories and having the responsibility not to harm certain interests of others and the capacity to make claims when they or their nationals are affected by illegality for which other states, corporations or international organisations are responsible. It is for this reason that a reasonably comprehensive if decentralised effort is made to connect every individual, corporation, vessel and aircraft with at least one territorial state. Nationality, in this sense, refers to the quality or character that arises from the

or indeed spacecraft in flight, nationality is the determinant of control. At this stage, the principle of nationality of aircraft alone will be examined. The nationality principle has two crucial applications. The first is in respect of the jurisdiction *ratione instrumenti* (i.e. over the aircraft itself) and that of jurisdiction *ratione personae* (i.e. over persons on board the flight). As regards the latter, clearly where there is a concurrence of jurisdictions, the quasi-territorial jurisdiction (or specifically jurisaction) of the state of registry takes precedence over the personal jurisdiction of any state whose nationals may be on board.

Just as in the case of maritime vessels and unlike any other land-based vehicles or craft (such as cars, tractors, cycles etc.) an aircraft must have a nationality. Nationality of aircraft is an unassailable legal principle the utility of which is reflected in the fact that it is well entrenched in several multilateral treaties regulating the airspace. For instance, in the Paris Convention of 1919,[214] it is stated that aircraft possess the nationality of the state on the register of which they are entered (Article 6). Furthermore, no aircraft shall be entered on the register of the contracting states unless it belongs wholly to nationals of such state. No incorporated company may be registered as the owner of an aircraft unless it possess the nationality of the state in which the aircraft is registered, unless the president or chairman of the company and at least two-thirds of the directors possess such nationality and unless the company fulfils all other conditions that may be prescribed by the laws of the said state (Article 7).[215] It is also stated that an aircraft may not be validly registered in more than one state (Article 8). The contracting states agree to exchange every month among themselves and transmit to the International Commission for Air Navigation referred to in Article 34 copies of registrations and of cancellations of registrations that shall have been entered on their official registers during the preceding month (Article 9). Last, all aircraft in international navigation shall bear their nationality and registration marks as well as the name and residence of the owner (Article 10).

The Havana Convention of 1928 also stated in similar terms in Articles 7 to 9 as follows:

Article 7: Aircraft shall have the nationality of the State in which they are registered and cannot be validly registered in more than one State.

Article 8: The registration of aircraft referred to in the preceding article shall be made in accordance with the laws and special provisions of each contracting State.

fact of a person's belonging to a nation or state. Nationality determines the political status of the individual, especially with reference to allegiance, while domicile determines his civil status. Nationality of individuals arises either by birth or by nationalisation. See *Black's Law Dictionary*, 6th edn (St. Paul, MN: West Publishing Co., 1990). See also Benedict Kingsbury, "Sovereignty and Inequality", 9, 4 *European Journal of International Law* (1998): 610.

214 *Supra*, note 198.

215 Article 7 was revised by a protocol dated in Paris 15 June 1929, which provides that registration of aircraft shall be made in accordance with the laws and special provisions of each contracting state.

Article 9: Every aircraft engaged in international navigation must carry a distinctive mark of its nationality, the nature of such distinctive mark to be agreed upon by the several contracting States. The distinctive marks adopted will be communicated to the Pan American Union and to other contracting States.

The Chicago Convention 1944 lends equal weight to the principle of nationality of aircraft. As Cheng puts it, the second important principle accepted by parties to the Chicago Convention 1944 is that enunciated in Article 17.[216] This Article states that: "Aircraft have the nationality of the state in which they are registered." Accordingly, Article 18 declares that "an aircraft cannot validly be registered in more than one state, but its registration may be changed from one state to another". Article 19 stipulates that the registration or transfer of registration of aircraft in any contracting state shall be made in accordance with its laws and regulations. Article 20 provides that every aircraft engaged in international air navigation shall bear its appropriate nationality and registration marks. Article 21 mandates a system by which states are obliged to supply to each other and to the International Civil Aviation Organisation (ICAO) any information that is demanded concerning the registration and ownership of aircraft registered in that state.

States translate these principles of air law into local legislation in different ways. As a general trend, however, it is always intended to give ultimate effect to the principles enunciated in the Chicago Convention especially the utility of the principles of nationality and registration. For instance, as far as British aircraft are concerned, the rules of nationality and registration of aircraft are important and have been incorporated into a plethora of legislation. The earlier legislative efforts include the Civil Aviation Act 1960 and the Air Navigation (General) Regulations 1960. While the 1960 Regulations operate against double registration (i.e. registration in more than one state), the 1960 Act regulates furthermore that an aircraft will be registered only if it appears to the minister that it is owned wholly by persons qualified to be owners of an aircraft registered in the UK.[217] Under that regime, the only persons qualified to be the owners of an aircraft registered in the UK are those incorporated in some part of the Commonwealth and firms carrying on business in Scotland.

The principal order currently in force in the UK is the Air Navigation Order 2009, which establishes a system for the registration and marking of aircraft and for the certification and licensing of aircraft airworthiness and makes provision in relation to air operators and crews, the rules of the air and air traffic service.[218]

216 B. Cheng, *The Law of International Air Transport* (London: Oceana Publications, Inc., 1962): 128.

217 Air Navigation Order 1960, Art 2.

218 This instrument came into force on 1 January 2010. To a great extent, English municipal air law is regulated by statute and by statutory instruments made under statutory powers. The principal statutes include the Civil Aviation Act 1982, which confers comprehensive enabling powers for the regulation of civil aviation, and the Airports Act 1986, which deals with the regulation and use of airport facilities. Much of the legislation gives effect in English law to international agreements: the Civil Aviation Act 1982 contains provisions for carrying out the requirements of

Registration and marking of aircraft remains mandatory under section 3 of the Air Navigation Order 2009, thus, an aircraft shall not fly in or over the United Kingdom unless it is registered: in some other part of the Commonwealth; in a contracting state (i.e. parties to the Chicago Convention); in a country with reciprocal arrangements with the UK; or it is a non-EASA glider or non-EASA aircraft not at any time making any incursion into foreign territory or merely a non-EASA kite or non-EASA captive balloon. According to Article 4, the Civil Aviation Authority is the authority responsible for the registration of aircraft in the UK and shall maintain a register for that purpose. Article 4 forbids double registration and registration for convenience. Article 5 states exhaustively those persons qualified to hold a legal or beneficial interest in an aircraft in the UK or a share therein.[219]

Not only must an aircraft possess nationality and be registered, it is the law in most jurisdictions that the registration mark must be displayed. The UK Air Navigation Order 2009 in Article 10 states clearly that an aircraft (other than an aircraft permitted by or under this order to fly without being registered) shall not fly unless it bears painted thereon or affixed thereto in the manner required by the law of the country by which it is registered, the nationality and registration marks required by that law. Deceptive marks are prohibited (Article 10(3) (a) and (b)).

Law courts appear to have interpreted these rules in a purposive manner and an example of this may be found under US jurisdiction where civil forfeiture proceedings against an aircraft alleged to have displayed a mark that was false or misleading with respect to its nationality or registration were dismissed as a result of a failure to allege that the aircraft in question was involved in air transportation. It was held that in so far as the aircraft registration listed the aircraft as "commercial-private", it was not apparent whether the vehicle was used only by its owner or used to provide services to members of the general public.[220]

It suffices to mention that a number of bilateral agreements between states also make provisions for the nationality of aircraft.[221] It is, however, important to note that there is still controversy among scholars on the subject of nationality of aircraft.

the Chicago Convention, whereas the Carriage by Air Act 1961 enacts in the law of the United Kingdom the provisions of the Aviation Security Act as amended at the Hague in 1955 and the Carriage by Air and Road Act 1979 including the provisions of that Convention as further amended at Montreal in 1975; the Carriage by Air (Supplementary Provisions) Act 1962 gives effect to the Guadalajara Convention; and the Aviation Security Act enables the rules of international agreements for the protection of civil aviation to be applied in the United Kingdom.

219 They are as follows: (a) the Crown; (b) Commonwealth citizens; (c) nationals of any EEA state; (d) British protected persons; (e) bodies incorporated in some part of the Commonwealth and having their principal place of work business within the European Economic Area; (f) undertakings formed in accordance with the law of an EEA State which have their registered office, central administration or principal place of business within the European Economic Area; or (g) firms carrying out business in Scotland.

220 *US v. One 1980 Cessna II Aircraft*, US District Court, Southern District of Florida 15 December 1997, 26 Avi 15. 459. For a thorough digest of this case, see xxiv, 6 *Air and Space Law* (1999): 333.

221 Other matters dealt with by bilateral agreements on the subject of jurisdiction over airspace and airliners in flight include: admission of civil aircraft, issuance of pilots licences and acceptance of certificates of airworthiness for aircraft imported as merchandise.

One view correctly holds that nationality of aircraft is based on registration; therefore, an aircraft may not be registered in two or more states at the same time.[222] An older opposing view argues that, in most countries, the nationality of the aircraft is determined by the nationality of the owner.[223]

It is necessary to present this controversy, because it is frequently assumed in accordance with the various treaty provisions discussed earlier that the nationality of ships and aircraft is invariably determined by their place of registration and hence by the flag they are entitled to bear. Cheng, however, aptly points out that this proposition ignores divergent state practice.[224] It is, for instance, a fact that the nationality of British ships is determined by the nationality of their owners. In Temperley's *Merchant Shipping Act*, [225] it is stated that:

> The term British ship is not defined in the Act. It would seem, however, that unless she is employed by a Government under Letters of Marque, the nationality of the owners is generally the criterion of the nationality of a vessel . . . Hence a British owned ship is a British ship for such purposes, even if she is not registered in this country or if she is registered in and carries the flag of a foreign country.

Thus, it is clear that the flag flown by an aircraft unfortunately offers no more than a *prima facie* presumption that the aircraft has the nationality of the state whose flag it carries. Schwarzenberger's caveat, then, is that only aircraft papers are real evidence of nationality. This is more so since some states still fall back on the nationality of the owner as proof of the aircraft's nationality. It is important to state that the preferred argument is the one that tallies with treaty law to the effect that the place of registration determines nationality (Article 77 Chicago Convention (1944)) and that it is within the domestic jurisdiction of every state to determine in accordance with its municipal laws to which aircraft it is prepared to grant its nationality. Thus, divergent practice as typified by the erstwhile British interpretation has to be brought in consonance with contemporary international law.

The major importance of the principle of nationality in relation to the incident of an aircraft in flight is that it opens the way for other rights and liabilities being attached to aircraft irrespective of their owners or operators.[226] For example, with the legal requirement of identification of the nationality of all aircraft in flight, states find it easier to permit a generally free use of their airspace for navigation. The mutual realisation is that any navigation over state territory inures as much as possible to the benefit and as little as possible to the distress of their citizens and other services.[227]

222 See Akehurst op. cit.: 183.
223 See Margaret Lambie, "Universality versus Nationality of Aircraft", V, 1 *Journal of Air Law* (1934): 46–7.
224 Cheng (1962) op. cit.: 129.
225 5th edn 1954: 3.
226 Cheng (1962) op. cit.: 128.

The operation of the principle of nationality of aircraft allows states to achieve the following:

- a reservation of commercial air traffic between points in the same states for nationals of that state – that is, the principle of cabotage, which has long been familiar in coastal shipping laws
- a protection of the public interest of the state itself against the possibility that its secrets of national defence might be unduly violated by the prying eyes of an observer while in flight over the aerial territory
- a means whereby the state may protect its citizens and territory against injuries resulting from improper or careless activities of aviators and/or enable its citizens to secure adequate redress if such injuries should occur. [228]

In short, the chief importance of determination of nationality of aircraft is to ensure cooperation and collaboration among states with respect to flights in air space. Without this basic understanding, it becomes impossible for aircraft to traverse state territories for various purposes. The detection and control of aerial trespass will be rendered more difficult and the provisions against unsafe aircraft and incompetent pilots will be even more difficult to monitor. The whole essence of the retention of state sovereignty over national airspace will be defeated. Ultimately, it presents an easy mode of determining which law governs and what tribunal or court has jurisdiction over the redress for, or punishment of, conduct in aircraft. According to one of the early authorities on the subject, diplomatic protection of the aircraft abroad; the right of requisition of the aircraft during war by the "state of the flag" foreign aircraft being exempt; and designation of civil and criminal jurisdiction over aircraft are sufficient reasons to at all times confer nationality on aircraft.[229] These observations remain true to this day.

2.3.1 Nationality principle and the question of what an aircraft is

Two questions require consideration. First, what is an aircraft? Second, which craft must possess nationality? Which "craft" fall within the provisions of the Chicago Convention 1944 and what laws govern those that fall outside this Convention? To many scholars at the inception of the last century when flight was at its beginning stages, an aircraft was, properly speaking, no more than a ship and, like a ship, it has peculiar need of national protection.[230] This sweeping generalisation would only lead to confusion if accepted *in toto*; for an aircraft is not a ship, unless

227 Hence the requirement of easily identifiable registration marks on all aircraft. See also Lambie op. cit.: 40.

228 Kingsley Rober, "Nationality of Aircraft", 3 *Journal of Air Law* (1932): 50.

229 A. De la Pradelle, 3 *Revue Juridique Internationale de la Locomation Aérienne* (1912): 116.

230 See Henry Conannier, "De Ia Nationalite et du Domicile does Aeronefs", 1 *Revue Juridique Internationale de la Locomotion Aérienne* (1910): 165. See also Lambie op. cit.: 41.

we speak in terms of an "airship". It is true that, as with ships, there is need for national protection of other vehicles engaged in international transport. This need has been extended to cover vehicles that traverse the airspace such as spaceships and space objects. This is surely not to say that there are no clear distinctions in legal terms between ships, airships and spaceships. Furthermore, we may enquire whether there are distinctions between an aircraft, which by international law must have a nationality, and other craft such as balloons and dirigibles.[231] The attempt to grapple with these distinctions will necessarily take us into comparative analysis of the aviation laws of different countries with differing approaches and solutions to this question and, of course, to similar questions with respect to space law.

The Chicago Convention refers in Article 3(1) to "civil aircraft" but offers no definition. However, the Council of the International Civil Aviation Organisation (ICAO) has defined an aircraft for the purpose of the annexes to the Convention as "any machine that can derive support from the reaction of the air". This is the same interpretation given in the annex to the Paris Convention of 1919. But, there are still significant objects, such as hot air balloons and gliders, that can violate airspace territory, which derive support from the reaction of air that properly defined are not "machines" as such. Are these classes of craft then aircraft and must the requirements of nationality and registration under Article 12 Chicago Convention 1944 be complied with in operating them?[232] Space-bound vehicles present another problem. They are no doubt also "machines" that "derive support from the reaction of the air when still within the atmosphere. Are these then aircraft, which must satisfy the nationality requirement and operate under all the provisions of the Chicago Convention? Cheng argues convincingly that:

> This definition of aircraft *senso stricto* while it includes both instruments which are lighter than air, like balloons and airships and those which are heavier than air, like gliders and aeroplanes does not apply to devices such as rockets, earth satellites and other space vehicles. Even though they may perhaps fall within a *sense alto* definition of aircraft as used in certain systems of municipal law, the term flight craft has the advantage of obviating any ambiguity.[233]

231 Balloons particularly have been considered as aircraft under UK law. See *Laroche v. Spirit of Adventure (UK) Ltd*, Court of Appeal of England and Wales (Mummery, Dyson and Jacob LJJ), 21 January 2009 [2009] EWCA Civ. 12. The Court of Appeal held that there was no reason why a hot air balloon designed for and capable of carrying passengers from one place to another should not be regarded as an "aircraft" for the purposes of the Non-International Rules of the Warsaw–Hague MP4 Convention: "The natural and ordinary meaning of aircraft was wide enough to include a passenger-carrying hot air balloon; and although it was necessary to bear in mind that the Warsaw Convention was originally applied only to international transport, hot air balloons are undoubtedly capable of being used as a means of transport." See Lawson Robert, "Balloons are Aircraft and Two Years Means Two Years", 34, 3 *Air and Space Law* (2009): 221–2.

232 Note that under the regime of the UK law discussed earlier, gliders and balloons are exempt from registration.

233 Bin Cheng, "International Law and High Altitude Flights and Man-Made Satellites", 6 *ICLQ* (1957): 491.

O'Connell, for his part, would appear to have fallen victim to sweeping generalisation. He writes: "[O]ne might conclude therefore that as a practical measure, the law relating to registration and nationality of space bodies in outer-space is the same as that of aircraft." [234] First, as will later be shown, it is not space bodies that are registered but spacecraft and space objects. Furthermore, the true position is that while the regulation of aircraft in flight falls under the purview of air law and the provisions of the Chicago Convention (1944), the regulation of space craft and other space objects falls under the fast developing rules of space law and the space treaties.[235]

The most pertinent provision on registration and nationality of spacecraft is enshrined in the Convention on Registration of Objects Launched into Outer Space of 1975.[236] This Convention states that when a space object is launched into orbit or beyond, the launching state shall register the space object by means of an entry in an appropriate registry, which it shall maintain. Each launching state shall in turn inform the Secretary-General of the United Nations of the establishment of such a registry.[237] Where there are two or more launching states in respect of a spacecraft, they shall jointly determine which of them shall register the spacecraft.[238] Each state of registry shall furnish the Secretary-General with an appropriate designator of the space object or its registration number.[239] Although the Registration Convention (1975) does not mention it clearly in any of its 12 articles, as in the case of the air treaties (particularly Article 17 of the Chicago Convention (1944)), a spacecraft bears the nationality of the state of registry of that spacecraft.

234 D.P. O'Connell, *International Law*, 2nd edn, Vol. 1 (London: Stevens & Sons, 1970): 540.

235 There are eight multilateral instruments, which constitute the *corpus juris* of space law. They are: (a) Treaty Banning Nuclear Weapon Tests in the Atmosphere, in Outer Space and Under Water 1963 also known as the Nuclear Test Ban Treaty; (b) United Nations General Assembly Resolution 1962 (xviii); (c) 1963 Declaration of Legal Principles Governing the Activities of States in the Exploration and Use of Outer Space; (d) Treaty on Principles Governing the Activities of States in the Exploration and Use of Outer Space, including the Moon and Other Celestial Borders (1967) (18 UST 2410, 610, UNTS 205); (e) Agreement on the Return of Objects launched in to Outer Space (1968); (f) Convention on International Liability for Damage Caused by Space Objects (1972); (g) Convention on Registration of Objects Launched into Outer Space (1975); (h) Agreement Governing the Activities of States on the Moon and other Celestial Bodies (1979) (GA Res. 34/68, U.N. GAOR, 34th Sess. Supp. No. 46 at 77, UN Doc. A/34/664 (1979).

236 Although outer space belongs to no one, the state of registry of a space object retains jurisdiction and control over it and any personnel on it while it is in outer space or on a celestial body. Ownership over space objects does not change because of their location and if found outside the territory of the state of registry, either on earth or anywhere else, it shall be returned to it after providing identifying data, if so requested (Article VIII Outer Space Treaty 1967). Similar provisions exist in Articles 1, 2 and 3 of the Astronauts and Space Objects Agreement (1969); in Article 7 of the Declaration of Legal Principles (1963) and Article 12 Moon Treaty 1979. See, further, *infra*, Chapter 9.

237 Article 11(1).

238 Article 11(2).

239 Article IV (b) and V

Thus, it is safe to conclude that although the applicable legal regime may differ, all spacecraft, aircraft[240] and, in fact, any other man-made flying object that is to be used for international flight must be registered by a state and must be invested with a particular nationality. Besides, if ever an interpretation is adopted by which air vehicles like gliders and balloons are not attributed with nationality (the value of such contraptions for aerial espionage must not be underrated) and if any aircraft flies without registration, international law is not helpless in coping with such flights. By analogy with the customary law of the sea where a ship is not prohibited from sailing without a flag, a glider, balloon or aircraft that flies without a flag may well be treated as if it were a stateless person with all the deleterious effects of such status.[241]

Unresolved issues concerning the legal regime of registration of aircraft and spacecraft exist presently. One of these relates to the special problem of the relatively newer class of aircraft, the X-15, which is capable of flying to heights previously considered supra-atmospheric. These hybrid rocket planes combine elements of the traditional aircraft and of spacecraft and, therefore, can fly above the lower airspace. The emergence of space tourism (dealt with later) has, in fact, spawned a new industry for the production of "hybrid crafts", which bring this issue to sharper focus. An aircraft is described in the air treaties as a machine depending on the reaction of the air as its means of flight. It is clear that aircraft that can function in an environment where all the aerodynamic features that give a normal aircraft the needed "lift" exist no more creates serious problems for aerospace lawyers. Should such an object be registered as an aircraft under the Chicago Convention rules? Or is it to be treated as a space vehicle, therefore, falling under the provisions of the space treaties?[242]

Noting that the pertinent international treaties are silent on this matter it can only be conjectured that it would be advisable that such "craft" be registered first as aircraft to satisfy the requirements of the Chicago Convention. Registration as a space object would appear to be necessary only on a planned launching into orbit or beyond. This interpretation falls on all fours with the precise wordings of Article II of the Convention on Registration of Objects Launched into Outer Space (1975),

240 Which includes (a) machines heavier than air that are mechanically driven (such as aeroplanes, sea planes or helicopters) as well as those that are not mechanically driven (such as gliders or even kites) and (b) machines lighter than air, whether mechanically driven (such as airships) or non-mechanically driven (such as captive or free balloons). See Cheng (1957) op. cit.: 111. See our discussion on space tourism in Chapter 3.

241 Thus, in the *Nain Malvan v. Attorney-General for Palestine* case, the judicial committee of the Privy Council stated; "[N]o question of comity nor of breach of international law can arise if there is no State under whose flag the vessel sails . . . Having no flag . . . the Asya could not claim that any principle of International law was broken by her seizure." See 1948 AC 351 at 369–70. See also Nwachukwu Okeke, *Theory and Practice of International Law in Nigeria*, 3rd edn (Enugu, Nigeria: Fourth Dimension): 173.

242 Particularly, Declaration of Legal Principles (1963) (Articles 7 and 8); Outer Space Treaty (1967) (Article VIII); Convention on Registration of Objects Launched into Outer Space (1975) (Articles II, III and IV).

which states that: "When a space object is launched into orbit or beyond, the launching state shall register the space object."[243] Note should be taken of the fact that the term space object includes launch vehicles (Article 1). Therefore, whether the launch vehicle itself proceeds into outer space or returns to earth after launch it must be registered as a *space*craft and not an *air*craft. This is particularly true if it will attain heights at which objects can be said to enter into orbit.[244]

However, since the decision to register the craft in question as aircraft or spacecraft will, in the first instance, belong to the state that owns it or its nationals, there will eventually be disagreements among states over which classification a particular vehicle should have been registered. Registration of a spy vehicle that can make space flights as an aircraft will, for instance, be a clever albeit illegal attempt to avoid the legal consequences of registration as a spacecraft. If a state successfully achieves this then it may not have to register the vehicle as a space object on the register of the UN as required by the space treaties and cannot be easily accused of using outer space activities to engage in unfriendly acts against other states. This again testifies to the need for international lawyers rapidly to address the separation in spatial terms the height at which the regime of air law ends and that of space law begins.

2.3.2 Nationality of aircraft and the question of "genuine link"

It is necessary also to consider if and to what extent the problem of "flags of convenience" exist in relation to aircraft and the jurisdictional problems this may create. The problem of flags of convenience is one that the maritime lawyer is more familiar with.[245] The tremendous growth in the aviation industry worldwide, however, threatens to reintroduce afresh the problem of flags of convenience in international relations. Nowhere is this more likely than in the developing states as a result of the increasing incidence of privatisation of national airlines and mushrooming private airline business.

243 The X-15 and such hybrid rocket planes make nonsense of these provisions. Such vehicle may not be "launched into orbit" but are capable of making space flights. It has therefore, been suggested that aerodynamic lift can no longer be considered a criterion to denote the boundary between airspace and outer space. See A.G. Haley, "Space Law and Metalaw – Jurisdiction Defined", 24 *Journal of Air Law and Commerce* (1987): 286; Pitman B. Potter, "International Law of Outer Space", 52 *American Journal of International Law* (1958): 305; Cooper op. cit.: 368, 370; A.G. Haley, *Space Law and Government* (New York: 1993): 77, 97–107. See *infra*, Chapter 11.

244 See *infra*, Chapter 11:8: The lowest point of orbital flight theory.

245 This problem arises out of the practice whereby some developing states notably Honduras, Liberia, Panama and Somalia bestow on foreign ships their flags, imposing minimal conditions for the acquisition of their nationality. They, in actual fact, exercise minimal control over such ships. The non-insistence on stringent standards and legislation by these states relating to matters of navigation safety; seamen's working conditions and skills translate to cheaper costs for the operators hence the attraction towards flag of convenience jurisdiction.

We may recall that the Paris Convention of 1919 stipulated clearly that registration could only take place in the state of which the owners of the aircraft are nationals. The Chicago Convention (1944), by way of contrast, does not make provision for this important requirement. It merely forbids dual registration (Article 18). Indeed, most of the rights exchanged under the Chicago Convention (1944) including the right of non-scheduled flights under Article 5 are in regard to aircraft registered in the contracting states, without reference to the nationalities of their owner or operators. Furthermore, transit and traffic rights for scheduled international air services are generally exchanged between the contracting states not in respect of aircraft bearing their nationality but of air transport enterprises or airlines of each other. This is, for instance, the case with both the International Air Services Transit Agreement (1944) and the International Air Transport Agreement (1944). Thus, the coast would appear to be clear for the problem of flags of convenience to repeat itself probably on a larger scale than it exists in the law of the sea. Certain states indeed appear to carry disproportionate number of aircraft on their registry. Although it appears that unlike the mercantile marine situation, the aeronautical "flag of convenience" is supposedly for legal and tax reasons only – and does not affect or reflect the maintenance and operation of the airline.[246] The Directors General of Civil Aviation Conference on a Global Strategy for Aviation Safety (DGCA/06) in 2006 recognised the trend and recommended in Recommendation 2/4 that: "States should eliminate flags of convenience and prevent illegal operations as well as the possible export of such activities from one State or group of States to another, and exchange safety information to this end."[247]

Fortunately, however, as Cheng notes many bilateral air transport agreements and some multilateral air transit and transport agreements incorporate a substantial ownership and effective control clause. These clauses ensure that airlines are vested in nationals of the respective contracting states. In this way, for now at least, the problem of flags of convenience can easily be excluded from scheduled international transport.[248] National laws also implement strict regimes to prevent this problem and in some cases attempts are made to make sure that foreigners are exempt from commercially exploiting an opportunistic registration.[249]

246 Access International LLC, "Aviation Flags of Convenience", *Air Safety Week* 30 September 2010, available at http://findarticles.com/p/articles/mi_m0UBT/is_9_21/ai_n27164832/ (accessed 1 October 2010).

247 See ICAO, Progress Report on the Issue of Flags of Convenience (presented by the President of the Air Navigation Commission) (AN Programme A1-SMP-ACT) C-WP/13133 ANC Report 20/02/08, available at http://www.icao.int/Hyperdocs/display.cfm?V=2&name=C-WP%2F13133&Lang=E (accessed 1 Oct 2010).

248 Cheng (1957) op. cit.: 203–4, 207–8, 398.

249 Cf. Air Navigation Order 2009 Article 5(2): If an unqualified person resides or has a place of business in the United Kingdom and holds a legal or beneficial interest by way of ownership in an aircraft or a share in an aircraft, the CAA may register the aircraft in the United Kingdom if it is satisfied that the aircraft may otherwise be properly registered; and 5(3): If an unqualified person has registered an aircraft under paragraph (2) that person must not cause or permit the aircraft to be used for the purpose of commercial air transport, public transport or aerial work while it is so registered.

The argument may be raised that among state parties to the Chicago Convention 1944 the combined effect of Articles 77 and 19 precludes any state party from contesting the nationality of an aircraft except where it relies on a substantial national ownership and effective control clause in an existing bilateral arrangement.[250] But there appears to be no reason why the genuine link rule under international law as enunciated by the International Court of Justice (ICJ) in the *Nottebohm Case* with regard to individuals and extended to ships cannot be further extended to aircraft and even spacecraft.[251]

Several innovative criteria have been formulated to detect non-genuine connection. Under US law for instance, following US registration, if the aircraft does not fly at least 60% of the time in the USA, the aircraft is disqualified from ongoing US registration. It must be conceded, however, that the application of a genuine link test to aircraft is by no means straightforward, as in the case of naturalisation of the individual. Brownlie and, earlier, Jennings note that registration of the aircraft is itself a presumptively valid and genuine connection of some importance.[252] We must, therefore, attempt to grapple with the role of registration. The pertinent questions remain whether registration merely certifies status under national law or whether it serves as a guarantee that the rules and regulations relating to the safety and legal operation of aircraft that engage in international flights would be enforced by the state of registration? An affirmative answer to the latter query is preferable and is definitely in consonance with the overall interests of aviation practice.

This is probably why when aircraft are leased or chartered for any length of time to an operator in a foreign country ("interchange of aircraft") international air law requires that the state of registry (i.e. lessor/charter) transfer its functions under the Chicago Convention (1944) to the state of the operator (i.e. lessees).[253] Thus, it has been the practice of the USA, as confirmed in the *Aerolinas Perunas S.A. Permit Case*, in bilateral treaties to reserve the right to refuse a carrier permit to an airline designated by the other contracting party in the event that substantial ownership and effective control of such airlines are not vested in nationals of the other contracting party.[254]

This system, which gives individual national control over aircraft in flight, has also meant that the regulatory system of international aviation depends for its

250 Cheng (1962) ibid: 128, 131.

251 In the *Nottebohm Case*, Second Phase (1955), between Guatemala and Liechtenstein, the ICJ propounded the "link theory", which has the effect that a state may validly not recognise naturalisation granted by another state to individuals with whom there is no social fact of attachment, a genuine connection of existence, interests and sentiments, together with the existence of reciprocal rights and duties. See *ICJ Reports* (1955): 4, 23.

252 Brownlie op. cit.: 427. See also R.Y. Jennings, "General Course on Principles of International Law", 121, 2 *Hague Recueil* (1967): 460–6.

253 Article 83 bis of the Chicago Convention adopted in 1980. (ICAO Doc. 9318), see also B. Cheng "Air Law", in *Encyclopaedia of Public Int. Law*, ed. Rudolph Bernhadt (Amsterdam: Elsevier Science, 1989): 9.

254 International Law Report, 31: 416; see also Brownlie op. cit.: 427.

effectiveness upon cooperation between states. Nicholas Mateesco Matte, therefore, correctly notes that this ensures that airworthiness, security and navigability of aircraft are of the highest standards worldwide. The organisation within which this cooperation has been facilitated so far is the International Civil Aviation Organisation (ICAO).[255]

The ICAO has been particularly strict (but rightly so) in applying the genuine link principle. This is in consonance with the task conferred on it under Article 77 of the Chicago Convention to "determine in what manner the provisions of this Convention relating to nationality of aircraft shall apply to aircraft operated by international operating agencies". This strict interpretation is more clearly seen in relation to joint ventures of airline ownership. Thus in 1960 when the ICAO Council received a request from the Arab League, which was contemplating the establishment of a Pan-Arab Airline, the Council convened a panel of experts to make a general study of the problems posed by Article 77. The panel found, inter alia, that unless an aircraft were registered in a sovereign and independent state, it would not have a nationality and would not be governed by the domestic law of any country.[256]

255 See Nicholas Mateesco, "Air and Extra – Atmospheric Space: Air", *International Law: Achievements and Prospects*, ed. M. Bedjaoui (Dordrecht: Martinus Nijhoff, 1991): 291. By an agreement, which came into force on 13 May 1947, the ICAO became a Specialised Agency of the United Nations Organisation. Article 37 of the Chicago Convention (1944) is headed "Adoption of International Standards and Procedures" and provides that contracting states undertake to collaborate in securing the highest practicable degree of uniformity in regulations and standards in relation to aircraft, personnel and airways to facilitate and improve air navigation. Article 47 grants the ICAO legal capacity in the territory of each contracting state to the extent that may be necessary for the performance of its functions. Article 60 provides that the ICAO shall be granted immunities and privileges, which are granted to corresponding personnel in other public international organisations. Tim Unmack comments that particularly "in view of the functions of ICAO concerning operational standards, the question of immunity from suit is important." See Tim Unmack, *Civil Aviation: Standards and Liabilities* (Gloucester: LLP Professional Publishing Co., 1999): 22–3.

256 See Cheng (1962) op. cit.: 131–2. Note should also be taken of Articles 79 and 83 (as amended). Article 79 provides that a state may participate in joint operating organisations or in pooling arrangements, through either its government or through an airline company or companies designated by its government. The Chicago Convention (1944) did not adequately specify the responsibilities of the state of operator where an aircraft of the state of registry is leased, chartered or interchanged. Therefore, on 6 October 1980 the ICAO Assembly decided to amend the Chicago Convention by introducing Article 83 bis. This provision deals with the transfer of certain functions and duties. When an aircraft registered in a contracting state is operated pursuant to a lease or charter agreement by an operator whose principal place of business or permanent residence is abroad in another contracting state, the state of registry may, by agreement with the other contracting state, transfer its functions and duties as state of registry in respect of that aircraft under Articles 12, 30, 31 and 32. It is important to note, however, that this provision does not apply to Article 77. Under Article 94(a) of the Convention, the amendment came into force on 20 June 1997 in respect of states, which ratified it. As at 30 June 2001 there are 127 ratifying states. Tim Unmack (op. cit.) suggests that the lacunae, which existed prior to the coming into force of Article 83 amendment, would not have proved to be a problem in the European Union (EU) because Article 10 of Regulation 2407/92 of 23 July 1992 applies in such cases.

In 1967 the Council of the ICAO further adopted a resolution requiring the constitution of a joint register in such cases for the purposes of Article 77 of the Chicago Convention and the designation of a state as recipient of representations from third states. The resolution applies to joint operating agencies and intergovernmental agencies alike. The position currently is still largely that which Brownlie describes thus: "In principle aircraft of joint operating agencies for example *Air Afrique* must be registered in one of the States involved."[257]

In sum, an international tribunal would look at the state of registration to determine nationality and to avoid the problem of flags of convenience.[258] In any case, the problem of flags of convenience never assumed serious dimensions with regard to aircraft as it did in the case of ships. One of the reasons for this may be that the "Form of Standard Agreement" recommended at Chicago as well as the Two Freedoms and Five Freedoms Agreements accompanying the Chicago Convention (1944)[259] all contain clauses authorising the revocation of permits when a state is not satisfied that the airline to which it has granted a permit is under the substantial ownership and effective control of national of the contracting state.[260] It will also be seen that the rules of nationality of aircraft demonstrate that like ships, aircraft and spacecraft are to some extent invested with "legal quasi-personality". That is to say, they are viewed as entities in themselves. In each case, the state of registration is responsible to other states for the conduct of the aircraft in question. The bottom line then is that nationality defines the incidence of control. It indicates which state has the right to exercise quasi-territorial control over the aircraft and is, therefore, liable for its actions under the Chicago Convention. To this extent, flags of convenience in relation to aircraft are a dangerous abstraction that must not be condoned. Therefore, it may be recommended that Article 17 of the Chicago Convention be amended to unequivocally contain a requirement of genuine link as in the rules governing nationality of ships and as recognised by the ICJ in the *Nottebohm Case*.[261] Furthermore the experience of the flag of convenience

257 Brownlie op. cit.: 427. *Air Afrique* had its headquarter in Abidjan, Côte d'Ivoire, and was established as the official transnational carrier for francophone West Africa. The airliner was dissolved in 2001.

258 Although the obligations imposed by Article 12 of the Chicago Convention raise the question of which state is to fulfil the requirements of registration, Article 77 of the Convention explicitly recognises the right of two or more contracting states to establish joint air transport organisations. Such organisations include the Scandinavian Airlines System (SAS) consisting of Swedish, Danish and Norwegian companies. See J.D. McClean, J.M. Balfour, Richard K. Gardiner, Jeffrey Goh and Rod D. Margo, *Shawcross and Beaumont Air Law*, Vol. 1, 4th edn (London: Butterworths, 1988): Chapter 11; McLean et al. op. cit. 3rd edition (1977): 15, 17–18. See also Nicholas Grief, *Public International Law in the Airspace of the High Seas*, thesis submitted at the University of Kent at Canterbury (1993): 196.

259 The two agreements refer to the Chicago International Air Services Transit Agreement 1944 and the Chicago International Air Transport Agreement 1944 (171 UNTS 387), respectively.

260 Johnson (1950) op. cit.: 75.

261 See for instance, Article 5 of the High Seas Convention (1958) (450 UNTS 82) and Article 91 of the Law of the Sea Convention 1992. Hereinafter called LOSC (1982) (UN Doc. A/CONF. 62/122 (1982) 21 ILM 1261).

problem as gallantly fought by the IMO has proved useful to those charged with the task of preventing the phenomenon in the airspace. This is clear from the many progressive measures already taken by ICAO.[262] Ultimately, however, the problems of aerial and maritime flags of convenience although comparable are necessarily different. These differences must always be factored into attempts aimed at dealing with the problems within the permissible use of pertinent strategies in international law and relations.

2.4 Obligations with respect to state aircraft, civil aircraft and piloted/pilotless aircraft

The Chicago Convention (1944) distinguished between state aircraft and civil aircraft. State aircraft are those "used in military, customs and police services" (Article 3). The test, therefore, is functional and does not depend on ownership at all. Any aircraft owned by a contracting state, which does not fall within this definition, is, for the purposes of the Convention, regarded as civil aircraft to which alone the Convention applies.[263]

Furthermore, it should be noted that the Chicago Convention (1944) for the purpose of conferring the right to fly distinguishes between commercial and non-commercial flights. Commercial flights are those that carry passengers, cargo or mail for remuneration or hire. They are further subdivided into scheduled and non-scheduled flights. The Convention grants a fairly liberal right for aircraft bearing the nationality of any of the contracting states to fly into the territory of other contracting states or to fly across it with or without a stop. No such right of entry or transit is given in respect of scheduled air services while that granted in respect of non-scheduled commercial flights is somewhat nominal.[264]

The Chicago International Air Services Transit Agreement 1944 and the Chicago International Air Transport Agreement 1944 both contain important provisions regarding obligations towards civil aircraft. In the former, each contracting state grants to the other states the following freedoms of the air in respect of scheduled international air services: (1) the privilege to fly across its territory without landing; (2) the privilege to land for non-traffic purposes. The latter agreement more ambitiously grants five freedoms, which, basically, are the two in

262 They include (a) the recognition that states have a responsibility to assure "themselves that foreign operators flying in their territory receive adequate oversight from their own State and taking appropriate action when necessary to preserve safety"; (b) the requirement to carry a copy of the air operator certificate (AOC) on board the aircraft; (c) an enhanced regime of surveillance of foreign operators; (d) the implementation of a system to provide states with pertinent data concerning aircraft registered in states pursuant to Article 21 of the Convention; and (e) the ICAO policies on transparency, disclosure and sharing of safety critical information including the procedure under Article 54(j) of the Convention. The ICAO Secretariat has also been in consultation with several states that have engaged in flags of convenience operations.

263 Bin Cheng, "State Ships and State Aircraft", 11 *Current Legal Problems* (1958): 225. See also Cheng, "From Air Law to Space Law" op. cit.: 238.

264 Cheng (1960) op. cit.: 238–9.

the Two Freedoms Agreement and additionally: (3) the privilege to put down passengers, mail or cargo taken on in the territory of the state whose nationality the aircraft possesses; (4) the privilege to take on passengers, mail and cargo destined for the territory of the state whose nationality the aircraft possesses; (5) the privilege to take on passengers, mail and cargo destined for the territory of any other contracting state and the privilege to put down passengers, mail and cargo coming from any such territory. It is, however, possible to question the commonsense of the freedom of transit for private aircraft through national airspace when most states simply do not have the technological prowess or investment capabilities to benefit from this right. Obviously, those states that own and operate large fleet of aircraft and have higher numbers of private and corporate investment in aviation have obtained valuable benefits for free.[265]

In connection with the duty of the flag state to register aircraft (whether civil or state owned), a little more must be said about pilotless aircraft and other pilotless flight craft such as rockets and earth satellites. Article 8 of the Chicago Convention (1944) states that:

> No aircraft capable of being flown without a pilot shall be flown without a pilot over the territory of a contracting State without special authorisation by that State and in accordance with the terms of such authorisation. Each contracting State undertakes to ensure that the flight of such aircraft without a pilot in regions open to civil aircraft shall be so controlled as to obviate danger to civil aircraft.

Cheng makes some useful suggestions regarding the scope of each contracting state's duty to control pilotless flights. He thinks it may be one or more of the following:

> (i) In respect strictly of its own territory. This is a literal but rather unlikely interpretation of the two sentences of article 8 taken together (ii) In respect of all aircraft bearing its nationality wherever they may be. This is possible though not the most probable interpretation of the intention of the parties, since it would have unregulated pilotless aircraft which have not been registered and therefore have no nationality (iii) In respect of all flights originating from its territory, which may take place wholly or within national airspace or partly within it and partly within free flight space and/or foreign airspace belonging to no contracting States to the Chicago Convention.[266]

It may, therefore, be said that Article 8 does not in any significant manner prohibit pilotless flights in regions open to civil aviation. The article merely requires

265 Note, however, recent introductions in state practice. Russia, for instance, has begun to obtain valuable consideration for allowing commercial airlines to make use of its airspace in order to shorten flight routes. See *infra*, 560.

266 Cheng (1958) op. cit.: 504.

that such craft are to be subject to control. This underscores the chief importance of the nationality requirement, which is that it serves as a verifiable means of determination of ownership and therefore, control and liability. Once the incidence of where control and liability lies are clear, air law does not prohibit pilotless flight. However, if it passes over national territory, prior permission in one form or the other must have been granted. Thus, the illegal use of spy aircraft is not permitted. Even if Article 8 were extended to apply to all types of flight craft, contracting states to the Chicago Convention may continue to permit such flights whether by balloons rockets or earth satellites, from their territories, so long as they are controlled in order to obviate danger to other civil aircraft. In any case, as will be shown, the regime for liability for space flight is equally based on adequate rules that aid the determination of ownership liability and control. It may be noted that operators in the developed states conduct the vast majority of pilotless flights, including earth satellite launches. Probably because incidents of interference with civil aviation in this manner is not common and have not led to disputes, there is also an assumption that works in the favour of the developed states and this is that, in the case of earth satellite launches, prior permission of the underlying states is a dispensable criterion. It is, however, likely that the increasing use of drones will reinvigorate debate in this area and this will be a good thing. While most drone flights conducted by the USA in the Middle East have occurred with some form of knowledge or tacit acknowledgment of the territorial states, there has also been much controversy surrounding these flights. It is hoped that stricter rules will eventually emerge to control the use and to generally strengthen the control over national airspace through international laws in order to forestall future disputes and tensions.

2.5 Summary and conclusions

The tridimensionality of state territory recognised under customary international law subsists to the present day. The idea of sovereignty and jurisdiction over the airspace has developed over the centuries and is older even than the history of human flight. First, there was the unduly generous position that the whole aerial space to an indefinite extent is subject to the underlying states sovereignty following the maxim *cujus est solum ejus usque ad coelum et ad inferos*. While the problem of the exact demarcation point between airspace subject to national sovereignty and outer space, which belongs to entire mankind, has not been solved, it may be safely concluded that under prevailing treaties on air law, particularly the Chicago Convention (1944), the principle of complete and exclusive sovereignty over the superincumbent airspace is unassailable. Airspace sovereignty is delimited *ratione loci* in respect of the space above national territories and not *ratione materiae* in respect of the air, which may at any given time, be filling this space. Quasi-territorial jurisdiction and personal jurisdiction may, however, be exercised by other states with respect to aircraft, spacecraft and their citizens which they have granted legal personality even when found in foreign airspace.

Innocuous as it may seem, the recognition in various multilateral treaties on air law that the territory of a state shall be understood as including the national territory, "both that of the mother country and of the colonies, and the territorial waters adjacent thereto"[267] is a fact that proves that air law was used as a means of legitimising or at least justifying the interests of the colonial powers. Without prejudice to the practicalities necessitating the inclusion of such provisions in the law it also serves as a pointer towards the need to re-examine contemporary air law and space law for all such relics of the old law of domination that may persist.

The nationality doctrine is a necessary and useful adjunct to the general rule of airspace sovereignty and jurisdiction. Since territorial sovereignty and jurisdiction extends upwards into the airspace it is a *sine qua non* of the continuance of international aviation that at any point in time the state of origin of each and every aircraft should be ascertainable. Nationality and registration of aircraft thus, becomes the simplest and surest way to ensure state security, compliance with good air navigation practice and at the same time respect for other rules of international air law. For purposes of identification in cases of damage to property, the distinctive mark of nationality may be of great significance. The nationality of aircraft as determined by registration is, therefore, a crucial concept in the determination of control over aircraft. The application of this principle involves ascertaining jurisdiction *ratione instrumenti* and *ratione personae*. The operation of the nationality principle in practice represents the hub on which respect for state sovereignty, jurisdiction, liability and safety of lives and property rests in the course of international aviation.

Although there are similarities in the legal requirements of nationality and registration of aircraft and spacecraft different laws and treaties are called into question. While air law governs the principle of nationality and registration of aircraft and all similar vehicles, which engage in airspace transport, space law dictates the rules with regard to spacecraft, rockets and all vehicles that can be launched into orbit. The existence of aircraft and launchers that can operate in both airspace and outer space necessarily introduces some confusion into the legal classifications. It is, therefore, suggested that to forestall any controversies in this direction an interpretation should be adopted, which makes such vehicles fall under the classification of registration as space vehicles. The basis of this suggestion is that most aircraft that are used for international transport do not need to make incursions into regions above the airspace where objects may be put into orbit. Therefore, the test should not only be functional but policy oriented. If an aircraft can make this sort of flight, it is better for the safety of outer space activities and to satisfy the security concerns of other states that it is registered on the register of the United Nations established for that purpose as a space object.

There ought to be a genuine link between the ownership of vehicles that travel through the airspace of other countries (including aircraft and spacecraft) and the state of whose nationality it bears. This is the best way to ensure that the reasons for operating the principles of nationality and registration of flight vehicles are

267 This was the formula used in Article 1 of the Paris Convention (1919). The Chicago Convention (1944) also repeats a substantially similar provision in its Article 2.

maintained. States ought to realise the mutual benefit of maintaining respect for the principles of sovereignty over national airspace as well as nationality and registration of flight vehicles that can engage in international or extra-atmospheric flights. However, to assume that the present regime is the fairest possible will be a questionable stance since it can be demonstrated that certain states with the technological and infrastructural capabilities are the principal beneficiaries of the regime, which allows private and commercial aircraft to fly over large numbers of national territories without financial charges. It may also be concluded that the development of the law relating to legal status of the airspace in the last century has very much reflected the dominant ideology of the time including the realities of the Cold War, the protection of the needs of the aviation powers and the security interests of nation states.

3 Jurisdiction over crimes in the airspace and on board aircraft

3.1 Development and patterns of national responses to crimes in airspace

> The law has yet to catch up fully with conventional aviation. . . This lag is nowhere more noticeable than in the field of criminal law and criminal jurisdiction as applied to civil aircraft.[268]

Crimes in airspace committed on board an aircraft in flight include; (a) common crimes (for example assault, theft and unruly behaviour); (b) aeronautical offences e.g. dangerous flying, flying unregistered aircraft, carriage of dangerous goods and munitions of war, flying an aircraft under the influence of intoxication, narcotics[269] and (c) unlawful interference with civil aviation e.g. hijacking, hostage taking and sabotage against aircraft. A common feature of these categories is that the rules of jurisdiction that deal with them are naturally of very recent origin. These rules are barely 60 years in existence and up until the present the exercise of criminal jurisdiction in relation to aircraft in flight is still a major source of controversy. A discussion of these developments is necessary for us to understand the nature of state jurisdiction in the airspace as well as to pinpoint possible paradigms to be adapted for the even less developed area of jurisdiction over crimes in outer space.

States had barely settled the question of sovereignty in the airspace and developed air safety regulations before newer expressions of criminal behaviour were introduced into the airspace. Early expressions of criminal conduct in the course of international flights exposed lacunae in air law, which international lawyers are still struggling to fill. Presently, newer forms of criminal conduct are revealed some of which are a result of increasing access to air travel as well as advancement in various areas of technological advancement. For instance, access

268 Bin Cheng, "Crimes on Board Aircraft", *Current Legal Problems* (1959): 177.

269 See, for instance, section 3 of the Nigerian Civil Aviation Act 1965 Cap. 51, LFN 1990; see also the UK's Air Navigation Order 1954 and section 11 of the Civil Aviation Act; Note also S. 139–144 Kiribati Civil Aviation Act 2004. Available at http://www.parliament.gov.ki/acts/2004/CivilAviationindex.pdf (accessed 10 October 2010).

to telecommunications and Internet facilities by passengers during flight opens up new vistas for the criminal mind in terms of financial crimes.[270] Therefore, fresh problems are presented for air lawyers. Familiar problems also present themselves in ever changing ways. For these reasons, the regime governing crimes in the air must be continuously reassessed and developed.

Two cases in 1950, one in the United States jurisdiction and the other in the English jurisdiction, drew attention sharply to this gap in the criminal jurisdiction laws of states particularly in relation to offences against the person. In *U.S.A. v. Cordoba and Santen*[271] the defendants were passengers on board an American Commercial Airliner flying from Puerto Rico to New York on August 2, 1948. While in flight over the high seas, a fight ensued between the two defendants over a missing bottle of rum. The defendant Cordova entirely lost his self-control, struck and bit the captain of the aircraft and the stewardess. He was finally restrained and locked up in the aircraft. Upon arrival in New York, the defendants were arrested. The U.S. District Court, Eastern District of New York, before which the two defendants were charged with assault, held that as a federal court, it had no jurisdiction to punish the alleged offences.[272] Presumably in reaction to this, the U.S. Congress passed Public Law 514 in 1952, which confers jurisdiction on Federal Courts over crimes committed on board American aircraft in flight over the high seas.[273]

A similar gap in English Criminal Law was exposed in Devlin J.'s decision in *R v. Martin and others*.[274] The facts of this case were that the defendants while serving as part of the personnel on board British aircraft allegedly carried raw opium from Bahrain to Singapore between January 1954 and August 18 1955. On being arraigned before the Central Criminal Court and charged , inter alia, with unlawful possession of drugs contrary to the Dangerous Drugs Regulations 1953, Regulation 3, the Court found that it had no jurisdiction. The Prosecution had unsuccessfully argued that though the relevant regulations of the Dangerous Drugs Regulations, 1953 were applicable only to Great Britain, section 62 (1) of the Civil Aviation Act

270 Rachael Jolley, "Email at a Mile High", *Times*, 6 May 2000.

271 (1950) USA v. R 1: 3 Avi 17, 306.

272 The prosecution had argued that Title 18 USCA 5. 451 provide the basis of the court's jurisdiction. This provision defines the admiralty and maritime jurisdiction of the federal courts and submits to federal jurisdiction, inter alia, crimes that are committed "on board American vessels on high seas or great lakes". It was the court's judgement that an aircraft is not a vessel within the meaning of that word in the said statute. Consequently, in the court's view, "the situation may call for correction or as the law now stands acts as those committed by Cordova may go unpunished" (Per Kennedy J) at pp. 9–10 and 17, 311 respectively. In short, it had been too readily assumed that criminal jurisdiction in airspace over the United States was that of states and that federal jurisdiction was at best interstitial. See Cheng (1957) op. cit.: 177–8; J.C. Cooper, "Crimes aboard American Aircraft", *American Bar Association Journal* (1951). On offences and certain acts committed on board or related to aircraft with relation to the USA, see Billyou De Forest, *Air Law*, 2nd edn (1946): Chapter 1.

273 This law was further strengthened in 1961. See Cheng (1961) op. cit.: 177–8 and Johnson op. cit.: 77.

274 [1956] 2 QB 272.

1949 was enough reason to deem the offence to have been committed in England. The provision reads thus: "(1) Any offence whatever committed on a British aircraft shall, for the purpose of conferring jurisdiction be deemed to have been committed in any place where the offender may for the time be." Devlin J., however, reasoned that section 62 (1) did not have the effect of extending the whole corpus of English Criminal law to British Aircraft abroad. He, therefore, held that it follows that the depositions do not show or disclose that any criminal offence had been committed, for this reason the committal was bad and on that ground the indictment had to be quashed.[275] According to this view, offences, which are under the Dangerous Drugs Act, were offences only if committed in Great Britain itself. Devlin J. warned, however, that the position might be different as regards common law crimes, such as murder and theft, which in his view were crimes wherever they are committed.

Today, it is clear that a British, American or indeed most other countries aircraft is far less of a flying oasis of lawlessness.[276] A substantial body of English and American aeronautical regulations and criminal laws follow aircraft bearing their nationality wherever they may be in order to ensure the safety of the aircraft and of persons and property on board and even on the ground. In England for instance, these aeronautical regulations which were found principally in the Civil Aviation Act 1949 and Order in Council are now incorporated under the Civil Aviation Act 1982 and the Orders in Council made by virtue of section 60.[277] Equally, English Criminal Law is applicable to (and English Courts have jurisdiction over) all acts committed within all aircraft in or over England, including the territorial sea, or

275 Ibid: 285.

276 Intoxication remains a common factor in the cases relating to unruly behaviour of passengers. On a United Airlines flight from Frankfurt, Germany, to Dulles International Airport in Washington, DC, a passenger shouted at a flight attendant, contending that the flight attendant had bumped him several times with the service cart. The attendant doubted bumping the passenger but nevertheless proceeded to apologise. This was obviously not satisfactory to the passenger who followed the flight attendant to the galley, threw him against an emergency exit and struck him severally on the head and face. On another occasion some English and Irish tourists had a food fight on the plane. A Saudi Arabian princess lost her cool as a result of perceived slow service in furnishing her a drink and she attacked a flight attendant. In another bizarre incident, an investment banker who was a passenger aboard a United Airlines flight to Buenos Aires and New York, wanted more wine, but the flight attendants refused to serve him, because he had already poured drinks on himself and other passengers. Prosecutors later alleged that he had started drinking before boarding, had continued during the flight and even helped himself to the alcohol instead of waiting to be served. When the flight attendants stopped the beverage service to begin food service, the passenger threatened one flight attendant and then pushed another into a seat. He then proceeded to climb on a food cart, lowered his pants and defecated on top of the food cart, after which he casually used the linen napkins as toilet paper. The captain suspended all food and beverage service, due to the possibility of bacterial infection. The American courts fined the defendant $48,000 (used to reimburse the ticket costs of other passengers), a further $5,000 punitive fine, $1,000 compensation to United Airlines as costs of cleaning the plane, 300 hours of community service and he was ordered to undergo counselling. See Stephen A. Mirmina, "Aviation Safety and Security – Legal Developments", 63, 3 *Journal of Air Law and Commerce* (1998): 561–2.

by persons on board such aircraft. This exclusive territorial jurisdiction includes all United Kingdom aeronautical regulations and laws.

In similar manner virtually all modern states have developed means to cope in their own ways with the different types of crimes in the airspace. Naturally there are both similarities and differences in the types of conduct that are prohibited as well as in substantive and procedural legislation. In Nigeria as in most West African countries, for instance, dangerous flying is an offence. Where an aircraft is flown in Nigerian territory in such a manner as to cause danger to any person or property on land or water, the pilot or other person in charge of the safe navigation of the aircraft and the owner of the aircraft shall be liable on conviction to a term of not less than two years or a fine of not less than N1,000,000.00 (1 million naira, i.e. 4000 pounds) or both. In any proceedings against the owner of an aircraft in respect of an alleged offence under this section, it is a defence to prove that the act alleged to constitute the offence was done without the fault, privity and consent of the owner (section 55(2)).[278]

Since the act also gives the Minister for Aviation the power to prohibit aircraft from flying over certain prescribed areas in Nigeria, it constitutes an offence to over fly such areas.[279] These and numerous other offences in relation to flight in Nigerian airspace have been spelt out under Nigerian air laws. They are applicable to pilots and persons who are Nigerians as well as to foreigners.

However, with respect to offences committed on board Nigerian aircraft in foreign airspace the development of Nigerian municipal law has been less specific. There is a vague provision in section 17 of the Air Navigation (Safety of Navigation) Act,[280] which empowers the Federal Government to make rules for the purpose of the Act. A Nigerian aircraft is defined as an aircraft registered in Nigeria in accordance with regulations made under the Civil Aviation Act 2006.[281] The only provision of substance regarding quasi-territorial jurisdiction over such aircraft is

277 Under section 60, orders in council may be made for carrying out the Chicago Convention 1944 including the general regulation of air navigation and other numerous specific purposes. British courts have held that powers conferred under that section should be exercised so as to give effect to and not conflict with that convention. See *R v. Secretary of State for Transport, ex p. Pegasus Holidays (London)* Ltd 1989 2 All ER 481.

278 It is a sign of the desirability of the Nigerian parliament to deal with this problem that it tries to keep up with the development in the area and increase the sanctions appropriately so that the deterrence value of the law in this important area of aviation law is not lost. Notably, the monetary and imprisonment sanctions have increased exponentially. Under the previous law, the punishment on summary conviction was a fine not exceeding 400 naira, imprisonment for a term not exceeding six months or both. It was also a valid defence for the owner (which includes any person by whom the aircraft is hired at the time of the offence) to prove that the alleged act was done without his knowledge and consent. See Civil Aviation Act 1964, section 3(1), (2) and (3). It, however, is arguable that even the current amount of about 4000 pounds in fines is insignificant given the seriousness of the offence and possible harm that can be caused by offenders. No. 30 Laws of Federal Republic of Nigeria.

279 Section 1(2) and (1).

280 Cap. 8 of the 1958 edn of the Laws of Nigeria.

281 Nigerian Civil Aviation Act 2006, section 17.

then prescribed in section 54(1). It states that any act done by any person on a Nigerian aircraft outside Nigeria which, if it had been done by him in any part of Nigeria, would have constituted an offence under the law in force in that part shall, for the purposes of any criminal proceedings against that person in respect of that offence be deemed to have been done by him in that part of Nigeria.[282]

However, paragraph 2 of the section exempts an offending foreigner from automatic punishment. This is because any action against a non-citizen of Nigeria is subject to the discretion of the Attorney General of the Federation. The Ministry of Justice must bring the offence and the intention to prosecute him to his notice. This gives room for delay and political considerations. For this reason alone, Professor Ajomo (one of the earliest authorities in the area of law in Nigeria), admits that Nigerian law is yet to catch up fully in the field of criminal law and criminal jurisdiction as applied to civil aircraft and its facilities.[283]

It is perhaps necessary at this point to consider whether trespass and illegal entry into a state's airspace constitutes *prima facie* a violation of the country's air safety laws. For instance, in the hundreds of records of airspace violations communicated to the UN by Cyprus with respect to Aircraft operated by the Turkish Air force, it is significant that Cyprus detailed with care the provisions of its Air Traffic Regulations that it considered were flouted. This may be evidence that Cyprus would in the event of capture of a pilot of an intruding aircraft embark upon criminal prosecution according to its laws based inter alia on aeronautical offences. Such a position will be entirely supportable under national laws and would be in accordance with good international practice. It is possible to infer that the rationale of exercise of criminal jurisdiction over conduct of aircraft and the persons in charge of them in the airspace includes the necessity to protect the state and its inhabitants from the physical harm that aircraft may cause to humans, buildings, flora and fauna. It is, therefore, necessary to adopt the view that intruding aircraft are by virtue of their unexpected presence a clear and present danger to the aviation and general welfare of the underlying state. Such aircraft and their occupants may, therefore, be subjected to the criminal jurisdiction of the offended state.

It is true, as we shall soon come to see that national regimes developed to cope with criminal conduct in the air must be as responsive as possible to emerging threats. The processes of apprehension and prosecution of offenders must not only be effective but must also be as timeously as possible. Therefore, there is much to be said in favour of streamlining of criminal jurisdictional laws along international standards. The existing situation is that some of the laws applicable in certain states are still of ancient origin arising from the regime developed for the high seas. In

282 As a federal state, the jurisdiction of courts over the offences have effects in all the component states Thus, section 54(3) reads: "Where it is alleged that an offence under this Act or regulations made by virtue of this Act has been committed, proceedings in respect of the offence may be brought in any court in Nigeria, which would have had jurisdiction in the manner if the offence had been committed in the part of Nigeria for which the Court acts."

283 M.A. Ajomo, "Hijacking or Unlawful Seizure of Aircraft", 7 *Nigerian Law Journal* (1973): 14–15. This arguably remains true in the new century despite Nigeria's increasing experience with acts of terrorism both in terms of unlawful interference with aviation and in other areas of life.

short, states have individually reacted to the challenges of air travel. As at 2002 three clear patterns had emerged:[284]

First, some states specifically pronounce territorial sovereignty over all aircraft in the country and express quasi-territorial criminal jurisdiction over all national aircraft abroad in a combination of four ways and, generally speaking:[285]

1 only when in flight[286]
2 only when not subject to territorial criminal law of a foreign state[287]
3 only when over the high seas or in *territorium nullius*[288]
4 if they are commercial aircraft.[289]

The second pattern of national laws regulating crimes on board aircraft reveals that the quasi-territorial principle applies to both national aircraft and foreign aircraft in the country subject to the following exceptions when national law applies territorially even to foreign aircraft in the country:

1 where there are specific provisions to the contrary[290]
2 if a national is involved or if the aircraft lands in national territory after the commission of the offence[291]
3 if the aircraft lands in national territory after the commission of the offence.[292]

Third, following an analogy from maritime law, several states refrain from exercising jurisdiction over foreign aircraft in national territory if it is merely a matter of internal discipline embarked upon on board the aircraft. Nonetheless, exceptions are made in those cases where the offence produces effect beyond the aircraft, local peace is disturbed or the assistance of the local authorities is requested:[293]

1 over national territory generally
2 over the territorial sea.[294]

284 Cf. Cheng (1959) op. cit.: 180–1; Gbenga Oduntan, *Sovereignty Jurisdiction and Control in the Airspace and Outer Space: Legal Criteria for Spatial Demarcation*, thesis submitted at the University of Kent (2002): 112.
285 Cuba (Code of Social Defence (1936)); Philippines (Penal Code (1930)); Poland (Penal Code (1932)); Uruguay (Aviation Codes (1942)).
286 Honduras (Aviation Law (1950)); Hungary (Penal Law (1950)).
287 Ecuador (Penal Code (1939)); Greece (Penal Code (1950)); Norway (General Penal Code (1902 as amended)).
288 Brazil (Air Code (1938)); Costa Rica (Penal Code (1941)); Guatemala (Penal Code (1936)), Italy (Penal Code (1930) and Navigation Code (1942)).
289 Switzerland (Federal Air Navigation Act (1948)).
290 Venezuela (Civil Aviation Code (1944)).
291 Lebanon (Penal Code (1943)); Luxembourg (Air Navigation Act (1948)); Syria (Penal Code (1949)). Subject to the provisions of Article 113-9 of the Penal Code, French Criminal law is applicable to felonies and misdemeanours committed on board or against aircraft not registered in France, inter alia, where the aircraft lands in France after the commission of the felony or misdemeanour. (Inserted by Act no. 92-1336 of 16 December Article 340 Official Journal 23 December 1992 into force on 1 March 1994.)
292 Belgium (Air Navigation Act (1937)); France (Air Navigation Act (1924)).
293 Guatemala (Penal Code (1936)); Romania (Penal Code (1936)).
294 Cuba (Code of Social Defence (1936)); Lebanon (Penal Code (1943)); Syria (Penal Code (1949)).

Some of these patterns prevail up to the present time and it can only be inferred that these varying positions have in one way or the other shaped the law governing crimes committed in the airspace as reflected in the air treaties which will shortly be examined. What is clear at this stage is that there are practically no reported cases of laws in any of the numerous Aviation Acts, which purport to govern acts committed in outer space or on board spacecraft. The advent of space tourism and the incremental deployment of aerospace vehicles like the XCOR Aerospace suborbital vehicle[295] and Virgin Galactic's Spaceshiptwo[296] that are designed to carry hundreds of fee paying space tourists per year opens new vistas in the discussion about the readiness of national criminal jurisdictional rules to regulate crimes onboard suborbital vehicles. For instance, according to Section II of the Penal Code of France dealing with, Offences Committed outside the Territory of The French Republic (Article 113-6 to 113-12) the territory of the Republic is said to include the territorial waters and air space which are attached to it (Article 113-1). Will a suborbital flight over French territory be outside the territory or is it within French airspace attached to it?[297] In the absence of any international agreement on the issue it will crucially have to be decided under various national laws whether such vehicles are spacecrafts (to which space treaties apply) or aircrafts to which only existing national aviation jurisdictional rules apply.[298] The fact that either of the regimes could apply does not necessarily mean that either would if nothing is done to ensure that the specific situation created by the existence of the new crafts is decided upon and legislated for.

3.2 Hierarchy of sources of jurisdiction over crimes committed in flight

There has already been a discussion about the concepts of territorial jurisdiction and quasi-territorial jurisdiction in relation to the two complementary concepts of

295 Mark Madler, "XCOR Ready for Liftoff: Space Entrepreneur Jeff Greason Aims His Rocket Company Toward the Stars", *San Fernando Valley Business Journal*, 13 September 2010, available at http://sfvbj.com/news/2010/sep/13/xcor-ready-liftoff/ (accessed 10 October 2010); Paul Baldwin Metro, "Space Tourism Entrepreneurs Want to Bring you to the Stars", *World News*, 17 March 2010, available at http://www.metronews.ca/ottawa/life/article/479385-space-tourism-entrepreneurs-want-to-bring-you-to-the-stars (accessed 12 October 2010).

296 Visit www.virgingalactic.com. Note also discussions at Chapter 10.3: Liberal commercialism and entrepreneurship as driving force of international space tourism.

297 One possible solution may lie in the provision of French criminal law, which states that national criminal jurisdiction is applicable to offences committed beyond territorial waters, when international conventions and the law provide for this. This is suggestive that in the case of a decision that a crime has been committed on board a suborbital craft this will be covered by French criminal jurisdiction where there are permissive provisions that exist in international conventions such as the Space treaties. French Penal Code Article 113-12. (Inserted by Act no. 96-151 of 26 December 1996 Article 9 Official Journal of 27 February 1996.)

298 Significant issues that arise include whether the powers of the suborbital aerospace vehicle commander are the same or similar to that of aircrafts. Are we back to pre-1964 in relation to powers of control over offenders? The ICAO had lamented in relation to Powers of the Aircraft Commander.

jurisaction and *jurisfaction*. What remains to be considered here is how to resolve conflict of criminal jurisdiction between states where common jurisdiction exists either *ratione personae* or *rationae instrumenti*. For instance, according to the active nationality principle a state may punish crimes committed by its nationals anywhere. However, the principle of territorial sovereignty operates to bar unrestricted use of this principle. How then can a state punish crimes committed abroad but on board its aircraft by its nationals or by other nationals?

It would prove useful to recall the concepts of *jurisfaction* and *jurisaction*. The former denotes the legislative power to prescribe rules and judicial powers to apply the rules and the latter explains the powers of enforcement and actual administration of justice. Cheng claims that although an aircraft moves from place to place thereby presenting itself under the *jurisaction* of several states, it can at any point in time or place be placed only under the exclusive jurisdiction of one state. In other words, in time of peace and subject to few exceptions an aircraft and the persons in it can be tried and punished only by a single state.[299] Thus, for instance, while an aircraft in Nigeria is subject exclusively to Nigeria's *jurisaction*, it will come under exclusive jurisdiction of the U.S. when it enters into American territory. This interpretation represents strict adherence to the territorial principle.[300]

As already said, the rule admits of certain exceptions. Apart from cases of condominium, leased territories, capitulation there is also the possibility of states agreeing by bilateral or multilateral treaties to the exercise in each other's territory of *jurisaction* over crimes committed on board their aircraft. Therefore, the powers of *jurisaction* may not always be exclusive in relation to crimes committed in territorial airspace.

The hierarchical order of state jurisdiction proffered earlier on in this work remains valid. Territorial sovereignty overrides quasi-territorial sovereignty, which in turn overrides personal sovereignty. But the Permanent Court of International Justice (PCIJ) statement in the *Lotus case* deserves closer scrutiny. The Court said in that case; ". . . it is equally true that all these systems of law extend their action to offences committed outside the territory of the state".[301] It could be argued that by 'action' the Court also includes the possibility of *jurisaction* in certain cases? This interpretation is highly probable. In any case the Court also pronounced that "the territoriality of criminal law therefore is not an absolute principle of international

At present, there are no international rules, such as those applying to captains of ships, which recognise the power of the commander of the aircraft to take immediate action if the safety of his aircraft or its passengers are endangered by the act of someone on board. The aircraft commander might find it necessary to restrain or arrest this person, and, under present circumstances, might then run the risk of being sued or even criminally prosecuted in some foreign country in whose territory the aircraft happens to be. See ICAO News Release, ICAO Drafts Air Law Convention on Crimes in Aircraft, available at http://www.icao.int/icao/en/nr/1962/pio196214_e.pdf (accessed 10 October 2010).

299 Cheng (1965) op. cit.: 183.

300 Cf. ibid.

301 Series A, No. 10 (1927): 20.

law and by no means coincides with territorial sovereignty".[302] Accordingly, under the passive-nationality principle claimed by some states they arrogate to themselves the right to punish crimes wherever committed of which their own nationals are victims.

As opposed to *jurisaction,* the universal and concurrent *jurisfaction* over crimes in the airspace is, however, a more settled notion. The power of *jurisfaction* may be (and usually is) shared by many states.[303] This is why a state may prescribe as illegal under its laws certain acts for any aircraft in its own airspace. It may, however, not prescribe how any other state's aircraft must behave in another country's airspace. A state may also prescribe what its nationals and others must do or not do in an aircraft that belongs to it. It may prescribe conduct for its citizens in any aircraft no matter to which state it belongs (nationality principle),[304] or even to non-citizens what not to do in any airspace if its interest or that of its nationals is affected (Protective Principle/Passive/Personality Principle).[305] Furthermore, a state's extra-territorial *jurisfaction* over its nationals in aircraft will normally be concurrent with the powers of *jurisfaction* of other states. Again this extraterritorial *jurisfaction* may also be concurrent with another states power of *jurisaction* over crimes, for instance, when the aircraft possessing the nationality of a state enters a foreign country.

Admittedly, the possibility of the proper exercise of *jurisaction* with respect to crimes in airspace defines the ultimate utility of the powers of *jurisfaction* described earlier. A state may, thus, find itself prescribing what it cannot possibly enforce. Whichever source of jurisdiction relied upon in dealing with any crime in the air, deference must be given to the *nemo bis in idem* rule according to which a person may not be tried twice for the same offence.

3.3 Jurisdiction over common crimes and unruly passengers

> In the last two years, however, it has become apparent that no rules exist for misbehavior on board aircraft in flight, at least no rules [*sic*] what to do with the misbehavers.[306]

It may be said that the rules governing the exercise of jurisdiction over common crimes in airspace and on board aircraft are complex, probably even unsettled. The term common crimes is used here in contradistinction to acts of terrorism and hijacking, which, it is argued are problems *sui generis* and of a special nature and of

302 Ibid.
303 See Cheng (1957) ibid: 183.
304 For example, a theocratic state may make it illegal for its citizens to consume alcohol on aircraft or anywhere at all.
305 For example, Article 694 of the French Code of Criminal Procedure earlier on referred to will apply to cover even a foreigner who on a foreign aircraft renders himself guilty of a felony or misdemeanor against France.
306 See Heere op. cit.: 82.

which separate discussion will be made later. The term common crimes as discussed here is also to be distinguished from that of aeronautical offences. As regards aeronautical offences, these are virtually under national jurisdiction and are not really dealt with by the Tokyo Convention of 1963. It is, however, of practical necessity that the laws prohibiting aeronautical offences are diligently observed because this class of offence generally raises serious safety concerns. As a result of this both nationals and foreigners are within the scope of application of these laws. An aeronautical offence is no less grave because a national rather than a foreigner commits it. Thus, a British evangelist who literally took his message to the heavens in violation of civil aviation rules found himself on the wrong side of the United Kingdom's aeronautical laws and was convicted by the trial court.[307]

It is important to note that while most states out of sheer necessity undertake the task of making aeronautical rules and regulations that are to apply to aircraft of their nationality even when navigating abroad, unfortunately, some states fail to extend the applicability of their general criminal law or that of their criminal courts in like manner. By token of this, the problem of the flying oasis of lawlessness even though reduced is still very much with us as no general criminal law applies to such aircraft when it flies outside the territorial jurisdiction of any state such as over the high seas or parts of Antarctica.[308] The regime of the Tokyo Convention (1963) on its part does not adequately solve the problem. It remains insufficient in relation to common crimes, first, because not all states are party to it and, second, because it unsuccessfully attempts to cope with two varied problems at the same time (i.e. offences against penal law and acts that jeopardise the safety of aircraft (Article 1).

What remains clear is that most states recognise and frequently express the desire to prosecute crimes committed in the airspace. When this occurs, the bases of jurisdiction relied on span nearly all the categories and classifications of criminal jurisdiction identified earlier.[309] The hierarchy of sources of jurisdiction over common crimes committed in the airspace may result in many contentious cases among states in future. The Chicago Convention of 1944 seems to offer inadequate guidance on this matter. All that the Convention requires is that each contracting state does not engage in any purpose inconsistent with the aims of the Convention

307 The evangelist, John Holme flew a motorised paraglider preaching to the people of Salisbury by megaphone. He found himself dodging electrified fences, trees and bird tables. His height on this maiden flight was sometimes as low as 6ft and astonished residents said he flew over so low they could see the look of horror on his face. There was not much opportunity for preaching and his efforts put him out of favour with the Civil Aviation Authority. The flight earned him a £1,050 fine and £250 costs when he appeared at Salisbury Magistrates' Court for flying too close to a populated area and straying into airspace over an airfield. It was the first case of its kind involving a foot-launched, powered flying machine. The position of the Civil Aviation Authority, as expressed by its officials was that, "[T]he rules state that the aircraft shall not be flown closer than 500ft to any person, vessel, vehicle or structure except while it is landing." See Helen Johnstone, "The Heavenly Host is fined for Low-flying", *Times*, 13 March 1998: 3.

308 Bin Cheng, "Air Law" in *Encyclopaedia of Public International Law*, ed. Rudolph Bernhadt (Amsterdam: Elsevier Science, 1989): 9. See also our discussions later.

309 *Supra*, Chapter 1.

(Article 4). Also that laws and regulations of a contracting state relating to the admission and or departure from the territory of aircraft engaged in international air navigation, including those relating to the operation and navigation of such aircraft while within its territory, shall be applied (Article 11). The Convention also insists that the rules of the air be obeyed. In other words, all aircraft carrying a state's nationality mark, wherever such aircraft may be, shall comply with the rules and regulations relating to the flight and manoeuvre of aircraft there in force (Article 12). Therefore, the rules the flouting of which gives rise to an offence would not be just every rule that applies on the land territory but those that have a bearing on aeronautical safety and, to some extent, state security.

The extent to which the Chicago Convention regulates jurisdiction over serious crimes against the person such as murder, rape, arson and theft is virtually negligible. In relation to common crimes, the governing rules and principles are to be found partly under municipal law[310] and, to some extent, the Convention on Offences and Certain other Acts Committed on Board Aircraft (14 September 1963).[311] The Tokyo Convention (1963) undoubtedly determines the incidence of control over unruly passengers and establishes the competence of the state of registry of the aircraft over offences and acts committed on board. Each state may take measures to establish its jurisdiction over offences committed on board (Article 3).

A contracting state that is not the state of registry may not interfere with an aircraft in flight in order to exercise its criminal jurisdiction on board except in five instances:

1 where the offence has effect on the territory of such state
2 where the offence is committed against a national
3 where the offence is against state security
4 where the offence is a breach of aeronautical rules of the territorial state
5 where exercise of jurisdiction is necessary to ensure compliance with multilateral agreements (Article 4).

These instances correspond with the principles of criminal jurisdiction that have been discussed earlier, respectively, protective principle, nationality principle, passive nationality, territorial principle and (potentially and in very limited situations) the universality principle.

The Convention provides the aircraft commander with the necessary authority to deal with persons who have committed, or who are in the process of committing, a crime or an act jeopardising safety on board the aircraft employing reasonable force. Thus, a violent, ranting passenger who has lost self-control may be restrained with actual physical force by or under the instructions of the aircraft commander. This may be done:

310 See *R v. Martin* discussed earlier. Cf. *R v. Naylor* [1962] 2 QB 527 and *Cox v. Army Council* [1963] AC 48.

311 Henceforth also referred to as the Tokyo Convention (1963) UKTS 126 (1969), Cmnd 4230; 704 UNTS 219. The Convention entered into force after the 12th ratification on 4 December 1969.

- to protect the safety of the aircraft
- to maintain good order and discipline on board
- to enable the delivery of such persons to competent authorities (Article 6(1)).

In fact, a cabin crew member may, *suo motu* and of his own accord, exercise restraints on an unruly passenger where he believes reasonably such action is necessary to protect the safety of the aircraft or of persons or property therein (Article 6(2)). It is suggested here that as long as there is reasonableness of action such powers given to the cabin crew, trained as they are, can be well justified. In any case, it is to be argued that when such discretion is exercised it flows from the delegation of the aircraft commander's powers. The reason for this view is that it can hardly be imagined that a crew member or indeed a passenger would act where there is an express prohibition by the aircraft commander.

The real problem, however, lies in that an ordinary passenger could indeed exercise the powers granted under Article 6(2). It takes little thought to see that this situation is fraught with danger. To request or authorise passengers to assist in the restraint of someone in the process of committing a common crime or being unruly is one thing but for air law to grant such powers in regard to normal passengers is to say the least excessive. In any case, it is unnecessary because such powers need not flow from a branch of international law since virtually all criminal laws recognise the powers of citizen's arrest. Thus, it may be argued that it is neater if not safer to let passengers act under municipal laws (i.e. that of the flag state or the territorial state) than to make them subjects of powers under treaty laws.

Of course, it is difficult not to consider the argument that prevailed at the Tokyo Conference, to the effect that, in an emergency situation in which danger of the aircraft or persons on board was clearly present, there is no special technical knowledge required in recognising the peril.[312] However, the right to prevent a felony or that of self-defence is one already entrenched in virtually all recognisable legal systems and there really is no need to revisit this under international treaties. The argument here is that the rights of private persons to effect arrest in the airspace can be located in the laws of the flag state of the aircraft.[313]

The powers of the commander enable him if the actions of the offender threaten the safety of the aircraft to forcefully disembark such a person in the territory of any state in which the aircraft happens to land and deliver the offender to the

312 See R.P. Boyle, "International Action to Combat Aircraft Hijacking", *Lawyer of the Americas* (1998): 340.

313 Under Nigerian laws, a private person may arrest any person who commits an indictable offence in his presence or whom he reasonably suspects of having committed a felony by night. (Criminal Procedure Act, section 12; Criminal Procedure Code S.28(d)) The only qualification to the powers of a private person to arrest is that the private person arresting without warrant must, without unnecessary delay, deliver the arrested person to a police officer or, in the absence of a police officer, must take such person to the nearest police station. Again, in this case, that will be police authority at the next airport. See also Oluwatoyin Doherty, *Criminal Procedure in Nigeria Law and Practice* (London: Blackstone Press Limited, 1990): 96–7.

competent authorities (Articles 8 and 9). It may be advanced that he may land at the nearest available airport for the sole purpose of disembarking the unruly person(s). In essence, it must be underscored that an unruly passenger may in addition to being unruly actually commit the more serious crime of endangering the safety of an aircraft in flight.[314] It can only be said that whosoever exercises the powers conferred by the Tokyo Convention (1963), reasonableness of actions to the perceived threat must hold sway. For instance, in a incident in March 2000 on an Alaska Airlines flight from Puerto Vallata to San Francisco, a six-feet tall heavily built man had taken off his shirt and socks and repeatedly disobeyed the cabin crew by switching seats. He eventually placed himself on a first-class seat from where he issued threats to fellow passengers stating that he was "going to kill all of you". In a short while, he made moves to carry out his threats by breaking into the cockpit struggling with the pilot and going for the throttle and fuel controls. The common threat rightly summoned spontaneous reactions from the cabin crew and passengers and the man was eventually overpowered and subdued until the plane landed.[315]

314 Article 1(1) Convention for the Suppression of Unlawful Acts against the Safety of Civil Aviation (1971). UKTS 81 (1983), Cmnd 9100 (1979) 18 ILM 1456. In force 1983.

315 In the typical case, cabin staff alone would be able to cope with the offender. In April 2000 a grandmother who punched an air stewardess in the face was convicted and jailed for six months. The 56-year-old care worker was so drunk on the Air 2000 flight from Manchester to Florida in March 1999 that she had to be taken off the aircraft in a wheelchair. Cabin crew refused to serve her any more alcohol after she had drunk three Bacardi and cokes. An almost empty bottle of rum was later found under her seat. As the aircraft approached Stanford Airport in Florida, she ignored the illuminated warning signs and stood to leave her seat. A stewardess went to tell her to sit down and managed to get her to sit back. But, as she tried to get her to fasten her seatbelt, the passenger punched her on the left side of the face three times. Testimony before the court revealed that the stewardess was so shocked by the attack that she suffered from nightmares, insomnia and was signed off work for three weeks. She also made moves towards seeking alternative employment. Judge Anthony Ensor, who has dealt with 12 cases of "air rage" between 1998 and 2000 in sentencing the convict said: "[I]t is a tragedy for you and your family that you should have acted totally out of character." But he added: "I have to have regard for the overall public interest." Under UK laws, reckless acts likely to endanger aircraft or persons therein are prohibited by Article 45 of the Air Navigation Order 1980 made under sections 60 and 61 of the Civil Aviation Act 1982. See, for instance, *Warton–Pitt* [1991] 92 Cr. App. R 136. Again, Judge Ensor (and a jury) recently in *R v. Whitehouse* (*R v. Whitehouse* (Neil) [2000] Crim. LR 172 (2000) 97(1) LSG 22 Times, 10 December 1999, Independent, 14 December 1999) adopted a strict view of the law representing a trend towards upholding the safety of air transport by discouraging misconduct in the airspace. It was held that the word "likely" in Article 55 of the Air Navigation (No. 2) Order (SI 1995 No. 1970), which provided that "A person shall not recklessly or negligently act in a manner likely to endanger an aircraft, or any person therein" should be construed as meaning "Is there a real risk, a risk that should not be ignored?" The Court of Appeal so held when giving reasons for dismissing, on 29 November 1999 an appeal by Neil Whitehouse against his conviction on 30 June 1999 in Manchester Crown Court, of an offence contrary to Article 55 of the 1995 Order on which he was sentenced to 12 months' imprisonment. The particulars of the offence were that he used a cellular phone to send text messages despite numerous admonitions to the contrary by cabin staff. See "Man Held in Cockpit Struggle", *Guardian Saturday*, 18 March 2000: 19; C.M.V Clarkson and H.M. Keating, *Criminal Law: Text and Materials*, 4th edn (London: Sweet & Maxwell, 1999): 177.

One further interesting point is that there is a distinction between the unqualified obligation to "take delivery" and the obligation to "take custody".[316] Any state in which the aircraft lands for this purpose would be under an obligation to allow the disembarkation and "to take delivery of any person whom the aircraft commander delivers pursuant to Article 9 paragraph 1". By the same token, paragraph 2 of Article 9 determines the obligation of the contracting state, after having taken delivery, to take custody and it states that custody may be taken "upon being satisfied that the circumstances so warrant". The way in which this would continue to work out in practice is surely going to be one of the more interesting areas of air law. The pertinent questions are: how long should it take the receiving state to take this decision? Besides what options are open to a passenger for whom it is later discovered that his forceful disembarkation and delivery was unwarranted or frivolous? This is quite significant since Article 10 of the Tokyo Convention (1963) gives an unqualified immunity from suits to the aircraft commander and the crew members as well as any passengers when they act against an alleged offender.

The framing of Article 10 is very generous in granting immunity from both criminal and civil jurisdiction. It states:

> Neither the aircraft commander, any member of the crew, any passenger, the owner or operator of the aircraft, nor the owner or operator of the aircraft, nor the person on whose behalf the flight is performed shall be held responsible in any proceedings on account of the treatment undergone by the person against whom the actions are taken.

It must be noted that the problem of the unruly passenger is here to stay and that human conduct will not necessarily get better when the body is airborne. In fact, with increasing access to air flights as a result of economic forces of demand and supply as well as sheer increase in world population, we are bound to witness a sharp rise in the occurrence of aerial crimes. Here again, the law must not only catch up but also must anticipate developments. A common observation in many of the recent literature on the topic is that, save for minor exceptions, both international and national laws remain anachronistic in effect.[317]

316 See R.I.R Abeyratne, "Unruly Passengers – Legal, Regulatory and Jurisdictional Issues", XXIV, 2 *Air and Space Law* (1999).

317 The problem of the disruptive or unruly passenger has become a major concern in the airline industry. The number of these cases is increasing alarmingly and international aircraft cabin associations have been calling for urgent reviews of the law. Several contemporary writers on the subject have alluded to the inadequacies of present international law. Although no precise statistics are available, there is a perception that the majority of cases of unruly passengers emerge from no less a place than in the first-class cabin, where celebrities, VIPs and high-powered professionals who are not used to assertions of authority by others frequently travel. Thus, a well-known American televangelist, Reverend Robert Schuller, physically assaulted a flight attendant because she would not remove the cheese from his hors d'oeuvres plate. See Stephen R. Ginger, "Violence in the Skies: The Rights and Liabilities of Air Carriers when Dealing with Disruptive Passengers", XIII, 3, *Air and Space Law* (1998): 106; R. Schmid, "Airlines Getting tough with Unruly Passengers", *Seattle Post-Intelligencer*, 1 May 1997: 17.

In contradistinction to anachronistic national laws applying to aerial crimes as that of the Nigerian situation described earlier, we have a crop of new and impressive legislative and policy responses in certain Western jurisdictions. In Britain, for instance, concrete legislation has been passed to fill apparent lacunae. Thus, section 92 of the Civil Aviation (Amendment) Act (1996)[318] was passed in response to police statistics showing that, each week, there were at least two or three cases when a foreign-registered aircraft landed at Heathrow with a serious offender on board and the police were incapacitated by lack of jurisdictional powers. By this provision, UK criminal jurisdiction extends to acts taking place on aircraft registered outside the UK (i.e. foreign aircraft) as well as on UK aircraft if two conditions are satisfied. First, the next landing must be in the UK and, second, the act must constitute an offence under the law of the state of registration if that act were to have been committed there. As a writer on the subject aptly puts it: "[t]he number of cases where the UK police are helpless will diminish, but will not disappear entirely".[319]

To combat the problem of unruly passengers the Dutch government, as from February 1999, began to place two police officers to accompany each Amsterdam Paramaribo flight to assist flight attendants if necessary.[320] KLM also announced special training for over 11,000 staff members who are in direct contact with customers. This came as a result of the fact that by the end of the 1990s there were on average 100 incidents of criminal and unruly conduct by air passengers on KLM flights alone, in one month.[321] Especially since the terrorist hijackings of 11 September 2001, many states such as Israel and the US have adopted both methods (i.e. airborne police escorts as well as specialised and standardised training) at least for their national airlines or leading operators.

Regrettably, it would appear that economic considerations have the greatest potential of hampering such enthusiastic formulation of jurisdictional competence as found in the UK and Dutch legal systems. Costs of prosecution and logistical problems are of crucial essence. Ironically, the problem of costs explains why both the territorial state (in which the foreign aircraft carrying an offender lands) and the offender's own state (capable of exercising personal jurisdiction) are often unwilling to prosecute in a majority of cases. The expanding scope of petty crimes complicates the situation for states.

For instance, in the last two decades and in response to ICAO recommendations, smoking on board aircraft has become an offence in most jurisdictions.[322] It would

318 Of 18 July 1996.

319 Heere op. cit.: 75.

320 It is not clear why this route is given particular attention. See ibid.

321 ITA Press No. 323 (November 1998).

322 In the USA, for instance, smoking is completely banned on aircraft having not more than 30 seats. In any case, no cigar or pipe smoking is allowed on any domestic aircraft. In 1988 smoking was banned on all domestic flights of less than two hours. In 1989 this was extended to all flights scheduled to last less than six hours. See Title 14 Aeronautics and Space 14 CFR Part 252—Smoking Aboard Aircraft. See also Mirmina op. cit.: 558–9. The ICAO passed a non-binding resolution in 1992 encouraging member states to progressively ban smoking on all international passenger flights. See *Smoking Restrictions on International Passenger Flights*, Res. A29-15 (1992) ICAO Doc. 9600-A29/RES, at 74.

not be difficult to imagine that Britain, for instance, would be reluctant to embark on a costly procedure to prosecute a Kenyan who smokes on board a Ghana Airways flight even though British courts would have jurisdiction if the next landing after the offence was committed were in the UK and if it is actually a statutory offence under Ghanaian laws. This is in consonance with the requirements of Section 92 of the Civil Aviation Amendment Act 1996. Contrariwise, Ghana understandably may be very wary of embarking on expensive repatriation and/or extradition procedures to bring such errant persons back within its jurisdiction. Add to this the difficulties that may be encountered in such cases in the determination of which airspace the offence took place and the near impossibility of securing the continuous attendance of witnesses. It should be noted that the vast majority of common crimes in the airspace are bound to be of such small economic significance. Therefore, there is no denying the fact that majority of offenders would (save for the occasional painful delay at the airport by officials) walk away without prosecution. They will then feel free to repeat same or similar offences in the future.

It must be noted that to judge one offence as serious and the other as not is not so easy a task when it comes to aerial crimes. Misbehaviour such as stowing too much luggage into the aircraft has the alarming but not apparent effect of threatening the safety of civil aviation. Overloading, simply put, can lead to a plane crash. Improper or negligent storage of items and luggage has continuously been a source of injury claims, compensation of more than US$1 million has been allowed in a series of cases and airliners have on many occasions been made financially liable for other criminal acts of passengers.[323] Smoking secretly in the lavatory on board aircraft has led to loss of lives.[324] A prosecution for outraging public decency

323 In US courts, for instance, the view has repeatedly been taken that where there is a special relationship such as that between passenger and airliner a duty of reasonable care is imposed and the potential for damage due to criminal/terrorist activity is treated as a "defect" in the process for which the airline may be liable if information or reasonable analysis suggests possible threats. See *Day v. Trans World Airlines*, 528 F. 2d 31 (2nd Cir 1976); *In re Air Disaster at Lockerbie, Scotland on December 21, 1988*, 928 F. 2d 1276 (2nd Cir), cert. denied 502 US 920, 112 S Ct 331 (1991). Here, the airline had advertised special security against terrorist bomb threats or attacks and the security system was not administered as advertised, which resulted in jury verdicts of wilful misconduct and unlimited damages. See also Carol E. Dubuc, "Potential Civil Liability Resulting from Terrorist Acts in the International Travel Industry", XXIII, 2 *Air and Space Law* (1998): 58–61; Heere op. cit.: 74.

324 In 1983, one passenger on an Air Canada DC-9 sneaked into the lavatory to smoke a cigarette. This led to the fire causing the death of 23 lives on board. As Mirmina insists: "[S]moking should be banned for several reasons other than flight safety. First, passengers on international flights fall asleep with lit cigarettes, burn flight attendants as they walk down the aisles and frequently extinguish cigarettes on the floor. Some flight attendants working on those flights suffer nausea, dizziness, severe headaches, fatigue, and loss of consciousness. And sometimes fights occur between smoking and non-smoking passengers." Interestingly, even where the ban against smoking is legally in place the same author notes: "People smoke in lavatories despite the presence of fire alarms, and some people try to disable the smoke alarms even though it is a federal crime to do so. Others attempt to cover the smoke detectors with a shower cap, while some unsuccessfully try to blow their smoke down the toilet." Mirmina op. cit.: 558–60. See further Matthew Wald, "Out of the Haze up in the Skies", *New York Times*, 30 June 1996: 5.

recently followed an incident in which two strangers performed oral sex on a transatlantic flight.[325]

In sum, it would seem desirable that a separate international treaty be formulated to govern jurisdiction over common crimes committed in the airspace.[326] Such a treaty would strike a balance between the jurisdictional claims of a flag state and those of the state in whose territory a crime occurs. What must not, however, be done is to adopt a piecemeal approach to this problem. This would only result in a cacophony of discordant legal rules and practices sometimes contradicting one another or creating further legal problems for the future. Instances of such developments already exist in the form of IATA recommended practices. For example, IATA Recommended Practice 1724, which many airlines have incorporated into their general conditions of transport, makes it possible to expressly refuse transportation on a second leg of a flight to a passenger who has misbehaved on the first leg. The question is if a passenger has truly "misbehaved' in a legal sense so as to amount to criminal conduct, should he not be prosecuted? On prosecution, he is proved either innocent or guilty. If innocent, he has as much right as any other person to free movement, which should not be curtailed by spurious bans. If he were guilty, he normally would be made to serve the required punishment or pay the required fines. Once this is done, the question of curtailing his freedom to board an aircraft on any other occasion becomes redundant, unless, of course, this is part of the judgment against the offender.

It becomes more important to adopt this position in the light of the prolific resort to temporary or indefinite blacklists in many jurisdictions worldwide. African indigenous airlines, like their European counterparts, for instance, have created blacklists that include passengers suspected to have assaulted or abused airline employees, especially during flights.[327] It must be mentioned that this aspect of aviation and airline security has begun to attract criticism and generate controversy especially with relation to human rights discourse. Human rights organisations such as the American Civil Liberties Union have correctly highlighted the potential for abuse.[328] The dangers of official extremism are revealed in the policy of one airline explained thus: "We would also request that the (regulatory) Nigerian Civil Aviation

325 See Gary Slapper, "Flight of Fancy", *Times* (Law Supplement), 11 April 2000.

326 Organisations of flight attendants are complaining more and more about the increasing violence they experience and witness on board aircraft. They are the unfortunate professional victims. It is worthy of note, however, that in realisation of the seriousness of these developments the Council of the ICAO has asked the Legal Committee to put on its agenda the formulation of an international Convention on "acts or offences committed on board aircraft not covered by existing air law instruments". On 6 June 1997 the Council of ICAO decided that a Secretariat Group should be established to study the problem; also at the 32nd Session of the ICAO Assembly in 1988, The IATA and the International Transport Workers' Federation presented a working paper for discussion to ICAO. See Heere op. cit.: 75.

327 Oyetunji Abioye, "Aero to Blacklist 'Air Rage' Passengers", *Punch*, 6 August 2010, available at http://www.punchng.com/Articl.aspx?theartic=Art201008060423643 (accessed 4 October 2010).

328 See Norberto E. Luongo, "Watchlists in United States and Canada: An Intricate Web", 35, 2 *Air and Space Law* (2010): 157, 162. See also Ruwantissa Abeyratne, "The NW 253 Flight and the Global Framework of Aviation Security", 35, 2 *Air and Space Law* (2010): 167–81.

Authority (NCAA) blacklists such a passenger, and the name of the passenger will be published in the newspapers."[329]

Serious issues of possible human rights violation, the right to privacy and respect for the rule of law as well as avoidance of the double jeopardy principle may be raised here. It may be suggested that there is a qualitative difference between a drunk who makes desultory comments about airline service no matter how ill timed and a person who commits or attempts to commit air piracy. While blacklists for the latter types of offender may be easily justified, the widespread maintenance of such blacklists between airlines for the former is not. Other issues that may have to be addressed under a new international treaty include the treatment of crimes committed on the high seas and other international spaces. The reality of the need for proper guidance on these matters is reflected in the submissions of Johnson that:

> Aircraft spend far more time than ships do in the territories of other States. They are, in this respect almost as much like trains and motor-coaches (for which a "law of the flag" would be absurd) as they are like ships. The consequence is that, in considering crimes committed on board aircraft, the jurisdiction of the Territorial State must be provided for as well as that of the Flag State.[330]

Abeyratne stated accurately: "[t]he international community must take cognizance of the fact that the Tokyo and Montreal Convention are ineffective if states do not make provisions in their own laws to combat . . . unruly passengers which may cause damage to persons and property on board aircraft".[331] Therefore, ICAO member states must fine-tune their national legislation and aviation procedures to cope with this problem. Yet care must be taken not to criminalise air travellers unnecessarily and the human rights of vulnerable people, who in many cases are far from their support systems and family ought to be of importance as well. Areas to be targeted include: facilitating immediate enquiry on disembarkation, the development of specialised rules on evidence, bilateral and multilateral extradition laws, education and enlightenment campaigns of both airline workers and passengers as to their rights duties and liabilities under national laws and treaty laws. Furthermore, stricter controls over consumption of alcohol on board and maybe even prior to international flight may well be within contemplation.

3.4 Control over unlawful interference with civil aviation

> Mentally unbalanced persons still use aircraft as vehicles for the expression of their psychoses.[332]

329 Africa News, "Nigerian Airline to Blacklist 'Air Rage' Passengers", *Afrique en ligne Actualités Africaines: Economie Politique Finances*, 6 August 2010, available at http://www.afriquejet.com/news/africa-news/nigerian-airline-to-blacklist-air-rage-passengers-2010080553995.html (accessed 4 October 2010).

330 Johnson op. cit.: 76.

331 Abeyratne op. cit.: 59.

332 Alona E. Evans, "Aircraft Hijacking, What is to be Done?", 66, 4 *AJIL* (1972): 819.

Apart from the general criminal acts that may occur on aircraft in flight discussed earlier, there exists a particular genre of offences that deserve separate discussion as a result of the crucial nature and implications they have on contemporary international relations. There are myriad ways in which free transport through airspace can be obstructed and endangered. Thus, the term "unlawful interference with civil aviation" encompasses a variety of criminal acts that jeopardise the maintenance of domestic and international civil aviation. The most common offences committed against the safety of civil aviation are hijacking, sabotage of aircraft on the ground or in the air and forced flights for the purpose of seeking territorial asylum in another state. It must be said that there is actually no single universally accepted notion of unlawful interference with civil aviation. The scope of the application of that term in legal literature and even in international instruments depends greatly on the particular definition provided therein.[333]

One of the reasons for this is that international criminal law in general has not grown out of broad principles but rather deductively, step by step, and in respect of particular offences that finally called for action of an international nature.[334] While it is true that problems of an unusual nature in respect of jurisdiction over offences that may be committed on board aircraft were considered as early as the first decade of the 20th century, it was only in the second half of the century that deliberate unlawful interference with civil air flight began creating new jurisdictional problems.[335] In retrospect it is not a wonder that on the first few years of the new millenium, offences committed on aircraft had come to create problems of such a spectacular nature that it may take up to a century for international relations to normalise.

Hijacking, for instance, started in the real sense with the breakdown of relations between the USA and Cuba.[336] It is reported that, in the 1950s, the majority of hijackings occurred for the purpose of securing political asylum.[337] This phenomenon Lissitzyn labelled hijacking for travel purposes.[338] By 1968 a considerable number of Cubans (over 295,000) had registered for services at the Cuban Refugee Center in Miami, Florida (in USA), many of whom had been resettled throughout the USA. They were encouraged to migrate from Cuba in the wake of Castro's revolution. Following a lack of agreement to regulate the return of these refugees to Cuba, there was another rapid increase in the number of hijackings witnessed during 1968 and in the first four months of 1969 in which many pilots of US

333 See Kay Hailbronner, "Civil Aviation, Unlawful Interference With", in *Encyclopedia of Public International Law*, ed. Rudolf Bernhardt (Amsterdam: Elsevier Science, 1989): 57.

334 Ajomo op. cit.: 13.

335 A.K. Saka, "International Air Law and Safety of Civil Aviation",12 *Indian Journal of International Law* (1972): 204.

336 Ajomo op. cit.: 15.

337 Nanay Douglas Joyner, *Aerial Hijacking as an International Crime* (Dobbs Ferry, NY: Oceana Publications, Inc., 1974): 4.

338 Oliver J. Lissitzyn, "International Control of Aerial Hijacking: The Role, of Values and Interests", 61 *AJIL* (1971): 83.

airliners were forced to divert their aircraft to Havana.[339] The chaotic situation was recorded by a writer thus: "Either U.S. flag aircraft were seized at home or abroad with the avowed intent of flying to Cuba, or foreign aircraft in Cuba were hijacked in an effort to reach American soil."[340]

Had hijacking remained confined to Cuban–American relations, it would not perhaps have attracted as much world attention as it has since, neither would it have posed so much danger to air travel. However, for the most part of the last half century, skyjacking and other unlawful acts against aircraft in flight have increased dramatically. The objectives for which hijackers commit their acts have also been changing continuously. The implications of these crimes on international relations are equally more complex. While initial incidents were directed by motives of political asylum with no *animo furandi* (robbery for private gains), other motives have also been manifested. Hijacking has been used as a means of escape from impending criminal proceedings or from prison sentence. It has been used illegally to extort large sums of money from states and airlines or for exacerbating ill-will between states. It is used for political fence mending, for drawing attention to liberation causes and many other motives including religious extremism.[341]

Sensational examples include that in which, on Christmas Eve 1999, five gunmen who were Moslem Kashimiri separatist fighters seized an Indian aircraft, which had taken off from Kathmandu, capital of Nepal, and diverted it to Afghanistan. The hijackers demanded $200 million and the body of a Kashimiri militant believed to have died while in custody of Indian security forces.[342] Terrorists threatened to detonate a device on board a Qantas flight travelling from Sydney to Hong Kong with 95 passengers and crew on board. They demanded $505,000 as ransom. In June 1997 an Air Malta flight bound for Turkey was illegally diverted to Germany. On 11 March 1997 a bizarre incident occurred on board Taiwanese flight FEAT 128 with 150 passengers and six crew members on board. A Taiwanese journalist doused himself with gasoline and demanded that the plane be diverted to mainland China. In November 1996, on board flight ET961 from Addis Ababa, Ethiopia, to the Ivory Coast, three hijackers, one wielding an axe, demanded that the pilot fly the plane to Australia, merely because the hijackers wanted to make history. The aircraft subsequently ran out of fuel and crashed into the sea near the Comoros Island, resulting in 123 deaths. In October 1996 a German court sentenced a Turkish male to a seven-year jail term for hijacking an aircraft with a toy pistol in order to draw attention to the plight of Chechen Muslims. During negotiations he released 108 passengers in return for a promise to have access to a radio reporter and a lawyer. In November 1995, on board Olympic flight 472 from Sydney International Airport, carrying 110

339 Ajomo op. cit.: 16.

340 Joyner op. cit.: 153.

341 For a fuller description of possible expressions of terrorism in the airspace, see Evans op. cit.: 819–20; Ajomo op. cit.: 16–17; S.C. Charturvedi, "Hijacking and the Law", 11 *Indian Journal of International Law* (1971): 89; Note also the 11 September 2001 terrorist hijackings discussed in Chapter 3.

342 See Zahid Hussein, "Taleban Tanks Surround Hijack Aircraft", *Times*, 31 December 1999.

passengers and bound for Athens, an Ethiopian journalist who had travelled to Australia from Greece on a false passport threatened a steward with a knife while the plane was still on the tarmac, demanding that the Greek government provide him with sanctuary.[343] In February 2000 about a dozen men who identified themselves as members of a group known as "Young Intellectuals", in an attempt to flee the erstwhile Taliban regime in Afghanistan, used guns, hand grenades and detonators they had smuggled into an Afghan Boeing 727 (carrying 173 passengers and 14 crew) to hijack the aircraft for asylum purposes. The aircraft landed in airports in Uzbekistan, Kazakhstan and Moscow before arriving at Stansted Airport leading to nearly five days of negotiation in Britain's longest hijack drama.[344]

The curious fact, however, is that while hijacking appears to be an easily identifiable act to the layman, to the international lawyer and indeed any prosecutor, a proper formulation of what is and what is not hijacking may be of crucial importance. That a criminal act resembles hijacking does not make it one as much depends on where, how and when the act or set of actions in question took place. In fact, at all times at which a state exercises criminal jurisdiction with respect to criminal acts relating to airspace activities a lot depends on the proper formulation of the facts in issue. To begin with, there are technicalities involved in the determination of which treaties cover any given set of facts. In sum, it is important to distinguish hijacking from other acts of unlawful interference with civil aviation.

The offence of hijack is defined in the Convention for the Suppression of Unlawful Seizure of Aircraft of 16 December 1970[345] as: the unlawful seizure or exercise of control of an aircraft "in flight", by a "person . . . on board" and "by force or threat thereof or by any other act of intimidation". Obviously, the scope of the offence could have been made wider.

The development of specific rules to cure the mischief began with the Tokyo Convention (1963).[346] This Convention drawn up under the auspices of the ICAO dealt primarily with jurisdictional questions relating to such crimes and the powers of the aircraft commander. In the face of dramatic increase in skyjacking, by 1968, the ICAO had initiated another convention, this time dealing extensively with unlawful seizure of aircraft. This resulted in the Hague Convention of 1970. Meanwhile, the UN General Assembly overwhelmingly adopted two resolutions: 2551 (xxiv) of 12 December 1969, condemning the forcible diversion of civil aircraft in flight, and 2645 (xxv) of 25 November 1970, condemning aerial hijacking or interference with civil air travel. In 1971 the Hague Convention was supplemented with the adoption of the Convention for the Suppression of Unlawful Acts against the Safety of Civil Aviation of 23 September 1971.[347] The latter convention is an

343 See Michael S. Simons, "A Review of Issues Concerned with Aerial Hijacking and Terrorism: Implications for Australia's Security and the Sydney 2000 Olympics", 63, 4 *Journal of Air Law and Commerce* (1998): 738–9.

344 Jamie Wilson, "Nine Afghans Guilty of Hijacking Jet to Safety", *Guardian*, 7 December 2001: 10.

345 To be referred to also as the Hague Convention (1970), ILM, Vol. 10 1971: 133. It was adopted in the Hague in 1970 and came into force on 14 September 1971.

346 *Supra*, note 311.

347 Also known and to be referred to henceforth as the Montreal Convention (1971).

attempt at giving the principles of the Hague Convention (1970) a broader application by defining acts of sabotage and violence related to offences interfering with the safety of civil aviation. However, it is noted that subsequent effort by the ICAO to develop international procedures and sanctions to ensure that states would observe their obligations under the three conventions failed.[348]

It needs to be said that hijacking as an act against the safety of traffic in the air is comparable to piracy.[349] Piracy is the oldest and perhaps only crime over which universal jurisdiction was generally recognised under customary international law.[350] Brierly noted that although there is no authoritative definition of international piracy, it is of the essence of a piratical act to be an act of violence.[351] In this sense at least, we can talk of air piracy. By 1991 authors including Shaw note that: "[I]t is likely that the law relating to hijacking will eventually turn that offence into a universal one on similar lines to piracy on the high seas."[352]

However, the analogy must not be carried too far. Although the act of hijacking is comparable to piracy, there is an agreement among jurists that international law principles applicable to piracy do not necessarily cover aerial hijacking. Furthermore, distinctions can be made between hijacking and other forms of interference with civil aviation. Writers from the developing world particularly stress the distinction. Ajomo, for instance, insists:

> If hijacking were indeed always an act of piracy, the duty of governments involved would be much clearer than it is now because piracy itself is a crime subject to universal jurisdiction. Under customary international and maritime law, pirates are offenders against the law of nations, *hostis humani generis*, and the enemy of the human race who may be arrested on the high seas by the warships . . . Thus the rule of customary international law regarding piracy would appear to have conferred a universal jurisdiction . . . The pirate loses the protection of his State and the nationality of the offender becomes irrelevant. Unfortunately it is not uncommon to treat as piracy acts that are not so in international law.[353]

The point raised here has been well taken. But it must be added that since there is no internationally accepted definition of piracy in any case, the true test may be to examine whether aerial hijack or the sabotage of aircraft constitutes an act that essentially makes the perpetrators *hostis humani generis*. If this were so, would it not be appropriate to regard persons engaged in such activity as essentially *de facto*

348 See Hailbronner op. cit.: 58.
349 Charturvedi op. cit.: 87.
350 Marlvina Halberstorm, "Terrorism on the High Seas: The *Achille Lauro*, Piracy and the IMO Convention on Maritime Safety", 82 *AJIL* (1988): 272.
351 J. Brierly, *The Law of Nations* (Oxford: Clarendon Press, 1928): 154.
352 M.N. Shaw, *International Law*, 3rd edn (Cambridge: Grotius Publications, 1991): 325.
353 Ajomo op. cit.: 19.

pirates? Indeed, it may be said that it is better for the safety of aviation activities that the law be brought in alignment with this view.

It is in this light that support may be found for the decision in *US v. Yunis*.[354] In this case, a resounding acceptance of the universal and passive nationality principles was established as the basis for a state to exercise jurisdiction over the crime of hijacking committed by an offender against its interests outside territorial bounds if the offender is later found in that state. Fawaz Yunis, a Lebanese national, was convicted for his involvement in the 1985 hijack of a Jordanian civil aircraft in the Middle East. His arrest was effected after he was enticed on to a yacht in the Mediterranean by Federal Bureau of Investigation (FBI) agents. He was then arrested when the yacht reached the high seas. The only connecting nexus of the aircraft to the United States was the presence of three American nationals on board. The aircraft was Jordanian registered; it carried the flag of Jordan and never at any point in time flew into or anywhere near US territory. The court overruled the defendant's claims that "[n]either hostage taking or aircraft piracy are heinous crimes encompassed by the (Universal) Doctrine" and that the USA itself does not recognise the passive personality principle as a legitimate source of jurisdiction. It was held that aircraft piracy and hostage taking are both subjects of international conventions, which demonstrates the international community's strong resolve to punish these crimes irrespective of where they occur. Furthermore, the court found that although the passive nationality principle is the most controversial of all five identified sources of extraterritorial jurisdiction,[355] it was ready to accept it because "the international community recognizes its legitimacy".[356] Interestingly, the court came to the conclusion that, in asserting jurisdiction over the defendant, it was acting in both national and international interests. Thus, "[n]ot only is the United States acting on behalf of the world community to punish alleged offenders of crimes that threaten the very foundations of world order, but the United States has its own interests in protecting its nationals".[357]

What remains unclear, however, is whether only one of the two bases of extraterritorial jurisdiction considered in this case would have been enough to ground jurisdiction. The court did not pronounce clearly on this issue. While it is suggested – *lex feranda* – that universal jurisdiction should be a sufficient basis to establish jurisdiction over aerial piracy, there is ample room for criticism. It is submitted that it is precipitate for US courts to conclude that it is *lex lata* that universal jurisdiction over hijackers already exists in international law. It is, of course, desirable, but that is a different thing from assuming with all certainty it exists presently.

Thus, on its own the universal doctrine would not have been sufficient to bring Yunis to book. As regards the passive nationality principle, it cannot be said that US courts will not forever be haunted by the fact that the shadow that exists over

354 681 F. Supp. 896 US District Court, DDC February 12, 1988.
355 *Supra*, Chapter 1.
356 681 F. Supp. At 901.
357 Ibid.

the potency of this principle is primarily due to the contentious objection of the USA against the Mexican court ruling applying the principle in the Cutting case.[358] The court in *Yunis* attempted to excuse this stating that "the United States has protested the assertion of such jurisdiction for fear that it could lead to indefinite criminal liability" for US citizens.[359] Thus, whether the passive personality principle alone can be used by a state to found jurisdiction over hijackers may depend on that state's attitude hitherto towards the principle and the protests if any by the suspect's own state and/or other states. However, it may be noted that this distinction may now have become academic in the light of the fact that a web of treaty laws now governs jurisdiction over air pirates.

Ironically, in an effort to combat the problems of unlawful interference with civil aviation within their jurisdiction, states can be accused of excesses. Certain legislative reforms in various jurisdictions have been identified as raising fundamental questions of constitutional and international law. For instance the Gore Commission's recommendations in the US jurisdiction raise such queries.[360] One central criticism is the use of passenger profiling, terrorism databases and "no-fly lists", which have since come into common use especially in the aviation practice of developed Western states. The use of profiles can potentially single out an individual in a discriminatory manner. For example, an Arab or Muslim would generally become suspect where airline workers in Western states take such profile into consideration. Indeed, lawsuits emanating within the USA in recent years are from Arab and Muslim Americans who claim their constitutional rights were infringed on as a result of the profiling regulations. The numbers of such complaints appear to be inexorably on the rise.

After the terrorist attacks of 11 September, leading Western states introduced the devices of terrorist watch lists and no-fly lists. Examples of these abound. The Canadian government created a number of national security programmes including the Advanced Passenger Information Program, Advanced Passenger Protect Program, trusted traveller programmes such as NEXUS and the Specified Persons List. The USA also introduced the Terrorist Identities Datamart Environment (TIDE), the Terrorist Screening Database (TSDB) and the Transport Security Administration (TSA), which has a congressional mandate to establish a programme that checks the names and dates of birth of passengers on domestic flights against the TSDB. The TSA also administers two lists namely a "no-fly" list and an "automatic selectee" list.[361] People on the former list will, as the name suggests,

358 *Supra*, Chapter 1.

359 681 F. Supp. at 902.

360 See White House Commission on Aviation Safety and Security: A Department of Transport Status Report Presented To The Vice President US Department of Transport News Release (July 1997) at 7, available 1197 WL 399309.

361 See the Canadian Aeronautics Act as amended in 2004; for the Nexus programme, see http://www.travelsense.org/pdf/TrustedTraveler_EN.pdf (accessed 21 May 2010); for material on the TSA visit http://www.tsa.gov/; TIDE was established under the Intelligence Reform and Terrorism Prevention Act of 2004 (IRTPA). See also http://www.nctc.gov/docs/Tide_Fact_Sheet_2010.pdf; Luongo op. cit.: 157–66.

not be allowed on board commercial aircraft in the first instance, while those in the latter list will receive additional screening at security every time they fly.

At any rate the limitations of these devices may have been exposed in the failed attempt to blow up Northwest Airlines flight 253 in December 2009. The name of suspect Farouk Abdulmutallab was already on US databases of suspected terrorists. Profiling, indeed, does not offer the intelligent solution it appears to represent in popular conception as its usefulness appears limited to assuaging the fears of the profiler rather than representing the realities of life. Existing criteria used for profiling may become instantly anachronistic or deficient with the changing fortunes of international politics and international relations. Nationalities and/or profiles that were considered rock solid and safe may, in the course of a single week, in reality change to represent more of a threat than received wisdom made allowance for. It is interesting to note the views of a writer on the topic in 1969:

> Given the incidence of hijacking, one must necessarily inquire as to who the hijackers are and what their motives may be. *The typical hijacker of a United States registered aircraft is a United States national.* Usually he acts alone, although there have been instances of two, three, or four hijackers taking over an aircraft. In at least six cases the hijacker has been accompanied by members of his family.[362]

Other criticisms include the development and use of devices that "can produce images of an individual's private bodily areas as well as reveal private conditions, ranging from mastectomies to catheter tubes".[363] Particularly controversial is the use of certain intrusive technologies including whole body imaging (WBI) units such as millimetre wave (MMW) screening technology and backscatter X-rays that have been deployed as a traveller scanning method at airport security checkpoints internationally, These devices are used to complement the more familiar metal detectors and are meant to detect threats to aviation security that metal detectors are incapable of identifying.[364]

The European parliament has mandated the European Commission to undertake a study of the impact of WBI devices from an economic, human rights and ethical perspective. More than 40 civil liberties human right groups under the

362 See Alona E. Evans, "Aircraft Hijacking: Its Cause and Cure", 63, 4 *American Journal of International Law* (1969): 700 (emphasis added).

363 For a treatment of the excesses of the new rules in the USA and the Gore Recommendations, see Michael J. AucBuchon, "Choosing How Safe is Enough: Increased Antiterrorist Federal Activity and its Effect on the Airport/Airline Industry", 64, 3 *Journal of Airlaw and Commerce* (1999): 903–905; see also Nadine Strossen, "Check Your Luggage and Liberties at the Gate", *Intellectual Capital*, 7 August 1997.

364 Office of the Privacy Commissioner, Privacy Impact Assessments: OPC letter in response to the privacy impact assessment (PIA) completed by the Canadian Air Transport Security Authority (CATSA) in anticipation of the deployment of millimetre wave (MMW) screening technology at selected Canadian airports, 29 October 2009, available at http://www.priv.gc.ca/pia-efvp/let_20100108_ e.cfm (accessed 25 May 2010).

Privacy Coalition have forcefully argued that this type of screening ought to be optional and for secondary screening only. In 2010 the German federal government rejected their use outright. Thus, there are enough grounds for states to move deliberately and very slowly on this matter. While there are sufficient considerations to be made under domestic laws alone the more significant breaches from an international law and relations point of view may be significant. It is not impossible to envisage the possibility of states to espouse citizens' claims on an international level where they are systematically targeted under what may amount to questionable practices.

The USA, particularly, has for decades displayed a readiness to employ certain means in the exercise of its jurisdiction to combat hijacking that are very much open to criticism.[365] Taken in the context of Joyner's thesis, the severe American legal and political reactions to the problem of aerial sabotage and hijack are a direct result of its peculiar and ever increasing vulnerability to international terrorism. The thesis as expounded by Joyner, and later on Cheng, is that there is a demonstrable connection between hijackings suffered by a state and the willingness to accede to international conventions dealing with the crime. Joyner, in his work in 1974, convincingly demonstrates with tables and statistics that there is a correlation in the pattern of exposure to hijacking attempts, the dates of signing the treaties and the commitment to eradicate the problem of hijacking. Cheng also reflects this stance when he wrote regarding the drafting of the Hague Convention (1970): "[W]hat was interesting to observe in the negotiations was that those States which believed that they were, for one reason or another, immune from hijacking were constantly dragging their feet. But as soon as one of their aircraft became the target of a hijack, they immediately turned into ultra-hawks."[366] Recent state practice, however, show that there is more cooperation in combating the problem of aerial hijack, which, of course, is a priority of the developed states, than other problem areas of unlawful interference with civil aviation such as aerial sabotage arising out of aerial trespass or the aforementioned growing problem of unruly passengers in the air. Another example of this sort of problem is shown in the way Israeli military forces destroyed the Gaza International Airport facilities on 4 December 2001 and 10 January 2002 rendering the airport inoperable. Israel, a state that to all intents and purposes takes the safety of aircraft very seriously, was found liable and condemned for the destruction of the airport and its air navigation facilities by the Council of the International Civil Aviation Organisation (ICAO) which adopted a resolution on the issue in Montreal on 13 March 2002. The resolution strongly condemned the act, stating that it amounted to unlawful interference against civil

365 In 1969 one legal writer notes: "In recent months a bantering remark to a member of a flight crew as to the prospects of a side trip to Cuba has earned more than one passenger a delayed flight, a conversation with an agent of the Federal Bureau of Investigation, or an appearance in court on charges ranging from disturbance of the peace to attempted aircraft piracy . . . In Boston a passenger who asked a stewardess 'how long does it take this plane to get to Cuba' was fined $200 on a charge of disturbing the peace." Evans (1969) op. cit.: 695–710.

366 See Joyner op. cit.: *et passim*; see also Cheng (1988) op. cit.: 33.

aviation and that Israel should take the necessary measures to restore Gaza International Airport so as to allow its reopening as soon as possible.[367]

Joyner's thesis may, indeed, be used to explain the policy reactions of the USA to the offence of hijacking generally but it certainly does not necessarily justify US policies in all cases.[368] There is, however, much truth in the observation of Cheng that: "[O]ne of the many menaces of our society is the single-cause crusader who puts the value he champions above all else. Important as the fight against international terrorism is, surely it cannot be placed above the need for all States to respect international Law."[369]

It must be said that states have a duty to give effect to the treaties governing crimes in the airspace and unlawful interference with civil aviation. International law, however, does not permit let alone require the application of those laws in a discriminatory manner or in a manner that, in effect, violates civil liberties. The lesson to be taught is that here as in other aspects of the law there must be proportionality not only between law and sanction but also between law and method of policing.

Much can, however, be said in favour of certain novel forms of punishment for perpetrators of aerial crimes that have emerged in the US jurisdiction. For instance, there may be a requirement that an individual convicted of aerial piracy pays an amount in restitution to victims of his crime. The methodology employed in calculating the amount of restitution includes the defendant's ability to pay as well as the financial impacts listed in the victim's impact statement. Thus, in *US v. Rezaq*,[370] on conviction, the defendant was ordered to pay $254 in restitution to seven victims. This sum is hardly excessive but, of course, stands as a precedent that may be useful in the future for exacting heavier sums from less necessitous convicts or the rich sponsors of terrorist hijacks. Apart from its deterrent value to would be offenders, this development partially remedies lacunae that have persisted since the beginnings of international regulation of the airspace,[371] which is the problem of a proper consideration of legal liability for aviation disasters involving terrorist acts. Issues of civil remedies are indeed much more closer to the general discussion of jurisdiction over aerial crimes and aviation offences than is commonly

367 PIO 03/2002, available at http://domino.un.org/UNISPAL.NSF/ (accessed 1 June 2010).

368 See, however, *infra* 3.7: The problem of state-sponsored crimes against the safety of aircraft, particularly the discussion of 9/11, which arguably confirms the fears of successive US administrations.

369 Cheng, "Aviation, Criminal Jurisdiction and Terrorism: The Hague Extradition? Prosecution Formula and Attacks At Airports", *Contemporary Problems of International Law; Essays in Honour of Georg Schwarzenberger on His Eightieth Birthday*, ed. Bin Cheng and E.D. Brown (London: Stevens & Sons Limited, 1988): 49.

370 US Court of Appeals District of Columbia Circuit 6 February 1998, Avi 15.404.

371 Cf. the fines discussed *supra*, notes 276, 278, 307 and 365. It is also significant to note that Libya paid "substantial" compensation to the families of those who died in the Lockerbie bombing. Although the Libyan government continuously maintains that it had no involvement in the attack, it deemed it fit to strike a deal that brought an end to the UN sanctions on the country, which were put in place by the Security Council.

realised. Unfortunately international regulation in this area is increasingly viewed as anachronistic. This underscores the need for better coordination of international legal policies relating to criminal and civil jurisdiction in airpsace law.

The Warsaw Convention[372] and the treaties regarded as the "Warsaw System"[373] regulate international liability for losses and accidents occurring out of air transport and have proved largely inadequate in governing this area of the law. These treaties imposed limits on damage liability and harboured substantial hurdles for recovery by grief-stricken families of victims. Levels of compensation available to victims were, notably, widely seen as inadequate.[374] Significant improvements to the liability and compensation regime for losses and damages may have occurred recently largely due to the efforts of airlines and the private sector.[375] Nevertheless, the treatment of liability for compensation of victims, particularly those of terrorist crimes, are still in need of serious overhaul. Without strict and proper guidance under international law it is no wonder that in most jurisdictions, liability for damage caused by hijackings remains quite an uncharted area. As a US court had cause to note "hijacking was probably not within the specific contemplation of the parties at the time of the Warsaw Convention".[376] The events of 11 September

372 The Convention for the Unification of Certain Rules relating to International Carriage by Air, signed at Warsaw on 12 October 1929.

373 The 1929 Warsaw Convention; The Hague Protocol 1955; Convention Supplementary to the Warsaw Convention for the Unification of Certain Rules Relating to International Carriage by Air Performed by a Person other than the Contracting Carrier, signed at Guadalajara on 18 September 1961 (Guadalajara Convention 1961); the Montreal Inter-Carrier Agreement 1966; the 1971 Guatemala Protocol.

374 Warsaw Convention 1929 (Art. 22: passengers = 125,000 francs; goods 250 francs per kilogramme); Warsaw Convention as amended by the Hague Protocol 1955 (Art. XI: passenger is limited to the sum of 250,000 francs; goods 250 francs per kilogramme); Warsaw Convention as amended by the Hague and the Guatemala Protocol 1971 (Art. 2: passengers = 100,000 special drawing rights; delay of persons = 4150 special drawing rights; baggage = 1000 special drawing rights).

375 There is a perception that the Warsaw Convention provided for limits of liability that are too low. When the US Senate failed to ratify the Montreal Protocol 3 the entire Warsaw Convention system appeared to be under threat of denunciation by the USA. The dissent of key players and the erosion of the integrity of the Warsaw system by differing national responses on the issue of liability risked putting the entire system in jeopardy. Some developed countries (Belgium, Denmark, France, Germany, Greece, Ireland, Italy, Portugal, Spain and the UK) unilaterally decided to increase their limits of liability over and above that dictated under the Warsaw system. Noting that the Convention's limits of liability, which had not been amended since 1955, are now grossly inadequate in most countries and international airlines acted together to increase them to the benefit of passengers These agreements are: the IATA Intercarrier Agreement on Passenger Liability (IIA) of 31 October 1995 and the Agreement on Measures to Implement the IATA Intercarrier Agreement (MIA) 1996. Signatories to this agreement include 132 international carriers as at 1 March 2009, representing more than 90% of the world's air transport industry. See list of carriers on the IATA website available at http://www.iata.org/whatwedo/Documents/iia_signatory_list_mar09.pdf (accessed 1 November 2010). The IATA agreement requires carriers to pay up to 100,000 SDR (approximately US$135,000) to accident victims, regardless of carrier negligence. Consequently, any accident victim having a claim against a carrier that was party to the second IATA agreement would have an absolute right to recover up to 100,000 SDR of proven damages.

376 *Husserl v. Swiss Air Transport Co. Ltd*, 12 CCH Avi.17, 367 at 17,370 (DCNY, 1972).

have led to some progress on the matter.[377] As one writer notes: "Osama Bin Laden probably does not know that one consequence of his war against the West has been a new set of procedures adopted by the international market for aviation in London."[378] Within one week of the event leading underwriters in London reached remarkable agreement with the leading international brokers. It is said that, although the final cost of 11 September may never be known, total insured losses are projected at US$32.5 billion, to which must be added over US$7 billion paid out by the Victim Compensation Fund in respect of 2,880 people killed and 2,680 injured in the attacks and in the rescue efforts.[379] Inevitably, since 2001 changes have also been implemented in the international aviation insurance regime to cope with the mischief of aerial and aviation terrorism.[380]

But it appears that these changes have not gone far enough and the real lessons of 9/11 for the aviation industry have not adequately imbibed. Progress has been timid and limited to pro-industry bureaucratic structures. Most of the notable changes have been spearheaded by Competition Directorate of the European Commission chiefly in the area of creation of an Aviation Liaison Forum (ALF)[381] (established in March 2005); a Crisis Response Protocol[382] (with the aim to maintain competition even in crisis situations); and an Aviation Insurance Clauses Group (AICG).[383] More importantly, the focus of much of the discussion and action in this specialist area are focused on Western business whereas the risks are global and emanate from the most unlikely corners of the earth. The exposure of the aviation industry to unacceptable risks continues. Scholars of the subject have suggested that the Convention on Damage Caused by Foreign Aircraft to Third Parties on the Surface Signed at Rome on 7 October 1952[384] has become outdated and needs to be replaced by a new treaty that is purpose built for the 21st century that seeks to protect the industry and particularly the direct victims. Yet the prospects of achieving this in the immediate future appear dim as the same parochial national interests that plagued the present convention and account for its relatively low ratification remain rife.

377 See, further, our discussions on state-sponsored crimes at 3.7.

378 Harold Caplan, "The Aviation Insurance Clauses Group: A Model for Other Markets", XXXI, 4–5*Air and Space Law* (2006): 254.

379 See the Insurance Information Institute, as quoted in OECD, *Catastrophic Risks & Insurance: Report No. 8 on Policy Issues in Insurance* (Paris: OECD, July 2005): 62; See also Caplan op. cit.: 257.

380 See, generally, Caplan op. cit. *et seq.*

381 Information and materials about the ALF are available at the website of the Lloyd's Market Association, www.lmalloyds.com.

382 Europa, "Competition: Aviation Insurers Commit to Reforms to Promote Competition and Transparency", Press Release (Brussels, 23 March 2005), available at http://europa.eu/index_en.htm (accessed 3 November 2010).

383 Information and materials about the AICG are available at /www.aicg.co.uk. It is notable that the AICG has begun consideration of Space Product Liability Policies in response to changes from Governmental to commercial involvement in outer space.

384 310 UNTS 181. The Convention entered into force on 4 February 1958. Status: 49 parties. Other scholars such as Caplan are, however, more optimistic and think that the changes witnessed so far in the aviation insurance can be seen as a successful model for other markets. See Caplan op. cit.: 254.

3.5 The regime of multilateral treaties

From the foregoing discussions it may be deduced that three main multilateral conventions regulate jurisdiction over criminal acts against civil aviation. They are the Tokyo Convention (1963), the Hague Convention (1970) and the Montreal Convention (1971). Other multilateral instruments of importance include the United Nations Convention against the Taking of Hostages of 18 December 1979,[385] the United Nations Convention on the Prevention and Punishment of Crimes against Internationally Protected Persons, including Diplomatic Agents (1973)[386] and Annex 17 of the Chicago Convention 1944, which prescribes standards for aviation security. There is also the Protocol for the Suppression of Unlawful Acts of Violence at Airports Serving International Civil Aviation Supplementary to the Convention for the Unlawful Acts against the Safety of Civil Aviation (1971)[387] and the Convention on the Marking of Explosives for the Purpose of Detection (1991).[388]

The Tokyo Convention (1963) applies in general to all offences against penal law and other acts that put aircraft safety into jeopardy. There are certain limitations to this instrument. It appears, for instance, that offences against penal laws of a political nature or those based on racial or religious discrimination are excluded from the scope of the Convention.[389] Neither does the Convention deal with offenders who are not on board aircraft and in the airspace. Thus, persons who place explosives on board the aircraft before takeoff are effectively out of the purview of this Convention.[390] The view taken by authors is that the Tokyo Convention (1963) was primarily a reaction to the discovery in cases such as *USA v. Cordova* and *R. v. Martin* (discussed earlier) that aircraft, when they are flying abroad especially over the high seas, were literally oases of lawlessness, with no ascertainable applicable law.[391] As a result, one of the central concerns of the Tokyo Convention (1963) as provided in Article 3(2) was not so much to do things for others, but to assert their own jurisdiction over aircraft of their own registration, wherever they may be. Thus, the wording: "Each Contracting State shall take such measures as may be necessary to establish its jurisdiction over offences committed on board aircraft registered in such State."

The question then is did the Tokyo Convention (1963) create a right that states did not previously possess? Again, it would be quite difficult not to yield to Cheng's view that it did not. As already mentioned, nationality is the chief determinant of jurisdiction over aircraft and the rules governing this date back to Regulation of

385 ILM, Vol. 18 (1979): 1457.
386 Of 14 December 1973; UNTS Vol. 1035: 167.
387 Done at Montreal on 23 September 1971; ICAO Doc. 9518. Reprinted also in XVIII-II *Annals of Air and Space Law* (1993): 245.
388 Signed at Montreal on 1 March 1991; ibid: 280.
389 Hailbronner op. cit.: 59.
390 Saka op. cit.: 205.
391 Cheng (1988) op. cit.: 31–2.

Air Navigation of 13 October 1919.[392] Thus, what the contracting parties to the Tokyo Convention (1963) had done in Article 3(2) is merely to undertake to exercise a right that they already enjoy under international law.[393] To hold otherwise would be to espouse the doubtful proposition that states that had exercised such jurisdiction prior to the Tokyo Convention (1963) or those that are not contracting parties to it presently are in breach of international law.

The Hague Convention (1970) is specifically concerned with aerial hijacking.[394] The Convention may be said to represent a remarkable milestone in the development of international criminal law in many ways. Parties to this Convention undertake to make unlawful seizure of civil aircraft an offence punishable by severe penalties. It is noted that, as far as hijacking and violent crimes are concerned, the obligation of the state of registration of the aircraft under the Tokyo Convention (1963) to establish jurisdiction extends to the state of landing and the state of the lessee of an aircraft leased without crew.[395] In other words, the Convention reinforces what the Tokyo Convention (1963) has achieved. This is in that it also requires the state of registry of an aircraft (and that of the operator) to exercise domestically its quasi-territorial powers (*jurisfaction*) and to ensure that its laws and the jurisdiction of its courts extend to the treaty offence committed on board such aircraft wherever it may be (Article 4(1)(a) and (c)).

The central value of the Hague Convention (1970) is the fact that it renders hijacking an international crime for the first time. This was no mean feat because at that time, due to the politics of the Cold War, the Soviet Union had objected to the use of terminology suggesting any notion of an "international crime" or even "international offence".[396] The internationalisation of the crime of hijacking was achieved in three ways. First, it was to make the treaty offence an offence punishable by severe penalties under written laws (Article 2). Second, states were required to exercise their territorial *jurisfaction* and make their laws and the jurisdiction of their courts relating to such offences applicable to any person committing such an offence wherever in the world, irrespective of the nationality of the offenders or of the victim. Third, and very important, with the intent to deny perpetrators of the offence of hijacking any safe haven anywhere in the world, the Hague Convention (1970) implemented the precept of *aut dedere aut punire* (i.e. either extradite or punish.)[397]

392 League of Nations, Treaty Series, 174,1919; *supra*, 2.3: Nationality principle and control over aircraft in flight.

393 Cheng op. cit.: 33.

394 By 1969 the problem of aerial hijack had reached epidemic proportions. Between 1930 and 1967 the total number of aircraft seizures in the air in one single year was an average of six. But in 1968 there were 38 hijack situations, of which the hijackers succeeded in 33. In 1969 the number rose phenomenally to 82 aircraft hijacks, 70 of these were successfully executed; see Cheng (1988) op. cit.: 37.

395 Hailbronner op. cit.: 59.

396 Cheng (1988) op. cit.: 35.

397 This innovation became known as the Hague extradition/prosecution formula and has been copied in a number of later treaties dealing with terrorism. Extradition has always been a very sensitive aspect of international relations and expectedly it proved to be one of the most intractable

Thus, Article 7 of the Hague Convention (1970) provides:

> The Contracting Party in the territory of which the alleged offender is found shall, if it does not extradite him, be obliged, without exception whatsoever and whether or not the offence was committed in its territory, to submit the case to its competent authorities for the purpose of prosecution. Those authorities shall take their decision in the same manner as in the case of any ordinary offence of a serious nature under the law of that State.

It would appear that scholars are divided as to the utility of the Article 7. Cheng, for instance, believes that the duty expressed in Article 7 falls short of ineluctable prosecution let alone prosecution.[398] This is because there is still an exercisable discretion, albeit carefully circumscribed, which remains with the prosecution authorities as to whether or not to prosecute. To "submit the case to competent authorities" is seen as not implying an absolute duty to diligently prosecute. Others, like Harris, however, would appear to believe that the alleged weakness is nothing but an essential safety valve. To him, the duty to prosecute or extradite not only leaves the choice to the state in whose territory the offender is but where that discretion has been exercised as in the *Lockerbie Case* (and under a similar formula in the Montreal Convention (1971)), a challenge to the exercise of discretion will only produce a confusion as to who is infringing the treaty provisions.[399] Libya, in that instance, it has been pointed out, was not merely the state in which the alleged offenders were located; it was also the state of which they are nationals. It could be regarded as having a specific interest of its own, on a par with that of the United Kingdom or the United States. Moreover, Libya's domestic law bars extradition of its nationals.[400] In such a situation, the argument that the *aut dedere aut judicare* rule as provided for in both the Hague and Montreal Conventions is not watertight enough becomes merely academic. This is particularly so where the state has discharged the duty of reference to competent authorities and has made moves to establish jurisdiction. Both positions have valid considerations. Another view, however, is to say that, in reality, whether the extradition/prosecution formula is drafted in a watertight manner or not, the treatment of the offenders will always ultimately depend on political considerations.

problems in the negotiations leading to the final draft of the Hague Treaty. The reasons for the reluctance of states to extradite or enter into extradition treaties are many, ranging from protection of sovereignty and political considerations to differences in the perception of the seriousness and punishment attached to specific crimes. In early 1987 the Federal Republic of Germany refused to extradite to the United States Mohammed Ali Hamadei, a Lebanese national, suspected of haven taken part in the hijacking of a TWA airliner in which a US national was murdered, unless the USA gave an undertaking not to impose the death penalty. See Cheng ibid: 34.

398 Ibid.

399 Harris op. cit.: 306. See *infra*, note 434.

400 M.C. Bassiouni and Edward M. Wise, *Aut Dedere Aut Judicare: The Duty to Extradite or Prosecute in International Law* (London: Martinus Nijhoff, 1995). See also I.A. Shearer, *Extradition in International Law* (Manchester: Oceana Publications, Inc., 1971).

The Montreal Convention (1971) is wider than the Hague Convention (1970) and encompasses acts such as the destruction of navigation facilities (where those facilities are used in international air navigation) if such act in any way endangers safety of aircraft "in flight". From a purely legal analysis, the mechanism of the Montreal Convention is identical to that of the Hague Convention. The difference between them lies in the differing mischief to be cured. While the Hague Convention (1970) addressed the hijacking mischief, the Montreal Convention (1971) was designed to cure the mischief of sabotage of aircraft and of air navigation facilities.[401] It, notably, does not cover acts against persons merely within airport facilities.[402] Under the Montreal Convention (1971), persons who attack or sabotage aircraft or air navigation facilities or pass on knowingly false information, thereby endangering the lives of people and the safety of an aircraft in flight, receive the same treatment as that meted out to hijackers under the Hague Convention (1970).

On the whole, it may be said that the three treaties discussed here represent a fair attempt by states to respond to contemporary problems of crimes committed in the airspace. The treaties complement one another in certain respects. It may be said that the central importance of the multilateral regimes created is that at least one state would be able to exercise jurisdiction over any alleged offender wherever the crime may have taken place in the air or on land.[403] The state that tries offenders of the class in question here does not have to be the registering state neither must it be the state in whose airspace the acts take place. A state in which the aircraft lands due to apprehension of danger or any form of diversion is also empowered to act. Such a state is required to inform the state of registry and the state of nationality of the offenders (if it considers it advisable or) any other interested state, of the facts of the arrest or detention and the intention to exercise jurisdiction.

What this means in respect of hijacking, for instance, is that if an American hijacks an Iraqi plane in South African airspace or indeed over the high seas and consequently escapes to Japan, he will find not only that he is subject to the jurisdiction of Japanese courts but also that as at the time of committing the offence, he was already subject to the jurisdiction of not only Japan but also of America, Iraq and South Africa, provided always that each of the states is, respectively, party to the Hague Convention (1970). Similar rules govern the act of aerial sabotage. It can, thus, be concluded that universal jurisdiction over hijackers and all those

401 It was hoped that the offence of sabotage would be simply drafted into the Hague Convention in 1970 but on account of ICAO standing rules, this would have led to a delay of the conclusion of the Hague Convention. Thus, there was the need to have separate treaties separated by a period of two years. This is probably another pointer to the fact that the law governing criminal jurisdiction in the air has developed in hotchpotch fashion.

402 Such acts are dealt with by the aforementioned Protocol for the Suppression of Unlawful Acts of Violence at Airports Serving International Civil Aviation (1971), which notes in its preamble that unlawful acts of violence are likely to endanger the safety of persons and jeopardise civil aviation.

403 See, for instance, Chapter II of the Tokyo Convention (1963).

who interfere with the safety of civil aviation is within contemplation as the number of contracting parties to the air treaties regulating criminal acts increases.[404]

The existing treaties, it would appear, indirectly encourage the development of specialised techniques and procedure in response to the common threat of hijack, aerial sabotage and recently (since 11 September 2001) the "weaponisation" of the aircraft. Whenever an act of interference, seizure or other wrongful exercise of control over an aircraft in flight has been committed or is about to be committed, state parties are to take all appropriate measures to restore control of the aircraft to its lawful commander. They are also to permit the continuation of the journey as soon as possible. This is a feature that first appeared in the Tokyo treaty (Article 11) and is shared (with minor differences) with both the Hague Convention (Article 9) and the Montreal Convention (1971) (Article 10). In the case of the Montreal Convention (1971), the duty of a state to establish jurisdiction where the alleged offender is present in its territory does not apply to all offences listed.[405] Furthermore, highly innovative mechanisms for coping with the international problem are infused into the treaties such as the extensive powers given to the aircraft commander and others on board to impose reasonable measures of restraint on hijackers (Articles 5 to 10, Tokyo Convention (1963)). Under this rule, the commander, crew and passengers have the right to take all appropriate measures to restore control to the aircraft and to facilitate the continuation of the journey and the return of the aircraft to the lawful owners.[406] The contracting state's obligation to handle the situation and to return control of the aircraft is, in practice, borne by the entire security apparatus at its disposal.

In fulfilment of these obligations, there have been very interesting responses in practice. In response to the hijack of a Nigerian Airways plane in Nigerian airspace

404 That the international society has been moving in this direction is evident from the initial efforts at international legislation over aerial crimes. It may be distilled from a close examination of the wide powers of contracting states in Chapters IV and V of the Tokyo Convention (1963) that universal jurisdiction was an aspiration of the drafters. There was the apparent desire to ensure that no lapses in jurisdiction create a safe haven for the class of offenders dealt with by the Convention.

405 Thus, for instance, the formulation of the Convention's Article 1(1). Offences in (a)–(c) relate essentially to acts affecting directly the safety of aircraft involved in international flights whereas (d) and (e) are of a different nature.

406 In order to protect the safety of aircraft as well as maintain good order and discipline on board an airline in flight, the aircraft commander may deliver to the competent authority of "any contracting state" where he chooses to land any person whom he reasonably believes has committed on board the aircraft an act, which, in his opinion, is a serious offence according to the penal laws of the state of registration of the aircraft (Article 9 Tokyo Convention (1963)). On being satisfied that the circumstances leading to restraining and arresting an offender are justified, a contracting state may cause him to be disembarked and place him under custody for such time as is reasonably necessary and indeed subject him to its criminal jurisdiction or extradition proceeding (Article 13(2) Tokyo Convention (1963)). Under the Hague Convention (1970), a state party is specifically required to establish jurisdiction in those cases where the alleged offender is present in its territory and it does not extradite him to a state possessing jurisdiction. This state party, once the alleged offender is found in its territory and not extradited, is also obliged "without exception whatsoever, to submit the case to its competent authorities for the purpose of prosecution".

by some terrorists in 1994 and the subsequent landing for refuelling purposes in Niger republic, 13 commandos shot their way into the aircraft ten hours before the hijackers ultimatum expired. In the process, three cabin staff and two hijackers were killed. A Nigerian security official on board had earlier passed out as a result of shock and fear.[407] Whereas in the case of a hijacked Ethiopian airliner, an Ethiopian security official who, by chance, happened to be on board acted legitimately (and as it would appear, in accordance with the aforementioned conventions) in opening fire on one of the offenders, killing him instantly, while the other one was overpowered.[408] The realisation always is that hijacking is "a nightmare, a vicious form of Russian Roulette in which the fate of the hijackers is inconsequential in comparison with the potential cost in life of passengers and goods, not to speak of the value of the aircraft itself".[409]

The problem in containing hijackers in such a manner is that it becomes a game of chance that may backfire with disastrous results. One possible future development might be the establishment of highly specialised forces to be maintained by each party to handle such incidents. It might also be that eventually specialised forces would be established at the regional level or by the UN to combat hijack hostage situations. This is, however, not to suggest that response to such situations must always involve military or paramilitary force. There may also be the need to make amendments to the existing air treaties.

The factor of violence must not only be reckoned with, but the cost must be assessed. Aircraft operators presently are placed in a precarious situation when faced with hijacking incidents in the air. Their agents in the air – commander and crew – must act timeously as security exigencies demand yet they must recognise the value of inaction where it would prove foolhardy to act. Terrorist attacks on airliners in the 1970s reveal the jeopardy facing the operators. A number of decided cases establish the right to compensation for mental distress arising out of an airline hijack. This recovery is possible under the Warsaw Convention as amended by the Montreal Agreement of 1966.[410] A carrier was also liable for injuries to passengers that occurred in a terrorist attack at Hellenikon Airport, Athens, at a departure gate.[411] In *Stanford and ors v. Kuwait Airways and ors*,[412] the US Court of Appeals considered the legal liability of Middle Eastern Airlines for having sold airline tickets to apparently suspicious-looking passengers who had interlined from the Middle East Airlines onto the flight of the first defendants (Kuwait Airways), which later

407 See Demola Abimboye, "Flying into Big Trouble", *African Concord*, 8 November 1993: 12–16.

408 Evans op. cit.: 820.

409 Ibid: 695.

410 See, for instance, the American case of *Krystal v. BOAC*, 403 F. Supp. 1322 193. (1975). See also Shaw op. cit.: 322.

411 *Day v. TWA, Inc.*, 528 F. 2d 31(1975), Cert. Denied 429 US 890. The basis of liability in this case is that the airline had not exercised due scrutiny during the boarding of passengers. Similarly, the US Federal Aviation Authority has fined airlines for careless scrutiny of boarding passengers that led to hijack situations. See Evans op. cit.: 821.

412 25 AVI 17, 511 1996; see also Unmack op. cit.: 396.

on suffered a hijack. The court decided to remand the case for a new trial and held that an airline in the position of Middle East Airlines could be liable in appropriate circumstances to other passengers on the Kuwait Airways flight even in the absence of contract. However, no liability was established in a case in which severe damage occurred as a result of an attack in the baggage retrieval area of an air terminal building while passengers were waiting for their luggage. This was because it did not fall squarely within the meaning of "disembarking" contained in Article 17 of the Warsaw Convention.[413] Unlawful acts must, therefore, be anticipated in aviation operations and, as one writer succinctly put it:

> [T]hey cannot be dismissed as an independent criminal act for which no innocent party can be responsible. Claims are made, successfully fought or settled by individuals against enterprises and authorities who are innocent of any involvement in an unlawful act other than having failed to prevent it.[414]

As regards extradition, *aut dedere aut punire* is firmly entrenched in terms of criminal jurisdiction in air law. The treaties discussed earlier, however, differ slightly in their provisions. It is common ground that offences committed on board and in the airspace of any state shall be treated for the purpose of extradition as if they had been committed not only in the place in which they have occurred but also in the territory of the state of registration of the aircraft. However, the Tokyo Convention (1963) states clearly that it is not designed to create an obligation to grant extradition (Article 16). By way of contrast, the Hague Convention (1970) moves towards encouraging extradition. Article 8 of the Convention deems that unlawful seizure of aircraft is an extraditable offence, in any extradition treaty existing between the states parties and that they undertake to include the offence of unlawful seizure of aircraft in every extradition treaty to be concluded between them. Furthermore, if a contracting state makes extradition conditional on the existence of a treaty and it receives a request for extradition from another contracting state with which it has no existing extradition treaty, it may at its option adopt the Convention as a legal basis for extradition in respect of the offence. And where a state does not make extradition treaties a condition, the offence shall *ipso facto* be recognised as an extraditable one subject to the conditions provided by the laws of the state on which the request is made (Article 8). This is *in pari materia* with Article 10 of the International Convention against the Taking of Hostages (1979).

413 *Hernandez v. Air France*, 545 F. 2d 279 (1976); *Mangrui v. Compagnie Nationale Air France*, 549. F. 2d 1256 (1977) Cert. Denied. 45 *Law Weekly* (1977): 380.

414 Unmack op. cit.: 396. Identifiable potential defendants include: the air carriers, the ground handling agents, security agents, airport operators, governmental intelligence agencies, security equipment contractors and maintenance outfits, and probably with the authority of the *Stanford Case* (*supra*, note 412) other enterprises that are indirectly concerned with the aforementioned classes.

3.6 The regime of bilateral treaties and other regional arrangements

States have, in addition to general multilateral treaties, tried to cope with the dangers of unlawful acts directed against the safety of civil aviation through bilateral arrangements and other regional responses. One of the early responses to this problem on the bilateral level is the UK–US Air Services Agreement in 1977, which includes a clause on aviation safety.[415] Since then, virtually every air services agreement concluded by the UK has contained an identical or near identical clause.[416] A similar clause exists in the UK agreement with Antigua and Barbuda, which came into force on 25 March 1985.[417] Article 8 of that agreement provides that:

> The Contracting Parties re-affirm their grave concern about acts or threats against the security of aircraft which jeopardize the safety of persons or property . . . The Contracting Parties agree to provide maximum aid to each other with a view to preventing hijackings and sabotage to aircraft . . . and aviation security. They will have regard to the provisions of the Tokyo, Hague and Montreal Conventions. The Contracting Parties shall also have regard to applicable aviation securing provisions established by the ICAO. When incidents of threats of hijacking or sabotage against aircraft, airports or air navigation facilities occur, the Contracting Parties shall assist each other . . . to terminate such incidents rapidly and safely. Each Contracting Party shall give sympathetic consideration to any requests from the other for its aircraft or passengers to meet a particular threat.

It can be seen that one of the important achievements of these bilateral agreements is that it reinforces the obligations to enforce multilateral conventions aimed at combating crimes in the airspace and on board aircraft.

Instruments of a regional scope to combat serious offences in the airspace also exist. In this category, we have the European Convention on the Suppression of Terrorism (1977)[418] and the Organization of American States Convention to Prevent and Punish Acts of Terrorism taking the Form of Crimes against Persons and Related Extortion that are of International Significance (1971).[419]

415 UKTS No.76 (1977) Cmnd 7016.

416 See Brian Yeomans, "Recognition of States and Diplomatic Relations, Law of the Sea, Air and Space Law: Some Recent Developments", 35 *ICLQ* (1986): 985. However, it is noted that the agreement with Korea has no security clause; UKTS No. 47 (1984) Cmnd 9263. Other agreements having security clauses include UK–New Zealand (UKTS No. 5 (1983) Cmnd 8784; UK–Egypt (UKTS No. 52 (1983) Cmnd 9025; UK–Cameroon (UKTS No. 4 (1984) Cmnd 9124).

417 UKTS No. 29 (1985) Cmnd 9556.

418 Done 27 January 1977; UNTS Vol. 1137, 93.

419 Done 2 February 1971; ILM Vol. 18 (1979), 1457.

3.7 The problem of state-sponsored crimes against the safety of aircraft

> International aviation is thus not just another problem in a changing economic system, though it is that; International Aviation is a serious problem in international relations affecting the way governments view one another, the way individuals view their own and foreign countries and a variety of direct and indirect connections the security arrangements by which we live.[420]

International relations in the 21st century has witnessed the unfortunate development of state-sponsored terrorism, including attacks on the safety of civil airliners. In fact, political motives and interstate rivalries have led particularly in the last decade or so to the problem of the refusal of some states to cooperate in the arrest and prosecution of offenders against the safety of civil aircraft. A criminal may escape into the protection of a state that is hostile towards the state of registry of an attacked airliner or, worse still, a state may actively sponsor crimes against the safety of aircraft belonging to the nationals of another state. The question here is how can jurisdiction be successfully established to bring such persons to book? The answers are not easy ones and they remain one of the most contentious issues in recent times.

It must be noted *ab initio* that "aerial hijacking and sabotage directed against civil aircraft generally do not qualify as acts of war committed by an organized armed force under responsible command fighting against the armed forces of a party to an armed conflict".[421] Therefore, it is out of contemplation for a state to claim that it is retaliating in a military manner or acting in such a manner against civilian aircraft. Indeed, under the laws of war, civil aircraft must not be subject to acts of reprisal or attack. Acts interfering with civil aviation, even when committed in the actual course of armed conflict may be subject to trial or extradition under the laws of war.[422]

However, it may be noted that newer problems for legal classifications on this issue have been introduced when, on 11 September 2001, in a coordinated attack against the United States, 19 terrorists hijacked four commercial aircraft. The men were nationals of several Arab or Islamic states (notably none of them is an Afghani). They flew two of the aircraft into the World Trade Center towers in Manhattan and one into the Pentagon in Virginia. The fourth plane crashed in Pennsylvania. Some 3,000 people died in the attacks; many others were injured and there was enormous destruction of property. On 12 September the United Nations Security Council adopted Resolution 1368 (2001), which, inter alia, condemned the terrorist attacks on the United States; expressed determination to combat threats to international peace and security caused by terrorists; called on all states to assist in the apprehension of the offenders; and decided that the Council is "to remain seized of the matter". On 28 September 2001 the Security Council

420 A.F. Lowenfield, "A New Takeoff for International Transport", 54 *Foreign Affairs* (1974): 34.
421 Hailbronner op. cit.: 58.
422 Ibid. See also our discussion in Chapter 5 on aerial trespass.

unanimously adopted Resolution 1373 (2001) calling for suppression of financing, improving international cooperation and also creates a committee to monitor implementation. The resolution reaffirms "the need to combat by all means, in accordance with the Charter of the United Nations, threats to international peace and security caused by terrorist acts". Primary suspicion for organising the attacks was ascribed by the American government to an Islamic militant terrorist group, al-Qaeda, which is dedicated to opposing non-Islamic governments with force and violence. The USA claimed Osama Bin Laden, a Saudi Arabian national assumed to be hiding in Afghanistan, founded this group. Osama Bin Laden and others, it is alleged, operated al-Qaeda from their headquarters in Afghanistan and forged close relations with the Taliban – the ruling theocratic regime in Afghanistan. In response to the 9/11 attacks, President George W. Bush declared a national emergency and announced the beginning of a "war against terrorism". On or about 5 October 2001 the Secretary of State declared al-Qaeda a "specially designated terrorist", pursuant to the International Emergency Economic Powers Act.

Afghanistan's Islamic ideological rulers, the Taliban, promptly condemned the terrorist attacks, but rejected the notion that Osama bin Laden could be responsible. After the Taliban refused repeated demands by the USA to turn over Bin Laden, the USA and Allied forces began retaliatory bombing of Afghan targets on or about 7 October 2001.[423]

While the term crimes against humanity (presumably demanding universal jurisdiction) has been generously applied to describe the actions of the perpetrators of the terrorist acts that took place on 11 September, it is more a description of the abhorrence of the crimes than a technical use of the term in international law. It is arguable that the specific crime that has been committed is the act of hijacking.[424] The offence of hijack is the unlawful seizure or exercise of control of an aircraft "in

423 This also led to significant loss of civilian lives and property as confirmed by media reports as well as independent sources such as the international Red Cross. As a result of American bombing on or about 9 November 2001, the Northern Alliance forces (a military coalition of various opposition groups in Afghanistan) began a series of military defeats, which led to the Taliban losing control over Afghanistan. The USA began a process of transporting allegedly captured members of al-Qaeda and Taliban forces numbering about 500 to the notorious Camp X-Ray detention facility consisting of cages open to the elements at the Guantanamo Bay, a territory it leased from Cuba since 1903. On 17 November the USA announced that there would be military tribunals to try the prisoners it holds in Guantanamo. The USA has signed each of the four Geneva Conventions on the laws of war and has ratified them with the exception of the two protocols of 1977 but has maintained that all its detainees will not be given prisoner of war status because they are either irregular combatants or have violated the laws of war. The USA made statements, signifying intention to expand the war on terror to other countries. It also identified an "axis of evil" involving three other states, Iraq, Iran and North Korea, which are also members of the United Nations. To date no definitive evidence has been presented before any international tribunal or United Nations body including the Security Council and General Assembly relating to the involvement directly or indirectly of these countries to the September 11 attacks.

424 Therefore, the international laws that govern jurisdiction over the perpetrators of the criminal acts include the aforementioned treaties: the Convention on Offences and Certain Other Acts Committed on Board Aircraft, 14 September 1963; the Convention for the Suppression of Unlawful Seizure of Aircraft of 16 December 1970; the Convention for the Suppression of Unlawful Acts

flight", by a "person . . . on board" and "by force or threat thereof or by any other act of intimidation".[425] It is, indeed, difficult not to agree with the Antonio Cassese argument that the terrorist attacks on the USA on 11 September 2001 have potentially shattering consequences for international law. It will, thus, be necessary to rethink some important legal categories and to emphasise general principles. Collective rather than unilateral measures should be taken as far as possible. Otherwise anarchy could ensue as a result and as much will be lost as was calculated to be gained.[426]

It is, however, likely that certain states would continue covertly to sponsor attacks on the safety of aviation. One likely indication of this is an apparent unwillingness in a number of cases to prosecute the suspected offenders and a refusal to extradite them to an aggrieved state. Those on the receiving end of such attacks are usually the developed Western states of Europe and America, which are particularly vulnerable in this area as a result of their massive private and public investments in aviation transport. It is no wonder then that close attention has been paid to this problem by leaders of seven major industrialised states in the Bonn Declaration in 1978.[427]

The Bonn Declaration is rather short as international agreements go but prescribes dire consequences for any state that actively supports terrorism on board aircraft and refuses prosecution and extradition requests. The Declaration reads in its entirety as follows:

> The Heads of State and Government, concerned about terrorism and the taking of hostages declare that their government will intensify their joint efforts to combat international terrorism. To this end, in cases where a country refuses extradition or prosecution of those who have hijacked an aircraft, the heads of states should take immediate action to cease all flights to that country. At the same time, their governments will initiate action to halt all incoming flights from that country or from any country by the airlines of the country concerned. The heads of state and government urge other governments to join them in this commitment.[428]

Although serious challenges may be raised in academic circles as to the ultimate legal or binding value of this agreement, it can be said that it binds the parties by

against the Safety of Civil Aviation of 23 September 1971 and the Bonn Declaration made in 1978 (*infra*, note 427).

425 See Article 1 of the Hague Convention (1971).

426 Antonio Cassese, "Terrorism is also Disrupting some Crucial Legal Categories of International Law", 12, 5 *European Journal of International Law* (2001): *passim*.

427 On 17 July 1978 at the end of an economic summit meeting in Bonn (then in West Germany) the leaders of Canada, France, West Germany, Italy, Japan, UK and the USA issued an unexpected declaration on aircraft hijacking. This declaration, commonly referred to in legal literature as the Bonn Declaration, specifically describes how the signatories intend to handle such cases. See Bonn Declaration on International Terrorism (1978) 17 ILM 1285; UKMIL 1978; (1978) Vol. 49 *BYIL* 423.

428 Text cited in James J. Busutil, "The Bonn Declaration on International Terrorism: A Non-Binding International Agreement on Aircraft Hijacking", 31 *Indian Journal of International Law* (1982): 474.

virtue of the principle of *pacta sunt servanda* and is actually evidentiary of contemporary international law.[429] For instance, it was effectively implemented on 21 July 1981 against Afghanistan.[430] It was also successfully used to put diplomatic pressure on South Africa when it refused to prosecute 45 white mercenaries who hijacked a plane from the Seychelles after a failed coup bid.[431]

One shortcoming of the Bonn Declaration is that the issue of sabotage of an aircraft in flight or other aviation facilities was not mentioned. For this reason, the declaration proves unhelpful in coping with instances such as the bombing of Pan-Am flight 103 over Lockerbie in Scotland by saboteurs, suspected to be Libyan agents. It would appear that this situation falls within Article I of the Montreal Convention (1971). This provision covers any person who unlawfully or unintentionally "destroys an aircraft in service or plans or cause to be placed in any aircraft in service by any means whatsoever, a device or substance which is likely to destroy that aircraft".

In an enthusiastic attempt to bring the suspects to book and as a result of the repeated denial by the Libyan government of its involvement in the bombing and refusal to extradite the suspects for trial in the UK, Western powers (UK and the USA) successfully spearheaded the imposition of sanctions against Libya through the Security Council in form of Resolution 731 (on 21 January 1992)[432] and Resolution 748.[433] Libya, in turn, instituted two contentious cases at the International Court of Justice (ICJ) against the USA and the UK.[434] The ICJ, however, turned down Libya's request for provisional protective measures against the punitive measures imposed by the Security Council, which was designed to be put into effect by all states and all international organisations.[435] In the declaration of Judge Shigeru Oda, then Acting President of the Court, it was stated that:

429 For a lengthy discussion on the legal validity of this Agreement, see ibid: 487. Harris adopts the view of that the status of the Declaration belongs in "soft law"; see Harris op. cit.: 299. This agreement was re-emphasised by the signatories in the Declaration of Montebello in 1981; ILM, Vol. 20 (1981): 956.

430 Statement on Terrorism issued in Ottawa by Prime Minister Pierre Trudeau on behalf of the participants in the Montebello Economic Summit, 81 Department of State Bill, No. 2053 (August 1981) on 16. The Statement reads, inter alia: "The Heads of State and Government are convinced that, in the case of hijacking of a Pakistan International Airlines aircraft in March, the conduct of the Babrak Karmal government of Afghanistan, both during the incident and subsequently in giving refuge to the hijackers, was and is in flagrant breach of its international obligations."

431 Seychelles initiated the action and worked through the support of the USA. See Busutil op. cit.: 475. See also Jere van Dyke, "Seychelles Newspaper asks Air Boycott on South Africa", *New York Times*, 20 December 1981: 12; "South Africa to try Mercenaries in Hijacking", *New York Times*, 6 January 1952: 49.

432 SCOR Resolution and Decisions, 1992: 51. Adopted unanimously.

433 Ibid: 52.

434 See *Case Concerning the Questions of Interpretation and Application of the 1971 Montreal Convention Arising from the Aerial Incident at Lockerbie (Libya Arab Jamariya v. United Kingdom)*; *Case Concerning Questions of Interpretation and Application of the 1971 Montreal Convention Arising from the Aerial Incident at Lockerbie (Libya Arab Jamariya v. United States of America)* ICJ Reports 1992.

435 See Request for the Indication of Provisional Measures Order of 14 April 1992 "Official Documents", Vol. 86, *AJIL*, July 1992: 638–67; see also Vera Gowlland-Debas, "The Relationship

> [I]t is a matter of general international law that while no state (unless by virtue of any Convention) is obliged to extradite its own nationals, any state may exercise criminal jurisdiction over crimes committed in its own territory or may claim criminal jurisdiction over acts done abroad by aliens which are prejudicial to its security or certain offences recognized by states as of universal concern.

The crux of the legal arguments presented by Libya was that it had complied with its obligations under the Montreal Convention (1971) by taking steps to prosecute the suspects in its own courts and has taken steps to ensure the presence of the accused in Libya. This view has received sympathy even on the bench of the ICJ where Judge Ajibola was of the opinion that Libya's right, under the Montreal Convention (1971) to prosecute its two nationals, if it wants, is a right recognised in international law and even considered by some jurists as *jus cogens*.[436] Libya also claims that particularly since the event the USA has been acting in breach of its obligations under that Convention. The question remains (even now, many years after a political resolution of the dispute) who among the parties to this dispute was acting in breach of the Montreal Convention (1971) and in excess of its jurisdiction? This would have to be answered in view of Resolutions 731 and 748.

This is more so as the case out of political expediencies was discontinued with prejudice by an agreement of the Parties', and the case was removed from the list on 10 September 2003. In a novel method of international jurisdiction introduced by the states parties concerned, the two Libyan nationals suspected to have committed the crimes were eventually submitted and tried by a Scottish court, which sat in Netherlands but applied Scottish laws in the case *Her Majesty's Advocate v. Abdelbasset Ali Mohmed Al Megrahi and Al Amin KhalifaFhimah Prisoners in the Prison of Zeist Camp (Kamp van Zeist) the Netherlands* in the High Court of Justiciary at Camp Zeist Case 1475/99.[437] This procedure opens new vistas in the law and practice of state jurisdiction in general and jurisdiction over aerial crimes particularly.

It was clear from the beginning that any eventual judgement reached by the Scottish court would be the subject of intense criticism. The court itself admitted:

> We are aware that in relation to certain parts of the case there are a number of uncertainties and qualifications. We are also aware that there is a danger that by selecting parts of the evidence which seems to fit together and ignoring

between the International Court of Justice and the Security Council in the Light of the Lockerbie Case", 88, 4, *AJIL* (1994): 644–6 ff.

436 [1992] ICJ Reports at 82, 187 (Ajibola dissenting).

437 The case report is available at http://www.pixunlimited.co.uk/guardian/pdf/0131lockerbie verdict.pdf (accessed 15 September 2010).

> parts which might not fit, it is possible to read into the mass of conflicting evidence a pattern or conclusion which is not really justified.

However, it went to on to conclude that:

> [H]aving considered the whole evidence in the case, including the uncertainties and qualifications and the submissions of counsel, we are satisfied that the evidence as to the purchase of clothing in Malta, the presence of that clothing in the primary suitcase, the transmission of an item of baggage from Malta to London, the identification of the first accused (albeit not absolute), his movements under a false name at or around the material time, and other background circumstances such as his association with Mr Bollier and members of the JSO or Libyan military who purchased MST-13 timers, does fit together to form a real and convincing pattern. There is nothing in the evidence which leaves us any reasonable doubt as to the guilt of the first accused, and accordingly we find him guilty.

The problem with this judgment is that the imputations made asserting the involvement of the Libyan government with the crime would appear to justify Libya's claims all along that the case is a political witch hunt and that a fair trial cannot take place if judged by a UK court. Sadly for international lawyers, the judgment completely ignores the question of international jurisdiction. The antecedents of the case are such that it is considered necessary for the judges to locate the basis of their jurisdiction over the case and to state this in the final judgment given. It will continue to be relevant in any discussion about the eventual solution given to this particular matter that Libya had expressed willingness to prosecute the suspects if provided with the evidence to do so.

However, the argument may still be advanced that the nature of sovereignty is fast changing and it is a trite observation that the overwhelming nature of sovereignty and jurisdiction must be tempered by the realities of an interdependent world. It may, indeed, have been better for the international legal order had the UK and the USA not insisted on the right of the UK courts to try this case since the Montreal Convention (1971) is the operative treaty and Libya was in the process of fulfilling its obligations under that treaty. A better option would have been to allow the ICJ to deliver an authoritative judgment as to which state(s) should exercise jurisdiction over the suspects. It would be unreasonable not to expect that the ICJ would take into full consideration the possibility of Libya being biased in favour of the accused if it tried the case. The UK and USA would, in any case, have done their best to prove this likelihood.

What also becomes clear from the preceding discussion is that the protective functions and jurisdiction of the state is usually what comes into play in dealing with perpetrators of crimes against the safety of aircraft whether they are state sponsored or not. In the nature of things, it will not be apparent what the motives or connection there are between the perpetrators and any state or political organisations yet states retain a legitimate right to exercise protective jurisdiction.

It is good international policy to thoroughly investigate, prosecute and punish crimes against the safety of aircraft and the airspace of independent states. Yet it must be recognised that the attempt to exercise protective jurisdiction may be fraught with danger and may have to pay attention to political and diplomatic sensitivities. Ryngaert correctly reflects this reality in stating the following caveat:

> The exercise of protective jurisdiction may also poison international relations and cause other States to retaliate, not only because other states might have concurrent jurisdiction over the crime, but also because crimes against the security of a state may, unlike common crimes, be supported or condoned by a foreign government . Claiming protective jurisdiction over the author(s) of the acts may imply passing judgment on the acts of a foreign State and could undermine the political independence of the latter State.[438]

Akehurst also warned that the protective principle loses its validity when it is used, "not to safeguard the political independence of the State seeking to exercise jurisdiction, but invoked to undermine the political independence of the other countries".[439] Where the author is not a state organ or an agent as may be determined by legal means, it becomes even more important to avoid international conflict in this manner by avoiding the exercise of jurisdiction. Of course, where the other state is involved in the perpetration of the crime, normal rules of dispute settlement known to international law are to be employed. Nowhere do these considerations come into issue more dramatically in the past decades than in relation to terrorist-inspired airspace incidents and crimes.

3.8 Summary and conclusions

National laws, on the one hand, and international law, on the other, govern jurisdiction over crimes in the airspace and/or on board aircraft. There exists a cacophony of national legislation governing aerial crimes. While some states have a sophisticated regime governing these crimes both in substantive and procedural terms, other states are still lagging behind in coping with the jurisdictional problems presented by international aviation in this century. It may indeed be predicted that lawyers everywhere will for a long time be kept busy with the task of interpreting and elaborating on the rules regulating crimes in the airspace as found both in international and national legal instruments.

There exist certain problems relating to criminal conduct in the air, which are not presently adequately regulated by international treaties. This refers particularly to the emerging problems relating to unruly passengers. The plans by the ICAO to address this issue should be actualised speedily. Any instrument drafted would

438 Ryngaert op. cit.: 97–8.

439 Michael Akehurst, "Jurisdiction in International Law", 46 *British Year Book of International Law* (1972–1973): 159.

have to include other acts or offences committed on board aircraft, which are not included within the scope of the existing air law instruments. It may be noted that the absence of a settled regime on the problem of unruly behaviour in the airspace also means there is very little to be learnt from air law by lawyers who may soon be called to fill similar lacunae with respect to outer space flight. In fact, it is significant to note that none of the air treaties dealing with criminal jurisdiction extends its application to events occurring on board spacecraft or to events occurring or having effects in outer space. Thus, the problem of flying oases of lawlessness may sooner than expected loom large again this time with respect to spacecraft and in outer space. The threat of this happening is very real, particularly with the advent of those aircraft capable of making flights through outer space and the onset of commercial space tourism.

The need for control over unlawful interference with civil aviation is a central feature of international legislation concerning air law. It would appear that states have developed international legislation relating to crimes committed on board aircraft and in the airspace with an obvious fire brigade approach. The result is a plethora of treaties and conventions all addressing problems identified with particular eras in international relations. This uncoordinated approach has produced dangerous gaps in the law. Jurisdictional questions relating to unlawful interference with civil aviation has been worked out with more seriousness by states in comparison with other forms of common crime committed in the airspace or on board aircraft. The reason for this is clear. Hijacking, for instance, is an act readily compared with (but not identical to) piracy – the abominable effects of which makes the perpetrators *hostis humani generis*. One central feature of the three main conventions regulating this problem is that at least the state of registry of the aircraft in which the criminal act takes place can exercise jurisdiction over offenders. Universal jurisdiction over hijackers and people who endanger the safety of civil aircraft may well be within contemplation in the near future. Such a development is, in fact, desirable. The positive development in the ratification of and accession to treaties regulating this category of offences should be noted. As at 2011 the Tokyo Convention (1963) was signed or ratified by 185 states, the Hague Convention (1970) by 185 states and the Montreal Convention (1971) by 188 states. The range of resolutions and conventions made under the aegis of the UN and its specialised bodies serve as a strong pointer to the competence and readiness of that body to cope with the increasing threat of hijacking and other aerial crimes.[440]

440 See, among others, UN Security Council Resolution 341 at 342 1970; 9 International Legal Materials 1291 (1970); UN General Assembly Resolution 2645 (xxv) (Doc. A/Res/2045 (xxxv); UN Press Release GA/4355 (17 December 1970), ICAO Assembly Declaration. Adopted 30 June 1970 Res. Al 7-1, ICAO Assembly, 17th Sess. (Extraordinary) 16–30 June 1970; 63 Department of State Bulletin 302 at 303 (1970); 9 International Legal Materials 1275 (1970) UN General Assembly Resolution 40/61. Adopted by the General Assembly on 9 December 1985. See "Official Documents", 80 *AJIL* (1986): 435–7; UN Council Resolution 579 (1985) adopted by the Security Council at its 2637th meeting on 18 December 1985 *AJIL* (1986): 437–8.

The following observations are, however, relevant. Unlawful interference with the safety of civil aviation is a problem of universal concern. In the final analysis, the law must be continually developed in a collective and coordinated manner. Individual reactions by states through dramatic policies or "single cause crusading" may prove inadequate. Aerial hijack, in particular, is becoming increasingly analogous to the crime of piracy in international law. In cases of conflicting claims of jurisdiction over people accused of the offence of unlawful interference with the safety of civil aviation, the conflict will be resolved by reference to the international instruments in force between the contending states. Ideally, the possibility of offenders in this category successfully escaping prosecution should be virtually negligible.

This is not to say that states and international lawyers can think that the mischief has been effectively cured. Evans rightly underscored the point when he wrote: "In the long view, aircraft hijacking and related offences are crimes of the aerospace age, controllable but not terminable until the function served by such attacks disappears."[441] Unfortunately, terrorist attacks on aircraft will remain a source of controversy. Certain political and religious interests in developing states are bound to continue to exert pressures on international issues through such unorthodox means.

It is significant to note that the preamble to the International Convention against the Taking of Hostages (1979) reaffirms the principle of equal rights and self-determination of people as enshrined in the United Nations Charter. It is patently clear that it is expected that nationals of the newer states would more often than not engage in aerial terrorism and hostage taking in the international system. While it may appeal to popular opinion in some quarters from within the developing states to see contemporary international law as geared against the interests of the developing world, it must be realised that engaging in unlawful interference with the safety of aircraft cannot be a means of participation in international politics. Tolerating or providing a safe haven for aerial hijackers is entirely unsupportable.

The use of watch lists and no-fly lists may be perfectly justifiable under the prescriptive jurisdictional powers of a state and under the reasonable exercise of state sovereignty. It is also necessary to recognise that the operation of such devices must be organised in a manner that causes fewest possible interruptions to other important legal and normative principles of international law such as human rights law construed in the widest senses. Lessons must be learnt from the findings of leading experts of constitutional and human rights law such as the Office of the Privacy Commissioner of Canada, contained in an audit report of the operation of Canadian watch lists:

> The Passenger Protect Program is a secretive program, with Transport Canada adding names of individuals to the List without those individuals' knowledge. The Program also involves both the collection and the disclosure

441 Evans (1969) op. cit.: 710, 822; cf. Evans op. cit. (1973): 671.

> of sensitive personal information from and to the Royal Canadian Mounted Police (RCMP) and the Canadian Security Intelligence Service (CSIS) without individuals' knowledge or consent . . . There is no requirement for airlines to report data breaches . . . Transport Canada has not verified that airlines are adequately protecting personal information.[442]

Reservations about possible human rights violations in the quest for aviation safety and aerial safety of states do not signify an underestimation of the threats. The point being made is that it is equally important that settled categories of law and human rights must not be needlessly endangered. It is, however, crucial that aviation security and aerial sovereignty of states must be respected now perhaps more than at any other time in history. A perceived inadequacy of the global framework of aviation security is the lack of an implementation arm. Considerable thinking has been done on some of the pertinent issues. The ICAO has taken extensive measures to introduce relevant international conventions as well as SARPs in Annex 17 of the Chicago Convention. A highly classified *Aviation Security Manual*, developed by ICAO, has been provided to states. Additionally, the organisation provides focused security training courses to its member states. The ICAO's role is largely confined to rule making and the provision of guidance and much of the implementation and domestication is left to the member states. There is the expectation that a global aviation security crisis management team will be instituted that could work towards effectively precluding acts of terrorism.[443] These developments are entirely supportable and are reflective of the strength of international coordination.

The problem of interference with the safety of aircraft is, unfortunately, likely to be of continuing nature in the course of the 21st century. Although a lot has been achieved in legal response to the problem particularly in the form of treaties and conventions, each event tends to be unique and even fraught with political dangers. This is why legal departments and legal advisers to states have to study in appropriate depth the position of international law in this area in advance of actual occurrences and dramatic scenarios to avoid mistakes in relation to legitimate options available to states.

442 See Audit of the Passenger Protect Program Transport Canada, Section 37 of the Privacy Act. Reports and publications of the Office of the Privacy Commissioner are available at http://www.priv.gc.ca/information/pub/ar-vr/ar-vr_ppp_200910_e.cfm (accessed 25 May 2010).

443 Abeyratne op. cit.: 181.

4 Jurisdiction and control in the airspace over international spaces

The jurisdictional issues raised in this chapter are both technical and of current academic interest. For instance, it may be asked: what is meant by "international space"? Which laws should govern the airspace of international spaces? Should it be the laws governing the specific international space in question or should it be the general principles of air law? Furthermore, there is the classic debate in academic literature as to whether the airspace above the high seas is also part of the common heritage of mankind.

Without intending to enter into technical details, which are considered not central to this work, it suffices to mention that the establishment of the international legal regimes for the high seas, Antarctica and outer space respectively has created a basic distinction between national spaces and international spaces in contemporary international law. International space, thus, simply put, is that environment that does not fall under any state's territorial jurisdiction. For our purposes, the international spaces to consider include the air space over the following areas:

1 non-sovereign maritime zones, i.e. international straits, the contiguous zone, the exclusive economic zone (EEZ), the continental shelf, the high seas
2 Antarctica
3 the polar territories.

The importance of understanding the jurisdictional issues raised when aircraft navigate in the airspace over these territories cannot be overstated.

There is, however, a concept with which we must grapple at this stage. That is the concept of flight information region (FIR) and it is a product of the ICAO rules and produces a certain blurring of the strict distinctions, which appear to exist between the maritime zones in international law. At the regional level, the ICAO has divided the high seas among contracting states. Each contracting state has responsibility for air traffic control and for control in general in its FIR. The FIR of each state is the airspace over its own territory and over its territorial waters; and over that part of the high seas that has been assigned to it. The airspace in the UK (including the territorial waters) is divided into two FIRs: London and Scotland.[444]

It must be noted, however, that the FIR principle does not confer any more substantive jurisdiction than a state already has in any given sphere. Where a state lacks substantive jurisdiction as in the airspace over the high seas, the workings of the FIR principle do not give jurisdiction. All a state does in its FIR is to offer air traffic control and see to it that all the rules of the air are obeyed. The rules over the high seas are exclusively the ICAO rules and no more. National legislation cannot be introduced to operate within the FIR where the region falls outside the territorial sea. Neither can a state deny access to foreign aircraft in the area within its FIR, when it is within international airspace. In any case, the ICAO rules to be enforced within the FIR apply to the contracting state itself.[445] With these considerations in mind, the view may indeed be taken that the FIR is a region established for the exercise of duties and not to claim rights. This view admittedly creates problems within the scope of a Holfedian analysis of rights and duties.

4.1 International straits

As regards the airspace above international straits, the first thing to note is that all aircraft enjoy the right of transit passage, which shall not be impeded. This is stipulated in Article 38 of the Law of the Sea Convention LOSC (1982)[446] in respect

444 To the west of the London FIR, air traffic is controlled by Dublin and Shannon ACCs. To the south, it is controlled by Brest and Paris ACCs in France and to the southeast by Brussels and Amsterdam ACCs. To the northeast, there is a link with Copenhagen ACC and to the east, over most of Continental Europe, aircraft in the upper air are controlled by Eurocontrol at the Maastricht ACC. Note: Maastricht does not control any air traffic in UK airspace. The aerial territorial control and area of responsibility of the UK is broken down as follows: the Area ATC services are supplied by National Air Traffic Services from three area control centres at London (LATCC), Prestwick (SCATCC) and Manchester. Traffic in the London FIR is controlled from LATCC and Manchester, and traffic in the Scottish FIR and oceanic traffic in the Shanwick oceanic control area is controlled from SCATCC. LATCC organisation: LATCC is split into various sections. There are two civil ops rooms, the ACR (area control room) and the TCR (terminal control room). Airways control is provided by en route in the ACR and terminal control services and approach radar for Heathrow, Gatwick and Stansted are provided in the TCR. The ACR is divided into two banks, north and south, and is further split into sectors. Each sector can also be split according to traffic conditions. North bank: Clacton sector – CLN East, West High and West Low. North Sea sector – Goles and Beeno Lakes/Wirral sector – Lakes and Wirral Daventry sector – DTY North and South South Bank: Bristol sector – Bristol, Strumble and Brecon Berry Head sector – BHD and Land's End Dover – DVR and LYD Worthing – SFD, Hurn High East/West and Hurn Low. London sectors: London middle sector, London upper sector. The TCR is also divided into north and south banks: North bank: TC Midlands – Cowley and Welin, Bovingdon, Lambourne Lorel NW departures NE departures TE East – SABER and DAGGA, Stansted approach. South bank: Heathrow approach Ockham. SE Low Biggin, Willo, Timba, Gatwick approach. See http://avism.com/atco/latcc/htm.

445 Heere op. cit.: 76.

446 The 1982 United Nations Convention on the Law of the Sea (to be henceforth referred to as the LOSC (1982) contains 320 articles and nine Annexes It was adopted by 130 votes to 4, with 17 abstentions. The pressures leading to the Law of the Sea Conference lasted between 1974 and 1982 and involved a very wide range of international organisations and states. Singh describes this document as "a charter for the world's oceans". It took 9 years to complete the instrument. It deals with almost every human use of the ocean – navigation and overflight, resource exploration and exploitation, conservation and pollution, fishing and shipping. It constitutes a guide for state

of straits used for international navigation between one part of the high seas or an EEZ and another part of the high seas or an EEZ. This is in contradistinction with what subsists with respect to the airspace above the territorial sea, where there is no right of innocent passage for aircraft.

It is correct to say that the concept of transit passage in the airspace over international straits excludes any activity by an aircraft in transit that is not a constituent part of the transit flight. Brownlie recognises the possible exception of warships from the general right of innocent passage for foreign ships through international straits.[447] The question may then be asked whether there is a similar possible exception of state aircraft (i.e. those used for police, customs or military services) from flying through the airspace of an international strait. By their very nature, straits are bounded by state territory (or territories), thus security considerations are expectedly important. Questions as to possible prescriptive authority and/or unilateral enforcement powers of the coastal state relating to transit passage of state aircraft are reasonable.[448]

It is, however, submitted that state aircraft should not normally be excluded from navigating over international straits. As to prescriptive authority, it is suggested that no such powers of *jurisfaction* by bordering state(s) exist over international straits. As to enforcement powers, Hailbronner's view is accepted in noting that:

> [A] breach of duties under the Convention or the municipal law by an aircraft in transit does not give the bordering state the right to take unilateral action to prevent the passage except where such action is designed for the protection of vital security interests against imminent and evident dangers resulting from activities of aircraft in transit (e.g. right of self-defence; vital interests).[449]

In any case, the general principle may be recalled as enjoined in various treaties that states should refrain from activities that may be harmful towards the lawful interests of other states.

4.2 Contiguous zone

The rule that national sovereignty and territorial jurisdiction should be limited to the territorial sea has been expressed in the Geneva Conventions of 1958 on the

behaviour in the world's oceans. See further Nagendra Singh, *International Maritime Law Conventions*, Vol. 4 (London: Stevens & Sons, 1983): 2646–7.

447 Brownlie, in fact, remains unconvinced that warships have any rights to innocent passage in territorial waters including situations "when the territorial waters are so placed that passage through them is necessary for international traffic". He based his position on both the lack of corroboration in the *travaux préparatoires* of the LOSC (1982) and because such "textual arguments advanced involve the unwarranted assumption that a question with a background of controversy was ultimately settled by leaving the issue dependent on inference". See Brownlie op. cit.: 194–6, 280.

448 Kay Hailbronner, "Airspace over Maritime Areas", in *Encyclopaedia of Public International Law*; Rudolf Bernhardt (ed.), *Comparative Law* (Amsterdam: Elsevier Science, 1989): 28.

449 Ibid.

territorial sea and the contiguous zone[450] and, finally, in the LOSC 1982. It follows, therefore, that sovereignty and territorial jurisdiction extends to the airspace above territorial waters. The fact that these Conventions do not extend state sovereignty to cover the contiguous zone is definitive of the nature of jurisdiction and control that states have in the airspace over the contiguous zone in international law. Thus, the rights that the coastal state may possess in the airspace over its contiguous zone cannot be more than what the law of the sea gives it over the underlying waters.

Indeed, we may recall that under Article 24 of the TSC (1958) all the coastal state may do in the contiguous zone is to exercise just that control necessary to: (a) prevent infringement of its customs, fiscal immigration or sanitary regulations within its territory or territorial sea and (b) punish infringement of said regulations committed within its territory or territorial sea. Under Article 33 of the LOSC (1982), however, a coastal state may claim a contiguous zone (for the same purpose as the 1958 provision) up to 24 nautical miles from the baseline.

One crucial thing to note is that while under the 1958 system the contiguous zone was part of the high seas, the LOSC (1982), it would seem, makes it part of the EEZ. Whatever the effect that may have, it would still be clear that in the airspace above the contiguous zone, there can be no sovereignty. The jurisdictional powers exercisable over such airspace (if any at all) would also have to fall within the parameters of the reasons why the zone was created. The question may be raised as to what happens when a foreign aircraft navigating over the territorial sea engages in acts for which Article 33 (a) and (b) of the LOSC (1982) was created. For instance, if parcels of hard drugs or toxic waste are dropped into the underlying territorial waters, it is clear that this will be a violation of international law. But can the right of hot pursuit vested on the coastal state under the law of the sea in relation to ships be exercised in relation to aircraft committing prohibited offences in the airspace above the contiguous zone? Or can an aircraft continue or commence the hot pursuit for offences committed by ships within territorial waters? It must be admitted expressly that at the present stage of international law there is no right of hot pursuit in relation to air law as there is in the law of the sea. Therefore, attractive as the concept may be, the use of aircraft to exercise the right of hot pursuit as enshrined in the law of the sea would not be easily supportable under contemporary international law.[451] Many states may, however, directly have within their national law and defence practice the right to repel and follow aircraft that stray so close to their territory as to threaten their security or engage in illegal unreported or unidentified fishing with national EEZ.

4.3 The exclusive economic zone

Due to the novelty of the concept of the EEZ, it presents a unique problem as regards the determination of the legal status of the overlying airspace therein. The

450 UKTS 3 (1965), Cmnd 2511; 516 UNTS 205; (1958) 52 AJIL 751.
451 See elsewhere in Chapter 4.

air law implications of the establishment of the EEZ were not dealt with by the LOSC (1982). Thus, the question of jurisdiction and control over the airspace above the EEZ was not delineated. This creates practical problems requiring legal solutions. For instance, wind energy exploitation technology involves devices with physical heights that may hamper aircraft navigation.[452]

A timely warning has been offered that:

> The establishment of the EEZ world-wide would absorb at one or several points all the major trading routes. Ships would have to navigate through the zones of a third state to communicate with most other states. Important air-routes would have to pass through the airspace covering a number of EEZ's. Unrestricted coastal jurisdiction within the 200 n.m. (nautical miles) EEZ could turn a strategically placed coastal state into a modern Venice, extracting political or economic advantage for the privilege of transit.[453]

It is accepted that much can be said in favour of the establishment of the EEZ. This is because it goes a long way towards placing non-renewable mineral resources within the jurisdiction and control of coastal states. Most of these states are developing and in dire need of such assistance. However, this advantage is in relation to the resources in the sea and under the seabed as the case may be but not necessarily in relation to the airspace over the EEZ or continental shelf. It is doubtful whether the drafters of the LOSC (1982) intended to create "air Venices". Article 78(1) of that Convention, in fact, provides that the coastal states' shelf rights do not affect the legal status of the airspace above.

There is, therefore, good reason to give a qualified acceptance for Attard's position that "it would be imprudent to expect a coastal state not to enquire about the flight of an aircraft, which might be engaged in the exploration of its EEZ resources".[454] Hailbronner expressed a similar opinion. He thinks that the use of aircraft to explore and exploit fishing resources as well as for prospecting in connection with economic exploitation of the EEZ must be regarded as the coastal state's exclusive right.[455] Heere misrepresents the actual words of the Law of the Sea Convention. He wrote: "Article 246(2) LOSC reads: 'marine scientific research involving aircraft in the EEZ can be prohibited by the coastal state'."[456] What the Convention actually states is: "Marine scientific research in the exclusive economic zone and on the continental shelf shall be conducted with the consent of the coastal state." This provision does not specifically mention aircraft. The only sovereign

452 Carl Q. Christol, "Law of the Sea: Neglected Issues", *Proceedings of the Twelfth Annual Conference of the Law of the Sea Institute, 23–26 October 1978*, ed. J.K. Garbie (The Hague: Martinus Nijhoff, 1978): 127.

453 Parenthesis added. See David Attard, *The Exclusive Economic Zone in International Law* (Oxford: Clarendon Press, 1987): 77.

454 Ibid: 80.

455 Cf. Ki-Gab Park, *La Protection de la Sommerait Aérienne* (Paris: A. Pendone, 1991); see also Nicholas Grief's review of this in *BYIL* (1992): 457–5. K. Hailbronner, "Freedom of Air and the Convention on the Law of the Sea", 77 *AJIL* (1983): 506.

456 See Heere op. cit.: 77.

rights granted to the coastal state in Article 56(1) (b) are for the purpose of exploring and exploiting, conserving and managing the natural resources, whether living or non-living, of the waters superjacent to the seabed and of the seabed and its subsoil.

The common pitfall into which these writers would seem to have fallen is their refusal to distinguish between "exploration" and "exploitation". It may be suggested that at least in respect of aerial territories above maritime zones, this distinction is highly significant. Thus, while it is true that the coastal state has rights barring foreign nationals from exploration in its EEZ, it does not necessarily have such rights with respect to the airspace over that zone. The correct view to hold is that at the bottom of the rights granted to coastal states in relation to the EEZ is the preservation of its natural resources from exploitation by others without its permission and/or benefit. Exploitation is, therefore, the most crucial economic right for which the zone was created. Accordingly, an aircraft, which, without making any connection to the underlying water through any device and which navigates over the EEZ, would appear free to do so even if its activities are in some ways exploratory, under the present state of the law. Therefore, it is consistent with legal reasoning that the consent of the coastal state required under Article 246(2) must not be unreasonably withheld.

For instance, it should be perfectly legitimate for an aircraft that is not flying over the territorial sea to monitor the movement of migrating fish so long as no danger is posed to artificial islands and installations. The desire may be to determine when such fish enters other maritime areas where they may be lawfully fished or for any other harmless scientific study. A coastal state may, thus, make laws and exercise the control necessary to protect its artificial islands and artificial installations located within the EEZ. The landing and takeoff of aircraft from such places without due permission would definitely impinge on the jurisdiction and control of the coastal state that places them there. Apart from this, exploration without more by any aircraft is perfectly legitimate. This includes activities such as aerial photography of the EEZ and remote sensing that are of a commercial nature. The simple rationale for this position is that these types of activity may not, in themselves, lead to the loss of one single resource. In any case, such activities are now conductible by means of satellite technology from outer space. In short, it must be accepted that the recent development of the EEZ concept does not significantly disrupt the rights and freedoms traditionally exercised by states in the airspace over the high seas, such as, overflight, space flights or maritime navigation and the laying of submarine cables.[457] It should be noted that the EEZ of a state or portions of it might also fall under its flight information region. In such a case, it has the duty to perform the roles for which that region was created. Further theoretical problems may be foreseen where the FIR of one state covers areas that are within the EEZ of another state.

457 See the views of B. Oxman, "The Third United Nations Conference on the Law of the Sea: The 1977 New York Session", 72 *AJIL* (1978): 57, 72 ff. See, however, our discussions relating to military activities over the EEZ.

4.3.1 Military activities over the EEZ

There is, however, much credit to the view that the extent of the rights enjoyed by a vessel or aircraft anywhere depends largely on the activity it is engaged in. Thus, for instance, a coastal state has a right under Article 216(1) to take enforcement action to protect its EEZ from pollution and dumping by foreign aircraft in its EEZ and continental shelf just as it does in its territorial sea. Furthermore, the legality of military reconnaissance conducted from the airspace of the EEZ is becoming a controversial issue.[458] International law abhors practices that have the potential to lead to international conflict or breach of the peace between states. It should be noted that in relation to the delimitation of marine airspace and the nature of jurisdiction and control exercisable therein there is an obvious lack of *opinio communis*. The creation of the EEZ concept further adds to the controversies surrounding the rule of freedom of the air above the oceans.

Military lawyers from developed states have been quick to point out that coastal states lack the competence to regulate military activities in the airspace above the EEZ. As stated by Raul Pedrozo: "Beyond the 12-mile limit is international airspace." Neither UNCLOS nor the Chicago Convention grants coastal states any authority over military operations in international airspace above the EEZ.[459] It is true that sovereign rights in the EEZ of coastal states are limited to the seabed and its subsoil as well as to the waters superjacent to the seabed. Apart from the obvious exception specifically mentioned in Article 56 regarding the production of energy from the water, currents and winds, it needs to be emphasised that the freedom of navigation and overflight granted by the UNCLOS is subject to a set of mutually applied conditions set out by the LOSC. While the coastal state should have due regard to the rights and duties of other states and act in a manner compatible with the provisions of the Conventions (Article 56(2)), other states can also only act within another state's EEZ by observing three conditions identified in Article 58. First, actions must give due regard to the rights and duties of the coastal state; second, states must be ready to comply with the laws and regulations adopted by the coastal state in accordance with the provisions of this Convention; and, third, all states must note the applicability of other rules of international law insofar as they are not incompatible with the Convention. Thus, for instance, deliberate acts of aerial sabotage of the coastal state in its EEZ pertaining to the rights granted over the EEZ under the Convention will certainly violate all three. Furthermore, even rights that do not percolate under EEZ principles (i.e. over the waters superjacent to the seabed and of the seabed and its subsoil) are caught by the requirement of compatibility with "other rules of international law in so far as they are not incompatible with this Part". While what is compatible with Part V

458 It cannot be taken for granted that all states have agreed to the practice of military aerial reconnaissance from the EEZ. See, further, *infra*, Chapter 5.

459 Raul Pedrozo, "Military Activities in and over the Exclusive Economic Zone" in Myron H. Nordquist, Tommy T.B. Koh and John Norton Moore (eds), *Freedom of Seas, Passage Rights and the 1982 Law of the Sea Convention* (Leiden: Martinus Nijhoff, 2009): 238.

may be interpreted to mean what is specifically provided for under the part, there is also the possible interpretation that compatibility with everything under international law precludes acts of military adventurism, preparation for aggression or, indeed, unfriendly acts that are inherently incompatible with the right of the affected coastal state. Under this interpretation, states may indeed legitimately seek to prevent espionage and/or remote sensing that goes against their safety and/or economic interests insofar that these may affect their ability to enjoy their rights under the law of the sea.

The fact that the errant flights (from the perspective of the coastal state) occur within the EEZ does not mean that it may not enquire into the safety and security interests it may have under other customary principles of international law. For instance, under the protective and or universal principles it may be interested in maintaining fundamental national security over aerial territory in the EEZ just as it may attempt to do anywhere else on earth that is not within the sovereign jurisdiction of other states. However, it must be said that states will be best advised to state quite categorically under which principle(s) they act in those instances where they exercise their jurisdiction over their EEZ airspace (i.e. under LOSC or other treaty rights, customary international law or under any requisite jurisdictional principles known to international law).

Yet we must accept the fact that there are some authors who cannot fathom any possible restrictions on military activities in the EEZ whether sea or aerial based. One such view vehemently argues that:

> First nothing in UNCLOS changes the right of military forces of all nations to conduct military activities in the EEZ. Second, state practice prior to and subsequent to the adoption of UNCLOS confirms military activities seaward of the 12-nm territorial sea without coastal State notice or consent. These activities include: task force maneuvering flight operations, military exercises, weapons testing and firing, surveillance and reconnaissance operations (and other intelligence gathering activities), and military marine data collection (military surveys).[460]

The professional instinct behind opinions like this is recognisable but international policy certainly does not encourage confrontations between air forces and state aircraft over international waters. Therefore, the pertinent question that arises is whether international peace is best served by a prohibition of reconnaissance missions over foreign EEZs. If the answer to that as we imagine it is in the affirmative, then military flights for reconnaissance purposes over foreign EEZs ought to be discouraged under the modern law of the sea. The question of how we can determine whether any particular flight is a reconnaissance or spying mission is another question all together and it is conceded that there is always scope for disagreement. It is also suggested that the answer will always lie in the particular facts

460 Pedrozo op. cit.: 242.

as they present themselves. Persuasive directions have been provided by the so-called Nippon Foundation Guidelines.[461] The directions are framed in exhortatory rather than obligatory language and are intended to be non-binding. The Guidelines indeed reinforce many of the duties that coastal states have regarding the respect that must be had to the freedom of other states in its EEZ including rights of overflight and the laying of submarine cables (Article 2(b)). Coastal states are exhorted to allow the conduct of all marine research that are designed for peaceful purposes in their EEZ (VII(a)). It is also required that coastal states must maintain a transparent and well- disseminated regime of legislation and policies relating to military activities in their EEZs (Article X(a)). Provisions within the Guidelines that appear to enhance the coastal state's jurisdiction and which are wholly supportable include the "dangerous or noxious cargo exception" by which a coastal state may, in accordance with international law, regulate navigation in its EEZ by ships carrying inherently dangerous or noxious cargo (Article III(a)); the reasonability and practicability criteria to be observed by all state vehicles and aircraft within the coastal state's EEZ (Article II(c)); right of coastal state to place temporary restrictions within special circumstances (Article II(d) and (e)); the duty on other states within the coastal states EEZ to avoid unreasonable and/or prejudicial activities to its good order and security or acts that interfere with the use and management of artificial islands, and other such structures (III(a–c)).

In terms of exercise of maritime surveillance, it is stated that the coastal state's right to conduct such activities must be recognised by other states and that the conduct of maritime surveillance by other states in the coastal states EEZ must be only for peaceful purposes. It is equally expected that states should develop arrangements for the sharing of the output of intelligence gathered from surveillance activities with the coastal state. Although it will be quite easy to do this where the surveillance was according to the guidelines conducted in the first place for peaceful reasons, it is suggested that there may be need for special arrangements of commercial payments where the nature of the surveillance was by expensive or commercially oriented means.

Perhaps the boldest propositions in the Nippon Guidelines relate to its provisions on military activities. While noting that military vessels and aircraft have the right to navigate in or fly over the EEZs of other states (Article V(a)), it is stated that:

> [S]hips and aircraft of a State undertaking military activities in the EEZ of another state have the obligation to use the ocean for peaceful purposes only,

461 The Nippon guidelines were prepared against the background of many international disputes over the EEZ including the collision between a US EP3 surveillance plane and a Chinese jet fighter over China's EEZ off the coast of Hainan in 2001, the Japanese Coast Guard shooting and sinking of a North Korean spy vessel in the East China Sea in December 2001 and the ensuing protest drawn from China since the incident occurred within China's EEZ. The Guidelines for Navigation and Overflight in the Exclusive Economic Zone were developed as a result of consensus among the jurists that participated at a series of meetings on the topic between 2003 and 2005. Guidelines for Navigation and Overflight in the Exclusive Economic Zone, available http://www.sof.or.jp/en/topics/05_02.php (accessed 14 July 2010).

> and to refrain from the threat or use of force, or provocative acts, such as stimulating or exciting the defensive systems of the coastal State. (Article V(b))

Furthermore, it is required that aircraft or warships of a state that intends to carry out a major military exercise in the EEZ of another state should inform the coastal state and the international community of the dates and times of such exercises and, if possible, invite observers from the coastal state to witness the exercise (Article V(c)). On the whole, any military activity in a coastal state's EEZ should generally not adversely affect search and rescue operations (V(d), the marine and other environment (e), disturb intensive fishing (V(g)(2), protected areas (4), sea lanes (5) or cables (5). All these provisions appear to be in line with the general policy directions of the international law of the sea and general international law. Nothing contained therein is likely to endanger the international system but will, rather, help in enthronement of a world of peaceful order in relation to the seas and the airspace over them.

4.4 The continental shelf

A geomorphological description of the continental shelf encompasses the gently sloping platform of submerged land surrounding the continents and islands, normally extending to a depth of approximately 200 metres or 100 fathoms, at which point the seabed falls away sharply. The legal definition of the continental shelf as contained in Article 76 of the LOSC (1982) reads: "The continental shelf of a coastal State comprises the sea-bed and subsoil of the submarine areas that extend beyond its territorial sea throughout the natural prolongation of its land territory to the outer edge of the continental margin, or to a distance of 200 nautical miles from the baselines from which the breadth of the territorial sea is measured where the outer edge of the continental margin does not extend up to that distance."[462] Aware of the immense resources that lay buried in the continental shelf, from the mid-1940s certain coastal states introduced declarations to secure a beneficial utilisation regime for themselves over this maritime zone. The USA was a forerunner in this area and issued the Truman Proclamation on the Continental Shelf (1945) by which it proclaimed: "The continental shelf beneath the high seas but contiguous to the coasts of the United States as appertaining to the United States, subject to its jurisdiction and control".[463] Although this

462 Note that, according to paragraph 3, the coastal state may also establish the outer edge of the continental margin wherever the margin extends beyond 200 nautical miles from the baselines from which the breadth of the territorial sea is measured, by either: (i) a line delineated in accordance with paragraph 7 by reference to the outermost fixed points at each of which the thickness of sedimentary rocks is at least 1% of the shortest distance from such point to the foot of the continental slope; or (ii) a line delineated in accordance with paragraph 7 by reference to fixed points not more than 60 nautical miles from the foot of the continental slope. In the absence of evidence to the contrary, the foot of the continental slope shall be determined as the point of maximum change in the gradient at its base.

463 Presidental Proclamation No. 2667 28 September 1945; 4 Whiteman 756. See also Harris op. cit.: 456.

proclamation (as well as similar provisions in some other declarations) went on to state that the character as high seas of the waters above the continental shelf and the right to their free and unimpeded navigation are in no way affected by the established regime, the status of the continental shelf doctrine was subject of much controversy. The UK, with much less continental shelf to claim (200 metres deep and about 300 miles off Land's End) compared with the USA (with up to 750 miles to claim in places like the coast of California) but with strong interests in international maritime navigation, was quick to point out it would not accept a continental shelf convention that did not clearly recognise the freedom of the superjacent waters of the high seas and that of the airspace above from any form of national jurisdiction.[464]

The Geneva Convention on the Continental Shelf (1958)[465] removed any possible ambiguity as to the juridical nature of the airspace above the continental shelf when it provided in Article 3 that the rights of the coastal state over the continental shelf do not affect the legal status of the superjacent waters as high seas or that of the airspace above those waters. Similarly Article 78(1) of the Law of the Sea Convention (1982) stated: "The rights of the coastal State over the continental shelf do not affect the legal status of the superjacent waters or of the airspace above those waters." The maintenance of the continental shelf doctrine, in contemporary international law, therefore, appears to be solely for the purpose of exploring and exploiting its natural resources. Even though states may create and maintain artificial islands and other permanent structures in furtherance of this purpose, they are not permitted to interfere with aerial navigation in any way so as to require that other states change their flight paths or suffer any restriction such as prohibition of overflight over artificial islands, installations or structures.[466]

Many writers rightly believe that the Geneva Convention on the Continental Shelf (1958) and the LOSC (1982) have attained the necessary balance between the rights of the coastal state in exploring shelf resources and the rights and freedoms of other states. Writers such as Brownlie would appear to have been too optimistic in thinking that, in practice, there are no further controversies or ambiguity. Contrary to his conclusion that: "[L]egislation of the United Kingdom and other states indicates that the shelf regime is not assimilated to state territory",[467] more circumspect enquiry has revealed that, particularly with respect to the rights of other states in the airspace, there is ambiguity in the practice of even

464 See Nicholas Grief, *Public International Law in the Airspace of the High Seas* (London: Martinus Nijhoff, 1994): 12–13; *YBILC*, 1953, Vol. 2: 267, Annex to comments by the Government of the United Kingdom; Lord Asquith in the *Abu Dhabi Arbitration* (1951) noted "there are in this field so many ragged ends and unfilled blanks, so much that is merely tentative and exploratory, that in no form can the doctrine claim as yet to have assumed hitherto the hard lineaments or the definitive status of an established rule of law"; (1951) 18 ILR 144.

465 UNTS Vol. 499: 311.

466 Grief (1994) op. cit.: 13.

467 Brownlie op. cit.: 215–16. Brownlie based his judgment on examination of the UK Continental Shelf Act 1964, c. 29 and cases such as *In re Ownership and Jurisdiction over Offshore Mineral Rights*, 65 DLR 2d (1967) 353; ILR 43, 93.

the UK.[468] Examples of this include the statements of a British government spokesman to the effect that unauthorised vessels and aircraft could not enter safety zones around oil and gas installations, whereas three months later it was declared that the UK had always accepted the principle of freedom of air navigation over all waters, outside the territorial sea and saw no reason to depart from the principle.[469] Another example of this equivocation can be found in Rule 5(1)(e) of the Rules of the Air Regulations 1991,[470] which prohibit all aircraft from flying within 500 feet of any person, vessel, vehicle or structure. By virtue of Rule 2, that applies to all "aircraft within the United Kingdom and . . . in the neighbourhood of an offshore installation". This arguably amounts to an attempt at extraterritorial rule making for aircraft belonging to other states in international space.

4.5 The high seas

The term high seas as defined in Article 1 of the Geneva Convention on the High Seas (1958) means all parts of the sea that are not included in the territorial sea or in the internal waters of any state.[471] However, the whole of section 1 of the General Provisions on the High Seas contained in Part VII of the (1982) LOSC is said to apply to "all parts of the sea that are not included in the exclusive economic zone, in the territorial sea or in the internal waters of a State, or in the archipelagic waters of an archipelagic State" (Article 86).

The freedom of the airspace over the high seas has had a comparatively long history. At the 1927 Lausanne conference of the Institut du Droit International, a declaration was adopted stating that: "The principle of the freedom of the sea implies . . . freedom of aerial circulation over the high seas." Article 2(4) of the 1958 Geneva Convention on the High seas recognised the freedom of aircraft to navigate over the high seas. Similarly Article 87(1)(b) of the 1982 LOSC recognises this freedom. A certain amount of ambiguity in relation to the concept of freedom of the airspace over the high seas was, however, introduced by Article 2 of the Geneva Convention. It provides that the freedom of the seas must be exercised with reasonable regard for the interests of other states in their exercise of the freedom of the high seas. As a result of this, a school of thought holds that customary international law, therefore, allows states the occasional exclusive use of the airspace over the high seas such as the establishment of military exclusion zones.[472] In fact, some states particularly the Western military powers, have established such zones. It is submitted that there is absolutely no support for this view under existing international law.

Thus, the US air defence identification zones (ADIZ), the Canadian air defence identification zones (CADIZ), the United Kingdom maritime exclusion zone (MEZ)

468 See Grief (1994) op. cit.: 13, particularly note 39.
469 Grief ibid: 13–14; Hansard, HL Debs, Vol. 388, col. 915: 2 February 1978; Cf. Hansard HL Debs, Vol. 391, col. 168: 2 May 1978.
470 SI 1991 No. 2437.
471 UKTS 5 (1963) Cmnd 1929; 450 UNTS 82 (1958) 52 *AJIL* 842.
472 See Heere op. cit.: 76. Note also the significance of the aforementioned FIR.

and the total exclusion zone (TEZ) (both established in the wake of the Falkland War and some aspects of which are still in operation at least in relation to Argentina) and the US 5-mile notice to airmen (NOTAM) zones established around US naval ships during the Iran–Iraq war are all products of international *Realpolitik* with little or no basis under international law. The fact that there have been heavy protests against these formulations at different times is good enough reason to hold that the institution of such zones cannot be successfully justified as arising from customary international law.

As to the right of aerial hot pursuit in the airspace of the high seas, it must be said that this is a right recognised in neither the Geneva Convention on the High Seas nor the LOSC. Some have suggested that the right already exists or ought to exist in customary international law.[473] In support of this view is the fact that no specific treaty expressly prohibits hot pursuit. In fact, Article 3(b) of the 1944 Chicago Convention (as amended) recognises the right of every state to intercept a foreign civil aircraft that is overflying its territory without authority.[474] Thus, presumably, there should be a right to pursue such aircraft from national airspace over the territorial sea into the airspace over the high seas for the purpose of escorting it back to the offended state. The Law of the Sea Convention does not grant military aircraft the right to visit foreign aircraft in the airspace of the high seas. In any case, the possibilities of an actual visit on board as is possible for intruding or suspect ships are very slim.

However, writers like Nicholas Grief make a distinction between pursuit and interception. He convincingly argues that the right to approach a suspect aircraft may be said to reside implicitly in the right of self-defence. State practice has also confirmed that military aircraft may approach and intercept foreign aircraft over the high seas in pursuance of the right of self-defence. Note should be taken that such interception is exercisable essentially as a factor of national interests rather than in the exercise of any international policing power.[475] In practice, however, it can scarcely be said that there is a "general practice accepted as law" that constitutes evidence of a rule of customary international law permitting the hot pursuit of foreign aircraft beyond national airspace. In conclusion, it is submitted that international law does not permit the hot pursuit of foreign aircraft in the airspace of the high seas. Such a right, it has been correctly noted, would be open to abuse and could not be exercised without jeopardising aircraft safety and endangering the lives of those on board.[476]

473 See M.S. Lasswell and I. Vlasic, *Law and Public Order in Space* (1964): 310. In 1956 a Chilean proposal to recognise the hot pursuit of an aircraft was not discussed by the ILC. See *YBILC* (1956) Vol. 2: 78 (Doc. A/3159). See also Grief (1993) op. cit.: 218–19.

474 23 ILM 705 (1984). Note, however, the injunction in Article 3 bis (a) to refrain from using weapons against civil aircraft in flight.

475 Grief (1993) op. cit.: 196.

476 Ibid: 222. The essential conclusions relating to the dichotomy between the juridical nature of the airspace of the high seas and the territorial sea was presented by Grief as follows: "Like the subjacent waters, the airspace of the high seas is not subject to the territorial sovereignty of any

4.6 Airspace over Antarctic territories

The airspace over the Antarctic continent deserves special mention and consideration. It needs be said that the international character of Antarctica also attaches to the airspace above the area.[477] However, it is submitted that in relation to the airspace over areas already subject to claims by the claimant states the position of international law is not clear. It can only be suggested that the airspace above the airfields and research facilities constructed by the claimant states should be utilised by other states in such a manner as not to disturb their ordinary usage.

Certain interesting considerations may yet be raised. A distinction can be made between ice shelves and ice islands of the Antarctic continent. Article VI of the Antarctic Treaty (1959) in delimiting Antarctica includes the fixed Antarctic ice shelves. Floating ice islands in this area, no matter how large, are excluded from the treaty by inference. Rights on the high seas are also expressly excluded. The distinction between the ice shelves and ice islands, thus, separate the Antarctic *terra firma* and the Southern Ocean, which falls under the law of the Sea.[478] Complexity, however, is introduced by the fact that the waters of the high seas flow beneath Antarctic *terra firma*. This problem as examined by Hanessian runs thus: "Although, ice shelves are carefully included within the scope of this Treaty . . . the intriguing question remains whether there are high seas underneath the ice shelves."[479]

The Antarctic Treaty (1959) in Article VI has already stated that the high seas applies to all parts of the southern ocean. Thus, there is a situation where the Law of the Sea Convention (1982) applies to the high seas waters which flow under Antarctic ice shelves and the Antarctic Treaty (1959) applies to the *terra firma* above these two sections. Kish would appear to conclude that the regime of the Antarctic ice shelves extends to the superjacent airspace based on the consideration that the airspace follows the legal status of the underlying surface.[480] It should, however, be pointed out that the underlying waters below the Antarctic surface are nonetheless to be taken into consideration in determining the juridical nature of the airspace above. This is particularly so with respect to areas of Antarctica already subject to claims. The argument that since the high seas flows beneath those sectors national

State. The freedom of aviation prevails there . . . The delimitation of the airspace of the high seas and that of the territorial sea is therefore inextricably linked with the question of the legal regimes applicable to those spaces" Grief (1994) op. cit.: 9; see also Hailbronner (1983) op. cit.: 506; see, further, *infra*, Chapter 5, especially the discussion on the aerial incident off the coast of China.

477 For the international regime governing Antarctica, see the Antarctic Treaty Signed at Washington, December 1959 UKTS 97 (1961, Cmnd 1535, 402 UNTS 71; 54 *AJIL* (1960): 477, Article 1. The treaty states in Article 1 that Antarctica shall be used for peaceful purposes only. Article IV(1)(a), however, states that nothing in the present treaty shall be interpreted as a renunciation by any contracting party of previously asserted rights of or claims to territorial sovereignty in Antarctica. Very significantly, paragraph 2 states that no acts or activities taking place while the treaty is in force shall constitute a basis for asserting supporting or denying any claim to territorial sovereignty in Antarctica or create any rights of sovereignty in Antarctica.

478 Howard J. Taubenfeld, "A Treaty for Antarctica", *International Conciliation* (1961): 285–6.

479 John Hanessian, "The Antarctic Treaty 1959", 9 *International and Comparative Law* (1960): 472.

480 Kish op. cit.: 35.

appropriation is forbidden may actually be used by states that oppose the existing claims as a contention to establish the common use of the airspace above.

Furthermore, with respect to all floating islands that are not fixed to Antarctica they are *prima facie* under the regime of the high seas. That is all floating ice islands, pack ice and fast ice that are not attached to Antarctic mainland, no matter how impressive they are in dimension, are not under the Antarctic regime and the legal status of the airspace above them cannot be determined by the Antarctic regime.[481] The significance of this is that where such floating territory of ice emanating from the Antarctic territories floats into the EEZ or the contiguous zone or the territorial sea of any state, the juridical nature of the airspace above such formation will naturally merge into that of the zone into which it falls.

4.7 Airspace over polar territories

The general regime of the high seas applies to the high seas of the Arctic Ocean by virtue of that fact all parts of the Arctic Ocean that are not under state jurisdiction and control form part of the high seas. Therefore, the glacial nature of the surface of the Arctic Ocean does not affect the legal regime of the high seas of the Arctic Ocean.[482] Therefore, the legal nature of the high seas determines the legal status of the airspace over the Arctic Ocean as international airspace. Many airlines currently make use of air routes across the Arctic and it is held to be preferable in comparison to the direct North Atlantic route. The airspace in this region is, therefore, an international resource, the freedom of navigation over which must not be hampered by ambitious claims, such as the sector principle that was developed by the Canadians in 1907 and contentiously espoused by the erstwhile Soviet Republic since 1926.[483]

4.8 Summary and conclusions

An international space in relation to the earth is any part of the earth's surface over which no state possesses exclusive sovereignty. The legal status of any such portion of the earth as international space attaches to the airspace above it. Thus, the laws governing a specific international space determine the legal rights in its airspace. It may, however, be necessary that a law of international spaces be developed. A treaty or international agreement regulating such places would be desirable. This would settle finally all controversies over the legal status of international airspace. It is notable that scholars from the Kent Law School Kish, Grief and the present author have over the years in essence argued in favour of an overarching law of international spaces.

481 See also R.D. Hayton, "The Antarctic Settlement of 1959", 54 *AJIL* (1960): 360.

482 Kish op. cit.: 28. See also Article 1 High Seas Convention (1958). See also our treatment of the Arctic resources *infra* Chapter 10.

483 The controversial sector principle is based on the argument that those states bordering the Arctic should possess territorial sovereignty over all adjoining lands and islands in the Arctic, within a sector to be defined in by the coastline of the territory concerned and meridians of longitude that intersect at the North Pole. See further Grief (1994) op. cit.: 23–5.

The maintenance and operation of air defence identification zones by a few states constitute a limitation on the rights of other sovereign states to common and equal use of the airspace over the high seas. The legality of these zones set up by certain Western powers is both questionable and unjustifiable. The creation and maintenance of the zones is, in fact, a reflection of the dominant interests of the powerful states. Similarly the maintenance of claims over sectors of Antarctica by certain states creates an unnecessary confusion as to jurisdictional rights over the airspace above those sectors. However, since the nature of the legal regime governing Antarctica is that which makes it an international common, it may be suggested that the airspace over all parts of Antarctica remains free from national appropriation.

An interesting situation would, however, seem to arise in relation to the airspace over Antarctica. This is because it remains unclear whether the legal status of the airspace above parts of Antarctic territory is determined by the legal nature of high seas that flow under parts of the Antarctic continent or by the legal status of Antarctica itself. If the former is true, then no exclusive jurisdiction can be claimed by any of the seven states making claims over certain sectors of Antarctica where the high seas flow under the ice. If the latter interpretation is accepted, then the airspace over Antarctic sectors already subject to claims would appear to be part of the exclusive jurisdiction of the particular claimant state. The absurd result of this would mean that airspace above parts of the high seas (even if covered by ice) would also be subject to sovereign claims. The preferred view is that the airspace over all parts of Antarctica and other international spaces is international airspace.

There is the need to revisit the right of passage of aircraft over the EEZ to bring it closer to reality. The present position that seems to be in favour of extending territorial jurisdiction and control over the EEZs airspace to coastal states would seem to be unfair particularly since the concept of innocent passage is simply non-existent under international air law. The vast riches conferred on coastal states with regard to the resources of the sea including the soil and subsoil of the EEZ is enough strategic advantage and air Venices need not be created. The common pitfall into which many writers would seem to have fallen is their refusal to distinguish between "exploration" and "exploitation". It must be asserted that, at least in respect of aerial territories, the distinction between exploration and exploitation is highly significant.

Since the airspace is defined in relation to the earth, the term international airspace does not include outer space. However, even in those areas that may be said to fall under the emerging law of international spaces, it is necessary to ascertain where precisely the airspace ends in legal terms and outer space begins. For instance, in the determination of liability for accidents, it is crucial to determine where the liability was incurred and which laws govern the incident – air law or space law.

5 Sovereignty and trespass in territorial airspace

> [I]f a genuine rogue civilian aircraft incident did occur, whether to shoot it down would be a terrible decision to have to take. And there would be very little time in which to take it . . . We firmly believe that a decision of this magnitude should not be delegated to officials, whether civilian or military, and that any decision to shoot down a suspected rogue civilian aircraft must be taken by Ministers.[484]

The contracting parties to the Chicago Convention 1944 recognise that "every State has complete and exclusive sovereignty over the airspace above its territory" (Article 1). In a sense, this provision reinforces sovereignty as a concept at the very heart of international rule of law and international relations. Indeed, without such agreement the Chicago Convention itself would not exist as it is an expression of the individual and collective will of the 190 sovereign states that have signed and ratified it as at 2010.[485] While it remains true that every state has complete sovereignty over the airspace above its territory, the question frequently arises as to the standard of treatment which may be meted out to aircraft which enter a state's territory without its permission. Since the first incident in 1904 when Russian soldiers shot down a German balloon,[486] there have been literarily thousands of

484 Select Committee on Defence House of Commons, Sixth Report: Defence and Security in the UK Session 2001–02 Publications on the Internet Defence Committee Publications, available at http://www.parliament.the-stationery-office.co.uk/pa/cm200102/cmselect/cmdfence/518/51802.htm (accessed 20 November 2010).

485 This is based on information received by the ICAO from the depositary, the Government of the United States of America, available at http://www.icao.int/icao/en/leb/chicago.pdf (accessed 15 December 2010).

486 The incident gave rise to considerable indignation, more so as it was alleged that the balloon was not naturally over Russian territory at the time. See D.H.N. Johnson, *Rights in Air Space* (Manchester: Manchester University Press, 1965): 70–1. The round-the-world balloon attempt by Richard Branson in 1998 brought into focus yet again the sensitive legal and political considerations involved in balloon flight over state territory. At one point Prime Minister Tony Blair, former Prime Minister Sir Edward Heath and the Foreign Office were all enlisted to try to persuade the Beijing authorities to allow the balloon a passage through China. Eventually, China reluctantly agreed to allow it to continue through its airspace. What it granted was travel through a limited portion of its airspace, south of 26° latitude and north of 43°. But the balloon missed

such recorded incidents, some of which have threatened international peace and stability. Many, mostly innocent, lives have also been lost in these incidents. Yet there has been no consensus in international law either in treaty or among *opinio juris* as to how exactly to deal with aerial trespass.[487] Indeed, many states have no settled policy on this important issue and are hostage, therefore, to the requirements of hasty decisions by ill-prepared air force officers or political decision makers. All these make inevitable the prospect of the perfect aerial storms that periodically unsettle national and international life.

The problem of airspace trespass remains one of the bugbears of international relations and threatens only to escalate in frequency and severity of consequences given technological developments and the prevalence of intractable political

the southern space by about 3°, some 250 miles. The balloon travelled through a narrow corridor, which took it seven miles north of Iran, 10 miles from Russia and 60 miles from Iraq – three of the four countries that had refused the expedition permission to enter their airspace (see Will Woodward, "China gives Branson balloon all-clear", *Guardian*, 23 December 1998: 5. By the same token, China refused any passage for the Breitling Orbiter balloon (see roving brief, "Breitling Orbiter Balloon over Rangoon", *Observer*, 8 February 1998: 9). Whereas, after frantic diplomatic exchanges involving the neutral Swiss government and the International Committee of the Red Cross, the balloon with its crew of two was eventually given approval to cross over Iraq and on to Iran. The permission came so late that it occasioned a 30-minute illegal presence in Iraqi airspace (Agence Presse, "Baghdad allows Balloon Crossing", *Guardian*, 2 February 1998: 13). US balloonist Steve Fossett, attempting the first circumnavigation of the globe, was also given permission to cross Libyan airspace. This was a remarkable feat considering the air sanctions against Libya championed principally by the USA and the UK (roving brief, "Balloonist to Cross Libya", *Observer*, 4 January 1998: 9.

487 For the purpose of this book, a chronology of the major military and diplomatic responses to aerial intrusions from 1946–2000 has been attempted (see Appendix I). As a result of the special and potentially continuing nature of conflicts arising from allegations of aerial trespass between Cuba and the United States of America, an attempt is also made to develop a chronology of allegations of Cuban airspace violations by aircraft with US nationality between 1992–2011 (see Appendix I). Both tables in Appendix I are original attempts to present reported incidents relating to aerial trespass as gathered from academic literature, press reports, internet sources and government official releases. Particular use has been made of the immense wealth of valuable official records kept by the United Nations Dag Hammarskjöld Library particularly under the searchable index of the United Nations Bibliographic Information System (UBISNET). It is to be understood that many of the claims have been disputed by one side to the crisis or the other and that the allegations and/or refutations are not proof in themselves of the truth of the matter. While a lot of effort was made to make the table as comprehensive as possible, it is not meant to be an exhaustive account. It is, indeed, a short sample of the actual number of occasions aerial trespass has been alleged to occur in international relations. The following sources were also consulted in compiling this list: Sichno Acosta, "Violating Cuban Airspace", *Guardian*, Thursday 27 June 1996: 10; *Aerial Incident of 10 August 1999 (Pakistan v. India)*, http://www.icj-cij.org; Richard Beeston, "Air Chief has no Tears over Downed Airliner", *Times*, 24 January 1998: 16; Michael Binyon "'Mercy pilot' held at Port Stanley", *Times*, 18 June 1998: 20; Michael Binyon and Ian Brodie, "US Fighters intercept Russian Jets", *Times*, 2 July 1999: 19; Cuban Ministry of Foreign Affairs, *Granma International*, 6 March 1996: 1–5; Cuban Ministry of Foreign Affairs, *Granma International*, 13 July 1996: 1 *et passim*; L. Gross, "Bulgaria Invokes the Connally Amendment", 56 *AJIL* (1962): 357; D.J. Harris, *Cases and Materials on International Law* (London: Sweet & Maxwell, 1983); Harris (1998) op. cit.; Hughes op. cit. (1998) op. cit.: 598–619; *Keesings*

differences that surround the practice. The mischief is very prevalent and affects states irrespective of size, relative military importance, ideology or population.[488] Yet despite the long history of state protestations against aerial trespass, it is quite inexplicably one of the most under-discussed areas of international law. Protestations range from the 30 November 1951 Soviet statement notifying the UN of a "violation of the state frontier of the Union of Soviet Socialist Republics by two United States military aircraft" to the Cypriot *note verbale* to the UN of 29 April 2010, which lamented: "well-known allegations of violations of international air traffic regulations and the national airspace of the Republic of Cyprus".[489] It is becoming increasingly clear that there is a serious problem of aerial trespass in the international relations of sovereign states.[490] This problem can only be ignored or underplayed at the peril of the international legal order. The frequency of occurrence and the vehemence with which states react to both proven and unproven instances shows that aerial trespass is something that sovereign states take extremely seriously. It is not alarmist to warn that aerial trespass may, indeed, become the flashpoint on which future wars will be fought.

Contemporary Archives 14359 (August 1955) (see text accompanying notes 52 and 53; *Keesings Contemporary Archives* 29060 (June 1978); Marian Nash Leich and Harold G. Maier, "Agora: The Downing of Iran Air Flight 655", 83 *AJIL* (1989): 319–41; O.J. Lissitzyn, "The Treatment of Aerial Intruders in Recent Intruders in Recent Practice and International Law", 47 *AJIL* (1953): 569–81.

488 On Tuesday, 9 March 2010: a grey Russian-built MiG17 Mexican military helicopter was alleged to have strayed into US airspace and hovered over homes on the Texas side of the Rio Grande. The aircraft appeared to have been involved in a hunt down of Mexican drug gangs. Several locals were reported to have spotted and snapped photos of the green helicopter as it flew about one mile into US territory southwest of Zapata, a town about 100 miles northwest of McAllen. The office of the US Assistant Secretary of Defence confirmed the incident. See Lynn Brezosky and Gary Martin, "Mexican Helicopter over Texas sparks Drug War Concerns", *San Antonio Express-News*, 11 March 2010, available at http://www.chron.com/disp/story.mpl/metropolitan/6909500.html (accessed 18 May 2010). Jared Taylor, "Defense Department confirms Helicopter Crossing over Zapata County", *The Monitor*, 1 April 2010, available at http://www.themonitor.com/articles/0in-37009-margin-county.html (accessed 26 May 2010).

489 Letter dated 4 December 1951, from the representative of the Union of Soviet Socialist Republics addressed to the President of the Security Council New York: UN, 6 Dec. 1951 UN Document Symbol: S/2430. UN Document Symbol: A/64/746 S/2010/196 Issuing Body/Session: A/64 S/65 Letter dated 2010/04/15 from the Permanent Representative of Cyprus to the United Nations addressed to the Secretary-General [New York]: UN, 20 April 2010 UN Document: A/64/746 S/2010/196; this study relies on the available records of official complaints to trespass in airspace available in form of searchable database at unbisnet.un.org.

490 Letter dated 4 December 1951, from the Representative of the Union of Soviet Socialist Republics Addressed to the President of the Security Council UN Security Council Doc. General s/2430 6 December 1951. English original, Russian available at http://daccess-dds-ny.un.org/doc/UNDOC/GEN/NL5/124/30/PDF/NL512430.pdf?OpenElement (accessed 2 June 2010); Annex to the letter dated 29 April 2010, from the Permanent Representative of Turkey to the United Nations addressed to the Secretary-General General Assembly, Security Council District: General 5 May 2010 A/64/772 S/2010/227 available at http://daccess-dds-ny.un.org/doc/UNDOC/GEN/N10/349/33/PDF/ N1034933.pdf?OpenElement (accessed 2 June 2010).

Between 1951 and January 2011 a total of 1,403 written state protestations (including some refutations) were reported to the United Nations concerning trespass in airspace (see Appendix I).[491] Many of these events were greeted by severe military consequences and some witnessed diplomatic and political solutions of various sorts. It is also apparent from a study of the official protestations to the UN that some groups of states are particularly susceptible to the tensions and occurrences of aerial trespass. This is true of Cyprus–Turkey, India–Pakistan, Iraq –USA, Cuba–USA, Lebanon–Israel (and, possibly, UK–France).

Unlike the regime of the territorial sea, the law of the air does not recognise a right of innocent passage over state territory.[492] Even over the territorial sea, there is no innocent passage for aircraft.[493] The reasons for this are clear enough. A state is particularly vulnerable from the air. The entire essence of sovereignty and the security of flight over state territory may be eradicated in one seemingly innocuous but illegal flight over state territory.

Nonetheless, it may be suggested that the crucial factors to examine with respect to the appropriateness or inappropriateness of response to aerial trespass are as follows: (a) was the incursion voluntary or involuntary? (b) Was the aircraft involved a civilian one or a state aircraft? (c) Was the flight over prohibited zones? (d) Was the aircraft warned that it was violating territorial airspace? (e) Was the aircraft given reasonable opportunity to cease the intrusion by changing course away from territory or to land for questioning?[494] Needless to mention that the advent of the era of drones and unmanned miniature flying objects open up newer horizons in the discussion of the mischief of aerial trespass.

5.1 Involuntary entry of aircraft

The right to penetrate foreign airspace and to land on foreign territory in the event of wreck or of unfavourable weather has been generally accepted and is based on analogous rights of entry for vessels in the law of the sea. Whether this right extends to state aircraft is debatable given that the Chicago Convention does not contain an express exception to Article 3(c) for aircraft in distress.[495] Article 25, which applies to civil aircraft rather than to non-commercial state aircraft, provides that: "Each contracting State undertakes to provide such measures of assistance to aircraft in distress as it may find practicable." In a sense, therefore, *bona fide* entry due to distress by a civil aircraft is strictly speaking not trespass.[496] It needs, however,

491 *Supra*, note 487.

492 Harris (1998) op. cit.: 185.

493 Nicholas M. Matte, "Air and Extra-Atmospheric Space", *Achievements and Prospects* (1995): 951.

494 Cf. Hughes op. cit.: 596.

495 Article 3(c) provides: "No state aircraft of a contracting State shall fly over the territory of another State or land thereon without authorization by special agreement or otherwise, and in accordance with the terms thereof."

496 Cf. Gerbard von Glahn, and J.L. Taulbee, *Law among Nations: An Introduction to Public International Law*, 8th edn (New York: Pearson Longman, 2007): 391. As Kirgis notes: "Customary international law recognises that ships at sea have a right to enter another state's port in distress. By analogy a similar right probably extends to aircraft in distress, including state aircraft." It need, however, be

be made clear that entry into foreign aircraft due to distress is very different from right of "innocent passage" as this concept simply does not exist in the regime of international air law.

The obligation to assist distressed aircraft under the Chicago regime is based on elementary considerations of humanity. It has antecedents in the law of the sea and is echoed in the law commanding assistance to astronauts and return of spacecraft and other space objects discussed at length later.[497] The unhappy conclusion reached in *Leiser v. United States*, which does not distinguish between entry due to distress and all other forms of entry into airspace and which led to the forfeiture of diamonds the appellant failed to declare regardless of the fact that he came into this country involuntarily and with no "intent to unlade", has to our knowledge not found, and will hopefully not find, resonance in the jurisprudence of other common law states and in international law.[498]

5.2 Deliberate intrusion by state aircraft

When unauthorised entry into foreign airspace is deliberately made, this is a clear violation of the complete and exclusive sovereignty recognised by Article 1 of the Chicago Convention (1944). Such an act constitutes an affront on the territorial sovereignty and jurisdiction of the underlying state. Such trespass also raises the question of the extent of the right of self-defence under contemporary international law.[499] One example of such violation of airspace rights that was of great political significance occurred in the U-2 incident. On 1 May 1960 a U-2 aircraft, a US high- altitude reconnaissance aircraft, was shot down at a height of 20,000 metres above the territory of the then Soviet Union. The USSR promptly protested about the flight and the USA did not justify its action by seeking a defence under any principle of international law. Neither was there protest at the shooting down or the subsequent trial of the pilot.[500] Indeed, after some hesitation, the United States' government and even Eisenhower himself accepted responsibility for the flight. When the Soviet Union sought to seek redress in the Security Council, the only justification advanced by the USA was one totally unknown to law. Its defence was

mentioned that the instance he wrote about was clearly outside the scope of flights covered by the Chicago Convention. Frederic L. Kirgis, "United States Reconnaissance Aircraft Collusion with Chinese Jet", available at http://www.asil.org/insigh66.cfm.

497 *Infra*, Chapter 9: Jurisdiction and control rationae instrumenti and rationae personnae in outer space.

498 The judgment read: "As we understand appellant's argument, he contends that the word 'arriving' as it appears in §§ 1496 and 1498 is to be construed in a limited technical sense, under the authority of various cases involving ships which he has cited, as meaning not mere physical arrival but rather 'a voluntary or intentional arrival of such goods with intent to unlade same . . ." in the United States. We cannot agree with this contention. *Samuel Leiser, Claimant, Appellant, v. United States of America*, Libelant, Appellee No. 5098. United States Court of Appeals First Circuit 13 June 1956.234 F. 2d 648.

499 Johnson (1965) op. cit.: 71.

500 Harris (1998) op. cit.: 241.

that it was necessary to effect that flight for the "free world" to protect itself against a government "well known for its expansionist activities and armed to the teeth".[501]

Unfortunately, due to the politics of the Cold War era, when the Soviet Union sponsored a draft Security Council resolution, which would have condemned "the incursions as aggressive acts", it was not adopted because only Poland supported it.[502] Probably due to such selective inaction by the Security Council, similar incidents have frequently been witnessed. Soon after the U-2 incident there was the RB-47 incident of July 1960 and in 1962 another US reconnaissance flight was shot down over Cuba. Such incidents continued until the late 1990s when the Cuban Air Force downed two US civilian Cessna aircraft over Cuba (see Appendix I).

Outside Cold War politics, the problem of aerial intrusion and the question of what is permissible response to it, remains a current legal problem in international relations. In response to a civil aviation complaint involving the Democratic Republic of the Congo, Rwanda and Uganda, the Council of the International Civil Aviation Organisation (ICAO) on 12 March 1999 adopted a declaration urging all states to refrain from the use of weapons against civil aircraft in flight and to be guided by the principles, rules, standards and recommended practices (SARPs) of the Convention on International Civil Aviation and its annexes and related aviation security conventions, for the safe and efficient development of civil aviation.[503] Between May and August 1999 several aircraft were shot out of the sky by both India and Pakistan, ostensibly on charges of aerial trespass by military aircraft. Pakistan shot down two of India's Russian-built MiG fighter planes over the disputed territory of Kashmir. Wreckage from the MiG21 and MiG27 fighters fell 4 miles inside Pakistani territory, according to that country's military authorities, who insisted that the two planes had been shot down with surface-to-air missiles after violating Pakistani airspace. India confirmed that it had lost two aircraft during the second day of strafing raids against Muslim infiltrators in Kashmir and declared that there would be no let-up in the use of air power in the disputed Himalayan region. It emphatically denied that its aircraft had violated Pakistani airspace. Later on in August 1999 India shot down a Pakistani military plane allegedly flying in Indian airspace.[504] On 1 April 2001 a US Navy EP-3 electronic surveillance plane, collided mid-air with a Chinese fighter jet shadowing it just off the Chinese Coast. The Chinese pilot died in the crash. The US surveillance aircraft made an emergency landing without permission on Hainan Island at Lingshui and China detained the crew for 11 days before allowing the Americans to dismantle the plane and ship it out more than three months later after a carefully worded apology from President George W. Bush. However, he declared that the United States would

501 Statement by US Ambassador Lodgee. See Johnson (1965) op. cit.: 74.

502 Johnson ibid: 74. It is not unusual for states to deny all knowledge of the offending flight. Thus, after the RB 47 incident the USA for 20 years denied all knowledge of the flight and would not even accept the dead pilot's remains.

503 PIO 03/99- ICAO Adopts Declaration on Unlawful Acts against Civilian Aircraft.

504 Note India and Pakistan are the world's newest nuclear powers. David Orr and Zahid Hassan, "India Says it shot Down Pakistani Plane in Indian Airspace", *Times*, 10 August 1999: 20.

continue surveillance flights off the coast of China, despite Beijing's demand that they be halted. Here, as in all such cases, truth is the first casualty of the incident.[505] The typical situation is one of accusation and denial. The country that shoots down an aircraft usually claims that the flight was intruding well into its airspace, that it was a reconnaissance flight/aircraft and that it had been warned to desist, while the state of registry usually issues a robust denial of such allegations.[506]

For instance, the view held by the Chinese government was that the act of the USA:

> constitutes a violation of the UN Convention on the Law of the Sea (UNCLOS), which provides, among other things, that the sovereign rights and jurisdiction of a coastal state over its Exclusive Economic Zone, particularly its right to maintain peace, security and good order in the waters of the Zone, shall all be respected and that a country shall conform to the UNCLOS and other rules of international law when exercising its freedom of the high seas.

505 There were two main issues here. First was the right of overflight by reconnaissance aircraft over EEZs and second was the intrusion and consequential landing in China by the US aircraft. For a comprehensive report of the US version of the incident, see Sean D. Murphy (ed.), "Contemporary Practice of the United States Relating to International Law: Aerial Incident off the Coast of China", 95, 3 *American Journal of International Law* (2001): 633–5. For the Chinese view, see China Ministry of Foreign Affairs Press Release on Solemn Position on the US Military Reconnaissance Plane Ramming into and Destroying a Chinese Military Plane (3 April 2001), available at http://www.fmprc.gov.cn/eng/ 9607.html (accessed 15 November 2003). See also China Ministry of Foreign Affairs Press Release on Spokesman Zhu Bangzao, "Gives Full Account of the Collision between US and Chinese Military Planes" (4 April 2001), available at http://www.china-embassy.org/eng/9585.html (accessed 15 March 2003).

506 Indian officials said the aircraft it shot down was a French-built Pakistani naval reconnaissance plane, which was flying near India's western border with Pakistan, 5 or 6 kilometres (2 or 3 miles) inside Indian airspace in Gujarat. Pakistani officials said it was merely a naval patrol aircraft on a training mission and that it was shot down well inside Pakistani airspace, killing all 16 crew members aboard in a "totally unprovoked aggression". Pakistani officials also claim that the wreckage was located near the town of Badin in southern Pakistan's Sindh province. Within a week of that incident Pakistan admitted opening fire on Indian jet fighters near the border but denied firing at Indian helicopters carrying journalists as fears grew that a fresh conflict could flare. It is, of course, not in all cases that such allegation of aerial trespass leads to employment of military force. For example, the sweeping flight through Greek Cypriot airspace made by Turkish fighter planes in August 1998 elicited no appreciable response to this infringement because Greece at that time was concentrating its efforts on joining the European Monetary Union. Turkey made the flights apparently to demonstrate its ability to destroy a sophisticated missile system to be sited in the Cypriot Paphos Airport. Again, in some cases, military tactics are used that fall short of actual combat. In a spectacular event showing that old habits die hard in international relations, in July 1999 American fighters were scrambled to escort Russian bombers out of "NATO airspace" around Iceland. The alleged Russian intrusion, the first since the end of the Cold War, was as a result of Russia's biggest military exercise for nine years, involving an estimated 50,000 troops, ships from three fleets and hundreds of aircraft. American F15 fighters from the Iceland Defence Force base at Keflavik flew within feet of the Russian TU95 Bear bombers in a confrontation reminiscent of the weekly encounters before 1991. At the same time two Russian TU140 Blackjack heavy naval bombers peeled away and flew down the Norwegian coast. They turned back before Norwegian Air Force jets were able to intercept them. Western diplomats said

What the Convention does provide in Article 58, which deals with rights and duties of other states in the exclusive economic zone (EEZ), is that in exercising their rights and performing their duties in the EEZ, states "shall have due regard to the rights and duties of the coastal State and shall comply with the laws and regulations adopted by the coastal State" insofar as they are not incompatible with the Convention. The duty imposed on the coastal state in Article 56 is to "have due regard to the rights and duties of other States" and to act in a manner compatible with the provisions of the Convention. The pertinent question is whether the US reconnaissance flights over China's EEZ were within the "rights and duties of the US under international law" or, put another way, whether by conducting reconnaissance flights over China's EEZ, the USA was not having due regard to the rights and duties of China as a coastal state. Does it also mean that by virtue of Article 58 China can make regulations binding on other states not to conduct reconnaissance flights over its EEZ?[507] Clearly there is scope for disagreement on these issues. It is for this reason that scholars including Cooper,[508] Kish and Grief[509] have at various times correctly called for specialised treaties that

that the confrontation may have been a Russian attempt to probe Western defences at a time of renewed tensions in the wake of NATO's Kosovo campaign. See Zahir Hussain, Coomi Capoor and Helena Smith, "India loses Two Jet Fighters in Kashmir Attack", *Times*, 28 May 1999: 17; Orr and Hassan op. cit.: 20; David Orr, "Pakistan opens Fire on Indian Jets", *Times*, 12 August 1999: 19; Helena Smith, "Athens loses Taste for Cypriot Missile Row", *Guardian*, 3 August 1998: 11. See also James Meek, "Russians to let Intruding Pilots take off for Home", *Guardian* 17 January 1998: 8.

507 It is worthy of note that the USA is not yet a party to the Law of the Sea Convention (1982). The US attitude to the question whether its flights in international airspace are in violation of China's security is reflected in the words of Colin L. Powell, the US Secretary of State at the time of the incident, as follows: "We understand what territorial integrity means in the concept of international law, not what some countries claim beyond what we think is appropriate. So we always fly these kinds of missions in ways that are consistent with the common understanding of international law and we will continue to do so." See Colin L. Powell, US Secretary of State, US Department of State Press Release on Interview on CBS "Face the Nation" (8 April 2001), available at http://www.state.gov (accessed 15 November 2003). See also Murphy op. cit.: 631.

508 John Cobb Cooper noted over three decades ago: "Too little consideration has been given to the legal control of flight above the seas which cover a large percentage of the earth's surface" (Cooper 1951 op. cit.: 195).

509 Grief believes that although there is a large measure of regulation in existing multilateral and bilateral agreements, as well as a body of applicable rules of customary international in certain areas of the airspace, what is needed particularly for those important sectors such as the airspace over the high seas is for international codification mainly as an exercise in consolidation and codification. The relevance of this thesis is immediately recognisable in relation to the aerial incident off the coast of China. There is little doubt that, in this case, both China and the USA have sought to exploit the grey areas relating to permissible state activity in the airspace above the high seas. With respect to aerial reconnaissance from the EEZ, Grief would appear to think that it is permissible because: "Article 58(1) includes the whole range of activities traditionally covered by the freedom of the high seas, including reconnaissance and military exercises subject to Part V of the Convention." Cf. Colin Powell's view op. cit.: *supra*, note 490. Without any express inclusion of military uses in this provision, it is obvious that China, just like any state that has sufficient interest in not having aerial reconnaissance conducted on its territory even from

will resolve comprehensively the question of jurisdiction over the airspace above seas and other international spaces.

The situation is not helped by the fact that there is no principle of *jus cogens* against aerial reconnaissance and espionage generally. Neither is there any legal obligation to inform ICAO of non-compliance by military aircraft with international flight rules.[510] In fact, it remains common practice among states for surreptitious intelligence collection to be conducted through varied and ingenious ways in one another's territory. Aerial espionage is of particularly desirable strategic advantage and remains a legitimate target for states. As a lawyer and commander in the US Air Force put it: "[O]ur spies are patriots. They take the risk of target country detection and punishment for espionage as a basic tenet of their trade, but the United States is under no obligation, domestic or international, to refrain from engaging in espionage."[511] While it is true that no international convention directly regulates espionage activities generally, it may be argued that the conduct of aerial espionage particularly in peacetime violates the basic principle that each sovereign state must have respect for the territorial integrity and political independence of other states.[512]

The rare combination of security, economic and ecological aspects of the airspace directly engages the national security interests, sovereignty and prestige of almost all countries of the world.[513] As a result, most states with the apparent backing of international law are clear as regards deliberate intrusion. Switzerland, for instance, reserves the right to resist such intrusions by all available means.[514] Indeed, the customary rule that states must refrain from resorting to the use of

international waters, will refuse to admit this understanding. From the perspective of international lawyers, it would indeed have been desirable for the dispute to be submitted to the International Court of Justice. Grief (1994) op. cit.: 10, note 16.

510 Heere op. cit.: 78.

511 (Commander) Roger Scott, "Territorially Intrusive Intelligence Collection and International Law", 46 *Airforce Law Review* (1999): 218. The United Kingdom also practised extensively the act of aerial reconnaissance especially at the height of the Cold War. See Tim Jones, "Balloon Spy Flights to Russia planned by MOD", *Times*, 10 August 1998: 4.

512 Contrariwise, it is necessary to accept that there is some truth to such views as follows: "In an era plagued by the threat of terrorism, the proliferation of weapons of mass destruction, rogue sovereigns and new threats not previously contemplated by international law, where hostile, closed societies will not participate in international arms control efforts or confidence and security building measures, the need for intelligence is still as compelling as it was during the cold war." See ibid. Yugoslav troops and paramilitaries engaged in "ethnic cleansing" in Kosovo were monitored by an array of Western surveillance technology in the sky. Michael Evans, "Airborne Cameras stalk Death Columns Balkans War: Air Campaign", *Times*, 8 April 1999: 4. This issue will remain one of the divisive controversies among lawyers it can only be hoped that states realise the importance to adhere to the principles of international morality and to the true spirit and letter of the Charter of the United Nations 1945. The advantages of so doing will obliterate the need to spy on one another's territory and the need to engage in acts of aerial espionage.

513 Christoper Jonsson, "Sphere of Flying: The Politics of International Aviation", 35, 2 *International Organisation* (1981: 274.

514 H. Weaver, "Illusion or Reality? State Sovereignty in Outer Space", *Boston University International Law Journal* (1993): 211.

weapons against civil aircraft in flight (which is codified in Article 3 (a) of the Chicago Convention (1944) does not apply to state aircraft on reconnaissance flights. Article 32 of the Paris Convention (1919) categorically provided that "no military aircraft of a contracting state shall fly over the territory of another contracting state nor land thereon without special authorisation". Thus, it becomes inescapable to come to the conclusion that necessary force (which may include military force) may be applied against state aircraft that deliberately fly into foreign territory without permission. This is more so in relation to flights over prohibited zones. The presumption of malicious trespass is higher if it occurs over an area that has been created and maintained as prohibited airspace. The power to designate prohibited airspace is within the sovereignty of states. It is, indeed, aligned with the practice of restricted zones in other areas of international law such as in the international law of the sea.

This is probably why the USA did not challenge the shooting down of the U-2 aircraft aforementioned. In fact, on those occasions when the USA protested the shooting down of the state aircraft, it was either claimed that the plane was actually not over state territory or that it strayed there accidentally. The attitude of the then Soviet Union on the true nature of such flights is based on the presumption that "a plane used for military purpose will always be regarded as a reconnaissance plane".[515]

On many occasions the USSR also maintained that the intruder was fired upon by interceptors only in response to unprovoked fire from the intruding plane. In any case, noting the inherent difficulties if not impossibility of determining the true nature of the intruding military aircraft even in time of peace, the mere fact of deliberate entry is usually seen as concrete proof of hostile intentions.[516]

A perusal of the tables in Appendix I will reveal that there are nearly always serious contentions as to whether trespass was deliberate or accidental.[517] The point should perhaps then be made that pilots of state aircraft particularly owe it as a duty for their own safety and in consonance with their duty under national and international laws to prevent accidental or mistaken trespass into foreign airspace. By the same token, there is the presumption that the territorial state would at least issue to the intruding state aircraft an order to land for questioning or to turn back and leave territory.

In those cases of entry due to distress or *force majeure*, there is also the expectation that instructions to land must be obeyed. Thus, even though the intrusion may on occasion be "intentional", it is legitimate if "the probable alternatives, such as crash-landing or ditching expose the aircraft and its occupants to such unreasonably great

515 Y. Korovin, "Aerial Espionage and International Law", *International Affairs* (1960): 49–50.

516 See the B-29 incident (1952) (Aerial Incident of 7 October 1952), *USA v. USSR* (ICJ Pleadings 29); the P-2-Y "Neptune" incident of 1954 (Aerial Incident of 4 September 1954), *USA v. USSR* (ICJ Pleadings 19) and the RB incident of 1960.

517 See further *supra*, notes 496 and 506.

risk that the entry must be regarded as forced by circumstance beyond the pilot's control".[518] Such an aircraft should not be shot down and the territorial sovereign may not subject its occupants to penalties or to unnecessary detention.

5.3 Aerial intrusion by civil airliners

It has been concluded both on functional and on legal grounds that the treatment of aerial intrusion by military aircraft be dealt with as distinct from non-military aircraft. However, there is an unwarranted assumption among writers on the subject that while the attitude of states toward military intruders show little consensus the attitudes toward civil airliners are uniform.[519] That is, civil aircraft must not be shot at or endangered by the security forces of the territorial state. However, in practice, states react with equal seriousness to cases of trespass by civil airliners as they do when state aircraft intrude.

The reasons are clear: intrusion, whether by civil or state aircraft, is a violation of state sovereignty and jurisdiction. They both have adverse security implications for the territory overflown. Thus, while it is easy to maintain an intellectual distinction, it must also be realised that intruding aircraft generally spend quite a short time in flight over state territory and the offended state usually has no prior warning. Therefore, military men and persons who are not skilled in international law take decisions under pressure of time. The harm that can be done to the corporate image and security of a state by even small and privately owned aircraft is great. In 1990, just before the disintegration of the Soviet Union, a small privately owned aircraft piloted by a 15-year-old German was deliberately flown into Moscow without permission and landed in the Kremlin Square. Although the culprit was arrested and prosecuted, the incident exposed unimaginable lapses in Soviet defence and general state of the then USSR.

As one author convincingly put it:

> [T]he fact that a violation of airspace or . . . "penetration" is sometimes effected as the U.S. affirms, by "unarmed" civil aircraft, does not alter matters. Whatever category a plane formally belongs to, its character is determined by the function it performs, a plane used for military purposes will always be regarded as a reconnaissance plane, just like a transport plane used as a bomber cannot expect to be treated as a commercial aircraft.[520]

Nevertheless, international law and the Chicago Convention (1944) reject the use of force against civilian aerial intruders as a primary remedy for the territorial state.[521] After the downing of a Korean Airlines flight 007 by the Soviet Union in 1983, with the consequential loss of 269 passengers and crew, an amendment to

518 Lissitzyn op. cit.: 588.
519 Hughes op. cit.: 600, 619–20 ff.
520 Korovin op. cit.: 49–50.
521 Hughes op. cit.: 630.

the Convention was adopted. This was in the form of an amendment to Article 3. The new Article 3 bis (a) provides that:

> The Contracting States recognise that every State must refrain from resorting to the use of weapons against the civil aircraft in flight, and that in case of interception, the lives of persons on board and the safety of aircraft must not be endangered. This provision shall not be interpreted as modifying in any way the rights and obligations of States set forth in the Charter of the United Nations.

It is in this light that it becomes pertinent to discuss the Declaration Adopted by the Council of the International Civil Aviation Organisation at the Ninth Meeting of its 156th Session on 10 March 1999. The Declaration repeats the preamble of the Chicago Convention (1944), which stipulates that the development of international civil aviation can greatly help to create and preserve friendship and understanding among the nations and peoples of the world, yet its abuse can become a threat to the general security (Declaration 1). Furthermore, the Declaration recalls that the Assembly and the Council affirmed in their resolutions that the unlawful seizure of aircraft and other acts of unlawful interference against civil aviation, including acts aimed at the destruction of aircraft, have serious adverse effects on the safety, efficiency and regularity of international civil aviation, endanger the lives of aircraft passengers and crew and undermine the confidence of the peoples of the world in the safety of international civil aviation (Declaration 2). More important, the Declaration notes that in accordance with Article 3 of the Chicago Convention, states must refrain from the use of weapons against civil aircraft in flight as being incompatible with elementary considerations of humanity (Declaration 4). States that have not yet done so are urged to ratify Article 3 of the Convention on International Civil Aviation as soon as possible and to comply with all the provisions of this Article (Declaration 7). Furthermore, the ICAO Council urges all states in exercising their authority under the Convention on International Civil Aviation and the aviation security conventions to be guided by the principles, rules, standards and recommended practices laid down in these Conventions and in the annexes to the Convention on International Civil Aviation.

Certain observations must be made. The protection of civil aviation from acts of unlawful interference has been enhanced by the Tokyo Convention (1963), the Hague Convention (1970), the Montreal Convention (1971) and the 1988 Protocol Supplementary to the Montreal Convention of 1971 as well as by Annex 17 to the Convention on International Civil Aviation. However, it must be noted that these instruments do not in any way purport to legislate on matters concerning aerial trespass. Thus, it remains an intriguing fact that the Declaration appears to rely on these treaties as a basis for prescribing that states refrain from the use of weapons against civil aircraft in flight (Declaration 5). The question of legitimate or illegitimate response to aerial trespass is different from the general problem of unlawful acts against civil aircraft. Clearly, the latter problem relates to illegal acts done by people or groups with the occasional suspicion of state-sponsored terrorism, whereas the use of force against intruding airliners is an act perpetrated by sovereign states. Thus, it will not do to lump these problems together or hope to use the solutions designed for the one problem to solve the other.

Besides this, it would appear that the Declaration has not gone as far as expected considering the enormity of the problem to deal with the precise issues that a state whose airspace is being violated may be expected to be guided by. It might have been expected that a specialised organisation such as the ICAO would be in a position to draw up a precise checklist of procedure a state may employ in a situation of aerial trespass. This was not done in the Declaration and it represents a lost chance to resolve the controversies in this area of the law. On the whole, the Declaration may be said to have avoided the main issues and it is unfortunate that it reads as if the entire instrument is a preamble to something else that, for political reasons, the ICAO cannot or has refused to legislate on.

Therefore, the question remains as to what may a sovereign state do in response to an intruding airliner? In such an event, the territorial state normally has two lawful remedies, one or both of which may be employed at once. First, the territorial state must indicate to the airline in an appropriate and effective manner, without causing an undue degree of physical damage to the aircraft and its occupants that it is engaging in an unauthorised act. The territorial state may then require the intruder to return to its authorised position, within or outside the airspace of the state in question. It may also request that the intruder aircraft submit itself for inspection at an adequate airfield within the territory of the offended state and effectively indicated to the intruder in an appropriate manner. Second, and usually subsequently, the territorial state may deal with the infringement of its sovereignty by making appropriate protests or demands through diplomatic channels.[522]

It is, however, true that ultimately the precise reaction that may be expected belongs to the territorial state. A lot will depend on the territorial state's preparedness for such situation, its territorial extents, alliances and the discipline as well as training of its forces and decision makers including political leaders. The defence of UK airspace, for instance, stretches from the coastal approaches to Norway and Iceland in the north to the southwest approaches and the Isles of Scilly in the south. For security reasons, the precise boundaries of such national defence zones are not clearly identified or verifiable. The UK operates air policing areas in conjunction with its European NATO neighbours. The precise zone apportioned to the UK is the APA9. This is the area for which the Ministry of Defence declares quick reaction alert (QRA) assets to NATO. The dimensions of APA9 are somewhat flexible, but, essentially, it includes UK airspace, the North Sea and the northern approaches and does not coincide with the FIR boundaries (discussed in Chapter 4). NATO Combined Air Operation Centre (CAOC) 9 (formed in 2000) is responsible for the activation of QRA assets from the UK in APA9. [523]

522 Ibid op. cit.: 619–20.

523 NATO members jointly and collectively conduct air policing to preserve the integrity of NATO's airspace. See, generally, Baltic Defence College, "Workshop on the New NATO Strategic Concept, 18 February 2010 by Baltic Defence College Faculty", 12, 1 *Baltic Security and Defence Review* (2010): 12–14.

The Select Committee on Defence House of Commons, Sixth Report in 2001–2002 written in the immediate aftermath of the 11 September terrorist attacks attempted taxonomy of considerations that remain valid to this day. Once a suspect aircraft is identified a quick reaction alert (QRA) aircraft may be launched to intercept and shadow the aircraft. An attempt may first be made to make it alter its course. Indeed, the aircraft may already be under NATO surveillance and may simply be handed over to UK authorities at the flight information region (FIR) boundary. The decision to scramble QRA aircraft would usually be taken by the duty controller at UK CAOC, as explained before the House of Commons. As a result of the possible graveness of the consequences of inaction the presumption is that if there is any doubt over whether an aeroplane should be intercepted, QRA aircraft are launched:

1 The use of lethal force against a rogue civilian aircraft will only be justified where it has been declared hostile.
A rogue civilian aircraft may be declared hostile where hostile intent is established. For these purposes, hostile intent can be expressed as a demonstration of an intention imminently to use the aircraft as a weapon and in a matter that will lead to a loss of life.
2 As this illustrates, establishing hostile intent would not be straightforward. It would also be necessary to weigh the consequences of shooting down a civilian aircraft, in terms of loss of life both of passengers and potentially of those on the ground, against the likely consequences of allowing it to proceed. That is, the action would have to be "proportionate". The MoD's view is:
If the following exceptional circumstances can be established, the use of force against a rogue civilian aircraft and the consequent risks to innocent lives could be considered proportionate:
   - that it is impossible to preserve the lives of those on the ground without bringing about the death of innocent persons on board the aircraft
   - that continued existence of the aircraft will inevitably bring about the death of those innocent people on board in a very short time, and
   - having regard to all of the circumstances, the loss of life which will result from the shooting down of the aircraft is not disproportionate to the consequences which are expected from not doing so.

In essence, the employment of force against intruding civil airliners is seen as narrowly limited by international customary law and in the practice of modern civilised states. Hughes sees firing on such an aircraft as lawful only when three criteria are satisfied:

1 It is necessary to effect a landing for the security of the offended territorial state.
2 The importance of discontinuing the intrusion by firing on the aircraft is in reasonable proportion to the danger to the territorial state arising from it.
3 Most important, that all other practicable means of discontinuing the intrusion have been exhausted – the aircraft has refused to comply with clear and

appropriate instructions to return to authorised airspace or follow interceptors to a designated airfield adequate for the type of aircraft involved.[524]

It is difficult to disagree with this line of argument. Intruding aircraft must, therefore, obey all reasonable orders of the territorial sovereign, including orders to land, to turn back or to fly on a certain course, unless where prevented by distress or other *force majeure*. Lissitzyn further enunciates the position by stating that intruding aircraft, whether military or not and whatever the cause of the intrusion, are generally not entitled to the special privileges and immunities customarily accorded to foreign warships. They and their occupants may be penalised by the territorial sovereign for an intrusion not privileged by mistake or distress.[525]

On the whole, it must be said that there should be limits on the enforcement of the rights of the territorial state in respect of the treatment of violating aircraft at least with respect to civil unarmed aircraft. Firing on such aircraft will often result in the loss of human life and such force should normally be exercised only in the most unavoidable instances.

5.3.1 Trespass by foreign-based dissident, terrorist and activist groups

There is, however, a category of intruding civil aircraft that deserves separate discussion. These are those aircraft that deliberately intrude into foreign airspace operated by political activists seeking to undermine the authority of the territorial regime. Where trespass is procured through the use of non-state agents by an independent state, the general rules of state responsibility may apply.[526] Accordingly, the state responsible for procuring or promoting the acts of trespass and aggression may become responsible for the consequences of such action and may be liable in damages and/or compensation. It may be argued that the event of the flights will have to be specifically imputable to the state accused of promoting trespass. Thus, if the facts reveal that the trespassing flights were made by non-state actors such as insurgent groups proving the involvement of the accused state can become problematic and the standard of proof may be high. This was the case with respect to the contras in the celebrated *Nicaragua Case* (*Nicaragua v. United States*). The ICJ

524 Ibid: 620.

525 Oliver J. Lissitzyn, "Some Legal Implications of the U-2 and RB-47 Incidents", 56 *American Journal of International Law* (1962): 135; see also Quincy Wright, "Legal Aspects of The U-2 Incident", 54 *American Journal of International Law* (1960): 836.

526 As Special Rapporteur on State Responsibility J. Crawford rightly stated, acknowledgement and approval by a state of conduct "as its own" may have retroactive effect. See International Law Commission, Fiftieth Session (1998), A/CN.4/490/Add., 5, paras 283–4). Where all the ingredients that establish responsibility are in place then there is an obligation to make reparations. See *Spanish Zone of Morocco Claims* 2 RIAA: 615 (1923), the *Chorzow Factory Case* (PCIJ Series A, no. 17, 1928: 29) and in Articles 1, 2 and 3 of the International Law Commission's (ILC) draft articles on state responsibility.

made an important distinction between merely furnishing insurgents or any other party with the means to engage in aerial trespass and the conduct of trespassing flights by a state directly. The position was explained thus:

> As to overflights of aircraft for supply purposes, it appears from Nicaragua's evidence that these were carried out generally, if not exclusively, by the contras themselves, though using aircraft supplied to them by the United States. Whatever other responsibility the United States have incurred in this latter respect, the only violations of Nicaraguan airspace which the Court finds imputable to the United States on the basis of the evidence before it are first of all, the high-altitude reconnaissance flights, and secondly the low-altitude flights of 7 to 11 November 1984,complained of as causing "sonic booms".[527]

This position would be quite unsatisfactory to an aggrieved state and the distinction may be lost to all but the most punctilious international lawyer in the foreign ministry of the accused state. It may well be argued that without the material support of the foreign state to rebel groups and their agents, the flights would not have occurred. The sponsoring state could be said to have conducted the flights much along the same arguments made about the culpability of states that harbour terrorist training camps from which terrorists then go abroad to commit abominable acts. These issues have become even more complicated with the advent of drones and the democratisation of access to such technology in recent years. Questions will arise as to whether trespassing drones operated by private companies are committing acts that are imputable to the state (a) from which the flight first emanated, (b) that procured the services of such companies or (c) harbour them. It is suggested that any of these or a combination will be sufficient to impute responsibility on a state where there is sufficient evidence of direct complicity and/or reckless abandonment of the duty to prevent such flights from emanating from national territory especially where this dereliction leads to systematic abuse.

Deserving of specific mention are the longstanding series of aerial incursions made by Cuban dissident groups based in the USA into Cuban territory with small civilian aircraft. As this research reveals (see Appendix I), there are allegations of at least 15 of these violations in the 1990–2000 decade alone. Mention must be made of a sensational incident that occured on 24 February 1996, the Cuban Air Force shot down two Cessna aircraft that had flown out of Opalocka Airport in Florida and moved into Cuban territorial waters five to eight miles north of Baracoa Beach to the west of Havana. Cuba immediately justified its actions based on self-defence. On Monday 26 February the UN Security Council met to examine the situation created by the shooting down of the two planes and came out with a declaration, stating that:

> The Security Council deeply laments the shooting down by the Cuban airforce of two civilian aircraft on February 24, 1996, which seems to have resulted in

527 *Nicaragua Case*, para. 91.

> the death of four persons. The Security Council recalls that in accordance with international law and in line with the provisions of Article 3A of the International Civil Aviation Convention of December 7, 1944, modified by the Montreal protocol of May 19, 1984, States must refrain from employing weapons against civilian aircraft in flight and must not endanger the lives of persons on board nor the safety of aircraft. States are obliged to respect international law and norms related to human rights under all circumstances. The Security Council calls on the International Civil Aviation Organisation to make an indepth investigation of the incident.[528]

It is curious, however; that the Security Council declaration makes no reference to whether the aircraft were actually in Cuban airspace by virtue of flying over its territorial sea. It is, therefore, difficult to understand whether the Security Council is applying a rule that, in spite of intruding aircraft deliberately entering national airspace and having been warned of this, the territorial state must not apply force. If this is what is meant, the rule will apparently reflect political undertones and the position of international law may, indeed, be different. In fact, the position of the Cuban Ministry of Foreign Affairs is persuasive. It reads:

> We must carefully define what is a civilian aircraft. Many crimes have been committed against our country with supposedly civilian planes originating in the United States. We should recall that counter revolutionary pilots in "civilian aircraft" have been utilised to bring spies and saboteuring into our country; and even more seriously civilian aircraft have been used to carry out biological warfare. As for the investigation of the ICAO . . . we accept it and urge that it take into account all the antecedents and circumstances of gross provocation that we have suffered, due to the reiterated violation of our airspace and the risks they entail for air navigation and our country.[529]

It is a well-known fact that the United States (i.e. the flag state of the downed aircraft) maintains an unfriendly disposition towards the Cuban government. Cuban authorities claim that the Havana Air Traffic Centre had warned the aircraft that the airspace zones to the north of the capital had been activated and of the risk the pilots were exposing themselves to. One of the crew was reported to have replied that it was clear that he could not fly within the zone but that he was going to do so nonetheless. The operators of the flights belonged to a Cuban exiled group known as "Brothers to the Rescue". Thus, while the exact facts of 24 February 1996 incident may remain forever in controversy, it may be asserted that similar fact evidence avails the Cuban government.[530] As a Cuban journal put it "the practice of violations of Cuban airspace is a constant feature in the policy of

528 See Cuban Ministry of Foreign Affairs op. cit.: 1.
529 Ibid.
530 See, further, Table AI.2 in Appendix I.

aggression against Cuba perpetrated or permitted by successive US governments throughout the 37 years of the Revolution".[531]

With such a catalogue of alleged violations of Cuban airspace, it is difficult to appreciate Lissitzyn's counsel that in time of peace intruding aircraft whose intentions are known to the territorial sovereign to be harmless must not be attacked even if they disobey orders to land, to turn back or to fly on a certain course.[532] To justify this position, he cited the killing of foreign nationals by US border guards, which constituted the basis of awards by the US–Mexican General Claims Commission under the Convention of 8 September 1923. In this case, the person killed was illegally crossing the border and the guards had no other means of stopping him. The Commission cited with approval the view that "human life may not be taken either for prevention or for repression, unless in cases of extreme necessity".[533]

It hardly needs to be mentioned that the deliberate infraction of national airspace by intruding aircraft cannot be so easily compared with that of an illegal immigrant who makes a dash across borders for asylum purposes. In the case of the last two US civilian aircraft shot down over Cuban maritime territory, it is clear that the Cuban authorities could not have been in a position to ascertain at once the reasons for the intrusion or the real nature of the aircraft.

Lissitzyn himself had correctly noted that:

> The increasing speed of aircraft and the tremendous destructive power of new atomic and other weapons, as well as the memory of Pearl Harbor, make it impossible to impose any rigid, restrictions upon the freedom of a state to guard itself against sudden attack or hostile reconnaissance. Among the many relevant factors may be character of the intruding aircraft and the probable motives for the intrusion, the proximity of the intrusion to important installations or to areas in which armed hostilities (whether or not legally amounting to war) are being carried on, the frequency and regularity of intrusions by aircraft of a particular state and the availability of means for controlling the intruders movements.

That the Cuban authorities accept knowledge of the fact that the two civilian aircraft belong to the "Brothers to the Rescue" is not necessarily fatal to Cuba's case. The said organisation was founded in the USA in 1991 and purports to be humanitarian in nature. It dedicates itself to rescue searches to save the lives of men and women who take to sea to reach the Florida coast in the USA, ostensibly for political asylum. The organisation is, however, considered counter-revolutionary by Cuba. Cuba has also alleged that the organisation drops subversive literature

531 Cuban Ministry of Foreign Affairs op. cit.: 1.

532 Lissitzyn op. cit.: 587.

533 See United Nations Reports of International Arbitral Awards, Vol. 4 (1923): 119, 121–2. See also United States–Mexican General Claims Convention 1923, 4 RIAA: 11.

over its cities and on occasion sprays chemical and biological weapons over its crops. It is submitted that it lies squarely within the rightful exercise of state sovereignty to use force in repelling such intruding aircraft when found within national airspace whether over land territory or over the territorial sea. It is further submitted that the USA has an obligation under international law to prevent the operation of such flights by aircraft bearing its nationality and flying from its territory. It is important to note that there are some other pairs of states that generate intense controversy in the area of serial aerial intrusions. Cyprus and Turkey alone account for up to 350 separate complaints lodged at the UN (see Appendix II). It is a sad reality that despite the susceptibility of all states to this problem and the particular history of certain states in this area, there is little to show that the UN has a robust mechanism for dealing with the specific issue of aerial trespass.

5.4 The controversial practice of no-fly zones and trespass over national territory

It appears that derogation from the rule that grants complete sovereignty to states in their airspace particularly the right to repel unwanted intrusion by military aircraft has been unwittingly created in the last two decades by a select few states. This stems from the enforcement of the so-called *no-fly zones* enforced against Iraq in its territorial airspace. The concept is essentially a creation of the Western industrialised and military powers, the USA, Britain and France. The origins of the no-fly zone device may have emanated from similar uses of air power between the two world wars by the British Royal Air Force (RAF) in air control operations over Somaliland, Mesopotamia and Aden. At that time, the Royal Air Force used air power to enforce colonial rule, ensure unmolested travel and sanctity of trade routes and generally maintain control among the tribes in the region.[534] There are, however, essential differences between these operations and the concept and operations of the no-fly zones developed in the last decade of the 20th century. For instance, the affected peoples of that era had no air forces, no air defences and no sovereignty. Perhaps, more important, the sophisticated treaties of air law including the Chicago Convention had not been created and were not in force. During the Falklands War in 1982, the British armed forces imposed a total exclusion zone in the airspace of their area of operations in the south Atlantic. However, this involved the application of force from all elements of military power – air, sea and land and it occurred mainly over disputed territory. Not until the end of the Gulf War in 1991 did no-fly zones assume their expanded, modern form.

The legality of the no-fly zones has been questioned by many legal writers, particularly those from the developing states including those states that originally stood against the invasion of Kuwait by Iraq, the occurrence of which led to the

534 See David A. Deptula "Air Exclusion Zones: An Instrument of Engagement for a New Era", paper delivered at 2000 Air Power Conference Aerospace Centre, available at http://www.defence.gov.au aerospacecentre/2000apc/Deptula.html#INTRODUCTION.

Gulf War. Immediately after the United States and the Allied forces liberated Kuwait, there was apparently tremendous protest within Iraq. The Iraqi government is alleged to have responded with brutality on the Kurdish Iraqis in the north, on the Shia Muslim in the south and there were tremendous humanitarian difficulties. The United States, through its major Western Allies, then engineered the creation of these zones through a circuitous route. What it relied on was a UN resolution (688), which essentially demanded that Saddam Hussein must stop repressing his own people. The resolution itself interestingly enough never mentioned the creation of no-fly zones. The position advanced by Western powers was that essentially the best way to make good on this resolution was to deny the Iraqi government the ability to fly planes over large areas of its own country. The zones were delineated in the north in the spring of 1991 and in the south in the summer of 1992.[535]

The UK Defence Committee of the House of Commons rationalises the existence of the no-fly zones thus:

> [T]he UK is making a valid contribution to stability in the Gulf, protecting the minority people of Iraq from Saddam Hussein and containing Iraq's ability to threaten its neighbours . . . We have no doubt that UK participation in the no-fly zone operations over Iraq is justified on moral and humanitarian grounds . . . We welcome in particular the Committee's recognition that military action is only ever undertaken in response to direct threats from Iraqi forces against coalition aircrew carrying out their humanitarian patrols. The Government remains satisfied that the no fly zones are legally justified as a measure to prevent a humanitarian crisis.[536]

The activity of US and British aircraft in the so-called no-fly zones led to dozens of severe military conflicts with Iraqi air and ground forces. During the flyovers over Iraqi national territory, missile bomb strikes were launched at Iraqi forces, including civilian targets. In December 1998 alone this allegedly resulted in 420 military casualties. Over 1,000 civilians were also wounded.[537] The argument that derogation from Iraqi state sovereignty is justifiable on humanitarian grounds rings hollow given the manner in which life and property of the Iraqi people had been endangered and destroyed. However, it will appear that politics rather than humanitarian considerations account for this, considering that no UN resolution,

535 Richard Haass "No Fly Zones", available at http://www.pbs.org/newshour/bb/middle_east/july-dec98/iraq_12-31.html (accessed 12 May 2010).

536 House of Commons Defence Committee Publications, Prepared 1 November 2000 Session 1999–2000 Publications on the Internet, http://www.parliament.the-stationery-office.co.uk/pa/cm199900/cmselect/cmdfence/930/93004.htm (accessed 1 June 2010).

537 Factsheet on the Patrolling by US and British Warplanes of the "No-Fly Zones" in Iraq Unofficial translation from Russian (368-07-03-2001), http://www.ln.mid.ru/WEBSITE/BRP_4.NSF/e78a48070f128a7b43256999005bcbb3/fe2f643ea36b13c043256a08005183b0?OpenDocument (accessed 15 May 2001).

treaty or agreement specifically authorised either creation or maintenance of no-fly zones over sovereign state territory.[538]

It may be argued that the maintenance of a no-fly zone by direct patrols is a clear derogation from the territorial state's sovereignty, which according to the Charter of the UN must be recognised by other states. From the perspective of a state that relies on the existence of an ongoing regime of no-fly zone outside such strict interpretation the flights into foreign airspace may be justifiable under other grounds even including humanitarian efforts as in the Iraqi no-fly zones scenario. The position, however, is that a no-fly zone significantly detracts from the right of independence of a state to independence within its territory. A territorial state ought to have unfettered access to all parts of its own territory following the usual tridimensional application of territorial jurisdiction. Territorial states are also entitled to a tridimensional monopoly of violence within national territory, subject, of, course to applicable humanitarian considerations. This is probably encapsulated in the submission that:

> Sovereignty implies "space", and what is more it implies a space against which violence, whether latent or overt, is directed – a space established and constituted by violence . . . Every state is born of violence, and state power endures only by virtue of violence directed towards a space. A founding violence, and continuous creation by violent means (by fire and blood, in Bismarck's phrase) – such are the hallmarks of the state.[539]

Elden also advises: "The control of territory is what makes a state possible. Thus, control of territory accords a specific legitimacy to the violence and determines its spatial extent. Those in control of territory – states – can act in ways those not in control cannot."[540] The exercise of any form of violence in the sphere of tridimensionality of a sovereign state by another state is *prima facie* an affront to that state's sovereignty just as much as if an entire brigade of guards invades its territory in a dawn advance. The potentials for escalation of disputes caused by policing no-fly zones is patently clear to the extent that a state that does not act at all or does not act quickly to blatant acts of aerial trespass opens itself to domestic criticism

538 Note that the Council of Europe and the European Court of Human Rights have found Turkey responsible for carrying out the following against the Kurds: "Burning villages, inhuman and degrading treatment, and appalling failures to investigate allegations of ill-treatment at the hands of the security force." The history of Turkey's war against the Kurds is too extensive to document here, but suffice to say in 1993–4 alone 3200 Kurds were reported killed and 3,500 villages destroyed. Between 1990–4 1 million Kurds fled from the countryside to Diyarbakir. Yet the continuing situation has not warranted the creation of no-fly zones to stop such events. See Marco Ciglia, "The Myth of "No-Fly Zones", available at http://www.google.com/search?q=cache:8ee3854056a4d113:ns.cnlcontact.com/delorca/enanalyse/iq7.htm+Iraqi+no+fly+zones&hl=en (accessed 15 May 2001).

539 Henri Lefebvre, *The Production of Space*, trans. Donald Nicholson-Smith (Oxford: Blackwell, 1991): 112, 280.

540 Elden op. cit.: p. xxxi.

from political rivals and the general populace. ICJ jurisprudence in the *Nicaragua Case* is instructive of the *erga omnes* nature of the prohibition of violation of national airspace especially where war has not been declared among states. The court noted that respect for state sovereignty in international law is closely linked with the principles of the prohibition of the use of force and of non-intervention:

> [T]he basic legal concept of State sovereignty in customary international law, expressed in, inter alia, Article 2, paragraph 1, of the United Nations Charter, extends to the internal waters and territorial sea of every State and to the air space above its territory. As to superjacent air space, the 1944 Chicago Convention on International Civil Aviation (Art. 1) reproduces the established principle of the complete and exclusive sovereignty of a State over the air space above its territory. That convention, in conjunction with the 1958 Geneva Convention on the Territorial Sea, further specifies that the sovereignty of the coastal State extends to the territorial sea and to the air space above it, as does the United Nations Convention on the Law of the Sea adopted on 10 December 1982. The Court has no doubt that these prescriptions of treaty-law merely respond to firmly established and longstanding tenets of customary international law.

Given the dangerous consequences of this device and the consequences it may have on civil aviation and the safety of civil populations it is imperative that a legal agreement is attained that will prevent further frivolous resort to it. Yet selective inaction of the ICAO and the Security Council has allowed a certain degree of permissiveness in this area of the law creating an unfortunate lack of certainty in an area in which uniformity of opinions is required. The meticulous reports made by Iraq to flagrant violations of its sovereignty to the UN were ignored in their entirety. Serious allegations, which, if established, are grounds for war crimes, can be found in Appendix III, which details Iraqi reports to the UN via official means. Some of these incidents are also backed by independent press reports and admissions by the governments of the participating states such as the UK Iraqi Enquiry.

The allegations of aggressive, dangerous and illegal actions engaged in by those states that enforced the no-fly zones in Iraq include aerial bombardment of villages resulting in loss of life and destruction of property,[541] endangerment of health by deliberate breaking of the sound barrier[542] and intimidating and illegal search of

541 A letter from the Minister for Foreign Affairs of Iraq was transmitted reporting alleged violation of Iraqi airspace and bombing of civilian and military sites in Iraq by United States and British aircraft in the period 18 December 2002 to 17 January 2003. See UN Database ref. no. S/1997/616; Date of violation: 16 July 97; Offended State: Iraq; Trespassing State: USA; Aircraft type: Military; Alleged actions: Dropped heat flares that fell on wheat and barley fields; Position of Aircraft: Dawblah area of Diyala Governorate; Iraqi response: Report to UN.

542 UN Database ref. no. S/1997/352 Date: 17 April 97; Territorial state: Iraq; Trespassing State: USA; Aircraft type: Military; Alleged actions: Broke sound barrier around Basrah on one occasion; Iraqi response: Report to UN.

vessels within national maritime zones,[543] harassment of civilian population and destruction of the livestock and the environment. It is indeed a disturbing fact and an indictment of the present stage of development of international law and international relations that official records of the UN contains over 1,400 reported cases of airspace trespass and very little has been achieved in bringing the offending states to account through international processes. Iraq officially communicated over 500 reported incidents that involved alleged violations of Iraqi airspace by the states involved in the use of the controversial no-fly zone device (see Appendix III). It is equally significant that states such as Saudi Arabia and Turkey were directly accused by Iraq of allowing their territory to be used as launching ground for the trespassing flights.[544] This, perhaps, attests to the potentials of the no-fly zone device to escalate international tensions and to involve a wide number of affected countries.

On the whole, the no-fly zone device in international relations has not received the authoritative treatment in international law that it deserves. In this way, international action is dictated by the exigencies of Western superpower influence and coordination. In much the same way that the USSR sponsored draft resolution to condemn the incursion of United States U-2 spy aircraft into Soviet airspace as aggressive received only the support of Poland complaints by the few states that have faced no-fly zones sanctions have received little support in the international fora. In contrast, the Cuban shooting of two Cessna aircraft that made deliberate and orchestrated forages into its maritime airspace in February 1996, was greeted by the Security Council's quickly pointing out (correctly) that states have an obligation to refrain from shooting down civil aircraft. It is unsatisfactory, however, that there was no examination of the legality or propriety of the continuous operation of the so-called "Brothers to the Rescue" flights emanating from United States' territory.[545] Since this problem, at least for now, is one faced by less powerful states in comparative terms to the usual enforcers of the no-fly zones regime, it is difficult to see how principled differences over the issue would receive the thorough consideration it deserves.

543 UN Database refb no. S/1997/28, Date: 18 September 1996; Territorial state: Iraq Trespassing State: USA Military; Aircraft type: Helicopter; Alleged actions: hovered over the Iraqi tug *Ninawa* while it was at anchor in the deep-water port at Mina' al-Bakr. Its master was ordered to assemble his crew. A number of soldiers were lowered onto the tug and they proceeded to search it, breaking all the locks on the cabins and tanks. The ship's papers and the identity documents of the crew were taken and information was demanded concerning the nationality of the crew members and the vessel's cargo.

544 See letter transmitted 4 November 2000 from the Deputy Prime Minister and Acting Minister for Foreign Affairs reporting that violations of Iraqi airspace by United States and British aircraft based in Saudi Arabia, Kuwait and Turkey continued over the period 24–31 October 2000; urges the Security Council to intervene with the governments of the countries in question with a view to inducing them to halt the violations. See UN Document Symbol: S/2001/725.

545 See Cuban Ministry of Foreign Affairs, *Cuba defends its Sovereignty*, *Granma International*, 6 March 1996: 1. This situation is best typified by referring to the longstanding series of allegations of aerial incursions made by Cuban dissident groups based in the United States into Cuban territory with small civilian aircraft that are registered in the United States.

This is not to say that there can be no situation under which no-fly zones may be legitimately envisaged. The point is that serious derogations from territorial sovereignty as this may arise only in a very limited category of cases. Such instances are best typified by the example of actions specifically undertaken with respect to Chapter VII of the UN Charter (Action with Respect to Threats to the Peace, Breaches of the Peace and Acts of Aggression). It is possible to locate the power of aerial blockade in Article 42, which provides:

> Should the Security Council consider that measures provided for in Article 41 would be inadequate or have proved to be inadequate, it may take such action by air, sea, or land forces as may be necessary to maintain or restore international peace and security. Such action may include demonstrations, blockade, and other operations by air, sea, or land forces of Members of the United Nations.

Actions taken specifically in furtherance of this provision as may be specifically and unequivocally requested by the Security Council would constitute an exception to the rule against aerial trespass in international law. It must, however, be pointed out that the foregoing analysis is one that the few states that employ this device in their international relations will find difficult to follow. Probably no instance reveals the disregard for international consensus in the shaping of air law better than the creation and expansion of the practice of so-called no-fly zones in Iraq by the United States, United Kingdom and France.[546] The concept is essentially a creation of these Western industrialised and military powers. It is yet another confirmation of the influence of the dominant forces that shape international legal rules. In that case, it is hoped that the practice not being founded on international consent may not find usefulness beyond the particular situations it was created for.

5.5 Summary and conclusions

Trespass into airspace over state territory remains a very serious problem in international relations. The legal and political quagmire in which states find themselves when allegations and counter allegations are traded deserves closer attention by legal scholars. The politically charged nature of disputes over trespass in the airspace makes it impossible in many cases to determine where the fault really lies. This, in turn, ensures that this problem remains one of the seemingly intractable problems in international relations. There is much controversy regarding the use of force against intruding aircraft particularly in relation to civil aircraft. It is, however, clear that unlike in the territorial sea, there is no right of innocent passage in the airspace over all parts of national territory. Therefore, it is advisable that in all cases the option to turn and fly back or to land for questioning at an indicated airport (or military airfield) should be communicated to all intruding aircraft (whether civilian or not) by an offended state. Where this is done, orders must be obeyed.

546 See Haass, 1998, op. cit.

The use of force against intruding aircraft in cases of deliberate intrusion is a lawful activity where the caution has been exercised and refused and where the territorial state is genuinely concerned about serious national security breaches. The right to self-defence, that logically inheres in the sovereignty that an independent state possesses, supports this position. The question of espionage in the airspace, particularly from the fringes of territorial airspace, must be addressed immediately by international law, as it is capable of undermining international peace and security. While international law remains silent on this issue, it might amount to naivety not to recognise that aerial reconnaissance, particularly, would more often than not be interpreted as a hostile act. If the reconnaissance takes place in territorial airspace this is clearly an act of trespass and the nature of the aircraft as a state spy plane aggravates the offence under national and international law. In that case, there may be much utility in the common recognition by states that aerial reconnaissance should be forbidden.

The discussion relating to aerial incidents reveals that certain states are more prone to generating conflicts relating to airspace trespass between them than others. General political hostility between these states has produced ongoing incidents of territorial airspace violations. Indeed, although the law needs to be further developed, many of the cases of intrusion into foreign airspace are the result of a deliberate policy (based on dual standards) to ignore existing international rules in favour of sheer demonstration of power or the pursuit of strategic or intelligence interests by powerful states. The imposition of no-fly zones against the Iraqi government in its own sovereign airspace is a legal abnormality. No-fly zones enforced against a sovereign nation particularly in peacetime and without specific UN authorisation remains a curious conception. This anomaly represents yet another creation of the dominant forces that shape international air laws. It is to be hoped that the practice not being founded on international consent and being directly in breach of international treaties including Article 1 of the Chicago Convention (1944) may not find usefulness beyond the particular situation it was created for. In any event, the imposition should in all cases be brought to a speedy end as soon as possible.

It would appear from the reported cases of aerial intrusion into Cuban airspace by aircraft of US nationality that the violation of Cuba's airspace represents a pattern of abuse of Cuba's sovereignty by the USA. The UN must monitor the pattern of disputes over airspace violations in order to identify those states that tend to generate these conflicts and direct particular efforts towards the affected parties to prevent further occurrences and the removal of such threats to international peace and stability.

The question of trespass, however, does not arise in relation to outer space. This is because there is no concept of territorial outer space. There appears to be recognition under customary international law (as evidenced in the opinion of scholars) that spacecraft have a right of passage through national airspace while ascending or descending.[547] Yet it must be significant that by 1996 at least the

547 This is generally thought to be one of the principles of international law that sprung up quite quickly despite short and scarce practice, because a substantial and representative quantity of

Republic of Korea had expressed the view that aerospace objects when in passage through the territorial airspace of another state may be subject to the relevant state's domestic law that can then be applied to the aerospace object in relation to the country's sovereignty and security problems.[548] It is suggested that unless such arguments are convincingly overturned by means of *opinio juris* and perhaps through the writings of eminent scholars it retains potency against spacefaring states (at least) in relation to a state that has officially expressed this view. Such a stance, if it gains ground, may introduce the problem of trespass by aerospace objects and, thus, threaten to endanger a fledging space launch industry that is spreading even into the developing world. It may be suggested that in the modern world where aerospace launches are increasingly common the right of ingress and egress of aerospace vehicles must be exercised *bona fide* by the launching state and that the territorial state possesses a right to impose safety restrictions.

In that case, it may be said that there is a right of innocent passage for spacecraft, whereas there is no corresponding right pertaining to aircraft. Furthermore there can be no right to repel aircraft movement in international airspace. This includes the airspace over international straits and the high seas. However, it must be realised that since it is within the inherent jurisdiction of every state to determine when to exercise its right to self-defence, any action taken against aircraft navigating in international airspace must be justified on other grounds and not on the basis of territorial sovereignty. The absence of agreement over the spatial demarcation boundary zone between outer space and airspace further makes the determination of the specific rules governing trespass in the airspace less effective. The day is soon to arrive when a dispute over the spatial distance of an object from land will be crucial in the determination of a dispute over airspace violation. The use of aircraft that have spacecraft features and performance further complicates the picture, especially with the impending advent of space tourism by private enterprises.

states support or acquiesce to the practice. Other examples include the principle of sovereignty over national airspace, the regime of the continental shelf and legal status of outer space. Jurists such as Mendelson *et al.*, however, argue that to state that the right of passage of spacecraft through airspace exists presently might be to pre-empt the rule. Apart from anything else, it is said to beg the question "whether (what might theoretically have been claimed to be) 'overflight' by a couple of States, but acquiesced in by many others, can properly be said to constitute 'scarce' practice". Indeed, it is possible to argue that this is another instance, where the convenience of the powerful states translates into law, examples of which include the principle that allows private aircrafts to benefit from use of national airspaces and the principle of aerial sovereignty over colonial possessions before that. However, because (as we shall later come to show in this book), the space treaties and many relevant resolutions of the UN General Assembly are in favour of international cooperation in outer space exploration, it is arguably wiser to interpret their content *ut res magis valeat quam pereat* (laws should be interpreted with a view of upholding rather than destroying them) and to adopt an interpretation which makes it possible for states to secure uncomplicated launches and re-entry for their space vehicles. See M.H. Mendelson *et al.*, "Final Report of the Committee: Statement of Principles Applicable to the Formation of General Customary International Law", Committee on Formation of Customary (General) International Law International Law Association London Conference (2000): 25–6 and note 64; information and materials about the International Law Association are available at www.ila-hq.org.

548 Republic of Korea (as contained in document A/AC.105/635/Add.1 of 15 March 1996).

6 Jurisdiction and control in outer space

Space Law has become a Reality.[549]

The matter (space law) has passed far beyond the stage of imaginative fiction.[550]

Earlier chapters of this book have demonstrated the manifestations of sovereignty, jurisdiction and control in the airspace. A central feature of the findings is that each and every state possesses absolute sovereignty and jurisdiction in its airspace, subject, of course, to specific rules of international law regulating the common use of the airspace for transportation. With the conquest of the final frontier (i.e. outer space), however, there is a fundamental change in the conceptualisation of the manifestation of state powers. The overused concept of sovereignty has not risen above the bounds of the earth's airspace, it would appear. In other words, it must be emphasised at this stage that it makes no sense in conventional terms to speak of sovereignty in outer space. This is because *ab initio* international legislation developed to govern outer space has been unequivocal on the prohibition of the application of state sovereignty in outer space. However, the concept of jurisdiction (*ratione instrumenti and ratione personnae*), by way of contrast, applies to outer space and is recognised in the entire legal framework for regulation of man's activity wherever it occurs in the entire universe. Therefore, the remaining chapters of the volume will focus on jurisdiction and control in outer space. Sovereignty is relevant only to the extent that activities in outer space are conducted either by sovereign nations or under the auspices of a sovereign nation in the case of corporations and international organisations. Requisite comparative and contrastive analysis will continually be made with the regime governing the airspace.

Lawyers, indeed, are said never to be too far behind the explorer. Thus, an elaborate web of treaties and conventions has been developed to govern man's activities relating to outer space. The following chapters will, therefore, be making reference to many of them, particularly the eight instruments that it may be said constitute the *corpus juris spatialis*. They are as follows:

549 Imre Anthony Csbaffi, *The Concept of the State Jurisdiction in International Space Law: A Study in the Development of Space Law in the United Nations* (The Hague: Martinus Nijhoff, 1971): xvii.

550 Parenthesis added; see W. Jenks, "International Law and Activities in Space", *ICLQ* (1956): 99.

1 Treaty Banning Nuclear Weapon Tests in the Atmosphere, in Outer Space and Under Water 1963[551]
2 United Nations General Assembly Resolution 1962 (XVIII)[552]
3 Declaration of Legal Principles Governing the Activities of States in the Exploration and Use of Outer Space (General Assembly Resolution 1962 of 13 December (1963))
4 Treaty on Principles Governing the Activities of States in the Exploration and Use of Outer Space, including the Moon and Other Celestial Borders (1967)[553]
5 Agreement on the Return of Objects launched into Outer Space (1968)[554]
6 Convention on International Liability for Damage Caused by Space Objects (1972)[555]
7 Convention on Registration of Objects Launched into Outer Space (1975)[556]
8 Agreement Governing the Activities of States on the Moon and other Celestial Bodies (1979).[557]

Other recent instruments of relevance to the study include: the Principles Relevant to the Use of Nuclear Power in Outer Space (1992)[558] and the Declaration on International Cooperation in the Exploration and Use of Outer Space for the Benefit and in the Interest of all States, Taking into Particular Account the Needs of Developing Countries (1996).[559] It is important to point out that a good number of national laws and codes directed towards outer space activities are now emanating from various jurisdictions. Some of these may indeed be of good use in establishing state prctice on aspects of space law.

6.1 Exploitation and use of outer space: achievements and prospects

The question that is usually raised by sceptics of space law is to ask whether outer space is of any real importance to the majority of states at present or even in the foreseeable future. Sceptics of space exploration, especially those from developing states, also question whether there is enough justification for the investment of colossal amounts of money into outer space exploration and activities.

551 Also known as the Nuclear Test Ban Treaty. UNTS Vol. 480 (1963): 45 ff.
552 GAOR, 18th Session, Supp. 15: 13 (1963).
553 Also known as the Space Treaty. 18 UST 2410, 610, UNTS 205.
554 Also known as the Astronaut Agreement or Rescue Agreement. UKTS 56 (1969), Cmnd 3997; (1969) 63 AJIL 382. In force 1968. 86 parties, including the 5 permanent members of the Security Council.
555 Also known as the Liability Convention. UKTS 16 (1974), Cmnd 5551; 961 UNTS 187; 10 ILM 965. In force 1973. 76 parties, including the 5 permanent members of the Security Council.
556 Also known as the Registration Convention. UNTS 187; 14 ILM 43; UKTS 70 (1978). In force 1976. 39 parties including the 5 permanent members of the Security Council.
557 Also known as the Moon Treaty or Moon Agreement. GA Res. 34/68, UN GAOR, 34th Sess. Supp. No. 46 at 77, UN Doc. A/34/664 (1979).
558 A/RES/47/68 85th plenary meeting, 14 December 1992.
559 A/RES/51/122 83rd plenary meeting, 13 December 1996.

The fact is that, as opposed to the airspace, the granting of air transit rights is not about the only way outer space can be exploited for economic benefits.[560] Celestial bodies including the Moon and earth-approaching asteroids, which may be accessible for exploitation in the near future, are rich in materials that would be useful for a variety of purposes on earth and in outer space.[561] Lunar surface materials are a possible future source of raw material that could be processed in space to produce structural metals, oxygen, silicon, glass and ceramic products. Lunar metals have potential for construction purposes. Titanium, which is a strong light metal that can withstand high temperatures, is in high demand for the aerospace industry and may also have applications in space construction. Processing lunar titanium may be easier (and possibly cheaper) than processing earth-based titanium, since titanium processing requires high temperatures, vacuum and large quantities of energy. Lunar silicon could be used to build photovoltaic systems in orbit or on the Moon. Furthermore, the oxygen from lunar materials could be combined with hydrogen from the earth to make water and could also be used in making an atmosphere for workers in space. Solar energy may also be intercepted and harvested to beam to specific points on Earth to supplement energy security.[562]

It has been scientifically concluded that most of the requirements for human activity and industry in space except water and hydrogen are available on the lunar surface.[563] Asteroids located in the belt between Mars and Jupiter are "thought to contain a rich variety of materials in sufficient quantities to 'support' a civilisation many thousand times larger than the Earth's population".[564] In fact, from a technical point of view, Mars can realistically be "colonised" by humans. Even scientists rather grimly speak of a "New World on Mars", which would offer people

560 An instance of the possible financial benefits to which a sovereign state might put the exclusive rights over its airspace is displayed in the way Russia recently allowed commercial airlines to make use of its airspace in order to shorten flight routes. In one demonstration, in July 1998, the first commercial passenger flight to land at the new Hong Kong airport was a Cathay Pacific 747, which had flown non-stop from New York over the North Pole. The journey took 15 1/2 hours compared with the usual 21. During the Cold War, the Russian Arctic and Far East – frontline defensive areas spiked with missile sites, naval bases and nuclear early warning stations – were forbidden zones for foreign airlines, as the Korean Airlines discussed earlier on (Chapter 5.3: Aerial intrusion by civil airliners) found to its cost unfortunately in 1983 when one of its jumbo jets, apparently off-course, was shot down by Soviet fighters, killing 269 people. Presently a less paranoid, much poorer Russia is anxious to open up new routes and derive as much economic benefits as possible from the ownership of its airspace. With each passenger plane paying about 60 pence a mile in transit fees, Russia hopes to earn £400 million a year to invest in its air traffic control system. As Leonid Shcherbakov, head of the country's airspace allocation organisation put it: "'It's just Russia's good luck to be sitting right where all the airways happen to go.'" See James Meek, "Arctic Route set to Shrink the World for Air Travellers", *Guardian*, 9 July 1998: 2.

561 Kurt Anderson Baca, "Property Rights in Outer Space", 58 *Journal of Air Law and Commerce* (1993): 1042.

562 See the United States Senate Committee on Commerce Science and Transportation, 96th CONG., 2D Sess., Agreement Governing the Activities of States on the Moon and Other Celestial Bodies, Part 4, 417 Comm. Print 1980.

563 Ibid: 416.

564 Grier C. Raclin, "From Ice to Ether: The Adoption of a Regime to Govern Resource Exploitation in Outer Space", 7 *NWJ Int'L & Business* (1986): 728.

who had no satisfactory role in society on earth opportunity to redefine their functions in a New World.[565] Of course, to make a place such as Mars habitable, it has to be "terraformed" and the frigid lifeless planet will thus be changed into a wet and warm one permitting the flourishing of life. As it is, Mars is endowed with all the necessities for the support of life and the actual development and the sustaining of a technological civilisation. Mars contains veritable oceans of water frozen into its soil as permafrost, as well as an abundance of carbon, nitrogen, hydrogen and oxygen, which indeed are valuable elements common in organic compounds. The physical aspects of Mars – its gravity, rotation rate and axial tilt – are close enough to those of earth to be acceptable.[566] It has been noted that virtually every element of significant interest to industry is known to exist on Mars. It remains the only planet that will accommodate large-scale greenhouses lit by natural sunlight. As Mars is rich in deuterium and other minerals, some writers predict that it will someday represent a commercially lucrative resource area.[567]

6.2 Jurisdiction and control in outer space: relevance of property and possession to the higher grounds

> "Property would in time be extended to almost every subject." (Adam Smith (1762)).[568]

With respect to the airspace as has been shown, three possibilities present themselves:

1 There can be national aircraft flying in national territory only.
2 National aircraft could fly in foreign territory.
3 National aircraft may navigate over international territory.

With respect to outer space, however, there is a central difference in that the proposition cannot be supported that national aircraft or spacecraft are navigating in "national outer space". That, as we shall come to see shortly, is a misnomer, a form of legal oxymoron. Simply put, while the airspace can form the object of property both in private municipal law and international law, the same does not hold true for outer space.

It is made clear in the Outer Space Treaty (1967) and the Moon Agreement (1979) that outer space including the Moon and its celestial bodies shall be the

565 Swanley Schmidt and Robert Zubrin (eds), *Islands in the Sky, From ANALOG, A Roadmap to the Next Frontier, Bold New Ideas for Colonising Space* (Chichester: John Wiley & Sons, 1996):125. See also Robert Zubrin and Richard Wagner, *The Case for Mars: The Plan to Settle the Red Planet and Why We Must* (Oxford: Free Press, 1996): 298.

566 Schmidt and Zubrin op. cit.: 125.

567 Zubrin and Wagner op. cit. See also Arthur C. Clarke, *The Sands of Mars* (Aylesbury: Hunt Barnard Printing Ltd, 1951); Ray Bradbury, *The Martian Chronicles* (London: Bantam Books, 1977).

568 Report of 1762 [i.53] in R.L. Meek, D.D. Raphael *et al.* (eds.), Adam Smith V: Lectures on Jurisprudence (Oxford: Clarendon Press, 1978): 23.

province of all mankind (Article 1 Outer Space Treaty; Article 4 Moon Agreement). Treaty law also assures that "there shall be free access to all areas of celestial bodies" (Article I Outer Space Treaty (1967); Article 4 and 8 Moon Treaty (1979)). Therefore, *prima facie* the Moon, outer space and celestial bodies are not subject to national appropriation by claim of sovereignty, by means of occupation or by other means (Article 3 Declaration (1963); Article II Outer Space Treaty (1967); Article 11(2) Moon Treaty (1979)). It may be posited here that were it not for these crucial provisions, state activity in space exploration might have proceeded on such a scale and in such a manner as to possibly degenerate rapidly into belligerency.

Nevertheless, certain allowances are made for some forms of control in outer space. In the Moon Agreement (1979), for instance, it is provided that: "Without prejudice to the rights of other States Parties, consideration may be given to the designation of certain areas as international scientific preserves for which special protective arrangements are to be agreed" (Article 7(3)). With the granting of such "special protective preserves", it may be argued that control and preclusion of intrusion is to some extent tolerated in outer space, at least as regarding lunar territories. This is also in line with the provision in Article 9(1) of the Moon Agreement (1979), which provides that: "States Parties may establish manned and unmanned stations on the Moon." It is probably important to note that "such stations must not exceed the Area which is required for the needs of the station" and that the Secretary-General of the UN must always be aware of the location and purpose of such stations. There is a danger, however, that these provisions of the Moon Agreement (1979) may be insufficient to deter states and persons who seek to introduce ownership, possession and the practice of appropriation of portions of outer space. This is particularly so since all that is required if a state creates preserves and stations is for it to "inform" the UN Secretary-General as provided in Article 7(2) and to "notify and report" as in Article 9(1).

Article 11(3) would, however, appear to remove all doubts as to the unsuitability of the practice of appropriation on the Moon or of the Moon itself. It states quite clearly that: "Neither the surface nor the subsurface of the Moon nor any part thereof or natural resources in place, shall become property of any state, international inter-governmental or non-governmental organisation entity or of any natural person." In order to remove the possibilities of any constructive appropriation, Article 11(3) states categorically that:

> The placement of personnel, space vehicle, equipment, facilities stations and installations on or below the surface of the moon including structures connected to its surface or subsurface shall not create right of ownership over the surface or subsurface of the moon or any areas thereof.

It is, thus, clear that to proceed surreptitiously to acquire territorial sovereignty on celestial bodies in space by placing equipment, machinery, stations there or through whatever ingenious means is contrary to international law. Furthermore there is no possibility of application of the principle of prescription as a root of title over the moon. This is somewhat comparable with the regime governing the deep seabed in that even the developed states preferred the security that a limited international regime of common ownership would offer their private and public undertakings to the hazards of a "free for all" scenario. Thus, the deep seabed has been recognised since 1970 as the "common heritage of mankind", to be used to the benefit of all states and not only for those states with the capital and technology to exploit them.[569]

Furthermore, it should be noted that after giving "reasonable advance notice" to enable consultations and safety measures to be conducted, representatives of one state may visit on a basis of reciprocity, the space stations, installations, equipment and space vehicles of other states which are located on the Moon or on a celestial body (Article XII Outer Space Treaty (1967)). This, of course, makes for easy detection of unlawful activities and creates an atmosphere for checks and balances necessary for the maintenance of the Moon and other celestial bodies as the "province of mankind". Regrettably it was not envisaged that there ought to be a specific scientific body within the framework of the UN that is to be charged with performing the duty of conducting inspections on stations and facilities established on the Moon.[570] This may be due to the enormous costs of space exploration, which largely removes it from the ambit of the activities of the UN. The need to have in place a serious and effective monitoring system on activities on the Moon is becoming more necessary with the impending possibilities of private enterprise participation on a large scale in activities conducted on the Moon. It may also be in the interest of the international community that the UN actively conducts future research activities in outer space. In the alternative, the present trend towards joint ventures into space exploration needs to be encouraged, as it will act as a bulwark against national aggrandisement.

As has been explained the absence of sovereignty in outer space is not tantamount to a total lack of jurisdiction. In any case, it will be absurd to contemplate a total lack of the applicability of jurisdiction in a sphere of activity involving

569 Note must be taken of the more recent significant changes that have been made to this regime at the behest of the developed states which suggests the triumph of parochial interests (discussed in Chapter 8). See Declaration of Principles Governing the Sea-Bed and the Ocean Floor, and the Subsoil Thereof, Beyond The Limits of National Jurisdiction, GA Res. 2749 (XXV), 17 December 1970 (1970); (1971) 10 ILM 220. See further D.J. Harris, *Cases and Materials on International Law*, 5th edn (London: Sweet & Maxwell, 1998): 471.

570 Interesting comparison can be made here with the system in respect of Antarctica. Unlike the Outer Space Treaty (1967) and the Chicago Convention (1944) regulating air law, the Antarctic Treaty (1959) did not make express provisions stipulating that all objects, instruments and stations placed on the Antarctic continent (whether by a state laying claim to a sector or not) remains within the jurisdiction and ownership of the state which places them there. However, the Antarctic Treaty, in Article VII(3), establishes a system of inspection that, by implication, indicates national authority over Antarctic stations and objects or instruments placed in them. This inspection system also indicates national authority over expeditions while underpinning the absence of national jurisdiction. According to this provision: "All areas of Antarctica, including all stations, installations and equipment within those areas, and all ships and aircraft at points of discharging or embarking cargoes or personnel in Antarctica shall be open at all times to inspection by any observers designated in accordance with paragraph 1 of this Article." This regime of inspection ensures that the national or joint Antarctic expeditions and stations conform with the international regime of Antarctica.

sovereign states. Just as state jurisdiction remains relevant in the discussion of the legal status of an aircraft in foreign airspace/territory so, too, is it relevant in outer space. In fact, as will later be shown, the scope of the discussion of jurisdiction in outer space may be wider. At this stage of analysis, it suffices to mention that although outer space belongs to no one and cannot be legally appropriated, the state of registry of a space object retains "jurisdiction and control" over it and any personnel on it while it is in outer space or on celestial bodies. Ownership over space objects does not change because of their location and if found outside the territory of the state of registry either on earth or anywhere in space it shall be returned to it after providing identifying data, if so requested (Article VII Outer Space Treaty (1967)). Similar provisions are contained in Articles 1, 2, 3 of the, Astronauts and Space Objects Agreement (1968); in Article 7 of the Declaration (1963) and Article 12 Moon Agreement (1979). Therefore, it is *lex lata* that states retain ownership, jurisdiction and control over objects and persons they employ for the conduct of outer space activities no matter where they may be placed in outer space. In this manner, spaceships are akin to aircraft in airspace but, of course, important distinctions exist between the two.

Contemporary rules of public international space law are based on time-tested principles of law recognised by civilised nations. This necessitates respect for the continuity of ownership and control. Thus, we have the continuation of the operations of rules of jurisdiction *ratione instrumenti* to cover spacecraft and all space objects in a quasi-territorial manner, in much the same way this principle was extended to aircraft and, before them, ships. As discussed previously, aircraft possess the nationality of the state in which they are registered. Therefore, just as an aircraft belonging to state A cannot fall under the ownership of state B because it is found in the latter's airport, so also is it impossible for ownership of a spacecraft or space object belonging to state A to be acquired by state B just because it now lies on Mars or indeed is found within the territory of state B on return to earth. Article 8 of the Liability Convention (1972) gives the state of registry jurisdiction over all space objects. Similarly, just as it is unthinkable for state A to claim jurisdiction over the airport or territory of state B just because its aircraft was parked there, it would be unacceptable for state B to claim ownership, possession, control or jurisdiction over lunar territory just because its spacecraft are situated thereon.[571]

Thus far our examination has dealt with the letters of the law. Clear as they appear to be, certain legal writers have at various times chosen to take the view that it is possible legally to possess parts of outer space or appropriate the resources found therein by a state or private corporations. Writers in this group include Baca, Christol and, once one of the leading authorities on air and space law, Professor Bin Cheng.[572] Matters are reaching a head with the advent of private speculators

571 It has been suggested that the best analogy in these respects would be found in the rules concerning ships. See Harris (1998) op. cit.: 249, 430. See, particularly, *infra*, Chapters 9–11.

572 Cheng wrote: "But extra-territorial bodies such as the moon and other planets must prima facie be regarded as *res nullius* which, like the New World and the continent of Africa at one time, are susceptible of being appropriate as national territory through effective occupation." See Cheng (1960): 235; Cheng (1965): 143–52.

in lunar properties in some Western states. The reason for this may be partly due to the fact that the concept of sovereignty and jurisdiction has been so much linked both in their history and practice with the concepts of property, ownership and possession that it has become impossible for some to disentangle the issues in the newer territories that have come to be regulated by the law. The jurisprudence developed over the centuries, particularly the influence of Roman law on these concepts, has become so deeply entrenched into legal tradition and in the minds of lawyers and academics that to discard them is, in fact, repudiated with indignation. It might even be suggested that nothing short of the development of new interpretations or meanings of ownership and possession at least in respect of outer space would resolve the controversy.

Therefore, an epistemological visit to the terms ownership and possession is required. It also becomes necessary to subject these terms to what Twining refers to as "high theory" and it is probably with reference to such a task that he declared that "there are some jobs for jurisprudence".[573] This is very true of the concept of ownership, as it has been described as being of both legal and social interest.[574] Dias, too, correctly notes that possession is both a juridical concept and an instrument of juridical policy. Possession as a legal concept is the actual physical control of an object with the will to exercise the control for one's purposes. Although possession has to do with claims of control over material objects of rights and a right of possessing may be an incident of ownership, it has no necessary connection with ownership.

Ownership is more than a concept of juridical policy in that it is also a social concept and an instrument of social policy. This is true, but it must be added expressly that from the position of international relations, ownership has additionally a political and capitalist role.[575] While it is clear that the term ownership has numerous senses, there is a general acceptance by jurists that ownership consists of an innumerable number of claims, liberties, powers and immunities with regard to the thing owned. Ownership is an institution that is generally recognised in all modern municipal systems as well as under the rules of public international law. Mansell et al. correctly note that: "[A]lthough we often equate property with private property (an exclusive individual right), there is no reason why this should be so."[576] Indeed, if ownership is to have relevance at all in certain respects as in outer space, we would have to adopt a conceptualisation that does not equate exactly with private property.

573 W. Twining, "Some Jobs for Jurisprudence", *British Journal of Law and Society* (1974): 149.

574 R.W.M. Dias, *Jurisprudence*, 5th edn (London: Butterworths, 1985): 292.

575 Social reformers particularly those of Marxist-Leninist leanings have been at pains to explain the evils that the concept of ownership has been put in capitalist systems both at the national and international levels. See Dias, ibid: 301; K. Renner, *Institutions of Private Law and Their Social Functions*, ed. El Kahn Freund (London: Routledge & Kegan Paul, 1949).

576 Wade Mansell, Belinda Meteyard and Alan Thomson, *A Critical Introduction to Law* (London: Cavendish, 1995): 49.

The term ownership has had changing connotations through the centuries. It can be said that just as each legal system has had to develop its own concept of ownership so also has each era of the development of mankind. The 19th-century French Civil Code conceives it as "[t]he right to enjoy and to dispose of things in the most absolute manner".[577] Jurists such as Holland say: "[P]roprietary rights are extensions of the power of persons over the physical world." He explains that the essence of all such right lies not so much in the enjoyment of the thing as in the legal power of excluding others from interfering with the enjoyment of it.[578] The essential thing to note is that the significant difference in the definitions offered in legislation and academic writing through the centuries (especially between the 17th and 20th centuries) is based on the fact that the older definitions do not recognise legal limitations of the owner's powers and rights of other persons other than the owner. The restrictions on or limitations to the liberties and powers of an owner, which germinated in the past and flowered in the last century, is bound to reach fruition in the 21st century. We might then be permitted to say that ownership, just like its grander cousin sovereignty, is receding from its absolute connotation. Therefore, it is preferred to hold as Salmond did that: "[t]hat which a man owns is in all cases a right. When as is often the case we speak of the ownership of a particular object, this is merely a figure of speech. To own a piece of land means in truth to own a particular kind of right in the land, namely the fee simple."[579] As to the so-called "right of ownership", Anglo-American juristic thinking regards it as a bundle of rights in the stricter sense. This includes powers, liberties and privileges, rather than a comprehensive right of absolute enjoyment and power of disposal, subject to restrictions imposed by law and rights granted by others.[580]

In all cases, however, the exact value of any instance of ownership will be affected by the extent of the advantages conferred and derivable over the subject matter. Thus, Dias counsels that we should speak in terms of a "right of ownership" as distinct from a collection of jural relations.[581] Salmond, for his part, states that ownership in its most comprehensive signification denotes the relation between a person and any right that is vested in him. That which a man owns in this sense is in all cases a right.[582] Indeed, ownership is needed to give effect to the idea of "mine" and "not mine" or "thine". Thus, a man by himself on a desert island has no need of it. It is when at least one other person joins him that it becomes necessary to distinguish between those things that are his and those that are not his. It is only then also that it is important to determine what he may do with his things, so as not to interfere with his companion.[583] By the same token, if the notion of statehood

577 Article 544, French Civil Code (1804). This section is a result of the 1789 revolution which ironically abolished feudal property from the Middle Ages. It survives to date, although it has limitations.

578 E. Holland, *Jurisprudence*, 13th edn (Oxford : Clarendon Press, 1924): 193.

579 J.W. Salmond, *Jurisprudence*, 1st edn (London: Sweet & Maxwell, 1902): Section 871: 268.

580 Roscoe Pound, *Jurisprudence*, Vol. II, Part 3 (Minnesota: West Publishing Co., 1959): 125–6.

581 Dias op. cit.: 292.

582 Salmond, *Jurisprudence*, 7th edn: 277.

583 Dias op. cit.: 297.

and territory did not exist in international law, then exclusive territorial ownership of the airspace would not have been developed in the 20th century. The question, however, is given the natural progression in the recognition of ownership rights (first over national landed territory and then national airspace), why are the concepts of property, ownership and possession not introduced in their normal senses to outer space?

To tackle this question, it is relevant to consider the interesting submissions and analogies given by Adam Smith in his lectures on jurisprudence in apparent defence of property, particularly by occupation. He wrote that there are four distinct states through which mankind passes. The first was "the Age of Hunters", the second the "Age of Shepherds", third the "Age of Agriculture" and, finally, the "Age of Commerce". Moving from this premise, he sought to develop a justification for occupation, that is the bare possession of a subject such as territory and the material benefits therefrom as a signification of the exclusive right to the subject so acquired.

He posed the pertinent question: "How it is that a man by pulling an apple should be imagined to have a right to that apple and a power of excluding all others from it – and that an injury should be conceived to be done when such a subject is taken from the possessor?"[584] To help grapple with this enquiry, Smith refers to "five causes from whence property may have its occasion". He lists and explains them as follows:

> Occupation, by which we get anything into our power that was not the property of another before-2dly [sic] Tradition by which property is voluntarily transferred from one to another-3dly [sic] Accession, by which the property of any part that adheres to a subject and seems to be of small consequences as compared to it, or to be a part of it, goes to the proprietor of the principal as the milk or young of beasts-4thly [sic] Prescription or Usucapio, by which a thing that has been for a long time out of the owner's possession and in the possession of another, passes in right to the latter-5thly [sic] Succession, by which the nearest of kin or the testamentary heir has a right of property to what was left him by the testator – of these in order.[585]

This, however, does not provide adequate explanation in answer to the question posed by Adam Smith himself. Occupation, accession, prescription and succession may at best explain why others respect ownership over, say, the apple and do not in themselves justify the right over the apple. What really gives the right over the apple it may be suggested is *acceptance*. Where there is no acceptance by others then a right does not exist or would have to be proved by extraneous means. Thus, when a society or even a community of states do not recognise or accept ownership over an object or thing, ownership over it becomes impossible.

584 Report of 1762–3 [i.27,i.32-i.38] in Meek *et al.* op. cit.: 14, 16–17.
585 Ibid: 13–14; cf. our discussions *supra*, in Chapter 2.

This classically represented is the basis of Western conceptualisation of property, ownership and possession. It must be added that these concepts have also formed part of the received legal system in most colonial and subjugated societies, which have at some point in time fallen under Western domination. So much so that property has become law and law has become property in some respects. Jeremy Bentham captured this classically when he stated that property and the law are born together.[586] In effect, up to the later part of the 20th century, wherever the activities of Western civilisation are carried out and in whatever ways, as long as there is a need to develop a body of laws to govern that area, experience has shown that the operation of the concept of property and possession has been carefully set up. Mansell *et al.* aptly sum up this reality by noting that so central is the idea to our comprehension of the world and to our reality that often to suggest that private property is not natural is to invite incredulity.[587] It is, therefore, not surprising that attempts have been made by some scholars, especially those from the spacefaring states to reintroduce the common notions of property and possession into outer space exploration. In fact, Sir Frederick Pollock considers that the common law abhors vacant property and "the law must needs reduce the properties of all goods to some men".[588] It must be pointed out that there is great danger in carelessly dismissing these arguments or in simply discountenancing them without carefully repudiating all attempts (no matter how small) to subject outer space or the celestial bodies therein to ownership regimes.

As has already been noted in our discussions of jurisdiction over international airspace, the appearance of many developing countries on the international scene from the last half of the 20th century has led to the recognition of certain territories as international commons. This development introduces strain on prevailing Western theories and connections established between the concepts of ownership, possession and *laissez faire* traditions. Developing countries constitute the majority of states and they are the most vulnerable to any adverse consequences in economic, environmental and geophysical terms as a result of outer space exploration. This puts the onus on them to be eternally vigilant regarding any threats towards sabotaging the existing legal status of outer space. The more the benefits of outer space exploration that advances in technology open up, the more there will be threats to the rules governing outer space exploration. There would also be increasing pressures to amend the existing rules of space law. At the very least immense intellectual effort will be exerted on developing highly innovative interpretations of existing rules with a view to recognising indiscriminate appropriation of resources for private use and profit.

The historic role of the use of the concepts of ownership and possession to secure hegemonic interests by states is a pointer towards possible future trends. The express recognition of ownership over particular things and the withdrawal of recognition in it have been deftly used as a sociopolitical tool especially in securing

586 Quoted in K. Gray, *Elements of Land Law* (London: Butterworths, 1987).
587 Mansell *et al.* op. cit.: 49.
588 Quoted in Pound op. cit.: 149.

hegemonic interests by the leading technological and industrial powers particularly since the Industrial Revolution.

If we take the concept of slave ownership as an example it would be noted that many countries, including the present Western industrial powers, actively recognised and promoted use of slave labour. Indeed, it may with some credibility be asserted that slave labour was the engine that fired economic prosperity and the Industrial Revolution in several Western states. Although it is generally accepted as being a gross simplification of the matter, the theory persists that eventually the leading Western states realised that slave trade and ownership in human beings had been exploited to its fullest by their own economies and that its continuance would be ultimately subversive of economic prosperity. Recognition of the right of property in human beings was thereafter withdrawn. Thinkers such as Adam Smith stated that: "The land can never be cultivated to the best advantage by slaves, the work which is done by slaves always coming dearer than that which is done by free men."[589] With time slavery was abolished in international law and it became illegal for any state to engage in slave trade.[590]

Of course, an enquiry into the inglorious history, causes and effects of slavery are beyond the confines of our study and may, indeed, be unnecessary. However, the example of slavery serves as an interesting example of how international law as an aspect of international relations serves as a tool to legitimise or render illegitimate ownership in certain things. There are also other examples of how technologically developed states dictate in accordance with national interests the legal ownership in property. As was pointed out earlier, the airspace was initially held to be free for all nations. This position rapidly changed in accordance with military expediencies after the First World War in conformity with Western interests. At the inception of the space age, the ideological divide between the main space powers in the Cold War era helped to ensure the legal regime of common ownership. However, in the increasingly unipolar world of today there are disturbing indications showing that the few space powers left may seek to import into space law the concept of ownership and possession over space-based resources in line with unbridled capitalist orientation. This is not to suggest that new entrants to outer space exploration from among the developing countries may not in the future equally pose a threat to existing egalitarian principles found in space law.

589 Adam Smith quoted in Meek *et al.* op. cit.: 579.

590 This was achieved both as a matter of customary law and as general principles common to major legal systems. Slavery is also outlawed by the constitution of virtually all states A convention to outlaw slavery was concluded in 1926 and one on forced labour in 1930. Note also the following treaties: the Universal Declaration of Human Rights (GA Resolution 217A (III), GAOR, 3rd Sess., Part 1, Resns: 71), Article 4: "Everyone has the right of life, liberty and security of person"; the International Covenant on Civil and Political Rights (1966) (UNTS 171; UKTS 6 (1977), Cmnd 6702), Article 8: "No one shall be held in slavery and the slave-trade in all their forms shall be prohibited"; the LOSC (1982), Article 99: "Every State shall take effective measures to prevent and punish the transport of slaves in ships . . . Any slave taking refuge on board any ship shall *ipso facto* be free."

So far this book has highlighted the predominance of the Western interpretations of the concepts of ownership and possession and pointed out the possibility of their expanding into outer space. It must be added that by no means can it be said that there are no opposing or different conceptualisations of the terms under review. Indeed, there are other constructs equally valid in logic and utility that are in opposition to the Western understanding of ownership and possession. In some societies, there is no need to define ownership in relation to land on earth at all, not to mention the possibility of seeking to extend its application into space. Such a proposition would be so utterly bizarre in conception as to be laughable in most African societies.[591]

Mansell *et al.* gave an insightful discussion about the offer made by Washington to an American Indian Chief Seattle in 1854 for the purchase of large tracts of ancestral land peopled by the Indians. The reported reply given by the Indian statesman exposes crucial differences about the conceptualisation of the terms ownership and possession among different societies especially over what may be regarded as commons in many native communities. He stated in essence:

> How can you buy or sell the sky, the warmth of the land? The idea is strange to us. If we do not own the freshness of the air and the sparkle of the water, how can you buy them? . . . We know that the white man does not understand our ways . . . He treats his mother, the earth, and his brother, the sky as things to be bought, plundered, sold like sheep or bright beads. His appetite will devour the earth and leave behind only a desert . . . Whatever befalls the earth befalls the sons of the earth . . .This we know. The earth does not belong to man; man belongs to the earth. This we know.[592]

Thinkers such as Jean Jacque Rousseau have also captured the ultimate undesirability of unbridled expansion of the institution of ownership over lands and territories. He wrote:

591 That is not to say these societies are incapable of developing or operating sophisticated legal constructs. The concepts of *res nullius* and *res communis* also exist in traditional African law. Taslim Elias, rightly, pointed this out, reminding us that: "When discussing the corporate nature of land holding in Africa and particularly the chief's role of allocator and reversionary on behalf of the land group, it is not often realised that from the earliest time, this apparently hide bound system has allowed for right of individuals acquisition of any part of the virgin bush. This means that it is entirely his to do with as he pleases to sell or lease or even pledge, without any family restriction or inhibition. But his children inherit such individually owned land as family property, possessing all the characteristics of customary tenure unless he disposes of it otherwise in his own life time or by Will." Under customary and Islamic law, the categories of land acquired for the use of the corporate unit such as kingdoms and the ceremonial land coincided to some extent with the concept of *res communis* in international law. Thus, the position of African countries and some other developing states in relation to Antarctica and other international territories is not based on any ignorance or unfamiliarity with basic legal concepts. The point rather is that their shared legal culture cannot comprehend why ownership should be claimed over resources that are so obviously the common heritage of all. See further, T. Elias, *British Colonial Law* (London: Butterworths, 1962): 235–7.

592 See quote in Mansell *et al.* op. cit.: 47. It must be added that this speech has a dubious provenance and may be no more than of anecdotal importance.

> The man who having enclosed a piece of ground bethought himself as saying "This is mine" and found people simple enough to believe him was the real founder of civil society. From how many crimes, wars, murders; from how many horrors and misfortunes might not anyone have saved mankind by pulling up the stakes or filling up the ditch and crying to his fellows "Beware of listening to this impostor! You are undone if you once forget that the fruit of the earth belongs to us all and the earth to nobody."[593]

It is probably in deference to such views and to forestall a repeat of the certain horrors and conflicts that would occur if ownership and possession were given free rein in outer space activities, that the treaty rules on space law were drafted and enacted into legislation. Indeed, we may add as an adjunct to Chief Seattle's view that outer space, like the earth, should belong to no man but that man belongs to the universe.

Last, we must note that there is much truth in the statement that the methods by which property is acquired will depend on the state or age each society is in at any time.[594] Returning to Adam Smith's analysis regarding the distinct ages through which mankind has progressed, i.e. age of hunters, of shepherds, of agriculture and age of commerce, the question that suggests itself is what age are we now in and what effect should that have on the notion of property? It may be suggested that, since 1957 when the first human was launched into space, we are in the space age. This, of course, cannot but have had an impact on the concepts of ownership. Hence we have the abolition of national ownership and possession in outer space.

593 Mansel *et al.* op. cit.: 47. Cf. C.B. Macpherson's treatment of Locke's theory of property right, which is, based on the justification of a natural individual right to property. "The great and chief end therefore, of Men's uniting into Commonwealths, and putting themselves under Government, is the *Preservation of their Property*." Even Locke began by accepting as the dictate of natural reason and the scripture that the earth and its fruits were originally given to mankind in common. His thesis, however, is that all these "being given for the use of men there must of necessity be a means to appropriate them someway or the other before they can be of any use, or at all beneficial to any particular man". Central to Locke's general political theory of appropriation and as it is probably believed by some today is the theory that private appropriation of property actually increases the amount that is left to others and that somehow appropriation by the well to do will necessarily translate to better living for others. Clearly, there is room for debate as to the relevance of this theory to the fortunes of states in the international system. In the world today, it is difficult to see the benefits of the richest states' productive capacity or material successes on the least developed nations. Hence it is difficult to appreciate how this premise can serve as a reason for developing states to acquiesce to uncontrolled access to the mineral resources that may exist outer space. Other political philosophers like Harrington have argued that accumulation is honourable and respectable and that estates are got by industry, not by "covetousness and ambition". Without prejudice to the correctness of this view in relation to individual societies, it is arguable that modern day theorists still need to engage in enquiry into the desirability of regulating the ownership over certain resources or resource areas which are by their very nature of international concern. See C.B. Macpherson, *The Political Theory of Possessive Individualism Hobbes to Locke* (London: Oxford University Press, 1975): 199–202.

594 Report of 1762–3 [i.53] in Meek *et al.* op. cit.:14.

As has been argued earlier where there is no acceptance by the majority of ownership or a right to possess, there is no right to ownership. The will of the international community as will soon be seen is not to recognise ownership over outer space. It may, thus, be suggested that in place of ownership and possession in outer space the best a state can be said to have is a *licence* to conduct activities in space. This is not necessarily a defeat of national sovereignty neither is it an unfortunate disregard for the right to ownership over conquered, discovered or acquired *res*, which has existed over centuries. Even *laissez faire* advocates like Smith who have argued that in time property would be extended to every conceivable subject readily admit that "yet there are some things which must continue common by the rules of equity".[595] By virtue of this reasoning it is also impossible legally for individuals or corporate bodies to create ownership over outer space or celestial bodies.

6.3 Summary and conclusions

The treaties that have been developed and adopted so far to govern outer space and its resources are impressive both in their scope and in their number. These treaties are the commendable creations of the United Nations, particularly the United Nations Committee on the Peaceful Uses of Outer Space (COPUOS). It must be said that due to the fast changing nature of developments in research and outer space activities, it is pertinent that further elaboration of the law is needed on a continuing basis and must be achieved in the coming years. The crucial nature of the task ahead of the UN in this field is attested to by the present and future possibilities for the derivation of valuable natural resources in outer space, especially on the Moon and other celestial bodies.

While national sovereignty and exclusive jurisdiction can be exercised over the airspace relating to all parts of national territory, sovereignty is completely inapplicable to outer space and its celestial bodies. Certain jurisdictional competencies are, however, exercisable in outer space in relation to scientific stations, instrumentalities and personnel. Central to the discussion of the application of jurisdiction and control in outer space are the concepts of ownership and possession. It is important that lawyers and writers on the subject come to an agreement that contemporary space law as expressed in the treaties gives very limited, if any, scope for the application of these concepts in relation to outer space-based resources.

There is presently no adequate and effective monitoring system on activities that take place on the Moon and other celestial bodies. The present regime, which requires states active in space research to report on their activities, may have to be backed up by a system of independent observation. This may be in the form of actual visits to *locus* where possible or by participation in all major space activities by internationally assembled teams of scientists. This would enable the entire world to ascertain that nothing prohibited (including commercial mining or exploitation,

595 Ibid.

dangerous experiments and space militarisation) takes place within space stations or on celestial bodies. These recommendations are becoming more necessary with the impending possibilities of private enterprise participation on a large scale in activities conducted in outer space, particularly on the Moon. It may also be in the interest of the international community that the UN actively conducts future research activities in outer space. In the alternative, the present trend towards joint ventures into space exploration needs to be encouraged, as it will act as a bulwark against national aggrandisement. In any case, it is necessary to put in place an effective system by which all space activities would have to be approved by the UN from the planning stages where possible to completion. Without these policy changes, it may become impossible to stem the unfortunate push towards private aggrandisement of outer space-based resources for the benefit of those states and persons who already possess the largest share of the resources that are based on earth.

Neither direct occupation nor constructive appropriation can in any imaginable way confer ownership over tracts of outer space, portions of celestial bodies or the resources based therein. In like manner, other traditional roots of title conferring ownership and right to possess such as prescription, accession and conquest are irrelevant in relation to outer space. Thus, such developments as witnessed in some Western states where tracts of lunar territory or plots of land based on celestial bodies are being sold by private enterprises as chattel are fruitless efforts or at best mere flights of fancy without any hope at all of translating into legal ownership and possession in the present or in the future. Similarly all registries of "lunar property" are baseless, null, void and of no effect whatsoever.[596]

An epistemological enquiry to the concepts of ownership and possession reveals that the concepts have been used as tool for the legitimisation of hegemonic interests throughout history. In reference to state ownership or sovereignty over super-incumbent airspace, there need be no form of overt effective occupation. Possessory rights reside implicitly in statehood. Thus, the correct airspace ownership is delimited *ratione loci* in respect of the space above national territories and not *ratione materiae* in respect of the air, which may at any given time be filling this space. The current attempt towards introducing these concepts in their municipal senses to outer space comes too late in the day to effect a change in the fundamental legal status of outer space as the "province of all mankind". Presently, therefore, the only

596 Note that such unsupportable claims have emanated from diverse sources. Two Yemeni citizens in 1997 filed a lawsuit against the United States National Aeronautics and Space Administration (NASA) for trespassing on the planet Mars, over which they claim sovereignty. Mustafa Khalil and Abdullah al-Amri claimed that they received Mars as an inheritance from ancient ancestors and that any landing on the planet should, therefore, be subject to prior notification and permission. Papers were filed with Yemen's prosecutor-general, which, the men say, prove their claim and they sought injunctions from the Yemeni judiciary and the assistance of the government to force the US government to stop the current mission to Mars "until justice has had its say". See Clive Schofield (ed.), "Yemen-Outer Space: Law Suit over Mars 'Trespass'", 5, 3 *International Boundary Unit Boundary and Security Bulletin* (1997): 27.

sense in which property has any relation to outer space is in the retention of right to ownership and possession over personnel and instrumentalities used in outer space exploration. The propertisation of outer space resources would surely lead to exploitation along the same lines existing on earth and experience has shown that this would invariably lead to serious pollution, environmental damage and cilmatic intervention. Furthermore in an era when efforts are being geared towards a new economic order that takes into account the right to development of all states particularly the developing states allowing space exploitation and the propertisation of outer space will further exclude the poor states and threaten their economy if cheap and abundant resources are brought in from outer space at the present time. Space mining may in this way harm the economic principle of comparative advantage. It is, therefore, the duty of all scholars of space law and indeed all states particularly the developing states to safeguard the non-applicability of national and private ownership over outer space and the resources based therein pending the development of the proposed international regime for exploitation. Until this equitable regime is in place any unilateral commercial exploitation by contracting parties remains illegal.

7 Legality of the common heritage of mankind principle in space law

This thesis has considered the application of the concepts of ownership and possession to outer space. The fundamental differences those terms connote with reference to other forms of territory such as in national airspace and other landed territory has also been noted. The central summation of the tentative conclusions is that those terms have no relevance with respect to outer space activities. It was, thus, argued that the term *licence* should be used to express a state's right to engage in outer space activities and to explain any form of exclusive use of territory or resources that are based in outer space. What remains to be considered is the exact legal regime that governs outer space activities. In other words, it is necessary to discuss the legality of the formula developed to govern the common ownership of outer space, i.e. the common heritage of mankind principle.[597]

The term common heritage of mankind is one that manages to appear both commonsensical and obscure at the same time. In reality it lends itself to myriad possible interpretations. Consequently, there is a situation in which both proponents as well as adversaries of commercial space activities use the term to advance their standpoints.[598] Analogies of this principle can be found in the legal regime governing virtually all the common spaces. Therefore, it is correct to note that "the common heritage principle has its main impact with respect to the establishment of an international administration for areas open to the use of all states (international commons)".[599] Impetuses for the extension of this principle into outer space would, however, appear to have come from analogies presented in the law of the sea. Although some writers find traces of the contemporary idea of the CHM in the thinking of Francisco de Vitoria[600] and even earlier St Thomas Aquinas,[601] the

597 To be referred to as the CHM principle.

598 H.L. Traa-Engelman, *Commercial Utilization of Outer Space: Law and Practice* (London: Martinus Nijhoff, 1993): 27.

599 Rudiger Wolfrum, "Common Heritage of Mankind" in Rudolf Bernhardt (ed.), *Comparative Law, Encyclopedia of Public International Law* (Amsterdam: Elsevier Science, 1989): 68.

600 Sylvia Maureen Williams, "The Law of Outer Space and Natural Resources", 36 *ICLQ* (1987): 144.

601 Ibid; see also Juan A. Travieso, "El Patrimonio Comun de la Humanidad en el Nuevo Orden International", 2 *Revista del Colegio de Abogados de Buernos Aires* (1981).

more popular opinion is that the CHM principle may have been introduced to the law of the sea as a result of a speech made by Ambassador Parado of Malta to the United Nations General Assembly (UNGA) on the future of the resources of the high seas in constituting the "common heritage of mankind".[602]

The principle consequently received recognition in the UN Declaration of Principles Governing the Seabed and the Ocean Floor, and the Subsoil Thereof, Beyond the Limits of National Jurisdiction.[603] By the time of the completion of the UNCLOS III in 1982, it was incorporated in Article 136 of the Law of the Sea Convention that: "[T]he Area and its resources are the common heritage of Mankind." However, it must be admitted that even in the law of the sea, the exact legal effect of this principle is subject to much debate.

In relation to space law, the CHM principle continues to be a subject of intense controversy pitting two forces against one another. As have been pointed out, the divide is between the developing states and the developed spacefaring states. Most of the former are presently incapable of directly reaping the benefits of space exploration and most of the latter are pushing aggressively for a favourable regime towards the commercialisation of space activities including extensive mining and appropriation rights. Indeed, it is probably right to say that the concept of the common heritage of mankind and its application still keeps the world community divided.[604] Opponents of the concept have ceaselessly attacked its legal validity from the time it was introduced in the law of the sea for predominantly the same reasons that it is today contested in relation to the law governing outer space activities. The chief reason is the incompatibility of the concept with unbridled capitalist exploitation of minerals and resources for private ends in a resource-rich zone. That is those states that possess the means to exploit resources in remote places do not see any reason why the spoils should be shared with other states that do not.

Many jurists (predominantly of Western inclination) have criticised any possible suggestion that the phrase expresses a legal concept. This is a very clever approach because once the legal validity in concrete terms has been successfully undermined, there presumably exists no need to respect any restrictions on the exercise of property rights. A member of this school of thought argues forcefully but not convincingly that:

> One caution lawyers, diplomats and statesmen should observe is to avoid trying to treat layman's language as if it were formulated in terms of technical legal concepts . . . on the other hand, the phrase, common heritage of mankind, a layman's formula if ever there was one should be given the greatest respect,

602 UNGA Official Records, 22nd Session, Agenda Item 92 (2), Doc. A/6695, 18 August 1967. Article 1 states that: "The sea-bed and ocean floor, and the subsoil thereof, beyond the limits of national jurisdiction (hereinafter referred to as the area), as well as the resources of the area, are the common heritage of mankind."

603 Reprinted in *International Legal Materials*, 220 (1971) Article 1. For an illustration of the application of the principle to the legal delimitation of the sea into zones, see Appendix IV.

604 Engelman op. cit.: 52.

> while it should not, indeed cannot be viewed as a prescription, it can be accepted as a kind of policy hortatory message, a kind of policy directive.[605]

In similar terms, Gorove insists that: "[C]ommon heritage of mankind no matter how well motivated, in a legally binding document carries no clear judicial connotation but belongs to the realm of politics, philosophy or morality and not law."[606]

It appears, however, that, on the face of it, there is nothing really confusing about the CHM principle. It can also be doubted that the view would ever be popular that outer space and the celestial bodies therein should be appropriated as national territory. The real heart of the dispute is whether or not the CHM principle will be able to accommodate an international regime based on commercial principles. That is whether there is a possibility of exclusive rights such as the age-old "miners right" as argued by M.L. Smith.[607]

To begin with, it must be noted that the common heritage principle is fast becoming part of customary international law. It constitutes a distinct basic principle providing general but not specific legal obligations with respect to the utilisation of areas beyond national jurisdiction. It inherently conflicts with the principle of sovereignty since it operates from the basis of regarding an environment as "international public utility" requiring the obligation to cooperate.[608] The CHM principle was first introduced to cover outer space by the words contained in Article 1 of the Declaration of Legal Principles (1962).

By the time the Space Treaty (1967) was drafted the resolve of states to render outer space a commons for all humanity had deepened. This led to the formulation of other interesting phraseology. In the discussion of the drafting of Article 1 of the Space Treaty (1967), the choice was between the terms "province of mankind" and "common heritage". Eventually the former was adopted because it was thought to reflect more closely the principles of the freedom of outer space and the prohibition of appropriation. However, it must be said that introduction of the newer phrase ought not to lead to any confusion neither does it prove that these phraseologies are mere declarations of intention as some writers have mischievously suggested.

Eventually, clear reference to this term was rendered in Article 11(1) of the Moon Agreement (1979). It reads that: "The moon and its natural resources are the common heritage of mankind." In addition to this, Article 4(1) of the Moon

605 L. Goldie, "A General International Law Doctrine for Seabed Regimes", 7 *International Lawyer*, (1973): 796, 819.

606 S. Gorove, "The Concept of Common Heritage of Mankind a Political, Moral or Legal Innovation", Vol. 9 *San Diego*, (1996). For further positions stating the alleged indeterminacy of the CHM principle see also Sylvia Maureen Williams (1987) op. cit.: 144; C.C. Joynes, "Legal Implications of the Common Heritage of Mankind", 35 *ICLQ* (1986): 190.

607 See M.L. Smith,"The Commercial Exploitation of Mineral Resources in Outer Space", *Space Law View of the Future* (Deventer: Kluwer Law and Taxation, 1988): 49–55.

608 See Wolfrum op. cit.: 68; see also Said Mahmoudi, *The Law of Deep Sea-Bed Mining* (Stockholm: Almkvist & Wiksell International, 1987): 1–5 *et seq.*

Agreement combines the two terms in the following manner: "The exploration and use of the moon shall be the province of all mankind and shall be carried out for the benefit and in the interests of all countries irrespective of their degree of economic or scientific development."

It would, therefore, appear that as used in the Moon Agreement (1979) both terms emphasise different things although they are geared towards achieving the same noble objective. Article 4(1) emphasises the cooperation of state parties in all their undertakings concerning the Moon and other celestial bodies; by the same token, Article 11 coupled with Article 5 in particular provide the CHM principle with legal teeth.[609]

609 Article 5 reads as follows: "States Parties shall inform the Secretary-General of the United Nations as well as the public and the international scientific community, to the greatest extent feasible and practicable, of their activities concerned with the exploration and use of the moon. Information on the time, purposes, location, orbital parameters and duration shall be given in respect of each mission to the moon as soon as possible after launching, while information on the results of each mission, including scientific results shall be furnished upon completion of the mission, including scientific results, shall be furnished upon completion of the mission. In the case of a mission lasting more than sixty days, information on conduct of the mission, including any scientific results shall be given periodically at thirty days' interval. For missions lasting more than six months, only significant additions to such information need be reported thereafter. (2). If a State Party becomes aware that another State party plans to operate simultaneously in the same area of or in the same orbit around or trajectory to or around the moon, it shall promptly inform the other State of the timing of and plans for its own operations. (3). In carrying out activities under this Agreement, state parties shall promptly inform the Secretary-General, as well as the public and the international scientific community, of any phenomena they discover in outer space, including the moon, could endanger human life or health, as well as of any indication of organic life." A question that may immediately suggest itself is why did the USA accept this? A possible answer would be that up until about two decades ago US policy regarding outer space matters was much less concentrated on commercial aims and more in tune with the realisation that outer space matters are inherently the concern of all states and peoples of the earth. In a piece of very interesting domestic legislation on extra-terrestrial exposure (Title 14, Section 1211 of the Code of Federal Regulations,) the USA took it on itself to establish in its space operations: (a) that it is NASA policy, responsibility and authority to guard the earth against harmful contamination or adverse changes in its environment resulting from personnel, spacecraft and other property returning to the earth after landing on or coming within the atmospheric envelope of a celestial body; and (b) other security requirements, restrictions and safeguards that are necessary in the interest of national security. This law makes it mandatory for a quarantine order of indeterminate period, to be issued on all people who have experienced extraterrestrial exposure by touching directly or indirectly extra-terrestrial matter, or by exposure to the atmosphere of celestial bodies if such person were on NASA manned and unmanned space missions that land or come within the atmospheric envelope of a celestial body and return to the earth. Whoever wilfully violates, attempts to violate or conspires to violate any provision of regulation or orders issued there under or enters or departs from the limits of a quarantine station in disregard of the quarantine rules or regulations shall be fined not more that $5,000 or imprisoned not more than one year or both. However, in 1991 Part 1211 was removed and reserved by the NASA administrator "since is has served its purpose and is no longer in keeping with current policy". See Fed Regulation, Title 14, Chapter V, Part 1211.104 Policy; see also Code of Federal Regulations, edition of 1 January 1997, Volume14, Part 1200 to end (Cat#AE2.106/3:14/P. 1200-end/997), Part 1211: 75.

7.1 Outer space – *res nullius* or *res extra commercium*?

In order to understand the legal status of outer space, it is considered important to determine, as much as possible, which of the Latin legal classifications relating to territory apply to it. Particularly reference is made here to the well-tested doctrines of *res nullius* and *res extra commercium*. Christol rightly points out that there may be a need to identify the characteristics of the CHM principle and to distinguish it from such other principles as *res nullius*, *res communis* and *res communis humanitatis*. Indeed, there is a host of other principles that may become relevant to our analysis.[610]

Although it has already been concluded in several places in this work that outer space is *res extra commercium*, it remains as relevant as ever to examine arguments to the contrary. This exercise will at once reveal the falsity of similar attacks on the settled CHM principle as well as strengthen our arguments in favour of the non-appropriation regime established for outer space.

In subtle attempts to befuddle issues, the suggestion that any of the qualifications *res communis* or *res nullius* or *res extra commercium* or *res communnis omnium* can apply at any time to outer space has been rebuffed as false by writers such as Quadri[611] and later even Lachs. Lachs starts off by accepting that "it is true that some of these definitions have been accepted in other areas of international law". He cleverly, however, sought to dismiss their application to outer space and celestial bodies by stating that their application is conditioned by a reply to a basic question: "Is outer space with the celestial bodies a 'thing' – *res* within the meaning of the law."[612] Quadri also argues that such qualifications are unwarranted because they stem from an assumption that space is a *res* and whichever of the adjectives tacked on lacks legal significance and is at best an indication of the preference of the author or the implications, which the term *res* might suggest. He thinks that: "[T]he proper procedure for approaching the question would be to study the possibility of applying the term *res* to space." Proceeding from this reasoning he, thus, concluded that cosmic space is not a *res*.[613]

Such strenuously made distinctions, however, serve no useful purpose. The bold thread that runs through the space treaties is that outer space and its celestial bodies should be explored and exploited in the interest of entire mankind and no one should be allowed to appropriate any parts thereof. In that case, it is more sensible

610 Roman law distinguished the following inter alia: *res communes*, things owned by no one the use of which was common to all, such as the air, running water, the sea and shores of the sea; *res publicae*, i.e. the property of the state – highways, rivers and harbours; *res universitatis*, property of a city such as theatres or race courses; *res sacrae, religiosae* and *sanctae* were *res nullius divini iuris* – that is no one owned them and neither could anyone legally acquire ownership of them; *res nullius humani iuris* neither owned nor could be acquired by any one. Examples include abandoned property and wild beasts. See C.Q. Christol, *The Modern International Law of Outer Space* (New York: Pergamon Press, 1982): 318. See also Pound op. cit.: 150.

611 Seara Vazquez, *Cosmic International Law* (Detroit: Wayne State University Press, 1985): 39.

612 M. Lachs, *The Law of Outer Space: An Experience in Contemporary Law Making* (Leiden: Sijthoff International, NV, 1972): 48.

613 Op. cit.: 39.

to hold that at least for now outer space is *res extra commercium*. It is important to this conclusion that no state has made incursions into space on the basis of acquisition of territory. In fact, the contrary view has always been maintained by all states that have participated in space exploration so far. Therefore, what is clearly property of all cannot be disposed of or used by any particular state or its private citizens (corporate or natural) as private property. Furthermore, once the status of *res extra commercium* has been conferred on any territory it becomes irrelevant to argue for a change in the legal status of the territory in question to make it *res nullius* considering that it already belongs to all.

Another fine distinction that has been advanced by proponents of the *res nullius* principle is that under customary international law, resources on the Moon and celestial bodies are, by their very nature, *res nullius*, therefore, appropriation is legally possible. Christol, for instance, is of the opinion that there is a difference between the spatial area of the Moon and other celestial bodies and their natural resources. To explain this unacceptable position the proponents seek to make a distinction between free space and pathways, on one hand, and celestial bodies, on the other. With regard to free space it is said that by its very nature and by analogy to the high seas there can be no appropriation since no sovereignty may be claimed without reference to dry land. Thus, the Moon and celestial bodies were merely *res nullius* whereas outer space, i.e. free space, *stricto sensu* was *res extra commercium* and the principles of non-appropriation and free access were valid both before and after the entry into force of the Outer Space Treaty on 10 December 1967.

This view is borne out of the classical but mistaken view of the nature of outer space that lawyers have. It is wrongfully assumed that outer space is a void in which solid celestial bodies float. The easiest way to puncture Christol's argument is to admit that while, of course, there are geophysical differences between the Moon's surface on which natural resources are presently to be found and the gases and cosmic dust that constitute the other "spatial territories" he refers to, however, that is the whole point of giving the widest interpretations to the scope of operation of the CHM principle. We cannot separate the spatial territory from the surface, not only because the law as it is written in the Space Treaty (1967) does not do so but because those very rarefied gases, cosmic dust and energy that constitute and fill the void that is known as outer space themselves may one day constitute valuable natural resources, if, indeed, they do not already do so. It is not when that day arrives that we would start to develop new laws to include further spheres within the operation of the CHM principle. Therefore, it is better to adopt the view that the CHM principle applies to the whole of outer space, including the celestial bodies, as well as their surface and subsurface.[614]

The truth, however, is that the difference between the legal status of celestial bodies and that of free space is a mere academic abstraction in the light of the rules that have so far been treated in both the Outer Space Treaty (1967) and the Moon Agreement (1979). The question that poses itself at this stage is whether *res extra*

614 Christol op. cit.: 318.

commercium sufficiently explains the regime governing outer space. Other writers such as S.M. Williams persuasively argue that the CHM principles goes even beyond that of *res extra commercium*. The preferable interpretation to give to this is that although *res extra commercium* (literally meaning something that cannot be the object of commercial trade, e.g. tombs under Roman law) is applicable, it lacks the element of pronouncing outer space as the property of all. In that case, *res omnium* (property belonging to all) is better. Having said that, however, that something belongs to all does not mean that it cannot be sold for profit, say, by the agreement of the parties. Thus, if the intention is to find a terminology that reflects both characteristics as closely as possible, then we must be speaking in terms of *res omnium extra communis* (property of all and not subject to sale). Cheng developed this theme even further by stating that the CHM principle is a new category to be added to the tripartite division of the world made by traditional law.

The relevance of the two terms ownership and possession to outer space law has been challenged and a preference for *licence* instead has been denoted. Again, it has been stated that there is a need to jettison the term *res nullius* and the insufficiency of even the *res extra commercium* formula has been alluded to. The obvious criticism such sweeping positioning is exposed to is that it may be said that in the enthusiasm of elaborating new terminology, old and tested doctrines of law are being discarded. There is, however, an appropriate defence to this criticism. If, indeed, new concepts have been created in space law by states in the 20th century in response to new situations that mankind has never faced before, then there is no plausible reason to limit current thinking to older doctrines, which the drafters of the pertinent space treaties had good opportunity to refer to but chose not to and, indeed, creatively developed alternatives for.

7.2 The scope of application of the CHM principle in space law

At this stage, it is important that the exact scope of the operation of the CHM principle is determined. The rationale for such an exercise cannot be lost to any scholar on the subject who labours to defend the existence and the legal validity of the principle along with its allied principles such as the non-appropriation rule and the absence of a property regime in space. For what will be the use of establishing these rules in space law if it can at any time be successfully argued by a dissenting state or author that a specific celestial body or area of outer space or, indeed, an entire galaxy is beyond the application of the principle?

It must not be assumed that it is an easy task to determine what part of outer space the existing law covers. As will become apparent, the answer has significance in the determination of liability for outer space activities and jurisdiction over space stations. As has been briefly mentioned the formula employed in the drafting of the Moon Agreement (1979) does not lend itself to sufficient exactitude. Admittedly the words of Article 1 limit the provisions contained therein to celestial bodies "within the solar system". The implications of this unnecessary limitation include the fact that once any activity takes place outside our solar system, it is outside the regime of space law, at least that enunciated in that instrument. The only real beneficiary of such a limitation will be either a rogue state, which seeks to find a part of outer space that is not covered by law over which it can exercise full sovereignty or another intelligence apart from the human race that exists outside the solar system, or both. This suggestion may not be as far fetched as it sounds if we consider the fact that just six decades ago it was largely held as impossible that man would engage in space flight or step on the Moon and that just over a century ago the first aircraft was built. Thus, only the imagination limits the possibilities of exploration beyond this solar system and the discoveries that the next 50 years might bring. This is the essence of the preference for the view that space law, particularly the provisions enunciating the CHM principle, apply not only to the solar system we exist in but to the entire universe of galaxies. Probably the apparent reason for the reference to the solar system in the Moon Agreement 1979 is that as the name of the treaty suggests the principal aim is to make legislation for the Moon, which is earth's natural satellite and of which there is only one in this solar system.

Let it be assumed that the limitation contained in Article (1) of the Moon Agreement (1979) is accepted. It will be discovered that, even then, the clear provisions of the Outer Space Treaty (1967) survive that limitation and still operate to cover (as it reads) "outer space, including the Moon and other celestial bodies" (Article 1). The term "other celestial bodies" is not limited to any given solar system. The CHM and the province of mankind principles thus, operate to seal forever the hopes of any space explorer to discover any spatial territory to which sovereign or private rights of ownership and control can be legally claimed.

Another way of viewing the scope of application of the CHM principle is to ask if the principle applies to all the contents of empty space. The question is does space law, especially the CHM principle, apply to the countless mass of meteors, rocks, rarefied gases etc. over and around the earth. The generic terms found in the space treaties (for instance, "celestial bodies" and "the Moon") make it difficult to tell whether these terms cover all natural objects in outer space irrespective of their size, structure or flight pattern.[615] It was, in fact, suggested once that smaller bodies should have a different status from outer space proper.[616] In other words, only "[t]he Sun and all planets and the moon" were not to be appropriated but "meteorites . . . any rock in space which can really be used and controlled" should belong to another class.[617]

615 Lachs op. cit.: 46.

616 Ibid. A list of these proposals was recorded by C.W Jenks in his Report preliminaire Institut du droit international: 109–201; cf. also M.G. Markov, "Moon Landing and International Law", III, 9 *Revista di Diritto Aereo* (1964): 9 ff.

617 E.L Fasan, "Law and Peace for Celestial Bodies", *Proceedings Fifth Colloquium on the Law of Outer Space, 23–29 September 1962*: 8 f.; Cocca also believes that "Planets are the only celestial bodies considered from a legal viewpoint; i.e. bodies admitting occupation if they are vacant." See A.A Cocca, "Basic Statute for the Moon and Celestial Bodies", 6 *Revista di diritto Aereo* (1963): 2nd quarter, para. v; cf. Mc Dougall, Laswell and Vlasic, *Law and Public Order in Space* (New Haven, 1963): 750 ff; J. Machowski, "The Legal Status of Meteors and Meteorites", 39 *Yearbook AAA* (1969): 101 ff.

The stance that smaller natural bodies should be subject to appropriation or regarded as *terra nullius* by virtue of their size is unacceptable. Such a proposition is as absurd as the corresponding theory among some air lawyers to limit sovereignty over national airspace to below dense clouds or those legal theorists who say that icebergs, which flow onto the high seas, should retain the sovereignty of the territory from whence they broke off. In the first place, the space treaties that pronounce the CHM principle did not establish this difference. Second, it is difficult to see how anyone could prescribe the minimum size below which an object would cease to be regarded as a celestial body. The preferred view is that which holds that, in the present state of man's knowledge, there is little that can serve as a basis for any distinction between a natural or physical definition of a celestial body, on one hand, and a legal definition, on the other.[618]

For all relevant purposes, therefore, the CHM principle applies not only to all "celestial bodies", no matter how small or large and no matter in which solar system in the infinity of space they are found, but also to all that may be considered "free space" including gases, particles and cosmic dust. The CHM principle, however, is not applicable at all to the airspace above national territory. As regards the airspace over territories on earth over which the CHM principle applies under another body of law such as Antarctica (the World Park concept) or the area (in the law of the sea) it may be suggested that the legal status of the airspace above those territories cannot be different from the status of the underlying territory.[619] Therefore, the airspace over the area is also the common heritage of mankind but it derives its status in being so not from space law but from the laws of the sea or Antarctic law as the case may be.

Controversial as these positions taken may seem, they are rational and in consonance with the legal rule of interpretation particularly that which dictates that laws should be interpreted to give effect to the intention of the drafters and to save it rather than it be destroyed. Last on this issue, it must be said that to engage in arguments that seek to limit the geographical or geophysical scope of the CHM principle in outer space as a method of curtailing the potency of the doctrine is a fruitless exercise. However, to engage in the intellectual exercise of determining the legal significance of the CHM principle remains a valid enquiry and is indeed a current legal problem relevant to the current century.

7.3 The CHM principle and the arguments for and against property rights in space

> No Moon, no planet shall fly a single nation's flag.[620]

618 Lachs op. cit.: 46.

619 A similar reasoning is found in the argument that the airspace over the high seas should be legally regarded as part of the common heritage of mankind. See, further on this theme, Nicholas Grief (1994) op. cit.: 9, 12–13.

620 Committee on the Peaceful Uses of Outer Space, 19 March 1962 A/AC. 105/PV. 2: 13–15.

One of the ways in which certain writers seek to attack and undermine the regime abolishing individual property rights in space is to argue that the CHM principle if ever it has any legal value at all does not, in fact, operate so as to block property rights in space. This argument, thus, necessitates a separate enquiry as to whether CHM principle in any way permits the operation of property over space-based resources. It remains settled law that outer space, including the Moon and other celestial bodies, is not subject to appropriation by claim of sovereignty by means of use or occupation or by any other means. [621]

At this stage, however, it is worth drawing a parallel between the early stages of the development of air transport and that of outer space exploration. In both cases, the uncertainties over the unfolding developments helped in different ways to avert the development of legal regimes that are solely for the interest of one or two states. In the case of air law, as mentioned in earlier chapters, the leading air powers recognised the importance of not allowing any one state to have unbridled access to the air space over other national territories. This was principally to contain the USA, which had a clear and distinct technological advantage in the air transport industry. Thus, the theory and practice of exclusive jurisdiction over national airspace by each state was upheld. In the case of space law, a similar conclusion as to the undesirability of the entrenchment of hegemonic interests within the new frontier was reached with a different prescription. Rather than grant all states equal sovereignty in outer space, no sovereignty was granted at all. The ideological Cold War that was at its height around 1957 produced an effect that was akin to the effects of the First World War on the shaping of air law earlier in the 20th century. The super powers and the leading states were not sure of the way events arising out of the space activities would turn out in the context of the prevailing Cold War. They were equally not certain of the particular benefits accruable from space exploration.

Thus, although the USSR was the first state to put a man in space in 1957, explicit statements were made renouncing all claims to outer space.[622] It was stated that: "No human activity on the Moon or any other celestial body could be taken as justification for national appropriation."[623] The USA also took this position long before it put a man on the Moon. The position as stated then was: "We have rejected the concept of national sovereignty in outer space. No Moon, no planet shall fly a single nation's flag."[624] In the words of US President Johnson: "The goals now within reach of the human race are too great to be divided as spoils, too great for the world to waste its efforts in a blind race between competitive nations."[625]

621 Article II Outer Space Treaty (1967); Para. 3 Declaration of Legal Principles (1963); cf. *supra*, last section and our discussions on the exploration and use of outer space, *infra*.

622 See *Pravda*, 18 November 1959, and United Nations 22 September 1960 (Official Records): 48, para, 58.

623 Legal Sub-committee, 20 October 1966, A/AC. 105/C.2/SR.63.

624 *Supra*, note 620.

625 See Adlai Stevensen in 1st Comm. statement on "International Cooperation in the Peaceful Uses of Outer Space", 2 December 1963, UN Press Release No. 4323, 2 December 1963. Statement

These noble postures along with the influence of the majority of developing states facilitated the eventual formulation of the CHM principle.

The problem is that for those states that invest heavily in space exploratory activities, the cost benefit of exploiting extensively space-based resources is quite real.[626] As time goes by and with the inevitable discovery of invaluable space-based resources as well as newer and cheaper methods of exploiting them, it is understandable that pressures are on the increase for the law to recognise and permit property rights and the commercialisation of outer space.

It is probably worthy of note that the USA would again appear to be at the forefront in the championing of commercialisation of space resources. This is probably comparable to the history of developments in air law where the USA developed and actively sponsored the "open skies" agenda in line with its business and hegemonic interests.[627] It is, therefore, no wonder that the United States National Commission on Space recommended that "steps necessary to undertake the development of . . . extra-terrestrial resources begin at once". A call was subsequently made for the establishment of pilot mining and production facilities on the Moon by the year 2007.[628] Western scholars such as Kosmo also believe that: "[T]he quality of America's future social and economic welfare is inextricably intertwined with the successful commercialisation of space by American private enterprise." Baca pushes the argument to extreme when he insists that: "the issue of sovereignty be reconsidered in space, as some form of sovereignty is an absolute necessity to the guarantee of the property rights required for the development of space resources".[629] Christol also thinks that there is a distinction between the ban of Article II of the Space Treaty concerning sovereign (i.e. national) appropriation of spatial areas and the right of legal persons to obtain property. It is also argued that the provisions of Article I and III in particular, of the Space Treaty (1967) as well as the other articles allowing free and equal exploration, use and exploitation of the space environment by states, must be contrasted with the rights of other legal persons to engage in such exploration, use and exploitation.[630]

It makes sense to consider at some length the most frequently cited justifications for the position adopted by those writers who believe that the CHM principle (if at all it has a legal value) does allow the existence of property rights in outer space. They are as follows:

also appended to the Educational Progress of NASA, Senate Hearings on Aeronautical and Space Sciences 88th Cong. 1st Sess. 21–2 November 1963. See also S. Bhatt, "Legal Controls of the Exploration and Use of the Moon and Celestial Bodies", 8 *IJIL* (1968): 36–8; A. Piradov and Y. Rybakov, "First Space Treaty", *International Affairs* (1967): 21–6.

626 Anderson K. Baca, "Property Rights in Outer Space", 58 *Journal of Air Law and Commerce* (1993): 1044–45.

627 *Supra*, Chapter 2.

628 Baca op. cit.: 1042.

629 *Ibid*: 1047.

630 Christol op. cit.: 318.

1 The term common heritage of mankind lacks any legal or scientific clarity and therefore, means everything and nothing at all.
2 It is claimed that the preamble to the Outer Space Treaty (1967) in fact recognises the exploitation of outer space.
3 Article 1 of the Outer Space Treaty (1967) (which contains the province of mankind formula a necessary adjunct of the CHM principle) is merely "a statement of general goals" and that the ratification of specialised treaties is necessary to create any specific obligations.[631] In the absence of such treaties Article 1(1) is seen to be more a moral and philosophical obligation than a legal requirement [632]
4 The general principle of non-appropriation is in effect circumscribed to a large extent by treaty provisions designed to facilitate the exploration and use of outer space. In other words, Article 1 specifically makes provision for use of outer space. Because the legal sense of the word "use" refers to the enjoyment of property often with an advantage or profit arising therefrom, by the occupancy, utilisation or exercise of the property, therefore, some form of appropriation must be permissible in order to facilitate the use contemplated in Article 1.
5 Since the Outer Space Treaty (1967) does allow for withdrawal, the non-appropriation principle would by the operation of the law of treaties simply not apply to any state that withdraws from it.
6 The Moon Agreement (1979), which introduces the CHM concept, has not been ratified by any of the space powers. Also, that it has not been signed by many states. Furthermore that it is not binding on any non-party state and the claim that it represents customary law is not credible.[633]
7 In respect of the geostationary orbit the characteristics of that flight path is not analogous to the situation on celestial bodies.

Thus, while the CHM principle and non-appropriation rules may work in the former they may be unworkable with respect to a lunar base, where investments will include not only equipment but site preparation and other modifications. It is

631 See N. Jasentuliyana, "Article 1 of the Outer Space Treaty Revisited", 17 *Journal of Space Law* (1989): 129, 139; Baca op. cit.: 1064.

632 See "Settlement and Sovereignty in Outer Space", 22 *UW Ont. L. Rev.* (1984): 155, 157–8.

633 Baca op. cit.: 1068. The Moon Agreement entered into force on 11 July 1984 with the ratification by the required fifth state, however, the record of ratification and accession to the Moon Agreement (1979) is, indeed, quite poor for both developed and developing states. Indeed as at January 2010 only 13 ratifying states and a further 3 signature only states were bound by the Moon Agreement (1979) whereas 126 states are parties to the Outer Space Treaty (1976) and it may be said that developing states particularly have not justified their interest in many of the principles they fought vehemently to have included in the treaty at the conference tables by ratifying it, or by persuading other states to accede to it. It is, however, possible to over emphasise this point because the number of parties is slowly rising and dramatic increases in the number of signatories to the instrument may be easily predicted if any threat to the common understanding states have as to the general nature of the legal regime for outer space emerges or if technological developments make the exploration of the moon easier.

argued that in such situations the limited possessory rights and the lack of a power to dispose the property may severely limit the value of any investment. In other words, space exploration may eventually suffer from space law to the detriment of mankind.

Such arguments as raised in the seven points just delineated may appear to be formidable and are, indeed, quite capable of attracting scholarly sympathy but again the correct view is that they are nonetheless insufficient. The arguments certainly do not justify any legal reasoning that limits the operation of the CHM principle in outer space in such a manner as to permit national or private appropriation and to recognise extensive property rights in space. Suggestions that sovereignty be introduced into outer space through a loose interpretation of the CHM principle or in any other form whatsoever is a form of legal heresy and should be dismissed for the following reasons.

In the first place, it is merely mischievous to overstate the obscurity of meaning shrouding the term CHM. Doing so is clearly an undisguised attempt to avoid the legal validity of the CHM principle. Indeed, it may be said with a lot of credence that specific semantic certainty has been afforded to this term in the works of many authors. R.P. Arnold impressively achieves this when he stated as follows:

> The word heritage suggests property or interests which are reserved to a person by reason of birth, something handed down from one's ancestors or the past. In defining mankind, it is necessary to make a distinction between mankind and man. Mankind refers to the collective group, whereas man refers to individual men and women . . . Mankind is not yet unified under one government, therefore the collective entity of mankind is represented by the various nations of the world. Thus the exercise of rights to the common heritage of mankind appertains to nations, representing mankind, and not individuals. The use of the phrase common heritage of mankind implies or prescribes worldwide ownership.[634]

Furthermore, due to the fact that the primary subjects of international law are independent states, it is logical that they should decide together and as a singular community, inclusive of all, fundamental matters that concern all. This is, therefore, what is legalistically referred to as mankind.[635] It has, thus, become possible to identify some basic elements of the CHM principle:

(a) That the areas constituting a CHM cannot be subject to appropriation.
(b) That the use of such area and the resources thereof shall be subject to a common management system.

634 Rudolph Preston Arnold, "The Common Heritage of Mankind as a Legal Concept", 9, 1 *International Lawyer* (1975): 154.

635 Neeru Sehgal, "The Concept of Common Heritage of Mankind Under the Moon Agreement (1979), 1979", 26 *INJIL* (1986): 108. See also A.A. Cocca, "Mankind as New Legal Subject – A New Juridical Dimension Recognized by the United Nations", *Proceedings of the Thirteenth Colloquium on the Law of Outer Space* (1971): 212.

(c) That the concept in question implies an active sharing of the benefits derived from the exploration and exploitation of those areas.
(d) That the area be used exclusively for peaceful purposes.
(e) That the area be preserved for future generations in perpetual succession.[636]

In the light of these definitions and assertions, it is highly unlikely that any possible interpretation of the CHM principle allows for property rights in space. The allegation that the existing space treaties recognise exploitation of outer space through the provisions permitting space exploration is yet another unsuccessful attempt to befuddle issues. The answer to this is that there is a clear separation in space law between the issue of the use of outer space resources in outer space for scientific experimentation, on the one hand, and that of exploitation or mining of outer space-based resources with a view to repatriating the resources to earth for economic and monetary gain, on the other hand. Regarding the utilisation of space-based resources in outer space itself there is little room for controversy. The reasonable use doctrine has been established in space law. The Moon Agreement in Article 6(2), for instance, permits the usage of minerals and other substances of the Moon in quantities appropriate for the support of their missions. This very much falls short of permitting mining for purely monetary gains. Furthermore, as will be later elaborated on, the right to collect and remove substances and minerals from the moon is limited to "scientific investigations and in furtherance of the provisions of the agreement" (Article 6(2) Moon Agreement (1979)). The phrase "in furtherance of the provisions of this agreement" covers many things. This includes, of course, the obligation to have due regard to interests of present and future generations as well as the need to promote higher standards of living and conditions of economic and social progress and development in accordance with the Charter of the United Nations (Article 4, Moon Agreement (1979)).

It might, indeed, be wondered whether the promotion of higher standards of living and economic progress would not be better served if those countries that can afford it are allowed to reap the benefits of their exploration by the granting of substantial mining rights in space law. The answer to this simply is that if that were what was intended, then the space treaties would have expressly stated so. However, what can be found in the treaties, particularly within the instruments dictating the CHM principle, is an intention not only to maintain outer space and its celestial bodies as common property until an exploitative regime is set up, but an obligation to share very generously benefits derived from scientific knowledge about outer space between all states irrespective of their degree of economic or scientific development (Article 4(1) Moon Agreement (1979)). This obligation is central to the workings of the CHM/province of mankind principles in space law so much so that states are advised to have regard to the desirability of making a portion of

636 See Williams (1987) op. cit.: 109; Dekanozov, "The Common Heritage of Mankind in the 1979 Agreement Governing the Activities of States on the Moon and other Celestial Bodies", *Proceedings of Twenty-Fourth Colloquium on the Law of Outer Space* (1981): 186.

such samples available to other interested state parties and the international scientific community for scientific investigation (Article 6(2) Moon Agreement (1979)).

It is, therefore, inevitable to conclude that states are free to determine all aspects of their participation in the exploration and use of outer space. However, for the CHM principle to operate effectively, all states particularly those with relevant space capabilities should contribute to the promoting and fostering of international cooperation. This dictates, as of now, an abandonment of property claims in outer space as well as the channelling of benefits of space exploration towards the interests of developing countries and countries with incipient space programmes (Declaration 2 and 3, Declaration on International Cooperation (1996)).

As to the allegation that the CHM principle does not bind a withdrawing state from the treaties that incorporate it and that it also does not bind any of the space powers that do not ratify the Moon Agreement (1979), it must be said that these submissions again are based on an insufficient premise. In any event, more and more states have ratified the Moon Agreement (1979) including at least one of the space powers. Furthermore, the regime of equal access to outer space created in the treaties has become part of customary international law. Therefore, a withdrawing party cannot legally gain ownership over what in effect already belongs to all. Just as a party to the Chicago Convention (1944) cannot by withdrawing from that treaty unsettle the principle of exclusive sovereignty and jurisdiction of states in their airspace; so also cannot any state(s) undermine the status of outer space as the common heritage of mankind by inopportune withdrawal from treaty law or opportunistic approach to treaty ratification and accession.

7.4 Summary and conclusions

The CHM and the province of mankind terminologies are two sides of the same coin. The principles exist in the space treaties to create legal obligations, which, in effect, dictate cooperation among state parties in aspects of their undertakings concerning outer space, the Moon and other celestial bodies, and in the sharing of the benefits obtainable therefrom. These principles represent a relatively new category of legal classification for the explanation of jurisdiction and control over international territory. Earlier analogies can be found in the law of the sea and the legal regime governing Antarctica. For all relevant purposes the CHM principle applies not only to all "celestial bodies" no matter how small or large and no matter in which solar system in the infinity of space they are found but also to all that may be considered "free space", including gases, particles and cosmic dust. It does not operate over the national airspace presently.

It is probably desirable that the applicability of the CHM principle extends to the airspace over the high seas as well. This is a logical consequence of the declaration of the legal nature of the high seabed and ocean floor (excluding the continental shelf) and the subsoil thereof as the common heritage of mankind. Furthermore, it is suggested that since the sovereignty and jurisdiction granted to states in their national airspace is delimited *ratione loci* in respect of the space above national territories and not *ratione materiae* in respect of the air that may at any given time be filling this space. Then there is scope for the separate determination of the legal status of the gaseous air itself (i.e. the gaseous envelope surrounding the earth). In that case, considering the central and irreplaceable nature of the air to the existence of human beings the sole conclusion that presents itself is that the air (*ratione materiae*) is best assimilated into the concept of common heritage of mankind. In other words, if there is at least one thing worthy of being regarded as the common heritage of mankind the air that we breathe would certainly qualify.

Of the older classifications known to law the CHM principle as it applies to outer space is best represented by the classification of *res omnium extra communis*. By virtue of this, the area covered belongs to entire mankind as represented by states. Sovereignty cannot in any way be legally enforced over outer space. Until a regime of exploitation is designed for it as was done in the case of "the area" in the law of the sea, outer space and its resources cannot be exploited on a commercial basis. It may, indeed, be said that it is better that no such regime of commercial exploitation is ever developed if it would inescapably entail environmental degradation, escalate global warming or lead to international conflicts.

International space law presently has enshrined the CHM principle and there is no convincing reason to abandon it or limit its applicability qualitatively or quantitatively. The arguments against the legal potency of the CHM principle are altogether insufficient to credibly cast any doubts as to the necessity and the validity of the principle in present day international law. The argument that it represents no more than a hortatory provision is unsupportable given its inclusion in the substantive parts of the Moon Agreement (1979) (Article 11(1). The fact that the principle has also enjoyed legal, obligatory and institutional validity in the law of the sea further proves that it was intended to and, indeed, has legal effect in space law.

8 Jurisprudential basis for common ownership

8.1 Jurisprudential basis for common ownership, possession and control over outer space

There are certain contradictions in the argument of those writers who expound the legality of unbridled private exploitation of resources on celestial bodies, which must be dispelled. Christol, for instance, admits that, "being unable to possess sovereignty, a State may not create exclusive property rights".[637] Yet he goes on to conclude as follows:

> *However, those public entities or those private institutions that have the capacity to engage in exploitative activities are fully competent to do so.* They are as required by Article VI of the Principles Treaty, to conform to the "authorization and continuing supervision by the appropriate State Party to the Treaty." As a result of this provision it is clear that parties may exercise important jurisdictional controls. Most importantly, the distinction between national sovereignty, and the right of a State to engage in jurisdictional authority, has been recognised. The extent of such jurisdictional authority will depend upon whether a State is bound by either or both of the 1967 Principles and the 1979 Moon treaty.[638]

But the real issue is not whether private organisations can engage in space exploration because, of course, they can; however, it is clear that no state may grant exploitative or exclusive property rights to public or private entities that go beyond that which the state itself possesses under the general principles governing space exploration in international law. In fact, the authorisation and continuing supervision required of states is there in order to ensure that the conduct of space exploration and exploitation proceeds in consonance with international law. Furthermore, it is important to stress that the jurisdictional duties imposed on states are not limited only to the Principles in the Outer Space Treaty (1967) and the Moon Agreement (1979) but also encompass duties that are laid down under the customary international law that has been developed in relation to outer space

637 Carl Q. Christol, "The 1979 Moon Agreement: Where is it Today?", 27, 1 *Journal of Space Law* (1999): 4.

638 Ibid; emphasis added.

activities. Thus, the fact that some spacefaring states, particularly the USA, Russia, Japan and China, have not ratified the Moon Agreement (1979) does not make it possible for them totally to ignore those rules of space law that are central to the regime created for the Moon since they serve as evidence of contemporary international law and may, in some cases, arguably have become part of customary international law.[639]

The effect of both the *res communis* principle adopted in the 1967 Space Treaty and the CHM principle adopted in the 1979 Moon Agreement (1979) is to produce a prohibition against the grant of exclusive right to private property. The argument that the *res communis* principle, which prevents a nation from exercising sovereignty on the high seas, but allows their fishermen to exploit fisheries and gives them proprietary rights, also applies to the natural resources in outer space is only correct in the sense that this will probably be the course the development of the law will have to take once commercial exploitation of outer space resources begins. Moreover, there are important distinctions. First, the practice of exploitation of the high seas for commercial fisheries has been going on for centuries and there is a settled recognition of that fact, prior to the development of treaties regulating the high seas in the last century, whereas the exploitation of outer space resources has hardly begun and the rules contained in the pertinent space treaties are largely in favour of sharing the benefits of exploitation between all states. Thus while the former may be located within the so-called lex mercatori, the rules governing the latter are just being elaborated under the shadow of the CHM principle. Second, as recognised by the United States delegate to the General Assembly Conference adopting the Moon Agreement in 1979, even though the Agreement did not specifically put in place a moratorium on the exploitation of natural resources, any such exploitation must be carried out in accordance with Article 11, paragraph 7, and Article 6, paragraph 2.[640]

Article 6(2) deals principally with the removal of samples for scientific studies. Article 11, paragraph 5, envisages that state parties to the Moon Agreement (1979) will establish an international regime to govern the exploitation of natural resources on the Moon and Article 11(7) provides that the main purposes of the regime shall include:

- the orderly and safe development of the natural resources of the Moon
- the rational management of those resources

639 China, for instance, was reported to announce plans for a lunar station to exploit valuable resources. Again a distinction may be made between exploitation of infinite resources and those that involve finite mineral resources. The former is typified by the ambition of the Chinese to collect sunlight in orbiting stations and beam either direct light or microwave energy down to earth-based collecting points. See John Gittings and Tim Radford, "The Moon – a Giant Leap for the Chinese who Spy a Business Opportunity in Space", *Guardian*, Tuesday 21 May 2002: 3.

640 UN Doc. A/SPC/34/19, 6, 7 November 1979. Note particularly Article 11(8), which stipulates: "All the activities with respect to the natural resources of the moon shall be carried out in a manner compatible with the purposes specified in paragraph 7 of this article and the provisions of article 6, paragraph 2, of this Agreement."

- the expansion of opportunities in the use of those resources
- an equitable sharing by all state parties in the benefits derived from those resources, whereby the interests and needs of the developing countries, as well as the efforts of those countries that have contributed either directly or indirectly to the exploration of the Moon shall be given special consideration.

In any case, Article 11(8) very importantly stipulates that all the activities with respect to the natural resources of the Moon shall be carried out in a manner compatible with the purposes specified in paragraph 7.

One possible argument that may be presented is that if commercial exploitation can only take place in accordance with Article 11(7) and that paragraph simply explains what is to be achieved by the envisaged international regime for the exploitation of natural resources on the Moon as demanded by Article 11(5) then commercial exploitation may only begin after that international regime has been put in place.

Even the Outer Space Treaty (1967), which is considered user-friendly by the proponents of the theory that exploitation for commercial benefits is currently permitted, expressly stipulates in Article II that: "Outer space, including the moon and other celestial bodies, is not subject to national appropriation by claim of sovereignty, *by means of use* or occupation, *or by any other means*" (emphasis added). This means that the drafters acknowledge that appropriation may arise by "use". Therefore, it may be argued that it is not possible even under this treaty,[641] for any state to exploit resources on the Moon for commercial benefits without at least by implication "appropriating" it.

The requirement in Article IX that a state about to conduct an activity that may potentially cause harmful interference with activities of other state parties should undertake appropriate consultation before proceeding with such activity also supports the argument that any state that wants to introduce commercial exploitation must first of all embark on international consultations. In order words, such a state even if not a party to the Moon Agreement (1979) ought to, under the rules of international comity, consult with the parties to that treaty as well as the parties to the Outer Space Treaty (1967) before commercial exploitation begins. In any case, one of the most likely candidates for such a move in the near future, the United States, has already committed itself on the conclusion of the Moon Agreement (1979) to future participation in negotiations respecting the establishment of an international regime for governing the exploitation of the Moon's natural resources.[642]

There is no doubt that the wish of the spacefaring states is to be able to carry out extensive commercial exploitation of available resources on the Moon and

641 To which, very importantly the, spacefaring states that have expressed the wish to embark on commercial exploitation (mainly the USA, China and Japan) are parties.

642 A representative of the USA also stated that the USA "would, when and if negotiations for such a regime were called for under articles 11 and 18, make a good faith effort to ensure that they are successfully concluded". UN Doc. A/SPC/34/19, 6, 7 November 1979.

eventually on other celestial bodies. This reality also informs the arguments of many writers on the subject. However, it may be said that pretending that the present laws allow unbridled commercial exploitation based on property rights is not the way to go about it because they clearly do not. The problem is also not with the Moon Agreement (1979) as many writers have sought to argue.[643] The real issue is that further consultations and international negotiations are still required before large-scale exploitation of the Moon's resources may begin. This has been envisaged by both treaties that have been considered and cannot be ignored by any state that wants to embark on space mineral exploitation. This is also a reality that must be coped with by statesmen, business interests and writers who advocate the concept of space "real property rights".[644] It is, therefore, possible to question the objectivity of views such as those of Cheng when he states that the Outer Space Treaty (1967) "while it precludes the space powers from appropriating territorially portions of outer space, the moon and other celestial bodies, leaves them free, *notwithstanding views to the contrary*, nevertheless to appropriate their resources".[645] If, indeed, the common heritage principle is in any way vague and imprecise then the right to real property on the Moon is even vaguer as no such thing is mentioned in any treaty.

The Aristotelian analysis of justice may still serve as a crucible into which we may pour the current problems of air and space law of the 20th and 21st centuries. Thus, it is sensible to adopt the distinction between particular justice and universal justice, on the one hand, and distributive and corrective justice, on the other.[646] While it may be taken for granted that justice has been achieved with respect to the airspace in that every state has exclusive jurisdiction in its national airspace, the enquiry remains particularly relevant and of contemporary significance with respect to the regime governing control over outer space-based resources. There is credibility in the jurisprudential premise that distributive justice is based on the principle that there has to be an equal distribution between equals and that

643 See, for example, Christol op. cit.: 4. Cf. *supra*, Chapter 7.3. The CHM principle and the arguments for and against property rights in space. Note particularly such views as that of Kosmo: "the quality of America's future social and economic welfare is inextricably intertwined with the successful commercialisation of space by American private enterprise" (quoted in Christol op. cit.: 318) and Baca's view that "the issue of sovereignty be reconsidered in space, as some form of sovereignty is an absolute necessity to the guarantee of the property rights required for the development of space resources". Anderson K. Baca "Property Rights in Outer Space", 58 *Journal of Air Law and Commerce* (1993): 1044–5.

644 See W.N. White, Jr, "Real Property Rights in Space", 40 *Proceedings Colloq. L. Outer Space* (1998): 380.

645 Ibid (emphasis added). It is obviously not enough for scholars to adopt the position of the proverbial ostrich that buries its neck in the sand. A lot of intellectual effort has been expended by some writers to proclaim property rights that simply are not there presently. Their position is very well captured in the opening quote to Christol's article, which, interestingly, attempts to dismiss the formidability of the Moon Agreement (1979) as an obstacle to the concept of space propertisation. It reads: "As I was going up the stair I met a man who wasn't there. He wasn't there again today. I wish, I wish he'd stay away" (Hughes Mearns, 1875). See Christol op. cit.: 1.

646 See Aristotle, *Nicomachean Ethics*, V. trans. Rackham (Cambridge: Harvard University Press, 1968). See also Dias, op. cit.: 65.

corrective justice restores equality whenever this has been disturbed (for example, by a wrongdoing). The relevance of these terms in relation to the ongoing debate about the legal status of outer space and its resources comes into sharper focus in the following.

To start with it may be necessary to recall the principle of the equality of states. Just as, in the municipal setting, justice connotes the legal equality of all persons so also among nations, equality of states reign supreme. One of the most opportune areas in which to test the doctrine of state equality and the obligation to take into consideration the interests of other states in resource management is found in relation to the special problem of the geostationary orbit.[647] Note that it has been concluded that there is no basis for excluding the legal nature of that orbit from the legal nature of outer space in general at least for the purposes of application of the CHM principle. The unfortunate situation has arisen in which the geostationary orbit is being clogged up by satellites that belong to a few states. Since the geostationary orbit is a finite resource, the *de facto* commandeering of slots must not be allowed to impede distribution and access to it by a few active states. It is clear that the present position with respect to geostationary orbit use, whereby the orbit is occupied principally by a few countries, accompanied by prompt replacement of spent satellites with newer satellites is unacceptable. Surely if it continues it may mean that other states may not in the future have orbital positions and related frequencies available.[648]

Significantly the CHM principle in at least this instance also works against the selfish instincts informing the usual positions taken by both developed and developing states. On the one hand, it renders untenable the central thesis of the Bogota Declaration (1976), in that no equatorial state can validly claim sovereignty over the orbit since it is the property of all. On the other hand, in line with the corrective aspects of justice, the 1985 Report of the Legal Committee on the Peaceful uses of Outer Space (UNCOPUOS) recognises that by reason of their geographical position the equatorial countries should be considered as having special rights to segments of the geostationary orbit superjacent to their territories.[649] Yet there is the likelihood in this century that an equatorial state may wish to launch its own satellite or group of satellites and would be told it may not do so by the International Telecommunications Union (ITU) because there are no

647 For further discussion of the issues relating to the geostationary orbit, see *infra*, Chapter 10; ITU Document WARC-BS (1977) 81 E of 17 January 1977. Text available in *Journal of Space Law* (1978): 193–6. The parties to the declaration are Brazil, Columbia, Congo, Ecuador, Indonesia, Kenya, Uganda and Zaire.

648 The geostationary orbit is a finite resource that can be "clogged up" in the sense that there are, in reality, only a few "parking spaces" in that orbit in which satellites can be placed along the same plane, for efficient coverage of the earth and without interfering or crashing into other satellites. What makes matters worse is that after a number of years some satellites wander off course and can very easily crash into nearby functioning satellites. See further Maurice N. Andem, *International Legal Problems in the Peaceful Exploration and Use of Outer Space* (Rovaniemi: University of Lapland, 1992): 162.

649 See A/AC.105/352 (11 April 1985): 32–4; see, further, A/AC.105/370: 19–27.

available positions or frequencies for it. Under its present rules, the ITU may be justified in placing precedence in favour of those states that have already launched satellites in accordance with its "first come first served" policies. But then, it may well be argued that it would be completely inequitable to expect an equatorial state to accept such a scheme as just. By virtue of geophysical realities there can be no equality of circumstances at least in a factual sense between such a state and the non-equatorial states, which monopolise the orbit.

A simple way of providing for the interests of these states is to make special slots available for them now and reserve them in perpetuity even if they do not yet have the technological capabilities to exploit the geostationary orbit. This it must be emphasised does not create ownership or sovereignty over the orbit as it is recognised for the airspace. It merely creates a licence to operate geostationary satellites which may indeed be sub-licensed for economic benefit. This position also recognises the importance of justly sharing the finite resource that the geostationary orbit constitutes.

This brings us back to the question of equality. Aristotle claims that justice is equality but only among equals, and inequality is just but only among the unequal. Therefore, he enjoins, that we treat equals equally and the unequal, unequally. Applying this to the regimes governing airspace and outer space, it must be said that both benefits and burdens must be shared equally among states. The benefits of the "equal" distribution of sovereignty in the airspace include the right to exclude unwanted foreigners, goods, flying objects, the assurance of state security, aviation safety, financial gain through the use of airspace as bargaining chips, etc. The burdens may be said to include the obligation to respect the sovereignty of other states over their own airspace, the duty to observe rules such as the privileges and duties exchanged in the Five Freedoms and Privileges Agreement.[650] In relation to outer space, benefits include the recognition of equal access to outer space (i.e. both orbital flight paths and celestial bodies). An adjunct of the right of access to outer space is the right to ascend into outer space and to descend. This operates as derogation from airspace sovereignty in that the airspace of a state might be traversed for this purpose. Other benefits include the freedom to engage in scientific experimentation and exploration, the removal of samples from celestial bodies, space tourism and the establishment of space stations.

Delineating the burdens to be shared may prove to be more difficult. Presently, some developing states seek an active role in different areas of space exploration. These include Argentina, Brazil, China, India, Indonesia, Iran, Mexico, Nigeria and Pakistan. Nigeria, for example, announced with fanfare in 1986 its plans to launch space-based telecommunication satellites in the 1990s.[651] In the early months of the year 2000 the president of the country announced that he was sorry but the scheme would have to wait, as there were more pressing priorities of development. Yet in a move that proves the point that the law and practice of outer

650 The Chicago International Air Transport Agreement 1944. BFSP 1, 171 UNTS 387, in force since 1945. 11 parties; UK not a party. *Supra*, Chapter 2.

651 Andem op. cit.: 165.

space exploration must proceed on the assumption that access to outer space and its potentials will become increasing democratised the Nigerian government made a *volte face* and started investing heavily in a space programme. Nigerian space policy is stated to be based on the realisation that there is no nation that can call itself developed in the 21st century that does not have indigenous critical mass of trained space scientists and engineers space scientists and engineers capable of contributing to a developed space programme.[652] In line with its policy statement to vigorously pursue the attainment of space capabilities as an essential tool for its socioeconomic development and the enhancement of the quality of life of its people, Nigeria has within the first decade of this century successfully embarked on two satellite projects through international collaboration – NigeriaSat-1 and NigcomSat-1. The country has made two further launches – NigeriaSat-2 and Sat-X spacecraft in the first quarter of 2011.[653]

Nonetheless, the prospect of serious participation in outer space technological activities remains beyond the reach of most developing nations. Save the obligation to assist in the return of space objects and astronauts that exists in treaty law, most states simply do not stand the chance of bearing the smallest burden neither do they make even the minimal capital outlay towards outer space activities. In this way alone, it becomes difficult not to see that following the Aristotelian analysis of justice there may be an amount of injustice in a regime that shares all benefits and burdens equally among transparently unequal states. If some states expend tremendous effort both in financial and intellectual terms in order to engage in outer space activities, it may be argued that they deserve some preferential treatment in the sharing of rights and liabilities. An alternative will be to ensure that all states have an active participation in outer space activities, say, for example, by making equal contributions to a common body that engages in space exploration. However, it would be unjust to share such a burden among handicapped or disadvantaged states that are patently unlikely to possess the necessary capacity to discharge them such as the Least Developed Countries (LDCs).

This brings us to the inescapable conclusion that scholars must locate the rationale/ justification for the prevailing regime of common ownership and control over outer space in something else apart from bare reference to the concept of

652 Federal Ministry of Science and Technology of Abuja, *National Space Policy and Programmes* (NASRDA, 2005): 3, 5, available at http://www.nasrda.net/NationalSpaceBook.pdf.

653 In September 2003 the observation satellite NigeriaSat-1 was launched on a sun-synchronous orbit from Russia. The satellite was designed to serve the remote sensing need of Nigeria and is also part of the world disaster monitoring constellations (DMC). In May 2007 NASRDA made another landmark achievement by launching a geostationary satellite, NigcomSat-1 into orbit. This satellite is designed to both Nigerian and other African nations' communication needs. Lanre M. Adetoro and Olalekan H. Aro, "Actual Problems of Aviation and Aerospace Systems", *Actual Problems of Aviation and Aerospace Systems*, 2, 29 (2009), available at http://www.kcn.ru/tat_en/science/ans/journals/rasj_cnt/09_2_4.html (accessed 11 January 2011); Economist "Nigeria's Space Programs Per Abuja ad Astra : A Boon or a Boondoggle? Nigeria's Space Programmes", *The Economist*, 11 November 2003, http://www.economist.com/node/2055248 (accessed 11 January 2011).

"equality". Obviously the CHM principle/province of mankind formulas are based on the idea of distributive justice and as Dias correctly notes justice is a process, a complex and ever shifting balance between differing factors, only one aspect of which is equality.[654] Therefore, the better view will be to state that the common ownership over outer space is a factor of universal justice. The prevailing principles operate on the basis of the common good of all states. It must be reiterated that just as it is makes for world order and peace that all states possess exclusive jurisdiction in national airspace, so also is it equally in the universal interest that all spatial territories above sovereign airspace should not belong to any state. Admittedly, this is no more than a value judgement but it is one that accords with international peace and harmony as well as the general tenor of the development of space law so far.

The reservation of mineral exploitation in outer space until a time in the future when an equitable regime of sharing has been established is a political and legal requirement. The right of all states to contribute to the development of this regime has nothing to do with the relative capacities of states to engage in scientific research. It is better to adopt the "theory of justice", used by John Rawls, to explain the fact that inequalities of wealth and authority are irrelevant to the imperatives of maintaining compensating benefits for everyone and, in particular, for the least advantaged members of society. This is because it is undoubtedly an intuitive idea that everyone's wellbeing depends on a scheme of cooperation without which no one could lead a satisfactory life. The division of advantages should be such as to draw forth the willing cooperation of everyone taking part, including if not particularly those who are less well situated.[655] However, much attention must be paid to Dias' view when he wrote that: "It is not enough to work out a just scheme of distribution, from whatever point of view but there is the further problem of getting it accepted and keeping it acceptable; which requires constant redistribution according to changing circumstances."[656]

It might be suggested, therefore, that rather than introduce the concepts of sovereignty or property into outer space what may be needed is a realignment of duties with respect to state participation. It may not be enough for states to send delegates to UN fora where legal and policy issues relating to outer space are deliberated on such as the Committee for Space Research (COSPAR) and the UN Committee on the Peaceful Uses of Outer Space (COPUOS) but they may have to contribute in small ways at least to actual space research and projects. This is more so since the benefits of space science allows developing states to leap frog several decades of technological and economic development. The modalities of this would have to be created under the aegis of the United Nations System.

654 Economist op. cit.: 66.

655 John Rawls (1972) quoted in M.P.A Freeman (ed.) *Lloyd's Introduction to Jurisprudence* (London: Sweet & Maxwell Ltd, 1994): 466.

656 Dias op. cit.: 66.

8.1.1 The significance of morality

The claim by some writers that there is no room for morality in the creation of international law deserves some consideration. It is thought, for instance, that moral considerations are unnecessary in space law since there have been no serious conflicts with respect to outer space. Also connected to this is the argument that the lack of a demarcation between the airspace and outer space has not generated any serious conflicts. Plausible as these arguments may sound, they are not acceptable because it is very possible that serious conflicts have been avoided so far as a result of the moral content and equitable considerations inherent in the law. In other words, military and political conflicts may have been defused well ahead by the existence of those very laws that critics of the present regime claim are unnecessary.[657]

The assertion of Sir Harold Nicolson that "[t]here does not exist such a thing as international morality" is inapplicable to air and space law.[658] The preferred view is that of Arnold Wolfers, who wrote: "[T]he 'necessities' in international politics, and for that matter in all spheres of life (that states) do not push decision and action beyond the realm of moral judgment." Earlier discussion in this book has shown that considerations of morality had an influence on the development of air law. It is sufficient to recall that examples of this include the universal response to the heinous crime of aerial hijack:[659] the formulation of the *aut dedere aut punire* principle and Article 3 of the Chicago Convention, which states that states must refrain from the use of weapons against civil aircraft in flight as being incompatible with elementary considerations of humanity (Declaration 4).[660]

Clearly, this is one of the reasons why the major air and space treaties are replete with provisions that recognise the imperatives of preventing economic avarice from making an inroad into spatial territories.[661] Rules of law, which permit commercial exploitation for private ends, were not advanced even though the Cold War was raging around the time the first space flight and the first Moon landings took place. Indeed, the United States delegate after the approval of the Moon Agreement by the COPUOS and Committee Four of the General Assembly in 1979 stated expressly that this "balanced" and "reasonable" agreement "would have to meet

657 The relation of law to morals was one of the three subjects most debated by 19th-century jurists, the other two being the nature of law and the interpretation of legal history. Jhering called it the Cape Horn of jurisprudence. The juristic navigator who would overcome its perils ran no risk of fatal shipwreck. Pound op. cit.: 215.

658 H. Nicolson, *Diplomacy*, 3rd edn (New York: Oxford University Press, 1973): 147. See Arnold Wolfers, *Discourse and Collaboration Essays on International Politics* (Baltimore, MA: Johns Hopkins University Press, 1973): 147.

659 *Supra*, Chapter 3.4: Control over unlawful interference with civil aviation.

660 Note also the Declaration Adopted by the Council of the International Civil Aviation Organisation at the Ninth Meeting of its 156th Session on 10 March 1999. See *supra*, Chapter 5.3: Aerial intrusion by civil airliners.

661 The preamble of the Chicago Convention (1944), for instance, stipulates that the development of international civil aviation can greatly help to create and preserve friendship and understanding among the nations and peoples of the world, yet its abuse can become a threat to the general security.

the approval of the United States Senate".[662] The United States also committed itself to future participation in negotiations respecting the establishment of an international regime for governing the exploitation of the Moon's natural resources. International law and politics is, therefore, rooted in ethics. States and non-state actors share a basic moral vocabulary. Therefore, if a sceptic of space law poses the question of what stops a state from acquiring outer space resources solely for its exclusive use and in an unbridled manner, the answer would be "international law forbids it". It may also be asserted that unbridled exploitation of the Moon's natural resources without reference to the expectation that it is an international commons also offends international morality. Similarly the weaponisation of outer space by covert or overt means also offends international morality. Needless to say, any state that disregards this thinking attacks the rationale of its own peaceful existence. This reasoning is further reinforced by the experience of the erstwhile USSR, which was a space power and the pioneer in manned space flight. As events turned out the USSR exists no more and Russia, the main successor to its outer space programmes, can hardly fund space exploration. In fact, it has recently lost its last independent space station – the Mir. Fortunately, the USSR had, from the beginning of its involvement with space activities, acknowledged outer space as *res omnium extra commercium.* If this had not been so, it would have secured for itself a merely transient victory.[663] The lesson to be learnt is that contemporary technological capability in any sector (aviation, Antarctica, high seas or outer space) is not good enough reason to advance positions that are not in line with the general international interest.

In essence, to ask whether it is fair and moral that the Moon should be free for all nations at all times is to beg the question. Naturally, a scholar adopting a capitalist, he-who-dares-wins approach would advance the position that if there were gold on the Moon, whoever can fetch it should keep it.[664] The truth, however, is that astronomically the Moon is the earth's natural satellite. Any adverse changes to the Moon's geophysical and environmental state will be of concern to the whole

662 UN Doc. A/SPC/34/19, 6, 7 November 1979.

663 *Supra*, 7.3: The CHM principle and the arguments for and against property rights in space. Note the position taken by Soviet scholar Y.A. Korovin. He eloquently submitted: "of possible conception of outer space – either as 'no one's', belonging to no one (*res nullius*) or as an object of common use (*res communis omnium*) we, in my opinion, should choose the second one, naturally, if the other states take the same stand". Quite prophetically, he continues: "proceeding from the conception of outer space as an object of common use for all mankind, it is necessary to recognise that forms and methods of this 'common possession' can be established only with the mutual consent of all 'users' i.e., as a result of international agreement among all the states interested in the exploration and use of outer space". Y.A. Korovin, "Conquest of Outer Space and Problems of International Relations", *International Affairs* (1959): 90. See also A.S. Piradov (ed.), *International Space Law* (Moscow: Progress Publishers, 1976): 86.

664 Cf. the views of President Dr. Mahithir the erstwhile Prime Minister of Malaysia: "I have heard that the South Pole is made of gold and I want my piece of it." See Michael T. Kyriak "The Future of the Antarctic Treaty System: An Examination of the 'Common Heritage' and 'World Park' Proposals for an Alternative Antarctic Regime," *Auckland University Law Review*, (1992), p. 117; Beck, "Antarctica at the United Nations 1988: Seeking a Bridge of Understanding," Vol 25 *Polar Records*, (1989) p. 329.

of mankind. Its resources may eventually be utilised but at this stage its use must be protected and managed in the interest of both present and future generations of mankind. Since no one is capable of laying claim to the earth then no one can own the Moon.

Another justification of the morality of the prevailing regime lies in the fact that international law particularly Article 2(4) of the UN Charter enjoins all states to eschew wars.[665] History has shown that many major wars have arisen from conflicts over territorial conquests.[666] The moral, therefore, is that the Moon and other celestial bodies must not become the theatre or subject of conflicts in the future. Andem is correct in noting that:

> It is logical and rational that anything common and general to all, calls for the general agreement of those concerned to formulate rules regulating its use and disposal . . . Any exploitation of the moon, for instance, through mining might affect the geophysical structure and composition of the atmosphere surrounding our earth, which would in turn have severe consequences not only on those states now actively engaged in the exploration and exploitation of outer space, but on all other states, developed as well as developing.[667]

There is no doubt that the entire world has an interest in the development of space activities as this writer correctly put it: "This notion of 'general interest' is not to be taken for granted and requires to be re-defined in reference to the fast development of modern technology that mostly benefit those (a few hundred million people) who control them while others (billions of people) still creep in the back, fighting for their essentials in life."[668]

8.2 Summary and conclusions

Outer space is the most recent to be conquered in the trilogy of most important international spaces. Before the utilisation of outer space-based resources can commence on a large scale or for commercial benefits, an elaborate legal regime would have to be developed. At this stage, there is no such regime in place. However, as a result of the CHM principle, which applies to outer space and the celestial bodies, commercial exploitation is presently forbidden. Due to the growing restiveness of certain developed states particularly those states that also have been the keenest to exploit the deep seabed and Antarctica, it is imperative that all

665 All members shall refrain in their international relations from the threat or use of force against the territorial integrity or political independence of any state, or in any other manner inconsistent with the purposes of the United Nations. Note also the 1970 General Assembly Declaration on Principles of International laws concerning Friendly Relations and Co-operation among States UNGA Resolution 2625 (XXV); note, further, Article 2 Moon Agreement (1979).

666 Particular note must be taken of the wars and conflicts resulting from the expansion of colonial territories by the European powers.

667 Andem op. cit.: 95.

668 Patrik A. Salin, "An Overview of US Commercial Space Legislation and Policies – Present and Future", XXVII, 3 *Air and Space Law* (2002): 209–10. 35 USC ssc. 101 *et seq.* (1982).

independent states should consider an exploitation regime shortly. Reasons for this include the potential for damage to the environment and the growing importance of outer space activities in the conduct of technological and scientific development. It is also important to put in place a progressive system before illegal or divergent state practice emerges in terms of space exploration and exploitation.

Before there can be any form of commercial exploitation of resources based in outer space an autonomous regime must be established under space law, with legal bodies of its own and in effective control of all activities. The enterprise that was created for high seabed mining provides a good model on which a similar organ for space exploitation may be based. The employment of "joint ventures" for outer space mining activities as is designed for the deep sea mining is also recommended. However, unlike developments in the deep sea regime the obligation of state parties to finance an Enterprise mining activities must be retained. The amounts to be contributed may, however, be calculated on means-related criteria. In the absence of this regime there can be no legal basis for the introduction of the concept of property or appropriation over resources based in space and on celestial bodies. It is hoped that when eventually such a progressive utilisation regime over space-based resources is put in place there would be scope for active participation in outer space activities, for all states irrespective of size and financial resources. A proportionate contribution system to the common body, which engages in Space exploitation, is desirable. It would clearly be unjust to share equally the burden among handicapped or disadvantaged states.

In terms of environmental concerns it would appear that the emerging space law has a lot to learn from the development of the Antarctic regime. An example, of this is the establishment of the Committee on Environmental Protection. The equivalent of this organ would also be necessary to take control over environmental issues arising from outer space exploration and exploitation. Surely, until such a body is created for outer space as well, there can be no assurance of effective policing of the international community's resolve in keeping outer space as free as possible from human contamination and harmful practices. The establishment of such a specialised body is also a *sine qua non* of the commencement of large-scale mineral exploitation of outer space-based resources.

It is important that an invidious system of special status for certain states such as the "consultative party" system that exist under the Antarctic system is not introduced into outer space law. All states must remain equal in all respects possible under the space treaties. This is to avert similar hostility to the concept of consultative parties and the hegemony they possess as found in relation to the Antarctic regime. The present system also provides the best possible checks on any potential excesses that may arise in the practice of space exploration. Suffice it to repeat that the repercussions of any dangerous activity in space exploration would more likely than not be felt by all states or other states apart from the particular state that conducts the activity. It is not enough to work out a just scheme of distribution, it is imperative that such a system be achieved through compromise and negotiation. This will entail getting it accepted and keeping it acceptable, which, of course, requires constant redistribution according to changing circumstances.

What must be avoided at all costs is a situation wherein a few states share the commercial, technological or scientific benefits that accrue from outer space exploration and exploitation between themselves alone without reference to the imperatives of the regime of international cooperation and equitable sharing stipulated in the major space treaties. Furthermore, it may be reiterated that it is better if no commercial exploitation were to take place on celestial bodies at all than for irreversible environmental damage to be done to the earth through the repatriation of resources from outer space. It needs also to be considered if indeed human exploitation should be allowed to cause irreversible geophysical or environmental degradation to other celestial bodies all in the cause of generating economic profit for the present generation. It may also be better that a moratorium on exploitation is established to cover the better part of this century somewhat along the lines of the 50-year moratorium placed on the exploitation of Antarctica's natural resources, rather than for the world to be drawn into such international conflicts as was witnessed in the scramble by colonialists for overseas territories, in Africa, Asia and Latin America. Last, it must be realised that *not all things that can be exploited should be exploited.* The fact that technology someday makes it possible to commercially exploit the air we breathe by, for instance, harnessing it in some form and making it scarce for resale does not mean that the law should lend legitimisation to such an abomination.

The jurisprudential basis for common ownership, possession and control over outer space can be said to be based on the simple logic that what concerns all must be approved by all. The principles of equality of states, justice and the theory of *nemo dat quod non habet* apply to outer space. Therefore, the better view will be to state that the common ownership over outer space is a factor of universal justice. The use of all potentially finite resources must be regulated tightly under an effective international regime. Thus, resources such as the geostationary orbit need to be regulated under more effective laws, which make the *de facto* commandeering of slots impossible, by a few active states. It is clear that the present position with respect to geostationary orbit use, whereby the orbit is occupied principally by a few countries, accompanied by prompt replacement of spent satellites with newer satellites without any allowance for the future interests of developing states is unacceptable and may eventually culminate in friction and disputes among states. It is not difficult to predict that both the technology and ability to place satellites into geostationary orbit will become feasible to very many states within the course of this century. The ITU policy of "first come first served" may not be adequate to cope with this eventuality and may, in fact, occasion indirect injustice in certain cases.

There is significant scope for the operation of the precepts of morality by states in their exploratory activities in outer space. Just as certain principles regarding the exercise of jurisdiction and control in the airspace have a moral basis so there is also a moral basis for the CHM and province of mankind principle in space law. International morality does forbid the appropriation of outer space for private ends either by the nation state or by private individuals and corporate bodies. This is why technological capability or superiority in any sector (aviation, Antarctica, high seas or outer space) has never been the sole necessary and sufficient reason to secure hegemonic interests over and above the general international interest.

9 Jurisdiction and control *rationae instrumenti* and *rationae personnae* in outer space

9.1 Jurisdiction and control over national and international space stations

It must be emphasised that the advent of space stations is a notable advance in the legal and scientific history of space exploration. The impending proliferation of national and international space stations in this century opens up new vistas for legal studies particularly in the area of civil and criminal jurisdictions. Space stations may be said to consist of two kinds: a long-life spacecraft generally geostationary, placed in free space or an established post or centre constructed on a celestial body.[669] Space stations can exist for a determined or fixed period or can be of a permanent and ongoing nature. There is an increasingly international dimension to the ownership and running of space stations. There is also an increasing involvement and participation at various levels of private organisation in space station activities. These factors cannot but render the legal regime governing space stations more complex compared to that of the national aircraft in foreign airspace or in international airspace.

The international dimension to the operation of space stations reflects in the definition and characterisation offered by many authors on the subject. In fact, as far back as 1974 writers such as Robinson wrote that the international space station is characterised in part as a "quasi-permanent habitat, with mixed sexes, representatives of various cultures, different races, alien life support systems, acute sensory deprivation/overload, etc."[670] Diederiks-Verschoor, in describing the salient features of space station, noted that:

> One characteristic they share is the high level of international co-operation required to assemble them and to ensure their operational efficiency: this is largely due to their multi-purpose activities and the complexity of the structures involved. Another thing they have in common is the size of the structures, a

669 J.E.S. Fawcett, *Outer Space New Challenges to law and Policy* (Oxford: Clarendon Press, 1984): 86.
670 George S. Robinson, "Scientific Renaissance of Legal Theory: The Manned Orbiting Space Stations as a Contemporary Workshop", 8, 1 *International Lawyer* (1974): 20–21.

necessity imposed by their wide-ranging functions. A third common factor is that space stations must be adequately equipped for many years' service.[671]

It should not, however, be assumed that the classification of what is and what is not a space station is an easy task. The differing and sometimes conflicting definitions found in legal literature attest to this. Zhukov states that a space station may be defined as any object or its component launched into outer space or constructed there for the direct exploration and utilisation of outer space, including the Moon and other celestial bodies and also the launch vehicle for such objects or any parts thereof.[672] This definition includes artificial satellites of the Moon, spaceships, orbital platforms, interplanetary stations and laboratories. For this reason, it is considered too wide a definition making it capable of bringing within the scope of discussion objects best treated separately, therefore, creating analytical confusion. A spaceship does not have to be considered under the definition of a space station unless, of course, by a layman whose understanding of what a space station is may be limited to the pop-fiction series "Star Trek". This may be just as inappropriate as defining aircraft and including airports.

For a suitable definition, Diederiks-Verschoor suggests that we must turn to the "Background Paper on Space Stations and the Law", prepared by the United States government. For the purposes of this report, a space station is "an object, or a collection of objects, which is in an intentional long-duration orbit and is, at least in part habitable". An explanatory note points out that this definition explicitly excludes space transportation systems such as the Space Shuttle.[673] It is important to adopt such a flexible definition. This definition is acceptable and has been adopted by this current work. Thus, structures such as Salut-Soyuz, Skylab, Spacelab, Mir, Freedom, Alpha and now the International Space Station (ISS) are all space stations. Nevertheless, some scholars have argued that Skylab was not a real space station because it was not a station that could have been used over a multi-year period.[674]

The functions space stations perform include data gathering, transmitting of information, astronomical observation, zero gravity experimentation, material processing, repairing facilities, energy generation, storage facilities and general scientific research. The construction of huge space stations capable of holding a large population of people is also well within contemplation.[675]

671 I.H. Ph. Diederiks-Verschoor, *An Introduction to Space Law*, 2nd rev. edn (London: Kluwer Law International, 1999): 90–1.

672 G. P. Zhukov, *Artificial Satellites for Meteorology and Radio Communication* (Moscow: Naula Publishers, 1970). See also A.S. Piradov (ed.), *International Space Law* (Moscow: Progress Publishers, 1976): 130.

673 US Congress, Office of Technology Assessment, Space Stations and the Law: selected legal issues, Background Paper, OT-ABP-ISC-41, August 1986.

674 See K.-H. Bockstiegel, "Legal Aspects of Space Stations", *Proceedings 27th Colloquium* (Lausanne, 1984): 225–9.

675 Individual space station components mentioned most in scientific and legal literature are as follows. Laboratory modules for scientific research; unmanned, remote controlled "orbital manoeuvring

9.2 Nature of jurisdiction over space stations

The special problem posed by space stations was correctly identified by the older authorities in space law. Fawcett observed in 1968 that a space station, whether manned or unmanned, on the Moon or Mars, would require freedom from interference with communications between it and the earth and with any observations, physical or astronomical it engages with. If the station is manned then there would be the need for free movement around it and for use of any mineral resources in its vicinity that might serve as fuel.[676] For space stations in free space such as the erstwhile Mir, its successor, Alpha and, of course, the ISS, the problem of space debris is of grave importance. This is because most man-made debris in outer space is found in the vicinity of space stations. It is, in fact, only a matter of time before damage to a space station caused by debris will lead to legal and political conflict.[677]

As was noted earlier, although the major powers are apparently prepared to date to accept the non-national regime created for the celestial bodies (despite recent attempts to introduce appropriation of natural resources) their view has always been that objects and stations placed on these bodies by them are to remain under national ownership, jurisdiction and control.[678] Indeed, it is difficult to see how a permanent station could be maintained without some form of tenure of the ground on or under which it is placed. The same goes for the area around the station sufficient for its maintenance and effective use including necessary rights of way. As a result of this, it may be noted that the closest analogies to the space station in jurisdictional terms are the Antarctic station and artificial islands on the high seas.

According to Fawcett, the essential elements of such tenure should be as follows:

1 that the establishment of the station and the area required for its operation should be notified to the secretary-general of the United Nations
2 that the area so notified be reasonably proportionate to the size, functions and needs of the station
3 that the station and area notified would be under the exclusive jurisdiction of the state of registry of the spacecraft bringing the component parts of the station
4 that the station should be permanent, in the sense that, whether affixed to the ground or not, it is not to be returned to earth again.[679]

vehicles" used to service instruments on platforms and free-flying satellites; orbital construction facilities, fuel dumps and "dry docks" for satellite assembly and maintenance; a reusable orbital transfer vehicle to ferry satellites into geosynchronous orbit. See Diederiks-Verschoor op. cit.: 91; see also W. Von Kries, "State Supervision and Registration" in *Space Stations, Legal aspects of Scientific and Commercial Use in a Framework of Transatlantic Co-operation, Proceedings of an International Colloquium*, ed. K.-H. Bockstiegel (Hamburg, 1984): *passim.*

676 J.E.S. Fawcett, *International Law and the Uses of Outer Space* (New York: Oceana Publications, Inc., 1968): 27.

677 It has been recommended that current space stations could be designed and used for debris-tracking purposes. See Dierderiks-Verschoor op. cit.: 98.

678 Houston Lay and H. Taubenfeld, *The Law Relating to Activities of Man in Space* (Chicago: University of Chicago Press, 1970): 99.

It would appear that all but the last two points are quite essential to the law governing space stations. It would also appear that the author's insistence on the last point arises out of a faulty interpretation of Article 8 of the Space Treaty (1967), which states that a state party on whose registry an object launched into outer space is carried shall retain jurisdiction and control over it. This provision is, however, not designed to deny the real owner of a space object or station the continued enjoyment of property merely because it is carried on the spacecraft of another state (this, of course, is the implication of Fawcett's third point). It is crucial to make this distinction in the light of the recent development of the space shuttle. This particular species of spacecraft has made possible the construction and operation of space stations by a state that cannot or does not want to invest in the building of launching crafts. The shuttle can assemble prefabricated modules and the docking of space shuttles with existing space stations presents unique opportunities of cooperation and specialisation, especially for developing countries. This should not be prevented by an unfortunate interpretation of the law. The important thing is that the owner of the space station or the space object must have registered it on its own registry and that of the UN as later on stipulated by the Registration Convention (1975).

In short, for the purposes of determination of jurisdiction it is the state, which registers the space station with the UN, and on its own register, that matters and not the state, which registers the spacecraft. As regards the thesis that the space station must remain permanently in space, this is a non-existent rule in any space treaty and it does not serve any useful purpose. Whether or not a space station or parts of it is returned to earth, the important thing is that the tenure of its existence in outer space should have been successfully and legally obtained before it is launched. Indeed, the introduction, withdrawal and reintroduction of the same space station would not be unsupportable by the law. Furthermore, it is reiterated that jurisdiction and control over all space object launched by a state follows such objects no matter where they proceed in the universe (Space Treaty Article VIII).

Particularly at this stage in the development of space exploration it is important to address the exact nature and scope of the powers of an operator (whether private business or state controlled) in the operation of a space station. In comparison to the jurisdiction and control over the airspace, jurisdiction over space stations is potentially a much more technical and complex area of the law. Unlike aircraft that have the sole purpose of transportation, space stations can be of much more value in scientific experimentation and exploitation including remote sensing activities. For instance, there is the question of legitimate mining and use of mineral resources on the Moon. Space manufacturing of drugs and other materials are engaged on in space stations. These problems have no analogy in the law of the air because very little if anything at all can be exploited in the airspace. Besides assuming it were even possible for an aircraft to stay stationary in the airspace for

679 Fawcett op. cit.: 27.

long periods of time, such permanence can never create any right over territory or present the same legal problems a space station can. If anything, such an aircraft can only create a continuous violation of territorial sovereignty and cannot claim a freedom from interference from the offended territorial state.[680] The only real similarities between an aircraft and the space station whether it is a simple orbital platform or a small space laboratory are the requirements of registration and nationality.

It has already been concluded that the idea of creation of property rights over space-based resources is not supportable under contemporary space law. But speaking particularly of proprietary or property rights over minerals found on celestial bodies on which a space station exists (at this stage in the course of things principally the Moon), a distinction would have to be made. This distinction is between the use of resources for the conduct of scientific exploration and for the sustenance of the mission on one hand and the mining of resources for the purpose of commercial repatriation to earth on the other. The former is expressly permitted under existing rules particularly Article 6(2)[681] of the Moon Agreement (1979) and the latter is expressly forbidden under the various rules that have already been considered.[682]

Therefore, it is a trite observation that prudence must be the watchword of any state that makes use of resources on a manned or unmanned space station based on the Moon. Due regard must also be given to the status of celestial bodies under the CHM principle and the province of all mankind formula. Contrariwise, where the resource made use of is of an inexhaustible class, the prohibition of national appropriation enshrined in Article II of the Outer Space Treaty (1967) would not apply. Thus, this prohibition will not apply to the spatial utilisation of solar energy. Any prohibition of such use would only be against good reason and commonsense.[683] In the absence of any assurance that states would continue to use good reason and commonsense in all matters, particularly where immense commercial gains are at stake, a clarification of inexhaustible resources would eventually have to be made by the UN Scientific Committee on Outer Space. This would have to be done taking into consideration present scientific knowledge. It is probably worthy of note that the principal spacefaring nations such as China, France, India, Russia and the USA, are all parties to the Outer Space Treaty and are bound by the reciprocity rule, whereas only Australia, Austria, France and India are the

680 The consequences of such hovering and trespass have been treated earlier. *Supra*, Chapter 5.

681 The Article provides that: "The States Parties shall have the right to collect on and remove samples of its mineral and other substances . . . States Parties may in the course of scientific investigations also use mineral and other substances of the moon in quantities appropriate for the support of their missions."

682 *Supra*, sections 4.1–4.4. It is also to be noted that, in the absence of an international regime to govern the exploitation of the natural resources on the moon envisaged under Article 11(5) and to be implemented under Article 18 of the Moon Agreement (1979), space stations must not be operated in a manner as to exploit natural resources.

683 See Stephen Gorove, 10, 3 *The International Lawyer* (1976): 534.

technologically advanced states that are parties to the Moon Agreement (1979). Thus, with the impending entry of China into actual space exploration on the Moon, the applicable rule relating to any proposed visit to an American space station thereon will appear to be that based on the principle of reciprocity alone. China would have to conclude special negotiations on these terms with the USA and may not rely only on advance notice of any visit.

It is perhaps very important to a discussion on the nature of jurisdiction over space stations to highlight the differences between the system of visits to space stations based in free space and those based on the Moon. The general rule is that space stations must be open for visits by the representatives of other states on the basis of reciprocity Article XII of the Outer Space Treaty (1967). This same provision requires that an advance notice of any visit should be given to the state of registry. This is in order that appropriate consultations may be held to secure safety and to avoid interference with normal operations. It should be noted that the Outer Space Treaty (1967) being a legal instrument, which applies to space stations generally, has the need to emphasise on the aspects of agreement and reciprocity. The Moon Agreement (1979), by way of contrast, disposes of the requirement of reciprocity. As long as reasonable advance notice is given, a state party may move in to other states' stations to assure itself that the activities therein are compatible with the provisions of the Agreement (Article 15(1)).[684]

With all these points in mind it is clear that the jurisdiction a state has over the portion of outer space occupied by its space station is in no way exclusive but functional. This is probably what gives birth to the concept of functional jurisdiction advanced by Ryszard Hara as a substitute for the concept of exclusive jurisdiction over space stations whether national or international. Functional jurisdiction is impressively described as encompassing:

> the right of persons to affect property, things, events and occurrences in designated zones in outer space or areas on celestial bodies, by legislative, executive or judicial means, to the extent and for the period of time that is necessary to safeguard and secure its rights to explore and exploit outer space including celestial bodies.[685]

9.3 Nationality and registration over space stations

Just as it is required of any aircraft that conducts international flights, it is important to note that the nationality principle applies to and determines jurisdiction over

684 For the number of states potentially subject to this regime, see *supra*, note 633. It may be envisaged that the USA and China will probably be the first states to put these provisions to test this century. See *supra*, Chapter 8.1 (particularly notes 639 and 641). See also Appendix IV.

685 See Ryszard Hara, "Jurisdiction of States in Outer Space", 17 *Polish Yearbook of International Law*, (1988): 80–1; see also Imre Anthony Csbaffi, *The Concept of State Jurisdiction in International Space Law: A Study in the Development of Space Law in the United Nations* (The Hague: Martinus Nijthoff, 1971): 24, 131.

space stations. This, in a sense, completes a legal tradition that, as noted earlier, began with the law of the sea in relation to ships and then moved on to apply to Antarctic stations and equipment as well as aircraft. The nationality of space stations as well as other space objects is established by the fact of registration by a state. Accordingly, the space station is subject under this principle to the authority of the state of registration. Every state is entitled to determine the conditions of granting its nationality to space stations and a state may indeed assign its rights over a space station to another state or international organisation by agreement, registrable under Article 102 of the UN Charter.[686] The rule of nationality and flag jurisdiction over space station is as important as it is in the law of the air because it determines international responsibility for national activities. Thus, the flag state has not just jurisdiction over but also responsibility for its national activities conducted on or in relation to space stations. This principle applies whether its private corporations or the state itself runs the space station.

Kish suggests that national markings of "space stations constitute the evidence of nationality established by registration".[687] This statement is far from being false, but, it must be noted that just as it is in relation to aircraft, the best evidence is to be found not just in the physical markings but in the fact of registration and inclusion in the prescribed register, in this case on the registry of the UN (opened for that purpose) and on the registry of the state itself. To begin with examination of the markings on a space station in the event of a dispute may have to be conducted *in situ*, an obvious difficulty not only because of the distance but also because as a symbol the markings may be difficult to locate. This is more so with the construction of some stations, which according to some authors may be up to five kilometres in size.[688] Again, markings on the space station just as on an aircraft may indeed be altered at any time. That is not, however, to suggest that the markings on space objects and on aircraft have little or no utility. Clear instances of this lie in the use of physical markings as identification in the case of aircraft trespass and identifying data in the case of crash landing into foreign territory of space objects and components thereof.

This, of course, brings us to a consideration of the issue of registration. While registration of aircraft operated by international operating agencies is dealt with under Article 77 of the Chicago Convention the principles of registration of spacecraft and space stations are enunciated in Article XI of the Space Treaty (1967); General Assembly Resolution 1721 (XVI) of 20 December 1961 (International Cooperation in the Peaceful Uses of Outer Space) and the mandatory system established by the Registration Convention (1975).

686 Fawcet op. cit.: 27; John Kish, *The Law of International Spaces* (Leiden: A.W. Sijthoff International, NV, 1973): 137.

687 Ibid.

688 J.E.S. Fawcett, *Outer Space New Politics and Challenges* (Oxford: Clarendon Press, 1984): 22.

689 Gorbiel, "Large Space Structures: The Need for a Special Treaty Regulation", *Proceedings 27th Colloquium* (Lausanne, 1985): 247–50.

Later it will be necessary to elaborate on the general issue of registration of spacecraft and objects. What must be done here is to draw attention to the peculiar problems presented by the registration of international space stations. Reference has already been made to the controversy presented over the years with respect to the registration of aircraft jointly owned by several states. The position of the law is that no matter how many states jointly own an airline the registration of the individual aircraft must be carried on the register of a particular single state. This position, however, is unsatisfactory within certain academic circles. The position of the law with respect to registration of spacecraft is, unfortunately, not as clear. The problem as noted by Gorbel is that the Registration Convention (1975) contains a gap as regards registration of space stations specifically.[689] A similar regime to that of aircraft is, however, dictated by Article II(2) of the Registration Convention with respect to "space objects". The question then is whether "space objects" include space stations.

The answer to this is contentious considering that several space objects may together constitute one space station. It is reasonable that the present trend towards evolution of multinational space stations would necessarily lead to a reassessment of the international instruments governing registration of space vehicles and objects. It has, in fact, been argued in certain quarters that the practical application of the principle of registration as determinant of jurisdiction as enshrined in Article VIII of the Space Treaty might prove to be too rigid to be generally accepted by the international community. This is probably what is responsible for the prevalent trend of supplanting existing international legislation with supposedly more flexible regime established by parties that are involved in the space station projects.[690]

For instance, an International Government Agreement (IGA) was developed in 1988 to regulate affairs between the partner states to the Columbus Programme under the International Space Station Project.[691] The partner states are mainly the USA, the European Space Agency, Canada and Japan. Article 5(1), which covers registration, states that: "In accordance with Article II of the Registration Convention each Partner shall register as space object the flight elements which it provides (listed in the Annex) to make up the station." The European partners having delegated the responsibility of registration to the ESA have that agency acting for them and in their collective interests. Furthermore, Article 5(2) stipulates that pursuant to Article VIII of the Space Treaty and Article II of the Registration Convention, each partner shall retain jurisdiction and control over the elements it registers in accordance with Article 5(1) and over personnel in or on the space station. With the admission of Russia into the space station programme in September 1993, it was agreed to replace the IGA (1988) with a new agreement,

690 Cf. *supra*, Chapter 2.3.2: Nationality of aircraft and the question of "genuine link". See also H.L. Van Traa-Engelman, *Commercial Utilization of Outer Space: Law and Practice* (London: Martinus Nijhoff, 1993): 54–5.

691 Done at Washington DC, 29 September 1988. See IGA Proceedings of the Colloquium on Manned Space Stations – Legal Issues, Paris 7–8 November 1989, ESA SP-305, ISBN 92-9092-062-9, January 1990.

which was signed on 29 September 1998.[692] The new IGA retained nearly all the original responsibilities in the management and control of the programme including registration.[693]

The question, however, is why must one single state of registry be appointed for a group of states when they commonly own an aircraft whereas it is possible for a single space station to be severally registered as if into shares?[694] Is it air law that needs to be brought to maturity on the reality of international cooperation and shared liability or is it space law that must proceed with caution in this guise? The position adopted by this thesis is that if a space station is to function as a single unit there is no point in the separate registration of the flight elements or the component parts of what is for all intents and purposes a single unit. The directive consideration already exists in the provisions of Article II(2) of the Registration Convention (1975) which states that: "Where there are two or more launching states in respect of any such space object, they shall jointly determine which one of them shall register the object in accordance with paragraph 1 of this article." While it cannot be disputed that there are factual differences if nothing else between an aircraft and a space station, it can still be said that the desire to determine where exactly liability lies when something goes wrong is the rationale for the requirement that dictates in air law and in the Registration Convention (1975) that one single member state be the state of registry of every aircraft or space object. This clarity may be jeopardised when a single functioning space station is registered in parts. It must, however, be admitted that prior to the docking together of the component parts in space there may be the need to register the parts separately. The registration achieved in this way reattaches to the space object if and when it breaks off and comes away from the entire space station for the purpose of a managed return to Earth. In that case, another registration may be necessary for the entire unit when it starts operating as a single body. There would then have to be appointed a single state of registry for the space station as a whole.[695]

On a last note on the issue of registration: it may again be stated that it is paramount that the old and familiar problem to the international lawyer, i.e. flags of convenience, must not be allowed to flourish or exist with respect to spacecraft and particularly space stations.[696] Concurrent with the increasing commercialisation of outer space activities in recent years the problem of flags of convenience even with respect to space stations is not far fetched. Therefore, it must be concluded with respect to aircraft that states wishing to register space stations

692 For text of the 1998 IGA, see 26 *Journal of Space Law* (1998): 90–98.

693 It confirms the leading role of the USA and most of the changes relate to technical realities of Russia's participation including the revision of the European contributions to the project. See, further, A. Farand, "Space Station Cooperation: Legal Arrangements" in *Outlook on Space Law over the Next 30 Years*, ed. G.L. Laferranderie and D. Crowther (1997): 90–98.

694 Cf. the fate of the Arab states attempts to register aircraft under the Pan-Arab Airline in 1960 and that of the registration of aircraft belonging to Air Afrique. *Supra*, Chapter 2.3.2: Nationality of aircraft and the question of "genuine link".

695 Cf. Gorbiel op. cit.: 248–9.

696 Cf. *supra*, the discussions on the problem of flag of convenience and need to pre-empt it in air law.

must be made to demonstrate a "genuine link" with the private organisations involved. This position is consistent with developments in international law since the *Nottebohm case*.[697]

9.4 Civil jurisdiction over space stations

Although we have largely left out civil matters in our analysis of jurisdiction over the airspace we nevertheless considered the aspects of civil liability for aviation damage. Therefore, it is necessary to mention briefly some aspects of civil jurisdiction in respect of the emerging law of space stations. Again, although jurisdiction *ratione personae* in outer space generally is to be treated later, certain considerations peculiar to space stations must be observed here. The basic problem presented by space stations both in civil and criminal terms is that of jurisdiction and control. To this extent, there is a similarity between space stations and aircraft in airspace. Space stations may be manned or unmanned, national or international, floating in open space or based on celestial bodies. Similarly, aircraft may be piloted or unpiloted, nationally owned or owned by two or more states and may be traversing in airspace or may have landed on some *terra firmae* or even on the sea. The connecting thread between these situations is that international law grants civil and criminal jurisdiction to the flag state based on the need for control and determination of liability. The extent of this control is always shifting and dependent on the advancement of technology and the prevalent mischief to be cured. George S. Robinson adopts a rather romantic view of the civil and criminal problems posed by the advent of space stations. He wrote:

> Legal relations among space station participants, alone while existing in a shared, long duration, confined, alien life-support environment, will rest upon a new theory of law, i.e. such space station participants will establish new value-forming processes and consequent judgments, based on the manifestations of totally different neurophysiological phenomena. Concisely, any legal theory evolved must consider such space station participants either as neo-colonialists or preferably, as "alien" life forms to evolve their own juridical systems while in long-duration flight, and to be dealt with on at-arms-length basis by Earth-indigenous institutions.[698]

These remarkable submissions open up the writer to criticisms of exaggeration but there are already a number of civil issues that have received judicial attention in some states having a bearing on the operation of space stations. For example, the provisions governing civil liability over mishaps arising from the operations of a space station are likely to become one of the most contested areas of space law. It is notable that Article 16(3) (a) of the IGA (1988) regulating the Columbus Space Station Project incorporated rules, which are now common practice in the drafting

697 ICJ Reports 1955: 4.
698 Robinson op. cit.: 28.

of international space contracts.[699] Very much unlike the practice in aviation law, this provision allows for a cross-waiver of liability in relation to claims based on damage, whatever the legal basis (including negligence of every degree and kind) that may arise out of a space station's operation.[700] Among the things that may go wrong on a space station is that a module or component part may fail to function altogether. This may affect the entire workings of the station. In any such eventuality, the cross-waiver signed by the parties will become definitive.

Prior to recent developments in space law and particularly with respect to aircraft the position of the manufacturer is largely defined by the concept of product liability. There is general agreement that this concerns the liability resulting from damage caused by a defective product. There is, in fact, no international convention regulating the rights and duties of a manufacturer, neither in space law nor in air law, although there exist regional agreements and directives of the European Community. The basis here both in air law and space law is always strict liability of the manufacturer.[701] If a product turns out to be defective after it has been sold, there are under Anglo-Saxon law two remedies available against the manufacturer: (1) breach of warranty and (2) tort. But when large-scale expansion of space activities started and with the advent of private manufacturers and users of space equipment and stations, questions regarding the liability of private manufacturers became important. This is what has led to the invention of purely commercial devices such as the cross-waivers referred to above.

Again closely linked to the position of the manufacturer in space law and air law is the position of the insurer. In neither sphere of law has the contract of insurance been regulated on an international level. Whereas particularly in space law this is a lacuna that needs filling considering that space operations insurance including those involving space stations has been provided mostly by private companies. The result of the apparent lacuna in international regulation of civil liability arising out of space contracts is that a patchwork of legal rules is being developed through the device of the Memorandum of Understandings (MOU) and national acts such as the US Commercial Space Launchings Act (CSLA) of 1978. A deplorable consequence of this is that legislation over matters of international concern is exclusively being shaped by a few states, as a matter of fact mainly by the USA. For instance, if a small state enters into a contract with a US launcher to place its space station in space, it would appear that if for any reason at all the launching fails and the space station is lost that state would have few or no remedies against the private

699 Especially in space contracts entered into in the USA. Notably, the cross-waiver provisions are also retained in the IGA (1998) dealt with later in our discussions on criminal jurisdictions in space stations.

700 The liability cross-waiver will, however, not apply to: claims made by a partner state and its own related entities or between its own related entities; claims made by a natural person, his/her survivors, subrogees estate for any injuries, death occurring to that natural person; or claims for damage caused by wilful misconduct (Article 16(d)).

701 For an air law civil case concerning the subject of "warranty", see *Helicopter Sales (Australia) Pty, v. Rotor-works Pty. Ltd.*, High Court of Australia; 1 Air Law: 189–90.

US launcher at least not in US courts. It is also clear that for a long time to come, the USA will always be favoured by the contracts that allocate insurance responsibility.

In *Martin Marietta Corporation v. International Telecommunications Satellite Organisation (Intelsat)*,[702] Martin Marietta contracted with Intelsat for the launching of two satellites on Titan II rockets. One of them failed to reach its proper position in the correct orbit, which resulted in substantial losses for Intelsat. The contracting parties were in agreement that the state with civil jurisdiction over the case is the USA and litigation centred over the questions of liability. Intelsat's position was that the contract on which Martin Marietta relied did not relieve it of liability for breach of contract. Intelsat also believed that through faulty programming and testing Martin Marietta had breached the contract, including its obligation to use its "best efforts" to secure the launching, that Martin Marietta had been negligent or grossly negligent, in failing in its "duty of care" and, last, that Martin Marietta had committed negligent or grossly negligent misrepresentation and failed to disclose material information.

Martin Marietta demanded confirmation and enforceability of (1) the exclusive remedy provisions available to Intelsat; (2) the so-called "cross-waivers" in the contract with Intelsat that were required under the US CSLA (1978). The decision reached by the Federal District Court dismissed the claims based on tort, because it found that Intelsat's damages arising from the satellite's failure were essentially economic in nature. Under Maryland law, a party cannot sue for purely economic loss unless an entirely separate duty of care exists. The court concluded that "equally sophisticated parties, who have the opportunity to allocate risks to third party insurance or among one another, should be held only to those duties specified by the agreed upon contractual terms and not by general tort duties imposed by state law". The court also dismissed Intelsat's tort claims on the basis that they were barred by the cross-waiver in the CSLA contract. It was stated categorically that the CSLA (1978) changed the law with the creation of an exception to the general rule that parties are not permitted to exclude liability for gross negligence.

Similar *ratio* have been followed repeatedly in the USA and legal experts predict it will be the law in other spacefaring jurisdictions.[703] The correctness and fairness of the *ratio* of this case will depend on which side of the divide the person examining it stands. To the tort lawyer, the decisions reached may seem reasonable. However, the decision may appear suspect to anyone who considers the peculiar needs and protection desirable for developing states presently involved in space activities and those who may in the near future summon up the necessary resources to engage in space station activities. The reality of the situation as it is dictates that US private concerns handle the highly technical aspects of production and launching of space stations. Accordingly, it is essential that any developing state, which participates in

702 See 19 *Journal of Space Law* (1991): 173–6. See also Diederiks-Verschoor op. cit.: 156, 160.

703 See, for instance, *Appalachian Insurance Co. v. McDonnell Douglas*, 18 *Journal of Space Law* (1990): 41–4. See also *AT&T v. Martin Marietta*, 23 *Journal of Space Law* (1995): 177–83. Note: this case was settled eventually.

commercial space ventures, protect itself to the fullest against unsuccessful operations caused by negligent and or accidental failures. This, however, is a Herculean task given the uneven bargaining power and prevalent practice of the application of the strictest limitation of liability, dictated by the practical commercial considerations under the civil laws of the USA and other spacefaring nations.[704]

9.5 Civil jurisdiction and intellectual property in the operation of space stations

Another intriguing aspect of civil jurisdiction over space stations is that which deals with intellectual property, where the layman perspective may find this difficult to relate with because of the territorial connotations of intellectual property regimes. Patent protection particularly is situated within the practice of territoriality and, therefore, presents special problems in the context of actions and events that occurred in outer space.[705] In truth, space activities and engagements nearly always involve various intersections with intellectual property. These range from the branding and copyright of spacecraft and logos to literally thousands of existing patents and design registrations and other intellectual property claims held with respect to space objects. It has been estimated that over 30,000 products and technologies have evolved from NASA's aeronautics and space programmes alone. These include graphite composites in tennis rackets, fishing poles and golf clubs, originally developed from spacecraft materials, heated ski goggles, which were adapted from helmets used for space walks, athletic shoes with special wedged heels design, movement detection burglar alarms and even freeze-dried foods, which was tried for the first time in 1962 for the John Glen's orbits.[706] Other derived inventions from space exploration activities include x-ray machines, solar heating systems, smoke detectors, solar calculators, automatic teller machines, liquid crystal watches, breathalysers, offshore oil rigs, monitoring exercise machines, metalised emergency blankets and airport luggage. This was all before the entrance of private enterprise into outer space activities. Now that commercial ventures have become more closely related to space exploration it is clear that specialist law will have to developed to cope with the weighty issues of intellectual property rights that will operate in relation to the zero gravity environment of outer space.

There are two possible directions that argumentation on the issue of international IP law for outer space activities may take. Free resource IP scholars would attempt

704 Note that the monetary requirements to engage in space station activities are mind boggling and crippling to struggling economies. The price for delivery of scientific material to Mir was about $20,000 a kilogram ($9,000 a pound). Dierderiks-Verschoor op. cit.: 99. See also R.V. Pino Jr; F.A. Silane, "Civil Liability in Commercial Space Ventures under United States Law", 21 *Air and Space Lawyer* (1993): 166–7.

705 Consider some of the arguments we traversed above in Chapter 1 about the difficulties that may attest departure from the general rule observed by states to restrict themselves to the maintenance of a strictly territorial legislative purview.

706 Alejandro Piera, "Intellectual Property in Space Activities. An Analysis of the United States Patent Regime", XXIX, 1 *Air and Space Law* (2004): 42.

to sustain the argument that space discoveries and inventions should enjoy universal access and that the benefits of space discoveries should not be constrained by the rules of international intellectual property. Similar views are discernible in the submissions of sceptics of the current international intellectual property regime especially those that consider the contents of the regime as predominantly geared towards protecting Western hegemony.[707] In other words, the zero gravity atmosphere of outer space presents the best possible opportunity to jettison the weight of the international intellectual property rights system and to adopt a more inclusive regime of sharing of knowledge and opportunities. The liberal capitalist ideology of IP should have no place in a place that, by both law and reason, belongs to all mankind. The flag state(s) intellectual property laws should not be allowed to move into outer space along with its space instrumentation.

A second approach and the more predominant view follows the practice of space going states particularly led by the USA to adopt the floating island theory by which national jurisdiction and laws follow the craft wherever it may venture in the universe. As elsewhere in the field of space law a continuum is, thus, followed from cases relating to the seas like *Gardner v. Howe* (1865)[708] and *Marconi Wireless Telco v. USA* (1942).[709] In these cases, the courts extended US laws to correct patent infringements that were made on board US vessels on the high seas. Hence the emerging consensus in academic writing is that as long as participants in space activities do not exclude others in access to space activities or put obstacles to the experimentation by other states in a manner that will be illegitimate or criminal in international law, there can be little contradiction in allowing states and commercial bodies to retain intellectual property rights in space.[710] Hence it appears that the view of the practising spacefaring states is that the general principles of international intellectual property will prevail on space stations and just because experimentation takes place in outer space would not allow actors whether state or private to do that which they are prevented to do on earth such as patenting forms of life or indigenous plants taken from any parts of the earth.

It is notable that the precise workings of the rules of intellectual property law in relation to outer space activities is very much made up along the lines of exigencies and in accordance with the wishes and interests of the spacefaring states that engage in space stations affairs. United Nations treaties on outer space contained no explicit provisions about intellectual property rights for things made or invented in space.

707 A growing body of scholarship insists that global intellectual property system is privatising humanity's common cultural heritage. It also argues that privatisation and monopolisation actually does discourage creativity and invention. See Alan Story, Colin Darch and Deborah Halbert, *The Copy/South Dossier: Issues in the Economic , Politics and Ideology of Copyright in the Global South* (Canterbury: Copy/South Research Group, 2006): 11–23, 154; see also A. Ngenda, "The Nature of the International Intellectual Property System: Universal Norms and Values or Western Chauvinism?", 14, 1 *Information & Communications Technology Law* (2005): 59–79.

708 9 F.Cas. 1157 (CCD Mass. 1865).

709 53 USP.Q 246 (Ct Cl 1942).

710 Piera op. cit.: 47.

However, successive inter-governmental agreements on the space station and the NASA Directive on Space Station Intellectual Property provide some useful guidance.[711] There is also no direct analogy or verifiable instance provided in air law but it might be said that when an invention takes place in a country's airspace it takes place for all intents and purposes in that country's territory and, therefore, is subject to its laws. By similar reasoning if an invention takes place on an aircraft bearing the nationality of a state, that state's intellectual property laws would normally operate subject, of course, to the inventor's nationality, choice of jurisdiction to register the invention as well as applicable pre-existing contracts.

The first provisions on the issue of jurisdiction over international intellectual property rights were presented in the form of Article 21 of the IGA (1988). This provision established a nationality basis for intellectual property and patent rights. The questions raised by this provision are many.

First, it is significant that it appears to have extended territorial jurisdiction directly into space. This is as opposed to the prior understanding of extraterritorial rights retained by states over flag vessels and instrumentalities when in foreign territory or in international spaces. In a sense, this jump in legal conceptualisation was made without any particularly convincing effort to acknowledge that monumental shift in legal categorisation of state jurisdiction. Questions may, thus, be raised as to whether the fiction of territoriality imported into space law in 1988 had any proper basis in international law. It was quite possible to achieve the desirable result of protection of patent rights over inventions and discoveries made on space stations without extending national jurisdiction into outer space. The IGA (1988) regime created certain problems throughout the period of its life. Although the agreement has been replaced by the 1998 Agreement, on the entry into force of which the 1988 ceased to be in force, it is still relevant to note the legal issues raised by the territorial jurisdiction approach to space invention:

1 An invention in space will establish the same priority as if it had taken place in the very country whose nationals makes the invention. This is in contrast with the position of an invention made on foreign territory. It is preferred wisdom to hold that such an invention not having taken place on national territory but in *territorium communis res extra commercium* takes place (at least in a loose sense) in foreign territory.
2 A space activity conducted *bona fide* by one state may evoke without its knowledge an infringement of another state's patent laws.
3 Legitimate scientific experiments and activities conducted in the environment of outer space may because of the fiction of territoriality run foul of national

711 Intellectual Property and the International Space Station: Creation, Use, Transfer, and Ownership and Protection, National Aeronautics and Space Administration, Office of the General Counsel (September 1999), available online at http://www.hq.nasa.gov/ogc/iss/ (accessed 19 February 2005); Henry R. Hertzveld and Frans G. von der Dunk, "Bringing Space Law into the Commercial World: Property Rights without Sovereignty", 6, 1 *Chicago Journal of International Law* (2005): 81–99.

laws and offenders could ultimately be treated as if their actions occurred within a state's territory.[712]

In the final analysis, Article 21 of the IGA (1988) constituted a threat against the spirit of cooperation and lack of territorial jurisdiction, which the main space treaties stand for, particularly the Declaration on International Cooperation in the Exploration and Use of Outer Space (1996).[713] The issues highlighted earlier underscore the dangers inherent when space law rules pertaining to jurisdiction and control are developed piecemeal through a proliferated arrangement by a select group of states. The emerging trend in both air law and space law as have been argued so far is that the technologically advanced states have sought to exploit any equivocation or lacunae in the law to advance national hegemonic interests. Not surprisingly, the US legislature purportedly acting under obligations to bring the US laws on patent rights and inventions in conformity with the IGA (1988) added a new section to the existing US Patent Act.[714] This section called the Patents in Space Act[715] stipulates: "Any invention made, used or sold on a space object or component thereof under the jurisdiction or control of the U.S. shall be considered to be made, used or sold within the U.S."

Note should be taken that the terminology employed in the Act is "jurisdiction or control". This obviously deviates from the formula "jurisdiction and control" used in the International Space Station Agreement (i.e. IGA (1988)) which actually conforms to the wording of Article VIII of the Space Treaty (1967). The

712 Traa-Engelman op. cit.: 298–9. Again, what seems to be of concern to some authors is that the space powers could through such domestic legislation be gradually introducing territorial jurisdiction and sovereignty into outer space. Salin formulates a balanced view of this development thus: "The United States is the predominant space power on earth, due to its sheer economic, technological and political might. But the business dimension does not explain the whole story. The United States also administers a full-fledged body of space laws and regulations that is unchallenged in volume, sophistication, and coherence by any other nation, or group of nations on earth . . . One cannot but observe the will of US lawmakers to grant their nation the legislative means to support a flourishing industry so that it can maintain its leadership imposition far ahead of its competitors, political ones in a recent past with the USSR, and commercial ones nowadays with Western Europe and Asia . . . In this last respect, we should not forget that Outer Space does not belong to anyone and should beware of inroads that are right now carved into this last common heritage of mankind." See Patrik A. Salin, "An Overview of US Commercial Space Legislation and Policies – Present and Future", XXVII, 3 *Air and Space Law* (2002): 236, note 72; see also Francis Lyall, "The Role of the World Interest in Space Communication Activities", 52nd Astronautical Congress, 1–5 October 2001, Toulouse (France), paper reference IISL-00-IISL.2.02.

713 A/RES/51/122; 83rd plenary meeting 13 December 1996.

714 35 USC ssc. 101 *et seq.* (1982).

715 The US House of Representatives on 20 July 1989 passed HR 2946, a resolution to amend Chapter 10, title 35, USC, with respect to the use of inventions in outer space. The text is reproduced in 18, 1 *Journal of Space Law* (1999): 89–91. Subsequently, a similar US Senate measure, Section 459 was passed in lieu – clearing the measure for the president. The text of version 5 of Section 459 passed on 7 November 1990 has been reproduced in the 2 *Journal of Space Law*. The regulation appears as Section 105 of 35 USC (1982).

significance of the wording of the US Act is that it underlies the possibility that the USA may, in fact, have jurisdiction over a space station but may not be in control of it. An example of this lies in Station Alpha jointly established by states including the USA and its arch rival Russia. In order to avoid conflict the following proviso was added to the aforementioned Act:

> Inventions made, used or sold in outer space on a foreign registered space object or any components thereof, shall not be subject to US patent laws, even if the object or component is at the time within the jurisdiction or control of the US, unless it is specifically so agreed in an international agreement between the US and the State of registry.

The fact is that through these provisions the USA again appears to have incorporated into its national laws what Traa-Engelman correctly refers to as the "fiction of territoriality"[716] introduced by the IGA (1988). There is also the implication that other national laws such as the US Invention Secrecy Act[717] also applies to outer space and other states must take them in to account. It suffices to query here the necessity for these rules in view of the fact that protection of rights to inventions and patents may be held to flow from Articles VIII and IX of the Outer Space Treaty (1967).

In 1998 a new Multilateral Space Station Agreement was executed involving the existing partners and a new partner, Russia.[718] This agreement strives to provide a clearer regime for the control of intellectual property rights but does not represent any radical departure from its predecessor. For the purposes of the 1998 Agreement, "intellectual property" is understood to have the meaning of Article 2 of the Convention Establishing the World Intellectual Property Organisation.[719] Therein "intellectual property" shall include the rights relating to: literary, artistic and scientific works; performances of performing artists, phonograms, and broadcasts; inventions in all fields of human endeavour; scientific discoveries; industrial designs; trademarks, service marks and commercial names and designations; protection against unfair competition; and all other rights resulting from intellectual

716 Traa-Engelman op. cit.: 299.

717 35 USC Sections 181–8 (1982).

718 Agreement among the Government of Canada, Governments of Member States of the European Space Agency, the Government of Japan, the Government of the Russian Federation, and the Government of the United States of America Concerning Cooperation on the Civil International Space Station Agreement signed at Washington 29 January 1998; entered into force 27 March 2001. With Annex and Arrangement signed at Washington 29 January 1998; entered into force 29 January 1998. Treaties and Other International Acts Series 12927 also available at http://www.spacelaw.olemiss.edu/ library/ space/International_Agreements/Mulilateral/ISS_IGA/1998%20-%20Agreement%20Among%20Canada%20ESA%20States,%20Japan,%20Russia,%20and%20the%20United.pdf (accessed 29 August 2010).

719 Done at Stockholm on 14 July 1967 and as amended on 28 September 1979, available on the website of the World Intellectual Property Rights Organisation www.wipo.org.

activity in the industrial, scientific, literary or artistic fields. Furthermore, for the purposes of intellectual property law, an activity occurring in or on a space station flight element shall be deemed to have occurred only in the territory of the partner state of that element's registry, except that for ESA-registered elements any European partner state may deem the activity to have occurred within its territory. As the ESA itself explains:

> [A]ny European Partner State may extend its national law to the European elements and elect to deem the activity to have occurred within its territory. In theory, an invention occurring in the European Laboratory could then be deemed to have occurred in France or Germany. An inventor having used the European Columbus Laboratory facilities may file for a patent anywhere in the world to protect his invention, but he will need to choose one of the European Partner States' territories to determine where his invention originally took place.[720]

A lack of elaborate rules on this important issue is quite endearing in itself and is probably the result of the predominantly science focused concern of the planners of the ISS. It has been shown in other areas of scientific exploration that we discussed earlier that scientific men have little patience for legal details and niceties. The current legal situation is, however, fraught with dangers as well. Even if an inventor chooses a particular partner state as the territory of invention it does appear that there is no precedent that binds all countries the world over to accept this fiction. It is possible to argue that intellectual property laws were designed for terrestrial application and not to govern activities that occurred on other planets or in free space. In this way, a possible refusal of recognition of the proprietary rights over ISS inventions by non-partner states is possible even if not at present probable.

For avoidance of doubt, participation by a partner state, its cooperating agency or its related entities in an activity occurring in or on any other partner's space station flight element shall not in and of itself alter or affect the jurisdiction over such activity provided for by the state of registry of the component. The temporary presence in the territory of a partner state of any articles, including the components of a flight element, in transit between any place on earth and any flight element of the space station registered by another partner state or ESA shall not in itself form the basis for any proceedings in the first partner state for patent infringement. In any event, this provision does not introduce any further certainty as to the right to retain control over all launched objects more than Article VIII of the Outer Space Treaty 1967 already does. Although no serious controversy has yet arisen regarding civil or criminal jurisdiction over patents and inventions made on international space stations, it must be said that in light of the commercial end to which space

720 ESA, "International Space Station Legal Framework", available at the website of the ESA at http://www.esa.int/esaHS/ESAH7O0VMOC_iss_0.html (accessed 17 June 2010).

activities are directed and the impending entry of hundreds of private actors, this area of the law is set to be one of the most contested jurisdictional issues space lawyers would face. The very interesting legal situation whereby the ESA module is in a sense quasi-European territory continues to raise certain questions. It is not yet clear how patent rights over jointly conducted research will be sorted out. Who gets reversionary rights to inventions? Although states such as Germany and the USA have already projected their intellectual property rights regime into space via domestic regulation, the question remains whether and to what extent such national legislation may affect the rights of other states outside the skeletal agreements on the issue under the IGA.

The broad principles in relation to IP issues on the ISS are that:

1 In relation to individuals, the ownership and the exploitation of any intellectual property – data or product – resulting from experimentation and activities on the space station utilisation will first depend on the type of contract the pertinent person executed with NASA, the ESA or any of the other partners.[721]
2 The place of invention or discovery in relation to the ISS space station is determined by the fiction of territoriality that attaches by virtue of ownership and fact of registration of the precise station's element in which the invention occurred (Article 21 of the Intergovernmental Agreement).[722]
3 It has also been correctly suggested by the ESA that the "country of invention" criterion is not proof of ownership of the invention. Nothing in the agreement and presumably under international property law precludes the right of an inventor to file for a patent in multiple countries. An inventor may, thus, file for a patent in any country he chooses. The main purpose of the territorial approach is only to satisfy the criteria required on intellectual property law to identify the location and country where the invention took place.

On the whole, the legal regime governing intellectual property on ISS and its modules (e.g. Columbus Laboratory) appears to be skeletal. In this way, the parties to the IGA appear to underestimate the possible jurisdictional and factual quandaries that can result out of the fast moving scientific events that occur on board the ISS and particularly on the European module.

Given the stress that extraterritorial jurisdiction is placing on international relations and particularly the increasing resort to this form or jurisdictional power by some of the states involved in the ISS, it may be envisaged that the future will be very interesting in the area of IP rights and space stations. It is, for instance, possible that there may be clash of registrations making priority difficult to

721 The ESA makes it a general rule that "the industrial and academic users who will have access to the Space Station through the European Space Agency will have their rights and obligations determined by the contractual framework they will have agreed on with the Agency". Ibid.

722 An invention made in the Kibo Laboratory within the Japanese Element will be deemed to have occurred in Japan – just as is the case with inventions on the US element.

determine. Simultaneous registration may deliberately or inadvertently occur. Given the expanding role of antitrust suits over technological products expensive litigation is near inevitable. Indeed, competition issues are bound to crop up in the operation of outer space activities. Despite the general tenor of scientific cooperation that underlies the whole ISS enterprise it is not difficult to foresee disputes relating to disclosure of formats and product makeups, design or patents much along the same divides in the Microsoft antitrust lawsuits. This will become even more likely once commercial production of biotechnological products begin in earnest.

It may be argued that there is scope for merging the contrasting positions represented in relation to application of IP rules to inventions in space. It is impossible to ignore entirely the significance of the province of mankind nature of outer space in considering this issue. The very unprecedented nature of the joint cooperation over the ISS shows that the parties have committed to an enterprise that goes beyond parochial national and/or commercial interests. Thus, for the ISS and other future cooperative space stations it is better to adopt a less national focused patent and commercial intellectual property regime beyond, of course, the moral rights of recognition for the invention. For instance, common ownership of all technological discoveries and patents or designs may be placed in the UN or any of its pertinent sub-organisations to be held in trust for the participating states in a space station. This will replace national and/or parochial claims to IP derived from outer space activities with an international regime of supervision and registration of space inventions. The system may preserve the commercial benefits to the successful scientific teams and their sponsors but for a shorter term than will be usually claimed under contemporary IP rules. The period of tenancy over IP patents could be reduced to five years only. The main advantage will be a reduction in the current race to the bottom approach to scientific design registration for patents and discoveries. A regime of shared IP ownership is inherently suitable for outer space exploration. Moreover, the idea is not so revolutionary given the ongoing example provided by the ESA cooperation in the area of recognition of country of invention.

At any rate, a separate treaty may be necessary to look at the IP issues in a holistic sense. The advent of private enterprises in space exploration would raise intellectual property rights questions with fresh vigour. Ethical issues will also be raised in relation to biotechnological creations in outer space. The law must not lag behind practice and intellectual property rights lawyers must become more imaginative in solving these issues before they arise. It is hoped that a similar system of shorter patent rights of no more than five years will be set for outer space creations so that tenant-seeking behaviour will not taint space science in the way it may have done on earth. Space research is too important to the destiny of mankind for international law to allow it to be rendered hostage to the profit line motivation of private interests.

9.6 Criminal jurisdiction over space stations

As to criminal jurisdiction on space stations, it suffices to mention that in the absence of elaborate rules in the space treaties this also is increasingly determined through the mechanism of agreement between the participating states in any international space station. If the space station consists of nationals of only one state the matter is more straightforward and the primary state with criminal responsibility is that which sends the astronauts. International joint space exploration is by its very nature still in its infancy and there are very few rules and bare legal jurisprudence to go by in understanding the nature of criminal jurisdiction in outer space. The most relevant instances with respect to multilateral space stations are contained in Article 5 of the IGA (1988),[723] which has been replaced by Article 22 of the IGA (1998).[724] The 1998 agreement would seem not to introduce any surprises in terms of registration, jurisdiction and control.

In Article 11, it is stipulated that all the partners in accordance with the MOUs will develop a code of conduct for the space station crew. In accordance with Article 22, specific provisions on criminal jurisdiction stipulate that specified states may exercise criminal jurisdiction on the international space station over personnel in or on the respective elements. In accordance with Article II of the Registration Convention (1975), the partner undertakes to register as space objects the flight elements constituting the station as listed in the annex. The European partners having delegated this responsibility to the ESA have that body acting in their name and on their behalf. Pursuant to Article VIII of the Outer Space Treaty (1967) and Article II of the Registration Convention (1975), each partner retains jurisdiction and control over the elements it registers in accordance with Article 5(1) and over personnel in or on the space station who are its nationals. Such exercise of jurisdiction and control is, however, to be subject to certain provisions within the MOU and other implementing arrangements, including relevant procedural mechanisms established therein. The mechanism of a code of conduct is retained and each partner, in exercising its right to provide crew, undertakes to ensure that its crew members observe the code of conduct.[725]

723 It provides, inter alia: "[T]he exercise of such jurisdiction and control shall be subject to any relevant provisions of this Agreement, the MOUs and the implementing arrangements, including relevant procedural mechanisms established therein." This refers to Article 8 of the Memorandum of Understanding between ESA and NASA, which entered into force on 3 June1985. It contains a large number of provisions on the Management Aspects of the Space Station Program Primarily Related to Operations and Utilization, elaborating, inter alia, on a Multilateral Coordination Board (MCB), a Systems Operations Panel (SOP) and a Users Operations Panel (UOP).

724 André Farand, "Signing of new Agreements on the International Space Station", available at ECSL News: Bulletin of the European Center for Space Law, available at http://www.esa.int/esapub/ecsl/ecsl17.pdf visited 17 August 2011.

725 Regarding liability, the utility of the Liability Convention (1972) is exploited in that it is provided that except as otherwise provided in Article 16, the partner states, as well as ESA remain liable in the event of a claim arising out of the Liability Convention. It is also envisaged that in practice the Partners (and ESA, where appropriate) may have to jointly redress any potential liability according to extent of apportionment of such liability and on the defence of such claim.

Article 22 of the IGA (1998) recognised the "unique and unprecedented nature" of multilateral criminal jurisdiction. It, therefore, ascribed criminal jurisdiction to Canada, the European partner states, Japan, Russia and the United States allowing them exercise criminal jurisdiction over their respective personnel in or on any flight element (Article 22(1)). In other words, national criminal jurisdiction over such personnel is not limited to the nationality of the flight element in which they are on when the pertinent act requiring criminal jurisdiction takes place. It may be noted that this provision ought to have included some indication of the situation governing jurisdiction over persons that do not have the nationality of any of the parties to the IGA but who are invited on board by any of the parties. In the absence of clear indications on this point, it is suggested that the national criminal jurisdiction will be retained over such person by the state party that invites such person on board. Where the invitation is perceived to be joint (for instance, ESA partners) then the criminal jurisdiction over such person(s) will be shared by the participating states.

Article 22(2) of the IGA does not lend itself to much clarity. It governs the case of alleged misconducts in orbit that: (a) affects the life or safety of a national of another partner state or (b) occurs in or on or causes damage to the flight element of another partner state. The provision allows the partner state whose national is the alleged perpetrator and the affected state to consult (at the request of the latter) as to which of the two states should prosecute. An affected partner state may, following such consultation, exercise criminal jurisdiction over the alleged perpetrator, either if the state of nationality concurs in such exercise of criminal jurisdiction, or if the state of nationality fails to provide within three months (90 days) assurances that it will submit the case to its competent authorities for the purpose of prosecution. *Lockerbie*-like jurisdictional and political quandaries are not completely avoided to the extent that indication of prosecution may be unsatisfactory to an affected state given the highly charged and sensational nature that such scenarios will have in both national and international media. To begin with, in such circumstances where prosecution is handled by the state of nationality, nothing short of a conviction backed by satisfactory sentencing or punishment to the required severity of the affected state (its media and public opinion) will suffice from the perspective of an aggrieved state. Furthermore, it is possible to envisage that there may be controversy or disagreement over the precise criminal charges that accused persons should face. It may be that there ought to have been inserted in Article 22 an indication requiring the necessary input of the affected state in the framing of charges where the state of nationality chooses to prosecute on its own. The framing of the entirety of Article 22 arguably suggests that it is preferable or at least more likely that the affected state will choose to exercise criminal jurisdiction.[726] In this manner, it can be seen that the thrust of the IGA 1998 rules

726 This is because the permission to prosecute in Article 22(2) is first given and the provisos follow later: "An affected Partner State may, following such consultation, exercise criminal jurisdiction over the alleged perpetrator provided."

is to create a regime that encourages rather than discourage multilateral criminal jurisdiction on the ISS. It clearly mandates that each partner state shall, subject to its national laws and regulations, afford the other partners assistance in connection with alleged misconduct on orbit (Article 22(4)).

On repatriation/scheduled return of the offender to earth, the issue of extradition to the territory of the affected state may arise. In this event, the provisions of Article 22(3) are applicable. Accordingly the affected state would have to determine whether the state of nationality of the offender requires that there has to be an extradition treaty between it and a foreign state that wants to exercise jurisdiction in such circumstances. If this is so, then subparagraph three invites the state of nationality, at its option, to consider the IGA (1998) as the legal basis for extradition in respect of the alleged misconduct on orbit. Extradition under such circumstances shall, however, be subject to the procedural provisions and the other conditions of the law of the requested partner state. The duty to prosecute or extradite not only leaves the choice to the state in whose territory the offender is but where that discretion has been exercised as Libya did in the *Lockerbie case* (and under a similar formula as in the Montreal Convention) a challenge to the exercise of discretion will only produce a confusion as to who is infringing the treaty provisions.[727] Furthermore, it appears that this particular provision appears to presume that the state of nationality of the offender may not on its own decide to punish the offender without recourse or promptings from the affected state. By way of analogy, if the misconduct physically takes place within the confines of another states element, this will be the equivalent of a national committing an offence abroad. In this context, it is not too clear whether there are enough jurisdictional grounds for the state of nationality to exercise jurisdiction where no complaint emanates from the affected state.

The important provisions of Article 22 are, however, not to be considered in isolation. Its provisions, for instance, do not limit the authorities and procedures for the maintenance of order and the conduct of crew activities in or on the space station in the code of conduct pursuant to Article 11. The code of conduct is not intended to limit the application of Article 22. Furthermore, a proper grasp of the issue of criminal jurisdiction over space stations will also include analysis of the various applicable national laws.

Canadian laws, for instance, exist to extend national criminal jurisdiction over its crew members for acts or omissions that would constitute an indictable offence as if such act or omission was committed in Canada.[728] In its Criminal Code (Part 1 Section 4 (2.31), Canada also insists a crew member of a partner state who commits an act or omission outside Canada during a space flight on, or in relation to, a flight element of the space station or on any means of transportation to and

727 Cf. the discussions on the Hague extradition/prosecution formula in Chapter 3.

728 Criminal Code (RS 1985, c. C-46) Part 1 Section 4 (2.3) (2.33). Again, in similar fashion to some other jurisdictions such as Nigeria with respect to crimes in the airspace, no proceedings in relation to an offence referred to in subsection (2.3) or (2.31) may be instituted without the consent of the Attorney General of Canada.

from the space station that if committed in Canada would constitute an indictable offence is deemed to have committed that act or omission in Canada, if that act or omission (a) threatens the life or security of a Canadian crew member or (b) is committed on, or in relation to, a flight element provided by Canada or damages a Canadian flight element. In this way, it is clear that what may be an indictable offence in Canada that is within the possibility of occurrence within the space station ought to be of interest to the entire personnel on the ISS no matter their nationality.

The complementarity of the IGA to national law has been explicitly referred to with regards to Spanish law. Romeo Melanda wrote:

> Spain arrogates competence to judge, for example, a citizen of the USA that has injured a Spanish citizen in the Japanese module, provided that after following the appropriate procedures (jurisdiction is established according to IGA principles) the USA accept Spanish competence or drop their claim to judge their national. The perpetrator must be in Spanish territory in order to be judged.[729]

The framing of charges against astronauts, scientific personnel and visitors to space stations may prove not to be quite straightforward in practice. For instance, each participant state must ensure that prosecution is made possible both by their substantive criminal law rules and by their national criminal practice and procedure forms. The compatibility issues extend to what must be found in the content of indictment. For instance, in England, an indictment must be in one of the forms set out in the Practice Direction and must contain, in a paragraph called a "count", a statement of the offence charged that describes the offence in ordinary language, and identifies any legislation that creates it; and such particulars of the conduct constituting the commission of the offence as to make clear what the prosecutor alleges against the defendant.[730] Although the same concern may exist in a space station relating to one state it is to be pointed out that in time more countries will become party to space station agreements. In this case, it will soon become apparent that the form of the indictment is such that its requirements will be difficult to fulfil in respect of charges against persons and incidents that occurred not only abroad but in outer space and with the difficulty of determination of the precise date and time of the events. For instance, a Nigerian criminal charge is supposed to contain (a) the name of the accused or accused persons, (b) date of the alleged commissions of the offence, (c) place of commission of offence, (d) statement of the offence committed and (e) name of the person and of the thing against whom or in respect

729 S. Romeo Melanda, "La Ley Penal applicable a los delitos cometidos en el espacio ultraterrestre y a bordo de vehiculos especiales", 34 *Actualidad Penal* (2001), quoted in Frans G. von der Dunk and Marcel Brus, *The International Space Station: Commercial Utilisation From a European Legal Perspective* (Leiden: Martinus Nijhoff, 2006): 214–15.

730 The Form of indictment (Criminal Procedure Rules, Part 14) shows that the following must be present: Indictment In The Crown Court At . . . The Queen V. . . . Charged As Follows: Statement Of Offence Particulars Date . . . Crown Court Officer.

of which the offence is committed.[731] Considering that space stations in orbit may not share the same dates and times with terrestrial records, it may be difficult to meet these formal demands.

In sum, criminal jurisdiction over persons on space stations will depend on (a) specific provisions within the multilateral intergovernmental agreement or MOU in force; (b) any applicable code of conduct drawn up for the instruction of all scientific or other personnel on board the space station; (c) the applicable national criminal laws of the state of nationality of the persons against whom criminal jurisdiction may be directed; and (d) the applicable criminal laws of the flag state(s) affected by the actions of the persons against whom criminal jurisdiction may be directed. The permutations of interactions that may lead to criminal action on the ISS as in any space station are incalculable and only limited by the imagination. There already appears some evidence of Robinsons "manifestations of totally different neurophysiological phenomena"[732] and the first major crisis involving criminal law is a matter of time. Note may be taken, for instance, of the toilet wars that have raged on the ISS. Gennady Padalka, a veteran Russian cosmonaut, complained in 2009 about human conflicts and lack of cooperation on the ISS. American astronauts had apparently been refusing Russian "cosmonauts" access to the use of toilets and gym exercise machines. The incidents may appear trivial but they do raise some interesting questions. Are boundaries and borders within space stations as strict as national boundaries and borders? Is there a presumption that the elementary considerations of humanity prevent astronauts from acting in such manner to each other? Will there be a duty to alleviate pain and discomfort in outer space? How are states to deal with assault and battery, homicide and sexual offences committed by scientific and other personnel on board state stations? These issues assume a pressing character in view of the many developments in the space tourism front and the imminent advent of permanent space hotels.

It is, however, not clear what will happen if several states other than the sending state of the astronaut seek to punish the same offence. Again what will be the exact recourse of the affected state(s) if the offender remains on board the station indefinitely with the obvious collusion of the sending state or if he is allowed to escape arrest on return to earth? Nevertheless, it must again be reiterated that space law is witnessing a shift towards the-extradite-or-punish regime found in air law. Although this formula in air law is reserved for the strict offences of hijacking and hostage taking, it would appear that in space law, lesser grave offences may trigger extradition. This is because a partner state, which as a legal practice makes extradition conditional on the existence of a treaty, may at its option consider the Agreement as the legal basis for extradition in respect of the alleged misconduct on orbit.

731 Nigerian Criminal Procedure Act Section 2. See also *State v. Okpegboro* [1966] All NLR 17; *Harunami v. Borno Native Authority* [1966] All NLR 22-23; *Ibeziako v. Commissioner of Police* 12 WACA 363; *Duru v. Police* [1961] 1 All NR 44. It is, indeed, the practice that a charge sheet should be as precise as possible in relation to the place and time of an offence.

732 Robinson op. cit.: 28.

A good indication of the apparent inadequacies of the seemingly detailed MOUs was revealed when Russia put into orbit a "non-professional" and allowed him on Space Station Alpha as a commercial space tourist. The US National Aeronautical and Space Administration (NASA) disagreed with the development and insisted that the passenger would be a safety risk. It also emphasised his trip was a one-time exemption. To win NASA's approval, the passenger, Dennis Tito, who happened to be a US national, had to sign an agreement that he would not wander through American segments of the station without an escort. He also agreed to pay for anything he broke. It is interesting to note that NASA administrator, Daniel Goldin, criticised this first space tourist before a congressional subcommittee. His pronouncement was that he has put "incredible stress on the men and women of NASA . . . Mr. Tito does not realise the effort of thousands of people, United States and Russia, who are working to protect his safety and the safety of everyone else."[733] This incident highlights the fertile ground for disagreement over criminal jurisdiction in space even amongst cooperating states. A visit that was properly and legally conducted according to the standards of one state was seen as incredible stress by another even though the visitor has the nationality of the complaining state. Space tourism, like air flight on commercial aircraft, will come in the natural course of things to be common practice. It is hoped that the 16 partners in the international Space Station Alpha would set reasonable and practical ground rules which may serve as precedents on which future excursions may be conducted.

9.7 Jurisdiction and control *rationae personae* in outer space

9.7.1 Terminological confusion

> The manned space station, characterised in part as a quasi-permanent habitat, with mixed sexes, representatives of various cultures, different races, alien life support systems, acute sensory deprivation/overload, etc., is too synthetically oriented to permit reliable application of empirically unverified legal fictions, such as those comprising the mechanical and jurisprudential mysticism by which the average Earth indigent is guided and controlled in daily activities.[734]

It is preferable to employ the phrase jurisdiction and control *ratione personae* in our analysis rather than the term jurisdiction over astronauts or cosmonauts as is common in most literature on the subject. This is because just like the terms pilot and cabin crew, the terms astronaut/cosmonaut have not been satisfactorily defined anywhere in any multilateral treaty.[735] Obviously, such a situation is fraught with

733 Washington (CNN), "Glenn: Tito Flight a 'Misuse' of Space Station", 6 May 2001, available at http://www.cnn.com/2001/TECH/space/05/06/glenn.tito/index.html; see also Washington CNN, "Russia 'Plans more Space Tourism'", 29 April 2001, available at http://www.cnn.com/2001/TECH/space/04/29/shuttle.tourists/index.html.

734 Robinson op. cit.: 28.

735 Cheng (1965) op. cit.: 40–43.

problems in that it can lead to analytical confusion. This is more so in those grey areas of jurisdictional discourse where air law and space law overlap. The term astronaut should have been defined when it was first employed in Article V(1) of the Outer Space Treaty (1967). But even if that occasion were missed it is unforgivable that in the more specific Astronauts Agreement in (1968) the term was yet again left undefined. This has led to differences of opinion among scholars and even states.

Cheng thinks that the term astronaut is descriptive rather than technical and that it refers to a person who ventures into outer space or who travels on board a spacecraft.[736] This position is probably based on common definitions found in dictionaries and may, therefore, be inadequate for legal treatment. *Webster's Third International Dictionary* defines an astronaut as "a traveller in interplanetary space" or/and "a student, devotee or advocate of astronautics".[737] It is quite easy to spot the flaw in the view that anyone found travelling through space is an astronaut. This is as absurd as saying that everyone on a ship is a sailor or everyone on an aircraft is a pilot or crew member. It makes sense to distinguish between (a) astronauts in the strict sense of the word, (b) mere passengers on a spacecraft or scientific personnel performing restricted experiments or operations in respect of the mission, (c) a journalist (as it has occurred at least once) and (d) a tourist (as will soon become commonplace). Jurisdictional powers over such persons as well as their rights and duties would differ from those of an astronaut just as there are legal differences between the jurisdictional competencies rights and duties of passengers on an aircraft and the pilot and crew members.

Whereas Western scholars favour the term "astronauts", the Soviet scholars favoured "cosmonaut". Attempting to explain the distinction, Piradov wrote that the term "cosmonaut" is wider in meaning, since it applies to people who make any type of flight in outer space, whereas the term "astronaut" is narrower and less definite (meaning a person who flies to the stars). This explanation is neither clear nor convincing. Others, such as Kamenetskaya, collapse the two words into one definition thus: "From the point of view of international law, cosmonauts/astronauts are people who carry out professional activities connected with the exploration and use of outer space in outer space itself and on celestial bodies, in accordance with the principles and rules of international space law."

Certain provisions of the Moon Agreement (1979) bring about further terminological confusion. In what may have been the clearest indication that space law, anticipated non-scientific visitors to outer space, within the first decade of outer space activities on the Moon, the Moon Agreement (1979) in Article 10 made provisions for "practical measures to safeguard the life and health of *persons on the moon*" (emphasis added). For this purpose, the Moon Treaty adopts the curious position that state parties shall regard "any person" found on the Moon as an

736 Ibid: 40.

737 Webster's Third International Dictionary of the English Language Unabridged (Springfield, IL: G. & C. Merriam, 1981).

astronaut within the meaning of Article V of the Outer Space Treaty and as "part of the personnel" of a spacecraft within the meaning of the Astronaut's Agreement (1968). To begin with, Article V of the Outer Space Treaty (1967) contains no description and definitely not a definition of astronauts. Then again it may be wondered whether in Article 10 the word "and" is used in the disjunctive sense, in which case "people" are either "astronauts" or personnel of spacecraft, or in the conjunctive sense, in which case they are both. But it should not be forgotten that people may be astronauts and not personnel of the particular spacecraft or space station – say, an astronaut launched into space on behalf of another state. Although the Moon Agreement (1979) is again unhelpful as to what it means by a state's personnel, Cheng persuasively suggests that this can be taken to refer to astronauts that are its nationals.[738]

The essential difference between the Space Treaty (1967) and the Moon Agreement (1979) is that while Article 12(1) of the Moon Agreement simply confers jurisdiction and control over astronauts who are nationals i.e. on the state of origin of any person in space, Article VIII of the Space Treaty (1967) confers jurisdiction on the state of registry irrespective of the nationality of all persons aboard the space vehicle. Both treaties, however, have somewhat failed to take into account the position of an astronaut who no longer forms part of the personnel of a space vehicle.[739] Should the state with overriding jurisdiction be his state of nationality or should it be the state on whose vehicle he was transported into space? In the absence of any agreement covering this situation, it is suggested that his state of nationality continue to possess overriding jurisdiction.

9.7.2 Cases of unsettled jurisdiction

It must be said *ab initio* that the exact workings of jurisdiction over people sent into outer space by whatever name they are referred to have not been as clearly worked out as that of jurisdiction over people in the airspace. Obviously, space travels have not had as long a history as have air flight. Besides, the scope and categories of people sent into outer space is increasing. The important hypothesis to test is whether all the categories of person that can be found on a spacecraft are subject to the legal jurisdiction of at least one state as is the situation with respect to persons aboard aircraft.[740] It is necessary to recall the principles of personal jurisdiction as discussed earlier under the overall doctrine of state sovereignty. It refers to the totality of powers a state has with respect to natural and legal persons possessing its nationality, enjoying its protection or owing it allegiance wherever they may be. The concept of nationality is the legal basis of personal jurisdiction. There must

738 Bin Cheng, "The Moon Treaty: Agreement Governing the Activities of States on the Moon and other Celestial Bodies within the Solar System other than the Earth, December 18, 1979", *Current Legal Problems* (1980): 225. See also Hara op. cit.: 82–3.

739 Say, for instance, when he completes his tasks and becomes so to speak *functus officio* and is not within a recognised space station.

740 See, generally, Chapter 3.

also be a genuine connection between the state and the people over whom it wishes to exercise personal jurisdiction. These rules found in the law of the sea and the law of the air apply with minor exceptions to jurisdiction over people wherever they may be situated in outer space.[741] Thus, it is a trite observation that spatial distance does not diminish the personal jurisdiction a state has over its citizens.

It is stated clearly under Article VIII of the Outer Space Treaty (1967) that states retain jurisdiction and control over personnel they launch into space on their own vehicles. Under Article VII it is also clear that they remain vicariously responsible for any damage caused to other people. The use of the term "personnel" in the wordings of Article VIII is instructive in that it covers any person no matter in what capacity he/she serves. However, it is interesting to raise certain questions relating to jurisdiction over two categories of person. They are (a) people on board spacecraft who are sent on the mission by private enterprises and (b) people charged with no functional purpose or carrying out no official functions on board a spacecraft.

As regards the first category, the situation is no different from the personal jurisdictional powers a state has over pilots of its privately owned aircraft who are nationals of that state. This principle has achieved such settled finality that even those states that have incorporated the principles of space law into local acts take it for granted and do not often make specific provisions pronouncing it. For example, the Australian Space Activities Act 1998 (Cth), which came into force on 21 December 1998,[742] creates a regulatory regime for commercial and other forms of private space activities where Australia would be responsible under the Liability Convention. However, this Act makes no specific reference to Australia's powers over astronauts and scientists on board any space flight (private or not) launched under the Act. This lacuna, however, does not avail Australia in the event that its citizens on board a spacecraft engage in acts that create liability for Australia. Where the person in question is not a national of the sending state, it may be suggested that the contract of employment between that person and the private enterprise establishes a linkage of protection and allegiance to the flag state of the spacecraft. In that case, civil jurisdiction is surely established and can be with some credit argued for depending on the circumstances. In any case, where personal jurisdiction cannot be found, any of the five principles or grounds of criminal jurisdiction would avail the state of registry of the spacecraft.[743] Again it must be stated here as in the introduction to criminal jurisdiction of states that it is advisable for a state to refer to the specific basis of jurisdiction relied on. For instance, the territorial or territoriality principle will not be useful where the acts in question took place in outer space.

741 A specific instance of this is the US jurisdiction over astronauts of other states in the in the Station Alpha under the IGA (1988).

742 For a discussion of this act, see Ricky J. Lee, "The Australian Space Activities Act: Creating a regulatory Regime for Space Activities", XXV, 2 *Air and Space Law* (2000): 56–61.

743 *Supra*, Chapter 1.5: Criminal jurisdiction of states.

As regards persons having no official functions on board spacecraft (these again may be sent by a private commercial arrangement), it is suggested that this category calls for no different consideration from passengers aboard aircraft in international airspace. Such persons may be a mere passenger, tourist or observer. Examples of this class of persons include Toyobuama, a Japanese journalist who was transported by special agreement to the Russian space station Mir as a commercial customer and US Senator Jake Garn also made a political flight on the space shuttle.[744] To highlight the impending possibilities of increased traffic by non-scientific persons, it is worth mentioning another US millionaire businessman who planned a trip to the Russian space Station Mir in 2001 had his trip rerouted to the international space station.[745] In these cases, it is suggested that joint jurisdiction over such people would be exercised by the state of registry and the state of nationality of the persons concerned. In which case, following the Chengian analysis of jurisdictional powers, which was adopted earlier on in this thesis, thc *jurisfaction* (ability to make rules governing the person) of both states would be applicable. As regards *jurisaction* (ability to enforce and concretise the rules made) it would appear that the immediate powers and possibilities to act belong to the state of registry of the spacecraft or space station. Where persons performing no official acts on board spacecraft are also not citizens of the state of registry but are physically in free space or are actually on a celestial body and not within a space station, then it may be argued that the state with jurisdiction over such people as regards acts done by them is the state of nationality. Liability in such cases will be personal and may be shared by any private companies and/or states on behalf of which they may have acted. Where such persons re-enter a spacecraft or return to a space station the immediate rights of arrest or detention will naturally be held by the state of registry.

In the interesting case of the American millionaire who visited the international space station by virtue of an agreement with the Russian participants it is instructive to note that the USA did not seek to exercise any control over him based on his nationality. Despite NASA's earlier opposition to the visit the only concrete jurisdictional demands were that the tourist should sign an undertaking waiving his rights vis-à-vis the USA to compensation for injury and death in the case of mishap and to pay for all damages he may cause while on board the space station. The experience of the visit by the American tourist to the ISS also revealed the inadequacies in the Memorandum of Understanding regulating the ISS. It is to be hoped that, in practice, bilateral or multilateral intergovernmental agreements or MOUs will always cover these matters in the future.

744 See N. Jasentuliyana, "Legal Aspects of Human Safety and Rescue in Space: Manned Space Flight Legal Aspects in the Light of Scientific & Technical Development", *Proceedings of an International Colloquium*, ed. K.H. Bockstiegel (Cologne: Carl Heymans Verlag, 1992): 168. See also Stephen E. Doyle, "Astronauts and Cosmonauts in International Cooperation in International Cooperation. A View of the American Experience", ibid: 55.

745 See Richard Stenger, "Mir-bound Tourist Detour to International Space Station", 4 January 2001, available at http://www.cnn.com/2001/TECH/space?01/04/tito.iss/index.html.

9.7.3 Liability over aerospace objects

It is also important to consider the issue of liability over aerospace objects. Liability of aerospace objects can relate to accidents and incidents affecting persons on board as well as persons and property on earth. This raises questions both *ratione instrumnti* and *personae.* Are aerospace objects while in airspace considered as aircraft and while in outer space as spacecraft, with all the legal consequences that follow therefrom? Does air law or space law prevail during the flight of an aerospace craft, depending on the destination of such a flight? Which of the two bodies of law governs an aerospace object that does not go into outer space but is used for solely or mainly for airspace activities? The definition of aerospace objects offered by Fiji may be considered adequate and perhaps indicative of the rising profile of this category of craft that the law must grapple with urgently:

> "[A]erospace object" . . . refers to an object that is capable of travelling through outer space and using aerodynamic properties to remain in airspace for a certain period of time. The Space Shuttle of the United States of America is a good example of this kind of object. During its missions it travels through airspace (space below the atmosphere) and remains there for a certain period of time before entering outer space (space above the atmosphere).[746]

Aerospace objects will continue to create problems for air and space law on many fronts until a specific treaty is drawn up which attempts a holistic and adequate treatment of the intersections between air law and space law regimes.[747] There are no specific rules on aerospace objects presently and the deciding factors will perhaps quite inadequately relate to the precise location that the aerospace object is as at when the relevant actions giving rise to liability occurred. The lack of resolution of the spatial demarcation issue adds to the problematic nature of aerospace objects.

The problem as it is discussed under the auspices of COPUOS is generally framed in terms of which body of the two specific bodies of law ought to apply to aerospace objects. States appear to be irrevocably divided on the issue as of present.[748] The answer to this of course is relevant to which liability regime is

746 See A/AC105/635/Add.10 of 21 January 2004. This is comparable with the Finnish view which states that: "An 'aerospace vehicle' could thus be defined as an aerospace object that is capable of 'travelling through' outer space and using its aerodynamic properties while travelling through airspace" as contained in document A/AC.105/635/Add.11 of 26 January 2005; see also the comparable views expressed on the question by Mexico as contained in document A/AC.105/635 of 15 January 1996 and that of Peru as contained in document A/AC105/635/Add.9 of 7 May 2003. The Philippines, in fact, reiterates the US shuttle as one of the best known examples of an aerospace object. See Philippines view as contained in document A/AC105/635 of 15 January 1996 as contained in document A/AC105/635 of 15 January 1996.

747 See, further, our earlier discussions about the ramifications of aerospace objects in relation to registration of aircraft and later in relation to new hybrid space tourist vehicles (Chapter 10.3).

748 There appears to be a predominant view that aerospace objects are "crafts" that are capable of operating in both airspace and outer space. This has certainly been the officially expressed position

applicable – that of space law and primarily the Liability Convention or those of air law including the Warsaw Convention? There is much persuasive force in the Indian view that states must be held to a very high threshold when involved in aerospace activities. India's stated position is that:

> Aerospace objects while in airspace are considered as aircraft, and while in outer space as spacecraft with all the legal consequences that follow therefrom, *provided that, as regards questions of safety and liability, the higher standards should apply.* However, where the passage through airspace is part of a direct and continuous journey to or from outer space, the object shall be considered as a spacecraft.[749]

It is perhaps important to note that, given the quite elaborate development given to liability for airline injuries and accidents and mishaps, it may indeed be wondered whether the air law liability regime is now not more favourable to injured persons than that provided by space law. Whereas air law has generally moved away from a fault-based requirement for compensation in the event of accidents there is still a fault-based criterion that may be said to apply with respect to damage being caused elsewhere than on the surface of the earth to a space object of one launching state or to people or property on board such a space object by a space object of another launching state (Liability Convention Article III).

of South Africa, Argentina and Benin. See A/AC105/635/Add.7 of 13 January 2003 (Argentina) views as contained in document A/AC105/635/Add.4 of 1 April 1997; Benin as contained in document A/AC105/635/Add.10 of 21 January 2004; Brazil as contained in document A/AC105/635/Add.10 of 21 January 2004; Colombia as contained in A/AC105/635/Add.5 of 5 February 1998; Czech Republic as contained in document A/AC105/635 of 15 January 1996. But as to what to do with this interesting category of objects there has been much scope for disagreement. Costa Rica views the development of aerospace objects as a problem: "The problem is that there are objects today that are capable of travelling through both airspace and outer space", as contained in document A/AC105/635/Add.7 of 13 January 2003. Algeria vehemently denies that an aerospace object can be defined as one capable of using its aerodynamic properties to remain in airspace for any appreciably lengthy period of time. The reason given for this view is that launchers do not have such aerodynamic properties (as contained in document A/AC105/635/Add.7 of 13 January 2003). The former state avoids the question entirely while the latter state answers a different question from the pertinent one. The issue is not whether launchers exist and how they operate but one of whether certain crafts can perform in both air and outer space environment and how to account for these. Chile has also expressed its preference for the terms "spacecraft" or "space vehicle" because they denote a man-made device, in order to distinguish natural objects from an "aerospace object" which is man-made (Chile's statement as contained in document A/AC105/635/Add.3 of 4 December 1996). This again answers other questions whether aerospace objects can be man made or natural but it does not resolve the conundrum of which body of law precisely governs aerospace flights at all stages. For the official statements and communications on the aerospace issue see the Questionnaire on Possible Legal Issues with regard to Aerospace Objects: Replies from member states available at website of the United Nations Office for Outer Space Affairs http://www.oosa.unvienna.org/oosa/SpaceLaw/aero/index.html.

749 India's views as contained in document A/AC105/635/Add.4 of 1 April 1997. See also our earlier discussions on the status of aerospace objects.

While a group of states such as Algeria[750] admit to the fact that they presently have no opinion on the matter and will prefer to investigate the question later, presumably in light of unfolding realities, a second group including Argentina,[751] Brazil,[752] Czech Republic,[753] El Salvador,[754] India,[755] Iraq,[756] the Lebanon,[757] Portugal,[758] Russia,[759] Rwanda,[760] Ukraine[761] and Yemen[762] believe that the general principle should be that aerospace objects moving through airspace may be considered to be aircraft and that if they travel through outer space they may be considered to be spacecraft. Nevertheless, bearing in mind technological advancement and the wide range of objects that can be encompassed by the given definition of an "aerospace object", a number of states welcome the possibility of elaborating a special regime the details of which may indeed be explored in the future.[763] In this case, the liability regime for aerospace objects would well and truly be indeterminable until then. A third view is that the original destination of the object should be the decisive factor in determining whether an object should be designated an aerospace object or an aircraft.[764] The planned destination will accordingly determine which liability regime applies. A fourth view is that space

750 Algeria as contained in document A/AC105/635/Add.7 of 13 January 2003.
751 As contained in document A/AC105/635/Add.4 of 1 April 1997.
752 As contained in document A/AC105/635/Add.10 of 21 January 2004.
753 The Czech Republic believes that those aerospace vehicles that would serve the purposes of air transportation, even it they should fly for a certain period in outer space, might essentially remain aircraft and vice versa those aerospace objects that fly through airspace for the purposes of their ascent to or descent from outer space might be considered as spacecraft. Czech Republic as contained in document A/AC105/635 of 15 January 1996. See also A/AC105/635/Add.7 of 13 January 2003.
754 El Salvador, however, also believes that it would be advisable to analyse the possibility of creating a special legal regime. View as contained in document A/AC105/635/Add.7 of 13 January 2003.
755 India as contained in document A/AC105/635/Add.4 of 1 April 1997.
756 Iraq's view as contained in document A/AC105/635 of 15 January 1996.
757 Lebanon's view as contained in document A/AC105/635/Add.5 of 5 February 1998.
758 Portugal's view as contained in document A/AC105/635/Add.11 of 26 January 2005
759 Russian Federation's view as contained in document A/AC105/635/Add.1 of 15 March 1996.
760 Rwanda as contained in document A/AC105/635/Add.11 of 26 January 2005.
761 Ukraine's view as contained in document A/AC105/635/Add.11 of 26 January 2005.
762 Yemen as contained in document A/AC105/635/Add.10 of 21 January 2004.
763 Ecuador's view as contained in document A/AC105/635/Add.7 of 13 January 2003; Finland as contained in document A/AC105/635/Add.11 of 26 January 2005. It may be noted that the Finnish view also has sympathy with the "destination-based" approach; Mexico as contained in document A/AC105/635 of 15 January 1996; Syrian Arab Republic as contained in document A/AC105/635/Add.3 of 4 December 1996.
764 Benin view as contained in document A/AC105/635/Add.10 of 21 January 2004; Chile as contained in document A/AC105/635/Add.3 of 4 December 1996; Colombia as contained in document A/AC105/635/Add.5 of 5 February 1998; Costa Rica as contained in document A/AC105/635/Add.7 of 13 January 2003; Pakistan's view as contained in document A/AC105/635 of 15 January 1996; Peru as contained in document A/AC105/635/Add.9 of 7 May 2003; South Africa as contained in document A/AC105/635/Add.7 of 13 January 2003.

law ought to apply to aerospace objects.[765] A minority view actually believes that it is safer to always apply air law to aerospace flights based on the near certain likelihood of entry into airspace of other states.[766] In this case, the air law liability rules will apply.

9.7.4 The legal status of astronauts

Unlike the situation found in air law where thousands if not hundreds of thousands of people are within the purview of states' jurisdictional powers and responsibilities, the main human subjects of rights and liabilities in outer space are astronauts. The basic distinction here is that astronauts are distinguished scientists performing some form of official duty or the other of a scientific nature. Astronauts, therefore, enjoy a special status in space law way beyond the status conferred on pilots of aircraft and their crew. No further proof of this may be necessary beyond reference to Article V of the Outer Space Treaty (1967), which confers on astronauts the status of "envoys of mankind". Apart from references to the powers of control over unruly passengers and persons involved in unlawful interference with civil aviation conferred on the commander and crew members of aircraft contained in the Tokyo Convention (1963) (discussed earlier) and the responsibilities of the pilot spelled out in the Chicago Convention (1944), international law is largely silent on the status of pilots and crew members of aircraft when in airspace. In fact, professional groups of airline workers are beginning to clamour for international legislation, which protects them from the peculiar dangers they face.

The precise import of the status of astronauts as envoys of mankind is that all possible assistance is to be rendered to such persons wherever they may be in distress in the entire universe. The right to the safe existence of astronauts when in outer space is assured under law. Even where the condition of distress is within a foreign state's territory as a result of accidents during ascent or descent to or from outer space such distressing condition must be removed or remedied. The Astronaut's Agreement (1968) elaborates on the protective status designed for astronauts. It provides that a state which receives information that astronauts are in distress or have unintentionally landed in its territory, on the high seas or in

765 Greece, however, admits that all air law rules concerning safety of air navigation should also be jointly applicable. See A/AC105/635/Add.3 of 4 December 1996; Madagascar as contained in document A/AC105/635/Add.10 of 21 January 2004; Morocco as contained in document A/AC105/635/Add.6 of 21 January 2002. The Moroccan view is interesting in that it allows that air law could be applicable if the object in question is used in the airspace of another state. However, it admits that such a dual regime could cause confusion; Philippines as contained in document A/AC105/635 of 15 January 1996; Slovakia as contained in document A/AC105/635/Add.9 of 7 May 2003; the Netherlands as contained in document A/AC105/635/Add.8 of 17 February 2003.

766 There is, however, the natural question what if the flight avoids entry to state's airspace. Republic of Korea's view as contained in document A/AC105/635/Add.1 of 15 March 1996; cf. Turkey's as contained in document A/AC105/635/Add.3 of 4 December 1996.

territory not under the jurisdiction of any state is to immediately notify the launching state or, if that is not possible, make a public announcement regarding the incident. The state is also expected to notify the Secretary-General of the United Nations who shall disseminate such information as widely and as expeditiously as possible using all appropriate means (Article 1). If astronauts land unintentionally in the territory of a state, that state is to immediately take all necessary measures to assist them and shall inform the launching authority and the UN Secretary-General of the action taken. The launching authority should where necessary assist and contribute substantially to search and rescue operations but overall direction and control over search and rescue operations lies with the territorial state (Article 2). To cover the eventuality of astronauts alighting onto a territory which is not under the sovereignty or jurisdiction of any state,[767] Article 3 provides that those states "which are in a position to do so" shall extend assistance in search and rescue operations and shall inform the launching authority as well as the Secretary-General of the United Nations. Jurisdiction and control *ratione personae* do not change as a result of rescue after unintended and emergency landings into an area belonging to no state. Such rescued personnel must be promptly returned to representatives of the launching authority (Article 4). It is clear from all these rules that the development of the law (especially the Astronaut's Agreement (1968)) has been much in favour of space exploring states. This is an instance of the law moving quickly to cover possible problems that the technological powers may face even before they arise. It may be noted that these principles have remained sacrosanct whereas effort is being geared by the principal beneficiaries to change other principles, which are for the benefit of all in favour yet again of the powerful states.[768]

The Moon Agreement (1979) also contains interesting provisions relating to the legal status of persons on missions to that planet. States are under the obligation to adopt all practicable measures to safeguard the life and health of any person on the Moon and to offer shelter in their stations or other installations to such persons that are in distress (Article 10). Article 12(3) states that "in the event of an emergency involving the threat to human life, States Parties may use the equipment, vehicles, installations, facilities or supplies of other States Parties on the Moon". In this particular manner, the Moon Agreement (1979) goes even further than the Astronaut's Agreement (1979) or any of the other major space treaties in securing the interests of humans in outer space. Thus, the earthly injunction to be your brother's keeper extends further and finds expression in space law.

It can be conclusively said that compared with air crew and the situation in air law the duties of states towards astronauts are much more clearly set out. This probably is one of the reasons why force has not been readily employed by states

767 That is, any of the international spaces that have been discussed earlier such as the high seas and Antarctica. *Supra*, Chapter 4.

768 The Astronaut's Agreement (1968) presently has 114 states that are parties to it and it remains of both strategic and practical importance to spacefaring states in that, it makes space exploration a less hazardous activity for astronauts and serves as evidence of international law even in relation to those states that are not party to it.

in reaction to aerial trespass by spacecraft, as has been the case with respect to aerial trespass by aircraft. As it has been noted previously, foreign pilots accused of aerial trespass have been repeatedly shot down by territorial states and when arrested they face prosecution. Cases of hostile treatment after unintentional entry into foreign airspace abound. These have on many occasions led to mass loss of life. The declaration adopted by the Council of the ICAO in 1999 goes a long way to prescribe a better treatment for aircraft passengers and crew based on elementary considerations of humanity (Declaration 4) but it falls short of the clear rights and duties spelt out in the space treaties for the protection of people engaged in outer space activities. Therefore, apart from the factual differences between the commander and crew of an aircraft and those of a spacecraft, there are also far-reaching legal differences.

It must, however, be pointed out that the legal protection given to astronauts and personnel of a space vehicle does not imply that such people are placed above the law. They are not exempted from bearing the consequences of any unlawful activities they may commit while, for instance, in the airspace of another state or for acts done after landing.[769] In short, as succinctly put by Ryszard Hara: "[T]he recognition of astronauts as envoys of mankind does not confer upon them any privileges other than those formulated by the legal instruments in question."[770] Thus, it will for instance be illegal under national laws for an astronaut just like a pilot to engage in aerial espionage while in the airspace.

It is advisable that academic attention be turned to the following salient points in the prevailing major treaties. In the first place, the Astronaut's Agreement covers people who are situated in outer space and not simply astronauts in the technical sense of the word. However, the question of the extent of protection to be accorded to persons or astronauts who are not in outer space legally is a debatable point. This may take the form of astronauts accompanying an unregistered vehicle or performing acts, which are by their very nature illegal in international law. For instance, with respect to military personnel engaging in military manoeuvres or activities that are against Articles III and IV of the Outer Space Treaty, it is submitted here that such persons whether they are astronauts or personnel of a space vehicle are not "envoys of mankind" and are not entitled to the special status and protection given by the space treaties. If they are on the Moon, they may (if possible) also be lawfully denied access to space facilities of others.

Article III stipulates clearly that activities in the exploration and use of outer space, including the moon and other celestial bodies, must proceed "in accordance with international law, including the Charter of the United Nations, in the interest of maintaining international peace and security and promoting international co-operation and understanding". In this way, the territorial validity of the Charter of the UN extends to outer space and celestial bodies. So also do the normal rules of public international law on the responsibility of states for the actions of persons

769 Lachs op. cit.: 72.
770 Ryszard Hara op. cit.: 82.

acting under their jurisdiction. The threat or use of force against a foreign spacecraft or any other space object in outer space would constitute a violation of the political independence of the flag state. Similarly the right of self-defence as enshrined in Article 51 of the Charter applies to attacks from outer space. It is thus possible for a state to subject any astronaut or other personnel to arrest and punishment for any illegitimate actions committed against it while such person were in outer space. Some authors, including John Kish, are of the opinion that, in the event of such attacks against foreign spacecraft or space objects in outer space, a counter-attack may be launched, as a measure of self-defence against the spacecraft or space station and presumably against the astronauts or personnel involved.[771] It is necessary to underscore the importance of the exercise of absolute care in such cases. The uniqueness of the environment in which these actions will take place alone marks it out as dangerous for states to resort unimaginatively to military actions. Indeed, since the Space Treaty has imported into outer space the contents of the Charter that means the provisions relating to the Pacific settlement of dispute in Article 33 enjoy a particularly significant position in terms of the options open to states in times of acute disagreements.[772]

Under Article IV states undertake not to place in orbit around the earth any objects carrying nuclear weapons or any other kinds of weapon of mass destruction, to install such weapons on celestial bodies or station such weapons in outer space in any other manner. The Moon and other celestial bodies are to be used by all state parties to the Treaty exclusively for peaceful purposes. The establishment of military bases, installations and fortifications, the testing of any type of weapons and the conduct of military manoeuvres on celestial bodies is forbidden. The use of military personnel for scientific research or for any other peaceful purposes is, however, not prohibited. The use of any equipment or facility necessary for peaceful exploration of the Moon and other celestial bodies is also not prohibited. Thus, the mere presence of a military man in space as an astronaut does not violate the Outer Space Treaty and such persons are to enjoy the full benefits and privileges accorded to astronauts in the major space treaties.

It must be added as a caveat here that, because the legality or illegality of persons in outer space may not be immediately determinable, it is better for state parties to the treaties always to grant all protection and duties incumbent on them in situations of emergency. But where it is clear beyond reasonable doubt that the presence of any person(s) in outer space was for an illegal or hostile purpose, the duty to hand them over to the sending state's representatives on return to earth becomes debatable. Indeed, it is possible to liken jurisdiction over such persons to that of pirates in international law.

771 Kish op. cit: 183.

772 Article 33 provides that the parties to any dispute, the continuance of which is likely to endanger the maintenance of international peace and security, shall, first of all, seek a solution by negotiation, enquiry, mediation, conciliation, arbitration, judicial settlement, resort to regional agencies or arrangements, or other peaceful means of their own choice.

Important as Article 12 of the Moon Agreement (1979) is to the safety of astronauts the implementation of that provision may eventually lead to intense contentious disputes. Central to the scheme is the fact that there is no need to obtain the consent of the launching state of any facility on the Moon in the event of emergencies. The astronauts involved are in themselves the sole determinants of what constitutes a "threat to human life". In fact, nothing in that provision categorically requires that the intrusion or trespass be reported to the real owners. In these contemporary times of cut-throat competition in the design and manufacturing of space equipment it requires only common sense to anticipate the possibilities of espionage on the Moon. The Astronaut's Agreement is also ominously silent on the question of compensation for damages and/or wastage that may be committed during the visit. Finally, it may be noted that these provisions are derogations from the jurisdiction *ratione materiae* that states possess over their installations and facilities on the Moon. With all these in mind it can be said that further elaboration of Article 12 is called for. In the meantime it can only be hoped that states will always remain circumspect in their operations on the Moon. Fortunately, however, most of these fears will be redundant if states adhere to the overall spirit and letters of the space treaties. Allowance has already been made for the continuous sharing of scientific knowledge and the reporting of observations and events.

9.7.5 Civil and criminal jurisdiction over envoys of mankind

The criminal jurisdiction of states in the airspace was discussed earlier in this book. Whereas the problem of human criminality has not manifested itself in the sphere of outer space activities with as much regularity or even seriousness as it has in the airspace and on board aircraft, there is an increasing sense of importance of the need to establish adequate criminal jurisdiction over persons in outer space. It should be recalled that though airspace activities began in earnest around the turn of the 19th century it was not until 1950 that the lacunae regarding criminal jurisdiction in the airspace were exposed in the cases of *R v. Martin* and *R v. Cordova*.[773] It took another 13 years before the first international convention that dealt with criminal jurisdiction was signed by states. A cocktail of conventions (a number of which have been dealt with) are now in place to govern crimes in the airspace. Each in its own way regulates jurisdiction over human actions in the airspace or on board aircraft. Even with these developments, it has already been concluded that there appears to be need for further conventions to deal with other forms of criminality in the airspace such as the problem of unruly passengers on board aircraft. If the legal history of airspace activities is anything to go by, we may be fast approaching the time when a crucial development of a criminal nature would involve astronauts or other persons in outer space or on board spacecraft. In *Space Law and Government*, Haley anticipated these problems when he wrote:

773 *Supra*, Chapter 1.

"[M]en on these bodies cannot be left completely free and unrestrained. Abuse of life-giving materials [oxygen and food supply] might well become a felony or even capital crime."[774]

From our treatment of jurisdictional issues so far, it may be seen that the sources of criminal jurisdiction over persons in outer space arise in three possible ways. First, criminal jurisdiction can be exercised by the state of registry of the space vehicle on which the person is transported into outer space.[775] Second, in the case of the Moon Agreement (1979), states simply retain criminal jurisdiction over their personnel (Article 12). In this case, it does not matter on whose space vehicle they are transported into outer space. Third, and very important, it must be argued that the kind of universal jurisdiction states have over *pirates jure gentium* also extends in very limited cases into outer space.

The principle that states that, unless otherwise provided for, the criminal laws of the state of registry applies to all astronauts and people on board a spacecraft is an extension of the law of flag jurisdiction found in air law and in the law of the sea. Thus, criminal jurisdiction accrues automatically to the flag state of a spacecraft under international law. But it may also be enacted into national law.

The USA, for instance, enjoys in practice both *jurisfaction* and *jurisaction* over its astronauts in outer space. This is exercised through the powers conferred on the mission commander contained in (subpart 1214.7) "Authority of the Space Transportation System Commander".[776] Section 1214.700 establishes the authority of the STS commander to enforce order and discipline during all flight phases of the STS flight to take whatever action in his/her judgement is necessary for the protection, safety and well-being of all the personnel and on-board equipment, including countdown; following crew ingress, the STS commander has the authority to enforce order and discipline among all personnel on board. During emergency situations prior to liftoff, the STS commander has the authority "to take whatever action in his/her judgement is necessary for the protection or security, or safety, and well-being of all personnel on board".

Thus, state jurisdiction in outer space can be exercised not only in terms of *jurisfaction* but also in terms of *jurisaction*. Personal *jurisaction* (i.e. ability to enforce laws) is in some ways realisable in outer space as attested to by the provisions of Sections 1214.702 "Authority and Responsibility of the STS Commander", where it is stated that:

> (a) During all flight phases of an STS flight, the STS commander shall have the absolute authority to take whatever action is in his/her discretion necessary to (1) enforce order and discipline, (2) provide for the safety and well being of all personnel on board, and (3) provide for the protection of the STS elements

774 A.G. Haley, *Space Law and Government* (New York: Meredith Publishing Company, 1963): 149.

775 Article 7 Declaration (1963); Article VIII, Outer Space Treaty (1967).

776 Authority Pub. L. 85-588, 72 Stat. 426 (42 USC 2473, 2455: 18 USC 799); Article VIII TIAS 6347 (18 UST 2410). Source 45 FR 14845, MNar. 7, 1980.

and any payload carried or serviced by the STS. The Commander shall have authority throughout the flight to use any reasonable and necessary means including the use of physical force to, achieve this end. (b) The authority of the commander extends to any and all personnel on board the orbiter including Federal officers and employees *and all other persons whether or not they are U.S. nationals.* (emphasis added)

These provisions are strengthened by Section 1214.704, which puts the authority of the commander as absolute and unquestionable. In this manner, as has been shown earlier on, his status is akin to that of a ship's captain and that of the commander of an aircraft under the Chicago Convention. The connecting thread in all these provisions is the obvious need to ensure the safety and survival of crew and passengers (if any). One remarkable aspect of Section 1214.704 is the imposition of a fine of $5000 or imprisonment of not more than one year on anyone who violates wilfully or attempts/conspires to violate the sub part by any form of disobedience. But as Doyle rightly notes: "[I]t is likely to be in the interest of any crew member to abide by instruction of the commander to ensure his/her own survival."[777] Therefore, in the final analysis the role of the "commander" is central not only in the maintenance of discipline and safety on board aircraft and spacecraft but also in the determination of which state is in control of the craft in question. Whereas recent academic opinion questions the factual control of "commanders", whether of aircraft or spacecraft for navigational offences in light of the increasing computerisation of both aircraft and spacecraft,[778] it is better to conclude that from the legal standpoint, the Chicago Convention and the provisions just discussed immediately, the pilot and spacecraft commander are in ultimate control of their vessels. They alone have the luxury of lawfully orchestrating the exercise of *juris-action* on behalf of their flag state(s) in the circumstances of an international flight and in any environment in the entire universe. [779]

9.7.6 Jurisdiction and control over mixed nationality crews

The present regime found in space law is unspecific and in any case may be said to be inadequate. An example of the contradiction between the Outer Space Treaty (1967) and the Moon Agreement (1979) as to which state exercises jurisdiction over people on board spacecraft has already been cited. The former bestows it on the state of registry i.e. *lex loci registratonis*, while the latter places jurisdiction in the hands of the state that places the person there. It suffices to mention that this kind of confusion is simply not found in air law. Clearly, in the event of a mixed nationality

777 Doyle op. cit.: 55.

778 See Ronald Schmid, "Pilot in Command or Computer in Command? Observation in the Conflict between Technological Progress and Pilot Accountability", XXV, 6 *Air and Space Law* (2000): 286–7 ff.

779 Appendix 6 No. 4.5.1 states: "The pilot-in-command shall be responsible for the operation and safety of the Traffic Regulations." See also Appendix IV.

crew on an aircraft jurisdiction *ratione personae* will be retained by the state of registry of the aircraft. In any case, the likelihood and significance of any conflict about jurisdiction over aircraft crew may be said to be predictably less than that of a conflict on jurisdiction over a mixed crew of astronauts on a space station. The advent of the formation of regional and sub-regional astronaut corps makes the resolution of all aspects of jurisdiction *ratione personae* in outer space even more necessary. For instance, the formation of the European Space Agency, which in the relatively short period of its existence has been increasingly active in sponsoring individual astronauts for space missions. This includes joint programmes with other states outside the region as well as regional programmes.[780] In fact, the ESA aims "to transform European citizens into European astronauts".[781] In the face of these developments and with the insufficiency of international rules designed to regulate joint crews, it has been suggested quite reasonably that with respect to crews comprising different nationalities, new rules of private law will have to be formulated.[782] It has also been correctly pointed out that private international law forms part of national law. Accordingly, national laws will apply in full on board space stations and spacecraft with crews of mixed nationalities. This is more so where there are no further binding agreements specifying a different distribution of jurisdictional powers by the participants in the particular mission. It has, however, been pointed out that unavoidable as the practice of separate agreements is, caution must be exercised. Where participants to a joint mission have drawn up a separate agreement to regulate jurisdiction over personnel, the rules contained therein must conform substantially to that found in the space treaties.

For example, where a state by agreement surrenders jurisdiction over its astronauts to another in a space mission, it cannot be said that by virtue of that fact it also escapes liability for the actions of such persons in outer space. Therefore, the assumption that contract is king in relation to joint crews in outer space operates within limits. The limits being that at this stage in the development of space activities states may have to ensure that when their nationals are in outer space they do not engage in illegal acts which may incur state responsibility. Jan Klucka remains correct in stating that: "Special agreements relating to private international law will constitute *lex specialis* and the scope of the conflict rules which apply to space objects with crews of different nationality will be determined by the agreements." However, the fundamental test of overall conformity to the rules of space law remains relevant.[783]

Whereas it occurs with more frequency nowadays that there are astronauts of different nationality on board a spacecraft or space station, they would be sub-

780 Doyle op. cit.: 55.

781 Kevin J. Madders, "The Formation of the European Astronauts Corps: The Legal Framework", in *Proceedings of an International Colloquium*, ed. K.H. Bockstiegel (Cologne: Carl Heymans Verlag, 1992): 25.

782 Jan Klucka, "The Role of Private International Law in the Regulation of Outer Space", 39 *ICLQ*, (1990): 920.

783 Ibid.

ordinated to the disciplinary authority of the commander. The commander in all likelihood will have been appointed by the state of registry of the spacecraft or space station. However, wherever the Moon Agreement (1979) is applicable (which includes the Moon and other celestial bodies within the solar system) it is the position of the present writer that jurisdiction and control is retained by the state of nationality of the astronaut(s).

The formula employed in the Convention on the Establishment of the European Space Agency[784] is of relevance here. The policy objectives of the ESA are said to be informed by the "novelties introduced by the International Space Station co-operation and by entering the business of flying 'aerospace objects'."[785] On board the Freedom ISS manned base, jurisdiction over the ESA team is determined by the code of conduct established under the IGA and MOU and this code applies to the ESA Columbus Free Flyer.[786] Another source of the law regulating mixed nationality crews, at least in relation to the European Astronautics Corps, is the special staff regulations. Issues elaborated on include: categories of astronaut (both grade and functional status), selection, training, assignment, applicability of codes of conduct, intellectual property rights, criminal jurisdiction, disciplinary procedures, special insurance, status during missions and powers of attorney. Doyle correctly notes that other examples of laws that are designed to regulate foreign astronauts on board national spacecraft can be found in the NAS Act.[787]

9.7.7 Socio-scientific considerations in the exercise of criminal jurisdiction in spatial territories

In a book such as this, it is pertinent to inquire whether there are any connections to be made between criminal behaviour in the air and criminal behaviour in outer space. If there are, the question that arises is whether this should have any bearing on the exercise of criminal jurisdiction in spatial terms. Any similarities found thereby can only enrich the analysis on the exercise of criminal jurisdiction in spatial territories as well as serve as a pointer as to potential areas of development in both air law and space law. As a matter of fact, it was fashionable at a time for some scholars to focus rather fixedly on arguments of a paranormal and psychological kind as a basis for the development of criminal jurisdiction over humans in outer space. Lawyers such as Robinson urge that international space law must not be allowed to apply shop-worn legal positivism in relation to the exercise of jurisdictional powers over people in outer space. He, therefore, postulates that the development and application of criminal behaviour should be based on a theory of "biochemical law". His position is that since nature was not made to suit man

784 See the ESA Convention May 1975, Basic Texts of the European Space Agency, Convention and Rules (1980); US Congress, US Congress, Space Law and Related Documents, 101st Congress 2 d Sess., Committee Print, S. Print No. 101-98, GPO, Washington, DC 1990.

785 Madders op. cit.: 26.

786 See the Columbus and Hermes Declaration set down in Annex III to the ESA Convention.

787 See Doyle op. cit.: 53.

but man made to suit nature; therefore, "[S]pace jurists must be acutely aware of the behavioural consequences of environmental changes permitted by technological manipulations." He concluded that a new juridical regime should be developed for astronauts on space stations with different and very specific standards for crew members vis-à-vis civil and criminal law.[788]

Christol is also of the opinion that account must be taken of the artificial environment and special human reactions, which may be anticipated under the novel conditions that exist outer space. Therefore, he insists that:

> [T]he lawyer, scientist, and technologist must jointly investigate the emotional, psychological and sociological problems created by such conditions as extended periods of weightlessness, artificial gravity, communal operation, in congested quarters, and reliance upon possibly uncertain supplies of life supporting substances. Their purpose should be to prepare acceptable legal norms for those embarking on extended space station activities. It is not too soon to think carefully about a normative code of space conduct which would carry fixed sanctions and which would be quite distinct from the operational rules and procedures designed to achieve safe passage.[789]

Lawyers trained in the common law tradition might find the exploration into extra-legal considerations in a discussion of spatial sovereignty and jurisdiction as unnecessary if not downright unacceptable. But it must be said that it would be avoiding reality to hold that the special conditions in which air flight and outer space flight take place will not have an impact on criminal behaviour. Examples of "perfectly normal and respectable persons" who assume appalling and morally as well as legally abhorrent behaviour while on relatively short air flights have already been shown (Chapter four). Whether and to what extent such conditions should reflect in jurisdictional competencies of states and particularly in terms of punishment of wrongdoers could become one of the sharpest points of divergence among jurists. One of the more innovative theories developed to understand the inevitability of violence among astronauts and persons in space goes thus:

> *Sensory Deprivation + Insecurity + Boredom = Potential Violence*[790]

The aim of this theory, as with others like it, is to make the lawmaker aware of the peculiar vulnerability of people in space towards uncharacteristic and potentially dangerous criminal behaviour. It is possible to disagree with this thinking. Robinson never does enlighten us on the applicability of his formula to crimes in

788 Robinson op. cit.: 27, 28, 30 ff.; see also Ernst Fasan, *Relations with Alien Intelligences: The Scientific Basis of Metalaw* (Berlin: Berlin Verlag, 1970): *et seq.*; *cf.* C. Voicu and T. Olteneanu, "Study of the Correlation between Flexibility of Attention and Dynamism of Nervous Processes", in *Biological Bases of Individual Behaviour*, ed. V.D. Nebzlitsyn and T.A. Gray (1972): 325–32.

789 Christol op. cit.: 494.

790 See Robinson op. cit.: 303.

the airspace. Indeed, most if not all of the constituent factors he claims may lead to violence may also be said to apply to people in the airspace. At any rate, it may be doubted that violence may be understood or excused in the law on the basis of predisposing factors. If the argument is pushed to its logical conclusion, then similar considerations will have to apply to people in confined spaces such as buses and offices.

The development of legal reasoning has shown that even under extenuating circumstances, the law eschews criminal conduct and states impose the strictest standards on their subjects to avoid crime. Thus, for example in the case of survival homicide, a situation that increasing outer space activities may soon lead to, there is no indication that space law will evolve different rules from pre-existing law. In isolated situations of extreme duress in outer space, self-sacrifice as opposed to survival homicide is recommended. It has been rightly noted that:

> In a space disaster the potential for rescue or abandonment is likely to be known with some certainty. When all available sources of oxygen have been totalled, and allowing for maximum narcosis of the crew there is simply too little oxygen for all to breathe, it is unlikely there is much room to wonder whether the next week will bring unforeseen rescue to the crew. But there are conceivable calamity situations, where the lives lost could be mitigated by sacrifice, and that the value of that sacrifice will be as predictable with as much certainty as humans can ever hope to obtain.[791]

This position follows British and American jurisprudence, which deal with survival homicide situations. In *US v. Holmes* the presiding circuit justice charged that; "it was the duty of the sailors to sacrifice themselves first to save the passengers".[792] Because of this, the defendant who assisted in throwing 14 people into the sea in order to save those remaining in a lifeboat was convicted. Also in *R v. Dudley and Stephens* where starvation and cannibalism occurred as a result of the sudden sinking of a yacht 1,000 miles from land, culpability was found for the consequent execution of the youngest survivor who was the weakest and near death. Lord Coleridge clearly stated that "self-sacrifice was the approved solution to such dilemmas".[793] There would seem to be no compelling reason to adopt any different rules for homicide in outer space or on board aircraft. In conclusion, in the absence of convincing sociological and scientific evidence, it is advisable that space law and air law should not be concerned with the socio-scientific reasons for criminal behaviour in spatial territories. What must be done is to continue developing the law to cope with newer challenges in terms of criminal jurisdiction in spatial territories in order to ensure that no lacunae exist.

791 See the Institute for Creative Studies in Washington DC, report entitled "Long Duration Manned Space Missions Certain Non-Engineering Aspects" quoted in Robinson ibid: 295.

792 Fed. Cases 360, No. 15, 383 (US Cir Ct E. Pa., 1842).

793 (1884) LR 14; 14 QBD 273 (1885). See also A.W.B. Simpson, *Cannibalism and the Common Law* (Chicago: University of Chicago Press, 1984).

9.8 Summary and conclusions

It is important to adopt a fairly flexible definition of space stations. Thus, we might say that a space station is an object, or a collection of objects, which is in an intentional long-duration orbit and is, at least in part, habitable. This definition explicitly excludes space transportation systems. Rockets and shuttles that go into space for transitory period (few days or weeks) are mere transport systems analogous to aircraft and deserve separate legal treatment from space stations.

The functions space stations perform are varied and increasing. Space law has to develop quickly to cope with the questions of jurisdiction and control that are presented by technological possibilities. Current use of space stations include (but are not limited to) data gathering, transmitting of information, material processing, repairing facilities, energy generation, storage facilities and scientific research. The construction of huge space stations capable of holding a large population of people is well within contemplation. The exact workings of jurisdiction over persons sent into outer space have not been clearly worked out as in respect of jurisdiction over people in the airspace. With the advent of space tourism and the development of space hotels and multi-purpose space platforms, the wholesale extension of criminal laws over people to cover activities in outer space is now a pressing necessity. In this way, the problem of oases of lawlessness that existed in respect of aircraft in international airspace prior to the legal developments starting from the 1957 Sputnik flight will be avoided in space law. Questions of civil jurisdiction over contracts and intellectual property among others will also have to be addressed soon.

The present laws governing jurisdiction over civil and criminal matters on existing space stations and spacecraft would appear to reflect the interests of the powerful spacefaring states. A good instance of this is found in provisions, which empower the USA with respect to the international space station to exercise criminal jurisdiction over misconduct committed by non-US nationals in or on a non-US element of the manned base or attached to the manned base or the personnel placed thereon. Similarly, the contemporary rules governing intellectual property over inventions and discoveries made in outer space are very much based on competitive capitalistic ideology without enough regard for the essentially cooperative nature of outer space activities. It is important that spacefaring states should not forget when enacting domestic legislation or making regional treaties that outer space does not belong to anyone. Therefore, particular care must be taken to avoid provisions that directly or indirectly contradict the rules laid down in existing space treaties. Most importantly all new legislation must respect the legal status of outer space as the province of mankind as well as the common heritage of mankind principle that applies on the Moon and other celestial bodies.

It is necessary to repeat the distinction regarding the right to collect in appropriate quantities and remove samples of mineral and other substances on celestial bodies in the course of scientific investigations and the right to conduct commercial mining on space stations in outer space. The former is expressly permitted under existing rules including the Outer Space Treaty (1967), whereas arguably the Moon Agreement (1979) has in effect forbidden the latter until state parties put into place an international regime for the exploitation. In the running and operation of space stations, due regard must also be given to the status of celestial bodies under the CHM principle and the province of all mankind formula. An exception may, however, be made where the resource made use of is of an inexhaustible class such as solar energy. In such cases, the prohibition of national appropriation enshrined in Article II of the Outer Space Treaty (1967) would not apply. However, even here commercial exploitation cannot be legally conducted until a suitable regime is developed which takes account of the CHM principle.

The principles of registration and nationality are of such utility in international law that they not only apply to spacecraft and space stations but also to aircraft, ships and Antarctic stations. If a space station is to function as a single unit there is no point in the separate registration of the flight elements or the component parts of what is to all intents and purposes a single unit. It must, however, be admitted that prior to the docking together of the component parts in space there may be the need to register the parts separately. In that case, another registration may be necessary for the entire unit for the purpose of its operation as a single body. There would then have to be appointed a single state of registry for the space station as a whole. Just as concluded with respect to aircraft, states wishing to register space stations must be made to demonstrate a "genuine link" with the private organisations involved. This position is consistent with developments in international law since the *Nottebohm case*. Only in this way can the determination of control over space stations and other space instrumentalities such as satellites and rockets be determined with the desirable certitude.

The rule expressed in Article 12(3) that in the event of an emergency involving the threat to human life, state parties may use the equipment, vehicles, installations, facilities or supplies of other state parties on the Moon goes a long way in revealing the true spirit of cooperation governing outer space activities. The earthly injunction to be your brother's keeper extends further and finds expression in space law. In this light, air law has a lot to learn from space law.

It can be said conclusively that, compared with the situation in air law, the duties of states towards astronauts are much more clearly set out. This probably is one of the reasons why force has not been readily employed by states in reaction to aerial trespass by spacecraft, as it has been the case with respect to aerial trespass by aircraft. However, the Astronaut's Agreement (1968) does favour sending states over territorial states. As has been noted previously, foreign pilots accused of aerial trespass have been repeatedly shot down by territorial states many times without adequate respect for human life. Cases of hostile treatment after unintentional entry into foreign airspace abound. These have on many occasions led to mass loss of life. In essence, it must be said that there are more prospects within existing international law for peaceful resolution of jurisdictional conflicts in relation to outer space activities than in airspace activities.

10 Contemporary trends and threats to the regime of outer space law

10.1 Illegality of the militarisation of space

The militarisation of outer space is prohibited but that has not stopped speculation on the usefulness of outer space as strategic military outposts and dominion of influence. Drumming up the language of war for a region that from the very inception of its legal regulation has been declared the province of mankind is not an easy task. Yet there is a strong field of American writers particularly in the Air Force schools that aggressively pushes this agenda in its academic publications. The argumentation strategy of those in this group include scaremongering, inventive reading of current international law on the subject and outright preference for the argumentation of force rather than the force of argumentation. An account goes:

> Until very recently, nations faced few constraints on uses of the space domain. Yet, despite the professed goal of cooperation in outer space and denouncement of aggressive use of force within that realm by many counties, "all space faring states today have military missions, goals, and contingency space-operations plans." Thus space is already a contested environment.[794]

The same writer warns "war is in the nature of man and, if history is a teacher, the issue is not if, but when war will reach outer space".[795] The admonition that "America must actively engage the international legal process in an effort to mould law in such a way as to enhance national security interests" is largely irrelevant. In truth, few states have, as has the USA, helped to mould the present shape of space law particularly as it relates to militarisation and propertisation of outer space.[796] The assertion that "international law may become one of the most potent weapons ever deployed against the United States" ought actually to be celebrated even by

794 J. W. Bellflower, "The Influence of Law on Command of Space", 65 *Air Force Law Review* (2010): 108, 109, 116.

795 Bellflower ibid; 109, 116.

796 See Adlai Stevensen in 1st Comm. Statement on "International Cooperation in the Peaceful Uses of Outer Space", 2 Dec. 1963, UN Press Release No. 4323, 2 December 1963. Statement also appended to the Educational Progress of NASA, Senate Hearings on Aeronautical and Space Sciences 88th Cong. 1st Sess. 21–2 November 1963.

the USA itself.[797] For if international law can successfully hold back the USA from space militarisation, this strong conceptual firewall will inexorably be the bulwark that will prevent other powers from successfully doing so in the 21st century. The idea that a "new" kind of international law is emerging that is "profoundly undemocratic at its core" and "has the potential to undermine American leadership in the post-Cold War global system" simply does not add up in respect of the use of outer space as in many other areas of international relations.[798] If there ought to be one single thing that qualifies to be bigger than even American or any other states ambitions it is the environment of outer space consisting as it does of unlimited and boundless universes. The alternative of a military space race in the modern era of increasing democratisation of technological attainments will hold unimaginable horrors and must be avoided.

Indeed, Bellflower had correctly discerned the position that the present regime of common ownership created for outer space means that, as with the high seas, powerful states: "cannot 'occupy' that is physically exclude neutrals – or enemies – from, space as one might with respect to territory on land".[799] The preference of those writers like Bellflower for the USA to engage in a "normative command of space" is illegitimate at law. Such definitions by the admission of Bellflower will support the acquisition of ownership and sovereignty whereas most writers in the American Air Force schools recognise and admit that "the very nature of a commons is that no state has sovereignty over it".[800] Therefore, if the aim of such normative struggle is to grant in favour of certain states authoritative control over outer space, the aspiration is demonstrably morally reprehensible.

The idea that outer space militarisation is inevitable is far from convincing. European nations involved in the ESA have not shown any interest in military space missions. If the definition of 'spacefaring state' includes states that procure satellite launchings through other states then it becomes clear that the predominant attention of states in relation to their use of outer space has been meteorological, telecommunications, commercial and not military.[801] The idea that the UN and

797 David B. Rivkin, Jr and Lee A Casey, "The Rocky Shoals of International Law", *The National Interest* (2000/01): 35.

798 See Charles J. Dunlap, Jr, "Law and Military Interventions: Preserving Humanitarian Values in 21st Century Conflicts", Carr Center for Human Rights Policy, Harvard Kennedy School Program on National Security and Human Rights, 2001 Workshop Papers: Humanitarian Challenges in Military Intervention: 5, available at http://www.hks.harvard.edu/cchrp/Web%20Working%20Papers/Use%20of%20Force/Dunlap2001.pdf (accessed 27 May 2010).

799 Bellflower op. cit.: 119.

800 Craig H. Allen, "Command of the Commons' Boasts: An Invitation to Lawfare?", 83, 1 *International Law Studies* (2007): 34.

801 The call to the instrumentation of the interesting concept of "lawfare" by pro space militarisation theorists shows their increasing desperation with the strong legal regime against space militarisation. Law as a method of warfare theorists include Bellflower op. cit.: 144. Such reasoning has more in common with Machiavellian traditions than with international law. In *The Prince*, Machiavelli admonishes leaders: "You should know, then that there are two means of contending: one by using laws, the other force. The first is appropriate for men, the second for animals; but because the former is often ineffective, one must have recourse to the latter." Niccolo Machiavelli, *The Prince*, ed. Quentin Skinner and Russell Price (Cambridge: Cambridge University Press, 1988): 61.

the COPUOS will abandon their very primal duties to maintain global peace and move towards the facilitation of a regime allowing militarisation of outer space is even by the standards of military academics overly ambitious. In view of all these, it may be concluded that "tactical lawfare", "strategic lawfare", "spherical battlespace", "command of space" are all fanciful flights of fancy with little or no chance of legitimation within the field of space law.[802] The power-realist approach to the exploration and use of outer space is prone to the projection of lawlessness and chaos into outer space. The introduction of a "playstation mentality" to the environment of outer space via space weaponisation will no doubt produce regrettable results. As Phillip Alston put it regarding the egregious abuse of the right to life through hi-tech instruments:

> The clearest challenge to this principle today comes from the programme operated by the United States' Central Intelligence Agency (CIA) in which targeted killings are carried out from unmanned aerial vehicles or drones. It is clear that many hundreds of people have been killed as a result, and that this number includes some innocent civilians.[803]

In view of such arguments, it would be reckless for the law to proceed in a manner that allows space weaponisation. The importance of establishing the illegality of space militarisation based on contemporary international law and refuting any suggestions as to lacunae on the topic is that it will remove all possibility of that old bugbear of international law intertemporal law rearing itself in space. It is clear that it is not permissible to weaponise space equipment and facilities under international law just as it is not possible to subject portions of outer space to exclusive jurisdiction. Therefore, it is not possible for states that have engaged in space launches to convert objects launched into military weaponry under the claim that there was no clarity upon the point at any time since the occurrence of the Sputnik flights.[804] The potential of a race towards space weaponisation race will

802 These ideas represent "harmful fantasy" that some legal sceptics refer to in their characterisation of international law. Robert H. Bork, *Coercing Virtue: The Worldwide Rule of Judges* (Washington DC: AEI Press, 2003): 39.

803 Philip Alston, "Promotion and Protection of all Human Rights, Civil, Political, Economic, Social and Cultural Rights, including the Right to Development", Report of the Special Rapporteur on extrajudicial, summary or arbitrary executions, United Nations A/HRC/14/24/Add.6, General Assembly, Human Rights Council Fourteenth session Agenda item 3, available at http://www2.ohchr.org/english/bodies/hrcouncil/docs/14session/A.HRC.14.24.Add6.pdf (accessed 4 June 2010); Declan Walsh, "Leading UN Official Criticises CIA's role in Drone Strikes", *Guardian*, 3 June 2010: 24.

804 The Japanese occupation of Korea from the forced Protocol on 23 February 1904 and formal annexation in 1910 to 1945 has, for instance, been justified under the workings of intertemporal law. Japanese writers point out that other major powers were also conquering weaker countries and annexing territory during this period, thus throwing into question whether the annexation of Korea by Japan was illegal. A similar scenario cannot be played out in space law because the treaty law that governs space law has been unequivocal on the point that outer spaces can only be used for peaceful uses and that it cannot be subject to exclusive use or sovereign claims. Dyke (2006) op. cit.: 215–17.

be inevitable if the laws prohibiting the activity are disturbed, just as surely as the race to acquire drones,[805] ship missile launchers and nuclear weapons has been unstoppable.[806] Collateral damage, human error and intelligence failure, matters that have become almost commonplace in the prosecution of defence operations in terrestrial conflicts, maritime blockades, drone attacks and the implementation of no-fly zones must be denied a new lease of life in outer space.

10.2 Jurisdiction and control over remote sensing operations: questions surrounding clandestine remote sensing from outer space

Remote sensing activities are one of the core areas of the utilisation of outer space science. It is difficult to overestimate the usefulness of this application to commercial and exploitative activities on earth. There are, however, security implications of remote sensing that are of concern to all states but to which developing states are particularly vulnerable. It would appear that the privacy of states has been lost in a fundamental way to remote sensing capabilities of a few technologically advanced states although access to the technology is improving remarkably for all interested states. Bin Cheng in 2004 gave a description of the impact of remote sensing activities on modern states that may be considered impressive in its analogical and figurative value. He developed the idea that hitherto a state's territory is its castle:

> A state's territory is its castle. No one is allowed to enter it without its permission . . . although aviation has added an extra dimension to the problem of states in controlling what goes on in their territory, their grip in law and in fact remains unaltered, so much so that from the legal point of view the world resembles a series of immense airtight petroleum storage tanks representing the various national States with their three-dimensional sovereignty . . . the arrival of the space age was as if the lid on the tank was suddenly ripped off. And, if we can change the image, it was like opening up an ant-hill with all the ants inside scurrying round wondering how to cover themselves and their secrets and stores.[807]

Where remote sensing is conducted by the mutual agreement between states or between private corporations and states there would be little controversy. The

805 Alston opines that the use of drones will spread and it will be more available to more and more states leading to chaos in the international system. He writes: "The appeal of armed drones is clear: especially in hostile terrain, they permit targeted killings at little to no risk to the State personnel carrying them out, and they can be operated remotely from the home State. It is also conceivable that non-state armed groups could obtain this technology." See Alston op. cit.: 9. Note also reports that Iran has provided weaponised drones to Hezbollah. Dan Ephron, "Hezbollah's Worrisome Weapon", *Newsweek*, 11 September 2006.

806 Over 40 countries have drones including the UK, Turkey, Russia, France, India and Iran have acquired drones. Walsh op. cit.: 24.

807 Cheng (2004) op. cit.: 573, 577–8.

legality of such activities would be manifest as long as the activities fall within the express or implied agreement between the pertinent parties.[808] In relation to areas within state territory or jurisdictional competence, the prohibition of clandestine gathering of data is irrefutable and the privacy of states is supported by international law and state practice.[809]

Remote sensing operations conducted through clandestine means, however, is the new bugbear of international relations. The problem of clandestine remote sensing may emanate in two basic ways: First, and perhaps most significant from the security of the territorial state's point of view, is espionage by remote sensing. This problem was first dramatically exposed during the twilight years of the Cold War era when a picture emerged in the *Jane's Defence Weekly* in August 1984 and in an edition of the widely circulated UK *Times* newspaper in the same month showing with extraordinary clarity the Soviet shipyard at Nikolaiev on the Black Sea.[810] Inset in the picture was the emerging jigsaw of the construction of the

808 Thus, for instance, the exact geographic position to be remote sensed would usually be identified. The particular features or resources to be searched for may also have been provided for. In this way, the body in charge of conducting the remote-sensing operations is bound by this agreement and ought not to go beyond it or retain unpermitted information that is derived in the course of the remote sensing. It is, thus, suggested that a remote sensing contract over national territory constitutes a kind of contract of agency. In which case, the principal is the state acquiring the required data and/or imagery and the agent is the state or corporate body conducting the scientific aspects of the task, and owning or operating the requisite satellites. In this manner, the normal duties of a commercial agent to his principal ought to apply and in performing his activities a commercial agent must look after the interests of his principal and act dutifully and in good faith. In particular, a commercial agent must (a) make proper efforts to negotiate and, where appropriate, conclude the transactions he is instructed to take care of; (b) communicate to his principal all the necessary information available to him; (c) comply with reasonable instructions given by his principal. For the common law jurisprudence on such agencies, see *Keppel v. Wheeler* 1927 1KB 557; *Chaudry v. Prabhakar* [1989] 1 WLR 29 (on reasonable diligence); *Boardman v. Phipps* [1988] 3 All ER 718 (no secret profits); *Initial Services v Putterill* [1968] 1 QB 396; *Gartside v. Outram* (1856) 26 LJ Ch. 113 (duty not to divulge confidential information); *Yasuda Fire & Marine Insurance Co. of Europe v. Orion Marine Insurance Underwriting Agency* 1995 2 QB 174 (duty to account to principal).

809 The general slant of international law is towards protection of the sovereignty and privacy of states. This is further buttressed by the important restrictions in the international regulation of various easements granted to foreign states in areas and zones that expose the territorial state to security concerns. Article 38 of the LOSC (1982), which regulates transit passage in straits used for international navigation, includes an important caveat namely – that in relation to research and survey activities during transit passage, foreign ships, including marine scientific research and hydrographic survey ships, may not carry out any research or survey activities without the prior authorization of the states bordering straits. Article 40, which deals with research and survey activities, further entrenches an anti-clandestine approach to collection of data by stating that during transit passage, foreign ships, including marine scientific research and hydrographic survey ships, may not carry out any research or survey activities without the prior authorisation of the states bordering straits. Relevant state practice may be seen in the reaction of the USA to the U2 incident highlighted in Chapter 5. Witnessing the flight of US aircraft over Soviet territory and the subsequent downing of the erring aircraft, the USA not only apologised for the event but made diplomatic assurances that such reconnaissance aerial flights will no longer be made. Bin Cheng, "The United Nations and Outer Space", 14 *CLP* (1961): 247, at 264–8; Cheng (2004) op. cit.: 557.

810 *The Times*, 8 August 1984: 26.

premier Soviet naval 75,000-ton nuclear-powered aircraft. Second is in the form of the gathering of data and images of the natural resources and environment of a territorial state. This includes collation of economically sensitive information about energy resources, hydrocarbon reserves, agriculture, fisheries, forestry, mining, shipping, cartography, wildlife migration patterns and human traffic flows.[811]

One of the options said to be open to states that are apprehensive of spying from above is that they should adopt domestic laws that make the remote sensing of their natural resources and any of the related processes, including the dissemination and use of the information derived therefrom, offences under national laws unless due authorisation are given. Presumably such laws will apply to offenders as Cheng said "wherever in the world the offences may have been committed".[812] Apart from the quick note that "wherever in the cosmos including the earth" would have probably been a neater formulation, the difficulty with this opinion is that it brings into discussion yet again the immense difficulties attending extraterritorial law making discussed in Chapter 1. This is more so with respect to the fact that such extraterritorial lawmaking will have in its purview the application of laws over foreigners and corporate bodies not within state territory and who may, in fact, be the alter ego of foreign government agencies and state organs.

Cheng himself had noted the limitations provided by the *Lotus Case* (1927) to the extent that the case, while seemingly allowing states to criminalise acts committed outside territory, does so on the proviso that enforcement may be attempted only when the perpetrators come within their territorial boundaries.[813] There is, of course, the possible argument that with respect to the small number of states that have declared their jurisdiction over portions of outer space up to several thousand kilometres away from earth under the so-called Bogota Convention unpermitted remote sensing satellite and activities could be argued to have occurred within territorial space. This would also appear to be compatible with the idea that a state's jurisdiction ought to extend up to wherever its security is being threatened. The Bogota Convention will be discussed in more detail in our final chapter in relation to the spatial demarcation question. It will later be seen that the providence of the Bogota view is still far from clear and has been attacked by many powerful states. Thus, this may not again be the solution required to safeguard the legitimate fears and interests of underlying states in relation to hostile or military remote sensing activities.

Why then would Cheng have placed himself in the position to recommend a solution that appears to contradict the clear jurisprudence of "effective *jurisaction*" he had espoused many years previously? The answer may lie in the fact that he and many others like him entrap themselves in the ropes of the conclusion that

811 See our later discussions on the views of states on the spatial demarcation. See also Cheng (2004) op. cit.: 587.

812 Cheng (2004) op. cit.: 583.

813 Note may also be taken of the very helpful concept of *jurisaction* introduced by Cheng himself and discussed earlier.

remote sensing by means of satellites where it takes place above 100 to 110 kilometres from the earth's surface is legal because it is then deemed to have taken place in outer space and is, therefore, for all intents and purposes lawful activity.[814] Of the many problems with this view the immediately relevant ones include that it ignores entirely the state security perspective to the spatial demarcation issue (also discussed in the last chapter). Furthermore, it reduces the entire question of the lawfulness of espionage activities from space to the simplistic question posed by Cheng: "Where are these data gathering satellites located, in international space or national space?"[815] The prevailing premise of the discussion ought to be the promotion of remote sensing activities without precipitating unwholesome practices and creating tensions and conflict among independent, sovereign states.

The idea that espionage from outer space is lawful or has received tacit recognition as an internationally legitimate activity just because the 1972 Treaty between the USA and the Soviet Union on the Limitation of Anti-Ballistic Missile Systems (ABM Treaty) stated that the parties shall each use "national technical means of verification at its disposal" in order to assure itself of the other signatory's compliance is wholly satisfactory.[816] To begin with, the language of the treaty insists furthermore that any such means of verification must accord and be consistent "with generally recognized principles of international law". It is important to note that such a principle cannot emerge out of the practice of two states no matter how powerful they may be or have been as in the case of the USA and the erstwhile Soviet Union (or Russia today). It is equally insufficient to dismiss the valid fears and concerns of the vast majority of developing states by adopting the view as Cheng did: "Military reconnaissance satellites have not only become a fact of international life that states just have to learn to live with, but also a vital instrument in the process of arms control and the preservation of international peace."[817]

There is ample evidence in treaties to indicate that unilateral lifting of the aerial veil of a state without its consent may be seen as hostile, offensive and/or even aggressive conduct in certain instances. A good place to begin the analysis will be the UN Charter. Article 74 provides that member states agree that their policy in respect of all territories under their jurisdiction "must be based on the general principle of good neighbourliness, due to account being taken of the interests and well being of the rest of the world, in social economic and commercial matters". In this way, one would struggle to see how clandestine study of another state's commercial and economic resources from outer space will fit within the necessary concept of good neighbourliness. Indeed, Cheng's conclusion on the matter is apposite stating that:

> There is no reason why this principle does not apply to data gathering from outer space . . . Although the import of the principle may not be altogether

814 Cheng (2004) op. cit.: 578–9, 581.
815 Cheng (1961) op. cit.: 579.
816 Cf. Cheng (2004) op. cit.: 585.
817 Cheng (2004) op. cit.: 586.

clear, its relevance to remote sensing is patent, especially in relation to the problems of dissemination and misuse of remote sensing data and information.[818]

In this manner, there is nothing about the "hi-tech" phenomena of remote sensing activities that ought to disturb the decisions reached on the binding nature of the obligation of good neighbourliness and respect for equitable conduct in the *Trail Smelter Arbitration* (1935),[819] *Corfu Channel Case* (Merits) (1949),[820] and *Fisheries Jurisdiction Case.*[821] Admittedly, it is a difficult proposition to state that specific rules exist under customary international law that prohibit espionage from outer space. It is, however, also difficult to prove that espionage activity from space is perfectly legal under international law in view of the spirit expressed in the provisions of the space treaties that place compelling emphasis on peaceful purposes as the guiding principle in the exploration of outer space. [822] It is, therefore, possible to conclude that although the matter is yet to be decided either way it accords with international policy that an eventual decision must take account of the need to prevent disputes among states. What is likely going to endanger international peace and security the most? Is peaceful conduct of international relations best served by allowing espionage or clandestine commercial exploration through remote sensing or not? There is already enough guidance in international jurisprudence that sways the argument in favour of an outright prohibition of all unauthorised remote sensing.

In sum, the direction of the moral compass on the issue of aerial to reconnaissance or covert remote sensing is the test of the king of the castle. According to this view, if all states were castles and their sovereigns were kings, the true test of legality ought to lie in the answer to the question of what will each king say on being told that the roof has been lifted and someone is peering into the castle without invitation. It is suggested that the king of the castle will not at all be pleased with the development. He may embark on a number of courses either to remove the threat or get even by some other means. The emergent scenario will tend towards instability rather than order and ought to be prevented if at all possible (Cheng 2004: 577–8).

10.3 Liberal commercialism and entrepreneurship as driving force of international space tourism

Recent trends in the development of space technology and space investment and practice of certain developed states show that space tourism is set to become the

818 Cheng (2004) op. cit.: 584.

819 3 RIAA: 1905 at p. 1965

820 ICJ Rep. 1949, p. 4 at p. 22.

821 ICJ Rep. 1974, p. 3, at pp. 30–31.

822 See, generally, the provisions of the General Assembly Resolution 1721 (XVI) of 20 December 1961 (International Co-operation in the Peaceful Uses of Outer Space); cf. Article IV Outer Space Treaty. The Moon and other celestial bodies are to be used by all state parties to the Treaty exclusively for peaceful purposes. The establishment of military bases, installations and fortifications, the testing of any type of weapons and the conduct of military manoeuvres on celestial bodies is forbidden; note also the common heritage principle which applies to outer space.

new frontier in air and space transportation. The development is bound to unsettle certain legal concepts and categories that took painstaking effort to put in place in the last century. It is possible to understand how Antarctic and Arctic tourism could have provided inspiration for those interested in space tourism. Antarctic and Arctic tourism revealed, even before space tourism could have been envisaged, the irrepressible curiosity of mankind to visit all corners of the earth and to visualise the universe. From 1958 to 1987, an average of a 1,000 tourists visited Antarctica each season. In 1999 to 2003, an estimated 15,000 tourists made landings in Antarctica and, during the 2003–2004 season, this number increased by 45% to more than 19,500. The estimate of total passengers for the 2004–2005 season, including those not landing, is over 27,000.[823]

No serious analysis of the phenomenon will fail to recognise the desirability of the democratisation of the outer space activity that allows unprecedented access to *hoi polloi*. A particularly inspiring account notes:

> [I]ndividuals in space experience the well-documented effect known as the overview effect . . . transformational experience that commonly follows observation of Earth from space-Earth free of borders and conflicts. When astronauts return to Earth, they all typically share the same transformational experience. A growing, successful space-tourism industry could bring perhaps millions to space who would, in turn, share this experience with others. This could have a powerful positive impact on our world. Space tourism is as important as ever, perhaps even more so than it was prior to September 11. Its importance goes beyond its potential economic value as a new industry when it can facilitate a new view of our world, bringing its people together and forming partnerships from former enemies as space remains outside the framework of human violence, hostilities, and war.[824]

The most striking feature of space tourism in the 21st century is that it is nearly entirely privatised. Indeed, it is fair to say that it is the free liberal economic model that governs much of recent development in the area of space activities and the regulation of space tourism will have to take this into account.[825] The principles of international space law are enshrined in the specialised treaties we identified in

823 Kees Bastmeijer and Ricardo Roura, "Regulating Antarctic Tourism and the Precautionary Principle", 98 *American Journal of International Law* (2004): 763–4.

824 D.M. Livingston, "Space Tourism after Dennis Tito Livingston", available at www.marssociety.org (accessed 15 September 2010).

825 The Intergovernmental Agreement of 1998 (IGA) is the primary legal document by which the nations involved in the ISS reciprocally bind one another to a common objective. And the IGA made references to commercialisation: "This civil International Space Station will enhance the scientific, technological, *and commercial use of outer space*" (emphasis added). Intergovernmental Agreement (January 1998), Article (1), available at ftp.hq.nasa.gov/pub/pao/reports/1998/IGA.html [hereinafter IGA] (accessed 12 September 2010). Rosanna Sattler, "US Commercial Activities Aboard the International Space Station", XXVIII, 2 *Air & Space Law* (2003): 70, 79–80, 230; see also Salin op. cit.: 79, 81.

Chapter 6, which are regarded as the *corpus juris spatialis* and are the first port of call in any enquiry about what rules should govern space tourism. The problem, however, is that most if not all of these were drawn up at a time when serious commercialisation of outer space and its resources was barely conceivable. Technological advances have democratised access to outer space not only vertically for and among states but horizontally among corporations and other private persons within states. The tensions and controversies that exist over certain other areas of space exploration and commercialisation particularly regarding the prospect of large-scale mineral exploitation by newer space actors have somehow eluded the issue of space tourism at least up to the end of the first decade in this century. Space tourism plans and actual flights by private entities appear to progress with little opposition by states. It is not helpful that legal writers on the subject have also largely ignored the development of space tourism.[826] In one sense, however, space tourism is part and parcel of the commercialisation of outer space activity and many of the arguments for and against private enterprise in outer space are applicable to the issue.[827] Perhaps the initial question that immediately poses itself is – what is space tourism? One likely answer has been supplied by the writer who broadly defined space tourism as "any commercial activity offering customers direct or indirect experience with space travel".[828]

Since the initial reluctance of the USA to its own national boarding the ISS on a pleasure trip, US authorities have made significant strides towards developing an active space tourism industry. It is notable that the architectural plan for US and other Western states' space tourism regimes are nearly entirely being designed around the idea of private participation in outer space activities. Indeed, Western states appear to have recreated space exploration very much according to their overall ideological image.[829] It is for this reason that, public–private partnerships

826 In describing the need to write about space tourism, Marietta Benko and Kai-Uwe Schrogl classified it perhaps erroneously as one of the "issues which are on the horizon but are still rather far away". Marietta Benko, Kai-Uwe Schrogl, Denise Digrell and Esther Jolley, *Essential Air and Space Law* (Amsterdam: Elsevier Science, 2005): 2.

827 The term "commercial", for the purposes of the US National Space Policy of the United States of America, refers to space goods, services or activities provided by private sector enterprises that bear a reasonable portion of the investment risk and responsibility for the activity, operate in accordance with typical market-based incentives for controlling cost and optimising return on investment, and have the legal capacity to offer these goods or services to existing or potential non-governmental customers. FAA, National Space Policy of the United States of America: 10, available at http://www.faa.gov/about/office_org/headquarters_offices/ast/national_space_policy/media/national_space_policy.pdf (accessed 10 August 2010).

828 S. Hobe and J. Cloppenburg, *Towards a New Aerospace Convention? Selected Legal Issues of Space Tourism*, American Institute of Aeronautics and Astronautics (2004).

829 As a consequence of the developments in law and economics, the characteristics of sovereignty have changed drastically in a way that reflects the new realities, both in their normative and institutional dimensions. In fact whether the focus is on exchange rates, monetary policy, arms control, chemical weapons, landmines, climate change, the ozone layer, endangered species, forest conservation, the rights of minorities, international trade or regional integration, the policy options open to states in any real sense have, in recent years, become increasingly constrained. With

have targeted funding schemes towards people who can develop space tourism vehicles and engage in tourism expeditions. The much discussed public–private participation devices known in many national jurisdictions have spurred on essential research and development.

Note may be taken, therefore, of the so-called X Prize Foundation, which spurs on dozens of entrepreneurs to engage in space flights and the building of commercially viable spacecraft for space tourism. On 4 October 2004, the privately built/operated and uniquely named "SpaceShipOne" made its second suborbital flight in five days at an altitude of about 112.2 kilometres. By performing this feat and with the vehicle being able to carry, apart from the pilot, the equivalent weight of two passengers, the US company Mojave Aerospace Ventures won the race to claim the coveted $10 million Ansari X Prize.[830]

The spirit of individual entrepreneurial involvement in outer space activities was energised further when Virgin Galactic, owned by the British airline entrepreneur Richard Branson, announced that it had teamed up with the US company Mojave Aerospace Ventures to create a space tourism business that would offer suborbital flights on a follow-up version aptly named "SpaceShipTwo". The proposed vehicle is to offer a space trip for $200,000 (£100,000) per passenger. Virgin Galactic, in the meantime, reported that as at 2010 up to 30,000 people have indicated their interest by signing up for the service and some 100 passengers were considered serious contenders for the first test flights that have started in 2008.[831]

Development has been so fast as to be nearly dizzying. Impressively named space vehicles have been built and introduced to fee-paying outer space enthusiasts.[832] There is an international groundswell of support to build spaceports. US financial muscle has been brought to bear on the task and spaceports are in various stages of completion in New Mexico, Oklahoma, Texas and Wisconsin among others. Spaceports are planned for Scotland and the United Arab Emirates (UAE) and

increasing frequency, economic policies, laws, regulations and directives are imposed on states sometimes contrary to the wishes of the national government's stated intentions. Liberal capitalism remains the favoured ideology protected by international laws across most fields of human endeavour. Philip Allston, "The Myopia of the Handmaidens: International Lawyers and Globalisation", 8, 3 *EJIL* (1997): 3; Andreas Follesdal, "Justice: Global and European", 14, 4 *Global Society* (2000): 600; Organisation of Economic Cooperation and Development (OECD), *Globalisation of Industry: Overview and Sector* Reports (Paris: OECD, 1996); A.-M. Slaughter, "The Real New World Order", 76 *Foreign Affairs* (1997): 183.

830 An X Prize is a multi-million dollar award given to the first team to achieve a specific goal that has the potential to greatly benefit humanity and is set by the X Prize Foundation. The X Prize is meant to incite innovation by tapping into competitive and entrepreneurial spirits. The $10 million Ansari X Prize won by the makers of spaceship one was for privately developed piloted spacecraft capable of reaching suborbital space twice in two weeks. For more information about this foundation visit the X Prize Foundation website at http://www.xprize.org/.

831 Peter van Fenema, "Suborbital Flights and ICAO", XXX, 6 *Air & Space Law* (2005): 396; Tariq Malik, "Virgin Galactic Unveils SpaceShipTwo Interior Concept", available at http://www.space.com/news/060828_spaceshiptwo_next.html (accessed 29 June 2011).

832 G. B. Leatherwood, "WhiteKnightTwo Rolls Out: Virgins Spaceplane Greets the World 28 July 2008", available at http://www.spacefuture.com/journal/journal.cgi?art=2008.07.28.white_knight_two_rollout (accessed 5 October 2010).

Singapore.[833] Despite the rapid pace of these remarkable developments and the natural euphoria that any member of the human race is expected to have towards the new opportunities it must be said that a proper scrutiny of the space tourism developments by writers on air and space law is imperative. The US government on its part has shown determination to assist its private sector to take a leading role in the development of space tourism among the many other commercial uses to which outer space activities can be put. This is, for instance, reflected in the many pronouncements and policy postures taken in the eight years of the Bush administration. A congressional report tellingly concluded nearly three decades ago that:

> Only when a large number of our citizens, representative of a broad cross-section of our society, begin to experience the "space adventure" directly, will the space domain and space activities gradually begin to move into the mainstream of our [non national security] interests and concern.[834]

The entrepreneurial and commercial value of space exploration that has now become particularly relevant to space tourism purposes have in such manner been written into the DNA of virtually all national and international instruments entered into by the USA as may be seen later: the *Commercial Space Act* of 1998 was persuasively described by an observer as an instrument that was clearly designed by US Congress for the purpose of "adding momentum to the drive for commercialization" and for the provision of "a legislative mandate for the development of privately funded space programmes" in the United States.[835]

On 23 December 2004 the Bush administration signed the Commercial Space Launch Amendments Act (CSLAA) into law.[836] The CSLAA established a charter

833 Tom Leonard, "New Mexico Town to Host World's First Spaceport. The New Mexico Town of Truth or Consequences is to Host the World's First Commercial Spaceport", *Telegraph*, 31 December 2009, available at http://www.telegraph.co.uk/science/space/6917074/New-Mexico-town-to-host-worlds-first-spaceport.html (accessed 12 October 2010); Marc Kaufman, "New Mexico Moves Ahead on Spaceport 2010 Opening Appears to Be Within Reach, Even With Remaining Hurdles", *Washington Post*, 10 May 2008, available at http://www.washingtonpost.com/wp-dyn/content/article/2008/05/09/AR2008050902508.html (accessed 10 October 2010).

834 Office of Technology Assessment, November 1984, "Civilian Space Stations and the US Future in Space", US Congress: 118.

835 Note that this Act has been repealed by the Commercial Space Launch Amendments Act of 2004. Two pieces of legislation supporting space tourism and a cost-effective US commercial space transportation system were proposed soon after the Tito flight. The first bill, HR 2177 – the Invest in Space Now Act of 2001 – was proposed in the House of Representatives on 14 June 2001. This bill was to amend the 1986 Internal Revenue Code, to support and encourage the development of a cost-effective, American space transportation system, to increase the competitiveness of the US commercial space industry and to expedite opening space to access by the American people. HR 2443, known as the Space Tourism Promotion Act of 2001, was also proposed in the House of Representatives on 10 July 2001. This bill specifically addressed space tourism as a significant new industry and elaborated on ways in which the US government can support this fledging market.

836 Public Law 108–492 108th Congress, 23 December 2004 [HR 5382]. An Act to Promote the Development of the Emerging Commercial Human Space Flight Industry, and for Other Purposes.

for private entrepreneurs in space. This includes, an "experimental permit" regime to allow reusable suborbital (passenger-carrying) launch vehicle developers to build and test their vehicles without undue regulatory constraints.[837] The Act and the ensuing regulations are clearly meant to foster commercial human space flight through a market-friendly legal, regulatory and safety regime.[838] The guidelines address in particular crew and passenger safety concerns and it is quite likely that its content will for a long time serve at least as a baseline and departure point from which any state seeking to modernise its legislation governing space activities will proceed.[839]

Yet the liberal economic model and capitalistic attitude to the use of outer space is not the only view possible, neither is it the only one to be found in the writings of concerned scholars. There have always been those who have condemned the increasing commercialisation of everywhere and have sought to expose the cultural basis for much of what happens in relation to outer space and other common resources. These views are significant but have been highlighted with perhaps less visibility.[840] The liberal economic, free market approach to space tourism is now reality. However, this does not mean that regulation of the activity must not be strong. Although the early signs appear to be that lesser regulation rather than more is the preferable policy from the perspective of Western business interests and entrepreneurs. Mr Tito, the first space tourist in history, announced before a US congressional hearing that he would "quite possibly" invest in a reusable launch vehicle company, but added that excessive government regulation could make investment undesirable.[841] "Under-regulation", however, must be avoided for the simple reason that the potential effects of space tourism are international particularly in relation to liability and damages for accidents. In a world in which American standards and rules have a peculiar tendency to translate into international law, deregulation would mean that by the time space tourism takes

837 Federal Aviation Administration, "Guidelines for Experimental Permits for Reusable Suborbital Rockets", Federal Aviation, http://www.space.com/media/pdf/ep_guidelines_ver1.pdf.

838 BBC News, "US Draws up Space Tourism Rules", 8 January 2006, available at http://news.bbc.co.uk/1/hi/sci/tech/4589072.stm (accessed 10 July 2010); the US Department of Transportation (DOT) and its FAA are the pertinent federal authorities charged with conducting and realising government policy in this area, and the FAA's Office of Commercial Space Transportation in the mean time issued a number of (draft) guidelines to give effect to the provisions of CSLAA.

839 Federal Aviation Administration, Office of Commercial Space Transportation, Draft Guidelines for Commercial Suborbital Reusable Launch Vehicle Operations with Space Flight Participants, 11 February 2005 Washington DC, 20591, available at http://www.faa.gov/about/office_org/headquarters_offices/ast/licenses_permits/media/FD_Passenger_Guidelines_2-11-05.pdf.

840 Note may be taken of the enduring attractiveness of the emotive statements of Chief Seattle in January of 1854 quoted Chapter 6. See quote in Mansell *et al.*, op. cit.: 47. It must be added that this speech has a dubious provenance and may be no more than of anecdotal importance.

841 108th Congress Report House of Representatives 2d Session 108-429 Commercial Space Launch Amendments Act of 2004: 33, available at http://www.faa.gov/about/office_org/headquarters_offices/ast/media/HR3257%20Congressional%20Report%20108-429.pdf (accessed 15 September 2010).

off on a global basis with many countries participating in it certain confusion will emanate from the practice.[842] Nowhere in contemporary international life is an activity that is primarily of international concern left to deregulation whereon the dangers will multiply for the sake of impressive profits to corporations and/or states. For instance, special measures to avoid the production of space debris are a *sine qua non* to any holistic treatment or regulatory framework of space tourism. While private space vehicles emanating from any jurisdiction must be subject to that country's legal jurisdiction, its obligations to observe all applicable space laws and recognise the international space law regime are beyond controversy.

The shortcomings of a solely national approach to this phenomenon apart of course from issues such as the requirements of registration and nationality are revealed in the manner in which SpaceShipOne was simply carried on the US national registry of space objects without any attempt to provide an entry on the UN Register. It has been suggested that this is understandable, since the requirements of the Registration Convention limit the launching state's obligations with respect to registration to objects launched "into earth orbit or beyond". Divergent practice exists elsewhere. It has also been noted that had SpaceShipOne been launched from Australian territory or by Australian owners, the requirements of the Australian Space Activities Act 1998 would have necessitated the registration of SpaceShipOne as a "space object".[843] In other words, some states will allow the assimilation of space law to their space tourism activities whereas others may not with perhaps deleterious consequences on the interests of other states as a result of accidents and mishaps that may occur.

The spatial demarcation issue discussed later is relevant here because, as explained by Fenema: "With the advent of space tourism as an industry using suborbital flights it will become necessary to determine which set of national and international rules apply to this activity."[844] There are still ongoing concerns as to whether the ICAO has a commanding role to play in relation to the suborbital space flights. A possible implication of the refusal of the USA to register SpaceShipOne on its national registry of space objects is that it may be argued that

842 The incremental influence of US policy on international regulation as well as other national systems is well known. It has been noted: "that for some years some of Australia's air safety standards have been written by Boeing Corporation in Seattle, or if not by that Corporation . . . by the US Federal Aviation Administration in Washington . . . Its telecommunications standards have been substantially set by the International Telecommunications Union. The Chair (and often the Vice Chair) of most of the expert committees that effectively set those standards in Geneva are Americans. The Motorola Corporation has been particularly effective in setting telecommunications standards through its chairmanship of those committees. As a consequence Motorola patents have been written into many of the ITU standards that we all must follow." J. Braithwaite and P. Drahos, *Global Business Regulation* (Cambridge: Cambridge University Press, 2000): 3–4.

843 Fenema op. cit.: 398.

844 Ibid: 399, 400. See also FAA, "Commercial Space Transportation: 2004 Year in Review", FAA/AST, January 2005, http://ast.faa.gov.

this amounts to a tacit recognition of the theory that outer space begins after about 100 kilometres. A decision that suborbital crafts should be considered space flights would have led to recognition that SpaceShipOne and objects that operate at its flight altitude are space objects that operate within the scope of the Space Liability Convention.

10.4 Summary and conclusions

The evolving regime of space law is constantly subject to developments from within and outside the law. The space lawyer must be prepared to continually address issues arising from international relations, progress in scientific research, and international commercial law among other areas of national and international life. Lord Denning's admonition to lawyers that: "I would use of international law the words, which Galileo used of the earth: 'But it does move'." "International law does change" remains true in respect of space law as well. This, however, does not mean that all changes are welcome. As a matter of international public policy arguments and developments towards the realisation of space militarisation are inherently negative, unsupportable and perhaps unfathomable given the destructive capabilities mankind has already needlessly created on earth. The prospect of environmental fallout from space militarisation and the inevitable clutter that further satellite placement of a military nature will create are just some of the reasons why this direction must be avoided by states. Even those states that have a present advantage in space technology must understand the logic of increasing democratisation of technologies. If the space militarisation route is adopted, despite the present prohibitions under international law it will be not be long before outer space becomes host to a space weapons race and the advantages sought will become illusory, much along the same lines of the arms and ammunition race to the bottom not least in the area of nuclear arms race. In the event, it is in everyone's interest that such a future must be avoided in the higher grounds in as much as it represents the last frontier of mankind's exploration. The prospect and possibility of unimaginable benefits that can arise from space exploration are such that it is not sensible to risk all in favour of the short-termism of military conquest.

The trend towards commercialisation of outer space activities, especially in terms of private participation by companies and even individuals, is difficult to avoid. There is, however, no reason why the involvement of private enterprise may not take place within the existing regime of international cooperation and with respect to the prevailing system of state sovereignty. Despite the many attractions of private enterprise in many areas of contemporary life, it is important to recognise the dangers and excesses that they may be prone to. This fact becomes clear in many areas including the unhealthy influence some multinationals represent to developing states, their role in the periodic collapse of the international economy and their overwhelming contribution to environmental damage and global warming. The penchant of private enterprise to engage in a race to the bottom for the profit motive calls for special scrutiny at this early stage of private involvement in outer space activities. Space tourism is, in fact, one of the areas in which private enterprise may be best involved in outer space activities. This area of activity must not, however, be left to develop haphazardly without international policy control or solely along the lines of self-regulation. It is crucial that specific rules guide space tourism – sphere of practice, methods, frequency and quality of service. It may be recommended that prior to the development of a specific space regime governing space tourism, the ICAO should have the mandate to manage the developments in this area given its experience in coordinating international rules and actions in the allied field of air law and aeronautic practice.

11 The never ending dispute: legal theories on the spatial demarcation boundary plane between airspace and outer space

> There is no universally agreed precise legal, technical or political definition of either the boundaries separating airspace from outer space or of the term outer space itself.[845]

If anything has become clear in this work, it is hoped that it will be the fact that the concept of territorial demarcation is a central feature of human communities and a central theme in human legal civilisation. The law has been employed since time immemorial to fashion out jurisdictional spheres along geophysical realities in relation to underground resources, land and maritime zones and the airspace as well as outer space. In all the territorial realities discussed so far, it has been shown that considerable effort has been put into delineating in the clearest terms possible jurisdictional extents usually by delimitation and sometimes by demarcation. It is to be noted that there are significant differences between the legal status of the airspace and that of outer space. Territorial sovereignty and exclusive jurisdiction is granted in the former for states whereas in the latter there can be no exercise of sovereignty. The legal distinction between airspace and outer space and the two bodies of law governing them is ultimately very necessary for the smooth conduct of air and space activities. In spite of the acknowledged commercial, strategic, political and environmental importance of air and space activities, the province and exact scope of the applicable laws have not been determined. This chapter seeks, therefore, to determine where in spatial terms exclusive sovereignty ends and where the province of all mankind begins. The determination of a demarcation line is considered primarily of legal significance. In a sense, the attempt to distil and formulate legal criteria for the resolution of the spatial delimitation dispute through a critical evaluation of the existing medley of ideas and theories on the subject is a logical necessity for a book like this. Exploration of the jurisprudence around airspace law and outer space law by jurists may be considered frivolous if lawyers, statesmen and decision makers of this century suffer from the same lack of precise understanding of the boundary between airspace and outer space that was true of the last century.

845 The Minister of State, FCO, *Hansard*, HC, Vol. 546 WA 66, 23 July 1993.

It is a trite observation that there are significant differences between the legal status of the airspace and that of outer space. In the former, states possess exclusive jurisdiction and, in the latter, there can be no exercise of sovereignty and territorial jurisdiction. The legal distinction between the airspace and outer space and the two bodies of law governing them is not only factual but ultimately very necessary. There is unanimity of opinion among scholars that the "airspace is that part of space subject to the sovereignty of a state".[846] McNair notes that "sovereignty in the superincumbent airspace reigns supreme".[847] Cheng sees the principle as "a well-recognised rule of international customary law".[848] For Hughes, the principle is now a fundamental tenet of international law.[849] This universal principle underlies other numerous bilateral and multilateral conventions particularly the Chicago Convention on International Civil Aviation (1944).[850]

The concept of sovereignty it would appear has not risen above the bounds of the earth's airspace. Indeed, it makes no sense in conventional terms to speak of sovereignty in outer space. As explained in earlier chapters, this is because *ab initio* international legislation developed to govern outer space has been unequivocal on the prohibition of the application of state sovereignty in outer space. Of particular importance on this point are the Treaty on Principles Governing the Activities of States in the Exploration and Use of Outer Space, including the Moon and Other Celestial Borders (1967)[851] and the Agreement Governing the Activities of States on the Moon and other Celestial Bodies (1979).[852] However, the concept of jurisdiction (*ratione instrumenti* and *ratione personnae*) applies to outer space and is recognised in the entire legal framework for regulation of man's activity wherever it occurs in the universe of galaxies. The concepts of "common heritage of mankind" and "province of mankind" have been developed in space law to govern outer space, thereby establishing outer space as an international public utility.[853] Yet there is no clear guidance in any treaty as to where outer space begins.

What remains to be achieved by international lawyers is to determine where exclusive sovereignty ends and where the province of all mankind begins. Patrick

846 Vazquez op. cit.: 27.
847 McNair op. cit.: 15.
848 Cheng (1960) op. cit.: 229; Cheng (1956) op. cit.: 208.
849 William J. Hughes, "Aerial Intrusions by Civil Airliner and the Use of Force", *Journal of Air and Commerce* (1980): 595.
850 78 UKTS 8 1953 Cmd 8742; UNTS 295. Article 1 reads: "The contracting States recognize that every State has complete and exclusive sovereignty over the airspace above its territory."
851 Also known as the Space Treaty. 18 UST 2410, 610, UNTS 205.
852 Also known as the Moon Treaty or Moon Agreement. GA Res. 34/68, U.N. GAOR, 34th Sess. Supp. No. 46 at 77, UN Doc. A/34/664 (1979).
853 Article 1 of the Space Treaty (1967) states that the exploration and use of outer space, including the Moon and other celestial bodies, shall be carried out for the benefit and in the interests of all countries, irrespective of their degree of economic or scientific development, and shall be the province of all mankind. Article 11(1) of the Moon Agreement (1979) also provides that: "The moon and its natural resources are the common heritage of mankind."

Del Duca[854] and Carl Q. Christol[855] rightly note that the demarcation point is still an open question and an unsettled issue in air and space law. This point arguably must exist somewhere in between the airspace, atmosphere and outer space. The determination of a demarcation line is primarily of legal significance. Scientific considerations are merely necessary to arrive at a suitable legal demarcation which would have a concrete and sensible basis, and around which the consensus of states can be built.

The core of the problem lies in the fact that air law (being the older body of law) has never come up with a definition of what the term "airspace" actually denotes. Also left unanswered is the question of where precisely its boundary lies in relation to "outer space".[856] The matter of the delimitation has been discussed since the beginning of space flight in 1957 and some even say discussion on it existed before then.[857] Views and literature on the subject abound. However, most of these concentrate on scientific and political considerations.[858] It is from this medley of ideas that scholars must distil and formulate legal criteria for the resolution of the spatial delimitation dispute.

To arrive at this point, it is possible to classify the existing theories into schools of thought. These theories range from the highly probable to the novel and the absurd.[859] The boundary problem involves a number of pertinent and distinct issues. Boundaries might be set in space for many different purposes. For example,

854 Patrick Del Duca, in a review of Gabrella Catalano Sgrosso's book: La Responsibilita Staki per le attivita svolte nello spazio extra atmosferica in 87 *American Journal of International Law* (1993): 355.

855 Carl Q. Christol refers to it as "the unsettled issue of formal boundary between sovereign airspace and non sovereign outer space". See ibid: 491.

856 Diedericks-Verschoor: op. cit.:17.

857 The views of Dr Bess C.M. Reijnen in the preface to Robert F.A. Goedhart, *Forum for Air and Space Law: The Never Ending Dispute: Delimitation of Air Space and Outer Space*, Vol. 4, ed. Marietta Benko and Willem de Graaff (1996). Other notable writers have stressed that international lawyers have an interest in assisting towards the development of clearly defined boundaries and frontiers. Prescott wrote: "Boundaries attract the interest of international lawyers because they mark the position . . . where international rights are determined and obligations assumed." Nicholas Grief more recently expressed similar views when he said: "To the international lawyer, in particular, the delimitation of national and international areas has vertical and horizontal aspects which require the application of legal principles and rules." International organisations that have consistently considered this problem to no avail include both scientific and legal or political organisations. These include the International Law Association; the International Institute of Space Law and The International Astronautical Federation (IISL of IAF); the Committee of Space Research (COSPAR) of the International Council of Scientific Unions (ICSU); International Civil Aviation Organisation (ICAO). See J.R.V. Prescott, *Boundaries and Frontiers* (London: Croom Helm, 1978) 20; Grief (1994) op. cit.: 7.

858 See the preface to Goedhart, op. cit.

859 It must be noted that it is not all the existing theories that have been discussed here. Indeed it is difficult to ascertain just how many theories there are. The schools are in some cases not sharply defined and the ideas of one may flow into the other or be subsumed in them. Therefore, the way they are treated and the classifications made herein will necessarily be different from those of other writers on the topic. What has been attempted is a general treatment of the existing theories.

spacecraft using nuclear fuels might be prohibited from operating below a certain altitude; launchers might be prohibited from discharging waste in certain layers of the atmosphere; spacecraft returning to earth or moving away from it might be required to control their flight in such a manner as may be dictated by the superadjacent state. The right of self-defence over superadjacent space might also be settled.

11.1 The no-present-need theory

Most of the theories on the issue of a demarcation line presuppose that a demarcation line must be drawn somewhere in space and the problem is to determine where. However, some authors like Jessup and Taubenfeld, simply assume that "at some point there is a limit to the extension of territorial sovereignties". It is only hoped that "in due course practical international necessities will lead to its definition".[860] Other authors belonging to this school, including Morennoff, believe that establishing a boundary altitude "might fetter space activities or needlessly interfere with the existing regime of international aviation".[861] Hurwitz also thinks that while the need for such delimitation is fast growing "it is not of crucial importance".[862] Cheng would prefer that such exercise be left to scientists to solve at a later date.[863]

The representatives of Canada, Great Britain, the United States and some other Western states also expressed such opinions in the early stages of legislative work at the United Nations Committee on the Peaceful Uses of Outer Space. At that stage, even the representatives of the Soviet Union commented that: "It is not possible at the present time to identify scientific or technical criteria, which would permit a definition of outer space."[864]

Recent responses and communications on the issue by the no-present-need states (Estonia,[865] Germany,[866] UK,[867] Saudi Arabia,[868] Denmark[869]) remain firmly

860 Jessup and Taubenfeld, *Controls for Outer Space and the Antarctic Analogy* (1959): 207.

861 Jerome Morenoff, *World Peace Through Space Law* (1967): 1.

862 Bruce Hurwitz, *The Legality of International Air Transport*, (1986): 31.

863 Cheng (1962) op. cit.: 121. It is surprising to note that the same author two years earlier wrote in respect of '. . .the identification of upper limits of national sovereignty' and concluded that '[s]uch a definition while hitherto unimportant in air law, is one of the first and most important problems that have to be tackled in Space Law'. See Cheng (1960) op. cit.: 230.

864 See UN Doc A/AC. 98/2 *passim*. See also A.S. Piradov (ed.), *International Space Law* (1986) 183–4.

865 See the response of 2 November 2009: "The Government of Estonia acknowledges the importance of the subject but does not consider it necessary to define outer space and/or delimit airspace and outer space at the present time. However, given the burgeoning space technology industry, the increasing spectrum of space activities and the growing role of private actors, there will certainly be a greater need for such definition in the future. For the time being, the Government of Estonia does not see the need for immediate action."

866 Germany believes that "[f]or the time being, it is not crucial to draw a fixed spatial borderline between outer space and airspace going beyond the status quo of the current practice. In that

of the opinion that nothing should be done to change the ongoing ambivalent situation of the law. Denmark's communication to the UN on the spatial demarcation is indicative of the resolve of some states to delay decision on the demarcation issue:

> The Danish Government acknowledges the importance of the subject, but does not consider it necessary to define outer space and/or delimit air space and outer space at present. The subject will be kept under close review, as it is under discussion in national as well as in European contexts.[870]

The arguments of this school can be summarised thus:

1 The absence of explicit agreement has not yet led to international tensions and does not appear likely to be able to do so.
2 An attempt to reach explicit agreement on establishment of an altitude boundary would invite many states to make claims to sovereignty that in analogous cases such as the high seas, have led to immoderate claims. In other words, a Pandora's Box situation.
3 Any boundary set might have to be set too high because fear of the unknown would lead states to claim as much as they could. By the same token, that future activity at lower altitudes may be acceptable if there is no explicit agreement on the extent of airspace.
4 An agreement reached later is likely to fix a lower altitude than an agreement reached now.
5 An agreed altitude once achieved will be next to impossible to reduce.[871]
6 An arbitrarily chosen upper limit could easily become a bone of contention. This is in that disputes may arise from boundary violations, which are all the more likely because space objects are in fact difficult to track or identify.[872]

Indeed, several authors have taken the position that the answer to the demarcation problem is primarily a political issue and that probably the answer

regard, it does not seem appropriate to anticipate technical developments. Germany is of the opinion that especially the current limited space tourism activities in the form of suborbital flights do not give reason to consider at present a more concrete borderline between outer space and airspace. The suborbital flights until now could be covered by air traffic law". A/AC.105/889/Add.3 (2 February 2009).

867 Response of [18 December 2009] A/AC.105/889/Add.4.

868 Committee on the Peaceful Uses of Outer Space Questions on the definition and delimitation of outer space: replies from Member States Note by the Secretariat A/AC.105/889/Add.4: 3

869 United Nations General Assembly, Committee on the Peaceful Uses of Outer Space, "Questions on the definition and delimitation of outer space: replies from Member States", A/AC.105/889/Add.1 (21 January 2008).

870 Ibid.

871 For these and other submissions, see Houston Lay and H. Taubenfeld, *The Law Relating to Activities of Man in Space* (Chicago: University of Chicago Press, 1970): 46.

872 Goedhart, op. cit.: 7.

lies in the political field with the law only rendering the possibility of assisting in the formulation of a solution.[873] This view is difficult to accept. Political resolution normally would have to take place before or at least contemporaneously with legal codification. Without things going in that order it is quite difficult to see how legal rules will be drawn up in the first place. It might, however, be suggested that the reason why the indecision over the issue of spatial demarcation has been allowed to fester so long is because the absence of a precise boundary is advantageous to the dominant interests in international space exploration.

Admittedly, however, the fault of a lack of a demarcation regime cannot be said to rest with the industrialised powers alone. Complacency on this issue is fostered by the fact that, prior to 1976, states have not protested at the passage of satellites over their territory. [874] Prior to the 1970s the call for a demarcation enjoyed much less popularity.[875] This is probably why the question was not dealt with in the seminal General Assembly resolutions and in the 1967 treaty. By the mid-1970s states that insisted on a demarcation spanned both the developing and developed state divide. Apart from the case of the erstwhile Soviet Union, there was a common factor linking the states making a call for demarcation and that was the apparent lack of capabilities to engage in large-scale space activities. Thus, states like Belgium, Egypt, France, Italy, Poland, the USSR and a majority of other states were unified in a call for spatial delimitation. As time went by the more developed states could be perceived to have become relatively cool towards the idea probably as the possibilities of space exploration opened up to them as well. Sometimes this took the form of joint space exploratory activity through such structures as the European Space Agency. The immutable US position is that there is no real usefulness to the various proposals to establish a boundary. This is because the region is devoid of physically observable landmarks and most countries are not capable of accurately determining the altitude of space objects and, therefore, have no way to monitor any agreed altitude boundary.[876]

Most states are currently agreed on the necessity for establishing a demarcation boundary line between the two territories. As may be seen in Appendix V: "States and their Position of Choice in Response to the Spatial Demarcation Boundary Plane Question", the majority of states that have responded to specific query from the UN on this issue have committed themselves to the idea that a demarcation point is both desirable and imperative.[877] A few states, like Mexico, however, persist

873 Ibid, preface.

874 Harris (1998) op. cit.: 253.

875 Diederiks-Verschoor, op. cit.: 17.

876 This was the reaction of the USA to a working paper submitted by the USSR in 1987 to COPUOS suggesting the 110 km above sea level limit as the demarcation point. See A/AC.105/C2/SR.316, paras 1–7; see also A/AC105/C.2/7/Add.1, para. 42, p. 15.

877 The table in Appendix V is derived from analysis of positions expressed by states in questionnaires administered by COPUOS. The significance of the questionnaires and the responses to them by states in our analysis lies in the fact that it is a product of the Legal Sub-Committee of COPUOS and this is the major forum where states are obliged to express a view on the subject of the

in sitting on fence on the issue.[878] It may, however, be noted that more stringent calls emanate from the ranks of developing countries. This may be a reflection of the fact that the relative quiet that exists on the matter presently may have been calculated by the states active in space to be a much safer situation than to open the matter up for multilateral treaty consideration. This indeed may establish a solution, which will not be in the interest of the spacefaring states. Contrariwise, the need to resolve the question would appear to be assuming a crucial dimension for the developing states as a result of the increase in traffic between earth and outer space and as a result of the increasing stakes, economic and political of outer space activities. By 1990 the tide in international opinion at least in the developing states was to achieve a solution to this never-ending dispute. Nigeria lent its voice to the matter when in June 1990, in an address at the 33rd session of the UN Committee on Peaceful uses of Outer Space, it called for "a clear definition and delimitation of the airspace of various countries as distinct from outer space".[879] This call reflected the swell of opinion among the non-spacefaring nations, which had no direct participation in outer space activities but are nonetheless rightly concerned about the questions of sovereignty and jurisdiction raised by contemporary developments in space.

As to the erstwhile absence of protest over the occurrence of space flights going through or flying above state territory this may be no more than evidence of a right of innocent passage.[880] One of the submissions by those who think there is no need to maintain a strict demarcation is that even in the event of an accident when the issue of liability is raised the defence of the state of registry will not depend on the place where the accident happened but will depend on the Outer Space Treaty

boundary demarcation plane. The responses given to the questionnaire supplied by COPUOS enjoy the added relevance that they are formal responses by the most competent experts within the respective states to a technical matter with the certain knowledge of all involved that this was going to represent the most authoritative and official response on the topic by the state on the matters raised therein. They, therefore, deserve the immense prestige and considered importance that they have received by COPUOS and other concerned bodies and writers. See Questions on the Definition and Delimitation of Outer Space: Replies from Member States at the 45th session of the Legal Subcommittee, available at http://www.unoosa.org/oosa/ SpaceLaw/national/def-delim/question.html (accessed 1 November 2010). Cf. Cheng op. cit.: 427–9.

878 It was stated in the questionnaire response that "Reflecting Mexico's strong conviction that undecided issues of concern to the international community should be settled by consensus among its members . . . to ensure that States are at some point able to satisfactorily dispel the uncertainty regarding the delimitation of outer space, it is necessary that the Legal Subcommittee of the Committee on the Peaceful Uses of Outer Space continue its consideration of the question." A/AC105/889/Add.4.

879 See A/AC 105. 105/C.2/SR.417-435. Summary record of the Legal Sub-Committee 45th session April–May 1990. See also Nigerian Institute of International Affairs, 5 *Nigeria Bulletin on Foreign Affairs* (1990): 6. See also *New Nigerian*, 14 June 1990: 8. Note that in 1987 the Nigerian reaction to the Soviet proposal of 110 km suggestion by the USA was to support the adoption of a linear delimitation. See A/AC105/PV.234: 58.

880 Cf. Harris, *supra*, note 16, at 253. Harris thinks this view is highly unlikely but recognises the possibility of this interpretation.

(1967) and the Liability Convention (1972). It is also said that, at any rate the obligations that ensue from these treaties will not make it necessary for the contracting state to delimit airspace from outer space.[881] This is, of course, a fallacy, for as soon as the fact of a case borders on uncertainties as to where in spatial terms an accident is caused or liability for damage or contamination arises, it can be expected with near certitude that lawyers for the defence will spring to attention and raise all possible doubts as to the regime that will govern the occasion.

Again, it should not be forgotten that two different registries exist for aircraft and space objects. This, of course, presupposes that different spheres of operation exist for them as well. Thus, the question really should not be whether there should be spatial demarcation but why it has not been achieved so far. Space objects particularly are a class of things that are difficult to trace and identify. That is the more reason to insist that a demarcation will make it necessary for spacefaring nations to obey very strictly the laws on markings, registration and provision of flight paths as well as other information.

As to the fear that states may begin to unreasonably veto space flights that might have to pass through national territory on ascent or descent, it is more reasonable to presume that, in view of the general tendency not to do so thus far, this fear may be more imaginary than real. Indeed, it has become customary practice to allow the ingress and egress of space vehicles through national airspace.[882] Rather than the delimitation of airspace from outer space having the effect of making space exploration operate under more difficult circumstances, it may be that a well-reasoned conclusion on the matter and a proper demarcation regime would, in fact, assure the development of space technology. Agreement reached now will buttress the settled nature of the main principles of space law. In any case, leaving things in a state of flux will more likely than not create a lot of tension, the groundswell of which we are beginning to see between states, which may, in turn, lead to the outbreak of war.[883]

Thus, it would appear that the only thing that the idea that there is no need to establish a spatial boundary demarcation plane has in its favour is that none has been established as yet. But, of course, not only is that not a good reason at all but it is a tenuous justification soon liable to change in the light of the recurrent discussions over this matter in various UN fora. What better way to dismiss the 'no-present-need' theory than to adopt unequivocally the view of Maurice Andem: "As a matter of fact, mankind cannot wait another 50 years in order to accumulate

881 Goedhart, op. cit.: 6.

882 Again this is an instance of the rules of international law being developed or tailored to take cognisance of the interest of the powerful nations. It is in some ways similar to the freedom of peaceful transit for private aircraft through national airspace. Although there are clear reciprocal benefits in an ideal scenario where all states have enough money and resources to run aircrafts, it is still necessary to consider the commonsense of the current situation where many states have neither successful airlines of their own nor private aircraft yet accept the existing servitude for nothing in return.

883 Witness the developments of the Bogota Declaration *infra* note 937. Cf. Goedhart, op. cit.: 7–9.

enough scientific and technical data before practical steps could be taken to select a specific altitude above sea level as a boundary between air space and outer space."[884] For sure, if it were premature at the time many of the "no-present- need" theorists put their ideas on paper some years back, it is no longer. There are many scientific and technical data that have been accumulated during the decades of practice of space flight. These data must, therefore, be sufficient to provide a solid, reliable and objective basis for the establishment of a frontier between air space and outer space.[885]

As a fledging discipline and an increasingly important area of international law, it is crucial that space law develop in a manner as to put its subject matter in an appropriately delimited context. It may, indeed, be better not to grant sovereignty over the airspace at all than to grant it without specifying precisely where it ends. For as we know there can be no limit to which such latitude can be exploited by humans. The exact vertical and horizontal airspace appertaining to each state must always be known. The fact that demarcation has been done thus far without any serious consequence is no reason why that position of things must continue. As Lord Denning once had occasion to say: "If you do not do a thing because it has not been done before then the world will stand still, law should develop."[886] The outer limit of the airspace must be fixed.

11.2 The present need school

The present need approach consists of states and scholars who recognise the desirability and, perhaps, even inevitability of the legal determination of the spatial demarcation boundary plane between airspace and outer space. A look at legal literature and the annals of the COPUOS will reveal that there are more states holding on to this view than there are states adopting the no-present-need approach. Interestingly, few authors can be found to have committed to this approach in pertinent literature on the topic. A possible reason for this is that literature on air and space law generally emanate from those states that have adopted the no-present-needs view. Scholars from these states, therefore, tend not to elaborate on the spatial demarcation issue at all. When they do their conclusions on the matter tend to simply re-echo the views of their states on this point. States that have openly committed themselves to the development of a legal solution to the problem tend to be developing nations and include Czech Republic, [887] Bangladesh,[888] Serbia,[889] Thailand[890] Tunisia,[891] Azerbaijan,[892] Qatar,[893] Belarus[894] Brazil,[895] Jordan,[896] Nicaragua,[897] Nigeria,[898] Ukraine[899] and Venezuela.[900]

884 Andem op. cit.: 153.

885 Ibid:143.

886 *Parker v. Parker* 1954 AC 15 at 22.

887 Response of 5 February 2010. United Nations General Assembly, Committee on the Peaceful Uses of Outer Space, "Questions on the Definition and Delimitation of Outer Space: Replies from Member States", 4 March 2010, A/AC105/889/Add.6, available at http://www.unoosa.org/pdf/reports/ac105/AC105_889Add6E.pdf (accessed 18 June 2010).

Although the states favouring this approach are largely from the global south, their stances are framed in terms of legal considerations and of policy.[901] Thailand, for instance, has consistently taken the position that this is undeniably a classic legal issue that needs urgent clarification. In terms of policy, some of the states are in favour of a rapid conclusion of the demarcation issue based on the need to ensure the right of equal access to outer space.[902] The reasoning appears to be that where there is ambiguity as to the spatial demarcation line there will be hesitation to embark on exploratory activities much along the same lines hesitation has been shown with respect to all other forms of territory where demarcation is controversial whether on land or sea. If a maritime territory is subject to dispute or has not been demarcated, corporations and state actors tend to be discouraged from investing in such areas.

888 Bangladesh communication to COPUOUS of 27 October 2009 as quoted in United Nations, General Assembly, Committee on the Peaceful Uses of Outer Space, "Questions on the Definition and Delimitation of Outer Space: Replies from Member States", January 2010, A/AC105/889/Add.5 11, available at http://www.unoosa.org/pdf/reports/ac105/AC105_889Add5E.pdf (accessed 18 June 2010).

889 Serbian letter of 17 November 2009, A/AC105/889/Add.5. "Yes. Owing to the increase in aviation activities and the number of satellites in low orbits, and with a view to having better regulations in the field of telecommunications, it is necessary to define more precisely and to delimit airspace and outer space."

890 See Thailand communication of 11 November 2009, A/AC105/889/Add.5. Thailand has consistently taken the position that this is an undeniably classic legal issue that needs urgent clarification. The concept of where airspace ends and outer space begins can no longer be swept aside as not being an urgent matter, because uncertainty in this regard can have a crucial bearing on sovereignty and the liability of launching states and of insurance companies. In addition, a clear definition of outer space can lead to a clearer definition of "space object". As a result, it is necessary to give clear-cut criteria for the definition and delimitation of outer space. Moreover, it is also clear to us that technology dictates the definition and delimitation of outer space. Suborbital space flight is a good example. Technological advancement has increased the altitude at which aircraft can sustain flight, which means the expansion of exclusive sovereignty over the airspace of a state's territory. Contrariwise, technological advancement has decreased the altitude at which the orbital flight of space vehicles is possible. Therefore, it is important to note that even though it is essential to define and delimit airspace and outer space, the continuation of technological improvement should be taken into consideration. In addition, collaboration with the International Civil Aviation Organization (ICAO) is necessary. To conclude, with respect to drawing the line between airspace and outer space, by either the spatialism or the functionalism approach, continuing technological advancement should be kept in mind, as well as the necessary cooperation with ICAO.

891 Tunisian communication of 11 November 2009, A/AC105/889/Add.5. "Regarding the first question, Tunisia considers it necessary to delimit airspace. The complete and exclusive sovereignty that every State has over the airspace above its territory should be recognized by all other States in conformity with the principles of international law. Outer space should be explored and used freely by all States without any form of discrimination, on equal terms and in conformity with international law. Given the current level of development in airspace and outer space, Tunisia believes that it is necessary to delimit airspace to guarantee national security and that outer space should remain accessible to all States. In view of the possible development of the space industry in Tunisia, it will be necessary to delimit outer space. In connection with the second question, in the opinion of the Tunisian Government there is no other approach to solving this issue."

Note may also be taken of the persuasive response of the Czech Republic to the demarcation issue. It stated inter alia:

> An appropriate resolution of this issue by a regulatory international instrument could avoid an eventual diversity of rules established by domestic legislation of individual States. It could also prevent international disputes that might arise from incidents involving this problem and would help avoid disparity in decisions on such disputes by national and international courts.

In other words, an agreement now will prevent ambiguity and tensions and disagreements in the future. A comparison of this stance with the argument of those who claim that an agreement now on a particular distance may be overtaken by future technological developments will reveal that the former appear to be more convincing considering that at least states will have a basis on which future modi-

892 Azerbaijan noted in its communication as follows: "Taking into consideration the existing global geopolitical situation, Azerbaijan considers it necessary to delimit airspace. The complete and exclusive sovereign right of a State over the airspace above its territory (both sea and land) should be recognized by other States according to the principles of international law . . . taking into account possible developments in space industry in Azerbaijan, the delimitation of airspace and outer space will be necessary, and relevant decisions will be taken." A/AC105/889/Add.4 (2009.

893 Qatar responded to its questionnaire in the following words: "The Government of Qatar believes that it is necessary to define airspace and to delimit airspace and outer space, as to do so would help to determine State responsibility, clarify the concept of national sovereignty and prevent any ambiguity with respect to relevant international laws and conventions. To do so would also fulfil the principle of the equality of States under international law." See A/AC105/889/Add.4 *supra* note 887.

894 It has been said that the government of Belarus: "considers the definition of outer space and the delimitation of airspace and outer space, and their appropriate incorporation into international legal instruments, to be an essential step on the path towards greater international cooperation in the exploration and use of outer space." A/AC105/889/Add.3 2 February 2009 *supra* note 887.

895 2 A/AC105/889/Add.2 February 2009.

896 Few states are as unequivocal in their written commitment to a spatial demarcation regime as Jordan has been: "Jordan has a firm interest in the definition and delimitation of outer space. The non-definition of outer space will result in ambiguity in the relevant laws and conventions. Moreover, the delimitation of outer space will be useful for the concept of national sovereignty, placing States on an equal footing before international law." See "Questions on the Definition and Delimitation of Outer Space: Replies from Member States", *supra* note 887.

897 Nicaragua maintains that: "Regarding the definition and delimitation of outer space and the character and utilization of the geostationary orbit, Nicaragua considers that equitable co-ordination should be undertaken by the International Telecommunication Union in accordance with the stipulations of its Radio Regulations." A/AC105/889/Add.1 *supra* note 887.

898 Nigeria believes that various criteria may also continue to be considered, in a technical context, to arrive at an accurate determination of the frontiers of territorial sovereignty. A/AC105/889, *supra* note 887.

899 A/AC105/889/Add.1 *supra* note 887.

900 Venezuela believes that: "In approaching the proposed questions, it is always advisable to begin with a definition, which by its nature is more lasting." A/AC105/889.

901 Note may, however, be taken that a few developing states are indeed within the no present need category such as Saudi Arabia which has expressed the view: "Saudi Arabia recognizes the importance of the subject but does not consider it necessary to define outer space or to delimit

fications or amendments may be built. Whereas an inability to reach agreement presently will probably concretise the confusion on the matter and states will not be accustomed to agreement upon the point. Having an agreement in place makes it easier to fashion out the parameters for further negotiations and modifications much along the lines of renegotiations on specific issues that attended the deep sea regime.[903]

The major fault of the present need school appears to be that although the adherents are of the firm view that something needs to be done they are inarticulate on how it should be done. None of the states has presented a coherent solution to the problem. In fact, it appears that membership of this school of thought is only the first step towards adherence to the precepts of one of the other theories (apart from the no-present-need school).

11.3 The criteria of space activities or the functional approach

Some writers have developed the highly interesting theory that states should not worry as to the fixing of a demarcation boundary plane but rather should concentrate on the regulation of activities in space, regardless of the location of these activities.[904] That is to say, the concept of outer space has to be defined on the basis of a definition of the concept of space activities, or at any rate in close relation with that term. The approach, therefore, is functional. Reduced to its simplest basis outer space is to begin where space activities can be said to have begun. Subsumed in this school is the theory of a uniform legal regime, which insists that both air flights and space flights should be subject to the same rules of law.

This school is populated with the likes of Schick, Goedhuis, Chaumont,[905] Quadri[906] and Vazquez, the last, for instance, claiming that if we are seeking a

airspace and outer space at the present time." Committee on the Peaceful Uses of Outer Space Questions on the definition and delimitation of outer space: replies from Member States Note by the Secretariat A/AC105/889/Add.4: 3, *supra* note 887.

902 See Azerbaijan and Qatari communications of op. cit. A/AC105/889/Add.4 (2009) *supra* note 887.

903 At the close of negotiations during the UNCLOS III, consensus was not attained between the Group of 77 and the Western industrialised states on a regime to govern the deep sea mining of manganese nodules. Remaining differences about the implementation of the seabed provisions were resolved in 1994 through the device of a supplementary Agreement relating to the implementation of Part XI of the Convention. The Convention and the Agreement then entered into force on 16 November 1994 and 28 July 1996 respectively. Note our discussions earlier. E.D. Brown, "Deep-Sea Mining: The Consequences of Failure to Agree at UNCLOS III", 7, 1 *Natural Resources Forum* (1983): 55.

904 The possibility of such an approach was referred to as early as 1959. See Ad Hoc Committee on the Peaceful Uses of Outer Space, UN Doc. A/AC, 198/2 General Assembly, June 1959: 8. See also McNair, op. cit.: 16.

905 According to Chaumont "splitting of the area above the earth would lead to a host of legal rules applicable to one and the same spacecraft in quick succession . . . wherefore it would be impossible to say clearly and exactly at any point of time which legal regime is relevant to the spacecraft concerned". Charles Chaumont, *Le Droit de l'espace* (Paris : Presses Universitaires de France, 1960): 37–61.

point in space to be governed by space law: "We must consider our planet as part of the universe and an insignificant one at that."[907] For theorists of this school, the area surrounding the earth should not be thought of as a place legally speaking but as a focus for activities. Thus, an expression such as "international cosmic law" is preferred, as it is non-spatial and could include all manner of activity.[908] Andem also appears to belong to this group, albeit in a not committed manner, because he recognised that the solution to the demarcation problem may not depend solely on this functional criterion. He wrote that it will "require the political will of all states to find a political solution by establishing a boundary between air space and outer space either by adopting the *functional or spatial approach*".[909]

Although the functional school may at face value appear to be *sui generis*, it, in actual fact, attempts to discount the contributions of the spatial theories and take them into consideration. The implications of the central submissions of the functional school may be represented thus:

- Space law covers among others the area of transport through airspace; therefore, it should be applicable to all transport from the earth to any point in space.
- Noting the definition of "aircraft" that exists in Annex 7 of the Chicago Convention, all other vehicles passing through and beyond the atmosphere should be classified as "spacecraft".
- Airspace extends to the maximum altitude attainable for aircraft, while outer space starts at the lowest point where spacecraft can orbit the Earth. It is, therefore, postulated that in between these two points there exists a "meso-space" for which authors like Wassenbergh have advanced a "right of innocent passage" of space objects through foreign airspace. [910]
- In the light of this, all space activities are best permitted at any level of altitude as long as the security of the underlying state is respected.
- Given the absence of a demarcation line in the Space Treaty (1967) and the lack of a definition of spacecraft in other space treaties, then the Space Treaty (1967) is by nature a functional treaty.

Putting all these together space law is seen as a functional body of laws and the definition of outer space must be a functional one.

The basic difference between the spatial approach and the functional approach is that while the former is based on the adoption of certain scientific and technical criteria, for example gravitational pull of the earth, lowest perigee of satellite orbits etc., the latter is based on the definition of space objects and their functions or

906 R. Quadri, "Droit international cosmique", 98, III *Recueil des cours* (1959): 505–99.
907 Fawcett op. cit.: 22.
908 Quadri, op. cit.: 521.
909 Andem, op. cit.: 143 (emphasis in original).
910 H.A. Wassenbergh, *Principles of Outer Space in Hindsight* (Deventer: Kluwer Law International, 1991): 18.

purposes and space activities.[911] The crux of the functional approach lies then in the nature of the activities displayed or to be displayed. Thus, there is no distinction between air flight and space flight as well as between aircraft and spacecraft.[912] By virtue of this reasoning, wherever space objects may be found to be in operation, outer space laws apply.

The fatal error in this approach is the over-enthusiastic attempt to put together in an untidy manner a jumble of considerations best treated separately and to hazard but one criterion from this. As will shortly be seen, acceptable and precise definitions of "aircraft" and "spacecraft" are just as elusive as similar definitions of air law and space law.[913] Having sought to include too many considerations into the development of the functional theory, the theory itself shares most of the criticism appertaining to those other theories from which it borrows heavily.

What is more when the functional theorists say they are not interested in the adoption of scientific and legal criteria for a spatial demarcation decision and that, therefore, they do not stand the chance of failing on that score, they are only correct to the extent that the little scientific considerations they do employ open that approach itself up to other cogent criticism. For instance, it is submitted that every movement with less than circular velocity (i.e. the launching velocity of a spacecraft amounting to 9.4 km/s) has to be considered a flight through airspace regardless of its height. That is why such a flight is subject to the jurisdiction of all states that are in such manner overflown. That said, every movement with escape velocity or one exceeding that velocity (i.e. 11.2 km/s or faster) should be considered a space flight, which, of course, by definition (presumably as a result of acceptance under customary law of the right of ingress and egress of spacecraft) is free from all state interference, irrespective of the height at which it is carried out. In other words, the speed of an object in itself is the distinguishing feature.[914] Note should be taken that the approach is supposed to take into account the security of the state from falling objects. While the security considerations are quite apt and necessary there is an apparent naivety in the functional theory argument because it fails to account for the following:

1 movements in outer space at less than circular velocity speed[915]
2 launching manoeuvres slower than escape velocity which thereby endanger the underlying state
3 the special problem of those aircraft that can also perform space flight
4 the possible harm that can be done by spacecraft on an ascent and descent trajectory through foreign airspace. This is because every flight with circular velocity or more will begin and end dangerously, at launch and at landing.

911 Andem, op. cit.: 133.
912 Goedhart, op. cit.: 91.
913 Cf. Diedericks-Verschoor, op. cit.: 8, 9, 20–21.
914 Goedhart, op. cit.: 82.
915 Such movements are still possible at an altitude of 1,000 km or even higher. See ibid: 89.

One shade of the functional theory is based on the assumption that since the largest part of the earth is covered by the sea, which is not subject to state sovereignty, there is no need to draw a boundary line between airspace and outer space. The one can be regarded as an extension of the other with a gradual transition for the purpose of conducting air and space activities.[916] This reasoning would have been more credible if most were not all launchings and re-entry of space objects take place solely at sea and outside state territory. The situation in practice, however, is that most space activities naturally emanate from national territory and involve the interests of other states. Therefore, justification of the functional approach on this ground fails. Also subsumed in this school of thought is the view that a uniform regime encompassing both air law and space law would in any case eliminate the need for demarcation all together.[917] Such a premise exposes the theorists of this school of thought to the accusation that their "thinking testifies to some naivety" and furthermore, as Verschoor put it, "there are compelling reasons supporting the opposite view".[918]

Even those states that do not want to see international resolution of the spatial demarcation plane issue any time soon recognise the problems that are presented by the functionalist approach.

The UK response to the COPUOS questionnaire was an excellent example of avoiding the issue whilst communicating dissent to the move towards a demarcation regime:

> The United Kingdom anticipates that the development of space transportation systems functioning seamlessly between airspace and outer space, relying on lift to fly through the air for part of their flight profile, will create uncertainties about the legal regime applicable to them. In particular, the distinct liability regimes applicable to each may be conflicting. The United Kingdom is currently reviewing its licensing process and how it could relate to commercial human spaceflight, where this will likely be an issue. The United Kingdom recognizes the need to avoid hybrid solutions and will seek a regulatory solution which provides seamless consideration and a degree of legal certainty for operators.[919]

916 Diedericks-Verschoor, op. cit.: 20.

917 This is the theory of a uniform legal regime. This theory makes both air flight and space flight subject to the same rules of law. Its cornerstone is the enactment of a single and uniform legal regime (i.e. a legal continuum) covering all space immediately surrounding the earth. The joining of air flight and space flight is chiefly inspired by the belief that air flight will be dwarfed by space flight as a result of technological progress. In that situation, the controversial concept of sovereignty as it exists today in state practice and under international law will become obsolete. See further H.T. Binet, "Toward Solving the Space Sovereignty Problem", in *Proc. 2nd Coll. I.I.S.L./I.A.F.* (1960). See also Goedhart, op. cit.: 91.

918 Diedericks-Verschoor, op. cit.: 17.

919 Questions on the Definition and Delimitation of Outer Space: Replies from Member States, *supra*, note 307 at 887.

By professing the need to avoid "hybrid solutions", the UK appears to repudiate one of the central tenets of the functional approach that is the preference for a uniform legal regime. The reference to "a degree of legal certainty" would at first appear to have signalled a possible shift away from previous UK policy of no present need but the problem with this view is that it betrays a predisposition towards a unilateral regulatory solution on a matter of international concern. At the very best, the promise of a regulatory solution communicated in this manner may be interpreted as one that envisages regulation within the UK's loyalties in the EU aerospace sectors.

Thus, despite its attractions, the criterion-of-space-activities view must be rejected in its entirety. Among the things it does not account for, even though it is supposed to be an all encompassing view, is whether or not the term space activities in its legal sense applies also to activities still in the planning stage or partially performed on earth, but directed toward space. In any case, the proposition that outer space law covers such activities happening on earth does not solve the spatial demarcation issue, neither does it remove the need to solve it. To say that outer space is not a place but a focus of activities is only a half truth. It is both a place and a focus of activities. To insist that outer space factually or functionally begins from earth is a conception colossal in its mistaken value. There is no compelling reason to adopt the position that all spatial space should be subject to a single legal regime. This would run counter to the natural inclination of states to preserve and even expand their sovereignty. It would run against most existing international treaties on air law and on space law. It would make nonsense of the provision of the Chicago Convention (1944) that every state has complete and exclusive sovereignty over its airspace.[920] Furthermore, it neglects the obvious value of developments in the law such as in Article II Outer Space Treaty (1967), which quite distinctly make outer space virtually a sovereignty- free area.[921] The principle of free and equal utilisation of outer space can only mean that there is a limit at some point to national sovereignty. In sum, the criterion of space activity is not of much help in determining the precise beginnings of outer space or a spatial demarcation line between airspace and outer space.

11.4 The aerodynamic lift theory

> The displacement of an aircraft through air space at a constant height meets a simple condition which can be expressed equation wise: weight = aerodynamic lift + centrifugal force. With increasing altitude the density of air, as well as the upward pressure of air, decreases. Beyond an estimated elevation of 83 km the air buoyancy would altogether disappear and only the centrifugal force or Kepler

920 Chicago Convention on International Civil Aviation (1944) 78.UKTS 8 1953 Cmd 8742; UNTS 295. Article 1 reads: "The contracting States recognize that every State has complete and exclusive sovereignty over the airspace above its territory."

921 "Outer space including the moon and other celestial bodies, is not subject to national appropriation by claim of sovereignty, by means of use or occupation, or by other means."

> force would remain, which could keep an aircraft in flight, if it can travel at a certain speed. To continue flight after the air lift has been reduced to zero, circular velocity (i.e. +/– 7,900 m/s) is required; in this way the aircraft would describe the demarcation line between two areas with legal regimes (i.e. air space and outer space).[922]

An aircraft is commonly described as a machine depending on the reactions of the air as its means of flight.[923] Therefore, a group of lawyers including Haley,[924] Potter, Hogan[925] and, at one time, Cooper[926] have concluded that airspace ends where an aircraft will no longer find sufficient aerodynamic lift to sustain a flight. This position exists in the stratosphere. It is held in scientific and legal circles that 25 miles above sea level is perhaps the maximum height for the practical use of aircraft requiring aerodynamic support to sustain flight and using breathing motive power. Fifty miles above sea level is perhaps the maximum height at which the atmosphere is sufficiently dense to provide any appreciable aerodynamic lift. At about 53 miles an object travelling 25,000 feet per second loses its aerodynamic lift and centrifugal force takes over. This is the Karman primary jurisdiction line,[927] which represents the highest distance the theorists of this school will admit as the point where sovereignty can no longer be enforced.

The lure of this school lies in the knowledge that sovereignty of the air granted in air law relates to the regulation of aeroplanes and other aviation craft, which, of course, need aerodynamic lift. Thus, once a point is reached where a vacuum exists and all the aerodynamic features that give a normal aircraft the needed "lift" exist no more, claims to sovereignty and jurisdiction should cease. Demarcation here is based on the aerodynamic features of flight instrumentalities.

The aerodynamic lift theory enjoys considerable support in scientific circles. This has translated into acceptance in legal academic opinion and, very importantly, in the position adopted by some states on the issue. According to the South African government airspace refers to the space above the surface of the earth and below the outer space. The country's Aviation Act 1962 (Act No. 74 of 1962) defines an aircraft as a machine that can derive support in the atmosphere from the reactions of the air, other than the reaction of the air against the earth's surface. In terms of

922 Goedhart, op. cit.: 61.

923 Fawcet, (1984) op. cit.: 22.

924 Pitman B. Potter, "International Law of Outer Space", 52 *American Journal of International Law* (1958): 305. Potter also reiterated the persuasive belief that "the functions of the physical scientist and the lawyer are inextricably intertwined".

925 John C. Hogan, "Legal Terminology for the Upper Regions of the Atmosphere and Space beyond the Atmosphere", 51 *American Journal of International Law* (1957): 362.

926 J.C. Cooper, "High Altitude Flight and National Sovereignty" in *Explorations in Aerospace Law: Selected Essays*, ed. Ivan Vlasic (Montreal: McGill University Press, 1968): 368, 370.

927 Defined as the height at which aerodynamic lift ceases and centrifugal force takes over; a suggestion put forward by Von Karma at a speech delivered in 1957 at the University of California later modified by Haley who applied the diagrams of Mascon and Gazely. See Haley op. cit.: 77, 97–107.

the Space Affairs Act 1993 (Act No. 84 of 1993), outer airspace is defined as the space above the surface of the earth from a height at which it is in practice, possible to operate an object in an orbit around the earth. From these two definitions, the position is taken that for the purposes of South Africa the airspace is the space above the surface of the earth up to a height where an aircraft is no longer able to derive support from the atmosphere.[928]

The aerodynamic theory it has also been said has a natural relation to air law. Air law, of course, is the older body of law in comparison with space law. Thus, the aerodynamic yardstick is mentioned in so many words in Annex A of the Paris Convention (1919) and in Annex 7 of the Chicago Convention (1944).[929] Buoyancy in the air is a feature of the atmosphere that may well serve the purpose of distinguishing between aircraft and spacecraft. The argument of the aerodynamic school, therefore, is that in the context of air law as enshrined in Articles 1 of both air treaties, the aerodynamic yardstick determines the scope of the "complete and exclusive sovereignty" a state possesses over its aerial territory. Sovereignty, therefore, does not exist beyond the uppermost height at which aircraft are capable of flying.[930]

After comprehensively reviewing the various schools of thought, Goedhart would appear to lend more credence to the aerodynamic theorists. He commits himself on this point after reviewing the aerodynamic theory by stating:

> In summary, it might be said that a height between 80 km and 90 km is most appropriate for drawing a legal boundary line between airspace and outer space. The lower and denser part of the atmosphere is as good as homogeneous in its chemical composition, whereas the upper part of it is in more than one respect equivalent to cosmic space, thus differing essentially from the deeper air layers. Luckily enough, this intermediate area which presents itself as a matter of nature, happens to coincide with the numerous proposals done in Western literature on international law: most of them are directed at choosing a height between 80 km and 100 km above mean sea level.[931]

This theory, however, is not without obvious shortcomings, not the least of which is the advent of a new class of aircraft, the X-15, which is capable of flying to a height previously considered supra-atmospheric.[932] These hybrid rocket planes combine elements of the traditional aircraft and of spacecraft and, therefore, can fly above the lower airspace. Countries such as Japan are now developing and

928 Depending on weather and other conditions, this height is put at approximately 30,000 metres above sea level. See the South African Government White paper available at http://www.transport.gov.za/docs/white-paper/airport-wp02.html (accessed 27 June 2011).

929 Entitled "Aircraft Nationality and Registration Marks".

930 Goedhart, op. cit.: 60.

931 Ibid: 59–60.

932 The X-15 is said to be able to attain heights up to 47 miles as opposed to the 25 miles that apply to conventional aircraft. See Harris, op. cit.: 252.

specialising on such space planes for their future transportation system. The space plane has several concepts in one technology and it is rather difficult to apply one legal regime to it.

Space planes may be categorised into "surface to surface" (STS) type and "surface to outer space" (STO) type, according to the purposes of their usage. These two types have different purposes, while both are based on the same technology. Therefore different legal systems, space law and air laws, are applicable. With respect to both there are problems that are not covered by present laws and regulations. These are problems that, admittedly, confuse many of the distinctions lawyers have sought to establish so far and with respect to which further research will be necessary.

However, one thing is certain: the aerodynamic lift planes need to function can no longer be a criterion to denote the boundary between airspace and outer space. It is also clear that states may consider 25 miles above sea level too close for security purposes.[933] Note that the U2 spy plane shot down in 1960, discussed earlier, was about 20 miles above Soviet territory.[934] In fact, it is very unlikely that states will ever remain content to restrict their claim to sovereignty to 20 miles when they might claim substantially more than that without unduly interfering with outer space activities. Commonsensical as the aerodynamic lift theory seems to be, it fails to offer a sufficiently precise criterion in law or in fact for drawing the line in the air between the airspace and outer space.

As to the utility of the so-called Karman primary jurisdictional line, it can only be said that the fate of that conception cannot be different from the fate of the aerodynamic theory itself. It should be stressed that the Karman line is no more than "an average outcome, comparable to the notion of the mean sea level, although more complicated than that".[935] Up to now, therefore, the Karman line is no more than a valuable reference boundary. The evolution of aircraft that are capable of navigating in the atmosphere above this line also diminishes the usefulness it has as a criterion to achieve legal spatial demarcation. Although some writers have tried to shore this theory up by stating that the line is subject to change in line with technological progress it is still not satisfactory.[936] This is because the desirable legal demarcation regime should ideally be of a near permanent if not final nature and not based on the possibility of change due to slight changes in technological progress.

933 Some, like Harris and Andem, even say 20 miles, whereas other accounts go up to 30 to 40 miles. This is again an indication of the scientific uncertainties that afflict research into this area. Ibid.

934 See Andem, op. cit.: 152. For further details, see *Amin V.G., Kosmicheskiye Apparaty I Mezhdunarodnoe Pravo* (1977): 55; NASA, *High Altitude Perspective*, NASA SP-427 (1978) 4.

935 Goedhart, op. cit.: 60

936 Diedericks-Verschoor, op. cit.: 18.

11.5 The Bogota Declaration view

In the Bogota Declaration of 1976,[937] eight equatorial states, Brazil, Columbia, Congo, Ecuador, Indonesia, Kenya, Uganda and Zaire, claimed sovereignty up to the geostationary orbit (GSO) above their territories, which is at a distance of 22,300 miles (i.e. 36,000km) away from earth. In the GSO, the orbit of a satellite around the earth is synchronised with the rotation of the earth on its axis. An object in that orbit over the equator travels at the same speed as the earth so that it appears to be stationary. The orbit is particularly essential for satellite telecommunications among other things.[938] With only three satellites placed in the geostationary orbit any state or operator can have satisfactory worldwide commercial coverage.

However, Article 2 sub. D of the Bogota Declaration 1976 stipulates that:

> Devices to be placed permanently on the segment of a geostationary orbit of an equatorial state shall require previous and expressed authorization on the part of the concerned state, and the operation of the device should conform with the national law of that territorial country over which it is placed.

In other words, these states claim that segments of orbit of geostationary satellites are not in outer space but are an integral part of the territory below.[939] So for them outer space over which the space treaties pronounce as the province of mankind begins after the geostationary orbit. Indeed, it may well be argued that when an object hangs permanently over a state it has a special relationship to it, which cannot easily be overlooked. Thus, lawyers from the developing countries like Umozurike counsel: "While the freedom of outer space exploit (sic) and the concept of common heritage to all mankind should be preserved, the special interest/risk to the subjacent states should not be ignored."[940]

The Bogota Declaration was obviously an attempt to alter the international legal status of outer space in favour of those underlying equatorial states. The fact that the Declaration was made at all lends credence to the idea that certain powerful states had failed to heed the warning expressed in such documents as the ITU Malaga–Torremolinos Convention of 1973, which stipulates inter alia: "Members shall bear in mind that radio frequencies and the geostationary satellite orbit are limited natural resources, that . . . must be used efficiently and economically." The enormity of the problems faced by developing states is reflected in the fact that even in such instruments as the ITU Convention (1973), the right of states to these finite resources is calculated to be based not on possible future competence or capabilities

937 For the text of the Bogota Declaration, see 6, 2 *Journal of Space Law* (1978): 194; see also Matte op. cit.: 341–4.

938 S. Gorove, "The Legal Status of the Geostationary Orbit: Some Remarks", *Journal of Space Law* (1985): 53.

939 L. Martinez, *Communication Satellites: Power Politics In Space* (Dedham, MA: Artech House, 1985): 53.

940 Umozurike op. cit.: 118.

but as expressed in this instance, "according to their needs and technical facilities at their disposal". From this perspective it can be seen that while such documents purport to ensure "equitable access" the premise on which this access is based is far from equitable since it is short-sighted and limited to present realities and to the neglect of future changes and needs which will surely take place. For instance, as at the time the ITU Convention was made in the early 1970s the expression space powers would refer mainly to the USA and the then USSR, today the term is said to include not only the major industrialised countries but others, including China, India and Brazil.[941] By similar reasoning, the list will surely continue to expand. The question is by the time it does, will there literally be any space left? It is for this reason among others that the parties to the Bogota Declaration insist that the ITU documents are impractical and unfair. Indeed they located support for their position within UN General Assembly resolutions.[942] The Bogota declarants have been careful to exorcise from their claims all portions of outer space that do not fall within their spatial territories. Thus, it is recognised that the international legal status of the segments of the orbit corresponding to the areas of the high seas beyond the national jurisdiction of states falls under the common heritage of mankind. Note should also be taken of the peculiar position of those equatorial states that had not ratified the Space Treaty (1967).

The recognition or maintenance of special interests of certain states over areas beyond their territory is one that enjoys substantial precedents. The special interests may be security, economic or environmental but the underling legal logic is such that it is seen as just and equitable to allow the maintenance of specialised zones which may reduce the rights of other states to enjoy access to what may be regarded as international space under treaty law, custom or usage. Essentially, the Bogota view may be seen as seeking the creation of a special zone in space. The law of the sea, for instance, has developed several concepts that provide special status and enhanced regulation for environmental protection throughout large areas of the high seas and EEZs. Notable among these are the concepts of the particularly sensitive sea areas; the marine protected area; special area; and the high seas large marine ecosystem (LME).[943] The growth in the creation of these specialised sea

941 Michael Laffaitur Bergquist and Kai-Uwe Schrogl, "A European View on UNISPACE III Follow Up", 16 *Space Policy* (2000): 193.

942 For instance, General Assembly Resolution 2692 (XXV) and even Article 2(1) of the 1974 UN Charter of Economic Rights and Duties of States (1974) GA Res. 3281 (XXIX) (1975) 14 ILM 251.

943 The so-called Particularly Sensitive Sea Area (PSSA) concept is, in fact, a management tool to reduce if not eliminate the most damaging impact of merchant shipping activities on certain areas of the oceans that require heightened environmental protection. Existing PSSAs include the Great Barrier Reef and the Torres Strait (Australia and Papua New Guinea); Sabana Camagüey (Cuba); Malpelo Island (Columbia); Florida Keys (USA); Wassen Sea (Netherlands, Denmark and Germany); Paracas National Reserve (Peru); Western European Waters; Canary Islands (Spain); Galapagos Islands (Ecuador); Baltic Sea Area; Papah_naumoku_kea PSSA (USA). See Myron H. Nordquist, Tommy T.B. Koh and John Norton Moore (eds), *Freedom of the Seas, Passage Rights and the 1982 Law of the Sea Convention* (Leiden: Martinus Nijhoff, 2009): 511, 513.

areas and the trend towards increasing national legal regulation of activities therein has been noted as giving rise to concern over their potential to impair freedom of navigation and overflight of foreign flagged vessels and aircraft.[944] In sum, international law does allow within the operation of an overarching legal regime the taking into account of the special relations that may exist between certain states due to their geophysical setting. Hence, the Bogota view is not without any basis at all in the logic of international law.

As would be expected, the claim by the Bogota Declaration has run into the most formidable brick wall of technically constructive and legally framed refutations by the industrial powers including the communist states. Reactions emanated both in the legal subcommittees and technical committee from the USA,[945] the Soviet Union,[946] the United Kingdom,[947] the German Democratic Republic,[948] Italy,[949] France,[950] Japan,[951] Poland[952] and Czechoslovakia.[953] While not exactly enjoying unanimous support among the developing countries the Bogota view received a more studied reception, not with a view to immediately declaring it as invalid but as a reflection of the special interests that must be taken into consideration in the development of a legal regime for outer space. Thus, countries like Brazil and Mexico and the Latin American states[954] have been quick to point out the need to place discussions over the use of the geostationary orbit on the agenda of the international community until it is resolved. It is also stated that any regime finally adopted should take account of those special cases in which equatorial countries might have particular need to use segments of the geostationary orbit above their territories.

Indeed, the 1985 Report of the Legal Sub-committee notes:

> Some delegations, though agreeing that a special legal regime should take account of the position of the developing countries, were unable to concur in

944 Ibid: 512.

945 See A/AC 105/C.2/SR-297 of 5 April 1978, paras 4–9. See also A/AC105/C1/SR.219 of 26 Feb. 1979, paras 7–1; A/AC105/ C.2/315 of 5 April 1979

946 Ibid: paras 30–35. See also, for example, A/AC105/ C.2/SR.314 of 9 April 1979, esp. para. 16.

947 Ibid: paras 24–7.

948 A/AC105/C.2/SR-297 of 5 April 1978, paras 28–9. See also A/AC105/C1/SR.219 of 26 February 1979, paras 7–11; A/AC105/ C.2/315 of 5 April 1979 paras 1–2.

949 See A/AC105/C.2/SR.297 of 5 April 1978, paras 19–23.

950 Ibid: paras 12–14.

951 A/AC105/C.2/SR.314 of 5 April 1979, paras 13–17. See also A/AC 105/-C.1/SR.199 of February 1978, para. 28.

952 A/AC 105/C.2/SR.297 of April 1978, paras 1–2; A/AC105/C1/SR.219 of February 1979, paras 16–20; see also A/AC105/PV.236, paras 23–5.

953 See A/AC 105/C.2/SR-297 of 5 April 1978, paras 10–11.

954 See the following: A/AC105/C.2/SR.297, paras 35–6. GAOR: 38th Sess. Suppl. No. 20 (A/38/20): 11, paras 60–4; A/AC105/320 7–11, paras 40–5; A/AC105/318: 15, paras 80–83. See also UNGA Res. 37/89 of 10 December 1983, paras 5 (b) (iii) and 7 (b) (ii); UNGA Res. 45/72 of 11 December 1990, paras 4(b) and 7(b) (ii); GAOR: 45th Sess. Supp. No. 20 (A/45/20), paras 18–19, 112–18. For the views of the Republic of Ecuador, see A/AC105/PV.234 (26 March 1982), paras 27–8.

> the view that by reason of their geographical position the equatorial countries should be considered as having special rights to segments of the geostationary orbit superjacent to their territories.

Very impressively the report continues by noting that: "Nor can the present system of 'first come, first served' be condoned if equitable access to the geostationary orbit is to be guaranteed to all countries. Moreover, the view was expressed that the geostationary orbit as part of outer space is a common heritage of mankind."

The Bogota Declaration also raises certain questions about the *consentment tacite* (tacit consent), which many writers have presumed about the practice of space flight over state territory, particularly the flight or placement of satellites through national airspace. As if to consign to the dustbin of history the right of non-spacefaring nations to object to any abuses or injustices inherent in the existing regime relating to outer space activities, Goedhart insists that it is a recognised principle that:

> [I]n particular circumstances a state must protest in order not to lose a right. A response from a state denoting disagreement (i.e. a protest) is always important if a state's violated right has been recognized in international law. Should a right, however, have a weak foundation, merely protesting will not suffice to maintain that right. In addition, objections against any infringement of law have to be made repeatedly: only if a state has objected from the outset to an international custom (i.e. the principle of the persistent objector). [955]

It may well be argued that the Bogota Declaration represents a veritable tool in the armoury of any state that, in the future, may seek to argue that the flight of satellites over its territory violates its airspace. This is particularly true where such state is a party to the Bogota Declaration and if the spatial demarcation problem persists. As to the condition that such objections must be made repeatedly,[956] it can only be asked what repetition is more potent than that the Declaration has not been unanimously withdrawn? The withdrawal of two states out of the eight evidently reduces somewhat the moral potency of this instrument but it does not remove the legal threat it poses. The statement that only if a state has objected from the outset to an international custom in the process of formation may it contract out of that custom (i.e. the principle of persistent objector) is not as damaging to the arguments of the Bogota declarants (or, indeed, any other state that challenges outer space activities in or over its territories) as it may at first appear. To begin with there is no agreement in international law as to how many years is sufficient for the formation of an international custom. Neither is there any prescribed time limit within which states must declare their objections to a legal or factual practice. It may, therefore, be suggested that in all cases regard must be given to the

955 Goedhart, op. cit.: 125.
956 Ibid.

circumstances surrounding the particular matter and to the nature of the particular state(s) involved.

In the nature of things, the time lapse between 1957 (time of the first space flight) and the making of the Bogota Declaration in 1976 may appear quite long but it must be mentioned that geostationary satellites did not immediately become fashionable. It is, therefore, fair in making any assessment to make allowance for the time it would have taken the states concerned to realise and comprehend the immediate and potential dangers they may be exposed to as well as calculate the potential benefits they may be forfeiting. With these considerations in mind, it must be said that from a logical point of view these are not the most damaging arguments against the potency of the Bogota Declaration (1976). In any case, the question may well be raised as to why the economically poor equatorial states should adhere to the treaty obligations of maintaining outer space as a common area for all mankind while those states that are economically well off already as things are reap the financial benefits available in the orbit and go ahead to arguably derogate from international space law by stealthily introducing the concept of private property rights over resources based even further away than the geostationary orbit and on celestial bodies.

However, while one may wish to romanticise the ideas propagated under the Bogota view, there is no escaping the fact that, on a general note, the claim is quite unpopular among non-equatorial states and the majority of space lawyers and it is especially unacceptable to the space powers. But again this is no compelling argument why the claims under it must be dropped. Therefore, it is still necessary to locate the real reason why the declaration cannot stand. A convincing view is that the declaration of sovereignty to a distance of 22,300 miles is a colossal proposition, which amounts to declaration of sovereignty over outer space, in violation of Article 1 Outer Space Treaty (1967) and Articles II and IV Moon Treaty (1979). It is, indeed, doubtful that such a distance can mark the spatial demarcation boundary between outer space and airspace.

This should not, however, be seen as a victory for the industrialised states' point of view. If anything, it is a victory for the generality of states. It will be a very powerful argument indeed, which will wrest from the equatorial states the rights to claim economic or strategic benefits over orbits literally hanging over their heads based on the common heritage principle and grant unrestricted property rights to the industrialised powers over space-based resources without international agreement as to the nature and extent of the regime for exploitation.

11.6 The *usque ad infinitum* theory

There are some scholars who hold steadfastly to the view that sovereignty extends *usque ad infinitum*. This is based on the exaggerated view expressed in the ancient Roman maxim *Cujus est solum ejus usque ad coelum et ad inferos*. It is no wonder then that it has few followers. As McMahon more correctly puts it: "Such a view may be more accurately characterized as *usque ad absurdum*."[957] It is agreed that any

957 J.F. McMahon, "Legal Aspects of Outer Space", 38 *British Yearbook of International Law* (1992): 339.

projection of territorial sovereignty into space ad infinitum will not only violate international law, but will be inconsistent with basic astronomical facts. The revolution of the earth requires that its position in relation to space and celestial bodies is never constant for the slightest conceivable fraction of time. Such a projection into space would give us a series of adjacent irregularly shaped cones of jurisdiction, continuously moving into themselves; with celestial bodies moving into and out of these cones ceaselessly.[958] In these circumstances, the concept of a space cone of sovereignty is both meaningless and a dangerous abstraction.

11.7 The national security and effective control theory

According to this theory, state sovereignty should extend as far out as the subjacent state could exercise effective control. The view among African scholars is that state sovereignty persists to any point in outer space if activities conducted therein affect state security or human welfare.[959] It is in fact posited that "a state can deny the freedom of outer space flight above its territory if the activity endangers state security or human life".[960] Cooper also suggested that: "[A]t any particular time the territory of each state extends upward into space as far as the scientific progress of any state in the international community permits such state to control Space above it."[961]

The appeal to realism of this school of thought is very strong but it is considered mistaken, harsh and unacceptable, in that the richest and most powerful states that possess the monopoly of space technology will inevitably acquire outer space both for military and other uses. It is better to be in agreement with the likes of Lachs and Schacter who see this view as fraught with serious dangers, for it is not only the degree and form of control that is in issue, but it is more a question of the age-old principle of equality of states. [962] Following this rule of effective control, states that do not possess adequate technological or military potential would be deprived of rights that should be theirs as equal subjects of international law. This will be an affront on the principle of equality of nations and is, therefore, rejected.

11.8 The lowest point of orbital flight theory

This is a widely popular theory that suggests that sovereignty should extend to the lowest height at which an object requires to enter into orbit and circle the earth. That point has been variously put at between 70 and 160 kilometres. This principle of the "lowest perigee demarcation" was adopted by the International Law

958 Wilfred Jenks, "International Law and Activities in Space", 5 *International Comparative Law Quarterly* (1956): 99, 102.
959 Umozurike, op. cit.: 264.
960 Ibid.
961 Cooper, op. cit.: 264.
962 Cf. Lachs op. cit.: 571. See also O. Schacter, "Legal Aspects of Space Travel", *Journal of British Interplanetary Society* (1952).

Association at its meeting in 1968 in Buenos Aires.[963] McMahon sees it as a sensible approach[964] and Harris admits that it would appear to be the most likely to be accepted but sets its limit lower (between 50 and 60 miles) than that indicated by other scholars.[965] Other notable lawyers in this school include McNair,[966] Jenks,[967] Cooper (at a later stage in his writings),[968] Jastrow,[969] Vosburgh[970] and, more recently, Grief.[971]

Expressed in scientific terms the central precepts of this school are explained by one of its proponents thus:

> The reference to orbiting vehicles, or satellites immediately introduces the possibility of a physically sound definition for the limits of airspace . . . I have in mind the fact that at low altitudes a satellite is quickly destroyed by friction. Therefore, I suggest that the boundary to the airspace of a nation should be defined as the altitude at which the density of the atmosphere is sufficiently low to permit the completion of one circuit by an orbiting vehicle, without destruction by atmospheric friction . . . Our calculations of satellite lifetimes indicate that critical altitude is 100 miles for a satellite of a typical weight and dimensions, i.e., a weight of one ton and a cross sectional area of 30 square feet. The critical altitude of 100 miles will vary by uncertainty of the density of the atmosphere at that altitude, and also for reasonable variations in satellite mass and cross sectional area, or more properly, the ratio of those last two

963 The word perigee is an astronomical term representing the point in the orbit of the Moon or an artificial satellite around the Earth when it is closest to the Earth. See L. Perek, "Scientific Criteria for the Delimitation of Outer Space", 5 *Journal of Space Law* (1987): 111.

964 McMahon, op. cit.: 343. He accepted the suggestion that a state should only exercise sovereignty over that area whose boundary is the lowest orbital at which an artificial satellite may be put in orbit at least once around the earth.

965 Harris, op. cit.: 253.

966 McNair, *supra*, note 3, at 16. He wrote "a more sensible approach is reflected in the view that a state should only exercise sovereignty over that area whose boundary is the lowest altitude at which an artificial satellite can be put in orbit at least once around the earth".

967 Jenks, op. cit.: 103–104.

968 J.C. Cooper, "Fundamental Questions of Outer Space Law" (lecture given at Leiden University, October 1960). Cooper, as has been noted, at an earlier time belonged to the Aerodynamic Lift School of thought as reflected in earlier papers written in 1951. See Cooper, op. cit.: 259. As late as 1958, he wrote: "I am convinced that the term airspace as used in the Paris Convention in 1919, was there meant to include only those parts of the atmosphere above the surface of the earth where gaseous air is sufficiently dense to support balloons and airplanes, the only types of aircraft then in existence." See Cooper op. cit.: 82. Cf. his views in Cooper, 'Legal Problems of Upper Space', *supra*, note 48, at 209–71.

969 R. Jastrow, Proceedings, 1st Colloquium on the Law of Outer Space (1958): 82.

970 J.A. Vosburgh, 56 *American Bar Association Journal* (1970), 134–6.

971 Grief surveyed the theories on the demarcation problem and showed preference for the arguments of the lowest orbital altitude school, noting that: "[A]lthough final agreement has not been reached, the lowest orbiting altitude of satellites commends itself as a logical basis for delimitation." He also suggested that the "von Karman formula" is very much in agreement with this view and both criteria, therefore, reinforce one another. See Grief, op. cit.: 45.

quantities. This figure of 5 miles represents the degree of arbitrariness in the proposed definition.[972]

Although it is clear that technological progress can also change things, modern writers on the subject like Goedhart and Kopal[973] are very much still in favour of the lowest perigee approach. Admittedly, there is something about this approach that appeals to the scientific mind, since it takes physical concepts and technological considerations into account. This is so much so that Goedhart found no difficulty in concluding that "[a]s a matter of fact, there are very few convincing arguments against the (lowest perigee) boundary criterion" and that "[a]t any event, it is hardly possible to exaggerate the acceptability of the lowest perigee criterion".[974] A closer examination of the central arguments of this school, however, reveals no overwhelming and convincing quality. In fact, it may be argued that its strengths and weaknesses are very much shared by the other demarcation theories based on scientific and technological criteria.[975] To begin with, proponents of this school regularly confuse it with the aerodynamic criterion. Thus, Goedhart appears to favour that argument as well.[976] Similarly, the South African perspective relies heavily on the lowest perigee criterion so much that it is not easy to say exactly which of the two approaches it has adopted.

However, the arguments of this school are not satisfactory. In the first place, the minimum perigee required for orbital flight apparently has not been determined with exactitude. The distances suggested vary widely. The exact distance cannot be given because of the vagaries of the atmosphere. Thus, no matter how sensible this approach may sound it leaves us still at the point at which we were, that is, no precise demarcation line separating territorial airspace from *res communis* outer space.

Furthermore, it is in complete contrast with the equally sensible aerodynamic lift theory in that the minimum height at which satellites can remain in orbit is at least twice the maximum height at which aircraft can fly.[977] Thus, an attempt to pick one of these theories will definitely mean a disregard of the obvious advantages in the other. Another possibility is to pick a middle distance between the two claims, but, of course, the distance that would be arrived at will not satisfy the security or

972 Jastrow, op. cit.: 82.

973 V. Kopal, *The Question of Defining Outer Space* (1980): 170–3; see also V. Kopal, "Issues Involved in Defining Outer Space, Space Objects and Space Debris", *Proceedings 34th Colloquium* (1991): 30–44.

974 Goedhart, op. cit.: 50–51.

975 These are the aerodynamic school (and its von Karman line variant), the gravitational effect argument and the atmospheric zone theories among others. The scientific basis category of schools is in contrast to the other categories such as the demarcation by arbitrary or conventional criteria theories; the security school (which some like Goedhart quite erroneously classify under the scientific criteria category) and the functional approach category.

976 It has been noted that Goedhart himself falls within the aerodynamic school.

977 Perek, op. cit.: 111.

effective control school. It is also to be noted that the lure of this theory previously was probably based on the nearly total acquiescence of states to the placement of satellites in space. Since no state complained over the placement of a communication satellite over its territory it was assumed that such distance is acceptable to the generality of states. However, with the signing of the Bogota Declaration (1976) by the concerned states this position has changed.

11.9 Theories of arbitrary distances

Since these basic schools of thought on the demarcation line between airspace and outer space have produced no overwhelming consensus and no international agreement, legal writers have suggested several arbitrary distances. The criteria for choosing these arbitrary distances vary and depend on the particular factors that appeal most to the imagination of its proposer.

One of the most intriguing suggestions was that which fixes outer space to a few metres above the tallest building.[978] It is sufficient to state that this is totally unacceptable as a taller edifice can always be built. Some writers break space into zones and establish different demarcations to suit different purposes. For instance, a distance may be suggested to serve as a limit to territorial airspace, in which states possess exclusive jurisdiction and control, and another intermediate zone (sometimes labelled neutral zone[979] or *neutralia*)[980] as an area of innocent passage and finally comes outer space.

Murphy suggested a height of 30 miles and another 4,000 miles for neutrals in wartime.[981] Azreges suggests 200 to 300 kilometres, being the supposed limit of air-filled space; Neuman thinks it is 250 miles (where there is too little air).[982] Cheng thinks it is between 310 to 610 miles[983] and later 300 to 500 miles based on assumptions as to where the atmosphere ends.[984] Danier, for his part, puts the limit of the atmosphere at 650 miles and thinks space begins there; Galina and Meyer citing some Western meteorologists put it at 7000 miles.[985] If we accept Westlake's immunity-from-falling-objects approach, then we must be willing to grant territorial sovereignty up to 327,000 kilometres or 161,000 miles, for it is at these distances that astronomic opinion holds that a rocket would leave the earth's area of attraction and pass under the predominance of the Moon and sun, respectively, thus, eliminating all possibilities of a fall back to earth.[986] In fact, between 1957 and 1960 alone the proposals made ranged from 20 to 1,500,000 kilometres.[987]

978 Vazquez, op. cit.: 34.
979 Lachs, op. cit.: 58.
980 Houston Lay, op. cit.: 49.
981 Ibid: 43.
982 Ibid.
983 Cheng, op. cit.: 208. Cheng, op. cit.: 23.
984 Cheng ibid.
985 Houston Lay, op. cit.: 49.
986 See Chapter 2.2. See also Cooper, op. cit.: 258.
987 For a tabulation of these proposals, see Goedhart, op. cit.: 3–4.

11.10 Developing a conclusive theory on a legal spatial demarcation boundary plane between airspace and outer space

From what has been argued so far, it would seem that all attempts at pinpointing the exact beginnings of outer space are doomed to fail logical tests. No matter which of the theories is finally adopted in international law, there will be obvious disadvantages and criticisms. However, as has been stated earlier this is no reason to leave the issue in the state of flux it is in now. The argument that the job should be left to competent scientists to deal with in the future is not cogent enough and is, therefore, unacceptable. Scientists, like lawyers, will remain undecided on this. In any case, any consensus reached now on the basis of science alone is at the mercy of the inevitable next scientific or technological development. Besides, it is more realistic to hold the view that the problem of the lack of demarcation is basically legal and political in terms of the problems and conflicts it would lead to.

Once national space is defined, the result will be that no vehicle whether aircraft or spacecraft may fly in, into or through another state's national space without its permission, acquiescence or tolerance. Thus, the demarcation line must not be too low, as this would put a space vehicle launcher at the mercy of surrounding states through whose airspace its vehicle must pass, on its way to or from outer space. Thus, all low demarcation line theories must be rejected.

At the same time, the demarcation line must not be too high, especially since the security of the state (which is the fundamental reason for seeking jurisdiction and control over airspace) can only be safeguarded by regulating activities rather than by an extensive projection of state sovereignty. In any case (at least for now), most states do not have the requisite technical and military ability to exercise any effective control or even detect intrusion.

With these considerations in mind, support is appropriate for a staggered demarcation regime in international law to regulate jurisdiction over spatial territories. This approach would have the advantage of softening the effects of any rigid demarcation. It is also suggested that an arbitrary distance will have to be chosen. Arbitrary as used here is not in the sense of a wild suggestion but on the basis of an attempt to synthesise the existing theories on the subject into one single legal theory. This spatial regime will, thus, not be based on one single consideration or criterion but will represent the smallest of all the evils that are represented in the other theories. Therefore, the following seems appropriate:

1 A lower demarcation line for territorial airspace of approximately 55 miles to be considered as the maximum height for the airspace, which will be subject to the complete and exclusive sovereignty of the subjacent state.
2 A buffer zone for the next 45 miles, which should be recognised as an area of innocent passage for all states.
3 An outer space demarcation line of 100 miles, which should mark the beginning of outer space (completely free from all claims of sovereignty and jurisdiction. For graphic clarity, the hypothesis may be represented in the following manner:

(OS = 100m) – (AS = 55m) = (45m BZ)

OS	=	outer space
AS	=	airspace
BZ	=	buffer zone
m	=	miles

The appeal of this recommended formula lies in the fact that it takes consideration of approximate estimations and it is a synthesis of several other theories on the subject. The general consensus of scientific opinion appears to speak of a 25-mile limit for sufficient aerodynamic lift for an aircraft; thus, for the "aerodynamic lift" theorists airspace ends there. To this, because of the vagaries of the nature of the atmosphere, has been added another 30 miles. In like manner, the generality of the "lowest orbital flight" theorists point at a distance of around 70 to 90 miles as the lowest points of orbital flight. To this has been generously included 10 miles; therefore, the suffocating feeling states have of the nearness of space objects literally "hanging over their heads" without permission would have at least been symbolically taken care of.

The creation of a buffer zone of 45 miles is justified for many reasons. First, it establishes a zone of innocent passage as recognised in the law of the sea, thus, making it possible for small and landlocked states to launch space rockets without having to seek express permission from neighbouring states before passing through that zone while ascending or descending. It is a fact that a rocket inclines in flight in such a way that it may need to utilise that area of space over other territories. Without the recognition of such a zone of innocent passage such states may in the future be particularly vulnerable to unnecessary veto of space activities. This, of course, means that there will be recognisable sanctions against non-innocent passage. The security theorists would be comforted to have such a zone in which suspect aircraft particularly those that can make space flights may be legitimately investigated. This might also involve the development of a positive right of hot pursuit in air law. Second, the creation of a buffer zone accommodates further scientific discoveries, which may necessitate an increase in the area recognised as airspace or a lowering of the precise limits of outer space. Third, the legal status of the atmosphere would be better elaborated in that the lower reaches of the atmosphere – that is, troposphere and some parts of the stratosphere – would be under territorial sovereignty. The upper parts of the stratosphere would constitute the buffer zone. The ionosphere (sometimes subdivided into the mesosphere and the thermosphere) and the exosphere would, thus, be legally in outer space. Fourth, the buffer zone can become a bargaining chip and negotiating weapon for states in their international relations for various purposes.

An international convention would ultimately be needed for the recognition of such demarcation regime as has been recommended. While conceding that physical and scientific information needed to reach a controversy-free decision is not yet available (and may never be available), this is no reason why the law should not anticipate scientific development. More so, once legal demarcations are fixed the law becomes specific irrespective of a probably eternal scientific indecision. Any frontier that is not unequivocal is bound to be a source of controversy.

These ideas put forward are only suggestions. They are in no way meant to be infallible. The hypothesis will, of course, attract all the usual arguments that any line-in-the-sand (or, in this case, line-in-the-air) solution will attract. However, given that the settled maritime zones in the law of the sea are no more than arbitrary lines in the ocean (there is really no logical reason why the sovereignty of a state should be limited to exactly 12 miles from baseline), the adoption of this hypothesis will be equally workable. States may adopt eventually another formula. Indeed, any equitable agreement among states would be a good starting point regarding this problem of legal demarcation in spatial terms. That this can be done against all odds and despite varying if not contentious opinion has been demonstrated in the delimitation of maritime zones in the law of the sea. But then even there the regime in operation continues to generate controversies and conflicts often and again.

Ideally, decisions finally reached should enjoy the greatest possible acceptance by all states. It is necessary that issues of sovereignty over airspace and outer space should be determined by all, in such a way that a balance is maintained between the interests of individual states and the general international interest. There is much wisdom in the Latin saying *Caveat humana dominandi, quod omnes tangit ab omnes approbatur*, i.e. what concerns all must be approved by all.

As noted earlier, the traditional concept of absolute sovereignty has become considerably eroded. So also has the concept of absolute freedom. States are under an obligation as provided for in international agreements and treaties to cooperate with one another to share the resources that are based in outer space in an equitable manner and to exploit outer space for the benefit and the interests of all mankind. The freedom of use of outer space and exploitation of its celestial bodies is not absolute and it must be exercised not only in such a way that the freedom of exploitation of others is not jeopardised but also the future of coming generations must not be threatened.

The space powers continue to play a leading role in the exploration and exploitation of outer space. They also influence considerably the drafting of space law. They must, however, realise that it is not sufficient to offer humanity a perpetual promise of respecting outer space and its celestial bodies as the common heritage of mankind. There is a basic obligation on all states capable of exploring and exploiting space now to be responsive to the interests of developing states. It is in this light that the General Assembly Declaration on International Cooperation in the Exploration and Use of Outer Space for the Benefit and in the Interest of all States, Taking into Particular Account the Needs of Developing Countries, adopted in 1996 (resolution 51/122) must be viewed as a particularly commendable development. This instrument recognises the importance of international co-operation in the exploration and use of outer space for the benefit and in the interest of all states, in particular, the needs of developing countries. The question of harmonising the interests of developed and developing states in the economic and technological benefits accruable from state activities in outer space is not merely a voluntary requirement or luxury with which the space powers can dispense. In it probably lie our collective survival as a race and the entire earth's survival.

While the political will and the legal backing seem to be in place among majority of states to achieve these purposes a lot still has to be done in respect of the monitoring of space activities and the enforcement of legal rules in space. In this era of possible total destruction due to environmental and military catastrophes, this is the least that is demanded from this generation, which has dared to penetrate the innermost sanctuaries of space. There is definitely no place for Machiavellian precepts in the building of space law. The continuing partnership of law, politics, science and technology in respect of space activities needs to be further consolidated in the interests of mankind.

12 General conclusion

> Two things fill my mind with ever increasing wonder and awe the more often and the more intensely the reflection wells on them: the starry heavens above me and the moral law within me.
>
> Immanuel Kant (1724–1804), *Critique of Pure Reason*

The problems that this book has sought to resolve may be described in terms of concentric circles. At the core of the analysis is the overall consideration about the fairness and adequacy of the past and existing rules of air law and space law as manifested particularly within the central principles of sovereignty and jurisdiction in public international law. The larger tasks involve comparing and contrasting the legal regimes governing the status of the airspace and outer space with a view to exposing existing lacunae and bias within the law towards national or group interests. At the outermost parts of the circle is the question of delimitation of the scope of applicability of both legal regimes. The aim was to suggest a fair resolution to the age-old spatial demarcation problem in a manner that neither reflects mainly the position of the dominant interests in international law, nor ignores the practical considerations of international business and scientific progress.

The methodology adopted and employed in the book's analysis involved:

1 extensive literature review of the standard works of reference on the subject area and analysis of the main international conventions and treaties having a bearing on sovereignty and jurisdiction in the airspace and outer space
2 epistemological approach to the treatment of the pertinent principles and legal issues relating to sovereignty and jurisdiction in airspace and outer space
3 comparative and contrastive approach to the major findings particularly between Chapters 6 to 11 (wherein the issues of space law are discussed in contradistinction to the regime governing the airspace)
4 analogical analysis calling on knowledge contained in relatively older or more mature bodies of law, such as the law of the sea (including the Arctic zones) and the Antarctic regime
5 treatment of significant issues and principles by simultaneously testing them against the theory that there may be proven bias in the general development of public international law relating to airspace and outer space

6 continual realignment of the pertinent issues and principles with general jurisprudential thought which ought to guide any legal regime, particularly the doctrines of fairness, equality, equity, justice and morals.

Although the conclusions that have been reached at the end of each chapter to this book remain valid, the following general conclusions are considered necessary. It is notable that the book has not treated in depth certain pertinent issues such as environmental damage to the airspace and outer space, space debris, liability for air and space accidents and space telecommunications. These issues are important but were largely excluded to focus the discussion and analysis to the specific problems of the study and for reasons of time and space.

Problems encountered during research into this book are many. However, certain problems deserve to be singled out at this stage because of their uniqueness. The first is the vacillation of leading scholars in the area on a few of the central issues in air law and space law. Two examples will suffice here. As pointed out earlier, some of the leading authors would appear to support two or more of the schools of thought on the resolution of the spatial demarcation issue at the same time or frequently change their opinions. Thus, Cheng could write in 1960 that although spatial demarcation was hitherto unimportant in air law it had matured by that date to "one of the first and most important problems to be tackled in law". Yet, by 1962, he would prefer that the matter be left to scientists to solve at some future date. Similarly, Cooper, at the drafting stage and in an article in 1950 considered that the definition of "state aircraft" is already contained in Article 3(b) of the Chicago Convention (1944) and is based on functional approach. Later in 1962 during a session of the ICAO legal committee held in relation to adoption of the Tokyo Convention (1962), he denied that the definition in Article 3(b) was restrictive and stated that other aircraft could also be state aircraft.

A second point, which may explain to some extent the reason for the first, is that a lot of ideological posturing may be said to account for much of the contribution of many authors in this area of the law. The writers from Western developed nations would appear to shy away from any position that might be against the interest of the development of free market principles in both air and space law. Therefore, their contributions are heavily influenced towards the facilitation of Western business in air and space activity. By the same token, writers from the developing states would appear instinctively to adopt certain intellectual positions on some issues, irrespective of the practical realities that may dictate different conclusions. In this way, it becomes difficult to conceptualise a consensus on many issues. A closer inspection of some issues on which there appears to be consensus would reveal that the prevailing position is no more than the views of regional or ideological bedfellows who have bothered to write on the issue.

A third problem relates to the dearth of contribution from authors from the developing states on most burning questions in air and space law. The bulk of their contributions are discernible only by combing through reports of various legal committees of the ICAO or other relevant fora within the UN dealing with space law matters, such as the UN Committee on Peaceful Uses of Outer Space

(COPUOS). This may, however, prove an insufficient method considering the general suspicion in legal; and political circles that many of the representatives that appear before such bodies are mere political appointees without the necessary legal expertise or experience on the highly technical matters that come up before such bodies.

The book has revealed that there are numerous instances in the law and practice of airspace and outer space activities that arguably constitute evidence of bias in legal development in these areas. Certain advantages have been retained by the leading technological and political powers, in respect of the contents of both bodies of law to the present day. It is envisaged that some of these will constitute grounds for severe tensions as well as political and legal conflicts in the future.

There is a clear advantage given and retained by those states that made the first steps towards developing the rules of air law since 1913. They had a unique opportunity to consider at length the legal, security and political ramifications of the development of air flight at a time when most of the presently existing states were no more than colonies and vassal states. The inclusion of colonies in the legal definition of national territory over which airspace sovereignty was granted in the major multilateral air treaties since 1919 stands as one of the best testimonies of the role of public international law in the legitimisation of colonial spoils. As at 1943 when the grant of complete and exclusive jurisdiction in the airspace was included in the drafting of Article 1 of the Chicago Convention (1944), only Liberia was an independent state in Africa. Thus, it is arguable that the general provisions of that Convention and the privileges exchanged in the Chicago Air Transit and Air Transport Agreements of 1944 were designed to facilitate the business of airspace activities for the richer states that possessed the necessary, political/ economic independence, flight instrumentalities and navigational infrastructure. In a sense, the jurisprudence espoused by the organs of regulation in air and space activities still reflects this reality.

A relevant example may be found in the allowance made in air law for the operation of pilotless aircraft over national territory. Although such flights may only be undertaken with the permission of the underlying state, it may be suggested that if the matter were to be decided today, it would be the natural inclination of the vast majority of states to discourage such flights in consonance with security considerations by imposing a complete ban on pilotless flights over any national territory. The impending possibility for misunderstanding and abuse is reflected in the current use of American pilotless, spy planes in the prosecution of the so-called "war on terror" or "operation enduring freedom". Note is taken of the shooting of suspected al-Qaeda terrorist suspects in Yemen via a pilotless Predator American spy plane in November 2002 and repeatedly on many occasions since 2009. The remote-controlled spy plane can lurk in an area for up to 16 hours, undetected at 15,000 feet, its cameras transmitting live video and infrared or radar pictures to military commanders or intelligence officials anywhere in the world. Although some of the drone flights may have taken place with the knowledge of the Yemeni authorities, it is envisaged that the American Central Intelligence Agency and the private companies it contracts such operations to will make expanded use of these contraptions in the future and in various states in the Middle East and indeed beyond. In a mere decade the US arsenal of drones has grown from less than a score to over 7,000.

The pre-eminent position that the advanced technological powers have in international relations and, significantly, in air law, have made it possible for them to exhibit agenda-setting functions by which they influence the development of air law. Instances of these identified within this book include the unbalanced attention the crime of hijacking has received in air law in comparison with other serious problems facing states in the airspace such as aerial espionage, aerial trespass and the drastic increase in other common crimes or penal offences committed on board aircraft.

Wherever disputes arise as to rights and liabilities in air law, it will appear that the more advanced the military and political clout a contending state has the greater the chances it has to have the dispute resolved in its favour. This is typified by the arm-twisting methods resorted to by certain Western states in the resolution of the dispute arising out of the Lockerbie incident and the seeming impotence of the International Court of Justice (ICJ) to adjudicate the matter according to the principles contained in the Hague Treaty (1970). The right of a state such as Libya to try its citizens suspected of executing heinous crimes has been ascribed as falling within the category of *jus cogens* by judge Bola Ajibola in his dissenting judgement in the *Lockerbie Case*. This fundamental truth was evaded in the legal history of this dispute. Libya was effectively arm-twisted into submission of its nationals to a foreign court against its own laws in a procedure that led to a predictable end.

Not only is there a discernible double standard in the application of air law in the practice of the international institutions, also there is a certain air of impunity surrounding the practice of certain developed states in their aviation practice and in relation to their actions in the airspace. On the one hand, the USA claimed recently that its conduct of reconnaissance flights over Chinese EEZ is legitimate; on the other hand, it continues to maintain its self-proclaimed Air Defence Identification Zones (ADIZ) over its own EEZ and even beyond that zone. In the past states such as Israel have displayed even more egregious attitudes to the rules of air law. In 1973 Israel in clear violation of Lebanese airspace sovereignty intercepted and forcibly diverted civil aircraft away from Lebanese airspace into Israeli territory, to land for the purpose of arresting suspected militants on board. Reports of such violations continue. Probably no instance supports the disregard for international consensus in the shaping of air law better than the creation and expansion of the practice of so-called *no-fly zones* in Iraq by France, the UK and the USA. No-fly zones have proven to be a veritable imperialistic tool in international relations. The satisfaction of this device in the case of NATO operations over Libya in 2011 by Security Council Resolution 1973 portends wider use against developing states.

Selective inaction of the ICAO and the Security Council to some of these developments has allowed a certain degree of permissiveness in areas of the law in which the most absolute certainty and unanimity is required. When the USSR sponsored a draft resolution to condemn the incursion of US U2 spy aircraft into

Soviet airspace as aggressive only Poland supported it. But when Cuba shot down two Cessna aircraft that made deliberate and orchestrated forages into its maritime airspace, the Security Council was quick to point out (correctly) that states have an obligation to avoid shooting down civil aircraft, whereas the Council refrained from examining the legality or propriety of the continuous operation of the so-called "Brothers to the Rescue" flights emanating from US territory.

It has been observed that wherever the interest of the developed technological powers are divided on issues of air law or where there are principled differences among them, then the particular issue involved would usually receive the most favourable and thorough consideration leading to the most equitable solution. Thus, for instance, the strong shipping interests of the UK have been opposed by the significant benefits of abundant natural claims to a shelf that the USA possesses. This has necessitated the curtailing of the continental shelf principle to the extent that the rights over the continental shelf do not affect the overlying airspace. Such differences may be found on other issues such as the initial suspicion of the European powers to the US Open Skies Agenda and the present coolness shown by the USA to the single European Skies.

With respect to space law, a clear line may also be established linking the wishes of the technologically advanced nations to the development of legal principles and at any rate the practice of space law. The championing of commercial rights in space property through occupation and appropriation represents a current and disturbing trend by certain scholars who are predominantly from a very few states that have advanced in outer space activities. The case for the so-called right to commercial exploitation of outer space resources is derived mostly through sheer practice led by the spacefaring nations. The entrance of private enterprise into outer space activities is not necessarily a bad thing but more effort ought to be put into aligning this development with the pre-existing rules of space law. Where necessary such as in relation to space tourism and indiscriminate or systematic remote sensing activities over foreign states (especially by corporations) for commercial purposes, further development of the law on a multilateral basis ought to be vigorously pursued. Most particularly worrisome are indications towards the propertisation of outer space and its planetary resources in the agenda of certain states. In reality, the letter and spirit of the major space treaties do not permit such a practice since a regime of common heritage has been created. Where the provisions of one treaty are clear on the point that treaty is maligned as irrelevant and a permissive interpretation is sought from another treaty. The problem is not in the law but in the desire to introduce a principle, which is against the spirit of the law. The antecedents for the current attacks on the CHM regime created for outer space are to be found in similar attacks launched against the concept in the law of the sea (particularly LOSC (1982)) leading to the near complete turnaround in relation to deep sea mining in the 1990s. The resort to the mere freezing of claims to Antarctica instead of a bold dissolution of territorial claims in the Antarctic Treaty System also testifies to the potency of certain vested interests in the regulation of resource control in international spaces. Discerning scholars and jurists have a duty to prevent myopic interests from successfully subverting *lex lata* relating to appropriation of resources in space law and to prevent space law from suffering the vacillating fate of the international deep sea mining regime. Similarly, developing states must remain vigilant towards the expected and sustained attacks on the idea of the common heritage principle and the aggressive push towards propertisation of the celestial grounds.

Because the consistent principle that governs the existing multilateral treaties preclude national appropriation of outer space by use or by any means whatsoever, nothing short of a collectively determined overall policy change in the form of a multilateral treaty of universal importance, may be allowed to trump this fundamental principle within the existing international regime of space law. In any event, it is presently unnecessary to make these changes in light of the unfolding evidence of irrevocable damage to the earth's atmosphere as a result of economic and commercial exploitation of mineral and non-renewable resources. The threats to atmospheric conditions and pollution represented by the intensification and increasing participation in space activities are not negligible. The law and science of climate change and global warming make it imperative that exploitative mining and extractive activities must be postponed with respect to outer space. This is not, however, to suggest that all debate on the possible directions the law may take in the future must cease. It is, in fact, very desirable that such discussions must continue among scholars, as well as, in the relevant international fora, particularly in the COPUOS.

Other concrete instances of the acute differences between developing and developed states in space law abound. In 1983, all Western governments voted against the General Assembly resolution 37/92 entitled Principles Governing the Use by States of Artificial Earth Satellites for International Direct Television Broadcasting, which calls for a notification to proposed receiving states before broadcasting may be directed therein. The question of remote sensing is likely to also remain a sore point between developing and developed states despite the adoption since 1986 of 15 principles by the General Assembly, which notably does not even require prior consent of states that are sensed. The development of Google aerial mapping and allied technology is bound to put further pressure on international relations. Cogent issues of national privacy from outer space and the rights of privacy of individuals are raised by these developments and have to be addressed with some level of alacrity. It is important for states to retain as much as possible their right not to be observed, particularly for commercial reasons without permission. There is no reason why states should needlessly give up their rights to privacy any more than there are for individuals to do same.

The clogging up of the geostationary orbit by a few Western states and the obviously inequitable policy of first come first served that has been the practice of the ITU represent a continuing injustice in space law. This is in the sense that it mortgages the interests of the majority of states to have access to that orbit and may particularly affect the inherent interests of the equatorial states to that orbit. The fact that eight equatorial states adopted the Bogota Declaration probably stands as good reason to suggest that not enough attention has been placed on the requirement in the ITU Convention 1973, which stipulates: "Members shall bear in mind that radio frequencies and geostationary orbits are limited resources." The drastic changes to national fortunes through economic fortunes such as that experienced by the BRIC states,[988] which is likely within a mere dozen or so years to include African states like Nigeria and South Africa (and perhaps becoming BRINKS), is an indication of possible strains on the current system guaranteeing access to outer space.

The argument that by retention of signature to any of the major space treaties, a state may retain its freedom to act in any way it chooses in relation to the fundamental principles of space law is wholly unconvincing, fanciful and, indeed, misleading, particularly when principles such as that prohibiting appropriation of outer space and its celestial bodies are concerned. It is suggested that such central principles have transcended the scope of mere treaty rules and have crystallised into customary international law. The non-appropriation rule, for instance, is not only repeated in all the major multilateral space treaties along with other central principles such as the prohibition of militarisation of outer space but it also represents a logical, factual continuation of a legal principle with roots back into the law of the sea, Antarctic Treaty System and even ancient concepts of *res communis*. By virtue of this reasoning any of the developing states that is a party to the Bogota Declaration but not a party to any or all of the space treaties will find that it may not derogate from the non-appropriation rule/CHM principle by exerting any form of territorial jurisdiction over the geostationary orbit. Equally, any developed state that is not a party to any of the space treaties will have no opportunity to derogate from the non-appropriation rule or the CHM character of outer space.

A great deal of legislation both multilateral and bilateral has been made on many crucial areas on air law and space law. There is also no shortage of scholarly literature in this area, although there is perhaps more on scientific and business commentary than on legal matters. It is desirable that in the interest of certainty and steady application of the law, drastic changes should not be made to the existing multilateral space treaties. Although the opportunity has arisen in the last few years for the review of virtually all the major treaties, it is more important at this stage that emphasis should be directed towards getting more states to accede to the existing treaties and increase ratification rather than to make drastic changes to them.

There are, however, certain undecided issues and grey areas having a bearing on sovereignty and jurisdiction in the air space and with respect to jurisdiction and control in outer space on which further work must still be done. These are areas on which there is pressing need for international legislation in the form of specialist treaties. These areas include: the propriety of determination of nationality of aircraft in accordance with place of registration as opposed to the nationality of its owners as in British shipping practice; the question of a conclusive definition of

988 This in economic and political parlance refers to the states of Brazil, China, India, Russia and that are deemed to all be at a similar stage of newly advanced economic development.

what constitutes an aircraft in legal terms, taking into consideration the diverse crafts that may need to be regulated in air law such as balloons, seaplanes, gliders, drones and the *sui generis* category of the X-15 and space shuttles; legality of aerial reconnaissance and intelligence gathering at high altitudes and from areas coterminous with state territory such as from the airspace above the non-sovereign maritime zones; scope and extent of applicability of space law in view of the ambiguity introduced by the "within the solar system" formula adopted in the Moon Agreement (1979) and the impending scenario of technological advancement making travel to other universes and long-term planetary visits possible; the regulation of damage caused by debris to space stations and satellites; and regulation of manned space flights and space stations, including international space stations. Last, it needs to be repeated that the spatial demarcation between airspace and outer space requires urgent attention in the form of a definitive international agreement. It has already been suggested that perhaps one of the main reasons why this issue remains unresolved in air and space law is because the absence of a delimitation and demarcation regime is advantageous to the interest of those states most closely related to intense aerospace activities. It is hoped that the solution suggested in this book will trigger useful debate on the issue and perhaps even constitute the basis of the eventual solution accepted by states and scholars.

Appendix I

Table AI.1 Chronology of notable military and diplomatic responses to aerial intrusions 1946–99

Date	*Type of Aircraft*	*Nation*	*Territorial State*	*Actions/purpose/ intended route*	*Military response and place of Incident*	*Consequence*	*Diplomatic response*
Aug. 9, 1946	State aircraft C-47	USA	Yugoslav	On regular flight from Vienna to Udine	Shot at by Yugoslav fighter planes over Yugoslav territory	Aircraft crash landed: Turkish officer wounded.	Disagreements over facts. USA alleges entry due to distress. Yugoslavia alleges that between July 16 to August 29 a total of 278 intrusions made.
Aug. 22, 1946	As above	USA	Yugoslav	Not known	Shot at by Yugoslav fighter planes over Yugoslav territory	All 5 crew members dead	Same as above
April 8, 1950	State aircraft: US naval B-29 bomber	USA	USSR	Not known	Shot down over Latvia in the area of the Baltic Sea	Aircraft personnel and crew perished	USA denies aircraft was armed, was not a B-29 and did not fly over Soviet territory. USSR alleges that intruder initiated exchange of gunfire. USA demands indemnity (22 Dept of State Bulletin (1950).
Nov. 1951	USA bomber	USA	USSR	Not known	Shot down	Aircraft and crew perished	Disagreements as to actual position of aircraft. USA denies intrusion and reports the incident to the UN (25 Dept of State Bulletin (1951) 905).

Nov. 1951	State aircraft C-47 (military transport)	USA	Hungary	Not known	Intercepted by Soviet fighters over Hungary	Successfully ordered to land in Hungary	USA alleges mistake. Crew of 4 detained and tried by Hungarian military tribunal and convicted of premeditated crossing of Hungarian frontier. Aircraft and cargo confiscated by order of court. USA pays under protest 30,000 dollars each on the crew and crew was released. USA closed Hungarian consulate in the USA.
April 29, 1952	Civil aircraft	France	East Germany	Scheduled flight from Frankfurt to Berlin via air corridor prescribed for flights from the West to Berlin	Fired on by a Soviet fighter aircraft within East Germany	Aircraft damaged but landed safely, two passengers wounded	Disagreement as to whether aircraft left prescribed air corridor. Allied High Commissioners in Germany jointly protest the shooting. France lodged separate protest on diplomatic level.
June 13, 1952	State aircraft: Swedish military DC	Sweden	USSR	Flight over the Baltic Sea	Not clear	Plane and crew missing	USSR admits two foreign aircraft were "driven off" on alleged day. Sweden asserted that both missing aircraft and rescue aircraft were shot over international waters (see Sweden Royal Ministry for Foreign Affairs, "Attacks Upon Two Swedish Aircraft over the Baltic in June 1952" Series II: 2 Stockholm 1952).

Table AI.1 Continued

Date	*Type of Aircraft*	*Nation*	*Territorial State*	*Actions/purpose/ intended route*	*Military response and place of Incident*	*Consequence*	*Diplomatic response*
June 16, 1952	State aircraft Catalina flying Boat	Sweden	USSR	Flight in search of missing DC-3 (above) along route over the Baltic Sea	Fired on and made to make forced landing on Baltic waters	Passing German vessel picked up the crew	
Oct. 7, 1952	State aircraft B-29 Bomber	USA	USSR	Not known	Shot down and disappeared over or near the Pacific Ocean in the vicinity of northern Japan and Soviet held islands	Aircraft and crew disappeared	USA refuses to regard Yuri as part of Soviet territory and denies overflight of same. Alleged also that the aircraft's guns were in operative and demanded compensation. USSR alleged intrusion into Soviet airspace over island of Yuri and that the aircraft initiated gunfire.
Oct. 8, 1952	State aircraft; hospital plane	USA	East German	Flight to Berlin	Machine guns used to force aircraft to land in East Germany	Investigations by territorial state	USA alleges that militant use of weapons constituted gross violation of agreed rules and procedures governing air traffic to and from Berlin.
Mar. 10, 1953	State aircraft; USA Jet fighter	USA	Czecho-slovakia	Not known	Shot down near the Czechoslovak/West German border	Pilot bailed out and landed safely in USA zone where wreckage was also found	USA charged that no warning given and aircraft was well within the West German airspace and demands compensation and assurances.

							Czechoslovakia asserted disobedience of orders to land.
Feb. 16, 1953	Two state aircraft, Soviet-type fighters	USSR	Japan	Not known	Fired on by US Air Force	Damage to aircraft but both fled to Soviet- held Kurile Islands	No report of official response by USSR.
March 12, 1953	State aircraft British Lincoln Bomber	UK	East Germany	On training flight, Route unknown	Shot by Soviet fighters near the British-Soviet zonal boundary. Wreckage found on both sides of the boundary	All 7 Crew members dead	Britain admits possible intrusion due to navigational error but states that aircraft carried no ammunition. Demanded compensation. Soviet Govt charged penetration into East German airspace, refusal of orders to land and initial firing by British bomber. French and USA High Commissioners joined their British counterpart in protesting through diplomatic notes.
March 12, 1953	State aircraft, British bomber	UK	East Germany	Not known	Mock attack by Soviet fighter aircraft	Landed safely	UK alleged that attack was over Kassel in West Germany. USSR charged that aircraft strayed out of corridors over East Germany.
March 12, 1953	Civil aircraft	UK	East Germany	Commercial transport to West Berlin	Same as above	Same as above	UK admits that the aircraft strayed from the Berlin–Munich corridor in East Germany.

Table AI.1 Continued

Date	*Type of Aircraft*	*Nation*	*Territorial State*	*Actions/purpose/ intended route*	*Military response and place of Incident*	*Consequence*	*Diplomatic response*
March 15, 1953	RB-50 weather reconnaissance aircraft	USA	USSR	Not known	Exchange of gunfire	No damage	USA alleged aircraft was on international water and at no time closer than 25 miles of the coast of Kamchattka. Demanded punishment for Soviet personnel. USSR alleged that USA aircraft initiated gunfire after violating Soviet national airspace twice, as far as 17 km inland.
July 29, 1953	State aircraft Air Force RB-50	USA	USSR	Not known	Shot by Soviet fighters	Aircraft crashed into sea of Japan off the coast in the area of Vladivostok crew of 17 dead or missing	USA alleged no warning was given and that attack was made 40 miles from nearest Soviet territory. USA demanded compensation for aircraft and lives lost. USSR alleged that the aircraft intruded Soviet airspace and fired in response to requests to depart.
July 23, 1954	Civil aircraft (Cathay Pacific)		China	Scheduled flight from Bangkok to Hong Kong	Shot down 10 miles east of China	Two passengers dead (drowned in sea), captain survived	Allegations that no warnings were issued. China accepts responsibility and right to compensation.
July 27, 1955	Civil aircraft (E1 A1	Israel	Bulgaria	Scheduled flight from London to	Shot down by Bulgarian fighters	All 51 passengers and crew of seven	Agreement as to fact that no warning was given.

	Company)			Israel via Paris Vienna and Istanbul	near the Greco-Bulgarian border	dead	Contentious disagreement as to fact whether aircraft was identified as a civil aircraft. Protest notes from Israel, UK, Canada, South Africa, USA, France. Dispute submitted to the ICJ Bulgaria accepts duty to compensate.
May 1, 1960	State aircraft U-2 high-altitude reconnaissance aircraft	USA	USSR	Took off from Pakistan and scheduled to land in Finland after taking aerial photos of Soviet territory	Shot down at 20,000 metres over Soviet territory	Aircraft destroyed and pilot arrested	USA did not justify its action in terms of international law or protest the shooting and the trial of the pilot.
Feb. 21, 1973	Civil aircraft. Libyan Airlines Boeing 727	Libya	Israel	Scheduled flight from Tripoli to Cairo over flew Cairo	Shot down 12 miles into occupied Sinai	108 lives lost	Disagreement as to whether warning was given. Israel justified its action stating the flight was over highly sensitiveness Israeli controlled area. ICAO Resolution of June 4, 1973 condemned Israeli action.
April 20, 1978	Civil aircraft Korean Airlines (KAL) Boeing 707.	South Korea	USSR	Polar flight from Paris to Seoul with scheduled stop at Anchorage	Intercepted and shot at by Soviet fighter aircraft, forced to land on frozen lake	Two dead, 11 injured and aircraft destroyed	No disagreements as to facts alleged by Soviet Union. South Korea in various messages expressed gratitude for speedy return of passengers and crew.

Table AI.1 Continued

Date	*Type of Aircraft*	*Nation*	*Territorial State*	*Actions/purpose/ intended route*	*Military response and place of Incident*	*Consequence*	*Diplomatic response*
Sept. 1, 1983	Civil aircraft. Korea Airlines (KAL 007)	Republic of Korea	USSR	From Anchorage Alaska to Seoul	Shot down by Soviet Fighter pilot with two air launched, heat-seeking missiles after straying a second time into Soviet airspace first over Kamchattka Peninsula and then the Sakhalin Islands	All 229 persons on board perished	USSR vetoed a draft Security Council resolution condemning and prohibiting force against civil airliners. USSR rejected calls for compensation for 60 USA nationals on board and other claims of other governments. ICAO seized the matter; gave resolutions. On Oct. 1, 1953 ICAO Assembly adopted resolution by the Council (see ICAO Doc. A24-WO49, P/38 and Ex/9, 26/9/83 and 27/9/83).
January 16–31, 1996	Various including TR-1 reconnaissance	USA, UK, France	Iraq	Reconnaissance and engaged in acts of provocation over Mosul, Irbil, Dohuk, Zakho, Aqrah, Amadiyah, Tall Afar and Ayn Zalah	Not available	Not available	Letter dated 10 February 1996 from the permanent representative of Iraq to the united nations addressed to the secretary-general.

January 14, 1996	2 military aircraft	Allied aircraft	Iran	Reported presence of Allied forces aircraft within Iranian airspace, Dec. 1995 and Jan. 1996	Not available	Not available	Letter dated 96/06/20 from the Permanent Representative of the Islamic Republic of Iran to the United Nations addressed to the Secretary-General. UN Document Symbol S/1996/454.
June 17, 1998	Private aircraft	Argen-tina	Falkland Islands (British colony)	Pilot Ernesto Barcella claimed to be on a humanitarian, mercy mission laden with 2,200 teabags, 80 oranges and 70 lb of flour	Fighter pilots scrambled to pilot intruder into the Islands' military airport. Pilot arrested and questioned	Landed safely	Argentine authorities contacted in Buenos Aires and pilot released to fly back on assurance by Argentine government that pilot would face prosecution for violating air traffic control and air safety rules.
May 1999	Two state aircraft: Russian MiG21 and MiG27	India	Pakistan	Indian aircraft on raid on "Muslim infiltrators" in disputed Kashmir	Both aircraft shot at by Pakistani fighter jets	Both aircraft wrecked. One surviving pilot captured by Pakistan held as prisoner of war	India denies violation of Pakistan airspace. India warns there would be further use of air power in the disputed Himalayan region.
July 1999	Several Russian TU 95 Bear and TU145 Blackjack heavy naval nombers	Russia	None But within NATO ADIZ (a 200 mile box) and close to the 12 mile Icelandic airspace	All Russian aircraft part of a big military exercise involving hundreds of aircraft, ships from three fleets and 50,000 troops	Several American F15 Fighters were scrambled from the Icelandic Defence Force Base at Keflavic and flew within feet of the Russian bombers to "escort" them as they flew clockwise around the Island	No casualties	White House states incident was a military and not diplomatic affair. No formal complaints from any party.

Table AI.1 Continued

Date	*Type of Aircraft*	*Nation*	*Territorial State*	*Actions/purpose/intended route*	*Military response and place of Incident*	*Consequence*	*Diplomatic response*
Aug. 10, 1999	State aircraft; Pakistan naval aircraft *Atlantique*	Pakistan	India	Routine training mission with 16 personnel on board	Fired on with air to air missiles by Indian Air Force planes	19 personnel on board perished and aircraft destroyed	Case submitted to the International Court of Justice Aerial incident of 10 August 1999 (*India v. Pakistan*).
October and November 30, 2000	Israeli warplanes	Israel	Lebanon	Reports on alleged violations of Lebanon's sovereignty that were committed by Israel on land, at sea and in the air between Oct. 30 and Nov. 30, 2000	Not available	Not available	Letter dated 2000/12/08 from the Permanent Representative of Lebanon to the United Nations addressed to the Secretary-General [New York]: UN, Dec. 11, 2000 UN Document Symbol: A/55/678.
April 1, 2001	Electronic surveillance US Navy EP-3 plane	USA	China	One in a series of Electronic surveillance missions made just off the coast of the Chinese territorial sea	Chinese fighter jets approached and followed US surveillance aircraft	Collision between a Chinese jet and the US aircraft. Both aircraft damaged. Chinese fighter jet plunges into the sea and pilot dies. US aircraft with 24 crew made emergency landing	After 11 days standoff US ambassador delivers letter to China stating, inter alia, "Please convey to the Chinese people and to the family of Pilot Wang Wei that we are sorry for their loss." April 12, American crew allowed to depart and aircraft dismantled and returned on July 3. Pentagon offers China

						without permission in Chinese territory and were detained	US$34,000 compensation and China rejects the offer and continued its demand for $1,000,000.
December 1–15, 2001	Military aircraft	USA and UK	Iraq	Policing no flight zones	Iraqi air defences on at least eight occasions engaged the aircraft and, drove them off	Not available	Identical letters dated 2001/12/25 from the chargé d'affaires of the Permanent Mission of Iraq to the United Nations addressed to the Secretary-General and to the President of the Security Council.
December 16, 2001 to January 15, 2002	Military aircraft	USA and UK	Iraq	336 hostile sorties, 84 of them from Saudi Arabia, 202 from Kuwait and 50 from Turkey	Not available	Not available	Letter dated 2002/02/11 from the chargé d'affaires of the Permanent Mission of Iraq to the United Nations addressed to the Secretary-General S/2002/171.
April 1–31, 2002	Jet fighters; reconnaissance aircraft helicopters	Israel	Lebanon	Air raids and bombardment of military outposts and important centre	Not available	Not available	Letter dated May 15, 2002 from the chargé d'affaires of the Permanent Mission of Lebanon to the United Nations addressed to the Secretary-General.
Aug. 23, 2002	Four Russian military aircraft	Russia	Georgia	Bombed the territory of Georgia, specifically the villages of Patara Borbalo, Ukana Pshavi, Tbatan and Bukhrebi and the area of the Ilto Gorge	No military response	Three Georgian citizens, including one woman, died as a result of this bloody act. Seven persons, including two children, were seriously wounded	Violation of airspace and bombing of the territory of Georgia allegedly by military aircraft of the Russian Federation, Aug. 23, 2002.

Table AI.1 Continued

Date	*Type of Aircraft*	*Nation*	*Territorial State*	*Actions/purpose/intended route*	*Military response and place of Incident*	*Consequence*	*Diplomatic response*
26 Jan. 26–Feb. 2, 2003	Israeli warplanes	Israel	Lebanon	28 such violations occurred. Reports issued by the United Nations Interim Force in Lebanon (UNIFIL) indicate that many of those violations involved deep penetration. Conduct includes flying at low altitudes over populated areas and breaking the sound barrier	Uncertain, however, Lebanon stated intentions to exercise self-defence, by opposing them with ground anti-aircraft fire	Flights according to Lebanon instil terror among Lebanese civilians, especially children	Letter dated 2003/02/04 from the chargé d'affaires of the Permanent Mission of Lebanon to the United Nations addressed to the Secretary-General A/57/722 S/2003/148.
October 5, 2003	Israeli Air Force planes	Israel	Syria and Lebanon	Missile attack carried out against a civilian site situated inside Syrian territory	Not available	Not available	Letter dated 2003/10/05 from the Permanent Representative of the Syrian Arab Republic to the United Nations addressed to the President of the Security Council S/2003/939. Requests the convening of an emergency

							meeting of the Security Council to consider the alleged violations of Syrian and Lebanese airspace committed on Oct. 5, 2003 by the Israeli Air Force and a missile attack on the same day against a civilian site inside Syrian territory.
Dec. 8, 13, 15, 16, 23, and 30, 2003; Jan. 7, 10, 14, 16, 21, 22, 25, 27 and 28; Feb. 6, 11, 12, 17, 18, 21, 22, 25 and 27; March 3, 7, 10 and 12, 2004	Cougar, C-160, CN-235, F-16 Turkish military aircraft of the Turkish Air Force	Turkey	Cyprus	Violations of the flight information region (FIR) of Nicosia and the national airspace of the Republic of Cyprus including flying over the occupied area of Mesaoria, and landings at the illegal airport of Lefkoniko	Not available	Not available	Letter dated 2004/03/16 from the chargé d'affaires of the Permanent Mission of Cyprus to the United Nations addressed to the Secretary-General A/58/739 S/2004/218. Reports alleged violations of the flight information region of Nicosia and airspace of Cyprus by Turkish military aircraft over the period 8 Dec. 8, 2003–Mar.12, 2004.

Table AI.1 Continued

Date	*Type of Aircraft*	*Nation*	*Territorial State*	*Actions/purpose/ intended route*	*Military response and place of Incident*	*Consequence*	*Diplomatic response*
March 12, 14, 21, 22, 23, 24, 26, 2004	Israeli military reconnaissance aircraft, helicopters	Israel	Lebanon	Overflew several villages the occupied Shaba' Farms, Naqurah, Hawla, Shaqra and the Saluqi valley and and then circled over Tyre and Beirut	Not available	Between 2150 and 2220 hours on March 23, 2004, two Israeli helicopters fired four air-to-ground missiles on the Saluqi valley, killing two Palestinian citizens and injuring another	Letter dated 2004/04/05 from the Permanent Representative of Lebanon to the United Nations addressed to the Secretary-General A/58/757.
S/2004/278							
July 4, 2005	Two American unmanned aircrafts (see annexes)	USA	Iran	Aerial reconnaissance	Not available	Unmanned aerial vehicle crashed 60 kilometres inside Iranian territory (in Ilam Province)	Letter dated 2005/10/26 from the chargé d'affaires of the Permanent Mission of the Islamic Republic of Iran to the United Nations addressed to the Secretary-General S/2005/692.
May 1–31, 2006	Military jet reconnaissance helicopter	Israel	Lebanon	Crossing of territorial waters, artillery fire and shooting of flares and firebombs over territorial waters; air raids,			Letter dated 2006/05/04 from the chargé d'affaires of the Permanent Mission of Lebanon to the United Nations addressed to the Secretary-General A/60/873–S/2006/363. Transmits statistical table

				artillery shelling, shelling of military positions and important posts			showing the number of alleged violations of Lebanese airspace, territorial waters and territory committed by Israel during May 2006.
January 15, 2007 (at 13.40 local time)	Two military helicopters	Uniden-tified but belong-ing to coalition forces operat-ing in Iraq	Iran	Violated Iranian air space in Pave region, Kermanshah Province, and entered 300 metres into Iranian territory	None but Iran concluded that "No doubt the Government of the United States of America is responsible for the consequences of such unlawful acts"	Not available	Letter dated 2007/02/15 from the Permanent Representative of the Islamic Republic of Iran to the United Nations addressed to the Secretary-General. Transmits *note verbale* dated Feb. 10, 2007 addressed to the Embassy of Switzerland (Interest Section of the United States of America) in Tehran from the Ministry of Foreign Affairs of the Islamic Republic of Iran; reports alleged violation of Iranian airspace by coalition forces operating in Iraq.
September 6, 2007				Crossing Syrian northern frontier from the direction of the Mediterranean, flying towards the northeast and breaking the sound barrier. As the Israeli aircraft were departing they dropped some munitions		No human casualties or material damage	Letters dated 2007/09/09 from the Permanent Representative of the Syrian Arab Republic to the United Nations addressed to the Secretary-General and the President of the Security Council A/61/1041 S/2007/537.

Table AI.1 Continued

Date	*Type of Aircraft*	*Nation*	*Territorial State*	*Actions/purpose/ intended route*	*Military response and place of Incident*	*Consequence*	*Diplomatic response*
Mar. 1, 2008	Israeli Air Force aircraft	Israel	Syria	Colombian military aircraft and army police personnel made incursions into Ecuadorian territory and took possession of a number of bodies and transported them back to Colombia in violation of Ecuador's sovereignty and territorial integrity	Not available	Not available	Identical letters dated September 9, 2007 from the Permanent Representative of the Syrian Arab Republic to the United Nations addressed to the Secretary-General and the President of the Security Council S/2008/146.
November 1–14, 2008	Israeli reconnaissance aircraft	Israel	Lebanon	Entering over al-Naqurah, Kafr Kila. Alma al-Sha`b, western Bekaa, Baalbek-al-Hirmil and Beirut	Not available	Not available	Letter dated 2008/11/26 from the Permanent Representative of Lebanon to the United Nations addressed to the Secretary-General and the President of the Security Council A/63/577 S/2008/747. Transmits statistical summary of alleged

							violations of Lebanese airspace and territory committed by Israel between Nov. 1 and 14, 2008.
July 16, 2009, at 0800 hrs	Two Chadian Sukhoi fighter jets and Chadian helicopter	Chad	Sudan	Sukhoi fighter jets bombarded the Um Dukhun area which is within the borders of the Sudan. A Chadian helicopter also bombarded that city at 11.00 hrs on the same day, dropping two bombs that fell some 500 metres from the market	Not available, however Sudan reserved its unrestricted and legitimate right to respond decisively to this attack and to previous aggressions and violations	Not available	Letter dated 16 July 2009 from the chargé d'affaires of the Permanent Mission of the Sudan to the United Nations addressed to the President of the Security Council.
June 18 and 27, 2009 at 0830 hrs	Two Mirage and two Jaguar fighter jets	Chad	Sudan	Violated Sudanese airspace over a distance of several dozen kilometres. They circled at medium altitude east of the city of Kulbus in Darfur (coordinates 1422-2246)	The Government of the Sudan reserved its full, sovereign and legitimate right to respond to those violations in such a manner as to preserve the sovereignty and national security of the country	Not available	Letter dated 2009/07/13 from the Permanent Representative of the Sudan to the United Nations addressed to the President of the Security Council S/2009/355. Reports alleged violation of Sudanese airspace on 27 June 2009 by military aircraft proceeding from Chad.

Table AI.1 Continued

Date	*Type of Aircraft*	*Nation*	*Territorial State*	*Actions/purpose/ intended route*	*Military response and place of Incident*	*Consequence*	*Diplomatic response*
Dec. 21, 2010 at 1030 hrs	Cessna aircraft	Costa Rica	Nicaragua	Flew from the Rio Colorado area of Costa Rica Aircraft over the El Delta border post and then returned to Costa Rican territory	Nicaragua views flight as acts of provocation that do not contribute to the search for frank and open dialogue		Letter dated 2010/12/22 from the chargé d'affaires of the Permanent Mission of Nicaragua to the United Nations addressed to the Secretary-General A/65/609 S/2010/622.
Sept. 1– Nov. 30, 2010	CN-235, B-200, CM-235, four F-16, C-160, one S-70, GLF-5, NF-5, C-130, S-92 one Kamov and two Cougar, one Turkish military air-craft of unknown type	Turkey	Cyprus	Violated air traffic regulations and the national airspace of the Republic of Cyprus over 132 times.	Not available	Not available	Letter dated 2010/12/05 from the Permanent Representative of Cyprus to the United Nations addressed to the Secretary-General A/65/609 S/2010/622 Cyprus, inter alia, cited one example of international recognition of sovereignty in the case of *Kibris Türk Hava Yollari (KTHY) and CTA Holidays vs. the Secretary of State for Transport [of the United Kingdom of Great Britain and Northern Ireland* – Turkey transmitted letter dated Dec. 31, 2010 refuting allegations concerning violations of international air traffic regulations and the airspace of Cyprus by Turkish aircraft (A/65/609-S/2010/622).

Table AI.2 Chronology of allegations of Cuban airspace violations by aircraft of US nationality 1992–96

Date	*Number of aircraft*	*Position of aircraft and actions*	*Type of aircraft*	*Registration number*	*Diplomatic response*
July 18, 1992	3	Reserved zone MUD-12 and MUD 52 MUD-42 and MUD-52 MUD-9 and MUD-15	C-337 C-310 PA-23	N-2432 S N-6737 T N-769 JH	Violations officially communicated to the USA Interests Section via Diplomatic Note 908 of July 21, 1994.
Dec. 28, 1993	2	Reserved zone MUD-9 and MUD-15	Not specified	Not given	As above.
Dec. 30, 1993	2	MUD-9	Not specified	Not given	As above.
Jan. 2, 1994	1	MUD-9	C-337	N-415 D	As above.
July 10, 1994 at 1000 hrs	1	Violated Cuban airspace 20 km north of Havana Province. This aircraft violated an airspace of 18km to a depth of 3 km abandoning Cuban national airspace to the north of city of Havana at 1000 hrs	Not specified	N-2506	No diplomatic response.
April 4, 1995 (between 1014 and 1057 hrs)	1	Violated Cuban airspace in zones to the North of the Western, between Santa Fe and Gunabo in City of Havana province, over a longitude of five miles, maintaining a distance from the Cuban coast that ranged between five and 10 miles	C-337 light aircraft	Not given	Officially communicated to the US Interests Section in Diplomatic Note 694 May, 25 1995.

TableAI.2 Continued

Date	*Number of aircraft*	*Position of aircraft and actions*	*Type of aircraft*	*Registration number*	*Diplomatic response*
July 13, 1995	4	Overflew Cuban territorial waters to the north of city of Havana, penetrating prohibited zone MU-P1, overflying city of Havana at a low altitude in a dangerous and negligent manner	Not specified	N-108 LS N-2506 N-54855 N-312 MX	Officially communicated to the US Interests Section via Diplomatic Note 1100 of August 21, 1995 together with a copy of the letter sent by the Cuban Institute of Civil Aeronautics (IACC) to the Federal Aviation Administration (FAA).
April 4, 1995 (between 10.14 and 2257 hrs)	1	Violated Cuban airspace in zones to the North of the Western, between Sante Fe and Guanabo in city of Havana province, over a longitude of five miles, maintaining a distance from the Cuban coast, which ranged between five to 10 miles	C-337 light aircraft	Not given	Officially commissioned to the US Interests Section in Diplomatic Note 694 May 25, 1995.
May 15, 1994	5	Violated Cuban airspace in the western region between Carden, in Matanzas province and the part of Mariel in Havana province between 15 to 80 miles maintaining a distance from coast of between 1.5 and 5.5 miles	Not specified	–	Officially communicated to the US Interests Section in Havana via Diplomatic Note 908 of July 21, 1994.
May 17, 1994	2	Same as above	Cessna-337 light aircraft	N-58 BB, N-108 LS	As above.
May 25, 1994	5	Same as above	Not specified	Not given	As above.

May 29, 1994	5	Same as above	Not specified	Not given	As above.
Jan. 9, 1996	1	Violated air territory over city of Havana dropping subversive leaflets inciting actions against Cuba's Constitutional Order	Light aircraft	Not given	Officially communicated to US Interests Section via Diplomatic Note 45 of January 15, 1996.
Jan. 13, 1996	1	Same as above	As above	Not given	As above.
Feb. 24, 1996	2	Five to 8 miles north of Baracoa Beach, west of Havana	Cessna aircraft	Downed over Cuban territorial waters as pirate aircraft that violated Cuban airspace	Disagreements over actual position of aircraft. Matter reported to the Security Council by the USA "Technical meeting" between (ICAO) team investigating the downing and delegations of Cuba and the United States of America; foreseen for two days, June 20 and 21, 1996, lasted only 20 minutes, and broke down. June 27, Council of the International Civil Aviation Organization (ICAO) adopted a resolution Cuba supports the letter, which Cuba supported but the USA denounced as unbalanced.
1 Jan 2000 (between 0800 and 0830 hrs)	1	Violation of the airspace of Havana, flying at heights of 30–50 feet over Miramar district including the National Hotel, Havana Bay and the Luis Diaz Soto Military Hospital	Cessna 172 M	N 9367 H	Letter dated 2000/01/14 from the Permanent Representative of Cuba to the United Nations addressed to the Secretary-General A/54/715 S/2000/44. Cuba believes this is a violation of Articles 4 and 12 of Chicago convention and also Article 3 bis.

Source: © Gbenga Oduntan 2011

Appendix II

Sample of letters of protest and denial between Cyprus and Turkey

(a) Letter dated 5 December 2010 from the Permanent Representative of Cyprus to the United Nations addressed to the Secretary-General

United Nations **A**/65/609–**S**/2010/622

General Assembly
Security Council

Distr.: General
9 December 2010

Original: English

General Assembly
Sixty-fifth session
Agenda item 43
Question of Cyprus

Security Council
Sixty-fifth year

Letter dated 5 December 2010 from the Permanent Representative of Cyprus to the United Nations addressed to the Secretary-General

Upon instructions from my Government and further to my letter to you dated 30 September 2010 (A/65/480-S/2010/502), I have the honour to draw your attention to ongoing violations of the international air traffic regulations and the national airspace of the Republic of Cyprus by military aircraft of the Turkish Air Force, recorded from 1 September to 30 November 2010, as follows:

On 1 September 2010, one CN-235 and one Turkish military aircraft of unknown type violated international air traffic regulations four times and the national airspace of the Republic of Cyprus four times.

On 2 September 2010, three Cougar Turkish military aircraft violated international air traffic regulations three times and the national airspace of the Republic of Cyprus three times.

11-20557 (E) 140111

On 7 September 2010, one B-200, one Kamov and two Cougar Turkish military aircraft violated international air traffic regulations six times and the national airspace of the Republic of Cyprus six times.

On 14 September 2010, two F-16, one CM-235 and one Turkish military aircraft of unknown type violated international air traffic regulations three times and the national airspace of the Republic of Cyprus.

On 15 September 2010, one CN-235 Turkish military aircraft violated international air traffic regulations twice and the national airspace of the Republic of Cyprus twice.

On 16 September 2010, two F-16 and one Cougar Turkish military aircraft violated international air traffic regulations twice and the national airspace of the Republic of Cyprus twice.

On 17 September 2010, one S-70 Turkish military aircraft violated international air traffic regulations twice and the national airspace of the Republic of Cyprus twice.

On 20 September 2010, one CN-235 and one Cessna Turkish military aircraft violated international air traffic regulations three times and the national airspace of the Republic of Cyprus three times.

On 24 to 26 September 2010, two F-16, one CN-235 and one Cessna Turkish military aircraft violated international air traffic regulations nine times and the national airspace of the Republic of Cyprus seven times.

On 28 September 2010, four F-16 and two CN-235 Turkish military aircraft violated international air traffic regulations three times.

On 29 September 2010, one CN-235 Turkish military aircraft violated international air traffic regulations twice and the national airspace of the Republic of Cyprus twice.

On 30 September, 1 October and 2 October 2010, two Cessna, one Cougar, two CN-235 and one Turkish military aircraft of unknown type violated international air traffic regulations nine times and the national airspace of the Republic of Cyprus eight times.

On 5 October 2010, two F-4, two CN-235 and one Cougar Turkish military aircraft violated international air traffic regulations six times and the national airspace of the Republic of Cyprus three times.

On 6 October 2010, one C-160 and one CN-235 Turkish military aircraft violated international air traffic regulations four times and the national airspace of the Republic of Cyprus four times.

On 7 October 2010, one Cessna Turkish military aircraft violated international air traffic regulations and the national airspace of the Republic of Cyprus.

On 9 October 2010, one CN-235 Turkish military aircraft violated international air traffic regulations twice and the national airspace of the Republic of Cyprus twice.

On 13 October 2010, one B-200 Turkish military aircraft violated international air traffic regulations twice and the national airspace of the Republic of Cyprus twice.

On 15 and 16 October 2010, one C-160, two CN-235 and two Cougar Turkish military aircraft violated international air traffic regulations seven times and the national airspace of the Republic of Cyprus seven times.

On 18 October 2010, two F-16, one CN-235 and two Cougar Turkish military aircraft violated international air traffic regulations three times and the national airspace of the Republic of Cyprus.

On 20 October 2010, one C-160 Turkish military aircraft violated international traffic regulations twice and the national airspace of the Republic of Cyprus twice.

On 21 October 2010, two F-16, and one CN-235 Turkish military aircraft violated international air traffic regulations twice and the national airspace of the Republic of Cyprus.

On 22 and 23 October 2010, one C-160, one CN-235, one Cessna and two Cougar Turkish military aircraft violated international air traffic regulations six times and the national airspace of the Republic of Cyprus six times.

On 25 October 2010, two F-16 and two Cougar Turkish military aircraft violated international air traffic regulations twice and the national airspace of the Republic of Cyprus twice.

On 26 October 2010, four F-16 and one CN-235 Turkish military aircraft violated international air traffic regulations twice and the national airspace of the Republic of Cyprus.

On 27 and 28 October 2010, one Cessna and one Turkish military aircraft of unknown type violated international air traffic regulations twice and the national airspace of the Republic of Cyprus twice.

On 30 and 31 October 2010, one GLF-5 and two Cougar Turkish military aircraft violated international air traffic regulations twice and the national airspace of the Republic of Cyprus twice.

On 1 November 2010, two GLF-5 and two Cougar Turkish military aircraft violated international air traffic regulations four times and the national airspace of the Republic of Cyprus four times.

On 2 November 2010, two Cessna and one Cougar Turkish military aircraft violated international air traffic regulations three times and the national airspace of the Republic of Cyprus three times.

On 3 November 2010, one C-130, one C-160 and two Cougar Turkish military aircraft violated international air traffic regulations five times and the national airspace of the Republic of Cyprus five times.

On 5, 6 and 7 November 2010, two F-16, three CN-235, one B-200, one Cougar and one AB-212 Turkish military aircraft violated international air traffic regulations eight times and the national airspace of the Republic of Cyprus twice.

On 9 November 2010, two Cougar Turkish military aircraft violated international air traffic regulations and the national airspace of the Republic of Cyprus.

On 10 November 2010, one CN-235, one B-200, one Cougar and one C-130 Turkish military aircraft violated international air traffic regulations six times and the national airspace of the Republic of Cyprus five times.

On 11 November 2010, two F-16, two CN-235, two C-130, two Cougar and one Cessna Turkish military aircraft violated international air traffic regulations nine times and the national airspace of the Republic of Cyprus seven times.

On 12, 13 and 14 November 2010, 10 NF-5, three C-160 and two CN-235 Turkish military aircraft violated international air traffic regulations 13 times and the national airspace of the Republic of Cyprus 13 times.

On 17 November 2010, one CN-235 and two C-130 Turkish military aircraft violated international air traffic regulations six times and the national airspace of the Republic of Cyprus six times.

On 23 November 2010, two F-16, one CN-235 and one S-92 Turkish military aircraft violated international air traffic regulations three times and the national airspace of the Republic of Cyprus.

On 24 November 2010, one CN-235 and one Cougar Turkish military aircraft violated international air traffic regulations twice and the national airspace of the Republic of Cyprus twice.

On 25 November 2010, one CN-235 and three Cougar Turkish military aircraft violated international air traffic regulations three times and the national airspace of the Republic of Cyprus three times.

On 26 and 27 November 2010, two F-16, one CN-235, one S-92, three Cougar and one Cessna Turkish military aircraft violated international air traffic regulations seven times and the national airspace of the Republic of Cyprus seven times.

On 29 November 2010, one Cougar Turkish military aircraft violated international air traffic regulations and the national airspace of the Republic of Cyprus.

On 30 November 2010, one CN-235 Turkish military aircraft violated international air traffic regulations and the national airspace of the Republic of Cyprus.

On behalf of my Government, I strongly protest the aforementioned continued abuses by Turkey and call for their immediate cessation. These systematic violations by Turkey of the sovereignty and territorial integrity of the Republic of Cyprus clearly violate international law and air traffic regulations and seriously threaten the safety of international aviation in the region.

The undisputable jurisdiction of the Republic of Cyprus over its sovereign territory, and hence the rejection of any claims by Turkey or its subordinate administration in the occupied part of the island to the airspace over Cyprus, has been determined on multiple occasions. Most recently, to cite but one example, in the case of "Kibris Türk Hava Yollari (KTHY) and CTA Holidays vs. the Secretary of State for Transport [of the United Kingdom of Great Britain and Northern Ireland]", the Court of Appeal of England and Wales upheld the earlier decision by the High Court of England and Wales that the Government of the United Kingdom of Great Britain and Northern Ireland was right to refuse permits to "KTHY" and "CTA Holidays" to operate direct flights from the United Kingdom to the occupied part of Cyprus. The Government of the United Kingdom had rightly ascertained that granting such permits would breach the rights of the Republic of Cyprus under the Chicago Convention on International Civil Aviation, and would cause the United Kingdom to be in breach of its own obligations under the Convention. In its judgement, the Court rejected the argument that the rights of the Republic of Cyprus under the

Convention were suspended due to the continuing occupation and de facto control of the northern part of its territory by Turkey. The Court reaffirmed the full and exclusive sovereignty of the Republic of Cyprus over its airspace above the whole of the island of Cyprus and the territorial waters adjacent thereto.

As I mentioned in my previous letter, these continuing provocations by Turkey put at risk the peace and stability in the entire region of the eastern Mediterranean and are unfitting for a country currently serving as a member of the Security Council. Moreover, such actions are especially unhelpful at the present juncture in the Cyprus question, in the context of the ongoing negotiations aimed at finding a just, lasting and peaceful solution.

I should be grateful if you would have the present letter circulated as a document of the General Assembly, under agenda item 43, and of the Security Council.

(*Signed*) Minas A. **Hadjimichael**

(b) Letter dated 10 January 2011 from the Permanent Representative of Turkey to the United Nations addressed to the Secretary-General

United Nations **A**/65/688–**S**/2011/12

General Assembly
Security Council

Distr.: General
12 January 2011

Original: English

General Assembly
Sixty-fifth session
Agenda item 43
Question of Cyprus

Security Council
Sixty-sixth year

Letter dated 10 January 2011 from the Permanent Representative of Turkey to the United Nations addressed to the Secretary-General

I have the honour to transmit herewith a letter dated 31 December 2010 addressed to you by Hilmi Akil, Representative of the Turkish Republic of Northern Cyprus (see annex).

I should be grateful if you would have the present letter and its annex circulated as a document of the General Assembly, under agenda item 43, and of the Security Council.

(*Signed*) Ertu#abgrul **Apakan**
Permanent Representative

Annex to the letter dated 10 January 2011 from the Permanent Representative of Turkey to the United Nations addressed to the Secretary-General

31 December 2010

Upon instructions from my Government, I have the honour to refer to the letter dated 5 December 2010, addressed to you by the Permanent Representative of Cyprus to the United Nations and circulated as a document of the General Assembly and of the Security Council (A/65/609-S/2010/622), which yet again contains well-known allegations of violations of "international air traffic regulations and the national airspace of the Republic of Cyprus", and to bring to your kind attention the points below.

In response to such pretentious allegations, I wish, once again, to reiterate that flights within the sovereign airspace of the Turkish Republic of Northern Cyprus take place with the full knowledge and consent of the appropriate authorities of the State, over which the Greek Cypriot administration in South Cyprus has no jurisdiction or right of say whatsoever. Furthermore, it should be emphasized that allegations of so-called violations of air traffic regulations are invalid, as the civil aviation authority of the Turkish Republic of Northern Cyprus is the only competent authority to provide air traffic and aeronautical information services.

As stated in our previous letters, such allegations are based on the false and illegitimate claim that the sovereignty of the Greek Cypriot administration extends over the whole island, including the territory of the Turkish Republic of Northern Cyprus. This claim by the Greek Cypriot side is divorced from the existing realities in Cyprus, namely, the existence of two independent States, each exercising sovereignty and jurisdiction within its respective territory on the island.

Attempts by the Greek Cypriot representatives, through often-repeated false claims, to confer legitimacy upon an illegal administration will be futile for as long as the Turkish Cypriot people refuse to give in to their demands. What would indeed be conducive to a better climate on the island would be for the Greek Cypriot side to stop arrogating for itself the rights and responsibilities it does not legally have, and to cease all hostilities towards the Turkish Cypriot people.

The Greek Cypriot administration should be reminded, once again, that its counterpart is, and has always been, the Turkish Cypriot side, not Turkey, and that its continued denial of the Turkish Cypriot sovereignty in the North of the island does not bode well for the prospects of a settlement of the Cyprus conflict in line with the established United Nations parameters, namely a partnership based on bizonal, bicommunal federation with the political equality of the two constituent States. The continuation of these allegations while the two sides are preparing to meet the Secretary-General of the United Nations in Geneva for a second time to achieve progress in the settlement negotiations, clearly weakens the spirit of trust and partnership between the two sides that will be necessary to achieve a lasting solution on the island.

I also deem it imperative to point out that the continuous allegations by the Greek Cypriot administration challenging the Turkish Cypriot sovereignty rights on the island, inspire and encourage hostility towards the Turkish people among the Greek Cypriot community, as exemplified by the increase in the number of violent attacks in the last months against the Turkish Cypriot people, even in peaceful social events such as concerts and basketball games. Instead of focusing its energy on generating further hostility against our people, the Greek Cypriot leadership must heed the call of the Secretary-General in his report (S/2010/603), and "improve the public atmosphere in which the negotiations are proceeding", including by "focus[ing] messages on convergences and the way ahead", and "deliver[ing] more constructive and harmonized messages".

I should be grateful if you would have the present letter circulated as a document of the General Assembly, under agenda item 43, and of the Security Council.

(*Signed*) Hilmi **Akil**
Representative
Turkish Republic of Northern Cyprus

Appendix III

Sample of letters of protest by Iraq against the USA, Britain and France.

Letter dated 11 February 2002 from the Chargé d'affaires of the Permanent Mission of Iraq to the United Nations addressed to the President of the Security Council

United Nations **S**/2002/171

Security Council

Distr.: General
15 February 2002
English
Original: Arabic

Letter dated 11 February 2002 from the Chargé d'affaires a.i. of the Permanent Mission of Iraq to the United Nations addressed to the President of the Security Council

On instructions from my Government, I have the honour to transmit to you herewith a letter dated 7 February 2002 from Mr. Naji Sabri, Minister for Foreign Affairs of the Republic of Iraq. The Minister calls attention to the ongoing wanton aggression against Iraq by United States and British aircraft in the unlawful no-flight zones and to the fact that in the period from 16 December 2001 to 15 January 2002 they carried out 336 hostile sorties, 84 of them from Saudi Arabia, 202 from Kuwait and 50 from Turkey.

The Minister reaffirms the Government of Iraq's condemnation of these acts of aggression against Iraqi territory, and he states that full international responsibility for them must be borne by the United States, the United Kingdom and the countries that provide the logistic support for this aggression, namely Saudi Arabia, Kuwait and Turkey. He further states that Iraq reserves its right, as established by the Charter of the United Nations and international law, to defend itself against this ongoing hostile, terrorist activity. He urges you to perform the duties assigned to you under the Charter by ensuring that this persistent aggression is halted and does not recur and that its perpetrators and the regional parties that associate themselves with it are made to bear full legal responsibility for it.

I should be grateful if you would have the present letter and its annex circulated as a document of the Security Council.

(*Signed*) Abdul Munim **Al-Kadhe**
Chargé d'affaires a.i.

Annex to the letter dated 11 February 2002 from the Chargé d'affaires a.i. of the Permanent Mission of Iraq to the United Nations addressed to the President of the Security Council

I should like to inform you that United States of America and the United Kingdom have continued their aerial aggression against the Republic of Iraq. United States and British warplanes based in the Kingdom of Saudi Arabia, the State of Kuwait and the Republic of Turkey have thus continued to violate Iraq's airspace. They flew 336 armed sorties in the period from 16 December 2001 to 15 January 2002, 84 of them from Saudi Arabia, 202 from Kuwait and 50 from Turkey, as shown in the statement enclosed herewith.

The enforcement by the United States and the United Kingdom of no-flight zones in northern and southern Iraq is a flagrant violation of the Charter of the United Nations, the established norms of international law and the Security Council resolutions urging States to respect Iraq's sovereignty, territorial integrity and political independence, and it constitutes ongoing armed aggression against Iraq. The international community has condemned the maintenance of the no-flight zones as representing an illegal use of force against an independent State. The United Nations has also done so, as exemplified by the statement of the Secretary-General at his press conference of 19 December 2001, when he said (press release SG/SM/8081): "[I indicated that] . . . I did not see anything in the Security Council resolution that authorizes the imposition or the enforcement of a no-flight zone".

The attacks being launched by United States and British aircraft on Iraqi towns and villages and on structures that are basic to life in the country, including healthcare and educational establishments and houses of worship, constitute blatant and continuing State terrorism and gross interference in the internal affairs of Iraq. When the 30-nation aggression of 1991 failed to break the will of Iraqis or to impair their freedom and independence, the United States and the United Kingdom proceeded to take the unilateral decision to impose the no-flight zones, first in northern Iraq on 7 April 1991 and then in southern Iraq on 27 August 1992, and they used armed force to attack Iraqi civilian and military installations with a view to undermining Iraq's stability and endangering the lives of its people. The maintenance of these zones and the use of force in them therefore represent a violation of the principle of non-use of force as enshrined in the Charter of the

United Nations and are in breach of the Security Council resolutions relating to Iraq, all of which affirm that Iraq's sovereignty, independence and territorial integrity must be respected. Since the no-flight zones were first imposed, there have been 211,154 violations by United States and British aircraft, including violations in which military and civilian sites have been bombed and destroyed, and 1,476 people have been killed and more than 1,320 injured.

Although the entire world has condemned this aggression and despite the letters we address to the Secretary-General and to you providing details of these acts of terrorist aggression, the United States continues to proclaim its contempt for the Charter of the United Nations and the resolutions of the Security Council, and the Security Council has taken no action with regard to this terrorist aggression being committed by the United States and the United Kingdom. This raises serious questions about the credibility of the United Nations and the Security Council and about their capacity to apply the norms of the Charter to all without distinction and without the use of double standards or to safeguard international peace and security and halt acts of aggression and intimidation that endanger them.

The Government of Iraq considers that the governments of the United States and the United Kingdom and the countries that provide the facilities for this terrorist aggression, namely Kuwait, Saudi Arabia and Turkey, should bear full responsibility for these hostile acts. It affirms Iraq's established entitlement under the Charter of the United Nations and international law to exercise its legitimate right to defend itself against this ongoing hostile, terrorist activity. It further expresses the hope that you will perform the duties assigned to you as they relate to the maintenance of international peace and security, that you will call upon the governments of the countries in question to halt their continuing aggression against Iraq forthwith and that you will ensure that those committing the aggression and the regional parties that are facilitating its continuation are made to bear full legal responsibility for it.

(*Signed*) Naji **Sabri**
Minister for Foreign Affairs
Enclosure

Violations of the airspace of the Republic of Iraq by United States and British warplanes, 16 December 2001–15 January 2002

1. In the northern region 50 sorties were flown at speeds of 720 to 780 kilometres per hour and at altitudes of 6,000 to 12,000 metres, as follows:

(a) At 1200 hours on 4 January 2002, United States and British F-14, F-15, F-16, Tornado and EA-6B aircraft coming from bases in Turkey and from Turkish airspace penetrated Iraq's airspace in the northern region. They carried out 12 armed sorties, were supported by an AWACS aircraft operating inside Turkish airspace and overflew the Amadiyah, Aqrah and Rawanduz areas. Our air defences, acting in exercise of the legitimate right to defend the homeland, engaged the aircraft and, at 1245 hours, drove them off.

(b) At 1215 hours on 8 January 2002, United States and British F-14, F-15, F-16, Tornado and EA-6B aircraft coming from bases in Turkey and from Turkish airspace penetrated Iraq's airspace in the northern region. They carried out 14 armed sorties, were supported by an AWACS aircraft operating inside Turkish airspace and overflew the Zakho, Amadiyah, Aqrah, Dohuk, Ayn Zalah, Dokan and Rawanduz areas. Our air defences, acting in exercise of the legitimate right to defend the homeland, engaged the aircraft and, at 1450 hours, drove them off.

(c) At 1250 hours on 14 January 2002, United States and British F-14, F-15, F-16, Tornado and EA-6B aircraft coming from bases in Turkey and from Turkish airspace penetrated Iraq's airspace in the northern region. They carried out 12 armed sorties, were supported by an AWACS aircraft operating inside Turkish airspace and overflew the Zakho, Amadiyah, Ayn Sifni, Baibo, Irbil, Dohuk, Ayn Zalah and Rawanduz areas. Our air defences, acting in exercise of the legitimate right to defend the homeland, engaged the aircraft and, at 1540 hours, drove them off.

(d) At 1150 hours on 15 January 2002, United States and British F-14, F-15, F-16, Tornado and EA-6B aircraft coming from bases in Turkey and from Turkish airspace penetrated Iraq's airspace in the northern region. They carried out 12 armed sorties, were supported by an AWACS aircraft operating inside Turkish airspace and overflew the Amadiyah, Aqrah, Dohuk, Ayn Zalah, Irbil and Rawanduz areas. Our air defences, acting in exercise of the legitimate right to defend the homeland, engaged the aircraft and, at 1420 hours, drove them off.

2. In the southern region 286 armed sorties were flown at speeds of 720 to 780 kilometres per hour and at altitudes of 9,000 to 13,000 metres, as follows:

(a) At 1320 hours on 17 December 2001, United States and British F-14, F-15 and F-16 aircraft coming from bases in Saudi Arabia and Kuwait and from Kuwaiti and Saudi airspace and territorial waters penetrated Iraq's airspace in the southern region. They carried out six armed sorties, two of them from Saudi territory with the support of an AWACS command and control aircraft operating inside Saudi airspace and four from Kuwaiti territory and by way of the demilitarized zone between Iraq and Kuwait with the support of an E-2C command and control aircraft operating inside Kuwaiti airspace. They overflew the Salman, Artawi, Busayyah and Jalibah areas. Our air defences, acting in exercise of the legitimate right to defend the homeland, engaged the aircraft and, at 1500 hours, drove them off.

(b) At 2044 hours on 20 December 2001, United States and British F-14, F-15, Tornado and EA-6B aircraft coming from bases in Saudi Arabia and Kuwait and from Saudi and Kuwaiti airspace and territorial waters penetrated Iraq's airspace in the southern region. They carried out 16 armed sorties, four of them from Saudi territory with the support of an AWACS command and control aircraft operating inside Saudi airspace and 16 from Kuwaiti territory and by way of the demilitarized zone between Iraq and Kuwait with the support of an E-2C command and control aircraft operating inside Kuwaiti airspace. They overflew the Ashbajah, Busayyah, Jalibah, Salman and Artawi areas. Our air defences, acting in exercise of the legitimate right to defend the homeland, engaged the aircraft and, at 2300 hours, drove them off.

(c) At 2000 hours on 21 December 2001, United States and British F-14, F-15, Tornado and EA-6B aircraft coming from bases in Saudi Arabia and Kuwait and from Saudi and Kuwaiti airspace and territorial waters penetrated Iraq's airspace in the southern region. They carried out six armed sorties, four of them from Saudi territory with the support of an AWACS command and control aircraft operating inside Saudi airspace and two from Kuwaiti territory and by way of the demilitarized zone between Iraq and Kuwait with the support of an E-2C command and control aircraft operating inside Kuwaiti airspace. They overflew the Busayyah, Ashbajah and Shinafiyah West areas. Our air defences, acting in exercise of the legitimate right to defend the homeland, engaged the aircraft and, at 2125 hours, drove them off.

(d) At 2100 hours on 23 December 2001, United States and British F-14 and F-15 aircraft coming from bases in Saudi Arabia and Kuwait and from Kuwaiti and Saudi airspace and territorial waters penetrated Iraq's airspace in the southern region. They carried out eight armed sorties, two of them from Saudi territory with the support of an AWACS command and control aircraft operating inside Saudi airspace and six from Kuwaiti territory and by way of the demilitarized zone between Iraq and Kuwait with the support of an E-2C command and control aircraft operating inside Kuwaiti airspace. They overflew the Nasiriyah, Busayyah, Jalibah and Ashbajah areas. Our air defences, acting in exercise of the legitimate right to defend the homeland, engaged the aircraft and, at 2210 hours, drove them off.

(e) At 1135 hours on 25 December 2001, United States and British F-14, F-15, F-16, Tornado and EA-6B aircraft coming from bases in Saudi Arabia and Kuwait and from Kuwaiti and Saudi airspace and territorial waters penetrated Iraq's airspace in the southern region. They carried out 16 armed sorties, four of them from Saudi territory with the support of an AWACS command and control aircraft operating inside Saudi airspace and 12 from Kuwaiti territory and by way of the demilitarized zone between Iraq and Kuwait with the support of an E-2C command and control aircraft operating inside Kuwaiti airspace. They overflew the Busayyah, Salman, Artawi, Jalibah and Ashbajah areas. Our air defences, acting in exercise of the legitimate right to defend the homeland, engaged the aircraft and, at 1315 hours, drove them off.

(f) At 1345 hours on 26 December 2001, United States and British F-14, F-15 and F-16 aircraft coming from bases in Saudi Arabia and Kuwait and from Kuwaiti and Saudi airspace and territorial waters penetrated Iraq's airspace in the southern region. They carried out 30 armed sorties, four of them from Saudi territory with the support of an AWACS command and control aircraft operating inside Saudi airspace and 26 from Kuwaiti territory and by way of the demilitarized zone between Iraq and Kuwait with the support of an E-2C command and control aircraft operating inside Kuwaiti airspace. They overflew the Busayyah, Salman, Jalibah and Ashbajah areas. Our air defences, acting in exercise of the legitimate right to defend the homeland, engaged the aircraft and, at 1530 hours, drove them off.

(g) At 1150 hours on 27 December 2001, United States and British F-14, F-15, F-16, Tornado and EA-6B aircraft coming from bases in Saudi Arabia and Kuwait and from Kuwaiti and Saudi airspace and territorial waters penetrated Iraq's airspace in the southern region. They carried out 30 armed sorties, 16 of them from Saudi territory with the support of an AWACS command and control aircraft operating inside Saudi airspace and 14 from Kuwaiti territory and by way of the demilitarized zone between Iraq and Kuwait with the support of an E-2C command and control aircraft operating inside Kuwaiti airspace. They overflew the Safwan, Busayyah, Jalibah, Salman and Artawi areas. Our air defences, acting in exercise of the legitimate right to defend the homeland, engaged the aircraft and, at 1330 hours, drove them off.

(h) At 1010 hours on 28 December 2001, United States and British F-14, F-15, F-16, Tornado and EA-6B aircraft coming from bases in Saudi Arabia and Kuwait and from Kuwaiti and Saudi airspace and territorial waters penetrated Iraq's airspace in the southern region. They carried out 20 armed sorties, six of them from Saudi territory with the support of an AWACS command and control aircraft operating inside Saudi airspace and 14 from Kuwaiti territory and by way of the demilitarized zone between Iraq and Kuwait with the support of an E-2C command and control aircraft operating inside Kuwaiti airspace. They overflew the Safwan, Nasiriyah, Busayyah, Jalibah, Salman and Artawi areas. Our air defences, acting in exercise of the legitimate right to defend the homeland, engaged the aircraft and, at 1140 hours, drove them off.

(i) At 0842 hours on 29 December 2001, United States and British F-14, F-15 and F-16 aircraft coming from bases in Saudi Arabia and Kuwait and from Kuwaiti and Saudi airspace and territorial waters penetrated Iraq's airspace in the southern region. They carried out 34 armed sorties, 10 of them from Saudi territory with the support of an AWACS command and control aircraft operating inside Saudi airspace and 24 from Kuwaiti territory and by way of the demilitarized zone between Iraq and Kuwait with the support of an E-2C command and control aircraft operating inside Kuwaiti airspace. They overflew the Jalibah, Busayyah, Salman and Ma'aniyah areas. Our air defences, acting in exercise of the legitimate right to defend the homeland, engaged the aircraft and, at 1020 hours, drove them off.

(j) At 0825 hours on 30 December 2001, United States and British F-14, F-15, F-16, Tornado and EA-6B aircraft coming from bases in Saudi Arabia and Kuwait and from Kuwaiti and Saudi airspace and territorial waters penetrated Iraq's airspace in the southern region. They carried out 22 armed sorties, 10 of them from Saudi territory with the support of an AWACS command and control aircraft operating inside Saudi airspace and 12 from Kuwaiti territory and by way of the demilitarized zone between Iraq and Kuwait with the support of an E-2C command and control aircraft operating inside Kuwaiti airspace. They overflew the Umm Qasr, Safwan, Jalibah, Busayyah, Salman, Ma'aniyah and Artawi areas. Our air defences, acting in exercise of the legitimate right to defend the homeland, engaged the aircraft and, at 1055 hours, drove them off.

(k) At 0905 hours on 2 January 2002, United States and British F-14, F-15, Tornado and EA-6B aircraft coming from bases in Saudi Arabia and Kuwait and from Kuwaiti and Saudi airspace and territorial waters penetrated Iraq's airspace in the southern region. They carried out 22 armed sorties, 12 of them from Saudi territory with the support of an AWACS command and control aircraft operating inside Saudi airspace and 10 from Kuwaiti territory and by way of the demilitarized zone between Iraq and Kuwait with the support of an E-2C command and control aircraft operating inside Kuwaiti airspace. They overflew the Jalibah, Busayyah, Lasaf, Salman and Artawi areas. Our air defences, acting in exercise of the legitimate right to defend the homeland, engaged the aircraft and, at 1025 hours, drove them off.

(l) At 0955 hours on 2 January 2002, United States and British F-14 and F-15 aircraft coming from bases in Saudi Arabia and Kuwait and from Kuwaiti and Saudi airspace and territorial waters penetrated Iraq's airspace in the southern region. They carried out 16 armed sorties, four of them from Saudi territory with the support of an AWACS command and control aircraft operating inside Saudi airspace and 12 from Kuwaiti territory and by way of the demilitarized zone between Iraq and Kuwait with the support of an E-2C command and control aircraft operating inside Kuwaiti airspace. They overflew the Jalibah, Busayyah, Ashbajah and Salman areas. Our air defences, acting in exercise of the legitimate right to defend the homeland, engaged the aircraft and, at 1150 hours, drove them off.

(m) At 1205 hours on 7 January 2002, United States and British F-16 aircraft coming from bases in Saudi Arabia and Kuwait and from Kuwaiti and Saudi airspace and territorial waters penetrated Iraq's airspace in the southern region. They carried out 10 armed sorties from Kuwaiti territory and by way of the demilitarized zone between Iraq and Kuwait with the support of an E-2C command and control aircraft operating inside Kuwaiti airspace. They overflew the Artawi, Jalibah, Ashbajah and Salman areas. Our air defences, acting in exercise of the legitimate right to defend the homeland, engaged the aircraft and, at 1315 hours, drove them off.

(n) At 1235 hours on 11 January 2002, United States and British F-14, F-15, F-16, Tornado and EA-6B aircraft coming from bases in Saudi Arabia and Kuwait and from Kuwaiti and Saudi airspace and territorial waters penetrated Iraq's airspace in the southern region. They carried out 17 armed sorties, six of them from Saudi territory with the support of an AWACS command and control aircraft operating inside Saudi airspace and 11 from Kuwaiti territory and by way of the demilitarized zone between Iraq and Kuwait with the support of an E-2C command and control aircraft operating inside Kuwaiti airspace. They overflew the Nasiriyah, Jalibah, Busayyah, Artawi, Ashbajah and Salman areas. Our air defences, acting in exercise of the legitimate right to defend the homeland, engaged the aircraft and, at 1400 hours, drove them off.

(o) At 0940 hours on 13 January 2002, United States and British F-14 and F-15 aircraft coming from bases in Saudi Arabia and Kuwait and from Kuwaiti and Saudi airspace and territorial waters penetrated Iraq's airspace in the southern region. They carried out 13 armed sorties from Kuwaiti territory and by way of the demilitarized zone between Iraq and Kuwait with the support of an E-2C command and control aircraft operating inside Kuwaiti airspace. They overflew the Safwan and Umm Qasr areas. Our air defences, acting in exercise of the legitimate right to defend the homeland, engaged the aircraft and, at 1110 hours, drove them off.

(p) At 1150 hours on 15 January 2002, United States and British F-14, F-15, F-16, Tornado and EA-6B aircraft coming from bases in Saudi Arabia and Kuwait and from Kuwaiti and Saudi airspace and territorial waters penetrated Iraq's airspace in the southern region. They carried out 20 armed sorties from Kuwaiti territory and by way of the demilitarized zone between Iraq and Kuwait with the support of an E-2C command and control aircraft operating inside Kuwaiti airspace. They overflew the Jalibah, Busayyah, Artawi, Ashbajah and Salman areas. Our air defences, acting in exercise of the legitimate right to defend the homeland, engaged the aircraft and, at 1345 hours, drove them off.

Appendix IV

Diagrammatic representation of sovereignty and jurisdiction over maritime, air and outer spaces

APPLICABLE LEGAL PRINCIPLES							
	OUTER SPACE AND CELESTIAL BODIES, GALAXIES AND THE UNIVERSES						
Sovereignty	-	-	-	-	-	-	-
Jurisfaction	-	-	-	-	-	-	-
Jurisaction	+	+	+	+	+	+	+
100 MILES MAXIMUM AIRSPACE DEMARCATION LINE							
	STATE TERRITORY	Airspace over 12 miles territorial sea	Airspace over 12 nautical miles CONTIGUOUS ZONE	EXCLUSIVE	Airspace over 200 miles ECONOMIC	ZONE	Airspace over HIGH SEAS
Sovereignty	+	+	-	-	-	-	-
Jurisfaction	+	+	-	-	-	-	-
Jurisaction	+	+	+	+	+	+	+
	COAST	12 nautical miles TERRITORIAL SEA	12 Nautical Miles CONTIGUOUS ZONE	EXCLUSIVE	200 Miles ECONOMIC	ZONE	HIGH SEAS
				Continental shelf	Continental slope	Continental rise	

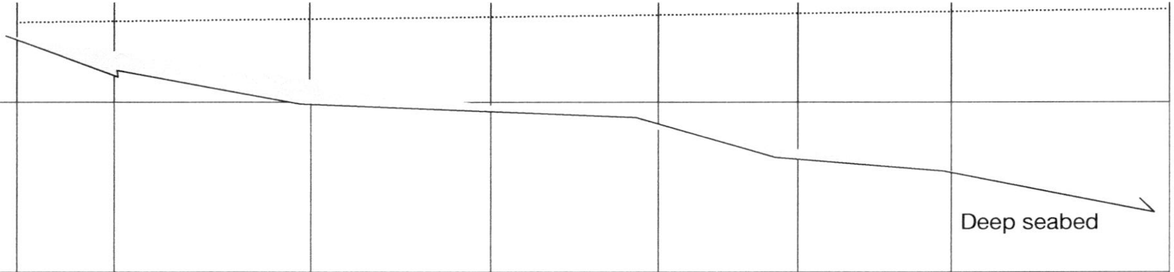

Sovereignty	+	+	-	-	-	-	-
Jurisfaction	+	+	-	-	-	-	-
Jurisaction	+	+	+	+	+	+	+
Right of hot pursuit	+	+	+	+	+	+	+
Jurisdiction over pirates	+	+	+	+	+	+	+
Application of the common heritage of mankind principle	-	-	-	-	-	-	+

+= applicable - = not-applicable

Appendix V

States and their position of choice in response to the spatial demarcation boundary plane question

Demarcation theory of choice	*Present need for delimitaition*	*The no present need theory*	*The Criteria of Space Activities or The Functional Approach*	*The aero-dynamic lift theory*	*The Bogota declaration view*	*The Usque Ad Infinitum Theory*	*The national security and effective control theory*	*The Lowest Point of Orbital Flight Theory*	*Theories of arbitrary distances*	*Delimitation will aid cooperation and promote peaceful relations*	*Delimitation will hamper technological development*	*Delimitation will aid the sovereignty and equality of states principle*
Azerbaijan	X						X					X
Bangladesh,	X											
Belarus	X									X		X
Brazil	X		X									
Czech Republic	X (2010)	X (2007)								X (2010)	X	
Estonia		X										
Germany		X										
Jordan	X							X				X
Serbia												
Thailand												
Tunisia	X						X					
Iceland		X										

Iraq	X			X (2009)	X	
Mexico		X				
Nicaragua	X		X			
Nigeria	X					X
Qatar	X					X
Serbia	X		X			
Saudi Arabia		X				
Thailand	X				X	X
Ukraine	X			X		X
UK		X		X		

Index

Abdulmutallab, F. 109
Abeyratne, R.I.R. 98, 102
advanced technological powers 317–18
aerial trespass: protestations 150–1
aeronautical offences 94
aeronautical rules and regulations 94
aerospace exploration 2
aerospace objects 250–2; liability 252–3
Afghanistan War 123
African Airlines Association (AFRAA) 66
air 57
air defence identification zones (ADIZ) 143–4, 147
air law 2, 4, 129, 299; controversy 8; double standards 317; treaties 61–2; *vs.* space law 20–1, 251
Air Navigation Order (2009) 68–9
air transport agreements 76–81
aircraft 71–2, 74–5, 260; civilian 80, 164; commercial flights 80; definition 71–2, 298–9; evolution 300; nationality 66–72; pilotless 81–2, 316; registration 320; state 80; trespassing *see* trespassing aircraft; US registration 77
airships 72
airspace 2, 57–8, 185, 283; conventions 257; legal status theories 60–1; ownership 58, 189; regulation 64; sovereignty 58, 82–3; transportation 5; *vs.* outer space 283
Ajibola, B. 126, 317
Ajomo, M.A. 89; piracy 106
Akehurst, M. 128
al-Qaeda 123
Alaskan Airlines flight incident 97
Allen, C.H. 267
Allied forces aircraft incident 329
Allied nations 30
Alston, P. 26, 268
American Indians 186
Andem, M. 217, 289–90, 294
Ansell, C. 24–5
Antarctic 145–7, 218–19; tourism 274
Antarctic Treaty (1959) 145
Anthony, C. 36
Arctic Ocean 146
Argentinean aircraft incident 329
Aristotle 212
Arnold, R.P. 203
asteroids 176
astronauts 244, 246, 265; criminal jurisdiction 258; definition 246; distress 253–4; envoys of mankind 253; legal status 253–5; protection 255; sacrifice 263; survival homicide situations 263; vulnerability 262–3
Astronaut's Agreement (1968) 253, 255, 257, 265
atmosphere 298–9, 311; height 309
AucBuchon, M.J. 109
Australian Space Activities Act (1998) 248; Australian liability 248
Authority of the Space Transportation System Commander 258–9
Aviateca, S.A. v. Friedman 34
Aviation Act (1962) 298
aviation industry 113; bureaucratic structures 113
aviation security devices 109–10

Baca, A.K. 201
Bangladesh: poverty 1
Beale, J. 32
Bellflower, J.W. 266–7
Bentham, J. 184
Bin Laden, O. 123
biochemical law theory 261–2
blacklists 101–2

Bogota Declaration (1976) 211, 272, 301–5; Article (2) 301; poor equatorial states 305; reactions 303; Report of the Legal Sub-committee (1985) 303–4; rich equatorial states 305; state withdrawal 304
Bonn Declaration (1978) 124–5; shortcoming 125
Borchard, O. 57
Bouve, C. 57–8
British courts 100
broadcasting 319
Brothers to the Rescue 164–5
Brownlie, I. 13, 79, 134, 142
Bulgarian territory incident 326
Burgess, M.: and Vollaard, H. 25
Bush, G.W. 123, 153

Canadian air defence identification zones (CADIZ) 143–4
Canadian Criminal Code (1985) 242–3
Canadian government 108
Canadian laws 242–3
Canadian watch lists 130–1
Caplan, H. 112–13
Cassese, A. 124
Cathay Pacific aircraft incident 326
celestial bodies 176, 189, 196, 198–9, 205, 218, 222, 256; private exploitation 207
Central Intelligence Agency (CIA) 268
Chadian aircraft incidents 337
Chayes, A.: and Chayes, A.H. 24
Cheng, B. 3, 36, 51–2, 58, 64, 92, 111, 210, 271, 283, 309; astronaut 246; crimes 85; definition of aircraft 72; hijacking 110; pilotless aircraft 81; prosecution 116; remote sensing 269
Chicago Convention (1944) 63–5, 68, 76–7, 80, 94–5; Article (1) 316; Article (3) 144, 159; Article (8) 81–2; Article (25) 151; Article (77) 78–9; contracting parties 148
Chicago International Air Services Transit Agreement (1944) 80–1
Chicago International Air Transport Agreement (1944) 80–1
Chinese airspace 153–5
Chinese EEZ 155
Chinese government 154
Chinese growth 5
Chinese space exploration 224–5
Chinese territory incidents 326, 330
Christol, C.Q. 195, 207, 262
civil aviation: unlawful interference 103
Civil Aviation Act (1996): Section (92) 99
Civil Aviation Authority 69
Cloppenburg, J.: and Hobe, S. 275
coastal states 140–1, 155
Cold War era 153, 200
Coleridge, J.K. 263
Commander, Space Transportation System 259–61
Commercial Space Act (1998) 277
Commercial Space Launch Amendments Act (CSLAA:2004) 277–8
Committee on Environmental Protection 218
Committee on the Peaceful Uses of Outer Space (COPUOS) 1, 199, 211, 285; Czech Republic response 292; UK response 296
common heritage of mankind (CHM) 191–206, 208–11, 217, 283, 312, 320; definition 203; *res omnium extra communis* 206
compensation 112
constructive presence theory 42–3
contemporary rules 180
contiguous zone 134–5
continental shelf 141–3; UK 142
control *ratione personae* 245–6, 254
control theory 52–3
Convention Establishing the World Intellectual Property Organisation 236
Convention on the Establishment of the European Space Agency (ESA:1975) 261
Convention on International Civil Aviation 159
Convention on the Law of the Sea (UNCLOS:1982) 23, 49, 138–9, 154–5
Convention on Registration of Objects Launched into Outer Space (1975) 73–5
conventions 64–5, 169
Cooper, J.C. 33, 155–6, 306, 315
corporate investment 52–3
cosmonauts 244, 246; definition 246
Costa Rican aircraft incident 338
Crawford, J. 18, 21, 35
crew members: mixed nationality 259–61
crimes 55
crimes in airspace 85–100; cabin crew powers 96; citizen's arrest 96–7; commander 96–7; common crimes 93–4; costs 99–100; overloading 100; unruly passengers 95–8

criminal conduct 85–6
criminal jurisdiction (principles) 39–50, 95; nationality 44–5; objective territorial 42–3; passive personality/nationality 48; protective/security 45–8; territorial 42–4; UK 99; universality 48–50
Csbaffi, I.A. 174
Cuban airspace 163–5, 170, 172, 317–18; Cessna aircraft 163–4
Cuban Ministry of Foreign Affairs 164–5
Cuban refugees 103–4
Cuban territory incidents 339–41
Cuban-American relations 103–4
Cutting Case 48
Cypriot territory incidents 89, 333, 338, 342–9
Czechoslovakian territory incident 324

Danish government 286
De Valles, A. 59
Defence Committee of the House of Commons (UK) 167
demarcation boundary line 282–315, 321; aerodynamic lift theory 297–300; arbitrary distances theory 309–10; buffer zone 310–11; equal access 291; formula 311; functional theory *see* functional theory; legal theory 310–11; lowest perigee approach 308; national security and effective control theory 306; no-present-need theory 290; orbital flight theory 306–9; present need theory 290–3; *usque ad infinitum* theory 305–6; zone of innocent passage 311; zones 309
Denning, A. 280, 290
Descartes, R. 12
developing states 5–6, 288, 318–19
developing *vs.* developed states 6
Devlin, P.A. 86–7
Dias, R.W.M. 181, 214
Diederiks-Verschoor, I.H.P. 220–1
Directors General of Civil Aviation (DGCA) 76
Doyle, S.E. 259
DPP v. Boot 43
drone flights 82
Dutch government 99

Earth: revolution of 306
Eichmann Case 37–8, 47, 50
Elden, S. 11–12, 40, 168
English aeronautical regulations 87–8
English Criminal Law 86–7
environmental damage 218–19
equality 211–12
espionage 156, 172; remote sensing 270–3
Ethiopian airliner hijacking 119
European Healthware 4
European Partner State 237
European Space Agency (ESA) 237–8, 260–1; objectives 261
European Union airspace 66
European Union legislation 65
Evans, A.E. 102, 109, 119, 130
exclusive economic zone (EEZ) 135–41, 147, 155; military activities 138–41
extradition 37, 120, 242–4

Falkland Island territory incident 329
Fasan, E.I. 198
Fauchille, P. 58, 61
Fawcett, J.E.S. 32, 222–3, 294
Federal District Court (USA) 231
Fenema, P.V. 279
flags of convenience 75–6, 79–80, 228
flight information region (FIR) 132–3
floating island theory 233
freedom 312
French aircraft incident 323
French Civil Code (1804) 182
French criminal law 46
French territory 91
functional jurisdiction 225
functional theory 293–7; flight velocity 295; problems 295; space activities regulation 293; *vs.* spatial approach 294–5

Garder v. Howe 233
Garn, J. 249
Gaza International Airport 110–11
Geneva Convention on the Continental Shelf (1958) 142
Geneva Convention on the High Seas (1958) 143; Article (2) 143
geographic entities 12–13
geometry 12
Georgian territory incident 331
geostationary orbit (GSO) 9, 211–12, 219, 301–5, 319
geostationary satellite 1
German territory incidents 323, 324, 325
Ghanaian laws 100
globalisation 23–5
Goedhart, R.F.A.. 297–300, 304, 308
Goldie, L. 192–3

Goldin, D. 245
Gorove, S. 193
Grief, N. 144; and Kish, J. 155–6
Griffiths, B. 38–9
Grotius, H. 58–9

Hague Convention (1970) 44, 106, 115–17; Article (7) 116; Article (8) 120; central value 115; hijacking 115
Hailbronner, K. 122, 134, 136
Haley, A.G. 257–8
Hanessian, J. 145
Hara, R. 225, 255
Harris, C. 116
Harvard Draft Convention (1935) 42, 47
Havana Air Traffic Centre 164
Havana Convention (1928) 67–8
Heere, W.P. 99, 136
heritage 203
high seas 143, 208
hijacking 103–31; aircraft operators 119; asylum purposes 105; combating 110, 119; definition 105; Ethiopian airliner 119; Indian aircraft 104; internationalisation 115; Nigerian Airways plane 118–19; offence 124; Taiwanese flight FEAT-128 104; universal jurisdiction 117–18
Hobe, S.: and Cloppenburg, J. 275
Holmes, J. 32
hot air balloon 60
Huber, M. 21
Hughes, L.N. 44–5
Hughes, W.J. 64, 161–2
human rights organisations 101–2, 109–10
human rights violations 131
humanity 152
Hungarian territory incident 323
Hurwitz, B. 285
Hussein, S. 167
hybrid rocket planes 74, 299–300

IATA Recommended Practice (1724) 101
Ibero-American Convention of Madrid (1926) 63
Indian aircraft hijacking 104
Indian aircraft incident 329
Indian airspace 153
Indian territory incident 330
indictment 243
intellectual property (IP) 232–9, 264; commercial ventures 232; inventions 232–4; ISS 238–9; patent protection 232; shared ownership 239
Intelsat 231; damages 231
international airspace 2, 147
international business transactions 52
International Civil Aviation Organisation (ICAO) 66, 68, 72, 78, 131; Council 78–9, 153, 159–60, 255; rules 132–3
International Congress of Aeronautics 61
International Court of Justice (ICJ) 14, 27–8, 125–7, 162–3, 169
International Government Agreement (IGA:2008) 227–30, 234, 240–2; Article (11) 240; Article (16) 229–30; Article (21) 234–5; Article (22) 241
international interest 312
international law 3, 111; customary 37; fundamental problems 7
International Law Association 61
international space 2, 4, 6, 18, 132, 146, 206
International Space Station (ISS) 227, 237–9, 244; IP 238–9; toilet wars 244; tourism 249
international straits 133–4
International Telecommunications Union (ITU) 211–12, 219; Malaga-Torremolinos Convention (1973) 301–2, 319
Iranian territory incidents 329, 334, 335
Iraqi airspace 170
Iraqi government 167
Iraqi no-fly zones 169–70
Iraqi territory incidents 328, 331, 350–9
Israeli aircraft incidents 326, 327, 330, 331, 332, 334, 336
Israeli Supreme Court 38, 50
Israeli territory 16–17, 110–11
Israeli violations 317
ITU Convention (1973) 301–2, 319

Jackson, J. 23
Japanese journalist space flight 249
Japanese territory incident 325
Jastrow, R. 307–8
Jenks, W. 174
Jessup, P.C.: and Taubenfeld, H.J. 285
Johnson, D.H.N. 17, 102
Johnson, L.B. 200
Jowitt, W. 21
Joyce v. DPP 45–6
Joyner, C.C. 103–4, 110–11
jurisaction 51, 92–3, 249

jurisdiction 8, 30–6; criminal *see* criminal jurisdiction (principles); definition 30–1; doctrine 31; personal 37–9, 41; quasi-territorial 36; sovereignty 54–5; territorial 33
jurisfaction 51, 92–3, 249; extra-territorial 93
justice 212–14

Kamenetskaya, E. 246
Kant, I. 314
Karman primary jurisdiction line 298, 300
king of the castle 273
Kish, J. 145, 226, 256; and Grief, N. 155–6
Klucka, J. 260
Korean aircraft incidents 327, 328
Korean Airlines flight (007) 158–9
Kosmo, J. 201

Lachs, M. 195, 198; and Schacter, O. 306
land boundaries 13
landlocked states 13
Lardone, F. 59
Law of the Sea Convention (LOSC:1982) 133–46; Article (76) 141; Article (78) 142; high seas 143
lawyers 262
Lebanese airspace 317
Lebanese territory incidents 330, 331, 332, 334, 336
Lefebvere, H. 168
legal writers 180
Leiser v. United States 152
Liability Convention (1972) 180
Libyan aircraft incidents 327
Libyan authorities 116, 125–7, 316–17
Libyan government 125–7
licence 191, 197
Lissitzyn, O.J. 162, 165
Livingston, D.M. 274
Lockerbie Case 116, 126–7, 317; Scottish court 126–7
Lowenfield, A.F. 122
lunar silicon 176
lunar territory 189

McGoldrick, D.: and Warbrick, C. 39
McMahon, J.F. 305
McNair, A. 60–1, 64, 283
Madders, K.J. 260–1
mankind 183, 203
Mansell, W.: *et al* 181, 184, 186
Marconi Wireless Telco v. USA 233
Marietta, M. 231
maritime exclusion zone (MEZ) 143–4
Mars 176–7
Martin Marietta Corporation v. Intelsat 231
Matte, N.M. 78
Melanda, R. 243
Middle East Airlines 119–20
Ministry of Defence (MoD) 160–1
Mir 249
misconduct in orbit 241–2
Montgolfier Brothers 60
Montreal Convention (1971) 117–18, 126
Moon 176–9, 196–8, 200–1, 208–10, 216–17, 221, 256; resources 210, 216
Moon Agreement (1979) 177–8, 193–4, 197–8, 202, 208–10, 264–5; Article (6) 204, 208; Article (10) 246–7; Article (11) 208–9; Article (12) 247, 254, 257–8, 265; astronauts 254; parties 224–5; reciprocity 225
morality 215–16, 219
Morennoff, J. 285
Multilateral Space Station Agreement (1998) 236
multilateral treaties 316, 319–20
Murphy, T.J. 309

NASA Directive on Space Station Intellectual Property 234
National Aeronautical and Space Administration (NASA) 232, 245
National Commission on Space 201
national space 310
nationality 37, 44–5; control 52–3; of craft 74–9, 83; double 44; foreign 45; public order 45
Nicaragua Case 162–3, 169
Nicaraguan territory incident 338
Nicolson, H. 215
Nigeria 288; space-based satellites 212–13
Nigerian air law 88–9
Nigerian aircraft 88
Nigerian airspace 65
Nigerian Airways plane hijacking 118–19
Nigerian government 212–13
Nigerian space policy 212–13
Nippon Foundation Guidelines 140
no-fly zones 166–72; Iraq 169–70; legality 166–7; origins 166
notice to airmen (NOTAM) zones 144

occupation 183
O'Connell, D.P. 48, 73

Oda, S. 126
open skies agreements 65–6
Ott, D. 43
outer space *see* space
Outer Space Treaty (1967) 177–8, 198, 209–10, 225; Article (1) 202; Article (V) 247, 253; Article (VIII) 247–8; Article (XII) 225
ownership 57–8; airspace 189; legal 185; space objects 180–90

Padalka, G 244
Pakistani aircraft incident 330
Pakistani airspace 153
Pakistani territory incident 329
Pan American Convention on Commercial Aviation (1928) 63
Paris Convention (1919) 76; Article (32) 157
Parker, H. 28
passive personality principle 107–8
Patents in Space Act (US Patent Act) 235
Pedrozo, R. 138–9
Permanent Court of International Justice (PCIJ) 42–3, 92–3
personal jurisdiction 37–9, 41
pilot 259
Pinochet Case 39
piracy 37, 49–50, 106
Piradov, A.S. 246
Pollock, F. 184
Pomponius 40
possession 181, 186–7
problems 315
profiling 109
prohibited airspace 157
property 177–87; legal ownership 185
property rights: space 199–206; space stations 224
protection for nations 7
protestations: aerial trespass 150–1
Pufendorf, S.V. 59–60

Quadri, R. 195, 294
quick reaction alert (QRA) 160–1

R v. Dudley and Stephens 263
R v. Horseferry Road Magistrates Court 38
R v. Martin and Others 86
Raclin, G.C. 176
Raustiala, K. 21, 24
Rawls, J.: theory of justice 214
regime 34
Registration Convention (1975) 227–8, 279; Article (II) 240
Regulation of Air Navigation (1919) 62–3
remote sensing 269–73, 319; capabilities 269; clandestine 269–70, 271; espionage 270–3; images 271; natural resources 271; state privacy 269–70
res communis 208
restitution 111
Robinson, G.S. 220, 229, 244; biochemical law theory 261–3
Roman law 58–9
Rousseau, J.J. 186–7
Royal Air Force (RAF) 166
Royal Netherlands Meteorological Institute (KMNI) 5
Russia *see* Soviet Union
Ryngaert, C. 30, 45–6, 49; control theory 53; nationality 53; protective jurisdiction 128

Salin, P.A. 217
Salmond, J.W. 182
satellite launches 82
satellite technology 3–4
Schacter, O.: and Lachs, M. 306
scholars 64, 315
Schwarzenberger, G. 22, 36, 41
scientific exploration 237
scientists 310
Scott, R. 156
sea areas 302–3
Select Committee on Defence: House of Commons 148
September 11th 113, 122–4
Shaw, M.N. 106
ships 72
Shuster, W. 20
Slaughter, M. 24
slavery 185
Smith, A. 183, 185, 187
Smith, M.L. 193
smoking on board aircraft 99–100
solar system 197–8
South African government 298–9
sovereign rights 52
sovereign states 7
sovereignty 2, 12–13, 21–31, 148; airspace 58, 82–3; domestic 22; equality 29–30; indeterminate 13; interdependence 22; international legal 22; jurisdiction 54–5; limitation 23; meaning 21–2; negative 22–3;

property rights 26–9, 55; special 12–13; Westphalian 22
Soviet Union 152–3, 157–8, 170; aircraft incidents 325, 329, 331; airspace 244–5, 317; naval nuclear vessel 270–1; property rights in space 200–1; space activities 216; territory incidents 322, 323, 324, 326, 327, 328
space 2–3, 8, 174–5, 283; activities 187; control 174; debris 222; disaster 263; equal access 205, 212; equal use 297; exploitation 175–7, 204, 208, 218–19; free space 199; instruments 175; invention 234–7; legal status 195; militarisation 266–7, 280, 320; national 177; powers 312; propertisation 318; *res extra commercium* 195–7; *res nullius* 195–6; research 188–9, 239; resources 189–90; territories 8; trespassing 172–3; *vs.* airspace 283; weaponisation 268–9
Space Affairs Act (1993) 299
space exploration 175, 184, 190, 220; multilateral 240; private enterprise 239
space law 4, 204, 290, 294, 318; *vs.* air law 20–1, 251
space objects 74–5, 289; ownership 180–4
space planes 299–300; surface to outer space 300; surface to surface 300
space property: commercial rights 318
space shuttle 223
Space Station Alpha 245
space stations 220–32, 264; civil liability 229–30; code of conduct 242–4; criminal jurisdiction 239–45; definition 220–1; extradition 242–4; free space 222; functions 221, 228, 264–5; humanity 244; insurance 230; intellectual property 238–9; manufacturing 223–4, 230; markings 226; multinational 227; nationality 225–8; operation 223; personnel 248; product liability 230; property rights 224; registration 223–8
space tourism 91, 245, 249, 264, 273–81; commercialisation 275–80; definition 275; development 275; free market 278; overview effect 274; privatisation 274–5; regulation 278–9; rules 275; technological advances 275
Space Transportation System Commander 259–61
space treaties 193, 199, 204–5, 223
Space Treaty (1967) 193, 223; Article (8) 223
spacecraft 73–5, 221, 276
spacefaring 267
spaceports 276–7
SpaceShipOne 276, 279–80
SpaceShipTwo 276
Spanish law 243
spatial delimitation 287–9; disputes 3
spatial territories 196
Stanford & Others v. Kuwait Airways & Others 119–20
state flag 36
state territory 56, 82; sectors 33–4
state-sponsored terrorism 122
states: fragmentation 18
Sudanese territory incidents 337
Swedish aircraft incidents 323, 324
Syrian territory incident 336

Taiwanese flight FEAT–128 104
Taliban 123
Taubenfeld, H.J.: and Jessup, P.C. 285
Temperley, R. 70
territorial jurisdiction 33, 39
territorial sovereignty 18, 20–1, 92
territorium 11
territory 11–14, 54; bounded space 12; controversy 14; delimitation 19; inaccessible zones 14; incidents 19; legal status 55–6; spatial 29; state *see* state territory; title 14
territory acquisition 13–18; abandonment 17; accretion 15–16; adjudication 17; annexation 16; avulsion 15–16; cession 15; conquest 16–17; discovery 17–18; disputes 18; flag-planting 15, 18; occupation 15; papal grant 18; prescription 17; relinquishment 17; renunciation 17; transfer 15
terror 40
terrorist attacks 119, 124, 130
Terrorist Screening Database (TSDB) 108–9
terrorist watch/no-fly lists 108–9, 130
terrorists 162–3
titanium 176
Tito, D. 245, 278
Tokyo Convention (1963) 95, 97, 105, 114–15, 120; Article (10) 98
Tomoya Kawakita v. US 44
total exclusion zone (TEZ) 144
Transport Security Administration (TSA) 108–9

treaties 112–21, 129, 159–60, 166, 188, 215, 255, 318; bilateral 121; multilateral 114–20; space 193, 199, 204–5, 223
trespassing aircraft 148–73; civilian airliners 158–60; deliberate intrusion 152; distress 152; drones 163; foreign pilots 255; hostile treatment 255; humanity 255; incidents 153; innocent passage 151–2, 171; involuntary entry 151–2; Korean Airlines flight-007 158–9; malicious 157; penetration 158; problem 149–50; shot down 153, 161; terrorists 162–3
Truman Proclamation on the Continental Shelf (1945) 141–2
Turkish aircraft incidents 333, 338, 342–9
Twining, W. 181

U-2 aircraft 152
Umozurike, U.O. 301, 306
United Kingdom (UK) 160–1; agreement with Antigua and Barbuda 121; air policing areas 160–1; aircraft 68; aircraft incidents 325, 331; airspace 64–5, 160; bomber incidents 325, 352–7; continental shelf 142–3; criminal jurisdiction 99; Defence Committee of the House of Commons 167; MEZ 143–4; police 99; QRA 160–1; response to COPUOS 296; ships 70; US Air Services Agreement (1977) 121
United Nations (UN) 24, 188; Charter 22, 29, 169, 255–6; Conventions 113, 129; resolutions 16–17; War Crimes Commission 50
United Nations (UN) Security Council 153, 163–4, 171; declaration 164; resolutions 105, 122–3
United States of America (USA) 110, 123, 152–7, 163–7, 216; ADIZ 143–4; aircraft incidents 322, 323, 324, 326, 327, 330, 331, 334, 339–41; airspace 64; Ambassador 152; bomber incidents 322, 324, 352–7; courts 38, 107–8; CSLA (1978) 231; Cuban relations 103–4; EEZ 317; Federal District Court 231; government 277; inventions 236; IP laws 233; jurisdiction 111; legislation 230–1; NOTAM zones 144; pilotless spy plane 316; piracy provisions 37; property rights in space 200–1; space law 266–7; surveillance flights 153–4; TWA 800 crash 19
Unmack, P. 120
US Patent Act 235
US v. Alvarez-Machain 38
US v. Holmes 263
US v. Rezaq 37, 111
US v. Yunis 107–8
U.S.A. v. Cordoba and Santen 86

Van Traa-Engelman, H.L. 234–6
Vazquez, S. 64, 283, 293–4
Verschoor, I.H.P. 296
vessels 36
Virgin Galactic 276
Virgin Galactic Spaceshiptwo 91
volcanic eruption (2010) 5
Vollaard, H.: and Burgess, M. 25

war 217, 266
war crimes 50
Warbrick, C.: and McGoldrick, D. 39
Warsaw Convention 112
Warsaw System 112
Wassenbergh, H.A. 294
western governments 319
Westphalian sovereignty 22
whole body imaging (WBI) 109–10
Wolfrum, R. 191

X Prize Foundation 276
X-15 aircraft 74, 299
XCOR Aerospace suborbital vehicle 91

Yemeni authorities 316
Yntema, H.E. 30–1
Yugoslav territory incident 322
Yunis, F. 107–8

Zhukov, G.P. 221

For Product Safety Concerns and Information please contact our EU
representative GPSR@taylorandfrancis.com
Taylor & Francis Verlag GmbH, Kaufingerstraße 24, 80331 München, Germany

www.ingramcontent.com/pod-product-compliance
Ingram Content Group UK Ltd.
Pitfield, Milton Keynes, MK11 3LW, UK
UKHW020023200926
475702UK00014B/2030

* 9 7 8 0 3 6 7 8 6 5 0 4 7 *